Another Fine Mess

A HISTORY OF AMERICAN FILM COMEDY

Saul Austerlitz

CHICAGO
REVIEW
PRESS

An A Cappella Book

Library of Congress Cataloging-in-Publication Data

Austerlitz, Saul.
  Another fine mess : a history of American film comedy / Saul Austerlitz. — 1st ed.
    p. cm.
  Includes bibliographical references and index.
  ISBN 978-1-55652-951-1
  1. Comedy films—United States—History and criticism. I. Title.

PN1995.9.C55A97 2010
791.43'6170973—dc22

                                            2010009010

Cover and interior design: Sarah Olson
Cover images: The Marx Brothers (The Kobal Collection); *The Life Aquatic with Steve Zissou* (Touchstone Pictures/The Kobal Collection/Philippe Antonello). Interior images: p. 1 © Roy Export SAS; p. 27 © The Harold Lloyd Trust; p. 39 © RHI Entertainment Distribution, LLC; pp. 51, 63, 75, 101, 163, 293, 319, 369 © Universal Studios, Inc.; pp. 87, 115, 229, 307, 333 © Warner Bros. Entertainment, Inc.; pp. 127, 189, 203, 255 © Sony Pictures Entertainment, Inc.; pp. 139, 151, 241 © Metro-Goldwyn-Mayer Studios, Inc.; p. 175 © Paramount Pictures Corp.; pp. 215, 345 © Twentieth Century Fox Film Corp.; p. 281 © Home Box Office, Inc.; p. 357 © DreamWorks II Distribution Co., LLC

Portions of this book have previously been published in the *Boston Globe*, Moving Image Source, and MyJewishLearning.

© 2010 by Saul Austerlitz
All rights reserved
First edition
Published by Chicago Review Press, Incorporated
814 North Franklin Street
Chicago, Illinois 60610
ISBN 978-1-55652-951-1
Printed in the United States of America
5 4 3 2 1

To Becky, who always makes me laugh

CONTENTS

· · ·

ACKNOWLEDGMENTS

Many friends and family members generously offered their assistance with this book. My father, Michael Austerlitz, and my father-in-law, Dan Silber, gave generously of their capacious movie collections, making the research process that much easier. Margaret Miller watched and discussed movies with me, and Ali Austerlitz, Reuben Silberman, and Dr. Ari Vanderwalde edited drafts of the book and offered their sage advice. Others provided comfort of a more intangible, but no less valuable, sort: Annie Austerlitz, Lisa Choueke Blank, Ari Holtzblatt, Jesse Kellerman, Josh Olken, Eli Segal, Carla and Dan Silber, Abby Silber, Rabbi Daniel Smokler, Adi Weinberg, Zev Wexler, and Aaron Zamost. Professor Michael Roemer of Yale University was, unbeknownst to him, the inspiration for this book, his mind-expanding course on the American comedy (which I took as a senior in college) first opening my eyes to the glories of the subject. My agent, William Clark, saw this project through from the original kernel of an idea, which began to form as my mind wandered during Rosh Hashana services back in 2007. My sincere thanks to Yuval Taylor, Mary Kravenas, Devon Freeny, and the entire staff at Chicago Review Press. My appreciation, as well, to the New York Public Library and Brooklyn Public Library for providing research materials, and a comfortable, quiet place to work. As always, none of this could have happened without the love and encouragement of my parents, Michael and Sarah Austerlitz. My deepest thanks go to my wife, Becky Silber. Her unfailing love and support, and invaluable *pro bono* service as a freelance repository of ideas, saw me through the oft-trying process of writing. This book is for her.

INTRODUCTION

John L. "Sully" Sullivan is the toast of Hollywood. The most dependable director in the business, Sully has just come off his latest triumph—*Ants in Your Plants of 1939*—and the studio is anxious to bankroll a sequel. Sully, however, has different ideas. He dreams of casting aside his status as a low-brow purveyor of yuks. He wants to make not another comedy, but a drama called *O Brother, Where Art Thou?* about people's genuine problems: unemployment, poverty, and inequality.

Sully hits the road in search of the real America, beset on all sides by studio bosses and flunkys pleading with him to abandon his quixotic quest. Having struggled in vain to escape his studio straitjacket, Sully suddenly finds himself all too free of their interference, assumed dead and languishing on a Georgia chain gang.

After a long day of backbreaking, soul-crushing labor, Sully and his fellow prisoners are taken to a local church to enjoy that most unrefined of entertainments: a Disney cartoon. Watching the faces of the other men as they sink blissfully into simple pleasure, Sully finally grasps the value of his low-brow craft. Neither mere mindlessness, nor blandly commercial calculation, it is the balm for wounded souls, offering catharsis through laughter. Comedy is what people need—not drama.

Sully is not a real director, and his credits exist only in the mind of Preston Sturges, the gleefully inventive writer and director of *Sullivan's Travels* (1941). *Sullivan's Travels*—Sturges's masterpiece—is a compelling argument in favor of that most maligned of cinematic genres from one of the all-time great American comic filmmakers. Sturges wrestles with his sense of comedy's inadequacy here—his nagging concern that, for all his effort, and all his genius, all he had managed to create was a handful of instantly forgettable *Ants in Your Plants*. In seeking to justify himself, Sturges asserts his claim for the genre he did so much to define.

Comedy is mostly without honor. Too often, comedy is treated as the bastard stepchild of American film. Rarely nominated for Academy Awards, or accorded the respect of a thoughtful newspaper review, comedies are considered the most disposable product of an industry dedicated to producing alluring but insubstantial goods. Drama, whatever its deficiencies, is granted the respect culture lends to noble intentions. Comedies, meanwhile, are seldom treated with the same deference bestowed upon the latest *O Brother, Where Art Thou?*

And yet, comedy has always been one of the richest veins of American cinematic culture. Beginning with the silent era, when Charlie Chaplin was, for a time, the most recognizable face on Earth, comedy (alongside those other evergreen genres, the Western and the musical) has been what American films have done best. Chaplin, Buster Keaton, Ernst Lubitsch, Sturges, the Marx Brothers, W. C. Fields, Mae West, Cary Grant, Billy Wilder, Jerry Lewis, Woody Allen, Robert Altman, Eddie Murphy, Albert Brooks, Ben Stiller—the list of standout comedic performers and directors overlaps with the list of exceptional American cinematic performers and directors, period.

This book is an attempt to redress that balance—to study the American comedy film in all its vigor and variety. *Another Fine Mess* is a tour through the history of the form as guided by some of its leading lights. It is a series of biographical essays on the luminaries of the American comedy film, arranged in loosely chronological order. The book selects the figures of greatest aesthetic, cultural, and historic interest, crafting a rough approximation of an American comedic canon. The essays—thirty in total—are supplemented by a further set of short entries on figures who did not quite make the first cut.

The resulting work is the record of a vital, vibrant genre continually in the process of reinventing itself. It is also a conversation among its practitioners. From Chaplin forward, the American comedy film has been an exclusive club whose members have engaged in a rollicking ongoing debate over what constitutes a good laugh.

Some have lavishly proffered their respect for their predecessors—witness Wilder's admiration of Lubitsch, or Jerry Lewis's love for Chaplin. Others have preferred to direct a vigorous raspberry in the direction of the past, like Richard Pryor's furiously comic inversion of the rancid stereotypes of the past. Whether the critics and historians have been paying attention or not, comedians themselves have always been keenly aware of their predecessors. Without listening to the dialogue among these artists, we easily lose track of much of what they have to say. Among other things, therefore, this book is a careful unwinding of the interconnecting filaments of the American comedy—the links that bind one generation to the next, one master to the disciples who follow in his or her wake.

As we progress through the history of the American comedy, from Chaplin to Judd Apatow, then, let us keep in mind Sturges's lesson never to underestimate the value of a good laugh. This book plays out against a ghostly landscape of unfurling American history, much of it tragic: wars and assassinations and depressions. These comedies are both a response to the grief and a salve for the wound. We laugh to forget, sure, but sometimes we laugh to remember, as well.

Of course, by its very existence, *Sullivan's Travels* reminds us that comedy is rarely purely escapist. Many of the films here are hardly comedies as we traditionally assume them to be. Is nuclear apocalypse funny? Is starvation? Is the Holocaust? If the resulting films are *Dr. Strangelove*, *The Gold Rush*, and *To Be or Not to Be*, then yes, yes, and yes. Since it is an open-ended category, in which a nearly infinite variety of styles and approaches are possible, we must maintain an open mind about what constitutes a good comedy. (Pretty much everyone agrees what constitutes a bad comedy; I'm looking at you, Rob Schneider.)

What makes for lasting comedy? There are no simple answers to that question, no easy means of predicting which films provide only fleeting entertainment and which are more durable, but in glancing backward, several patterns emerge from our story. American comedy is the story of the little man transcendent, be it Chaplin's Tramp or Albert Brooks's small-minded, self-obsessed yuppies. It is also the story of the outsider, the stranger triumphant. Many of the figures included here are expatriate Brits, like Chaplin, Stan Laurel, Cary Grant, and Peter Sellers; even more are Jews, knowing interlopers like Groucho Marx, Billy Wilder, Woody Allen, Albert Brooks, and Ben Stiller. Some—too few—are women, their very presence a rejoinder to some of the sexist dunderheads who have written about comedy in the past. A smaller handful are African Americans, reminders of the restless ghosts of the past, and the belated integration of the American film.

It is also a genre that finds its consolations in the small pleasures of the everyday. Comedy is about—has *always* been about—the way we live now. We turn to drama to experience a heightened version of the world as we know it—life, puffed up. Comedy releases all that hot air; our laughter is a bemused acknowledgement of our own collective foibles and inadequacies.

All comedy scrambles desperately to answer a single question—what would be funny? And its inspiration springs from a single impulse—wouldn't it be funny if . . . ? Comedy has always been the loosest of genres, allowing Chaplin, Fields, Groucho Marx, Marilyn Monroe, Bill Murray, and Will Ferrell to comfortably coexist, as long as they each pay close attention to the sign on the wall (with attribution to Donald O'Connor, from *Singin' in the Rain*): "Make 'Em Laugh."

Before we begin, a few notes on methodology. In selecting the subjects for the chapters, I sought to strike a balance between the past and the present. I also sought a rough chronological parity, with approximately the same number of chapters covering each era.

I intentionally did not, however, attempt to balance out the overwhelming abundance of white men here. The American film comedy has been, for much of its century in the limelight, their nearly exclusive playground, and no amount of creative manipulation can change that reality. (In fact, the only minority group *over*represented here is Jews.) The reasons for the relative absence of women, African Americans, and other minorities have more to do with the history of film, and of American culture, than with my own aesthetic preferences. In seeking to tell as broad a story as I could here, I also sought to avoid rendering an unrecognizable portrait of my subject.

Film is, even in this multimedia, multiplatform era, a defiantly distinct medium, and calls for discrete treatment. The inclusion of stand-up and television comedians, in particular, would have made for a far more diverse assemblage of talent, but alas, that is a subject for another book. In addition to keeping Lucille Ball, Jerry Seinfeld, Lenny Bruce, and Bert Williams from its pages, it also means that in considering figures like Richard Pryor and Woody Allen, whose careers ventured far beyond film, I overwhelmingly emphasized the cinematic aspects of their stories.

This should not minimize the cross-pollination between theater and film, and television and film in particular; where would Mae West, or W. C. Fields, or the Marx Brothers be without vaudeville? And what would the past thirty years of comedy be without the overwhelming influence of Lorne Michaels and the graduates of *Saturday Night Live*? Rather, in writing about these figures, I sought to place their film work front and center. In some cases, this is a no-brainer; in others, perhaps, less so. But this is a conversation that took place, overwhelmingly, onscreen, and I wanted to be receptive to all of its nuances. And it doesn't mean *Freaks and Geeks* is anything less than brilliant.

I had particularly hoped to include more contemporary female actors and directors, but in many ways comedy today has returned to its roots in the silents. Women are increasingly irrelevant to the boys-only treehouse that dominates today's comedy, present as girlfriends or scolds and little more. One can only hope that some future edition of this book will include the numerous female comic giants to come of the twenty-first century.

Any book of this kind will, by its nature, be incomplete. So as much as I wanted to include Sandra Bullock, and John Bunny, and Danny Kaye, and Gregory La Cava, and Barry Levinson (and on and on), there simply was not room for everybody. In some cases, individuals I had hoped to discuss were left out entirely; in others, figures who might otherwise have been the subject of their own chapters (like Howard Hawks) were pushed to the back because there would have been too much overlap between them and an already extant chapter.

All of which should serve as a necessary reminder that this book is, more than anything else, intended to serve as the beginning of a fruitful discussion. It is not meant to close off debate, but to spark it. It is only one possible history, selected from an infinite number of potential permutations. The rest, dear reader, are up to you.

1

CHARLIE CHAPLIN

THE MOST FAMOUS
MAN ON EARTH

"There's something about working the streets I like. It's the
tramp in me, I suppose." —Charlie Chaplin, *Limelight*

We begin, contrary to all of Hollywood's most cherished rules of thumb, at the very pinnacle of our narrative. Stories, we have been told, have three acts: conflict, complication, conclusion. Charlie Chaplin's life had three acts, just like the screenwriting gurus suggest, but his life—his work—stands at the undoubted apex of the American comedy. For the American comedy

---

The Tramp enjoys a shoe-leather steak in *The Gold Rush*.

film, there is no build-up, no steady accretion of powers, no development. There is only the sudden, unheralded arrival of absolute genius, of a kind never to be matched. "What Shakespeare is to Elizabethan theater, Dickens to the Victorian novel, and Picasso to modern art, Chaplin is to twentieth-century cinema," says film historian Jeffrey Vance. There has never been, and will never be, another Chaplin.

Charlie Chaplin's life had more than its share of tawdry spectacle—sexual, political, professional—but Chaplin's is a hero's story. It is the story of a man—the most famous man on earth, for a time—who created the most indelible character in the history of film. Think about this for a second: when Chaplin burlesqued Adolf Hitler as Adenoid Hynkel in 1940's *The Great Dictator*, more people in the audience would have known who Charlie was than the man whom he was parodying.

If we must begin at the pinnacle, let us begin with the pinnacle of the pinnacle, the greatest comedy ever made: *City Lights*. And if we are to talk of *City Lights*, should we not begin with its most enduring moment? Chaplin's Tramp has, in the guise of a benevolent millionaire, paid to restore the sight of the impoverished flower-seller (Virginia Cherrill) whose plight had so moved him. Only just released from prison, he walks down the street visibly diminished: pants split, jacket sleeves ragged and torn, hat crumpled. He turns, and there she is.

Amused and repulsed by this unkempt ragamuffin, she chases him to press a coin, and a flower, into his hand. She catches up with the Tramp, grasps his hand, and from the familiar feel of his palm, recognizes the shabby vagrant as her savior. He gazes at her, his face filling the entire frame, and the film ends on a sustained note of transcendent yet troubling emotion. It is, without question, one of the most transporting moments in the American cinema, mingling terror, ecstasy, and an overwhelming pathos. "It is enough to shrivel the heart to see," observed James Agee, one of Chaplin's most steadfast critical champions, "and it is the greatest piece of acting and the highest moment in movies." Let us now freeze that image in our minds, and rewind a ways, to catch up on the plot. Having wound all the mismatched threads of his life and art together into one enduring, perfect instant, we must now reverse the process, unraveling the strands back to their origins. How had the Tramp come to this?

"There is only one way of making comedy richer, and paradoxically, funnier," Walter Kerr opines in his superb book *The Silent Clowns*, "and that is by making it more serious." Chaplin's career is a story of natural growth, with each gag growing organically out of its predecessor, and tragedy birthed out of comedy. Retracing the steps of his career—from Keystone to Mutual to Essanay to First National, from one-reel to two-reel to feature-length—is to glimpse the astonishingly rapid growth of an unparalleled inventor. Chaplin arrived at *City Lights*—at that moment of ecstatic perfection—having begun by aiming for something else entirely.

It is a biographical commonplace to refer to the childhood of Charles Spencer Chaplin as Dickensian. Still, the comparison is apt, communicating both the squalor of his early years and a reminder of the era in which he was reared. We think of Chaplin so readily as a product of the twentieth century—its technological prowess, its speed, its ready commodification—that it is easy to forget that the man himself was a child of the nineteenth century, born in London in 1889.

Any trace of Victorian romanticism in Chaplin's persona was extremely hard-won, and protected against all the depredations of his childhood. His parents were both stage performers. Charles Sr. was a popular singer, and Hannah—known professionally as Lily Harley—was an occasional performer after the fashion of then-popular chanteuse Eva Lester. Hannah fell sick, and Charlie shuttled between brief stays with relatives and longer stints in the workhouse. Charles Sr., a shell of his youthful self, died of cirrhosis and dropsy at the age of thirty-seven, and Hannah had developed the mental illness that would haunt her for the rest of her life. At the tender age of fourteen, Charlie was, for all intents and purposes, alone.

After some small roles on the legitimate stage, he came to the attention of Fred Karno, the music-hall and burlesque entrepreneur who had hired his half-brother Sydney in 1906. Charlie was grudgingly given a two-week trial in 1908, and taken on permanently when he received far more laughs than the ostensible headliner. Karno's troupe mingled the comic and the sentimental, with a laugh, and sometimes a tear, for audiences—a combination later revived for use in Chaplin's own cinematic work. In 1913, on an American tour with Karno, he was summoned to a lawyer's office in New York for a meeting. Chaplin assumed it was regarding a bequest from a wealthy aunt, but it was a contract from Mack Sennett's Keystone film company. They offered him the princely sum of $150 a week to come to Los Angeles and act in their films.

The pieces came together rapidly. The costume—too-large pants, too-small jacket, little hat and big shoes—were grabbed out of Keystone's wardrobe closet for an early short. The duck-footed waddle was borrowed from a figure remembered from his London childhood. The raucous mayhem was the trademark of Sennett, creator of the Keystone Kops, but the jaunty tone of exuberant politesse—the tipped hats and twirled canes—were Chaplin's own.

Chaplin's first cinematic efforts are lost to us, though they still exist. They are unintentionally unsettling. We know they are meant to be funny—we can almost sense the punch lines—but, as Kerr astutely observes, all humor has been leached from them, evaporated by the passage of time. In their hectic slapstick, punches are thrown, kicks are delivered, and chases pursued with manic intensity, but the pace and the format seem all wrong to us. We seek explanation, and they give us an unstinting diet of sameness. Did people once laugh at this untrammeled mayhem? We watch them as if their silence were a foreign language, tantalizingly familiar but ultimately incomprehensible.

These difficulties of translation from the past taken into account, it would be mistaken to dismiss out of hand the shorts Chaplin made at Keystone. Their belief in physical motion as the linchpin of all comedy stuck with Chaplin; even after decades had passed, and his work had been rededicated to the principles of internationalism and world peace rather than the comic possibilities of a swift kick in the ass, Chaplin assembled his films in similar fashion. The ideas grew more grandiose, but the methods hardly changed.

As Chaplin grew accustomed to not only starring in but also directing his own films, he grew tired of Keystone's serial manhandling. He still wanted the Tramp to physically engage, to kick the ass of an uncaring world, but sought to explain—to contain—the violence.

He began to succeed with efforts like *The Bank* (1915), where Charlie is a lovelorn bank teller who thwarts a gang of thieves. Emotion was the mortar smeared between the bricks of comedy, solidifying the structure, allowing Chaplin to build more sturdily than he ever had before. When the Tramp awakens from his dream of a passionate clinch with his love, and finds himself kissing his mop, the reversal of fortune is heart-rending. It is also uproariously funny.

When fond remembrances are traded of Chaplin shorts, they are almost invariably of his work at Mutual, where he settled in 1916 after a year at Essanay. Unlike the Keystone machine, which ground out one new Chaplin short each week, and sometimes two, the Mutuals were produced at a slower, steadier pace. They are the finest examples of Chaplin's virtuosic physical gifts, of the unexpected reversals and inversions that are the heart of his humor, and of his deft sentimental touch. The Tramp is heroic, and heroically self-serving, and his manipulations of the physical world are magnificently cunning. The films' plots are the artificial limits placed on Chaplin's seemingly limitless ingenuity, the net that turns anarchy into a civilized game of tennis.

Charlie does nothing in the expected fashion: In *The Rink* (1916), he mixes a cocktail by doing a natty little rumba in which everything shakes except for the drink itself. We take our delight in brief, gulping snatches, charmed by his enthusiastic repurposing of the familiar, in which a dishrag can become a ukulele, and a gingham shirt a tablecloth. We see the world through his eyes, and are enriched by his boundless imagination.

We count on the Tramp to behave as we would, or as we would hope to. The slippage between those two roles—hero and charming cad, savant and dolt— gives him a schizophrenic quality, as if Chaplin could not decide whether his Tramp were role model or reflection. In truth, he is both. When he dives into the water to rescue a drowning woman in *The Adventurer* (1917), we are proud to bear witness to the Tramp's heroism. When, spotting her nubile daughter, he abandons the mother to rescue her more attractive offspring instead, we roar with recognition, acknowledging the calculation inherent in valor. There was little room for flesh-and-blood supporting characters in Chaplin's films because the Tramp himself was so much larger than life. Like Hamlet, or Falstaff, he contained multitudes.

From amidst Mutual's embarrassment of riches, a handful of efforts stand out for particular praise. *One A.M.* (1916) is a solo act, a vaudeville-inspired routine about a drunken tippler's return home that demonstrates Chaplin's infinite creativity, with only a fishbowl, a swiveling table, and a grandfather clock for company. *The Pawnshop* (1916) is perhaps the most perfectly formed of his early works, its inventiveness so voluminous as to nearly overwhelm any semblance of plot. In the film's most memorable sequence, Charlie confronts and demolishes an alarm clock, his pantomime transforming it from invalid to rusty can of sardines to diamond, and back again. Sweeping the now-mangled pieces back into the clock, and then into his customer's hat, Charlie shakes his head mournfully, the doctor once more, informing the family that while everything had been done, the patient could not be saved. *Easy Street* (1917) was a chase film with social content, shoehorning violence, poverty, drug addiction, and domestic abuse into a Keystone-style routine that put the Tramp on the beat. Chaplin was experimenting with films that were greater than the sum of their routines. But if a comedy were more than just a comedy, could it still be funny?

The answer was an unambiguous yes. *The Immigrant* (1917), the greatest of Chaplin's shorts, is a film whose herky-jerky rhythms match those of the boat the Tramp takes to America: the Cy Young windup Chaplin uses to throw dice, the soup bowls skidding from one end of the dinner table to the other, serving two diners simultaneously, the alternation of whimsical and heart-rending sequences. As a director, Chaplin nurtures an irony and delicacy that complement his balletic physicality as an actor. Along with the other immigrants, the Tramp catches a brief glimpse of the Statue of Liberty before an official herds the hordes behind a rope—the symbol of freedom negated by its defenders.

From Keystone to Essanay to Mutual to First National to his own United Artists, from $150 per week to $670,000 per year: Chaplin's rise was meteoric, and unprecedented. There were Tramp dolls, toys, and books. There was an animated cartoon series, newspaper cartoons and poems, and a song by fellow comedian Lupino Lane, "That Charlie Chaplin Walk." Celebrity attracted its concomitant share of controversy; Chaplin's 1918 marriage to sixteen-year-old Mildred Harris, pregnant with his child, unsettled some of his admirers, as did the baseless but persistent rumors of "slacking" from military service during the First World War.

"The way he is able to mount stairs," a fatuous editorial in Britain's *Weekly Despatch* argued, "suggests the alacrity with which he would go over the top when the whistle blew." As soldiers readily testified, Chaplin was doing far more to boost military morale with his filmmaking than he ever could as a grunt, but the link between Charlie and the war persisted; numerous editorial cartoons during those years pictured Chaplin facing off with the Kaiser, or crouched in the trenches. He had become, for many, the representative of the bedraggled common man at war—a role he would reprise in the service comedy *Shoulder Arms* (1918).

The last handful of Chaplin's shorts, made for First National before the shift to feature-length films, are a profoundly mixed lot. Some, like *A Day's Pleasure* (1919), are skilled runs through the knockabout style, while others, like *Sunnyside* (1919), are lopsided, incoherent messes. There are brilliant moments—the drunken Tramp boarding a food cart that he takes for a trolley car, gripping a salami like a subway strap, in *Pay Day* (1922), or Chaplin using his artfully deployed arms to turn an unconscious crook into a marionette in *A Dog's Life* (1918)—but the films themselves lack the concise wallop of the Mutual films. They are neither here nor there, torn between laughter and pathos without settling firmly on an approach, or a style.

Chaplin had demonstrated an infinite number of variations on a well-worn routine with his Tramp shorts. The only direction left to take his character—

the direction he had been unconsciously heading, even as he loudly protested that it was impossible—was toward a feature-length film. Chaplin had long argued that comedies, by their nature, could be no longer than they already were, that the requirements of the feature film would inevitably distort any such attempt. The director, though, had been subtly shifting the nature of what a Tramp short could be; after all, *The Immigrant* or *Easy Street* had hardly been the stuff of Keystone comedy. The emotional tug of Chaplin's late shorts demanded a broader canvas.

Maybe it is not the First National shorts that come up short, but the lone feature Chaplin made for the company in 1921—his first—whose glow paradoxically cast its neighbors into relative darkness. "A picture with a smile—and perhaps, a tear," *The Kid* is a visible extension of the great Tramp's powers, fully embracing the undercurrent of emotional vulnerability that had coursed through his earlier work. It is the most heartfelt of Chaplin's films, the interlinking strands of sentiment and playfulness giving this work its undiminished emotional pull.

The Tramp stumbles upon an abandoned baby in a filthy alleyway, and soon synthesizes the Kid (Jackie Coogan, brilliantly mimicking Chaplin's restless energy) into his makeshift life. The Kid smashes the windows that Charlie, a glazier, repairs; he makes flapjacks as lazy Charlie loiters in bed. More than any of the women after whom he helplessly pines in his other films, it is the Kid who is the ideal complement to the Tramp's buoyantly hardscrabble existence. When the authorities snatch the Kid away, the Tramp becomes a boys'-adventure gallant, scrambling across rooftops to rescue his son. The finale, when the Tramp, the Kid, and the other denizens of the ghetto are transformed into angels, is a touching non sequitur, a paper heart Scotch-taped to the body of the narrative. At this still-formative stage (he had been making films for less than a decade), Chaplin's instinct was to punctuate all serious bits of business with a joke. He had not yet grown entirely comfortable with sentiment himself.

A Woman of Paris (1923) was the first Chaplin film made under the imprimatur of United Artists, the collective he had formed with Douglas Fairbanks, Mary Pickford, and D. W. Griffith to counteract the studios' clumsy attempts to monopolize the film market. It was also the first Chaplin picture not to feature him as the star. Instead, it is a sophisticated French romance whose indirect, glancing approach would greatly influence the work of Ernst Lubitsch. Chaplin wanted to prove a point—that he could be more than just the Tramp—but *A Woman of Paris* is, by any contemporary standard, a terrible slog. The Tramp did not belong in elegant Paris apartments, and neither, it turned out, did Chaplin.

Inspired by the story of the Donner Party, *The Gold Rush* (1925) is comedy of unparalleled rigor. Charlie is a starving prospector, one of the thousands of men drawn to Alaska by the promise of riches. Hunger is the film's sole motivating factor—a hunger for companionship, and the even more elemental hunger for nourishment. The Tramp furtively snacks on salted bits of candle wax, his hiccups giving him away to his famished associates. Having feigned passing out from hunger, the Tramp stills the hand of his rescuer, pouring coffee down his throat, to stir in some sugar. At one particularly desperate moment, Charlie serves up his own boot for Thanksgiving dinner. Chaplin slurps up the laces like strands of spaghetti, sucking the boot's nails like succulent chicken bones. The realistic principle is essential for Chaplin: having eaten his own shoe, the Tramp walks around with one boot for the rest of the film.

Charlie is infinitely resourceful and terribly vulnerable, all at once. The sentiment, and the danger, heighten the comedy, its wit—Charlie shooting a bear and immediately setting the table for dinner, or strategically opening the cabin door to blow an opponent out with the wind—sharpened by its place on the knife's edge of catastrophe. The entire film, not merely Charlie's cabin, teeters on the edge of a precipice. But the Tramp remains as heedless as ever, his insensitivity—to stalking bears, or that treacherous cabin—the punch line to every joke. The hilarity of Chaplin's famous dance of the dinner rolls, a brief pantomime in which twin loaves of bread briefly take on the appearance of tiny, elegant feet doing a high-kicking step, is intensified by its placement in the film: it is intended as an entertainment for the dinner-party guests who have stood him up. The hunger pangs echo from the heart, not only the stomach. The gags are as swift and sure as any Chaplin had attempted before, or would introduce after, but there is a yawning emptiness to the film—an appetite that cannot be sated.

Left out of his autobiography, given short shrift by critics, *The Circus* (1928) is Chaplin's portrait of the artist as accidental genius. The Tramp stumbles into a circus and entertains the audience with the unintentional wit of the maladroit. He has no idea he is capable of being funny. When he attempts any sustained routine, the Tramp is a terrible flop—albeit a remarkably amusing one for those of us who are not proprietors of a circus. The match with Chaplin himself is inexact—the man did nothing accidentally—but the gags are priceless. Charlie's utter lack of timing in his attempted run-through of an onstage barbershop sequence is itself a masterpiece of timing.

The setup—cruel fathers and headstrong daughters under the big top—is straight out of W. C. Fields, but as with *The Gold Rush*, Chaplin's unbounded wit in *The Circus* is tempered only by a romanticism that would be sappy were it not for its sublimity. The caravan pulls away at the end of the film, and the Tramp is alone once more, at the center of a hollowed-out circle where a circus once stood. The commotion has all gone, and all that remains is a crumpled star drawn on a piece of paper. The Tramp vigorously kicks it with the back of his foot and trundles off. Waddling in the direction of the horizon, Chaplin embodies the guardedly optimistic romantic fatalism of his Victorian stories; rarely assured of a happy ending, the Tramp triumphs by keeping on keeping on.

And so we complete the circle, returning to 1931 and *City Lights*. Hannah Chaplin had died in 1928. Second wife Lita Grey (whom he had impregnated while she was filming *The Gold Rush* with him) had divorced him, the lurid sexual details of her allegations spilled across the front pages of newspapers worldwide. By virtue of its release date, *The Circus* had narrowly skirted the issue, but four years after *The Jazz Singer*, the question was unavoidable: what did the Tramp sound like? Alone among his fellow comedians, Charlie Chaplin refused to answer. The Tramp was silent, and would remain so, far beyond the advent of sound. Other than some *Peanuts*-esque nonsense sounds, and the whistle Charlie accidentally ingests, *City Lights* defiantly, triumphantly clings to silence.

After nearly two decades of practice, slowly climbing from one-reelers to features, Chaplin had mastered the silent comedy's economy of means. The Tramp is never again so resourceful, so kind, or so genial a figure as he is here. His politesse is matched by his powers of self-preservation. He is forever doffing his cap at an incomprehensible world, his jaunty step out of sync with the ugliness around him.

Chaplin is unfailingly tender, even as the world treads all over him with muddy boots. This is the source of his comedy, of his frustration, and of his eventual ambiguous triumph. Each scene introduces a new challenge, which the Tramp greets with geniality and tact. Part aristocrat, part bum, Charlie straddles the gap between royalty and poverty. In the film's marvelously apt symbolic conflation of roles, he cruises the streets in a Rolls-Royce, on the lookout for stray cigarette butts to pilfer. *City Lights* depends on our familiarity with Chaplin's past; we laugh even before the routines have been explained, confident that the Tramp will rope-a-dope his way to unexpected success.

The comedy is a new sapling grown out of Chaplin's Mutual roots, born of misapprehension and confusion. The Tramp confuses a streamer of confetti for an endless strand of spaghetti; takes a man's bald head for an appetizing entrée; and sits silently as his girl unravels his underthings, mistaking them for her ball of string. The comedy is melded seamlessly with the drama, for what is the girl's taking Charlie for a wealthy benefactor other than another humorous confusion squeezed until tragedy drips out like sap?

City Lights is an unending reel of magnificent moments. It is the Tramp's apotheosis, a full-dress demonstration of his infinite jest for an audience whose head had already been turned by the magic of sound. As if intent to prove that such trickery was unnecessary, Chaplin seizes this unlikely moment, well after the death knell for the silents had already been sounded, to reveal the fullness of his capabilities. Each scene is a marvel, a perfect stand-alone two-reeler, but the strands are weaved too diligently to be pulled apart.

Unlike *City Lights*, *Modern Times* (1936) is essentially, as critic Otis Ferguson noted in his penetrating review of the film, four separate one- or two-reel shorts. Fearful that technology was rendering him a has-been, Chaplin was ensuring his own obsolescence by acting as if 1936 were 1916 all over again. He was clinging to silence nearly a decade after its place had been usurped by sound. His anxieties are writ large in *Modern Times*, transposed from a lone filmmaker to all of humanity: it is the machine that is mankind's true opponent, deadening the senses and twisting flesh into steel.

Of these hastily patched-together bits, only the opening sequence, with Charlie as a factory automaton, tightening bolts and women's dress buttons with equal facility, is the equal of his best work. The Tramp, normally master of the inanimate, is here its helpless plaything. All manner of machines have their way with Chaplin, from the auto-feeder that shoves hors d'oeuvres and metal bolts into his mouth with equal facility, to the assembly line, which demands his unblinking, unstinting attention. The Tramp is menaced by technology. Chaplin's revenge is only partial and symbolic, but essential nonetheless: after his friend gets stuck in the gears of the menacing behemoth they work on, the Tramp feeds him his lunch by hand, stuffing a hard-boiled egg into his waiting mouth, and using a chicken as an impromptu funnel. Chaplin is, in essence, placing his own genius in competition with modernity, asking audiences to root for his improvisatory brilliance over the simple-minded dutifulness of the unthinking machine.

The rest of the film is like a remake of the Mutual short *The Rink*, with its skating and waitering sequences amplified by a strongly felt but maddeningly vague political awareness. Labor dissatisfaction and unrest is ever-present in *Modern Times*, but Chaplin cannot corral it into any recognizable shape. The film's political consciousness, like the red flag the Tramp picks up off the ground, waves proudly but meaninglessly. Chaplin had once seamlessly integrated comedy and pathos, but this was a tougher fit, as if he were unsure just how nonchalant one could be when the subject turned to matters of state.

The political itch, for Chaplin, was an insatiable one. A committed, if intellectually uncertain, leftist, his intense disgust at the rise of European fascism found expression in the unlikely decision to play the dictator of Nazi Germany in his next film. Chaplin had previously given thought to a Napoleon biopic, going so far as to shoot screen tests in full uniform, but the prospect of throwing down the gauntlet to his evil doppelganger—the tyrant with the Tramp mustache, born only four days after him, bewitching Europe with his crowd-pleasing routine—was too tempting to ignore. It would also mark the beginning of the political trials which would test Chaplin's grace under fire after the Second World War.

In *The Great Dictator*, Chaplin is both Tomanian dictator Adenoid Hynkel, and his near-twin, a meek Jewish barber. Released in 1940, *The Great Dictator* has the profound misfortune of being made before Auschwitz. Many of the pleasures of *The Great Dictator* are lost in the gap between the film's knowledge of world affairs and our own. Chaplin himself acknowledged that he would not have made the film as he had if he had been aware of the full extent of Nazi criminality. Knowing, as Chaplin could not have, the genocidal horror of Nazi evil, *The Great Dictator*'s satire feels fatally tepid. Chaplin appears to sincerely believe that his film could be enough to topple Hitler from power—a sentiment not shared by Ernst Lubitsch's similarly minded *To Be or Not to Be* (1942), which has the wisdom of its somber pessimism. *The Great Dictator* is nonetheless an act of profound personal courage, a rare attempt by an entertainer to use his gifts to comment on (and potentially influence) current events as they were occurring.

The Jewish barber is the more Tramp-like of Chaplin's two characters, but most of the film's attention is lavished on the buffoonish Hynkel. Chaplin has located Hitler's Achilles' heel: his burning need for respect. Chaplin undercuts his authority at all points; Hitler's strongest weapon—his mesmerizing speeches—are transformed into Hynkel's gibberish-German outbursts. Hynkel's foil is not the barber—for how could the little Jewish fellow keep up with world leaders?—but Jack Oakie's barrel-chested Napaloni, dictator of Bacteria. This Mussolini manqué brings out the schoolboy in Hynkel. As they exchange aggressive salutes, or swivel in matching barbers' chairs, each seeking the upper hand on the other, the fate of nations has been reduced to a playground brawl between two petulant, spoiled brats.

For at least one moment, as Hynkel spins a globe on his finger, tosses it from hand to hand like a balloon, and frolics with it tucked under his arm in some perverse inversion of modern dance, Chaplin has perfectly married symbol and reality, capturing Hitler's megalomania and craving for world domination in one indelible image. Pity, then, that the rest of the film could not match its inspired whimsy. Audiences particularly resented the seven-minute closing speech, in which Chaplin delivered a rousing oration on peace and brotherhood. Informed that the scene might cost him one million dollars in lost box office, Chaplin was unflustered: "I don't care if it's five million. I'm gonna do it." *The Great Dictator* is principled, tenacious, and clever; it is also, in the decidedly relative terms of Chaplin's matchless career, a flop.

Chaplin had been a dedicated advocate of the Allied cause in World War II, appearing at a mass rally in San Francisco to agitate for opening a second, eastern front to the war. After the war's end, such sentiments were confused by many with sympathy for Communism, and public opinion hardened against the once-beloved clown. Chaplin was attacked by know-nothing journalists for a perceived lack of loyalty to his adopted country, and scrutinized for alleged Communist ties that existed nowhere other than within the fevered minds of his persecutors. At a 1947 press conference for his next film, *Monsieur Verdoux*, Chaplin was mercilessly assailed for his perceived Communist allegiances, lack of patriotic fervor, failure to vote, and insufficient veneration of the war dead. The transcript reads like a rejected scene from one of his own scripts, too exaggerated by half to play as comedy.

Verdoux itself is a record of a harsher, angrier Chaplin—the Tramp after the twin traumas of depression and war. Henri Verdoux is a bank clerk turned serial killer, romancing and dispatching lonely women with pitiless efficiency in order to provide for his family. For our purposes, though, Verdoux's most notable traits are those he shares with the Tramp: delicacy, chivalry, and a physical grace that is itself a kind of wit. Aware of the audience's abiding love for the Tramp, Chaplin now implicates us in Verdoux's crimes. In one scene, as he is about to serve a poisoned glass of wine to a penniless female drifter, Chaplin's eyes flick to the glass, up to the camera, and then back down, curious whether we will intercede. We cannot, and *Monsieur Verdoux* argues that, in the era of the atomic bomb, murder has become the international lingua franca. "Upon leaving this spark of earthly existence," Verdoux tells the court, a dark glimmer in his eye, "I have this to say: I shall see you all . . . very soon."

Verdoux is a political screed, when it remembers its instructions from Chaplin. More farce than thriller, it is a funnier film than it prefers to let on. Its laughs are all the Tramp's, but the notion of that lovable scamp having grown up to become a mass murderer was too unsettling for audiences to handle. *Verdoux* is the strangest entry in Chaplin's filmography, a maddeningly inconsistent hodgepodge of tones and approaches that nonetheless achieves a perversely luminous grace.

In 1952, Chaplin and his family (he had married again, to Eugene O'Neill's daughter Oona) boarded the *Queen Elizabeth*, en route to Britain. They were two days at sea when word came that U.S. Attorney General James McGranery had invalidated Chaplin's re-entry permit, calling for the INS to hold hearings on his fitness to reside in the country. McGranery hinted at secret documentation that would reveal much about the actor and director's "unsavory character." Chaplin and his family resettled in Switzerland. He would not set foot in the United States for another twenty years.

Exile was a kind of living death, making *Limelight* (1952) a valedictory to the Tramp, and to Chaplin's own past, entirely apropos for that dark year. *The Circus* had imagined the artist as accidental genius, and *Modern Times* had recreated the birth of a performer. *Limelight* is a farewell to the unpredictable inspiration of comedy, an autumnal romance that also functions as a final good-bye to the most beloved character to ever appear onscreen. Chaplin had long treated the sound film as a nuisance, searching for dodges that would allow him to avoid speaking, but *Limelight*'s script is beautifully concise. Chaplin has finally found a rough verbal approximation of the Tramp's effortless physical brilliance. His Calvero is an aristocrat of a fallen world. The fleeting May-December romance with dancer Claire Bloom is tender, but Chaplin's true sympathies are with the aging comedian, his audience depleted, his wisdom born of terrible suffering. "Time is the great author," he tells an accompanist. "It always writes the perfect ending."

Limelight would have served as the perfect capstone for Chaplin's own career, its melancholy tempered by his marvelous, touching stage routine with that other great silent clown, Buster Keaton (about which more later), but exile had prompted other, less generous feelings. *A King in New York* (1957) is his riposte to the bullies who had banished him from his adopted home. *King*'s America is a plastic world of salesmen, hacks, and courtiers, but the tone is amused, not hectoring, and the comedy is as inviting as ever.

The political hectoring of the film's final third is only amplified by the jarring presence of Chaplin's son Michael as a pint-sized Trotsky, but who wouldn't gladly sit through it for the sight of Chaplin's exiled King Shahdov pantomiming an order of caviar and turtle soup for the benefit of a passing waiter?

There would be one final, forgettable Chaplin film, *A Countess from Hong Kong* (1967). A lugubrious, overly madcap farce, *Countess* offered the dubious pleasures of Marlon Brando, looking like a mackerel stuffed into a wool suit, as an international diplomat trapped in a ship's stateroom with voluptuous dancehall girl Sophia Loren. The spectacle of adults behaving like overly frightened children at the thought of seeing each other unclothed, in this year of *The Graduate*, was dispiriting, and the comedy was shockingly inept. Chaplin makes only the briefest of appearances in the film, but is not Loren's stateless waif, searching for a safe port of entry, an autobiographical portrait in disguise?

In April of 1972, some forty-three years after the Academy had first issued him an honorary award for *The Circus*, Charlie Chaplin was summoned back from his Swiss exile to receive its lifetime achievement Oscar. The applause was thunderous, a tribute both to the comic who had once been the most famous man on earth, and to the martyr who had endured two decades of banishment over half-baked lies and politically motivated innuendo. The citation read: "To Charles Chaplin, for his incalculable effect in making motion pictures the art form of this century." For once, the Academy's praise was, if anything, understated.

Five years later, on Christmas Day, 1977, Sir Charles Chaplin was dead. The tributes were copious, the praise fulsome; those mourning his loss understood that Chaplin had been a giant in their midst. It was Bob Hope, of all people, who issued the pithiest, most heartfelt encomium to the man the world still knew as the Tramp: "We were fortunate to have lived in his time."

2

BUSTER KEATON

THE CAMERA MAN

"Tragedy is a close-up; comedy, a long shot." —Buster Keaton

Tragedy, or comedy? It is a question we will find ourselves asking numerous times in reviewing the lives of the great American comedians. Comedy is a funny business, but something in the genetic makeup of those who make us laugh is primed for tragedy. Or is it merely that, in being so funny, they emphasize, once the cameras have ceased rolling, the misfortune and humiliation doled out to all of us in roughly equivalent doses? Buster Keaton once noted that "tragedy is a close-up; comedy, a long shot," but a convincing

A rebel hero peeks inside a pesky cannon in *The General*.

argument could be made that, when it comes to his own biography, precisely the opposite is the case. It is the close-ups—the individual moments, some preserved on film, some not—that provide the comedy, and the long shot—the life, as it was lived—that possess the tragic arc. Let us begin, then, with one of the close-ups, and enjoy the sight of a young man, his eyes dilating with excitement, taking in the limitless potential of a medium still in its swaddling clothes. The tragedy will come soon enough.

In March 1917, Buster Keaton was twenty-one years old, a lifelong vaudeville veteran taking his first steps away from the family act he had performed with his entire life—literally. He had just signed on with the Shubert organization's latest spectacle, *The Passing Show of 1917*, promised the lavish sum of $250 a week, when a friend offered to take him to visit the studio where a rising star named Roscoe "Fatty" Arbuckle produced his short films. Arbuckle invited Keaton to watch him at work, and the young comedian, whose stage training had heretofore inculcated a native hostility to the moving pictures, peppered his host with questions. Buster studied the cameras, the lights, and the cutting rooms, inspecting the equipment with an engineer's eye for detail. Toward the end of the day, Arbuckle summoned Keaton to shoot a handful of scenes together. Thoroughly taken by the new medium, Buster would tear up his theater contract and take a job with Arbuckle at less than one-sixth the salary. The Shuberts never had a chance.

Joseph Frank Keaton VI had practically been born onstage. His mother Myra and father Joe had been itinerant performers, their act a combination of the acrobatic and the exotic. Joe would kick and leap furiously, and Myra would accompany his exertions by bleating out tunes on the alto saxophone. When their first child was born, they swaddled him inside an open trunk during their performances, but the toddler always preferred the limelight—whatever dangers might lurk there—to the quiet and safety found offstage.

Keaton made his first stage appearance before his first birthday, interrupting one of his father's routines, to the great amusement of the audience. The toddler was happy nowhere quite so much as on that stage, and his parents were happy to make use of his evident skills. By age five, he was the youngest member of his parents' act, now called the 3 Keatons. He also had been granted a nickname that would stick with him for the rest of his life. Watching the youngster take a vicious tumble down a flight of stairs, Harry Houdini (who toured with the Keatons for a number of years) exclaimed, "That's sure a buster!" The name stuck. What was more, it would fit the man, whose career would be built on a steady routine of well-planned falls, dives, and tumbles.

His most astonishing buster had been an entirely unplanned one. At twenty months of age, an approaching cyclone swept Keaton out of a second-story window and onto the street, where he landed safely a full block away from home. Enormous danger and paradoxical safety; young Buster's brush with death would set the tone for his work as a filmmaker, serving as a primal scene he would re-create as the finale of one of his best films.

The 3 Keatons' routine was simple. Joe would play the agitated father, tossing his son across the stage—and sometimes into the crowd—with impunity. Little Buster's coat even had a handle sewed onto its back for his father to grip. Buster had learned how to take a buster in stride, rarely if ever injuring himself, but rumors spread nonetheless. Some said he was no child at all, but an adult midget; others, that his body was covered in bruises from the onstage beatings his father gave him. There were no bruises, but the mark of his father's grip stayed with Keaton. There was to be no smiling, and no laughter, while performing. The audience laughed hardest when Buster's face remained impassive. A smile seemed to spoil the effect. Try as they might, no director or producer was ever able to get Keaton to smile, no matter how boffo a finale they thought it might provide. He knew better.

After a forced two-year hiatus from New York (the anti-child labor Garry Society had finally been successful in banning the Keatons from Broadway), Buster returned to acclaim in 1909, and a renewed sense of focus. Too big to be tossed across the stage, Buster now slid and dove across the floor at his father's instigation. (He was, he told a reporter, giving polish to the American stage.) Joe Keaton's drinking and violent temper had meant the dissolution of his marriage, and the Keatons' act too. Buster was now the star of the show, and Broadway renown was firmly in his grasp—at least, until he threw it all away after an afternoon with Fatty Arbuckle.

By the standards of Keaton's later work, his initial cinematic collaborations with Arbuckle were rudimentary. Keaton was sidekick and crony, his straight-faced sluggishness a welcome accompaniment to Fatty's childish petulance. In shorts like *The Garage* (1920), the last and possibly the best of their collaborations, Keaton and Arbuckle are pie-tossing, water-spraying, motor-oil-drinking pump jockeys. Their antics are straight Keystone, but there is a hint of something Keatonian in the mathematical purity of the gags, like when Buster, having lost his pants to a rabid dog, is lifted up bodily by Arbuckle, sliding his legs into a pair of trousers hanging on a store rack.

In 1920, Arbuckle was bounced upstairs to produce his own feature films, and Keaton was granted the opportunity to take over his production team.

Chaplin had become the exemplar of the new form without ever showing much interest in how it all worked. Detractors argued that Chaplin was always a handful of years behind the times, never proficient in the technical side of filmmaking, and with little desire to grasp the possibilities of his medium. Meanwhile, Keaton had spent his teenage summers designing elaborate Rube Goldberg contraptions intended to wake a perpetually tardy friend, and always said that had he not been a performer, he would have been a structural engineer. Those proclivities led him to ask questions that had not been asked before: Just what was this new medium? What was its potential? Chaplin was an artist whose chosen medium, incidentally, was film; Keaton was a filmmaker, first and foremost.

Keaton arrived, with his first solo short *One Week* (1920), a fully formed actor and filmmaker, though little evidence of the extent of his talents had dribbled out during his time with Arbuckle. His two-and-a-half-year stint writing, and occasionally directing, his own two-reelers was an apprenticeship for the even more accomplished features to come, and a triumph in its own right. Having been taught by his stage experience that a delayed response was always funniest, Keaton's films incorporated the artful pause into their own rhythms.

Keaton's shorts require our thinking, at some length, about the medium itself; he is among the most self-reflexive of filmmakers. Keaton resides somewhere in the gap between the rigidity of the real world and the flexibility of the screen world. His films are a series of intricate problems presented for the camera. He is simply wondering, in the course of these films, whether people and objects behave differently when we watch them on a screen than they would in real life. The answer, of course, is yes.

Objects, for Keaton, take on an aura of mutability, their instability a product of the movie camera's presence. Keaton paints a hook onto the wall in *The High Sign* (1921), then proceeds to hang his hat on it. The rowboat of *The Balloonatic* (1923) is transformed into a wooden skirt, or an appendage to a balloon, through Keaton's skillful manipulation of the material world. When nine dancing Busters fill the frame in the vaudeville spectacle of *The Playhouse* (1921), laughter bubbles up simultaneously with a wondrous sense of "how'd he do that?" (In this case, the answer was a camera with nine identical tight-fitting lens caps and a very precise sense of cinematic space.)

There are remnants of Arbuckle's blackjack-wielding slapstick in Keaton's eighteen shorts, but anarchy has mostly given way to a giddy delight in invention. Chaplin had proffered a laugh and then a tear, but Keaton offered neither—at least, not openly. Keaton is not the sanguine Tramp, nor is he Harold Lloyd's middle-class striver. His face is famously impassive, a product of his father's childhood tutelage, and so are his movies. The plots are schematic, familiar, mostly secondhand, but the gags, contraptions, and routines are all Keaton's, and entirely original. The films are less organic units—nothing much ever seems to happen to Keaton—than structures housing the elaborately-worked-out set pieces: haunted houses, runaway balloons, crafty Western parodies. Sometimes, Keaton makes no effort to hide the strings: *The Scarecrow* (1920) and *The Playhouse* (1921) are brilliant burlesques padded with lackadaisical supporting material.

The best of Keaton's shorts integrate narrative with comedy, presaging the precisely amalgamated feature films he would make later in the decade. *One Week* (1920), the first of Keaton's solo shorts, is a marital farce, a parody of technological innovation, and a rip-roaring physical comedy, all at once. Newlywed Buster and his wife attempt to assemble a prefabricated house by following the detailed instructions, and wind up with a contraption that more closely resembles a Dalí sculpture than a Cape Cod. The house, in the process of being dragged to its final resting place, gets caught on the tracks as a train rushes headlong in its direction. Buster and his wife breathe an enormous sigh of relief after it passes by harmlessly on the next track, only to watch helplessly as the house is blindsided by another train, approaching from the opposite direction, which smashes it to bits.

Cops (1922), perhaps the most acclaimed of Keaton's shorts, is essentially a two-reel chase scene, with Buster facing off against an ever-swelling phalanx of police officers. The knockabout comedy of his youth, and of the childhood of the silent comedy, is here inflated to a point of hallucinatory intensity; Buster, pursued by a nightmare army in blue, swarming the screen and enveloping the lone man in the porkpie hat. Where did realism end and surrealism begin? With Keaton, the one folded into the other; one could, in fact, be so thorough a stickler for exactitude that the final result would verge on the dreamlike.

Keaton's features, which began with 1923's *Three Ages*, are an extended footrace between verisimilitude and the faint air of homegrown numinousness that clings to his work. On the surface, all is dedicated to realistic meticulousness. Locations, costumes, chases—the vaudevillian's desire never to trick the audience demanded a rigorous approach to filmmaking. If there was a fall to be taken, it would be Keaton—and not a stand-in—who would take it. If an effect was intended, Keaton preferred shooting dozens of takes to get it all in one master shot than use the most basic editing techniques to achieve the same result. Realism is bred in the bone of these films, which rightly demand our respect for their deceptively simple rigor. The new feature length required a retreat from the cartoonish. A two-reel short could be sustained on a steady diet of ludicrous or impossible gags, but a feature required realism—albeit a tempered, limited version of realism.

Three Ages is an extended burlesque of D. W. Griffith's *Intolerance*, with man's perpetual chase after women replacing man's injustice to man as history's thematic through-line. Keaton is the runt in romantic competition with beefy Wallace Beery in prehistoric times, ancient Rome, and modern-day America. The Griffith comparisons were intentionally sought. *Three Ages* was a tentative first step toward a new comedic style, one where stunts could be punch lines, and laughter could stem from the wonder of a well-executed routine.

Our Hospitality, released only two months later, is Keaton's first truly authoritative feature. It is an affectionate parody of Southern mores—a subject, and region, he would eventually return to for his most fully realized film, *The General*. Buster is a Northerner caught up in a clan war between the Hatfields and the McCoys—pardon me, the Canfields and the McKays. Keaton was simultaneously naif and expert, his initial credulity giving way to a remarkable aptitude for slithering away from danger. We laugh at McKay heir Keaton's gormlessness when, early in the film, he momentarily borrows a revenge-minded Canfield's pistol and fixes the malfunctioning trigger, or when he opens an umbrella while standing under what turns out to be a Niagara-size waterfall.

Keaton appreciates this laughter, but it is all building to another, deeper kind of amusement. Keaton's perfectly timed leap, at the film's climax, catching his girl as she is about to plummet over the falls, and swinging her back to safety, is comedy with pretensions to the dramatic—even the epic. Keaton put himself in grave danger during *Our Hospitality*. He was nearly swept away by the raging river during the filming of one sequence, grabbing onto a branch just before crashing into some jutting rocks. This being Keaton, he inserted the shot of his near-calamity into the final film. What could be more realistic than the accidental?

Filmmaking had become, like vaudeville once had been, a family affair, with Keaton's father, wife, and even newborn son starring alongside him. Keaton had married Natalie Talmadge, sister to two stars and an actress in her own right, in 1921, but the marriage had been dogged from the outset by his wife's lavish spending habits, the meddling of his mother-in-law, and the nagging sense that he was considered, by the extended Talmadge clan, to be one of its lesser lights. Keaton's films are not quite misogynist, but his affection for women is distinctly limited—a product, one must surmise, of his unhappy marriage. They are the object of pursuit, but the prize is booby-trapped; the boy-gets-girl ending of his film *College* concludes with three quick shots (child-rearing, miserable old age, and twin gravestones) that indicate that happily ever after is a mere figment of the cinematic imagination. The look on Keaton's face in *The Navigator*, when his crush has strategically fainted to avoid having to climb a rickety ladder, speaks volumes: he wanted to kiss them, but Buster also occasionally—as in *The General*—wanted to throttle them too.

Keaton was never the box-office draw Chaplin or Harold Lloyd were, but his films were steady moneymakers, made frugally and earning healthy profits. Joe Schenck, married to Keaton's sister-in-law Norma Talmadge, was his producer, shielding him from the unpleasant scrum of business affairs. Keaton's dependence on Schenck, and lack of familiarity with financial matters, left him dangerously open to changes in the industry weather. A technical wizard, Buster Keaton was hardly an expert manager of his own career.

The Playhouse and *The Love Nest* had experimented playfully with cinematic technique, but *Sherlock Jr.* (1924), Keaton's funniest—and arguably most accomplished—picture, was a master class in filmmaking doubling as a comedy. Walter Kerr described it as "simultaneously brilliant film comedy and brilliant film criticism." Buster's motion-picture projectionist dreams himself onto the big screen, emulating his favorite detectives while solving crimes with panache.

The effect would be repeated numerous times by other filmmakers (most notably Woody Allen with *The Purple Rose of Cairo*), but *Sherlock* is uniquely consumed by the fundamental oddity of the motion picture as an art form. Buster leaps onto the screen and finds himself at the mercy of the capricious cutting of the unseen filmmaker. He sits on a pedestal in a garden, and crashes into the street; he paces the sidewalk, and discovers himself perilously perched atop a cliff; an onrushing train brusquely interrupts a placid desert scene. (Even later, when he has returned to the waking world, it is the dream world's wisdom he seeks. Unsure what to do with the girl in his arms, Buster peeks out at the screen, taking instruction from the lovers and proceeding accordingly.)

Other filmmakers would study this near-miraculous sequence too, wondering just how Keaton had managed to perfectly match the framing of the parade of images so effortlessly. Always meticulous, Keaton had completed and printed each shot separately, with the camera operator using the last frame to direct the placement of the actor for the next image.

If *Sherlock Jr.* was a feature-length exploration of the possibilities of montage, *The Navigator* (1924) was a study of the comic potential inherent in the long shot. Keaton's camera is immobile, fixed in place by the desire to objectively record—really, to document itself. *The Navigator*'s unmoving camera is itself a testament to its honesty. What we see is what actually took place. The French film critic Fereydoun Hoveyda once observed that all films are documentaries of the conditions of their making, and nowhere is this truer than with Keaton. Filmed aboard an oceangoing vessel scheduled to be scrapped, it is the closet autobiography of a comic, documenting the transition of a hapless Bertie Van Alstyne (Keaton's bumbling trust-funder from 1920's *The Saphead*) into a marvelously efficient Buster Keaton protagonist.

Trapped aboard a large, empty ship with love interest Kathryn McGuire, Keaton emphasizes his character's initial infelicity, the better to dazzle with his later aptitude. He uses an industrial-size drill to open a can while preparing breakfast, and tenderly, tragically attempts to rescue some boiling eggs from the bottom of a colossal pot, striking a match to search its depths for any survivors. Time passes, weaknesses become skills, and a second breakfast sequence serves as an impromptu rehash of *The Scarecrow*'s magnificent system of kitchen pulleys and levers, breathtaking in its effortless efficiency.

It is Keaton's malleability—his ability to adapt, smoothly and effortlessly—to any state of affairs that gives *The Navigator* its buoyant charm. When in danger of imminent attack from cannibals, he puts on a diving suit and floats on his back, transforming himself into a rowboat McGuire can paddle to safety. Keaton's fluidity is his strong suit; there is no pause during these transformations from man to machine.

Seven Chances (1925) is bright and clever, like *Cops* if the pursuers had been—even more frighteningly for Keaton—a horde of desperate brides-to-be. After the technical and comedic triumphs of *Sherlock Jr.* and *The Navigator*, though, it could not help but feel like a regression. Keaton's physical agility, dodging love-hungry women and falling rocks in the finale, is masterful, his pratfalls each small masterpieces of technique, but the plot feels slight, and the comic set-pieces not plentiful or multifaceted enough to make up the difference. *Go West* (1925) is a further step backward, a mock Western whose putative love interest is a cow named Brown Eyes. There are isolated moments of brilliance in *Go West*—a train journey measured by shots of a steadily decreasing loaf of bread, the miniature revolver Buster keeps in his oversized holster, tied to a string—but the film itself feels shapeless and unfocused, a loose string of horse-opera gags tied to nothing at all.

Battling Butler (1926) is the last of Keaton's warm-ups before his masterpiece, *The General*. By all measures, it should have been another *Go West*. Keaton lacks the preternatural physical expressiveness of Chaplin's prizefighter in *City Lights*, but *Battling Butler* is one of the warmest of Keaton's pictures. You can take the boy out of the upper crust, but you can't take the upper crust out of the boy; some of *Battling Butler*'s most charming moments come from his trust-find dingbat turned boxer's attempts to preserve his routine in the most unlikely places. He dresses in a tuxedo for dinner while camping; his tent is appointed with an absurdly lavish bathroom; training for the big fight, he strips off his sweat suit to reveal—wouldn't you know it?—another tux.

The General (1926), the film Keaton's career had been building to, is simultaneously Keaton's epic and the most unadorned of all his films. The plot is austere: Keaton's Civil War–era railroad engineer Johnnie Gray sneaks behind enemy lines to steal back his locomotive from the Union soldiers who had swiped it from him. The film is a feature-length chase sequence (or really two of them, first hurtling forward and then backward), but the chase has been elevated to sacred cause, in perfect lockstep with the emotional center of the film. (Incidentally, in a statement that surely deserves enshrinement in the hall of fame for ludicrous utterances, Keaton argued, regarding his playing a Confederate, that "you can always make villains out of the Northerners, but you cannot make a villain out of the South.").

The General is not a comedy, per se. It is a comic epic, a film of panoramic landscapes shrunk to human size by Keaton's ever-alert responses to danger. The fusion of widescreen action and close-up emotion is inscribed into the design of the film itself, with the camera mostly poised just above Keaton's head, taking in Johnnie, the train, and the surrounding landscape all at once. Its fidelity, as Walter Kerr observed, was itself epic. Keaton has elevated realism to a guiding principle, and unearthed comedy from the unlikeliest material. When Johnnie is too busy chopping timber to spot not one, but two entire armies on the move, or is followed by a naggingly persistent cannon, the comic peaks are inseparable from the dramatic arc.

The General was the culmination of Keaton's ambitions, its scope and mood reflecting Keaton's desire to transcend knockabout comedy. How strange it was, then, that his next film was not only a drastic reversion, but also a fairly blatant knockoff of Harold Lloyd's *The Freshman*. *College* (1927)—even the title was bland—is Xeroxed Lloyd, with Keaton fumbling around his school's athletic fields to no particular purpose. Between his tasteless turn as a waiter in blackface here and the Confederate pride of *The General*, there was a nagging sense that Keaton wanted to emulate not only Griffith's technique, but also the unabashed racist pride of *Birth of a Nation*.

The rebel gray was replaced, in *Steamboat Bill, Jr.* (1928), with another kind of uniform: beret, bowtie, and striped sports coat, the image of bohemian dilettantism completed by the ukulele he carries. Keaton is again a Lloyd-esque hero—the shrimp belatedly made good—but the humor is his alone. *Steamboat* is a masterful comedy that crescendos into an even-more-masterful comic adventure, which is, in its own right, the finest extended sequence Keaton had ever done.

Steamboat's cyclone finale (inspired by Keaton's childhood brush with death) is simply breathtaking, and, with some knowledge of its production, harrowing. Buster, trapped outside in the storm, stands motionless as the façade of a building rips away from its foundation and crashes to the ground. An open second-story window passes directly over his head, the cavity just wide enough to allow Keaton to escape unscathed. The clearance for Keaton's head was all of three inches. Had Keaton been positioned a foot to the left or right, or the wall fallen unpredictably, he would have been instantly killed by the two-ton mass. On the set, crew members turned away from the action (some resorting to prayer), and director Charles Reisner stayed in his tent rather than risk watching his star's death.

Keaton, always true to his scruples, makes no special attempt to underscore the danger. Perhaps the key to understanding this remarkable moment comes just a few minutes later in the film, when Keaton leans against a door labeled "STAGE DOOR," only to find that it, too, has toppled, an unstable opening to a nonexistent wall. There was no safety in performance. Buster Keaton had devoted his career to courting danger; this stunt was only the latest, and most extreme, manifestation of a life spent teetering at the precipice.

It is perhaps best, for all parties involved, if we draw the curtain here, and presume that the real Buster Keaton, for all intents and purposes, ceased to exist after 1928. Schenck moved the production of Keaton pictures to MGM, and the resulting efforts (with one notable exception) were nothing short of a travesty. Production head Irving Thalberg was amiable enough to his new star, but refused him permission to establish his own filmmaking unit, preferring to awkwardly cram him into the MGM system. Keaton began drinking heavily and sleeping around, and his wife left him. After the divorce, a terribly bitter one, she went so far as to change their children's last names to Talmadge, erasing all vestiges of Keaton's involvement in their lives. There were still ideas for new films—an Oregon Trail comedy with Marie Dressler, an all-star parody of *Grand Hotel* with Laurel & Hardy and Edward Everett Horton—but Thalberg refused them all.

Before that, there was one last Keaton masterpiece, produced under the aegis of MGM. The studio had not yet settled on a strategy regarding the production of his pictures, and so allowed *The Cameraman* (1928) to proceed in similar fashion to its predecessors. It is, like *Steamboat Bill*, an action comedy. Buster, an aspiring cameraman, bats, fields, and runs the bases at Yankee Stadium, as if executing a baseball-themed revival of *The Playhouse*. His virgin attempts at filming for the newsreels, with their hapless double-exposed shots of battleships steaming down Broadway, are self-reflexive gestures in the vein of *Sherlock Jr.*: reminders that this, too, is only a film. Keaton's hero is a dolt who becomes a dashing cameraman, cheerfully oblivious to the perils of his task. Any symbolic resonance with his own career was only too purposeful. MGM, typically, wanted Keaton to smile at the end of the film—something he had never done before. He reluctantly agreed on the condition that it be tested with audiences first. They uniformly disliked it. The Old Stone Face was not intended to smile.

Let us assume, then, that following *The Cameraman*, Buster Keaton was replaced by some helpless, mirthless doppelganger, doomed to insipid productions that understood nothing of Keaton's magic. Playing a series of overly chatty bumblers in films like *Speak Easily* (1932), he was disastrously paired with the mugging Jimmy Durante, who robs Keaton of whatever dignity might have remained. Sound was a disaster for Keaton. His speaking voice could never match the dignity of his silence, but MGM perversely insisted that he was ideal for drawing-room comedies and romantic farces. The studio eventually terminated his contract in 1933. Buster Keaton was thirty-seven years old, and unemployed.

After two European flops, Keaton was reduced to two-reelers for the decidedly minor Educational Comedies, and occasional gag work for MGM. The man who had done so much to create the American film comedy was now writing bits for performers nowhere near his equal. Keaton eventually scrabbled his way back to a major studio, albeit in a tenuous role, shooting a series of modestly amusing shorts for Columbia in the late 1930s and early 1940s. He was still a young man, but like his onetime mentor Arbuckle, Keaton was a man who had deliberately been forgotten by Hollywood.

Real-life stories are rarely as neat as those up on the screen, and Keaton's exile was so thorough, his deletion so complete, that rediscovery was nearly inevitable. New prints of his classic films, once thought lost, were struck, and a new generation of postwar audiences discovered *The General* and *Sherlock, Jr.* Keaton was rewarded with steady television work, and the occasional supporting role in films like Billy Wilder's *Sunset Blvd.* (1950) and *It's a Mad Mad Mad Mad World* (1963), but the greatest, and most lasting, tribute to his genius came from fellow comic legend Charlie Chaplin, hiring Keaton to play his onstage partner in his 1952 film *Limelight*.

No longer the pale, rail-thin wraith of his youth, Keaton had grown fuller-cheeked, more absent-minded professor than action hero. The two titans of the silent comedy, their faces ravaged by age, momentarily join forces for a theatrical number that is itself essentially silent. Keaton plays the piano for this musical number, his attention distracted by a continually slipping pile of sheet music. Chaplin sets the driving pace on his violin, and Keaton must race after him, his body splayed out on the floor, his fingers stretching for the keys.

Critics carped that Chaplin had edited the scene to favor himself, but if anything, the opposite was true. The scene is a tribute to the glories that were, and a testament to the silent icons' undiminished capabilities, with Chaplin embracing Keaton as an equal. The comedy number was impeccable, but the moment that lingered was a brief shot of the two men in their shared dressing room—Chaplin applying eyeliner, Keaton affixing his mustache. "If anybody else says it's like old times," Keaton warns, "I'll jump out the window!" It was not at all like old times. Instead, the brief union of Chaplin and Keaton was a painfully bittersweet nod of recognition from one giant to another. The moment was unbearably intimate, its tragedy—that of time's passage—unstated, but only too tangible.

3

HAROLD LLOYD

THE STRIVER

"There is more magic in a pair of horn-rimmed glasses than
the opticians dreamed of. With them, I am Harold Lloyd;
without them, a private citizen." —Harold Lloyd

It was, in the end, all due to the glasses. Without them, Harold Lloyd had been merely another in the anonymous mass of second-tier silent comedians, Chaplin substitutes whose efforts were reluctantly screened those weeks the Tramp had no new entertainment in theaters. Lloyd had been known as Willie Work, his name more question than statement, and

---

Lloyd hangs for dear life from the minute hand of a clock in *Safety Last*.

then Lonesome Luke. Luke was less Chaplin fill-in than imitator, his slavish devotion clumsily masked by a series of physical and sartorial inversions of the Tramp's style. His pants were tight, his eyebrows a pair of arched triangles, and his mustache twin dollops of greasepaint on either side of his mouth. Luke was an adjunct to the Keystone style of slapstick, his world sharply delineated by beat cops and the hot pursuit of girls, his cinematic style little more than the collective tramping of cast and crew to a nearby park, scenario nowhere in sight, to cobble together a hodgepodge of modestly amusing sequences.

The empty space in the middle of Lloyd's face was where the Tramp's own mustache would have gone, and the ghostly absence was telling. Harold Lloyd was indebted to Charlie Chaplin for his very existence. He was a second-rate Tramp, at best, and he knew it. The story, at least as he told it, was that Lloyd was checking out one of his own Lonesome Luke pictures when he heard one young moviegoer tell a friend, "Oh, here's that fellow who tries to do like Chaplin." Lloyd went back to his producer and collaborator Hal Roach, and told him it was time to put aside the Tramp imitation. The mustache and tight pants were jettisoned, replaced by a pair of horn-rimmed frames.

The glasses, by their simple presence atop his nose, imposed a new type of scenario on Lloyd. He was now just plain Harold, the quintessential middle-class striver. The glasses suggested the characteristics he was to adopt: shy, bookish, ambitious, and romantically clueless. The glasses were, in some elemental fashion, the essence of Harold; without them, as Lloyd once proved, he could stroll down Manhattan's Fifth Avenue in the middle of the day, at the height of his success, without a soul recognizing him. Lloyd's new films turned Chaplin inside out. The Tramp's effortlessness would be replaced by the comedy of great effort. Success would come, but at a price. The fun would be in the striving.

It would also come in the posing. "The glasses character," as Lloyd would dub him, would become a master of mistaken identity. We are forever confusing Harold with his betters, or watching as he contrives to convince others—women, usually—that his climb has been faster, more effortless, than it has actually been. Chaplin had secured our instant identification through the plasticity of his face, which begged our sympathies. Keaton had been the still point amidst the chaos. Possessing only a fraction of their gifts as comedians, Harold Lloyd required the assistance of an indelible persona, easily created and instantly identifiable. He was average—no, more than that: he was the epitome of averageness. Harold Lloyd was averageness raised to the level of a national trait, lovable precisely because of his utter ordinariness. Chaplin's Tramp had succeeded through the mysterious workings of fate, but Lloyd's triumphs were achieved only through his own extraordinary efforts. We want him to succeed, but we must see every accumulated drop of flop sweat along the way.

Lloyd may have ditched the Tramp shtick a few years in, but his career is still, inexplicably, measured by the yardstick of Chaplin—and of Keaton, to whom his later work bears some resemblance. It is as if there were only room for two great silent comedians, and Lloyd's presence in the company of comedy's all-time greats was an explicit rebuke of Charlie, or Buster. Harold Lloyd is dismissed lazily as being Chaplin's inferior, and no more.

Lloyd, indeed, is no competition for Chaplin. Then again, neither is anyone else in this book, and the prospect of a hall of fame for comedy whose membership requirements are so stringent would make for a (pardon the pun) lonesome gathering. So here we have Harold Lloyd, unquestionably the bronze medalist of the silent comedy, his oeuvre running a distinct third behind the two unquestioned geniuses of the era. Hardly a soul would argue otherwise. But Lloyd is a significant figure in his own right, and a more charming, multifaceted one than memories might allow for. A genius he wasn't—not quite. A wonderfully inventive Everyman? Indubitably.

Harold Lloyd was born in small-town Nebraska in 1893. His mother had once entertained hopes of a career as a singer, and his father bounced from job to job—from Singer sewing-machine salesman to shoe-store manager, from photo-gallery owner to restaurateur. Harold was himself an entrepreneur from an early age, overseeing a small newspaper-delivery empire and hawking popcorn to passersby on the street. In later years—the successful ones—Lloyd would compare his youth to Tom Sawyer's, but in truth the better comparison would likely have been to Huckleberry Finn's: peripatetic, unstable, with an unsteady father. He took to theater instantly, befriending a local impresario named John Lane Connor and taking small roles in his troupe. Harold even put on productions in his own basement, charging three cents for front-row seats.

Lloyd's parents divorced in 1910, and after winning a sizable settlement from a drunken driver, his father moved out to Southern California, eager for a fresh start. Harold appeared as an extra in Edison Film Company Westerns being filmed in Long Beach, and when local theatrical work dried up, headed north to Los Angeles, where the film industry was only just settling in. Universal, one of the fledgling Angeleno film companies, engaged a steady stream of extras for its productions. Employing some of his later characters' on-the-spot ingenuity, Lloyd noticed that security guards would only check extras' IDs in the morning, but not the afternoon. He carefully applied his own makeup and did his best to blend into the crowd of extras returning from lunch. After a few days of this ruse, he had successfully passed himself off as one of the gang. Consider it the first Harold Lloyd gag, his first successful attempt at climbing the ladder of success.

One of Lloyd's fellow extras was a former mule skinner and Alaskan prospector named Hal Roach who saw a future in low-budget comic one-reelers. After some false starts, Lloyd and Roach would go into business together in 1915—the year of Chaplin's emergence as a superstar. Roach would produce and occasionally direct, and Lloyd would be the star, his lack of any comic experience or training apparently no obstacle to success. The early Lloyd-Roach films were made for a few hundred dollars, with story and characterization at a bare minimum. With names like *Luke's Society Mixup* and *Luke Joins the Navy*, the titles fairly telegraphed the film's contents. Chaplin could not be said to be an influence so much as a ghostwriter on these pictures. *Fireman, Save My Child* and *Lonesome Luke in Tin Can Alley* make no effort to mask their borrowings from the Tramp. There would be a new Lonesome Luke every week—sometimes two—and what they lacked in Chaplin's ingenuity, they made up for in sheer presence. As Chaplin was working more infrequently, taking months and then years between pictures, Lloyd was a steady toiler. Lloyd would make his protagonists strivers—epitomes of 1920s up-from-the-bootstraps success stories—because he was one himself.

His slow, steady rise to prominence was nearly halted by a terrible accident that could have been a gag from one of his films were it not for the horrific aftermath. Posing for a new set of publicity photographs in August 1919, Lloyd was handed what he took to be a prop bomb outfitted with a long-burning fuse. He was attempting to light a cigar with the smoking fuse when the bomb—only too real—exploded in his hand. Doctors were concerned that he might permanently lose his sight, and the actor was petrified that his face would be scarred from the incident. His vision was not impaired, nor were there any permanent scars, but the bomb had torn away the thumb and forefinger of his right hand. After a lengthy recovery, the ever-resourceful Lloyd had a prosthetic thumb and finger, easily flexed and controlled, designed from soft rubber. The artificial fingers were sheathed in a flesh-colored leather glove. The eagle-eyed will occasionally spot Lloyd favoring his left hand, but he preferred to keep his disability a private matter. What kind of all-American boy—at least in the 1920s—would have a mangled hand?

After an eight-month hiatus, Lloyd would return to work, armed with a new contract paying him five hundred dollars a week and 50 percent of the profits from his films. Later, after he and Roach amicably split, Lloyd would own his work outright and retain nearly all the profits from his films. Savvier about money than many of his compatriots, he understood that it was not enough to make the films. Without a stake in their profits, as Keaton had learned, there could be no stability; without complete control of their content, the comedian always ran the danger of being forced into inferior vehicles. Always the entrepreneur, Lloyd eventually parlayed his success into one of the largest personal fortunes in Hollywood—a status reflected in his forty-four-thousand-square-foot Beverly Hills estate, Greenacres, complete with Olympic-size swimming pool and nine-hole golf course.

"The glasses character" was developed in 1917, for the one-reel comedy *Over the Fence*, but it took Lloyd a number of years to leave behind the exuberant slapstick of Lonesome Luke. The two-reel pictures of 1919–1921 are the first real flowering of Lloyd's gifts, albeit in tenuous and compromised form. The additional production time removed some of the frenzy from filming, and allowed Lloyd and his writers the luxury of working with characters, not mere outlines.

Many of these films, like *Bumping into Broadway* (1919), are one-note chase films of the sort that Roach made with his other, less talented stars. These anarchic tendencies would occasionally rub up against something else, something still unformed, like in *High and Dizzy* (1920). An uninspired doctor's-office setup leads to a brilliant finale where Harold, trapped in a room with love interest (and Lloyd's future wife) Mildred Davis as her father bangs terrifyingly on the door, escapes his predicament with an ingenious ruse. Smashing the window of the minister's office one floor below with a vase, Harold tempts the clergyman out with some greenbacks on a string, and cajoles him into marrying them immediately. A circular pull from the window curtains serves as an impromptu ring, and the happy couple dangle over the ledge as they are joined in holy matrimony.

His last, and best, short, *Never Weaken* (1921), is essentially an extended suspense sequence set atop a floating girder with a brief comic prelude. The construction of its climactic scene—its steadily mounting anxiety, its carefully composed series of challenges and scares—is impeccable. We understand, without needing to be explicitly told, that Lloyd proves his aptness as a romantic suitor by surviving this trial-by-girder. The moment is thrilling, invested with the exuberance of a job well done—both for the character, and the mind that had devised the dare.

Lloyd employed a large team of gagmen (including many veterans of Keaton's team) to write for his films. As one sequence was being shot, another was being assembled, with ideas batted around with astonishing fluidity. Gag piled atop gag, with Lloyd employed as arbiter and quality-control manager. Plots were loose, informal, and incidental. Occasionally (especially after the switch to sound), Lloyd would forget to adequately explain a critical plot point, accidentally making a hash of the story. Lloyd was no sentimentalist, like Chaplin; we only felt for Harold because of his elaborately exaggerated travails. When his films worked, which was most of the time, they were elaborate mechanical contraptions whose interlocking pieces clicked smoothly together. When those sequences were heavy-handed, or lacking in wit, the resulting films felt sodden, like Keystone sequences inflated to interminable length.

In film after film, Lloyd disguised himself as a lump—in a mail sack, or under a tarp—to hide out. The repetition was indicative of Lloyd's crafty recycling of successful gags, but it also offered a certain metaphorical resonance: here was Harold Lloyd, hiding his light under a bushel. Lloyd was sometimes the moneyed idler, sometimes the impoverished climber, but he was forever being challenged by circumstance, required to doff his lumpishness and don the togs of the hero. Lumpishness was not so easily ditched; much of the hilarity of Lloyd's silent features finds its source in his sustained denseness. Arrested by revolutionary forces in *Why Worry?* (1923), Lloyd invites his jailers to lunch, and signs what he takes to be the hotel's register—actually the list of prisoners to be shot at sunrise. He is a cloddish writer of romantic fantasy who believes himself to be the reincarnated William Shakespeare in *Girl Shy*, and the buffoon who takes himself for a god in the campus comedy *The Freshman*. The currency of Lloyd's world was humiliation, and Harold was always a very wealthy man.

The feature-length Lloyd is the comedian at his apex, confident in his abilities and comfortable with his adopted rhythm. Not every film is memorable; as a general rule of thumb, the character-driven films are stronger, and funnier, than the gag-heavy pictures. If no one sees *Why Worry?* or *Hot Water* (1924) much anymore, it is because these films provide little emotional foothold for viewers.

Lloyd had been too unflappable, too cool in *A Sailor-Made Man* (1921), his first feature, in which he clambered up the walls of a palace, and clubbed a rajah's henchmen into submission. *Grandma's Boy* (1922), by comparison, turns him into a shrinking lily, disdained by a world demanding prompt action. *Grandma's Boy* is a domestic comedy with pretensions to the epic. Harold, in need of an infusion of courage, is given an amulet that, his grandmother informs him, had protected his grandfather on a daring incursion into Union territory during the Civil War. (What is it, anyway, with comedians and the Confederacy? Was there no humor to be found in Lincoln's Army?)

Inspired by his grandfather's sterling example (Lloyd plays his ancestor in an extended flashback, his glasses modified only slightly for period authenticity), and with the amulet in his hand, Harold heroically overcomes the bully and wins the girl. Lloyd's burgeoning forcefulness as a comic filmmaker finds symbolic expression in the late-blooming vigor of his protagonists. No matter that his grandmother's story is entirely fabricated, and the amulet is actually her umbrella handle—Harold's strength grew with his confidence, and Lloyd's did too.

Has there ever been a more potent metaphor for the pitfalls of the long ascent to success than Lloyd hanging off the side of a building, feverishly gripping the minute hand of a clock? *Safety Last* (1923) is unmistakably an elaborate setup for its human-fly climax. But what a setup, and what a glorious payoff! The film is an increasingly audacious series of impersonations. Harold feigns unconsciousness to cadge an ambulance ride to work, poses as a mannequin so he can be carried past his watchful boss, and bluffs his way behind the general manager's desk to impress his girlfriend. Harold's last boondoggle requires him to climb to the top of a skyscraper, his path beset by belligerent pigeons, dangling ropes, and falling tennis nets.

The tension is ratcheted up with each slip, each faulty foothold; the sequence's realism is affirmed by the perpetual presence, in the background of nearly every shot, of the street far below. We know now, from interviews and biographies, that Lloyd made artful use of camera angles and mockups for the sequence, but this knowledge hardly detracts from the mounting tension. At one point, Harold clambers onto a ledge, and a mouse crawls up his leg. Doing a frantic two-step to dislodge the unwanted intruder, he receives a healthy round of applause from the crowd gathered at street level, which believes him to be dancing a jaunty jitterbug. Lloyd was betraying a healthy skepticism in his audience. Did they see the mouse, or just the jitterbug?

In *Girl Shy* (1924), Harold was the lummox once more, a stuttering, virginal loner convinced his fraudulent tales of romantic passion have the makings of a literary masterpiece. The romantic interludes and professional humiliations are all prelude to one of Lloyd's most inventive mad dashes, this time to keep Harold's girl from reaching the altar with a rival. Commandeering cars, police vehicles, horses, fire trucks, trolleys, and motorcycles, Lloyd demonstrates his own desire to always top his own topper. The stunts are only too real; watch for the moment when Lloyd, atop a pair of horses, takes a gruesome, unplanned fall, only to rise again a moment later and continue racing through the streets. Harold arrives in time to break up the wedding, and, too tongue-tied to explain, carries the bride off without a word. *The Graduate* would reprise Lloyd, with only minor alterations (and minus the trolley), forty years later.

Anticipating and besting Keaton's *College*, *The Freshman* (1925) offers the most acute of Lloyd's many humiliations. The figure of Harold Lamb, sacrificial offering to the undergraduate gods, is the nearest to Chaplin among Lloyd's heroes, a figure of quivering (if only occasional) pathos. This Lamb's wounds are entirely self-inflicted, though, a product of an overabundance of credulousness and one too many collegiate entertainments. "I'm just a regular fellow," he tells everyone he meets at school, echoing the banter of his favorite campus-idol movie. "Step right up and call me Speedy." Harold's new catchphrase comes with a matching step—a debonair Irish jig. We wince, knowing that so ripe a target will undoubtedly be pricked by the arrows of countless others.

The bulk of *The Freshman* (the second highest-grossing silent comedy of all time, after *The Gold Rush*) is turned over to these abasements: the impromptu speech delivered to the entire student body, the hastily tailored suit that falls to pieces at a dance. Harold sobs in his girl's arms when he discovers his own wretchedness—a note of despair that Lloyd removed from later reissues of the film, believing it to be too maudlin for a later, savvier generation of moviegoers. The moment is actually just right, its agony the necessary lead-in to the ecstasy of the climactic football game. The game is the entire film rendered in miniature, with initial failure paving the way for last-ditch success. After browbeating his coach to let him in the game, Harold fumbles away an easy touchdown before being granted an unexpected second chance and bulling his way face-forward into the end zone. He looks up, a beard of goal-line chalk on his face, and sees other, younger students doing the Speedy jig—this time in genuine tribute. We will return to this moment of triumph later, with a question that, once asked, would linger over all of Lloyd's triumphant adventures: what comes after glory?

The Kid Brother (1927) is an explicit attempt to match *The Freshman*'s heartfelt success. This male Cinderella story was another opportunity for

Lloyd to play the shrimpy upstart who bests his macho rivals, and was a success on those terms, but it lacks the numerous scraps of comic business, strewn throughout the film, that had made *The Freshman* such a thoroughgoing success. As Walter Kerr had said of Chaplin, a comedian could only get funnier by growing more serious—but not if the drama came at the expense of the comedy.

The last of Lloyd's silent films would commingle his raucous and sentimental streaks more skillfully than ever before. *Speedy* (1928), issued some months after Al Jolson told audiences "you ain't heard nothin' yet" in *The Jazz Singer*, would join Keaton's *Steamboat Bill, Jr.* and *The Cameraman* as masterpieces of the waning form, dictated as the silent film lay on its deathbed. Harold "Speedy" Swift is Lloyd's fastest-thinking, nimblest hero yet, a ne'er-do-well too good for the numerous jobs he holds ever so temporarily. Speedy is endlessly, charmingly self-sufficient, capable of turning a manhole into a makeshift wheel, or making use of a dollar bill attached to a hook to lure subway riders out of their seats. Working as a soda jerk, baseball nut Harold surreptitiously updates the kitchen staff on the Yankees game by deploying doughnuts as an impromptu box score. The Yankees score three runs, and Harold's predicament is obvious: how will he record the score? He grabs a pretzel, bites it in half, and displays the remainder, which takes the form of a perfect 3.

Speedy eventually adopts the cause of his girl's father's horse-drawn trolley, which is in imminent danger of having its license revoked if it fails to run its route every twenty-four hours. Utilizing a mannequin dressed in a policeman's uniform, rigged to crisply salute at the tug of a string, Speedy maneuvers his unwieldy, archaic contraption for one last run across the city. Whether intentionally or not, Lloyd was writing the obituary—a romantic one, but an obituary nonetheless—for the silent film.

Speedy interrupts its main plotline for a trip to Coney Island that plays out like a Lonesome Luke one-reeler transposed to 1928. During this interlude, there is a brief moment where Speedy and his girl hitch a ride back to the city in a moving van, and fleetingly, movingly, set up a home in someone else's borrowed living room as it floats through the metropolis. All this scrambling was to preserve that evanescent glimpse of a place that might be called home. Winning the girl was not reserved for the movies; Lloyd had married costar Mildred Davis in 1923, as her contract was up for renewal. Davis quit acting to raise a family, and they would be married for forty-six years, through three children, Lloyd's numerous infidelities, and her battles with alcoholism.

Unlike Keaton, for whom it spelled a hasty and unmourned commercial death, Lloyd survived the transition to sound, retaining some measure of his success for nearly a decade after the switch to talkies. Understanding the nature of his appeal, he preferred not to tamper—at least not at first—with the formula that had been so successful. The trajectory is easily traced. As soon as Lloyd's characters stopped being named Harold—as soon as Lloyd felt the need to play a different kind of character to boost his fading box office—the quality of his work fell off precipitously, and never recovered. Lloyd was Harold. He may have been the most actorly of the silent comedians, but there was only one character he could truly, effortlessly embody.

Lloyd's first sound film, *Welcome Danger* (1929), is an unmitigated disaster, but one suspects that technology, not feeble inspiration, is primarily to blame. The film had been shot and edited as a silent picture before Lloyd decided it would be best to release it with sound. The resulting effort is slipshod at best, offering compelling testimony to the technical difficulties of working in the new medium. *Welcome Danger* is painfully, exaggeratedly slow—something no Lloyd film had ever been before—and much of the dialogue is very obviously dubbed onto otherwise-silent sequences.

Whatever the defects of his virgin sound effort, Lloyd learned quickly. The solution was in matching the dialogue to his plots, not—as Keaton had so blunderingly done—building his films around their talk. His next film, *Feet First* (1930), is essentially a reshuffled version of *Safety Last*, but with a pleasing, if rudimentary, frisson of verbal sophistication. Lloyd plays another go-getter clambering to success, a shoe salesman passing himself off as a rising industrialist. It is an underappreciated gem, unfairly ignored by those who assumed that sound spelled Lloyd's doom the same way it had for Keaton.

Lloyd is as fiendishly inventive as ever. A stowaway on a cruise ship, he wheedles his way into a big breakfast by professing to illustrate the faux-pas of another diner, dunking his toast, slurping his coffee, and catching food in his mouth. Spotting an incriminating photograph of himself attached to a passenger's rear end, Harold borrows a cigar and casually lights it on fire, all the while chatting amiably with his boss.

Feet First's big finale, though, is the *Safety Last* climb wired for sound. The sequence lacks some of *Safety Last*'s excitement, its unity of action broken up by obtrusive interior shots, but is nonetheless a more-than-worthy variant on one of Lloyd's classic moments, dreaming up entirely new obstacles to be encountered and overcome.

Dialogue had not killed off Lloyd's appeal, but it had led to a peculiar haziness in his plotting. Some confusion about Lloyd's love interest (is she his boss's daughter, or his secretary?) in *Feet First* was never adequately explained, and *Movie Crazy* (1931) is also marred by the fog surrounding leading lady Constance Cummings's motivation in posing as a tempestuous Spanish actress. This film-world satire was a clever spoof of Hollywood, and of Lloyd's bumbling wannabe screen idol. Like *The Freshman*'s Harold Lamb, he cannot be swayed from the ironclad belief that everything he touches turns to gold.

After that, Lloyd's focus began to slip, with predictably mediocre consequences. *The Cat's-Paw* (1934) was moderately amusing, with Lloyd as the son of Chinese missionaries returned to the United States to find a bride, heroically naive and dedicated to the ancient philosophy of Ling Po. There was little to take hold of here, though, other than the film's vague, quasi-fascist belief in maintaining order through violence. *The Milky Way* (1936), directed by master comic craftsman Leo McCarey (who had done so much for the Marx Brothers, W. C. Fields, and Mae West), promised more, but it too sought to make Lloyd over in the manner of his successors. His milkman-turned-pugilist Burleigh Sullivan is more Harpo Marx than Harold, borrowing much of the plot of Keaton's *Battling Butler* to boot. Lloyd's well-intentioned halfwit had at least retained one aspect of his storied past: *The Freshman*'s jig had been transmuted into an effective boxing side step.

Following 1938's *Professor Beware*, another absent-minded academic farce in the manner of Keaton's *Speak Easily*, plummeting box-office revenues convinced Lloyd to retire from moviemaking. Dedicated to hobbies like photography and increasingly involved with the Shriners (he would become their Imperial Potentate, appearing on the cover of *Time* magazine, in 1949), Lloyd pulled his early films from circulation, waiting until the 1960s to issue a series of compilations of his best gags. There was, however, one last film, this one a tribute to, and a repudiation of, Lloyd's most admired film. Director Preston Sturges, having left Paramount for the ample bankroll of Howard Hughes, approached Lloyd about shooting a screwball sequel to *The Freshman*, catching up with the football hero some twenty-two years after his triumphant touchdown.

The idea of using Lloyd's own past as prologue was inspired, as was the new film's beginning—the last reel of *The Freshman*, lightly edited and reworked for sound. As the presidential calendars on the wall of his office flip from Harding to Coolidge to Hoover to Roosevelt to Truman, Harold (his last name now Diddlebock, not Lamb, in tribute to Sturges's fondness for ludicrous, vaguely lewd names) remains at the same desk, crouched over the same book of figures. Fame has come and gone, and left behind only regrets and dashed hopes.

The first third of *The Sin of Harold Diddlebock* is a promising hybrid of Lloyd's and Sturges's approaches, plunging the silent star into this hyper-literate chatterbox of a film. Its remainder, though, is shrill and raucous, favoring Sturges's dialogue over Lloyd's traditional gags, or any sense of character development. There is an escaped lion, and a tense crawl along the ledge of an office building, but Sturges and Lloyd have offered us no amusement, and no drama, to keep us involved. It is only the outline of a Harold Lloyd scenario, with none of the humor or terror that had once made them memorable. The fault lies primarily with Sturges's direction, which does Lloyd no favors, and his script—or lack thereof. This melancholy farce about failure was itself a failure. It bombed at the box office too, pulled from distribution by Hughes, and recut and reissued in 1951 under the title *Mad Wednesday*. It would be no more successful in its second incarnation.

The Sin of Harold Diddlebock was a movie about what happens after the great moment has passed, and its time frame jibed noticeably with that of the film comedy itself. The silents had had their moment of glory, only to find the cheers fade to silence. The crowd roared no longer. Harold Diddlebock was simply Lloyd himself, and the other greats of the silent era. The glories of the past could not be recreated—only temporarily revisited. The silent greats had departed from the scene, but who would come along to replace them?

4

LAUREL & HARDY

STRAIGHT MAN
AND LITTLE BOY

"This is the first mistake we've made since that fellow sold
us the Brooklyn Bridge." —Stan Laurel, *Way Out West*

In the winter of 1910, the Fred Karno company left England for a tour of
the United States. The troupe was made up of English music-hall performers, their on-the-job training the endless cycle of British theaters and vaudeville houses. They were not only veterans of the music hall; they were actually transporting the spirit of the music hall across the Atlantic. The Karno

---

The duo together in bed with their new furry friend in *Angora Love*.

troupe's most prized sketch, called *Mumming Birds* for local audiences, was renamed *A Night in an English Music Hall* for Americans. The unquestioned star of the troupe, soon to take America, and the world, by storm, was *A Night in an English Music Hall*'s leading man, Charlie Chaplin. Meanwhile, Chaplin's understudy and roommate Stanley Jefferson settled for bad pay, bit roles, and limited prospects. Stardom seemed as unlikely as it had on that night in 1906 when young Stanley snuck out of his father's house, in his father's clothes, to compete in a local amateur night. Stanley was right—stardom was indeed quite far off. It was so far off, in fact, that by the time it came, another decade and a half would pass, and Stanley Jefferson would be known by a new name—Stan Laurel.

Meanwhile, Oliver Hardy was working as a projectionist at a movie theater in his hometown of Milledgeville, Georgia, dreaming of a career in the pictures. When word arrived of a burgeoning film colony in Jacksonville, the onetime vaudeville singer known as "the Ton of Jollity" made his way south to Florida. An overweight comedian in the Fatty Arbuckle tradition, Hardy was featured as the heavy in dozens of instantly forgettable shorts. Personable, charming, and engaging, Hardy was a raw talent in search of a shaping force.

The team of Laurel and Hardy was so perfect that it seemed preordained, and yet a substantial portion of their careers would elapse before anyone had the bright idea of pairing Laurel with Hardy. Before we get to their partnership, then, we must first explore the winding paths that brought them together. The task is not simple; Hardy alone acted in nearly three hundred shorts before his first pairing with Laurel. But some sense of how they got along solo—not all that well, as it turns out—will help to illuminate the magic of their union.

To watch Stan Laurel's and Oliver Hardy's solo work is to bear witness to a single mistake, repeated time and again. Burdened with the gift of hindsight, we cannot understand why Laurel and Hardy insist on the clumsy scenarios, the ill-suited roles, the improper costumes. Above all, we struggle to comprehend why Laurel and Hardy insist on keeping their distance from each other, unable to sense the magnetic attraction that should have been pulling them together. Their paths, as we will see, would cross more than once.

After departing the Karno troupe, Laurel stayed in the United States, hoping to follow in Chaplin's footsteps. Chaplin was an inspiration, and an albatross. What could any English music-hall comedian do that would not be burdened by comparison with the most famous performer in the world? Embracing his own obscurity, Laurel transformed himself into a Chaplin imitator, tirelessly working vaudeville houses. Hardy, meanwhile, modeled himself after Chaplin's chief heavy, Eric Campbell. Playing a menacing brute in dozens of films, Hardy made a habit of twirling his mustache and looming threateningly over renowned Chaplin imitator Billy West. The roles made use of Hardy's commanding bulk, but little else.

Laurel, meanwhile, had ventured out to Los Angeles, summoned by producer Hal Roach to work for his studio, Pathé. Laurel was a foil to Larry Semon in films like *Huns and Hyphens* (1918), where he plays the world's least likely German saboteur, and *Frauds and Frenzies* (1918). Semon's work is largely forgotten today, but Semon was once considered a legitimate peer to Chaplin, Keaton, and Lloyd, his raucous, freewheeling chase films enormously popular with audiences.

Laurel is almost entirely unrecognizable in these early efforts. He is less stooge than cad, the lazy man of leisure ill-equipped for mundane life. He is cruel like the early Chaplin had been, careless and unthinkingly brutish in films like *The Lucky Dog* (1919). Hardy actually appeared in *The Lucky Dog*, too, as the goon who holds up Laurel, but their joint presence onscreen cast no particular glow, and was buried in the avalanche of shorts featuring either Laurel or Hardy, but never both. Hal Roach, who employed them both, tried practically every permutation when casting his films, but Laurel and Hardy remained resolutely separate—almost perversely so, as when they were later both featured in *Sailors Beware* (1927) without appearing in any scenes together. (Laurel even directed Hardy in 1925's *Yes, Yes, Nanette*—a film he did not appear in himself.)

Laurel moved on in 1919, and was replaced by—wouldn't you just guess it?—Oliver Hardy. Hardy was Semon's official second banana in films like *The Bell Hop* (1921) and *The Sawmill* (1921). Billed as Babe Hardy, he was a simple man playing a simple role, his main task never to tread on his leading man's aura.

Laurel was only marginally better off. Starring in his own solo shorts, he became known for a series of broad parodies of then-familiar hits. In *Mud and Sand* (1922), Laurel is Spanish matador and all-purpose twit Rhubarb Vaselino, sleepwalking through a farcical inversion of the hit Rudolph Valentino film *Blood and Sand*. Laurel was a poor man's Chaplin, aping the great man's physical eccentricities in films like *Mandarin Mix-Up* (1924) and *Detained* (1924), without summoning any measure of his grace or nobility.

It is not until 1927, with *Duck Soup* (not to be confused with the Marx Brothers classic of the same name), that Stan and Ollie finally arrive at the beginning of their journey. Laurel was thirty-seven and Hardy thirty-five, and both had labored in Hollywood for over a decade, with only minor success. From the very first moment they are thrown together, there is something charged in the air, as if two powerful but unstable elements had unexpectedly set off a chain reaction. Laurel, the comic inventor, plays second fiddle to everybody's favorite sidekick, Hardy, and contrary to all expectations, the formula clicks. Laurel and Hardy discover an empty mansion, and pose as master and maid, in order to rent it out to a pair of stuffy Brits. Hardy is the man of the house, his smoking jacket and sleeping cap suggesting an unshaven fairy, and Laurel is saucy and impudent, a man doing a pitch-perfect impression of a flirty parlor maid.

We may be able to feel the electricity, but their boss did not—at least not at first. Roach kept them apart for another handful of films, but starting with *Do Detectives Think?* and *Putting Pants on Philip* (both 1927), Laurel and Hardy were a permanent team. (Hardy would act in a small handful of films without Laurel later in his career, but Laurel would never appear again without his partner). Traces remain of the caddish, Tramp-like Stan, but collaboration makes for something greater, and something stranger, than either had been able to accomplish alone. There is something of Keaton in Laurel's newly stoic expression and perpetual air of puzzled curiosity, as if this were an alien planet whose ways were unfamiliar to him.

During their long partnership, Stan—who wrote many of their gags, sweating over new scripts while Hardy entertained himself on the golf course—was often frustrated by an uncomprehending world that laureled Hardy, insisting that all the inspiration had been his alone. But Laurel required Hardy—his hail-fellow-well-met charm, his rotund good humor, and his gift for physical comedy. Stan Laurel helped to create Oliver Hardy because he needed him—because he could do the things a Laurel could not. Laurel and Hardy made for a great comic partnership, but in some elemental sense, they are merely two sides of the same creator.

From the outset, Stan and Ollie are more like life partners than friends. Joint operators of a private-detective agency in *Do Detectives Think?*, they also share a room—and a bed. There is no doubt, however, who is in charge; Laurel may have been the genius of the pair, but onscreen, he takes a back seat to Hardy, preferring to be guided rather than to guide. (How different that made Laurel from his silent predecessors, who tended to accentuate their genius by surrounding themselves with a cast of cardboard cutouts.) Laurel and Hardy are both childlike, but it is Stan who is the infant of the pair, regularly bursting into tears when faced with unexpected obstacles.

The anarchic good cheer of *Putting Pants on Philip* is instantly recognizable as Laurel & Hardy's preferred mode; after only a short time together, they have settled on a deceptively simple style of juvenile aggression. Stan is Ollie's Scottish nephew, visiting America. Unfamiliar with native ways, he wears a kilt while chasing the ladies, which causes unforeseen complications. A powerful sneeze causes Stan to lose his drawers, leading to the moment when he stands over a sidewalk grate, enjoying the breeze, anticipating Marilyn Monroe's impromptu show in *The Seven Year Itch*. As funny as this all is, the more intriguing component of *Philip* is Uncle Oliver's attempt to clothe his nephew in trousers. A tailor attempts to take the measure of his inseam, and Stan panics, tearing down the shop's drapes and dashing down the street. What, exactly, is he worried might happen?

This, then, might be the ideal moment to delve into the thorniest issue in the field of Laurel & Hardy studies: what to make of the relationship between Stan and Ollie? Stan enjoys dressing up in women's clothing, favors a good cry, and is often found in the kitchen; Ollie wears a mustache, regularly boils over with rage at Stan's clumsy excesses, and prefers shouting to all other forms of emotion. Laurel and Hardy are found—not once, but time and again—sharing the same bed, enclosed in cramped spaces, attempting to change clothes in unison, or caring for a helpless creature: a baby, or a pet. In *Liberty* (1929), they struggle to swap pants on the street, and get caught by passersby in a variety of compromising positions. In the astounding *They Go Boom!* (1929), they are asleep in their joint bed, their domestic bliss interrupted by a series of rackety disruptions. Stan opens his shirt to nurse a foundling in *Their First Mistake* (1932), a bottle strapped to his chest in motherly imitation.

Should we assume that Laurel and Hardy were—dare we say it?—gay? The suggestion is written into the films themselves—*Liberty* is about gay panic, if nothing else—but the duo elides so blunt a classification. They are less homosexual than pre-sexual, overgrown children aware of sex but unfamiliar with its particulars. Even marriage is not enough to sway them from their innocence; their wives, shrews one and all, are more like the perpetually agitated mothers of wayward toddlers than sexual beings. One can no more picture Stan or Ollie having sex than fellow silent comedian Harry Langdon, once known as Baby; their world precludes such base desires.

If there is a desire that truly motivates Laurel and Hardy, it is revenge. Action must be followed by reaction, and punishment meted out, equitably and forcefully. Revenge, and its inevitable devolution into chaos, is essential to the appeal of silent shorts like *Battle of the Century* (1927), *The Finishing*

Touch (1928), and the epochal *Big Business* (1929). What is unique to the slapstick menace of Laurel & Hardy is their circumspection. They watch, impassively, as their bodies are mangled, and possessions trampled, patiently awaiting the moment when they can wreak their own vengeance in response. Hardy stays calm as he is clobbered by a pie in *Battle of the Century*, and betrays no anger when an angry Christmas-tree customer wrecks his car in *Big Business*. The humor stems not so much from the action as their reactions; we watch Stan and Ollie dispassionately biding their time for the next attack, and chuckle at their Zen-like dedication to destruction.

Chaos spreads like an oil slick, polluting the atmosphere everywhere Laurel and Hardy go. Pies end up everywhere in *Battle of the Century*: on Ollie's face, the mayor's shoes, down a manhole, inside the mouth of a dental patient. (A pretty young woman even slips on one, and gingerly walks away, her splay-legged shuffle like an impromptu audition for a Chaplin-imitator contest.) In *You're Darn Tootin'* (1928), Stan and Ollie's squabbling sets off an orgy of uncontrollable pants-ripping among passersby. Laurel and Hardy stand outside the circle, watching the free-for-all with detached amusement. Their mania is contagious.

The plots of these shorts are the barest coat of logic applied to a rambling edifice of violent disarray. Laurel and Hardy are avatars of entropy, with few films documenting their delight in pandemonium better than the marvelous *Leave 'Em Laughing* (1928). Ollie takes Stan, suffering from a toothache, to a dentist. Both end up receiving extra-strength doses of laughing gas, and set off in their car, where they are reduced to helpless laughter at each fender bender and traffic tie-up. *Leave 'Em Laughing* explicitly states what their other films only imply: that nothing pleases Laurel and Hardy quite so much as leaving a giant mess in their wake. Laurel, the fop no longer, has become an idiot-sprite, and Hardy his minder, cursed to eternity with enduring his pal's mindless lapses. Stan's eternal stupidity and Ollie's bumbling are perfectly matched, the one enabling the other.

The later silent shorts move beyond Keystone-style pandemonium, adopting a homegrown surrealism that showed they had been influenced by the work of Luis Buñuel and Salvador Dalí—or was it the other way around? In *Wrong Again* (1929)—the title already hinting at the general direction of the plot—racetrack trainers Stan and Ollie confuse a horse from their stable named Blue Boy with the Thomas Gainsborough painting of the same name. Hearing that a wealthy gentleman has been offering a sizable reward for the return of his "Blue Boy," they drag their recalcitrant horse to the man's house.

Buñuel and Dalí had surreally juxtaposed a cow and a piano; Laurel and Hardy, with the assistance of director Leo McCarey (the best of their collaborators), stick a horse atop a piano.

The setup of *Big Business* (1929), the unquestioned masterpiece of Laurel & Hardy's silent period, and quite possibly the best film they ever made, is similarly brilliant in its simplicity: Laurel and Hardy are door-to-door Christmas-tree salesmen in southern California. They clash with surly homeowner (and regular foil) James Finlayson, who takes umbrage at their aggressive sales technique. He clips their tree apart with pliers, and in response, Stan carves off slices of his front door like a Christmas ham. *Big Business* is a faultless marvel of one-upsmanship, with Stan and Ollie taking out their frustration on Finlayson's house as he methodically vandalizes their car (doesn't quite seem like a fair trade, does it?). Laurel and Hardy remove their coats and commence wrecking, tossing furniture out the window, and using a shovel to smash vases like so many softballs. Finlayson, meanwhile, yanks out their steering wheel, and rips out the front headlights before using them as projectiles to smash the windshield. All the while, a police officer watches, licking his pencil as he prepares the epic ticket to end all tickets.

Chaplin elided it, Keaton was broken by it, and Lloyd was scarred by it, but the arrival of sound hardly impeded Laurel and Hardy. Having only just begun to truly introduce themselves to audiences, Laurel and Hardy were better equipped to adapt to the new demands of sound. The truth is that not much adjustment was required. Stan and Ollie simply kept on doing what they had been doing—in some cases, quite literally, as many of their silent-era plots were reworked for sound. Dialogue actually helped Laurel and Hardy to clarify their roles—Stan the Cockney bungler and strangler of language, and Hardy the Southern gentleman, his "gaucherie," according to biographer Simon Louvish, "clad in a repertoire of cautious smiles and finger twiddles."

Sound allowed them to revisit many of the themes of their silent two-reelers, confident that the addition of dialogue, and the short memories of fans, would make for a smooth transition. *Hog Wild* (1930) is a revamped version of *The Finishing Touch*, and *Berth Marks* (1929) a revival of *You're Darn Tootin*'s pants-ripping mania. Laurel and Hardy were never slowed down by sound, like Keaton and Lloyd were, incorporating it seamlessly into their arsenal of idiocy. It was only when pressure from their fellow comedians, and a changing film industry, pushed them into feature-length films that Stan and Ollie faltered. One wishes, instead, that the shorts could have gone on forever.

Retreads they may be, but early sound efforts like *Angora Love* (1929), *Bacon Grabbers* (1929), and *They Go Boom!* (1929) are among the finest examples of Laurel and Hardy's quirky wit. There is a faint aura of the adult slumber party to these films. Laurel and Hardy are rowdy little boys sharing a bedroom, playing with their pet goats (in *Angora Love*), or squabbling over Ollie's uncontrollable sneezing. Their landlord, in the guise of an angry father, must come in and mete out discipline. Even when alone, as in the train picture *Berth Marks* (1929), they are like two petulant kids trapped in a cramped space, bickering over their mutually frustrated attempts to undress for bed. *Brats* (1930), where Laurel and Hardy play both themselves and their own children, only literalizes their metaphorically childish ungovernability.

Theirs is a cinema of eternal recurrence: the same scenarios, the same altercations, the same conundrums repeat with dependable regularity. The cop, the landlord, the shrewish wife—they all stand unblinking watch, forever present to police the misbehaving boys. The point has been made before, by Louvish and others, but the bare simplicity of their comedy makes Laurel and Hardy slapstick Beckett characters, Vladimir and Estragon played for laughs. They are Beckett's prisoners of fate stripped of the existential anguish.

All of which leads, in roundabout fashion, to *The Music Box* (1932), the *Big Business* of their sound shorts. Stan and Ollie are movers lugging a heavy piano up an enormous flight of steps leading from the street. They are continuously interrupted by a series of immovable obstacles—a nursemaid with a baby carriage, a skeptical police officer, an imperious European professor insulted by their brash American impudence. Like Sisyphus with his stone, Laurel and Hardy watch helplessly as the piano repeatedly goes lumbering down the steps, all their efforts for naught. *Big Business* had been about destruction; *The Music Box* similarly fetes frustration, with the foiling of Laurel and Hardy's plans elevated to an eternal principle. In its second half, *Music Box* echoes *Big Business*'s furious roundelay of carnage. Stan and Ollie become a two-man wrecking crew laying waste to the house of Billy Gilbert's snooty academic. Resistance was futile; the second law of thermodynamics stipulated that, just as Laurel and Hardy had always suspected, entropy was always on the increase in the world.

Laurel and Hardy had experimented with the feature form as early as 1931, with *Pardon Us* the first of their longer films. But the transition was gradual (their last short, *Thicker Than Water*, was made in 1935), and the two-reeler, of which they had demonstrated so thorough a mastery, still beckoned. The violent spats with dyspeptic Charlie Hall in *Them Thar Hills* (1934) and *Tit for Tat* (1935) are distilled Laurel & Hardy, adapting *Big Business*'s eye-for-an-eye ethos. They are among the most tightly plotted of their films, and also the loosest; with story a mere afterthought (even more than usual!), these films dedicate themselves wholeheartedly to the joys of destruction.

In *Them Thar Hills*, the healthful mountain water the boys guzzle thirstily turns out to be moonshine. Out of their minds on mountain water, an encounter with Hall's angry vacationer turns into a brutal melee. They cut off a hank of his hair and glue it to his chin with molasses, then, for the pièce de résistance, tar and feather him.

Ollie nods his head forcefully, pleased to see that justice has, for once, been meted out. *Tit for Tat*, a sequel of sorts to *Hills*, has Laurel and Hardy distracted from opening their new store by a tête-à-tête with their next-door neighbor (Hall again). Stan and Ollie win the match by not only exceeding their opponent's vigor, but by eclipsing him in pugnacious creativity. While Hall burns Ollie's nose with hot pincers, and grinds a tray of pocket watches into a mechanical milkshake, they drench him in whitish goo, slather him with lard, and fill his cash register with honey. Oh—and meanwhile, all of Stan and Ollie's new merchandise is stolen by a crafty thief. Who cares, though, when revenge is served?

Features were the future, and Laurel and Hardy dutifully switched over to making sixty- or seventy-minute films rather than the twenty-minute shorts they had perfected. The longer format was hardly ideal for them. There was never quite enough plot to go around, and Stan and Ollie, so charming in smaller doses, grew wearisome when their visits lasted longer than an hour. Padding, never before a problem, became an issue for Laurel and Hardy's features. Part of the difficulty lay with Roach, who insisted on plugging Stan and Ollie into whimsical genre pictures like *The Devil's Brother (Fra Diavolo)* (1933) and *Babes in Toyland* (1934), surrounded, in Marx Brothers-at-MGM-style, by dashing romantic heroes and trilling singers.

Laurel and Hardy were far better when they were left to their own devices. *Sons of the Desert* (1933), the best of their features, tinkered only slightly with their evergreen formula. Stan and Ollie are living in adjoining Southern California homes, each tyrannized by their shrewish wives. (Ollie must ask his wife's permission for Stan to even set foot in their house.) Stan is, to be fair, a dreadful nuisance, unmasking himself early on as the culprit who has been eating their wax fruit. Laurel is masterful in this scene; each bite is a new, unpleasant adventure, punctuated by a dry, labored swallow, but Stan brooks no thought of quitting with only half-a-bellyful of wax. Laurel has, if anything, grown yet more muddle-headed with the passage of time. Stan's signature gesture, agitatedly fluffing his thatch of hair, is an expression of his eternal confusion. His stupidity has been elevated to an organizing principle.

Laurel and Hardy collude in the hopes of escaping their wives and attending the annual convention of the Sons of the Desert. Ollie fakes an illness, and recruits Stan for the prescribed ocean journey. We enjoy Stan and Ollie's childish pleasure in their deception, skipping the cruise and heading to the convention instead. Our mirth increases exponentially when it is revealed that the voyage they were supposed to be taking has met a tragic end, the ocean liner sinking with nearly all passengers aboard. *Sons of the Desert* ends with Laurel & Hardy's trademark complaint—"Another fine mess you've gotten us into!"—and Stan and Ollie are forced to return with their tails firmly tucked between their legs. Stan tells the truth about their deception, and is rewarded; Ollie stubbornly insists on sticking to his foolish story about "ship-hiking" home, and is pelted with a complete set of dishes as a reward.

Way Out West (1937), the only other Laurel & Hardy feature to live up to the promise of their shorts, is even looser and woollier than *Sons of the Desert*. The Western lampoon has a delicacy at odds with its violent slapstick. Stan and Ollie find the time to sing together: a rare moment of amity in their frequently disputatious world. Stan shows off an unexpectedly deep baritone during their duet "The Trail of the Lonesome Pine"—at least until Ollie clubs him with a mallet, at which point he turns into a fluting soprano.

The boys are on a mission to deliver the deed to a gold mine to its rightful owner. Along the way, they become embroiled with a pair of unadulterated Western stereotypes—a crooked saloon owner named Mickey Finn (Finlayson) and his scheming girlfriend. The boys are children let loose in the Wild West, blissfully unaware of their surroundings, consumed as they are by their own childish preoccupations.

Chaplin had turned his shoe into food in *The Gold Rush*; Laurel turns food into an essential part of his footwear. "I can't eat that meat," a saloon customer shouts. "It's as tough as shoe leather." Stan's ears perk up, and he pounds the hunk of beef against the counter to test it out before slipping it into the hole in his sole. *Way Out West* ends, as you'd suspect, with a knockdown, drag-out fight that is nonetheless a model of decorum when compared to the fisticuffs of *Big Business* and *Tit for Tat*. At the film's conclusion, Stan and Ollie are riding along once more, bonding over their shared Southern heritage—Ollie from Georgia, Stan from the South of London—and harmonizing once more. The moment is as near to sublimity as Laurel and Hardy would ever get, a song on their lips, and a melody in their hearts as they continue on their merry way.

Oh, that the air of merry abandon would have lingered a bit longer! *Way Out West* is not quite the apex of Laurel and Hardy's hilarity, but watching the increasingly belabored attempts at humor in their later work is a dispiriting enterprise. Paradoxically, just as they were losing their grip on their own work, in the mid-1930s, Laurel and Hardy's popularity was growing once more. Many of the rough edges had been sanded away, making Stan and Ollie a kid-friendly institution. As it turned out, however, it was precisely those rough edges that had given Laurel and Hardy their remarkable durability. Without them, they became just childish rather than charmingly scattered.

Not all the films are terrible; *Block-Heads* (1938), which builds on the silent *Should Married Men Go Home?* (1928), is actually half of a great one, before petering out in a loud, angry fizzle of a conclusion. Stan is the last soldier standing from the First World War, still in the trenches two decades after the war's end. Dedicated old friend Ollie, convinced that Stan is an amputee, carries him everywhere on his return home before discovering the truth: "Why didn't you tell me you had two legs?" Stan responds, truthfully: "You didn't ask me." James Agee raved about the surrealist brilliance of Stan and Ollie being confronted by a lumbering gorilla while lugging a piano across a suspension bridge in *Swiss Miss* (1938), but neglected to mention that the rest of the film was hardly the equal of its brief moment of inspiration.

Roach briefly fired Laurel in 1939, tired of his contract demands. Laurel was replaced by onetime silent star Harry Langdon (who also cowrote *Block-Heads*), but the lone Langdon & Hardy picture was a flop, and Laurel was soon back in his place. Laurel & Hardy moved to Fox, where they worked with second-rate technicians on third-rate stories. They imported other fading stars for assistance—Marx Brothers foil Margaret Dumont for *The Dancing Masters* (1943), Buster Keaton as a gag-writer for *Nothing but Trouble* (1944)—but their efforts were mostly for naught. The magic of Laurel and Hardy was to be found in Stan and Ollie themselves, and no one else. When it ran out, no amount of studio-supplied grease could get the machine running again.

In 1939's *The Flying Deuces*, Ollie, jilted by a woman, contemplates suicide. Stan, distraught at the notion of life without his bosom friend, agrees to kill himself, too. Ollie expects nothing less, for what sort of tenuous, half-cocked friendship extends no further than the grave? As it turned out, Stan and Ollie did not commit suicide in *The Flying Deuces*, or in any of their other films. Our relief at their continued well-being is only matched by our having escaped the fraught issue of just what the afterlife might have looked like for Laurel and Hardy. How could it be anything more than what they already had? Given that their final film was *Utopia* (1951), I propose that we envision eternity, for them, as being granted the privilege of never having to say good-bye. For Stan and Ollie, being together was like heaven.

As I noted earlier, after their first film together as a team, Stan Laurel never again acted without Oliver Hardy. This is, literally speaking, the truth, but the ghost of Laurel (still very much alive) is nonetheless present in Jerry Lewis's *The Bellboy* (1960). Lewis's Stanley (note the shared first name) runs into the not-quite Stan (actually played by the film's cowriter, Bill Richmond) in the lobby of his hotel. The two men—one a young Turk of postwar American comedy, the other an unquestioned titan of the form—keep turning and facing each other, an unspoken word hanging in their air. Laurel smiles, searching his pockets, then shakes his head, as if whatever he had in mind was no longer feasible. Stanley shakes his head too, and Laurel heads for the door. Lewis summons Laurel in order for him to pass the torch to the next generation of comedians. His exit is a final bow for the golden age of comedy, which Lewis was in the process of revamping for a new generation. Stan bows, and an entire era makes its final farewell.

5

THE MARX BROTHERS

BROTHERS OF ANARCHY

"Well, that covers a lot of ground. Say, you cover a lot of ground your-self. You better beat it—I hear they're going to tear you down and put up an office building where you're standing. You can leave in a taxi. If you can't get a taxi, you can leave in a huff. If that's too soon, you can leave in a minute and a huff. You know, you haven't stopped talking since I came here? You must have been vaccinated with a phonograph needle."
—Groucho Marx, *Duck Soup*

The silent comedy had come and gone, far quicker than its adepts might have expected. The movies had grown talkative, and comedy, too,

From left: Zeppo, Chico, Groucho, and Harpo prepare for attack in *Duck Soup*.

would have to learn how to speak. Enter, from stage left, heralded by angelic choirs and a lone harp, three brothers, late of New York's Lower East Side and the illegitimate theater, named Julius, Leonard, and Adolph Marx. The movies wanted sound? Well, they would get more than they would know what to do with.

These Brothers Marx were less communists than anarchists, wreckers taking a hammer to a world of privilege that excluded them. If all comedy is devoted to the destruction of property and propriety, the Marx Brothers are its Stakhanovite champions, dedicated unstintingly to the cause of undoing established orders. They embody the comedy of the foreigner—the immigrant—putting one over on the well-heeled natives.

In thirteen features spanning two decades, Groucho, Chico, and Harpo—as Julius, Leonard, and Adolph would dub themselves—would remain surprisingly consistent. Groucho was the comically inappropriate public figure—Professor Quincy Adams Wagstaff in *Horse Feathers*, Captain Spaulding the African explorer in *Animal Crackers*, President Rufus T. Firefly in *Duck Soup*—with the silver tongue, stringing together non sequiturs into lunatic scraps of nonsensical poetry. Tie undone, hair disheveled, suit rumpled, a cigar jammed deep into the corner of his mouth, crab-walking through scenes in a simian crouch, Groucho never needed to pause for breath, or thought, before striking. Chico was the tin-eared immigrant on the make, his English as woeful as his confidence schemes were brilliant. And Harpo was a malevolent Pierrot, impish and undaunted. Childishly expressive, communicating primarily in yelps, pouts, exclamations, taunts, and smiles, he was a silent-era carryover, smuggling a tiny piece of Chaplin's artistry into the era of sound. Leaping into women's laps, handing strangers his thigh for safekeeping, swiping their silverware, and dunking his feet in their lemonade, he acted out what Groucho could only verbalize.

There are moments that we expect in every Marx Brothers film: the opening musical number, like "Whatever It Is, I'm Against It" in *Horse Feathers*; Groucho's verbal shadow-boxing with designated punching-bag Margaret Dumont; Groucho and Chico's tongue-twisting bouts of spiraling linguistic confusion; the emptying of Harpo's remarkably capacious pockets (which seemingly contain everything from an alarm clock to a fish); the harp-driven musical interlude (or as I prefer to think of them, "popcorn breaks"). It would be easy enough (though mistaken) to think of their work, from 1929's *The Cocoanuts* to 1949's *Love Happy*, as a single work, whose separation into component parts is nothing more than an optical illusion.

The Marx Brothers were expert in the overturning of established orders, not the least of which was the Hollywood studios' gentlemen's agreement that explicitly Jewish material was verboten. Eastern European Jewish immigrants with a yearning for wholesome American mores, the lords of the studios frowned upon Jewish characters, stories, and material, tainted as it was with the odor of the old country. (These were the same studios, after all, that would soon make movies about the Nazi threat that scrupulously avoided mention of the word *Jew*.) The Marxes' humor, meanwhile, positively reeked of herring and the shtetl. "All along the river, those are all levees," real-estate speculator Groucho points out to Chico in their first film together, *The Cocoanuts*. "That's the Jewish neighborhood?" Chico wonders. Groucho acknowledges as much. He is not, nor has he ever been, an all-American hero. "Well, what do you think I am, one of the early settlers?" he asks in *Animal Crackers*.

The humor—anarchic, absurdist, ebullient—was Jewish, but the characters they played were not. Of the three brothers, Groucho was the lone explicit Jew. Chico was Italian, and Harpo was vaguely Irish (that curly red wig). In *Monkey Business*, occasional fourth Marx brother Zeppo swipes Maurice Chevalier's passport, forcing each of the brothers in turn to do their best imitation of the zees-and-zoes singing voice of Ernst Lubitsch's leading man. (Harpo, in case you were wondering, does it by surreptitiously cranking a phonograph behind his back.) The Marx Brothers, and their perpetually cynical attitude toward romance, were a vigorous raspberry blown in the direction of Lubitsch's brand of sentimental romance. A troupe of Maurice Chevaliers they weren't.

Harpo scrabbles after unsuspecting women, hoping to ensnare them in his embrace. Groucho's snares, in comparison, are all verbal. He drizzles a steady trail of honey for his perpetual foil, wealthy patron Margaret Dumont, in the hopes of digging deep into her capacious purses. "Will you marry me? Did he leave you any money? Answer the second question first," Groucho demands of her in *Duck Soup*. As Groucho romances Dumont's dowagers, he maintains a steady line of side patter, intended for our ears only. It is one of the unstated rules of the Marx Brothers films, along with the guaranteed crowd-pleasing capabilities of a Harpo harp solo, that Groucho be granted the right to insult Dumont unrepentantly.

The Marx brothers were not, as it turned out, early settlers. Growing up in modest comfort on Manhattan's Upper East Side and East Harlem in the waning years of the nineteenth century, the boys were guided in the direction of the stage by their mother, Minnie Schoenberg, and their uncle, Al Shean (a vaudeville veteran). There were ample diversions along the way. Leonard was a school dropout, pool hustler, and gang hanger-on. Adolph also preferred work to the classroom, finding occasional employment as a cigarette boy and bellhop. Leonard took piano lessons (or so he claimed) from a one-handed woman, who instructed her pupil in how to coax a pleasing sound from the instrument with just the right hand.

Julius, younger than Leonard and Adolph, took to performing from the beginning, singing in a church choir for a short time before joining a vaudeville act. Soon, the Marxes formed their own singing troupe, touring such bastions of commerce as Trenton, New Jersey, and Mansfield, Ohio, first as the 3 Nightingales (Groucho and younger brother Gummo accompanied by singer Mabel O'Donnell), then the 4 Nightingales when Harpo joined. Harpo couldn't sing a lick, so his mother told him to simply keep his mouth open silently during their numbers. Between songs, the brothers would entertain audiences with a brisk line of patter.

Eventually, the Marx brothers realized that bright futures as singers were not awaiting them, and that audiences actually preferred the patter to the harmonies. Legend has it that a runaway mule, disturbing a show in Nacogdoches, Texas, gave them license to jettison the pre-packaged material and jazzily riff instead. They wrote a sketch known as "Fun in Hi Skule," in which the brothers played malaprop-prone youngsters with ethnic handles. Groucho was the latest in a long line of "German" comedians poking genial fun at the ways of Teutonic immigrants. By 1912, when oldest son Leonard/ Chico was twenty-five, the Marxes were touring the country on the prestigious Pantages theatrical circuit with their shows *Mr. Green's Reception* and *Home Again*.

World War I spelled a hasty demise for all brands of genial German comedy, so Groucho made himself over as a Yiddish-inflected comic, rebranded (more honestly) as Jewish. Soon, the Marx Brothers had ascended into the stratosphere, their shows famous for their boundless energy, verbal ingenuity, and ad-libbing ingeniousness. Harpo was drafted as an auxiliary member of the Algonquin Circle, trading bons mot with Alexander Woollcott and chauffeuring George Bernard Shaw around the French Riviera. Other than a brief detour to make a first film (1921's *Humor Risk*, now lost), the Marxes spent the 1920s touring the country with a series of plays that were all only variations on a theme. The brothers' shows incorporated musical comedy, verbal humor, and slapstick—every kind of laugh, for every kind of audience. Hollywood was soon to come calling.

The Marxes' first sound film, *The Cocoanuts*, is a filmed version of one of their plays, and is paced and staged as one. There are brilliant moments, but they are mostly the ones impermeable to damage of any kind. "I kill *you* for money," Chico tells his crony Harpo, demonstrating his financial desperation, before patting him on the back, and laughing. "Ah, no, you my friend. I kill you for nothing." Groucho's spiels mingle the flowery and the mundane, their comic force stemming from the unlikely cohesion of their mismatched parts. One can see where future Jewish comics, and Woody Allen in particular, got their inspiration from Groucho's sallies. "Your eyes! Your eyes!" he tells Dumont at a romantic moment. "They shine like the pants of a blue serge suit." Groucho later regales an audience with the tale of his childhood home. "And it was in that little house that Abraham Lincoln was born—much to my father's surprise."

The Cocoanuts is raucous, chaotic—and too slow. Groucho speaks with deliberate slowness, dragging his feet in the hopes that the audience will keep up. Directed by the lead-footed Robert Florey and Joseph Santley, *The Cocoanuts* undercuts its occasional glimpses of brilliance with inept staging. The Marx Brothers had always given the impression of inventing their routines on the spot, but the truth was that every line had been carefully polished in advance, tested on the stage before being preserved for posterity. The Marxes were using material that they had perfected in front of hundreds of audiences in dozens of cities, and the wear and tear was evident. It is also worth remembering their ages: Chico was forty-two, Harpo forty-one, and Groucho thirty-nine. Their youths had gone unrecorded. They had spent more than half their lives onstage, and the adjustment to filmmaking was a complex one.

They would not make the same mistake twice. Their next effort, *Animal Crackers* (1930), is infinitely faster than its predecessor. There is more dialogue in its first fifteen minutes than most entire films, and the jokes arrive without letup for every one of its 97 minutes. Groucho is the intrepid Captain Spaulding, feted in song: "Hooray for Captain Spaulding, the African explorer!" "Did someone call me *schnorrer*?" Groucho interjects, reminding audiences (in case they had forgotten) that the only jungles he had ever explored had been those within walking distance of Delancey Street. "All the jokes can't be good," Groucho warns us after a clunker. "You've got to expect that once in a while."

The truth is that *Animal Crackers* has vanishingly few failed riffs. Pens run dry of their ink and pencils shrink to nubs in the attempt to jot down every brilliant witticism in Morrie Ryskind's literate, lightning-speed script.

Chico, as itinerant musician Signor Ravelli, informs Groucho that he charges ten dollars per hour for playing, twelve dollars an hour for not playing, and fifteen dollars an hour for rehearsing. "What do you get for not rehearsing?" Groucho wonders.

"You couldn't afford it. . . ."

"How much would you want to run into an open manhole?"

"Just the cover charge."

"Well, drop in some time."

"Sewer."

The relatively rigorous narrative logic of *The Cocoanuts* has evaporated. Groucho begins *Animal Crackers* as an explorer, and ends it as a private eye. We already know Groucho is a fraud, and his brothers are chiselers and crooks. Who needs to know more?

Monkey Business (1931) is nothing less than breathtaking. The Marxes are stowaways aboard an ocean liner, drafted into a war between dueling gang bosses. The plot, needless to say, is beside the point; whole scenes are devised as elaborate setups for verbal or physical payoffs. Groucho is maniacal, a whirling dervish of Dadaist wordplay. "You know who sneaked into my stateroom at three o'clock this morning?" he asks a ship steward. "Nobody! And that's my complaint. I'm young—I want gaiety, laughter, ha cha cha." Later, he tells an object of his lust to ditch her marriage: "You take the children, your husband takes the house. Junior burns down the house, you take the insurance, and I take *you*." Groucho's brilliance stems from the head-scratching quality of his nonsense haikus, which never end up precisely where they had begun. At times, Groucho appears to be channeling another film entirely—one only he has the script for. "Come Kapellmeister, let the violas throb!" he shouts at no one in particular, appealing to his girlfriend for a lone night of passion. "My regiment leaves at dawn." Often, his warped mantras screech to a halt before they've even started, making perfect sense only until their meaning sinks in. "How many Frenchmen can't be wrong?" is a question that only works in Marx-world.

"Is this stuff on the level, or are you just making it up as you go along?" Groucho wondered in their next film, *Horse Feathers* (1932). They were, indeed, mostly making it up—or at least it felt as if they were. Groucho was president of a football-mad college, but the film was mostly Harpo's. His pockets, stuffed with hot cups of coffee, fish, and candles magically burning at both ends, were never more capacious, his whimsy never more charming. "Oh, Professor, you're full of whimsy," a coed coos to Groucho, and he apologizes. "Can you notice it from there? I'm always that way after I eat radishes." The password here is *swordfish*, and it provides entrance to a gleefully demented madhouse dominated by Groucho's flights of verbal fancy, and Harpo's willful confusion.

For the climactic football game—you knew there was going to be one, right?—Harpo rides a garbage cart onto the field like a Roman chariot. He pauses during a touchdown run to grab a hot dog from a vendor, and uses banana peels to scatter the defenders in his way. Chico, meanwhile, plays without removing his trademark dented fedora, and Groucho dashes onto the field to execute a crushing tackle on a runner: "That'll teach him to pass a lady without tipping his hat."

Too quick for their dim-witted persecutors, the Marxes had unleashed a barely controlled chaos over the course of four films. They had yet to meet a foil agile enough to parry with them, or a director able to corral their energy. Leo McCarey and *Duck Soup* would change all that. It is the Marx Brothers' masterpiece, and one of the small handful of undying works of comic genius produced by the American cinema. It channels their peculiar genius and mobilizes it for prescient, biting satire. Battling paper tigers no longer, *Duck Soup* finds the Marx Brothers unleashing the dogs of war.

McCarey, working from a script by Bert Kalmar and Harry Ruby, wrestles the Marxes into an actual scenario, with a distinct beginning, middle, and end. Groucho is Rufus T. Firefly, the "progressive, fearless fighter" the country of Freedonia breathlessly awaits. Margaret Dumont is Mrs. Teasdale, the country's grande dame, sure that Rufus T. Firefly is the man to solve her country's ills. (By the way, why does no one ever think to question Dumont's sanity? In film after film, she is convinced that the solution to all her problems lies in bringing in Groucho Marx to take care of everything.) Groucho parries with Mrs. Teasdale, asking after her husband.

"He's dead."

"I'll bet he's just using that as an excuse. . . ."

"I held him in my arms and kissed him."

"Oh, I see. Then it was murder!"

Once in office, Groucho demonstrates his usual perspicacity. "Clear?" he rumbles at an underling. "Why a four-year-old child could understand this report. Run out and find me a four-year-old child. I can't make head or tail of it." Eventually, Chico and Harpo come to work for President Firefly. Groucho conducts a rigorous job interview. "Now what is it that has four pair of pants," he quizzes them, "lives in Philadelphia, and it never rains but it pours?"

The mind boggles at the sheer genius of the man who came up with that line, as it does with one of the most beloved Marx sequences of all. Firefly is summoned to Mrs. Teasdale's room in his pajamas to take back some secret plans for war. Chico and Harpo follow closely behind, dressed in matching white nightcaps and pajamas, hoping to pass themselves off as Firefly and intercept the plans. There is a classic round-robin chase around Mrs. Teasdale's room, with Chico and Harpo doing their utmost to pass themselves off as the president. Soon enough, Harpo, having accidentally smashed a full-length mirror, must pose as Groucho's shadow.

Groucho, suspecting something is afoot, scrutinizes his mirror image before putting it to a series of tests. He crouches on the floor, he skips, he pogos, he does a series of Russian leg-kicks, he jitterbugs, he hallelujahs, his arms raised in praise to heaven. The magic is in the sheer creativity of Groucho's experiments, and the miraculous dexterity of Harpo's responses. Groucho pulls out a white hat from behind his back, and Harpo, who has a black hat similarly posed behind his back, emerges with a white one as well. Providing the topper to the topper, Chico belatedly arrives, and three Grouchos momentarily confront each other.

Duck Soup is an ordinarily extraordinary Marx Brothers effort until approximately halfway through, when something unusual happens. Groucho, having slapped a foreign ambassador for his impudence, has declared war, and is unwilling to consider peaceful alternatives: "It's too late. I've already paid a month's rent on the battlefield." From here to its conclusion, slapstick yields the stage to Brecht. Chico is on trial for his life for treason ("Sure, I sold the code—and two pairs of plans," he remarks in typical Chico fashion, before turning to Groucho and asking, "That's some joke, eh, boss?") and Groucho is his prosecutor.

The Marxes' brand of illogic shakes hands with the avant-garde, turning a hectic farce into a savage indictment of warfare. *Duck Soup* turns war into a theatrical spectacle, conveyed in a series of military-themed tableaux. In a sequence of rapid-fire sketches, Groucho ventures through American military history, fighting the First World War (he asks for shoulder-high trenches: "get 'em this high, and our soldiers won't need any pants") and the Civil War, where he adds a Stetson hat and a broad southern drawl to his repertoire. At the conclusion of the film, Groucho and his brothers find themselves trapped in a crumbling house in the Freedonian countryside, bombed and under siege. Is what we are watching still a comedy? "Send help at once," Groucho broadcasts over the radio. "If you can't send help, send two more women." I suppose it is, but *Duck Soup*'s scabrous denunciation of war's eternal pointlessness—change the costumes, but everything else stays the same—is unstinting, and prescient.

A Night at the Opera (1935), the Marx Brothers' first film for MGM, is a confusing masterpiece, marking both the apotheosis of their house style, and the beginning of their decline. MGM boss Louis B. Mayer had actually objected to production supervisor Irving Thalberg's acquisition of the Marx Brothers, seeing their humor as too Jewish for mass consumption. If *Duck Soup* had brilliantly tinkered with audience expectations, the MGM films began to tamper with Marx magic. The onetime anarchists were declawed, rendered polite comic relief for bland lovers. Director Sam Wood and screenwriters George S. Kaufman and Morrie Ryskind (with an uncredited assist from then-MGM gag writer Buster Keaton) craft some of the Marx Brothers' most memorable moments, but they also (under pressure from the studio) fundamentally misunderstand the nature of their appeal.

With all that noted, and with the unnecessary bloat of MGM's "classy" Marx films suitably deplored, *A Night at the Opera* is still one of the Marx Brothers' gems—mysteriously so. The plot, revolving around lovebird opera singers, and the machinations required to wangle a chance at stardom, is eminently forgettable, but the film could care less for plot. It is a double-time greatest-hits performance, revisiting the Marxes' favorite routines and setups for one last dazzling run-through.

Groucho and Chico haggle over a singer's contract, objecting to the party of the first part and the party of the second part, alternately tearing out sections until neither is sure what remains. "Now what do we got left?" Chico wonders. "Well, I got about a foot and a half," responds Groucho. Harpo, called upon at the last minute to deliver a speech, delays the inevitable by guzzling glass upon glass of water: "We're alright as long as the water supply holds out," Groucho cracks.

The astonishing middle section of the film is like an extended retake of *Monkey Business*'s shipboard antics. Chico and Harpo stow away in Groucho's postage-stamp-sized room, signaling their meal preferences via horn. "It's either foggy out," Groucho tells a steward, "or make that twelve more hard-boiled eggs."

This rollicking interlude transitions smoothly into the most legendary of all Marx Brothers sequences: the stateroom scene. Groucho, Chico, and Harpo are crammed into a tiny room already dominated by Groucho's enormous trunk ("Wouldn't it be simpler if you just put the stateroom in the trunk?" he

asks a steward). They are soon joined by a maid to make up the bed, a mani-
curist, a woman in search of her aunt, and a janitor. The somnolent Chico
paws at each new entrant, prompting Groucho to note admiringly that "he
does better asleep than I do awake."

Groucho welcomes the arrival of chaos, only truly in his element when in
its midst. A woman pops her head in the door: "Did you want a manicure?"
Groucho demurs: "No, come on in." The stateroom scene, like the similarly
celebrated mirror scene in *Duck Soup*, succeeds by virtue of its can-you-
top-this? daring. The joke builds and builds, adding new layers with each
entrance, and each addition.

A Day at the Races (1937) is the last Marx Brothers film to contain flashes
of genius. Soon enough, terminal velocity would kick in, and the Marx Brothers would slog on, mere shadows of their former selves. Weighed down as the
film is by racially dubious cliches and an overabundance of trilling operatic
numbers, there is less room for the Marxes to do what they did best. The
illogic that had once been so thrilling has now been replaced by a stultifying
literal-mindedness. We've always known Groucho was a fraud, but it is only
now that the deception must be carefully explained: Groucho is a horse doctor, not an MD. Hijinks ensue.

The only scene that ascends to the level of Marx mythology is an encounter between Groucho and Chico at the racetrack. Chico is an ice-cream vendor peddling hot tips for the fourth race, and Groucho his designated sucker.
Groucho must buy more and more books to decipher his encoded tip, and
Chico keeps pulling out new, absolutely essential volumes from his depthless
cart. "All I wanted was a horse, not a public library," Groucho complains. He
winds up with books jammed under his arms and between his legs, with more
yet to come: "Nine more? Say, you don't handle any bookcases there, do you?"

There are a handful of splendid moments in *A Day at the Races*: Groucho's
malicious, ceaseless repetition of the phrase *thank you* ("thank yew"); Groucho
taking Harpo's pulse ("Either he's dead, or my watch is stopped"); his warning to Harpo, who is snacking on a mercury thermometer and searching for
something to wash it down with: "Hey don't drink that poison! That's four dollars an ounce!" If only there were more such moments. Instead, *A Day at the
Races* puzzlingly transforms itself into a minstrel musical, with the brothers
blacking up with axle grease and leading a crowd of stereotypical happy darkies in a shuffle-step. Not even taking into account the shameful racial politics
of this sequence, this is shopworn material of the kind that the older, ruder
Marx Brothers would have gleefully demolished. Here they lead the parade.

The films after *A Day at the Races* mark a painful diminution in the comedians' once-considerable powers, and MGM was mostly to blame. The studio violated the unstated first principles of the Marx Brothers' world, transforming Groucho into a lummox, and his brothers into numbskulls. They would increasingly be shoved to the margins in their own films, fighting for screen time with inept singers, crude racial bromides, and utterly pointless plots.

Harpo and Chico suffer the worst indignities. The pair had been twin masters of duplicitous scheming and linguistic confusion, but *A Night at the Opera* begins the process of transforming them into heartwarming, well-meaning kooks. The balance of power between the brothers had always depended on Groucho's fear of Chico and Harpo's unpredictable antics. He knew that no matter what cushy gig he may have landed, they would show up and spoil it. "You don't have to send for them," he notes in *A Day at the Races*. "You just rub a lamp and they appear." Rather than clashing, the brothers were now entertaining different audiences. Groucho was for the adults, and Chico and Harpo for the kids. Doing stupid piano tricks to the amusement of a youthful audience, they had been rendered that worst thing of all for a comedian: polite. By the time of *A Day at the Races*, Harpo was a flute-playing Pied Piper, leading the children (and the film's rancid portrayal of happy, smiling darkies) in song. There was even whimsical music as an audience prod for his brief interludes—a terrible indignity for so brilliantly inventive a physical comedian.

For devotees of the Marx Brothers, watching their later films—*Room Service* (1938), *At the Circus* (1939), *Go West* (1940), *The Big Store* (1941), and *A Night in Casablanca* (1946)—is like watching the decline of a beloved relative. The desire remains, but the energy and skill necessary to execute has permanently receded. Even the assistance of none other than Buster Keaton, hired as a gag-writer for *At the Circus*, and future Jerry Lewis director Frank Tashlin, assisting Harpo for *A Night in Casablanca*, could not save the terminally ill patient. *The Big Store* plays out like a Keystone Kops chase comedy, a quarter of a century too late and with the wrong stars. *Go West* is a pale imitation of Laurel & Hardy's enormously successful *Way Out West*, and *A Night in Casablanca* turns the Bogie-Bergman classic into a particularly by-the-numbers episode of *Scooby-Doo*.

The Marx Brothers had never been chase comedians, or parodists; their magic was found in the carefully calibrated blend of the cerebral and the physical, the endearing and the menacing. These late Marx Brothers had been neutered, stripped of their ability to do real damage. Without that threat, the comedy, too, fell away. There are isolated moments of cleverness in these movies—one thinks of the elaborate preparations of private detective Wolf J. Flywheel (Groucho) and his assistant (Harpo) to create the illusion of a busy office in *The Big Store* (1941)—but they are few and far between.

Seeing Groucho, Harpo, and Chico put through their paces in such dismal surroundings is yet further reminder that the professional lives of comedians are dismayingly short, and that the tail ends of even the greatest comedians' careers are often dismal. After making their last film together, the Marx Brothers mostly went their own ways, other than the occasional bland television appearance. Chico formed a jazz combo called Chico Marx and His Ravellies, which toured frequently throughout the 1940s. Harpo recreated the mirror scene from *Duck Soup* with Lucille Ball on the television program *I Love Lucy*, and wrote a well-received memoir called *Harpo Speaks*. Groucho had the most success, hosting the enormously successful game show *You Bet Your Life* from 1947 to 1961, first on radio and then on television. As it turns out, he never told a woman with 20 children that he loved his cigar, too, but took it out every once in a while. It makes for a great story, though, doesn't it?

6

W. C. FIELDS

THE JUGGLER

"The jockey was a very insulting fellow. He referred to my proboscis
as an adscititious excrescence. I had to tweak his nose."
—W. C. Fields, *The Bank Dick*

Forty-five. An age by which most comedians have retired, or been hustled
offstage, resigned to their easy chairs and the memories of that one special gig in Rochester. It is not, for the most part, an auspicious age for debuts.
Unless, that is, one's name is William Claude Dukenfield—better known as
W. C. Fields—and the time has finally arrived for Hollywood to catch up with

The Bank Dick on the lookout for crooks.

an ornery genius. The year is 1925, and D. W. Griffith, approaching the end of a legendary career as a director, has cast Fields in his latest film, *Sally of the Sawdust*. The story of a fairground confidence man one short step ahead of the law, whose saving grace is his boundless love for an adopted daughter, *Sally* was an adaptation of Fields's own play, *Poppy*.

Along with Chaplin, Griffith was the last of the Victorian filmmakers, his artistic and emotional sensibility formed by that bygone era's mores, and W. C. Fields, both in *Sally* and his enormously successful films of the 1930s and 1940s, was a living link with an era of American entertainment—medicine shows, Wild West extravaganzas, circuses, and minstrel shows—whose fragments, shored against the ruins, would be recycled time and again by Fields in his films. Under his guidance, half-forgotten nineteenth-century temperance dramas, the stage routines of his youth, and the rhythms of his own misbegotten home life served as the brick and mortar of his eternally fresh, unaging comedies.

Although photographs still exist, and witnesses are available to offer their testimony, it is hard to imagine W. C. Fields as a young man. In the mind's eye, he appears perpetually middle-aged, lugging a substantial spare tire around his midsection, his nose ballooned to comically exaggerated proportions by eczema and a taste for strong drink. One imagines a middle-aged baby emerging from his mother's womb, gripping a cigar between his teeth.

Fields had begun performing as a teenager, billed as a "tramp juggler" with a series of limber comic routines. Like Chaplin would later do, W.C. would come onstage dressed as a tramp, outfitted in a battered top hat and a shabby, shapeless overcoat. Part of the joke was Fields's frustration with uncooperative props. "He always talked to his 'properties,'" remembered a colleague. "He would reprimand a particular ball which had not come to his hand accurately, whip his battered silk hat for not staying on his head . . . mutter weird and unintelligible expletives to his cigar when it missed his mouth."

By twenty-three, Fields had toured the great capitals of Europe, sharing stages with Harry Houdini and the Marx Brothers. According to a 1908 article in the London *Sunday Chronicle*, Fields was "probably the most copied man on the vaudeville stage." In 1915, when he was thirty-five, he was asked to join what was then the most prestigious vaudevillian troupe in the world—producer Florenz Ziegfeld's Follies. The class of 1915 featured an exceptional array of gifted performers, among them Will Rogers, Fanny Brice, Eddie Cantor, and Bert Williams. Fields became a Ziegfeld regular, and eventually a Broadway star in his own right. Fields had arrived on vaudeville's greatest stage in time for its golden age—its last flowering before the movies and radio would kill it off for good.

It is difficult to envision a silent W. C. Fields, but that was the essence of his act for a great many years. Fields's juggling routine was wordless—in part to remain accessible to foreign audiences—and when the movies first beckoned, the silent film was still in its first flowering. The man who turned the muttered aside into an art was required to keep his mouth shut.

Fields's first, abortive sojourn in Hollywood in 1915, when he acted in two shorts for producer Mack Sennett before returning to the stage, was hampered by the very absence of what would become his most distinctive comedic trait. While Fields was a gifted physical comedian, adept with the pratfall or the magic trick, what did he do with all the excess verbal energy, the sheer torrent of wit, that are the greatest attribute of his sound-era comedies? He must have had grips and extras biting their lips until they drew blood in a desperate attempt to keep from laughing. Fields was a juggler performing with one hand tied behind his back.

In order to become W. C. Fields, technology would have to catch up with him. Late in arriving, his creative pinnacle would also be longer lasting than those of his contemporaries; Fields was still dominating the box office when Harold Lloyd, Buster Keaton, and the Marx Brothers were rapidly fading from sight.

The Fields we know and love, though, is as consistent, as unchanging, as Chaplin's Tramp or the Marxes' scamps. He is a hustler, a schemer, a man with a line of patter and an inexhaustible capacity for putting one over on his fellow man. He is a lovable mountebank, a crooked Babbitt fleecing the rubes of an innocent America. This troupe of Dickensian grifters—Larson E. Whipsnade, Dr. Eustace McGargle, Egbert Sousé (pronounced *Soo-zay*)— must endure the incivility of a nightmarish domestic life, hounded by shrewish wives, nagging mothers-in-law, and barbaric children. This setup—an outer world of suckers, and an inner one of hecklers—would be the fundamental dichotomy of his films.

Fields never directed his own films, like Chaplin or Keaton did, nor did he ever collaborate with first-rate screenwriters, like the Marx Brothers had (although he was a gifted writer in his own right). Years of stage experience had left him with one gift critical to his big-screen success: a well-honed personality. By the time he reached the screen, Fields was no babe in the woods but a grizzled veteran, with two and a half decades' experience onstage. For the purposes of his film career, Fields *was* born middle-aged, and our collective unfamiliarity with him as anything other than a permanently hammered, cynical sourpuss gives his persona a solidity it might otherwise lack. For Fields, life was a performance; and each movie another chance to play "W. C. Fields."

Fields starred in a number of silent films (some of them lost), but it is the early sound shorts that give us an impression of what it might have been like to see W. C. Fields on the vaudeville stage. Modeled as they were on well-honed stage bits, these two-reelers are essentially single gags, padded with brief opening and closing material. In these shorts, Fields was often a harried middle-American shopkeeper, using his store of homegrown ingenuity to please customers and stay out of trouble. A man enters the store in *The Pharmacist* (1933) and whispers a request—presumably for liquor. Casual as ever, Fields removes a fan from beneath the counter and turns it on, blowing the man's coat open to reveal a policeman's badge. He flinches, switches the fan off, and turns on his attempted tormentor: "Certainly not! Do you think I'd break the laws of this great, grand, and glorious United States of ours, just to satisfy your depraved tastes?" Crisis averted.

The Golf Specialist (1930) is a rendering of Fields's legendary golf routine (resuscitated for 1934's *You're Telling Me*), with Fields a duffer whose tee shot is perpetually interrupted by nuisances: a caddy nervously folding stray sheets of construction paper, a squeaky pair of shoes, a society lady walking an enormous dog. "That's a beautiful camel you have with you," Fields attempts by way of veiled critique, before turning on his caddy. "Don't you know I'll smite you in the sconce with this truncheon?" he shouts, wielding his 3-iron like a deadly weapon. Fields's language is deliberately archaic, even mock-classical, while his bit is essentially a slice of Mack Sennett slapstick.

The Fatal Glass of Beer (1933), Fields's most fully realized short, is a loose parody of *The Gold Rush*, burlesquing the frontier setting of Chaplin's masterpiece. "It ain't a fit night out for man or beast," Fields solemnly observes each time he opens the door of his Alaskan cabin, his musings rewarded, time and again, with an icy slap of snow in his face. *Fatal Glass* revels in what would come to be a familiar sight: W. C. Fields, perpetually frustrated in his petty ambitions. At the dinner table, he grasps a giant slab of French bread in his fist, dipping it into the soup with relish, but continually interrupted in his attempt to bring it up to his mouth. The jokes are repeated to the brink of excess, but something about Fields's demeanor—his air of perpetual optimism, crushed by petty circumstance—makes each repetition more side-splittingly funny than its predecessor.

The shorts had introduced an already-recognizable Fields—ludicrous, conniving, inept—but it was not until the uninterrupted run of features beginning with 1932's *Million Dollar Legs* and ending with his final film, 1941's *Never Give a Sucker an Even Break*, that the Fields aesthetic would crystallize. Fields was the writer on many of these films, which was less a matter of putting pen to paper than savvily adapting his stage act for a new medium. W.C. was a Falstaffian raconteur, good-naturedly mumbling his way along a path studded with hazards. Many of these were adaptations of his silent work; *It's the Old Army Game* (1926) would become *It's a Gift*, and *Sally of the Sawdust* was transformed into *Poppy*. The silent W. C. Fields had made little impact; when Fields was amplified by sound, the result would be notably different.

The Marx Brothers had tormented a cloddish and uncomprehending world; W. C. Fields was, in turn, tormented by those very same clods. Fields is harangued by an unending series of shrewish wives (all presumably modeled on his estranged wife Hattie), abused by children and household pets, and perpetually accused of crimes he has no interest in committing. "Harold," the tyrannical Mrs. Bissonette demands of Fields, harassed by a persistent insurance salesman in *It's a Gift*, "if you and your friend wish to exchange ribald stories, please do it downstairs." Summoning the police to his aid after discovering a troupe of burglars singing in his cellar in *The Man on the Flying Trapeze*, Fields ends up being the one arrested, for brewing illegal applejack. There is a hint of Kafka's *The Trial* in Fields's ludicrous dilemmas, with order regularly giving way to nightmarish chaos. Unlike Kafka's heroes, Fields takes a perverse pleasure in his misery. He has come to see it as the natural order of events.

Fields's genius was to elevate the minor annoyances of family and professional life into a poetry of irascibility. A gleefully impudent tyke dips his pocket watch in molasses in *The Old Fashioned Way*; in *It's a Gift*, his daughter's primping forces him to dance a one-man tango around a spinning hand mirror hanging from the ceiling, shaving in quick, blunt strokes; a much-deferred sleep in *Flying Trapeze* is immediately extinguished by a ringing alarm clock ("Quite a snooze!," Fields bleats on arising). The butt of all this hostility, Fields resigns himself to muttered asides and the occasional half-hearted attack: the child booted in the ass in *The Old Fashioned Way*, or the threats ("Quiet, or I'll throw a woodpecker on you!") lobbed at ventriloquist's dummy Charlie McCarthy in *You Can't Cheat an Honest Man*.

We enjoy seeing Fields's parade being rained on, but we especially cherish his brief, hushed rebellions. In the opening scene of *The Man on the Flying Trapeze*, Fields's Ambrose Wolfinger sneaks off to the bathroom to brush his teeth, cleaning his molars with a healthy swig of his homemade applejack. In *It's a Gift*, he shouts at his daughter, demanding her respect: "You've all got to realize one thing: that I," dropping his voice to a near-whisper when he realizes his wife might be able to overhear him, "am the master of this household."

Fields is nothing if not resourceful: he can, like Chaplin or Keaton, turn a seemingly impossible situation to his advantage. Chaplin and Keaton did it with their physical gifts; Fields achieves the same results with his florid verbal gifts. The difference is that those silent geniuses always managed to dance between the raindrops. Fields, meanwhile, gets splattered with every drop.

A little-seen precursor to the Marx Brothers' *Duck Soup, Million Dollar Legs* (1932) is a Ruritanian romance with an unexpectedly ribald streak. Fields is here as the president of Klopstokia (chief exports: goats and nuts). He is the politician as charlatan, inhabiting a role one could easily imagine Groucho playing. Introducing his arrival for a cabinet meeting with a spectacular one-man-band performance, Fields gives his underlings the fish-eye: "Any of you mugs been playing my harmonica?" There is an air of ludicrous futility to Fields, though, that is his and his alone. Practicing governance by arm-wrestling, continually losing his hat and searching fruitlessly for it, the president is an amiable idiot, a suitable figurehead for this anarchic republic. Fields is only a supporting character here, but his spirit of dithering buffoonishness infects the surroundings, so that even the romance between his daughter and Jack Oakie's traveling salesman is possessed by the mood of genial anarchy.

You're Telling Me (1934) begins with a moment swiped directly from Chaplin's *One A.M.*, with Fields the sozzled paterfamilias sneaking home after a night of revelry. His Sam Bisbee is both a harried proprietor—another in the long stretch of homegrown philistines Fields would embody—and the first of his shambling dreamers. In this remake of his 1926 silent *So's Your Old Man*, Fields is an inventor with a puncture-proof tire to market. A demonstration goes predictably awry, with Sam shooting out the tires of a police car, and even his halfhearted suicide attempt is stymied by the powerful fan that keeps the lethal dose of iodine from reaching his anxious mouth. With scenes of Fields's lugging around a recalcitrant giant turkey as a gift for his wife, there is a vague whiff of Buñuelian surrealism to the comedy—*Un Chien Andalou* and *L'Age D'Or* having been released only a few years prior.

The Old Fashioned Way (1934) makes the salvaging of fondly remembered routines its explicit theme. Fields is the Great McGonigle, proprietor of a shabby traveling troupe of actors. The shabbiness *is* the joke, with Fields chuckling at the ludicrousness of the old-time performers as he lovingly pre-serves their routines for posterity. The show that McGonigle's actors put on, the temperance spiel *The Drunkard*, was a real play, a nineteenth-century chestnut staged by P. T. Barnum and other legendary hucksters of the distant past. *The Old Fashioned Way* does more than reference *The Drunkard*; it actu-ally stages the show, with every stilted line of dialogue and awkward physi-cal gesture lovingly preserved. There was always something Victorian about W. C. Fields, beginning with his baroque, sonorous way of speaking, and *The Old Fashioned Way* cannily makes him a purveyor of old-time entertain-ment—a living exemplar of the bygone variety show.

The Great McGonigle leads his fleabag company with bluff good cheer, escaping the summons of agitated sheriffs and the imprecations of vengeful landladies with equal aplomb. Sneaking up behind a sheriff holding a sum-mons for his arrest, McGonigle sets the papers on fire, lighting his cigar from their smoldering ashes. Aboard a train, he steals the sleeping-car ticket of a stranger, and then shouts from his lofty perch when the man has the audacity to complain to a conductor: "Quiet, please, quiet! What is this, a cattle car?"

McGonigle always lands on his feet; his company may have folded, but he rapidly finds new employment as a medicine-show pitchman, enthusiasti-cally hawking a cactus juice remedy guaranteed to cure all hoarseness . . . HOARSENESS, that is. *It's a Gift* (1934) sentences Fields once more to his domestic prison. The film may not be a model of narrative consistency (none of Fields's pictures were), but it is an undoubted classic of American comedy. Fields is Harold Bissonette (pronounced *Bisson-ay*, at least when his wife is nearby), local shopkeeper, husband, and father. Each of these roles provides its own small, sharp agony. Even his attempts at revenge—the icepick wielded over the head of the nightmarish Baby Leroy, the cold cuts swiped from his son's sandwich—are symbols of Fields's ineffectuality. He is the Babbitt beaten down by family life, only capable of small acts of sabotage against the tyranny of domesticity.

The routines—blind man accidentally smashes up the merchandise, early-morning bedlam disturbs Harold's sleep—are inventive, but what lifts them into the realm of genius is Fields's weary brilliance in responding to these per-secutions. The blind man, Mr. Muckle, pops into the store wielding his cane, while an impatient gentleman cholerically demands ten pounds of kumquats. Harold shuttles between his customers as Mr. Muckle jostles lightbulbs and knocks over glassware, muttering "coming coming coming" as a mantra to ward off disaster.

It's a Gift's back-porch sequence is also a small, self-contained masterpiece of lunatic ingenuity, with Fields's nap on an outdoor swing interrupted by the rattle of milk bottles, the patter of an obstreperous insurance salesman, the squeak of a clothesline, and the shouts of an Italian vegetable seller. "No," Harold mutters to the insurance man with barely suppressed fury, "I don't know Karl LaFong—capital L small A capital F small O small N small G." Harold, who begins the scene muttering futilely about "those sleigh bells," ends it wielding a shotgun, hoping to draw a bead on the wily vegetable man.

It is a source of continual surprise, for those unfamiliar with W. C. Fields's oeuvre, to be reminded of the sheer volume of unpleasantness in his films. Domestic life is no more idyllic in *The Man on the Flying Trapeze* (1935). In the film's opening scene, his wife demands that Fields (swigging whiskey in the bathroom as he scrapes his toothbrush against the medicine cabinet) stop futzing around and come to bed. She silently steams through his tortoise-like preparations, during which he carefully unrolls each sock, blows into it as if it were a balloon, and gently rolls it up. The entire routine is repeated in reverse, just as meticulously, when he must arise and investigate the singing burglars in his cellar. The film eventually devolves into a shaggy-dog tale of a lost wrestling ticket, but this extended opening routine is every bit the equal of anything in *It's a Gift*, and proof that for all of Fields's seemingly unquenchable desire to revisit past glories, he had his finger firmly on Americans' funny bones in the present.

One might think, given the mellifluous excess of his dialogue, that the character of Mr. Micawber, from Dickens's *David Copperfield* (1935), had been written precisely with W. C. Fields in mind. Each line of dialogue sounded like something Egbert Sousé, or Dr. Eustace McGargle, might have offered as an observation. "I have thwarted the malevolent machination of our scurrilous enemies," Micawber announces after crawling through a skylight to avoid his creditors. "In short, I have arrived." The influence of Dickens's humor on Fields's linguistic contortions was obvious and long-standing, which made it all the more surprising that he had been required to lobby so hard for the role of Micawber in George Cukor's adaptation of the novel.

Replacing Charles Laughton after he dropped out of the film, Fields turns in an indelible performance—the only real job of acting in his career, playing a character not of his own design. Nonetheless, Fields's Micawber is reminiscent of no one so much as himself, and much of the charm of this otherwise staid *Copperfield* is to be found in his performance. Micawber's weakness for flowery aphorisms makes him an ideal Fields character, for whom Dickensian orotundity was always second nature. Belying his curmudgeonly reputation, especially regarding child performers, Fields's Micawber betrays a palpable fondness for Freddie Bartholomew's young David. Granted the opportunity of playing a dramatic role—albeit in his own cockeyed fashion—W. C. Fields proved indubitably that he was not only a brilliant comedian, but an actor as well. He would rarely be given the opportunity to demonstrate it again.

Instead, he returned to what he knew best. *Poppy* (1936) is a revisiting of his acclaimed stage show, and of *Sally of the Sawdust*, retaining some of Griffith's sepia-toned sentimentality while restoring its droll hijinks. *Poppy* is amiable enough, but like the Marx Brothers' MGM films, these later Fields efforts (*You Can't Cheat an Honest Man* follows nearly the identical template) are weighed down by thoroughly unnecessary romantic and musical sub-plots. Fields is still the center of attention but is also drafted into duty as a romantic jester, his antics the counterpoint to a saccharine love story. Pro-fessor McGargle is the latest in Fields's string of mountebanks, selling talking dogs to unsuspecting bartenders, and overpriced bottles of restorative tonic to country yokels. Meanwhile, his daughter Poppy has cast a spell on the scion of a local blueblood family, who disdain the McGargles' common roots. McGargle is a crook with pretensions to grandeur, but his memories of lazy afternoons playing croquet in far-off Darjeeling are cast into doubt by his evident lack of familiarity with the game: "What lazy lout left these wires all over the lawn?"

Poppy had retained some of Fields's traditional speed and efficiency, but *You Can't Cheat an Honest Man* (1939) is frightfully, inexplicably slow—the *Room Service* to *It's a Gift*'s *Duck Soup*. Worse, it is dragged down by the presence of Charlie McCarthy and ventriloquist Edgar Bergen, about whom the best that can be said is that he is marginally less wooden than his dummy. Fields is Larson E. Whipsnade, crafty proprietor of a flea-bitten circus, whose profits derive primarily from hoodwinking his customers and fleec-ing his employees. There are some clever touches—the ten-gallon hat Whip-snade wears to introduce the world's tallest midget, the impromptu shower under an elephant's trunk—but too much of the film is given over to Fields's exchanging insults with a lifeless block of wood. *Honest Man* is also marred by its racially charged humor, with Fields's rancid quips about "Ubangis" and Charlie's donning blackface for a musical number two of the most repellent examples. The result of all this miscalculation is a diminishment of his natu-ral gifts, rendering him more an object of pity than one of amusement—the kiss of death for any comedian.

By all measures, *You Can't Cheat an Honest Man* should have marked the beginning of the inevitable slide into irrelevancy that marks nearly every American comedian's career. Instead, W. C. Fields's last three films (not counting a few cameos and walk-on appearances) count among the highlights of his filmography, and include at least one undisputed comic classic.

My Little Chickadee (1940) crudely slapped together two 1930s comic icons—Fields, sixty, and Mae West, forty-seven—and left them to wrestle for supremacy. Fields's ever-increasing belly, magenta-colored snout, and ridiculous tan top hat make him a walking punch line, but he surprisingly holds his own, and then some, when pitted against West.

The screenplay, cowritten by the two actors, is a clash of dueling sensibilities: West's simpering sensuality, in which every line, no matter how vanilla, serves as a double-entendre, and Fields's trademark non sequiturs. "During one of my treks through Afghanistan," he remarks to no one in particular, "we lost our corkscrew. Had to live on food and water for several days." Neither Fields nor West is particularly at home in the Western—even a comic Western like this one—and both play against the plot (which has something to do with romantic masked bandits). For all its flaws, and the delicate tap-dance Fields does around West's coarse come-ons, *My Little Chickadee* is near-prime Fields: a portrait of the middle-aged man as boozer and bon vivant. "Sleep, the most beautiful experience in life," he enthuses as he climbs into bed, before remembering a lone exception. "Except drink."

The Bank Dick, also from 1940, is yet superior, and ranks alongside *It's a Gift* as the pinnacle of W. C. Fields's cinematic efforts. The plot is once again ragged, loose to the point of disjointedness. Fields is Egbert Sousé, a barfly unexpectedly hired as a last-minute replacement director, sitting in for alcoholic has-been A. Pismo Clam. Sousé prefers to while away his hours at his favorite watering spot, the Black Pussy Cat, getting quietly soused. "In the old Sennett days," Sousé declares, "I used to direct Fatty Arbuckle, Buster Keaton, and Charlie Chaplin," and promptly goes about turning this English drawing-room drama into—wouldn't you just know?—a circus picture. The self-reflexive film-set ambience is only a diversion, though, an appetizer before the entree.

Having flamed out as a director, Sousé is hired as a bank security guard, where he apprehends a boy wielding a toy pistol: "Is that gun loaded?" he demands of the boy's mother. "Certainly not," she retorts, "but I think you are." Fields is once more the accidental not-quite-hero, taking credit for collaring a team of bank robbers before being unveiled as a fraud. Eventually,

Sousé becomes embroiled in a stock-purchasing scam (between *The Bank Dick*, and *It's a Gift*'s barren southern California orange grove, Fields's characters fall victim to every swindle known to mankind) and must keep bank examiner J. Pinkerton Snoopington (played by master character actor Franklin Pangborn) from investigating the books too closely. Sousé torments the weak-stomached Snoopington with florid descriptions of nauseating dishes: breaded veal cutlet with tomato sauce, or coconut custard pie with saveloy pudding.

In this unexpectedly sunny film, all the traditional Fields elements—suspicious bosses, embittered wives, impossible children—are present but have been declawed. Sousé is allowed to serve as both butt and hero. It is Fields's equanimity, his refusal to panic, that is his making in *The Bank Dick*. The drink-addled buffoon is also the savior, and as in *It's a Gift*, is amply rewarded for his gullibility. Lounging in his beautiful home, surrounded by servants and loving family, Egbert is served his cafe rum for breakfast before heading out to the bar—er, the office. "What a changed man!" his mother-in-law moons.

Fields is once more the great man in his last film, 1941's *Never Give a Sucker un Even Break* (a favored motto of the actor's; Fields pictured theater marquees nationwide reading "W. C. Fields—Sucker"). This shaggy dog of a film features Fields as a movie star named W. C. Fields pitching an increasingly bizarre screenplay to the president of Esoteric Pictures. Fields is a star without honor, razzed by children as he tips his cap to a poster of *The Bank Dick*, and tormented by the waitress at a flyblown cafe he frequents. "No extra charge for the cold shower, I hope?" he wonders after she accidentally pours water down his pants. The food is hardly any better: "I didn't squawk about the steak, dear. I merely said I didn't see that old horse that used to be tethered outside here." W.C.'s equanimity is preserved, even when the censor's scissors interfere with his plans. W.C., parched, enters a drugstore and orders an ice cream soda. Fields turns to address the camera. "This scene was supposed to be in a saloon, but the censor cut it out. It'll play just as well," he mumbles to himself, blowing the head off his soda.

The film-within-the-film—the script presented by Fields and his niece (Gloria Jean)—is yet weirder. A passenger on an enormous airship, W.C. leaps out after a stray bottle of whiskey and ends up on the secluded estate of Mrs. Hemogloben and her nubile daughter. (In an unsettling act of cinematic cross-breeding, Mrs. Hemogloben is played by none other than Margaret Dumont, butt of a thousand Marx Brothers routines.) W.C.'s screenplay is a nonstop collision of frantic non sequiturs, but each line is kissed by Fields's gift for mix-and-match wordplay. "Don't you want to live in this beautiful nest," he asks his niece, "have a personal maid, wear diaphanous gowns, and eat regularly?"

W.C. is past his romantic sell-by date, more attracted to the bottle than the hourglass figure: "I was in love with a beautiful blonde once. She drove me to drink—that's the one thing I'm indebted to her for." Handed a glass of goat's milk at a bar, W.C. haltingly lifts the glass to his lips, as if about to imbibe poison. "Someday, you'll drown in a vat of whiskey," a secretary warns him, and W.C. warms to the notion: "Drown in a vat of whiskey? Death, where is thy sting?"

While W. C. Fields, the amusing lush, was entertaining America, Bill Fields was slowly, steadily drinking himself to death. His mottled, discolored nose was not merely a cinematic sight gag, nor had it been acquired from playing ping-pong, as one wag in *Never Give a Sucker* had noted. Fields spent his last years resting and recuperating at a southern California clinic, alternating periods of abstinence with drunken revels. Arthritis and cirrhosis of the liver were the tangible marks of a lifetime of heavy drinking, and W. C. Fields, only just past his sixtieth birthday, found himself forcibly retired from feature filmmaking, still near the peak of his comedic powers. Fields would die on Christmas Day 1946, only sixty-six years old, but driven into a premature grave by a lifetime of boozing. His life may have been cut unnaturally short, but W. C. Fields was also spared what so many of his fellow comic luminaries were not: a tragic wasting away of their powers. Fields left the game while still on top; how many others would be able to claim the same?

7

MAE WEST

"IT'S ALL BEEN DONE BEFORE, BUT NOT THE WAY I DO IT"

"Sex didn't begin in Hollywood. It just went
there to get in the movies." —Mae West

"**G**oodness, what beautiful diamonds!" A typical hat-check girl, a typical nightclub, a typical Hollywood production of the early 1930s—but the woman with the diamonds around her neck is anything but typical. "Goodness has nothing to do with it," she simpers, a lascivious smile stealing across her face, and the movie—and the history of American comedy—would

---

W. C. Fields eyes costar Mae West suspiciously in *My Little Chickadee*.

never be quite the same again. *Night After Night* (1932), directed by studio craftsman Archie Mayo, was an utterly unremarkable gangster picture, with George Raft as a tough guy longing to go straight. The dewy Constance Cummings is the polished finishing-school girl he yearned for, and an already-notorious ex-vaudevillian, Broadway actress, and writer named Mae West plays Maudie, Raft's defiantly unpolished onetime flame. West puts the match of her burning ambition—and simmering sensuality—to this polite effort in the commonplace, her brassy, trashy, boldly unrespectable Maudie hinting at untapped depths of transgression. "Mae West stole everything but the cameras," Raft would later note approvingly of the actress, whom he had personally recruited for the part. The audience wanted more, and so did Mae West. She would never take fourth billing in a film again.

Every time breeds its own heroes, and its own oppositional figures. In the repressive Hays era, when the movies were policed by puritanical former postmaster general Will Hays in cahoots with the Catholic Church, someone had to represent the unfettered sexual urge. In the 1930s, this role was filled (and I do mean filled) by Mae West, whose one-track mind had a broken track. Mae is a carnivore whose favorite dish is men, and her movies are feature-length attempts to capture a few specimens for her personal collection. They are dazzling inversions of the accepted order, in which the woman was the voracious predator, and men the pursued. Mae West's world was designed to her specifications: the men flutter around her like butterflies, and every stray line of dialogue only masquerades as plot, its true function being to set the table for her next bon mot. Like Groucho Marx, with whom she shared a gift for clever wordplay and a taste for the off-color, West never met a setup line she didn't like.

West is more myth than legend; for a woman with so healthy a figure, there is surprisingly little to wrap your arms around in her work. There is only one character in her films. West is so much larger than life, so thoroughly demanding of our attention, that her supporting cast—the hustlers and whores, gangsters and politicians, maids and chauffeurs—are wooden dummies, coached to walk and talk in the precise manner designed to best display the star. There is a reason why West's most famous movie, *My Little Chickadee*, is also her most schizophrenic: sharing a stage with another star was hardly her strong suit.

This is not to say that West is undeserving of the accolades directed her way. Mae was the vessel that launched a thousand raunchy remarks. She was also, her famous legal troubles notwithstanding, the right star at the right time, as she well understood: "I lived at just the right time for me," West would tell writer Charlotte Chandler toward the end of her life. "A big part of luck in life is you've got to get your timing right. A little earlier and they would've put a scarlet letter on my forehead or burned me at the stake. A little later and I couldn't have shocked people anymore." Hays, Joseph Breen, and the rest of the repressive prudes were her true costars, their spotlight casting the richest possible glow on her scandalous spectacle. "Maybe censorship was my best *friend*," she later observed. "You can't get famous for breaking the rules unless you've got some rules to break."

Mae West had never shied from breaking the rules. Born in Greenpoint, Brooklyn, in 1893 (not 1900, as she would later claim), Mary Jane West grew up in relative comfort, the beloved older daughter of a German immigrant and an Irish ex-prizefighter turned livery-stable owner. Even as a child, the stage beckoned, and by age seven she was singing and dancing at the Royal Theater in her native borough, billed as Baby May. "My first love affair?" West would later ask rhetorically. "I fell in love on that stage. It was with my audience, and it's lasted all my life. . . . No man could equal that." Soon, West was winning amateur contests across the city, and hungry for bigger challenges. Opportunity promptly arrived in the form of actor Hal Clarendon, who hired her for his traveling troupe of actors. Mae played a series of little-girl roles until puberty struck, and no one could mistake her for a child anymore.

As a teenager, West followed in the footsteps of W. C. Fields, Stan Laurel, Charlie Chaplin, and other future cinematic luminaries by elbowing her way onto the still-thriving vaudeville circuit. West actually got her start in burlesque, a down-market vaudeville whose subject matter and clientele were grubbier than that of the glittering downtown palaces of the respectable theater. The star-in-waiting explicitly modeled herself on vaudeville icon Eva Tanguay, whose career was peaking when West was getting her start. Tanguay's repertoire included such bawdy, double-entendre–rich songs as "Go as Far as You Like" and "It's All Been Done Before but Not the Way I Do It" (could there be a more perfect motto for West's own career?).

Burlesque gave way to the legitimate theater: first the show *A La Broadway*, produced by future Hollywood mogul Jesse Lasky, and then the well-established Keith circuit of regional theaters. West formed a sister act with her younger sister Beverly. Beverly, naturally, was the straight man of the duo.

Timing was everything for Mae West. It was the defining trait of her stage act, which depended on the lazy, sidelong sting of her jibes. West summed up her style perfectly, quoting one of her favorite numbers: "It isn't what I do, but how I do it. It isn't what I say, but how I say it, and how I look when I do it and say it."

Timing was also West knowing how far she could push, and how notoriety could be a new kind of fame. She was a hit in impresario Arthur Hammerstein's 1918 show *Sometime*, playing a man-hungry, love-starved thrill seeker named Mayme. West rewrote some of her dialogue, spicing up Mayme's tame thrills, and the show's success gave her the necessary push to try her own hand at writing. West began creating her ideal role: crass, glittering, sexy, and untamable. Sex was no longer merely subtext, the doubled entendre; it was now the prime subject matter of all West's work.

The Ruby Ring, whose protagonist wins a bet with her friend that she can wheedle five marriage proposals in five minutes each from five different men, was her first attempt at playwriting, but it is *Sex*, from 1926, that truly set the tone for what was to come. With its pimps, hookers, and corrupt cops, *Sex* is at home in the urban demimonde. West was Margy La Mont, a prostitute hoping to go straight, in search of unsullied love.

It was not only the frankness of West's play that violated the moral sensibilities of the censorious; it was the lack of remorse. The "fallen" women of *Sex* were profoundly lacking in shame. "It's just a matter of circumstances," Margy (West) tells her high-society nemesis, suggesting that any woman might find herself turning a trick to change her luck.

Sex was "*the* scandal of the New York stage in 1926," West's biographer Simon Louvish notes, and "scandal" is not meant frivolously. The show was raided by the police in February 1927, and West was arrested, charged with "producing an immoral show and maintaining a public nuisance." The charges also meant an early curtain for her second show, then also running on Broadway: a melodrama about homosexuality called *The Drag*, which may have been the only play of the decade capable of surpassing *Sex* in shock value. West was found guilty and sentenced to ten days in jail. Her silk stockings were taken before booking, but West was allowed to keep her silk underwear.

Having attracted so much notoriety for her Broadway endeavors, West soon came to the attention of Hollywood. Her arrival coincided with the studios' adoption of the repressive Hays code, designed to curb the influence of amoral entertainers like—well, like Mae West. "The sympathy of the audience shall never be thrown to the side of crime, wrong-doing, evil or sin," the Hays code had pronounced, unceremoniously tugging down the curtain on a freewheeling era of promiscuous, naughty, disarmingly honest sound films.

Mae West arrived in California just in time to bear the brunt of the backlash, armed with a contract from Paramount and a play named *Diamond Lil* that was guaranteed to shock.

Collaborating with the Hays Office, Paramount tiptoed around *Diamond Lil*, suggesting tweaks and cuts. No mention of white slavery, no Salvation Army uniforms for Cary Grant's Captain Cummings, no kept women—not even any use of phrases like "for God's sake!" in the dialogue. And yet, the studio and the censors had both neglected to heed West's own warning. It was less about what she said than how she said it. Mae West didn't need to spell it out for us to get the message.

She Done Him Wrong (1933), as the film was eventually titled, was batting practice for West, its script a series of softballs tossed her way, each smacked out of the park with lackadaisical assurance. Grant is the official straight man here, representing the massed forces of overbearing gentility, but truth be told, there are nothing but straight men here. Their lines all serve as setups to West's punch lines, which are less funny than ingenious. Language is playfully bent to her purposes, with sound, not just words, treated as pregnant with unstated meaning. "*Ohhh*-wa," West's Lady Lou exclaims on first being introduced to elegant Russian emigré Sergei (Gilbert Roland), the fricative hinting at untapped, unexplored depths of sensual pleasure.

Hint is all *She Done Him Wrong* can really do, hemmed in as it is by the code's stringencies, but a decade on Broadway had equipped West with all the tools necessary to gesture in the direction of indecency without making any directly incriminating statements. The censors' senses were dulled, squabbling over taking the Lord's name in vain, but allowing West to belt out "A Guy What Takes His Time" and "I Wonder Where My Easy Rider Has Gone," both, as their titles more than suggest, littered with writhing double-entendres. "I wonder where my easy rider's gone," West sings, her voice somewhere between a simper and a bray. "I never saw that jockey trailing anyone before." And for those who think that song is about thoroughbreds, West has a bridge to sell you, in just a film or two.

Set in "the Gay Nineties . . . when they did such things and they said such things on the Bowery," as the film's opening titles have it, *She Done Him Wrong* is an amoral spectacle whose unsavoriness is safely contained by its time frame. Diamond Lil no longer, West's Lady Lou holds court in a downtown saloon, watching over her flock of fragile girls. Diamonds and brothels, the high life and the low life; West shamelessly intertwines glitz and grit—her two favorite interests.

The plot is helpful for West's purposes, but is ultimately irrelevant; for all they matter, the sets and backdrops might as well be made of painted cardboard. They exist only to provide an excuse for West's string of inverted aphorisms. She is not, like Groucho Marx or W. C. Fields, providing sardonic sideline commentary. Instead, she is a wisecracking philosopher, imparting her hard-fought wisdom with devilish panache. Her delivery is clipped but muddy, her words slurred, as if by an excess of desire. "When women go wrong," she tells an anguished good-time girl, "men go right after them."

Lady Lou, we are made to understand, knows a little something about going wrong herself. "It was a toss-up whether I go in for diamonds, or singin' in the choir," she chortles, pausing for effect. "The choir lost." Just like the Marx Brothers, West was scoring points off the world. Only here, everyone *thinks* themselves as wised-up as she is.

Stripped of their low-life accoutrements, West's films were actually women's pictures turned inside out and emptied of melodramatic affect. The code of the women's film, which stipulated that the worst crime of all was to wrong a fellow woman, remained in place, but the hokier aspects of the form were eliminated. No hankies were necessary for these films. West was a lone woman struggling to make her way in hostile territory, but was decidedly not a victim herself.

Mae West drips sex, but she shares surprisingly little with another ribald blonde who would follow in her footsteps, Marilyn Monroe; contrary to the impression given by a later West film, *Go West Young Man*, West is hardly an erotic figure. With her oversized parasol and peaked feathered cap, she is already comically exaggerated—less a sex object than an overripe parody of one. Unabashedly about sex, these films are hardly sexy at all. Instead, it is West herself who is doing the lusting, with not only her dialogue but her body language offering the impression of an insatiable desire. When Lady Lou gives Captain Cummings a frank once-over, the role reversal is dizzying, and marvelous. It is the woman doing the assessing, and the man who provides the eye candy. "Why don'tcha come up sometime, see me?" she purrs to Grant, in the most famous of her many famous come-ons.

Grant, clad in black uniform and cap, like a Norwegian postman, is as drab as his color scheme. In later years, after his ascent to superstardom, West would take the credit for Grant's success. Having spotted him on the Paramount lot, she told various journalists and hangers-on, she demanded him as the star of her next picture: "If he can talk, I'll take him." The story is a nice one, but fundamentally false; Grant had already starred in a handful of pictures before *She Done Him Wrong*. It is false, too, because in some elemental way, the cloddish actor West was starring opposite was not Cary Grant—at least not yet. Studying his performance in *She Done Him Wrong*, one would never guess that this attractive lump, seemingly incapable of blinking convincingly onscreen, would turn out to be the greatest comic actor Hollywood would ever produce.

The West-Grant duo would return that same year for *I'm No Angel*, a typically fast-moving endeavor that begins as a circus picture, briefly pauses for an Art Deco romantic interlude, and wraps up as a courtroom drama. West is a sideshow attraction named Tira whose down-home Dance of the Seven Veils attracts a loyal male following. After a jealous boyfriend nearly kills an admirer, Tira heads for New York, where she becomes a sensation with a new act that has her placing her head inside a lion's mouth. She continues ascending the social ladder horizontally, ditching her pickpocket boyfriend for a rich playboy, and then for his equally wealthy, but far more dashing attorney (played by Grant).

I'm No Angel is less a sequel to *She Done Him Wrong* than a paraphrased remake. West is once more the tart-tongued siren, luring men to their fates while taunting them with their helplessness. Like the stage spectacles from her vaudeville days, it hopscotches from one set to another, linked only by the most tenuous of plot devices. No one went to a Mae West comedy for its plot, as she well knew, and her script for *I'm No Angel* is little more than a thin filament linking unrelated wisecracks. "I had to shoot a lion once," Tira offhandedly remarks to a society lady. "Really? Was he mad?" she asks. "Well, he wasn't exactly pleased."

One develops the sneaking suspicion, on watching *I'm No Angel*, that the wisecracks predate the plot, which is constructed out of jury-rigged leftover parts. West's philosophy of life emerges, one carefully packaged and delivered bon mot at a time. "When I'm good, I'm very good," she tells Grant, patting him on the shoulder, "but when I'm bad, I'm better." West, like Groucho Marx (who was busy shooting *Duck Soup* on another Paramount lot around the same time), was making the familiar unfamiliar. Shopworn phrases and sentiments slick with overuse suddenly slip free of their bonds, and become capable of surprising once more. Where Marx always gave the impression of having thought up his free-associative rants on the spot, West never does. Each witticism is lovingly, meticulously polished.

Tira struts into her apartment after a rough encounter with a jealous girlfriend, and calls out to her maid: "Oh, Beulah, peel me a grape." West herself admitted she wasn't quite sure what the line meant, but its air of dissolute leisure, and the actress's insouciant delivery, ensured that it, of all *I'm No Angel*'s lines, stuck in the audience's minds. In the midst of a decade of unprecedented economic misery, perhaps the idea of such profligate luxury provided a thrill of its own. Along with Fred Astaire and Ginger Rogers, West was offering the vicarious thrill of opulence to financially strapped moviegoers; unlike Fred and Ginger, her characters had always clawed their way up from the bottom.

West herself had ascended to the pinnacle of American show business; she was the highest-paid performer in the United States for 1934, earning more than double the man in second place, W. C. Fields. In the process, she had become her big-screen persona; fans expected Mae West to be the same onscreen and off, in a way that Julius Marx or Charles Chaplin were exempted from permanently embodying Groucho or the Tramp. West's third film as star, *Belle of the Nineties* (1934), maintains and extends her box-office-tested formula. Once more, vaudeville and liquor and old-timey sin were blended into a cocktail of song and salaciousness. Leo McCarey (who had directed the Marx Brothers and W. C. Fields, and would go on to work with Harold Lloyd and Cary Grant) was hired to direct, although West, who contributed the script once again, saw him as essentially a hired hand. West's ego may have gotten the best of her, but she also had a point; each West picture had a uniform style that no director could tamper with too much.

Now an established superstar, West's persona grew ever more exaggerated with each film. West's delivery is brassier, the gowns dripping with yet more spangles, and the feathers on her hats are large enough to keep entire apartment blocks in the shade. In *Belle*, Mae is Ruby Carter, "The Most Talked About Woman in America" (a true enough proposition), whose stage act culminates in an appearance as the Statue of Liberty. Liberty is at stake in the film, too, with Ruby exiled from St. Louis to New Orleans to give her prize-fighter swain a shot at the title. "You certainly know the way to a man's heart," her maid tells her, and since Ruby doesn't know how to boil an egg, it's safe to say that it's not through his stomach.

Bluesy musical numbers like "A Good Man in Memphis," along with the presence of jazz legends Louis Armstrong and Duke Ellington, and actresses Hattie McDaniel, Gertrude Howard, and Libby Taylor as West's maids, gave her films a distinctly African American tilt. Blues and jazz were a natural fit for West, whose scripts echoed the blues' unapologetic libidinousness and plain-spoken honesty, but her films never mustered the same respect for

African American performers that they naturally displayed toward African American music.

West saw herself as a trailblazer—"I fought for gay rights before it was the thing to do," she would later say about her play *The Drag*—but the black characters in her films have more in common with the troublesome pickaninnies of Harold Lloyd's shorts, or W. C. Fields's dim-witted sidekicks, than they might be comfortable allowing for. The slew of maids *yes, ma'am*–ing West linger in the mind longer than they should, their unquestioning obedience distractingly, dismayingly servile. And yet, the offscreen Mae West may not have been so arrogantly superior; Libby Taylor, who played her maid in *I'm No Angel* and *Belle of the Nineties*, had really been her maid before West cast her as one. Taylor went on to other roles—almost all maids, but as McDaniel once said, "I'd rather play a maid and make seven hundred dollars a week than be a maid and make seven dollars."

Goin' to Town (1935) flouted the Hays code even more flagrantly than its predecessors. Little-regarded, with journeyman Alexander Hall as director, it may be the best of West's films—that is, if any distinction can be made among them. For *Goin' to Town* shares nearly everything with its predecessors. Bouncing around like a steroid-addled bunny rabbit, the film veers from the Wild West to Buenos Aires, from cattle rustling to oil to horses to high society. Playing the arriviste, defending her territory against all comers, West crackles with nervous energy. Her Cleo Borden is the kind of lady who refers to her palatial mansion as "the old j'int," and lets her pet monkey run free on the Louis XIV furniture. Respectability beckons, but Cleo refuses its call. "For a long time, I was ashamed of the way I lived," she tells a friend. "You mean to say you reformed?" her friend wonders. "No, I got over being ashamed," West retorts.

The double-entendres are so numerous, so rich with barely buried meaning, that the enforcers of the code must all have been attending the annual censors' convention when the script came in. "You did consent, didn't you?" a judge asks Cleo, seeking confirmation of her brief marriage to a cattle thief. West responds, with a barely repressed smirk, "I certainly did—twice."

Cleo is not only a sexual colossus, but an unabashed blue-collar gal mingling with the bluebloods. "You'd like to have my ancestors go back and come over on the *Mayflower*," she tells one breeding-obsessed aristocrat, and tells another asking after her forebears that they had been traced, "but they were too smart. They couldn't catch 'em." West is proud of being nobody in particular, descended from a long line of crooks and hustlers. Cleo, like West's other heroines, is a slob who wants to become a dame, while reserving the right to opt out if she finds it not to her liking: "I'm gonna take a shot at this lady business." She sings an aria from Saint-Saens's *Samson and Delilah* in her new incarnation as an opera singer. Her nasal voice sounds like Maria Callas as played by Bugs Bunny.

Was West poking fun at herself, or providing accidental fodder for lampoonists? Judging by the evidence of the self-referential (note the title) *Go West Young Man* (1936), a little of both. After the censor-butchered religious fable *Klondike Annie* (1936), in which West used showbiz savvy to jazz up the Holy Trinity, she plays a version of herself in *Go West*, the first of her star vehicles not written by the star herself. Mavis Arden, the star of overblown melodramas like *Drifting Lady*, seeks to escape the clutches of her overbearing press agent. When their car breaks down in the middle of nowhere, Mavis's exasperation is quickly softened by the arrival of hunky Bud Norton (Randolph Scott). Suddenly, a day in the country looks a lot more appealing. "I can't tell you the number of men I helped to realize themselves," Mavis tells aspiring inventor Bud, and he presses on with describing his ideas, convinced she is more interested in his designs than her own.

West took over the Jean Harlow role for this loose remake of *Bombshell*, which lacks that Frank Capra film's tartness. Mavis has something of Harlow's gift for the charming malapropism, but West's heart is not entirely in the comedy. When she first spots Bud, Mavis rolls her eyes and hums to herself, amused by her own tastes, but she might as well be rolling her eyes at this film, which lacks its predecessors' bite.

Go West was too tame by half, and *Every Day's a Holiday* (1937), her most lavish enterprise yet, seeks to return the actress to her native turf. We are back in New York at the very tail end of the nineteenth century, and West is legendary con woman Peaches O'Day, whose business is selling the Brooklyn Bridge, time and again, to naive immigrants. The atmosphere of cheerful corruption is a precursor to Preston Sturges's *The Great McGinty*, but *Holiday* is blatantly uninterested in its proceedings. It is a series of monochromatic stage sets intended to allow West's wit to sparkle brightest. Unfortunately for the star, her witticisms are in disrepair here, the humor damp and musty. Fleeing the police, Peaches passes herself off as French diva Mlle. Fifi, putting on an elaborate stage show nearly identical to those of previous West heroines. (Her moans and indistinct murmurs mean the same thing in French they do in English, it seems.) West's accent is terrible, and A. Edward Sutherland's direction indifferent, but *Every Day's a Holiday* is inoffensive, if unremarkable.

If West's routine was all about sex, how would it be to star opposite a jovial lush whose only interest in women appeared to be as drinking partners? And, to really ramp up the degree of difficulty, why not make it a western? *My Little Chickadee* (1940), the last of West's major films, appeared at first blush to belong in the hall of fame for terrible movie scenarios. What could West's sashaying seductresses have to say to W. C. Fields, that charming, irascible buffoon? And indeed, there are numerous moments in *My Little Chickadee* where the two stars appear to be acting in two entirely different comedies accidentally spliced together by an editor who himself had imbibed too deeply of the grape. Fields is his typical orotund, jocular self, and West is sneaky and self-absorbed. Slowly, the joke sinks in: Fields and West's characters behave as if they have vanishingly little in common, too.

My Little Chickadee is one of the unlikelier pairings in the history of the American film, with only the union of Chaplin and Keaton in *Limelight* a comparable commingling of comedic firepower. In that film, Keaton had been a walk-on player, a Proustian madeleine summoning memories of the silent film. Here, who was the star? Fields and West wrestle for control of the picture, and end up reaching an equitable split: Fields gets most of the best lines, and West most of the screen time.

After retreating into near-tameness on her previous few films, *My Little Chickadee* finds West in fine fettle, energetically trading barbs with all comers. West marries Fields out of convenience, and then spends the film fending off his advances. Every sound out of her mouth has a sexual ring; even when she expresses her concern over the local schoolhouse's lack of books, she makes it sound lewd. "I was in a tight spot," she says of a narrow escape from danger, "but I managed to wriggle out of it." West wriggles out of embarrassing herself here, as well, and while the peace between *Chickadee*'s stars is a cold one, they charmingly swap their trademark lines like graduates signing each other's yearbooks. "You must come up and see me sometime," he tells her, and she responds in kind: "Oh, I'll do that, my little chickadee."

Afraid of her costar's reputation, West had a clause in her contract forbidding Fields from coming to the set drunk, and enforced it; she had him physically removed when he arrived inebriated, and did not allow him back until he had sobered up. The film was an enormous success, but West swore never to act onscreen with Fields again. The experience of sharing the screen was too demanding.

As it turned out, *My Little Chickadee* would essentially serve as West's big-screen swan song. After an ill-fated return in 1943 with the misguided *The*

Heat's On, made as a favor for producer Gregory Ratoff, West abandoned film acting for a quarter of a century. She returned to the stage, toured the world with a revived version of *Diamond Lil*, published her autobiography, and developed an interest in Eastern mysticism. She supposedly rejected an offer to star in Billy Wilder's Hollywood farce *Sunset Blvd.*, and was miffed when Wilder gave Gloria Swanson all that business with pet funerals: "They stole the idea of my monkey from me," she told Chandler.

As time passed, and the censors' chokehold loosened, Mae West came to represent an earlier generation of undercover heroes. Whatever boundary the new generation of American actors and directors wanted to push in the late 1960s and early 1970s, it turned out Mae West had been there already. The ageless diva had aged, but plastic surgery and a careful personal regimen had kept the septuagenarian star in fine fettle.

After a quarter of a century away from the screen, she made a grand re-entrance as talent scout Leticia Van Allen in the 1970 adaptation of Gore Vidal's gender-bending novel *Myra Breckinridge*. Nearly eighty years of age, West still buzzes with barely contained energy, even as her face remains strangely immobile. "Hi cowboy," she purrs to one potential client. "How tall are you without your horse?" "Well, ma'am, I'm six feet seven inches," he responds. "Never mind about the six feet," she retorts, "let's talk about the seven inches."

A dirty blonde to the very end, Mae West never outgrew the interests of her youth. Amidst the *Midnight Cowboy*–esque happenings and end-of-Hollywood musings of the legendarily discombobulated *Myra*, West did not look aged, or decrepit; she looked right on time.

8

ERNST LUBITSCH

THE TOUCH

"How would Lubitsch have done it?" —Billy Wilder

W hen the great man died, the directors William Wyler and Billy Wilder—his friends, countrymen, and colleagues—were leaving the funeral service, when one turned to the other. "No more Lubitsch," Wyler said mournfully, as if finding it difficult to believe that the world could go on without him. "Even worse," Wilder replied, "no more Lubitsch movies." The shock and dismay at losing the most talented and remarkable of their fellow directors is palpable, but Wilder's point should not be missed: Ernst Lubitsch

---

Margaret Sullavan and James Stewart wait for Matuschek & Co. to open in Lubitsch's *The Shop Around the Corner.*

was the movies he made. They could not easily be separated from his own zest and vigor in making them, or from the experiences that informed them. They were the best of him.

They called it the Lubitsch Touch, but they could never provide a definition to go with it. Like Louis Armstrong said of jazz, if you had to ask what it was, you'd never know. What they all knew, though, was that only Lubitsch could provide it. Coming of artistic age in the early 1930s, when the restrictive Hays code was in full force, Lubitsch was forced to improvise. The style he had perfected in Germany, in his American silents, and even in his early sound films was now persona non grata in the United States. In its place, Lubitsch crafted a style that hinted at sex, that was playfully adult in its themes, without ever crossing the invisible boundary line that separated smut from genius.

To watch a Lubitsch movie is to be ushered into a perfect world, where the drinks are cold, the clothing is perfect, the decor is timeless, and the women (and men) are gorgeous. Unlike their cohorts, Lubitsch films left the door open for you, too. You weren't just watching; you were a part of the fun, able to enjoy the joke by virtue of cracking the code. Maybe that is what the Lubitsch Touch, at the last word, was: the ability to make you feel you were as clever as the people onscreen. No one has been able to do it since. As Wilder noted many years after Lubitsch's death, "If one could *write* Lubitsch touches, they would still exist, but he took that secret with him to his grave. It's like Chinese glass-blowing; no such thing exists anymore. Occasionally, I look for an elegant twist and I say to myself, 'How would Lubitsch have done it?' And I come up with something and it will be *like* Lubitsch, but it won't *be* Lubitsch. It's just not there anymore."

Born to a secular Jewish family in Berlin, Lubitsch was drawn to performance from the outset. His merchant father wanted him to learn a respectable trade, preferably joining the family business, but the allure of acting was too strong a temptation. Lubitsch wangled his way into the theater group of director Max Reinhardt—then the first name of the German stage. The roles young Ernst played were primarily stereotypical "Jewish" roles—lazy, greedy, callow youngsters. One photo from the era shows Lubitsch in ill-fitting suit and bowler hat, like a Teutonic Tramp, wielding a briefcase and rolled-up umbrella to fend off the advances of a mangy-looking dog.

Lubitsch never became a famous actor in Germany, but some scrap of his best-known roles must have stuck in the country's collective consciousness: when the anti-Semitic documentary *The Eternal Jew* was being put together after Hitler's rise to power, the parade of "foreign Jews" polluting German society included the actor Ernst Lubitsch. Lubitsch became a director in Germany, and a successful one, making pictures like *The Eyes of the Mummy Ma* (1918) and *The Doll* (1919), and when he went to the United States, he left Germany for reasons of commerce, not politics.

In many ways, Lubitsch was an anomaly in the German-expatriate community in Los Angeles. He was neither an intellectual nor politically attuned; a committed anti-Fascist in principle, Lubitsch once attended a Hollywood dinner given for the son of Italian dictator Benito Mussolini out of sheer ignorance. While a Jew, Lubitsch had not been driven out of Germany. The person responsible for his emigration was not Adolf Hitler, but Mary Pickford—the child superstar who had invited him to Hollywood to direct her in 1922. As life in the real Europe grew increasingly fractious and murderous, Ernst Lubitsch was engaged in the lifelong project of building a brighter, cleaner, more perfect Europe—the Europe of Americans' dreams, and his own—on a southern California soundstage. And while his own romantic life was rocky at best, his films were effortless, tantalizing fantasies of passion without fetters.

Lubitsch had been brought to Hollywood to assist Pickford in making the tricky transition to adult roles after a smashingly successful career as an energetic pixie, but found his true calling a few years later, after the transition to sound. Lubitsch's early sound films are an opportunity to see not one, but two genres being born simultaneously: the musical and the romantic comedy. Birth is an appropriate metaphor, too: things get a bit messy, and it is the passage of time that brings maturity to Lubitsch's sound work.

Musicals had been the very bedrock of the sound film from the outset; the first major sound film, *The Jazz Singer*, was a musical. But where *The Jazz Singer* was a heavy-handed melodrama interrupted by invigorating bursts of music, Lubitsch had a different kind of musical in mind. Beginning with 1929's *The Love Parade*, starring Maurice Chevalier and Jeanette MacDonald, Lubitsch sought to craft an integrated musical, in which the music both commented on and advanced the plot. Lubitsch made the musical the essential genre of the sound film by keeping it jazzy and off-the-cuff, employing a string of low-key leading men capable of building a rapport with audiences. Taking a page from Chaplin's groundbreaking *A Woman of Paris*, Lubitsch preferred to tell his stories by inference, coming to the same points from new angles.

Lubitsch films were like soufflés: purchase all the proper ingredients and follow the instructions, and the results would be delicious, but skip any one of the steps and the result would be a soggy, inedible mess. Cursed with Paramount's shallow roster of employable stars, Lubitsch had to turn time and again, in these early years, to actors who could not pull off the delicate blend of sex and sensitivity that the roles required. A single bum performer was enough to sink an entire film.

In short, *The Love Parade* and 1930's soggy *Monte Carlo* are records of what life was like before Samson Raphaelson. As Lubitsch himself acknowledged, the "Lubitsch Touch" was mostly a collaborative process, with the brilliant but un-intellectual Lubitsch needing a skilled writer to provide the bones of the material, and to understand what he was aiming for. But it was Lubitsch who was the skilled rewrite man—who would go through a well-honed script and add toppers and clever touches everywhere, like the sign posted in a European department store in *Bluebeard's Eighth Wife* (1938), next to "Se Habla Espanōl" and "English Spoken Here": "American Understood."

That's how Lubitsch's brain worked; he was merely telling the same old story of boy meets girl, but every aspect of it—even the signs on the wall— had to somehow be fresh. And so Lubitsch films are singularly difficult to describe. Their charms are all evanescent—gossamer-thin—and are pleasurable insomuch as they appear casually tossed-off. Watching *Trouble in Paradise*, or *Heaven Can Wait*, one is blessed with the delicious sensation that the film—the product of innumerable hours of work—is the merest fluff from Lubitsch's collar.

His collaboration with Raphaelson on *The Smiling Lieutenant* (1931) is the first of his sound films to truly click: where the ingredients of sex and romance and humor and music are baked properly, and avoid premature collapse. Chevalier plays a military man whose maneuvers take place primarily between the sheets. An officer in "the boudoir brigadiers," as Max Robin's song wittily has it, Chevalier effortlessly romances Claudette Colbert, the bandleader of a traveling all-ladies' group, the Viennese Swallows. (Lubitsch was enamored of bawdy double-entendres.) Shortly thereafter, he falls into the orbit of a clueless princess (Miriam Hopkins) who snookers him into marriage.

For the first time, the music advances the plot, rather than stopping it dead in its tracks. And with Raphaelson on board, even the dialogue sounds like music: "Someday we may have a duet," offers Colbert, and Chevalier parries, "I love chamber music." Colbert avers, saying, "First tea, and then dinner, and then maybe—maybe breakfast." Cut to the next morning, with eggs sizzling in a pan.

One Hour With You (1932) has a famously convoluted history, only partially cleared up by the credits, which list the film as directed by Lubitsch,
with assistance from George Cukor. In actuality, Cukor was initially assigned
to direct *One Hour* before Paramount executives (and Lubitsch himself) realized that Cukor was stepping on the comedy. Lubitsch suited up and replaced
Cukor on set, and the final result is one of the most Lubitschean of his films,
and easily the best of his early musicals.

One Hour reunites Chevalier and MacDonald as a married couple who
have magically retained their sexual spark—they open the film making out
on a park bench. Chevalier's fidelity is challenged when he meets his wife's
best friend Mitzi (Genevieve Tobin), a flirtatious scamp who refuses to take
no for an answer. "I don't want to mix business with Mitzi," he complains to
his wife, but Chevalier is shoved into compromising situations with her until
he can no longer resist.

One Hour with You is a surprisingly adult drama, risqué in ways that contemporary films would be leery of, but it is melodrama with a punch line
and a chorus. The sumptuous Art Deco decor echoes the cool suavity of the
characters, never caught short for a retort or a snappy song. They are lovers as
we would like to be—debonair, charming, passionate, and ultimately faithful, more or less. Lubitsch makes flawlessness seem easy, as if it were merely
a matter of the right actors saying the right lines on the right sets. *One Hour*,
a neglected masterpiece in its own right, is an opportunity for audiences to
escape into perfection, and get away from the unpleasant realities of 1932
America into Ruritanian bliss.

For Lubitsch too, work was an escape from the unpleasant reality of his
own personal life. His first wife Leni left him for his friend (and occasional
collaborator), Hans Kraly, and his second wife Vivian was a well-born gold
digger embarrassed by her husband's gauche ways. Vivian once told Raphaelson, "I'm all in favor of mixing the blood of the aristocrat with the blood of
the peasant." Ever loyal, Raphaelson responded by saying that he completely
understood the metaphor: that she was the peasant and the brilliant Ernst the
aristocrat.

Perhaps as a result of his often-unhappy personal life, Lubitsch's early
American films had a recurring interest in bringing powerful women to heel,
as male surrogates like Chevalier and *Monte Carlo*'s Jack Buchanan engage
in elaborate schemes to take back the upper hand from the powerful, self-
sufficient women played by Jeanette MacDonald. Woman on top was not a
position these films were comfortable with, and so the rightful order of the

world is restored, in which even queens and princesses are dutifully subordinate to their husbands.

Equality created far more comic opportunity than patriarchy, and so in Lubitsch's first mature masterpiece, *Trouble in Paradise* (1932), the men and women were all equally carefree, equally flirtatious, and equally nimble. The heavy-handed moralizing of Lubitsch's early musicals has been replaced by a delightfully cheerful amorality. Gaston (Herbert Marshall) and Lily (Miriam Hopkins) meet by picking each other's pockets, each complimenting the other on their good form and execution. He returns her pin, only to discover his watch is missing. Never at a loss for a topper, he asks if she minds if he keeps her garter.

Gaston and Lily form a company of thieves and make wealthy entrepreneur Mme. Colet (Kay Francis) their first target. Gaston rapidly insinuates himself into her affairs, public and private. A metrosexual *avant la lettre*, Gaston offers advice on everything from lipstick shades to corporate governance, and his plans for theft are complicated by his burgeoning feelings for his target. Gaston speaks in a low, slow murmur, as if muted by too much lovemaking, and the film is notable for a similarly insinuating frankness, whereby little is said and much implied.

In one of the legendary Lubitsch set pieces, and a perfect example of the Lubitsch Touch, the film indicates a blissful night of romance by a montage of clocks striking ever-later hours as, offscreen, phones go unanswered, champagne corks pop, and lovers whisper sweet nothings into each other's ears. Since sex must remain forever offscreen, Lubitsch invests objects with sexual meanings. Clocks, doors, bottles of champagne: each becomes a representative from the Republic of Love. Lubitsch's desire to give his audience pleasure extends to the desire to lend them sophistication by proxy. There is little heartache or betrayal here; just the maneuverings of three crafty dealers each seeking to get their fair share of love and money.

Lubitsch's next film similarly required the delicate avoidance of the fundamental point of its story. Where *Trouble in Paradise* is about a man caught between two women, *Design for Living* (1934) is about a woman with two lovers, each more or less satisfied with their unorthodox arrangement. Lubitsch's embrace of oblique storytelling, and his innate desire to tantalize rather than satisfy, gave him the freedom to tackle a story whose foundation had to be shrouded in mystery because of the censors' strictures. Gilda (Miriam Hopkins) reaches a "gentleman's agreement" with two starving American artists in Paris (played by Fredric March and Gary Cooper) to serve as a joint artistic collaborator and muse to the two men, with no sex involved. Still, at the first inkling of romance, her hastily built facade of monasticism gives way: "It's true we have a gentleman's agreement, but unfortunately, I'm no gentleman."

Because of the delicate nature of the material (how could a mainstream film of 1934 comfortably allow a woman two lovers?), *Design* hints rather than shouts. March's wearing a tuxedo to breakfast is indication enough to Cooper that his time with Hopkins has come to an unexpectedly abrupt end. When Hopkins impulsively decides to marry the sexless Edward Everett Horton (a man who keeps his marriage license filed next to his dry-cleaning bills), Cooper and March send her two distinctly phallic flowers as a reminder of what Gilda is giving up. The next morning, after a failed wedding night, Horton storms out of the bedroom and kicks over the flowers—a demonstration of jealousy as witty as it is indirect.

The true sophisticates prefer comedy to melodrama and burlesque, and so Cooper and March assess their setbacks and betrayals with an equanimity and good cheer born of the knowledge that one is not always the protagonist of every story—an insight severely lacking in the graceless Horton. Ben Hecht's script is occasionally heavy on the pedals, but *Design for Living* captures the blithe good cheer and carefree spirits of early 1930s Lubitsch as well as any film other than *Trouble in Paradise.*

The mid-1930s marked a period of tumultuous change in Lubitsch's work, a middle period of mixed-bag efforts, halfway between the insinuating comedies of his early American work and the more emotionally attuned efforts of his maturity. *The Merry Widow* (1934) was a semi-remake of *The Love Parade*, reuniting Maurice Chevalier and Jeannette MacDonald for an amiable romantic farce. Chevalier is as dashing as ever—the film's shrieking Jujus, Dodos, and Fifis testified as much—as a blithe gigolo summoned to save the Marshovian monarchy by wooing MacDonald—and her fortune. "Have you ever had diplomatic relations with a woman?" Edward Everett Horton's royal courtier asks, and Chevalier chuckles knowingly. Lubitsch playfully tweaks the censors; in one charming scene, the camera holds on an unbroken two-shot of Chevalier and MacDonald's faces as all the action ("give me back my shoe!") takes place below the frame line.

The Marlene Dietrich vehicle *Angel* (1937) was a premise without a plot, and *Bluebeard's Eighth Wife* (1938) rapidly peters out after a brilliantly risqué comic opening (contributed by screenwriter Billy Wilder), where Gary Cooper and Claudette Colbert meet cute in a department store: he wants to buy only the pajama tops, and she requires the use of just the bottoms.

Ever uninterested in politics, Lubitsch found that politics had a funny way of catching up with him. In 1935, his German citizenship was revoked, and shortly afterward, the Nazis included him in the array of Jewish "parasites" whose photos were displayed around Berlin. In September 1939, Lubitsch's beloved daughter Nicola was on board the *Athena* when it was torpedoed by the Germans. For a number of hours, Lubitsch anxiously awaited news of his daughter's fate from Los Angeles, sure that she had been killed, before learning that she had miraculously survived the explosion. Lubitsch the fantasist, the dreamer of beautiful dreams, discovered to his chagrin that the apolitical man was a contradiction in terms, at least in the 1930s.

After the release of *Bluebeard's Eighth Wife*, Lubitsch was particularly distraught over an otherwise positive review that raised the question of whether people struggling through the Depression could enjoy a film whose protagonists didn't work. But where so much "committed" work from that era was fatally self-serious, more intent on speechmaking than entertaining, Lubitsch managed to integrate the real world—scarred and blemished as it was—into his fantasies without undue harm to either.

Maturation was not merely a process of life's catching up with Lubitsch; it was also a result of finding the right collaborators. The magnificently melancholy character actor Felix Bressart was essential to the success of both *The Shop Around the Corner* and *To Be or Not to Be*, and the transition from engaging but limited performers like Hopkins and MacDonald to the likes of Greta Garbo, James Stewart, and Carole Lombard allowed Lubitsch to aim higher, and achieve more.

Late Lubitsch is a blend of the audacious and the autumnal, the romantic and the black-comic. Romance now takes place amidst Communist and fascist tyranny, or is plagued by the goblins of self-doubt and miscommunication. In short, real life has encroached on Lubitsch's fantasies, but rather than pour cold water on them, fantasy has been invigorated by the human touch. Unruffled by brute reality, Lubitsch's later films redouble their commitment to pleasure of all kinds. In a world splintering apart with centrifugal force, it is the only freedom left. As Ninotchka learns, it is also the only freedom worth savoring. Freedom is the ability to wear a ridiculous traffic cone of a hat, if for no other reason than it being spring in Paris. "Bombs will fall, all civilization will crumble," Ninotchka says with a grimace, "but not yet—please!"

Ninotchka (1939) was the first of Lubitsch's films to burden weightless fantasy with the weight of the world. Leon (Melvyn Douglas) is a Parisian lawyer and quasi-gigolo who finds himself overwhelmingly attracted to his paramour-client's intractable opponent—a frosty, sexless Soviet bureaucrat. Ninotchka (Greta Garbo) has been summoned to Paris to clean up the mess left by her three predecessors, who have been lured away from the Marxist fold by wine, women, and song.

Ninotchka is standard-issue high-level Lubitsch romance, frothy and evanescent in matters of the heart, but the film demonstrates a similarly effortless wit when it comes to global affairs. Ninotchka shouts at a porter who offers to carry her bags: "That's no business—that's social injustice!" Unflustered, the porter retorts: "That depends on the tip." In a restaurant, the owner, shocked at her claim that she never thinks about food, asks what she does think about. "The future of the common people," she answers, a haughty, Lenin-esque gleam in her eye. "That's also a question of food," the restaurateur replies. *Ninotchka* inspired reactions as funny as the film itself. At one preview screening, a member of the audience wrote that it was the "funniest film I ever saw. I laughed so hard, I peed in my girlfriend's hand."

Ninotchka's blend of the serious and the comic, the romantic and the bittersweet, paved the way for what remains Lubitsch's singular masterpiece, and quite possibly the single greatest film ever produced within the studio system. If aliens ever come to Earth and demand a fuller understanding of the moving pictures that seemed to occupy so much of our time in the twentieth century, it would be best if we cut directly to the chase and screen *The Shop Around the Corner* (1940) for them. Lubitsch ascended many peaks in his career, and each has its charms, and its adherents. There will be few capable of making arguments against *Ninotchka*, or *Heaven Can Wait*, or *Trouble in Paradise*. *The Shop Around the Corner*, however, is in another category entirely. It is pure cinematic magic: the kind that, seen once, is indelibly burned into our brains, stored in the grottoes of recollection with the care and sentimental affection normally accorded only to our own fondest memories. *The Shop Around the Corner* is simply perfect.

The Shop Around the Corner is actually two conjoined films, each lovely and bittersweet in equal measure. In the first, clerks at Matuschek & Co., a Budapest department store, seek to hold on to both their jobs and their sanity in the midst of economic chaos. In the second, two brittle, self-possessed Matuschek employees—Mr. Kralik (James Stewart), and Miss Novak (Margaret Sullavan)—bicker at work while spiritually communing through an anonymous exchange of pen-pal letters.

It is Lubitsch's supreme control of the material that papers over the fundamental division in the film, and the change in focus that takes place around its halfway point. The critic's complaint about *Bluebeard's Eighth Wife* had been taken to heart. For Lubitsch, there could no longer be a film about lovers that was unaware of the brute necessity of money.

The first half of *The Shop Around the Corner* is consumed by uncertainty and economic panic. Miss Novak practically begs Kralik and Matuschek for a job, and only receives one when she proves her worth as a saleswoman, selling a musical cigarette case to an overweight woman as a candy box with built-in musical calorie counter. The threat of deprivation—of going without—is what moves the characters of *The Shop Around the Corner*. No longer do Lubitsch's lovers exist in a fanciful never-never land where luxury flows like tap water; here every pengö is earned by the sweat of one's brow.

Loneliness and joblessness are equated, allowing Lubitsch to incorporate the economic into his finely honed emotional spectrum. The terror of unemployment written on the face of Felix Bressart's Pirovitch is balanced by Mr. Matuschek's fear of being alone on Christmas Eve. The stupendous array of supporting characters in *The Shop Around the Corner*—Lubitsch's best ever, led by the inimitable Bressart—provide a milieu in which Stewart and Sullavan insert themselves. *The Shop Around the Corner* is a melancholy romantic comedy that takes place on the brink of an abyss, and while Lubitsch is too much the comic raconteur to send his film over the edge, he pauses long enough for a sustained look.

The Shop Around the Corner exists entirely in a muted emotional register. Lubitsch succinctly underscores each scene with deftly nuanced shifts in mood and mise-en-scène. Stewart in particular is marvelously charming—proud and sheepish in precisely equal doses. When he is fired, Stewart is stunned, quiet, and still, and his round of handshakes to each of his colleagues is just right—the exact action a proud man like Kralik would take in a profoundly humiliating situation like that.

When Stewart and Sullavan finally do come together, it is the embrace of two battered boxers who, having fought ten rounds, are too tired to keep fighting. The bittersweetness is balanced out by the magnificent comedy of Raphaelson's script. Every line, and every character, is perfect in its own right, but also forms another strand of the web of economic and emotional uncertainty that makes up the film. When Kralik and Pirovitch discuss the financial feasibility of taking a wife, and Kralik wonders about the cost of entertaining friends, Pirovitch tells him, "Listen—if someone is really your friend, he comes after dinner." Kralik tells Pirovitch that he has discussed love with his pen pal, but only from an intellectual viewpoint. Pirovitch retorts, "Why, what else can you do in a letter?"

Even the smallest characters are convinced, like Edward Everett Horton in those 1930s Lubitsch comedies, that the story belongs to them alone. "It was a terrible shock," teenage errand-boy Pepi tells Stewart in the hospital after Mr. Matuschek attempts suicide. "Well, I have to get over it." Perhaps that is ultimately Lubitsch's secret: there are no supporting characters here, only protagonists with less screen time.

Having rhetorically conquered Communism with comedy in *Ninotchka*, Lubitsch next sought (after 1941's disastrous *That Uncertain Feeling*) to take on fascism with a different kind of firepower—the undying narcissism of actors. *To Be or Not to Be* (1942), scripted by Edwin Justus Mayer, is blood brother to Chaplin's *The Great Dictator*—a knockabout WWII-era Nazi comedy whose tone (the Mel Brooks–starring 1983 remake notwithstanding) could only make sense before Auschwitz.

A troupe of Warsaw actors, led by ham extraordinaire ("What you are, I wouldn't eat," Bressart's Jewish understudy sneers at him) Josef Tura (Jack Benny) and his flirtatious wife Maria (Carole Lombard), are thrust into the midst of political intrigue when Maria is drafted to prevent Professor Siletsky, a Nazi spy, from sharing damaging information with the Gestapo. Maria, already enamored of a young Polish fighter pilot (who "can drop three tons of dynamite in two minutes"), must feign attraction to Professor Siletsky in order to win his trust and slay the Nazi dragon. "Oh, I'm terribly frightened, and terribly thrilled," she purrs at their first meeting, offering a dazed "Heil Hitler" after they exchange their first kiss.

To Be or Not to Be is not exactly a film noir; even nighttime scenes, where characters wield flashlights, are bright and evenly lit. Nonetheless, it possesses a nuanced sense of wickedness (if not quite evil) and a sympathy for human frailty. Maria Tura is a serial philanderer who cannot keep her dress buttoned, so to speak, but rather than condemn her, as an earlier Lubitsch film might have done, *To Be or Not to Be* allows her to triumph from it. Josef is indeed a terrible ham, guilty of strangling Shakespeare with overacting, but it turns out that this is exactly the quality needed to combat the Nazis. It is the shallow, self-aggrandizing, self-obsessed actors who emerge triumphant.

The Nazis, too, are little more than hams: bad actors spoiling an entire nation with their dreadful performances. "So they call me Concentration Camp Ehrhardt?" a Nazi flunky asks Josef with a laugh, exactly echoing

Tura's own line earlier in the film, when he had been passing himself off as Ehrhardt. ("I thought you'd react that way," Tura responds, pleased with his actorly sagacity.) The Turas and the rest of their troupe play at being courageous, tough, and principled, and succeed the way all actors do: through lying. Actors being actors, the primary concern is always the audience's response: the highest form of praise offered by Bressart's actor is "that would get a terrific laugh" —even when the performance at hand is a matter of life and death.

By the time of *Heaven Can Wait* (1943), the mood was distinctly autumnal. The spirit was born of Lubitsch's recurring health problems (he suffered his first heart attack in 1943), and the pressure that the ongoing war placed on the imaginary Europe of his fantasies. *Heaven Can Wait* is weighed down by a newfound sense of mortality. With thoughts of his own death gloomily filling his mind, Lubitsch made a film whose playful sense of fun is haunted by its own sense of an ending. Henry Van Cleve (Don Ameche) is a lover, not as we would like to be, but as we are: foolish, overly sentimental, misguided, and predictable. He is also, for all his faults, remarkably charming. He is a rogue whom we wish to forgive for all his excesses.

Heaven Can Wait—the first of Lubitsch's films to be set in the United States—walks a remarkably narrow line between broad comedy and sentimentality. Henry and his wife Martha (Gene Tierney) have a storybook romance, but life proves to be more than "happily ever after." A pampered layabout before he marries Martha, Henry mostly remains one after taking marital vows. He chases after other women, neglects his wife, and is financially and emotionally irresponsible. For all that, his marriage is—in its patchwork way—a happy one. *Heaven Can Wait* finds poetry in the prose of daily life. Its characters are neither dukes nor thieves—merely everyday Americans whose youth is steadily worn away by the worries of maturity, and the irrepressible movement of the hands of time. As Andrew Sarris noted about the film: "the form is very light, but the essence is very dark."

For all that, *Heaven Can Wait* is a remarkably funny film, providing yet further evidence of Lubitsch and Raphaelson's joint wizardry. Nearly every line of the film is quotable: Henry's cousin Albert describes Martha's father as "one of the great meatpackers of our time," and Henry's naughty grandfather writes a rhyme (to the tune of the meatpacker's ad jingle) to commemorate Henry's theft of Albert's bride: "She was packed by E. F. Strabel/to be served at Albert's table/but that Henry changed the label." Lubitsch carefully stacks *Heaven Can Wait* to cast his protagonist in a favorable light, surrounding him with prigs like Albert, and buffoons like his father, who appears to still be unclear on the details of the birds and the bees at age forty-three.

Henry and Martha have their troubles, as we can clearly see; but Lubitsch subtly emphasizes the always-replenishing affection Henry feels for Martha through camera movement. When Henry sees Martha for the first time, the camera tracks in for a close-up of his face; and when Henry informs us, in voiceover, that the dance we are watching (at their twenty-fifth anniversary celebration) would be the last they would ever dance, the camera pulls up and away from them as they swirl around the floor. *Heaven Can Wait* is about Henry, not Martha; but Martha's presence attracts the camera, and her absence pushes it away. Without her, there are still good times to be had, but she takes the heart of the film along with her when she dies.

Cluny Brown (1946), the last film Lubitsch would complete, offers a reduction of his style to its essence. The subject is still romance, and the manner whimsical, but the idealized protagonist has taken on a new form. He is no longer merely the charming seducer; he is now Adam Belinski, Czech philosopher and anti-Nazi dissident. Belinski (Charles Boyer) must acclimate himself to the unusual ways of the English gentry—their prejudices, their snobberies, and their particular blind spots. In this film, what they hate to acknowledge, more than anything, is the reality of their clogged internal plumbing.

Cluny Brown (Jennifer Jones), a working-class lass with a taste for the wrench and hammer, enjoys reminding the high-minded swells that everyone—themselves no exception—has pipes that need maintaining. Cluny is a beautiful woman who likes nothing more than banging away at a good joint—double-entendre fully intended. Cluny is symbolically rubbing her clients' faces in the reality of sex whether they like it or not, and Belinski is a bemused spectator to the hash she makes of prim English morals.

Toward the end of his career, and the end of his life, Lubitsch sought to paint a self-portrait in celluloid. Playfully adapting himself to his new country, adrift from the continent he once called home, Belinski is a romanticized version of Lubitsch, or the Germans with whom he often barbecued in his Bel Air home on Sundays. Coming at the end of a brutal war between his adopted country and the country of his birth, Lubitsch's last film is an ode to the exile, simultaneously home everywhere and nowhere. Belinski's love for Cluny is an expression of Lubitsch's love for his new home. The film may be set in England, but it is a love letter to Lubitsch's own America.

Having suffered from a variety of heart-related ailments since the late 1930s, Lubitsch had been fearful for his health for a number of years. The director suffered a heart attack at the 1947 Academy Awards, and was afterward under the regular close monitoring of a doctor. It was during the filming of *That Lady in Ermine* that Lubitsch suffered a fatal heart attack, dying in November 1947. There would be no more Lubitsch films—not even *That Lady in Ermine*, which was completed (some might say polished off) by Otto Preminger. Others would take up the mantle of Lubitsch, including his onetime screenwriter Billy Wilder, but no one could truly succeed him. Once Ernst Lubitsch was gone, there would be no more Lubitsch films—ever.

9

PRESTON STURGES

THE COCKEYED CARAVAN

JOHN L. SULLIVAN: I want this picture to be a commentary on modern conditions. Stark realism. The problems that confront the average man!

LEBRAND: But with a little sex in it.

JOHN L. SULLIVAN: A little, but I don't want to stress it. I want this picture to be a document. I want to hold a mirror up to life. I want this to be a picture of dignity! A true canvas of the suffering of humanity!

LEBRAND: But with a little sex in it.

JOHN L. SULLIVAN: With a little sex in it.

HADRIAN: How 'bout a nice musical?

—Joel McCrea, Robert Warwick, and Porter Hall, *Sullivan's Travels*

Hollywood hobos Joel McCrea and Veronica Lake in Sturges's *Sullivan's Travels*.

To hear about his life, Preston Sturges sounds like someone out of a Preston Sturges movie. Peripatetic bohemian mother, picaresque European childhood, stint running a cosmetics firm, marriage to heiress, stint as an inventor. Oh yeah—and for a few years in the 1940s, the funniest man in Hollywood. Sturges was the first studio screenwriter to graduate to directing—except when he did it, there was no such thing as a writer-director. Sturges had to beg his way into the director's chair, offering Paramount what amounted to a free script (this when he was one of the highest-paid writers in Hollywood) for the opportunity to direct. His gamble paid off, with a run of blockbuster successes and brilliantly inspired, utterly original comedies. But like so many other American comic geniuses, Sturges's winning streak was short-lived, and never to recur.

A charming failure before and after his years of triumph, Preston Sturges was the real-world equivalent of one of his own characters: *The Great Moment*'s W. T. G. Morton experimenting with laughs instead of laughing gas. It also makes Sturges only the most notable of the Mount Rushmore figures in the laugh-today, cry-tomorrow world of comedy, where the question is not "What have you done for me lately?," but "What are you doing for me right this very second?" Like Dr. Morton, Sturges stumbled, then succeeded, before finding himself cruelly dismissed by the bean-counters. Comedy, as always, was short-lived.

Born in 1898, Sturges's childhood was a blur of exotic European locales interrupted by brief visits to various educational institutions. His mother Mary D'Este (later Desti) considered herself the closest bosom friend of dancer Isadora Duncan—she painted the scarf that would get caught between the wheels of Duncan's Bugatti and strangle her in 1927. Mary wanted her son to find himself as an artist—a great painter, perhaps, or a brilliant poet—but all Preston wanted to do was be a stockbroker like his stepfather Solomon Sturges.

Mary eventually found a career as the proprietor of Maison Desti, which offered an array of perfumes and face powders for discerning women. By the age of fifteen, Preston was living on his own in Deauville, France, overseeing a new Maison Desti store. After a brief stint in the Army Signal Corps during World War I, Sturges married and was managing Maison Desti's New York affairs.

Sturges wanted to be his stepfather—rock-solid, dependable, consistent—but instead he was a carbon copy of his mother: flighty, mercurial, and lacking commitment. Marriages (including one to Post heiress Eleanor Hutton) came and went, and Sturges's devotion to Maison Desti was similarly short-lived. For a time, Sturges lived on his wife's opulent estate and tried his hand at being a full-time inventor. He came up with some wonderful gadgets (a lightweight car, an airplane that took off vertically), echoing the gift for discovery that had led Sturges to design a kiss-proof lipstick for Maison Desti. Invention, like its eventual successor songwriting, was mostly a bust as a career move, and the onetime teenage entrepreneur was now divorced for the second time, at a loss as to what to do with his life.

It was then, in 1927, that Preston Sturges had a case of appendicitis that would change his life. While recuperating in the hospital, Sturges, inspired by a book on writing, decided to try his hand at playwriting. Sturges had never been lacking in short-lived enthusiasms, but writing was a different matter entirely. One of his plays was produced in Provincetown, then another in New York. Suddenly, and with much fanfare, Preston Sturges was a well-regarded young playwright, churning out comic farces and domestic dramas with remarkable speed.

Soon enough, Hollywood came calling, and Sturges became a hired typewriter at Paramount, then Universal. He was underwhelmed by Los Angeles ("like Bridgeport with palm trees," he dubbed it), but the work was steady, and good. He adapted Tolstoy's *Resurrection* and penned a Diamond Jim Brady biopic, but Sturges became famous for a wholly original screenplay he wrote called *The Power and the Glory* (1933). Jesse Lasky called it the most perfect original script he had ever read, and Orson Welles credited the film (which starred Spencer Tracy) as the inspiration for *Citizen Kane*.

Having mastered the art of the screenplay, Sturges found himself increasingly irritated by what happened to his finished product. Like many other writers-turned-directors, Sturges was impelled to get behind the camera by seeing what a hash others had made of his words. In his case, Mitchell Leisen's pointless, niggling cuts to his script for *Remember the Night* (1940) propelled Sturges to action.

Directing, for Sturges, meant an opportunity to protect his words from being mangled (a lesson well learned by a later devotee of Sturges's, Billy Wilder). Sturges's greatest gift as a director was the ability to get out of the way of his script. His four-year run from 1940 to 1944, in which he wrote and directed seven films, is the most remarkable string of successes ever put together by a Hollywood filmmaker. In it, Sturges remade the American film comedy in his own anarchic, democratic image. His films were the antithesis of the era's reigning Capra-corn—well-scrubbed Americana with a populist bent, like director Frank Capra's *Mr. Smith Goes to Washington*, or *You*

Can't Take It With You. Roaming the same terrain, Sturges's films spread the wealth, with protagonists forced to share valuable screen time (and space) with all manners of walk-on schnooks, kooks, and weirdos. Sturges reveled in the abundant variety, and absurdity, of America, as only one who had been schooled abroad could.

Sturges wanted to dedicate his first film as a director, *The Great McGinty* (1940), to the filmmaker who, more than anyone else, helped him find his voice: Ernst Lubitsch. *McGinty* indisputably announced the arrival of a major talent, although Sturges could have afforded a few more lessons at Lubitsch's knee on the complexities of mingling hard-boiled comedy and soft-hearted sentiment. As it stands, *The Great McGinty* is half of a brilliant film, with an IOU for the remainder.

McGinty was the first time that the same name appeared in a film's credits as solo writer and director (although Ben Hecht and Charles MacArthur had cowritten and directed four films together in the 1930s). Never a believer in the factory model of film production ("I for one can think of no surer way of stamping out originality, initiative, pride of achievement, and quality," he once said of the studio system), Sturges was convinced that quality films could only be made by a single writer and director, able to implement on the set what he had imagined on the page. Nonetheless, Sturges was never a commanding visual stylist—not with this first effort, nor with any of his subsequent films. Lubitsch-style sight gags and elegant decor were not his forte.

The false-start opening of *McGinty*, with a shambling drunk telling his story of embezzlement and social disgrace, gestures at normalcy before veering into Sturges's preferred mode of idiosyncratic comedy. Contrary to first impressions, *McGinty* is to be a political film, but a Tammany Hall picture, not a Franklin Delano Roosevelt–WPA type of effort. It is like a fictional adaptation of the memoirs of Tammany's George Washington Plunkitt, full of graft, chicanery, and corruption. It is also rip-roaringly funny, and possessed of a furious intellectual energy that only the Marx Brothers, among Sturges's contemporaries, possessed. McGinty (Brian Donlevy) is a bum who enters the voting booth on Election Day in exchange for the two dollars promised by the incumbent mayor's cronies. McGinty is not content with one payday when so many are in the offing, and offers his services as a full-time voter. The bum may lack status, or a meal beyond the chicken leg hidden up his sleeve, but he also lacks all fear of the political elite. "How's my back hair, Flossie?" he shouts at the city's mayor, insulting him on election night for refusing to celebrate with a man's stiff drink.

Swiftly ascending the political ladder, McGinty serves as a bill collector ("It's $2.50 or Madame La Jolla doesn't jolla any more") before being tapped as a future star by the Boss (Akim Tamiroff). McGinty is duly elected mayor, but first he must pass that most essential litmus test for any aspiring politico, past or present: he must marry. A man without a woman, notes the Boss, "is like a coat without the pants." McGinty duly covers his ass, and weds his secretary Catherine (Muriel Angelus), a polite Barbara Stanwyck type without Stanwyck's verve, or charm.

It is here that the film, seemingly purposefully, veers off the rails, never to return. A rollicking comedy of down-and-dirty politics becomes a corny domestic drama of the slowly awakening heart. Having inherited a family (and an elegant Art Deco apartment, to boot), McGinty sheds his preference for bear-skin rugs and loneliness, and throws himself into being a father and husband. Catherine wants McGinty to use his office for the good, but as soon as he is elected governor and plans to put a halt to the graft, the Boss pulls the plug on his career. Soon enough, both men inhabit the same jail cell, later to be exiled to the same run-down South American bar. Sentiment replaces savvy, and *McGinty*, which had burst out to a world-record start, sags noticeably near the finish line.

Sturges had not quite hit the target with his first effort, but he was close enough to a bull's-eye for Paramount to realize how lucky it had been to give him a chance. *McGinty* won an Academy Award for its screenplay. (He jokingly told the Oscar audience that "Mr. Sturges was so overcome by the possibility of winning an Oscar that he was unable to come here tonight, and asked me to accept in his stead," forgetting that hardly anyone in Hollywood knew what he looked like.) Sturges's next film, *Christmas in July* (1940), turns the same ingredients into a more successful cocktail of sharp wit cut with a dash of melodrama. Like *McGinty*, *Christmas in July* is a Depression movie, its protagonist a lowly clerk too poor to marry his girlfriend Betty (Ellen Drew) and dreaming of a quick payday. Luckily for him, coffee company Maxford House is holding a slogan contest, and office clerk Jimmy MacDonald (Dick Powell) has a killer one: "Maxford House: if you can't sleep at night, it isn't the coffee, it's the bunk." Jimmy erroneously comes to believe that he has won the contest, and turns his life upside down in celebration.

Trained by the theater, Sturges was a dialogue man, and the conversation in *Christmas in July* positively glitters with wit. If there weren't so much more to come, one might speculate that Sturges had saved every good line he had ever thought of in his life and inserted it into his script. *Christmas in July* knows only one speed—faster—and its shifts in tone, from bittersweet to celebratory to sentimental back to bittersweet, take place at warp speed. Jimmy glows with the news of his victory, bursting with new ideas and ambitions. His prize is taken from him, along with his promotion, but the worst loss is the sense of accomplishment. "He belongs in here because he thinks he belongs in here," Betty tells their boss, and one can hear Sturges, the forty-year-old failure suddenly, unexpectedly made good, speaking directly through her. Nothing stings like the withdrawal of approval.

McGinty and *Christmas* had been romances in which the chorus was as significant as the lovers, but even when above-the-title stars replaced no-name Paramount players, Sturges maintained the democratic style. By this time, Sturges owned the Players, a restaurant on the Sunset Strip that served as a clubby hangout for the filmmaker and his friends. Sturges's films became extensions of the Players's back room, where all the directors' favorites could entertain themselves and each other. For Sturges, who was as much European as American, the fundamental truth of his native/adopted homeland was its cacophony of competing voices. The lovers were occasionally drowned out by the valets and ship-hands. Sturges had taken Lubitsch's fascination with character performers and elevated it to a philosophy of filmmaking. The background had become the foreground, and Sturges was often more interested in these heretofore invisible actors—their lumpy bodies, misaligned faces, and nasal voices—than his well-proportioned, pleasing-to-the-ear leading men and women.

The Lady Eve (1941) is the Sturges film that comes closest to standard romantic-comedy fare, but Sturges has too little of the sentimentalist in him to approach matters in battle-tested fashion. (This is a film in which a tender love scene is repeatedly interrupted by a horse nuzzling the leading man.) In this battle of the sexes, we root for the scoundrel to hoodwink the naif. Charles "Hopsie" Pike (Henry Fonda) is a scholar of snakes, and heir to the Pike's Ale fortune. He is only just back from a year up the Amazon when he meets the intoxicatingly alluring temptress Jean Harrington (Barbara Stanwyck) aboard a cruise liner. She promptly and efficiently woos him, all in the name of a quick windfall for her and her con-man father Colonel Harrington (Charles Coburn). In this retelling of the Biblical story, it is Stanwyck's Eve who is the snake in the garden, with Adam too dim-witted to realize just what he's taking a bite out of.

Fonda is quite good in the only purely comic role of his career, but Stanwyck is nothing less than brilliant. With a bare midriff and plunging décolletage, she effortlessly maneuvers Hopsie into a kneeling position during their first meeting, and he never manages to rise again. We believe Eve's scheming more than her emotions; it is hard to picture someone so fully in control of her surroundings surrendering to love. But we never like her more than when she is fighting for Hopsie. The scene in which Stanwyck and her father silently duel over cards, each topping the other's tricks in a battle royale over Hopsie's money, is perhaps the most charming in a film of unyielding suavity.

Stanwyck glows with pleasure in every scene of *The Lady Eve*. First, it is the joy of seeing the sucker fattened for the kill; later, after her disappointment in love, it is that of the plotter seeking vengeance. "I need him," she intones, her mouth slightly open in anticipation, "like the axe needs the turkey." When Jean makes her second-act entrance as visiting British aristocrat Eve, she practically dares Hopsie to recognize her. He doesn't. As he says later in the film, "If she didn't look so exactly like the other girl, I might be suspicious." She extracts her revenge and wins her man, all in one fell swoop. Theirs is a love story that transcends all plausibility, but for Sturges, plausibility is the garlic-clove of small minds, wielded in the hopes of warding off the bite of comic rapture.

The remarkable allure of *The Lady Eve* is its shimmering, undiminished ebullience. No matter how many twists the plot takes—Hopsie and Jean in love, then out of love; Jean as herself, then convincing Hopsie to fall in love all over again with her doppelganger—the film maintains an even keel of bemusement at this collision of starchy American moralism and an equally all-American brand of knavery. Jean is a crook, and her father is a thief, but their honest scheming, in Sturges's eyes, is far preferable to hypocritical uprightness. And might there not be a parallel with the director's own preference for honest, lowbrow comedy over puffed-up drama?

Lady Eve was Sturges's biggest critical and commercial success yet, but his remarkable run was only beginning. For his next effort, romantic comedy gave way to a dazzling mélange of genres and styles that could hardly be pigeonholed. Was it a Hollywood comedy? A romance? A tragedy? A Warner Bros.–style realist film about the Depression? The answer was "all of the above." *Sullivan's Travels* (1941) was to be Sturges's most remarkable accomplishment, and the richest statement ever made in American film about the nature and purpose of comedy.

Like Bob Hope and Bing Crosby's *Road* series, or the work of the Marx Brothers, *Sullivan's Travels* is a Hollywood effort aware of its own movieness. Small reminders are buried like land mines every few feet, beginning with the very first scene, in which a life-and-death struggle atop a moving train is interrupted by a title card: "The End." John L. "Sully" Sullivan (Joel McCrea) is screening a film for the bosses at his studio in the hopes of teaching them a little something about real moviemaking. Sully is worn out from the Herculean task of providing ninety minutes of the same escapist drivel to an audience too exhausted to demand better. It is time to make serious films, on serious topics, for a serious audience. The execs are far from convinced. "Who wants to see that kind of stuff?" one exclaims. "It gives me the creeps!"

Sullivan is unswayed, and sets out on a mission to unearth the real America—its poverty, its strife, its suffering. Problem is, he can't seem to find America. His first journey (there are four, just like in the film's explicit model, *Gulliver's Travels*) is a romantic farce, with Sullivan escaping spinster sisters intent on keeping the handsome stranger all for themselves. The second is a comedy of errors, with Sullivan and his newfound companion (Veronica Lake) riding the rails like a pair of hobos who just happen to have a paid staff, a well-stocked land yacht, and a pair of butlers calling the railroads to ask the time of the next freight train's arrival.

Suddenly, the tone shifts, with flickering lights and gloomy shadows as the couple tour a ramshackle encampment. McCrea and Lake stand in line for a hot dinner, and shiver with cold in an unheated church, as the camera roams row after row of hard-luck, unkempt men. All this takes place in a silent montage, with cloyingly sentimental music laid atop. Sturges is counting on our gag reflex kicking in; if we haven't screamed "baloney!" at least once during this sequence, he hasn't properly done his job. This, we come to understand, is the film Sully would make, if given the opportunity, complete with the gauzy ending of the couple staring at the moon-dappled water.

And here the story seems to end. It's "the greatest expedition of modern times," one hyperbolic press agent pronounces. Sully is a hero, and a national icon, and his movie—which he plans to call *O Brother, Where Art Thou?*—a surefire smash. Sully heads out one last time, to pass out five-dollar bills to some hard-luck cases, and is brutally attacked by a tramp.

Sully is dead, or so the world thinks. The bottom has dropped out of this safe, amiable film of studios and grosses and delusional directors, and suddenly trouble—real, unadulterated trouble—hangs in the air like a threat. Sully, groggy and suffering from amnesia, brains a tyrannical railyard bull with a rock, and is sentenced to six years at hard labor for his crime. Sully is now the star of his own version of *I Am a Fugitive from a Chain Gang*, with the back-breaking labor, vicious overseer, and aura of racial harmony through mutual suffering all borrowed from that earlier landmark of social realism. We have grown accustomed to the quicksilver moods of *Sullivan's Travels*, but Sturges is dead-serious now. He has rigged the entire film—every pratfall, every misstep, and every deliberately unconvincing moment—in order to arrive at this moment.

The chain gang's work is unforgiving, and their overseer brutal. The only respite is a weekly trip to a nearby church, where a sympathetic preacher hosts a film screening. The film is no *O Brother, Where Art Thou?*, or *I Am a Fugitive*, for that matter, but that most escapist of lightweight comedies—a Pluto cartoon. (Sturges had wanted to use a Chaplin short, but couldn't get the rights.) Sully, the cultural sophisticate, looks around, confused, studying the audience's reaction, and then asks the trusty: "Am I laughing?" Tired, dirty, and disheveled, his face blackened with soot, no longer distinct from the yearning masses he had once ached to instruct, Sully laughs. Comedy may be lowbrow; it may lack the intellectual heft of socially engaged drama; it may be little more than a momentary escape from real problems. It is also, at the most elemental level, a superb balm for those very same problems. As Sully later puts it: "There's a lot to be said for making people laugh. Did you know that's all some people have? It isn't much, but it's better than nothing in this cockeyed caravan."

The Palm Beach Story (1942) is a return to form, with Sturges—having made his dramatic point—reverting to the charmed romantic farce of *The Lady Eve*. It is an Art Deco comedy about genteel poverty, with Joel McCrea as an idealistic but underemployed architect, and Claudette Colbert his underappreciated wife, who suggests divorce as a means of career advancement. McCrea is the audience surrogate here, flummoxed by his wife's scheming, and Colbert our guide into *Palm Beach*'s loopy romanticism. The dialogue is acid, the film's romantic glow cut by the wicked bite of its characters. Colbert fends off her husband's accusations of infidelity when a wealthy benefactor—the Weenie King of Texas, if you must know—provides her with an unexpected windfall: "You'll die laughing." McCrea is unmoved: "All right, convulse me."

She is a shameless flirt, planning to attract a wealthy new husband to bankroll McCrea's designs, and Sturges provides her with an ample array of foils. First, there is the Ale & Quail Club, a traveling circus of millionaires (played by some of Sturges's favorite male character actors), who smuggle her aboard the train heading to Florida and send out a shotgun-wielding search party when she goes missing. They are replaced by the Rockefeller-esque baron played by Rudy Vallee, who courts Colbert assiduously as his sister (Mary

Astor) lures the reluctant McCrea. "You never think of anything but Topic A, do you?" McCrea marvels, and Astor is puzzled: "Is there anything else?" *Palm Beach* is a comedy about sex, money, and success, its easy romance burdened by the pain of unfulfilled dreams. It is a backwards romance, in which husband woos wife while fending off her other suitors—and some prospects of his own. McCrea gets the last, appropriately Sturgesian word: "Everybody's a flop until he's a success."

The Great Moment (1944) reunites Sturges and McCrea, this time in a dramatic mood. Sturges's attempt at hagiography was still riddled with comic asides—McCrea smashing up a medical-supply store, the attempted experimentation on the family dog, his bungling efforts at dentistry—but the tone was elegiac. Dr. Morton, who discovers ether as a pain suppressant, sacrifices fame and fortune to save a servant-girl from the discomfort of an anesthesia-free operation. McCrea is charming, but Sturges's script is unsure of itself, and Paramount's butchering of the final cut, over the director's strenuous objections, hardly helped. The studio ended up sitting on *The Great Moment* for over a year; shot before *Miracle of Morgan's Creek* and *Hail the Conquering Hero*, it ended up following them into theaters.

Coming after a decade of tasteful drawing-room comedies and chaste romances, Sturges's films drastically pushed the envelope of comic acceptability. Some had protested the Ale & Quail Club's overzealous use of ammunition, considering wartime shortages, but they would have been better served reserving their outrage for Sturges's next two films. Demolishing the rickety edifice of wartime piety, *The Miracle of Morgan's Creek* and *Hail the Conquering Hero* (both 1944) took a sledgehammer to virginity, marriage, military service, and the idyllic small town. Little was left standing once Sturges had his way with American mores. "The Hays Office," James Agee observed about Sturges's wartime films, "has been raped in its sleep." The two films were enormous successes, but given their subject matter, could there be any surprise that they were to be Sturges's last such hits?

Joel McCrea—the quintessential all-American hero—had been Sturges's stand-in for three films, exuding boyish charisma and manly assurance. Now, Sturges replaced him with pint-sized neurotic Eddie Bracken. McCrea bent the world to his will, or charmed it into submission. Bracken, in stark contrast, could hardly convince his own extremities to comply with his orders. Nervously chattering, slumping in his seat, his eyes popping with shock and dismay, Bracken is the preyed-upon American male, at the mercy of forces greater than himself.

Sturges's comedies had always been loud, competing to be heard above the din, but *The Miracle of Morgan's Creek* approached new levels of cacophony. Bracken's 4F Norval Jones is drafted to serve as a surrogate husband for his longtime crush Trudy Kockenlocker (Betty Hutton) after she gets married to a departing soldier. Trudy cannot remember the name of the man she married—Ratzkiwatzki?—and has lost her marriage certificate, but has definitive proof of her newfound marital status growing in her belly. *Knocked Up* before its time, *Morgan's Creek* improbably manages, with a few necessary hedges, to be a comedy about an unmarried floozy who gets shitfaced and pregnant, then enlists a well-intentioned cretin for a face-saving marriage. Agee was hardly exaggerating; one wonders what manner of bribe (free meals for life at the Players?) Sturges must have offered for a film this eye-popping to be cleared for conservative American moviegoers. I mean, really: Kockenlocker?

Like Sully Sullivan, Norval has the misfortune of having his fondest hope come true. "I almost wish you could be in a lot of trouble sometime," he tells Trudy, hoping to prove his loyalty to her. Soon enough, Norval is riding to the rescue as Trudy's unwitting savior, agreeing to marry her and take responsibility for her forthcoming offspring. Norval is a sibling to *The Lady Eve*'s Hopsie, preyed upon by sharp-eyed women in search of a patsy. Norval is there to be snookered "like the ox was made to eat and the grape was made to drink," Trudy's teenage sister (Diana Lynn) argues. Hopsie was a turkey, and Norval is an ox, but both are not long for this world. Norval is pressganged, hoodwinked, accused, imprisoned, and ultimately feted, all for reasons beyond his control. He is fate's fool, and Sturges is his puppetmaster, jerking him hither and thither with merciless whimsy.

Stuttering, goggle-eyed, his pomaded hair quivering with intensity, Bracken is a one-man special effect—a jangling open nerve. Bracken is so over-the-top, in fact, that he manages to distract audiences from the film's astounding sexual frankness. At a time when even married characters were required to sleep in separate beds, *Morgan's Creek* genially barrels over well-honed statutes of marital propriety. The Governor and the Boss from *The Great McGinty* make appearances, too, hoping to turn the miracle of Morgan's Creek to political advantage. Being a Sturges character means joining an exclusive club—one where you're always invited back for an encore.

In *Hail the Conquering Hero*, Bracken is Woodrow Truesmith (Sturges has a true gift for ridiculous names, doesn't he?), son of a WWI hero. Rejected from military service, Woodrow is working in a California manufacturing plant and sending letters home filled with imaginary stories of Pacific derring-do. Discovered in a bar by a passel of salty working-class Marines, they are struck by an idea: what if one of them lends him a uniform, and some medals, and they escort him home to his mother?

Hail is an interlocking spiral of ever-escalating disasters, with one unexpected calamity leading to another. The townsfolk, hungry for a hero, strike up an impromptu welcome-home rally, then draft him to run for mayor. His mother's mortgage is ritually burnt, and his ex-fiancée (Ella Raines) casts longing glances in his direction. And quasi-psychotic Marine Bugsy (Freddie Steele), comically overprotective, won't allow Woodrow to tell the truth to his mother.

The addition of Bracken twisted the antic spirit of *Palm Beach Story* into something positively excruciating. With Bracken as the central node in a revolving axis of absurdity, every twist and turn of the plot registers on his face. Bracken is forever mugging for an unseen audience, his mouth and eyes registering mute horror at the depths of his degradation. *Hail* is a group film, with Bracken always surrounded by his admirers. That a sea of boosters could become a lynch mob is the subtext of Sturges's deeply subversive film, which echoes Sturges's career-long distrust for, and fascination with, public opinion. This is essential to the story—Woodrow is literally hemmed in by his well-wishers—but it is also representative of Sturges's raucous democracy.

Comedians' stories rarely end well, and Sturges's was no exception. His last three films at Paramount had him butting heads with new production chief Buddy De Sylva, who eventually let his most successful director depart the studio. Sturges signed a lavish contract to work for Howard Hughes, but only managed to make three increasingly mediocre films for him: the Harold Lloyd comeback *The Sin of Harold Diddlebock* (1947), the painfully unfunny fantasy *Unfaithfully Yours* (1948), and the Betty Grable vehicle *The Beautiful Blonde from Bashful Bend* (1949).

Sturges asserted his authority over Lloyd to disastrous effect on *Diddlebock*, making a Harold Lloyd picture that sounded like Sturges and went precisely nowhere. *Unfaithfully Yours* was even worse, a disastrous comedy of revenge cued to classical music. The murderous scenario was darkly promising, but *Unfaithfully* lacked the charm of Chaplin's *Monsieur Verdoux*, released the previous year. Rex Harrison's dreadfully unpleasant performance was partially to blame, but Sturges's instinct for skirting the edge of artistic calamity had abandoned him. And Betty Grable, who had starred in Ernst Lubitsch's abortive last film, *That Lady in Ermine*, hammered the final nail into the coffin of Sturges's career with her wooden performance in *Bashful Bend*.

Without the support of Paramount's lavish studio facilities, and the deep bench of character performers essential to the success of his films, Sturges had to concentrate his attentions on individual actors—never his strong suit. Without the full roster of Sturges accomplices, his late films feel curiously empty, and silent. *Diddlebock* was not only Harold Lloyd's artistic epitaph; it was Sturges's, too. A melancholy farce about failure, it wondered what it felt like to know that your best days were behind you.

10

CARY GRANT

THE PICTURE OF
ARCHIE LEACH

"I pretended to be somebody I wanted to be, and
I finally became that person." —Cary Grant

T he American comedy has reached a state of perfection only twice: first
with Charlie Chaplin, and then with Cary Grant. Besides British ances-
try, and an adolescence spent in the music halls, what Chaplin and Grant
shared was a sense of having burst onscreen already fully formed. Chaplin grew and grew as an artist, his palette expanding from Sennett slapstick

Grant and Katharine Hepburn confront the perils of *Bringing Up Baby*.

to the brilliant inventiveness of his Mutual shorts to the still-unparalleled union of the physical and the spiritual that marked his feature-length work, but always appeared to be merely unfolding another corner of a portrait already fully sketched. Cary Grant, too, gave the impression of having simply arrived; here he was, cartwheeling across the screen, lightly bantering with generation after generation of leading ladies, never aging, never weakening, never growing weary of the burden of reminding all of us out there sitting in the dark of whom we might become, if only we, too, could be as carefree as Cary Grant.

But that both was and was not the whole story. Even after shedding the remnants of Archie Leach—his miserable Bristol childhood, his years of vaudevillian servitude—Cary Grant was not, yet, "Cary Grant." Grant was a leading man from the start—tall, dark, and handsome—but in his earliest films, sparring with Mae West in *She Done Him Wrong* (1933), he is all wrong: gawky and reticent. Watching him grapple with West, fending off her onslaught of sexual sallies, we are struck by his gormlessness. Who is this man posing as Cary Grant? With the benefit of hindsight, we know there is a formidable comic intelligence lurking behind those hooded eyes, trapped beneath those silly costumes, but for the life of us, we cannot find the slightest trace of it. If Grant's career had consisted solely of his two collaborations with West, he would still be remembered, if only for being the recipient of the most famous come-on in screen history, but for little more.

Then Claudette Colbert hiked up her skirt and crooked her thumb in *It Happened One Night*, and the walls of Jericho came crashing down, opening a gap for Cary Grant to batter his way through. Screwball comedy did not begin with Grant, but its essence—of gleeful frivolity and effortless charm— was made to serve the actor's strengths. Grant had initially been hired by Paramount as a Gary Cooper manqué—a fill-in when the more famous screen star was busy and a potential replacement if Cooper ever grew too big for his britches. The concept seems absurd to us now; how could anyone have confused Grant with the stolid, slow-moving Coop?

Paramount clearly had no idea what to do with him, which is why it agreed to loan him out to RKO in 1935 for a patchy venture called *Sylvia Scarlett*. Grant was a Cockney grifter who teams up with, and takes advantage of, Katharine Hepburn and Edmund Gwenn's father-daughter team of amateur criminals. *Sylvia Scarlett* is an impossible jumble of moods, genres, and styles, leapfrogging from farce to tragedy with nary a warning, and yet there is magic in the film that no amount of narrative turmoil can stifle. Hepburn and the film's director, George Cukor, had loosed something in Grant. Ambiguity was the order of the day; *Sylvia Scarlett* was a terrible box-office flop in large part because of the film's playful indistinction about genders, roles, even sexual preferences. Nonetheless, the gifted actress, so skilled at imprinting her ebullient good cheer on celluloid, had spurred Grant to be better than he had ever been before. Sprinting for the first time to keep up with a world-class runner, he discovered what he might be capable of.

Paramount still did not understand what it had on its hands, so when his contract expired in 1936, Cary Grant became a free agent, picking his own projects without proper affiliation with any studio. The punishment for his reckless individualism was tallied with the Oscar ballots: the Academy Awards, serving as the industry's coronation of its own favorites, perpetually snubbed Grant's best work (nominating him only twice, for his treacliest dramatic performances). Like Chaplin and Keaton, and most everyone profiled here, Cary Grant was never awarded a competitive Oscar.

Grant's unparalleled run as a leading man and comedian owes an enormous debt to the remarkable directors—Leo McCarey, George Cukor, and above all, Howard Hawks—with whom he had the intelligence and good fortune to work. But it is also testament to the man, who more than any other figure in this book, except Chaplin, embodies American film comedy at its best. If Mount Rushmore were dedicated to comedians instead of statesmen, Cary Grant would have found himself climbing across his own face in *North by Northwest*. His sheer presence made for a new kind of comedy, one never before attempted. The great comics who came before Grant had mostly been runts: shrimpy underdogs with a gift for coming out on top. But what if the romantic leading man was also the comedian?

Born in Bristol, England, in 1904, Archie Leach had been a child of the music hall. Archie had seen Chaplin perform with the Fred Karno troupe as a young boy. At age thirteen, when an assistant teacher brought him backstage at the Bristol Hippodrome to tour the theater's switchboard and lighting systems, he was mesmerized, and hooked. A misfocused spotlight that inadvertently revealed a magician's best trick cost him the Hippodrome job, but Leach's acrobatic ability won him a spot in Bob Pender's troupe, touring the length and breadth of Britain. Home life was something to be endured, and escaped; Archie's mother had vanished one day when he was ten years old. He was eventually told she had died of a heart attack. It was only decades later, when Cary Grant was already a world-famous actor, that he learned she had been institutionalized and was still very much alive.

Leach made his American debut in 1920, when Pender's company was invited to New York by impresario Charles Dillingham. On tour with Dillingham's revue *Good Times*, he met the Marx Brothers, who were also making the rounds of the Keith theatrical circuit. (Oddly enough, he was most taken with Zeppo, studying that most anonymous of Marxes' fashion sensibility.) When the show closed, he chose not to go back to England, preferring to test his luck in New York. There were tough times; for a while, Archie peddled his roommate's neckties on the street. Leach assisted mind-readers, jugglers, and unicyclists, and did some stilt-walking as well. He had a stool at Broadway hangout Rudley's, where the other patrons included Moss Hart and Preston Sturges, but no real career to call his own.

Slowly, walk-on Broadway roles turned into a long-term contract with the Shubert Organization, which tided him over during the fallow years after the stock market crash of 1929. Eventually, the movies came calling. After a successful screen test, Paramount general manager B. P. Schulberg suggested changing his name to something more mellifluous. How about Cary Lockwood—the name of a character he had played onstage? Not liking the sound of Lockwood, the actor scanned a studio-prepared list of preferred last names, and picked Grant. A Hollywood star was born.

The Cary Grant we knew made his first appearance in 1937's *Topper*, an amiable fantasy of the afterlife in which his prematurely deceased playboy, accompanied by wife Constance Bennett, embarks on a shambling crusade to improve the fortunes of the banker who had been in charge of managing their fortune. *Topper* had the charm of screwball, but without its savage wit. It did not uncover the essential conflict of the form: the battle of the sexes, knowing and calloused. These comedies of remarriage, as Stanley Cavell would dub them, were close combat between competitors all too aware of their opponents' weaknesses. They knew where all the dirty socks were buried. For such an enterprise, Cary Grant was the ideal star: even knowing his faults, what woman could refuse him permanently?

The real fun begins with *The Awful Truth* (1937), where Grant crashes his ex-wife Irene Dunne's staid romance and enjoys the ensuing havoc. "Ever since I was a small boy," Grant purrs to her new flame, Ralph Bellamy, with mock-sincerity, his smile dripping with good-natured condescension, "that name has been filled with magic for me: Oklahoma." Twisting the knife one turn further, he lets his enthusiasm for Oklahoma City spill over: "And if it should get dull, you can always go over to Tulsa for the weekend." Grant narrowly avoids choking on "Tulsa," savoring this moment of supercilious mockery.

Love, in these movies, is a shared conspiracy. Screwball cracks the door open just enough for us to get a glimpse of what happiness might be: a private joke for two. Grant wrecks Dunne's dull future, and she returns the favor, but all along we know that they are only meant for each other. Who else would know when to laugh?

The Awful Truth is screwball with a touch of Lubitsch, all mismatched hats and lovers hiding behind closed doors. Grant treats every scene as an opportunity to score points off Dunne, enjoying the competition more than the marriage. Grant and Dunne would essentially remake *The Awful Truth* three years later, as *My Favorite Wife* (1940). Leo McCarey (who had won an Oscar for *The Awful Truth*) had been scheduled to direct before falling sick, and was replaced at the last minute by screenwriter (and future Hepburn-Tracy hagiographer) Garson Kanin. Grant is torn between ex-wife Dunne, unexpectedly returned after being lost at sea for seven years, and his fusspot new wife (Gail Patrick).

There are echoes of *Awful Truth*'s cunning, with Grant marvelously professing mock-befuddlement over Dunne's desert-island companion (Randolph Scott), but Lubitsch's smoothness has been elided, replaced by a klutzy, anxious energy native to Cary Grant alone. Patting his brow apprehensively as Scott shows off on the diving board, knocking a glass of water onto a judge's brief, Grant was displaying chinks in the armor of his allure. Cutting against the bias of his own flawless good looks, Grant had discovered that bungling suited him well.

Would it have changed matters at all to know that Cary Grant himself, if forced to choose, might have selected neither Dunne nor Patrick, but Scott's Tarzan-esque muscleman? Rumors had bounced around Hollywood in the 1930s that the two actors, roommates in a Santa Monica beach house, were more than friends—rumors that apparently had more than a shred of truth to them. Cary Grant, though, could be said to only truly exist onscreen; this man showing up at parties dressed as a woman, or posing in matching aprons with Scott, was someone else entirely, someone we didn't know at all. "Everybody wants to be Cary Grant," the actor once mused. "Even I want to be Cary Grant." The offscreen Cary Grant—the one who lived with Scott, who married five times, who experimented with LSD—was a shadow, a mere speck obscuring our view of the flawless giant on the screen.

Crawling on all fours like his dog Mr. Smith, wrestling with an ill-fitting hat, Grant revealed a heretofore unknown gift for physical comedy in *The Awful Truth* which prepared him well for *Bringing Up Baby* (1938), the most ebullient of Grant's screwball pictures, and a shining example of the form. Dunne had been a worthy screwball foil for Grant, her honeyed drawl a useful counterpoint to Grant's brusqueness, but it was Katharine Hepburn who unquestionably summoned his untapped genius.

Throughout *Bringing Up Baby*, bumbling scientist David (Grant) and WASP princess Susan (Hepburn) speak at cross purposes—she airy and flighty, he bumbling and increasingly agitated. She has swiped his golf ball and sideswiped his car, and has inveigled him into stealing another woman's purse. Grant, for one, is not amused. "It isn't that I don't like you, Susan, because, after all, in moments of quiet, I'm strangely drawn toward you, but—well, there haven't been any quiet moments." Nor would there be. Hawks's film is a masterpiece of maniacal frenzy, a screwball adventure whose mismatched protagonists dance a two-step of attraction and repulsion. Grant's paleontologist, obsessively fixated on the final missing bone for his brontosaurus, is the helpless plaything of Hepburn's dizzy dame, dragged off to the wilds of Connecticut to chase a runaway leopard, find his missing intercostal clavicle, and salvage the funding for his research. No amount of wriggling can free him from her stifling embrace; one of the most pleasurable aspects of *Bringing Up Baby*, which amuses as it discomfits, is watching Grant vainly attempt to slither out of her clutches.

David does not appear to be enjoying the show much, but this, we come to understand, has been a put-on as well. "I just discovered that was the best day I ever had in my whole life!," he tells her at the very end of the film, only belatedly realizing that turmoil, not calm, is his fuel of choice. The same was true for screwball.

To describe *Holiday*, from that same year, as a lesser collaboration is to imply an entirely unfounded mediocrity. Grant has less to work with, his character an upwardly mobile grind in search of relaxation who discovers that his fiancée's sister (Hepburn) is far more likely to provide it than his overly practical betrothed. Grant and Hepburn bat their effortless banter back and forth like a badminton birdie, each anxious not to let it drop. Practicing their cartwheels (Grant's adolescent training as a tumbler had come in handy), rehearsing together for a parental interrogation, the two stars speak a language comprehensible to no one else on screen.

Bringing Up Baby is, among other things, a celebration of speed, but its velocity pales in comparison with Grant and Hawks's breathless *His Girl Friday* (1940). Ben Hecht and Charles MacArthur's play, updated by Charles Lederer, was sentimental about its motor-mouthed cynicism, its ink-stained wretches redeemed by their uncynical affection for their ragged trade. As newspaper editor Walter Burns (a role inhabited with equal gusto, if less flair, by Walter Matthau in Billy Wilder's *The Front Page*), Grant is marvelously insincere. Oozing phony earnestness, Walter is a snake, and his ex-wife Hildy Johnson (Rosalind Russell) is only too familiar with the oil he peddles. Bellamy is here again, with the promised land of Oklahoma City replaced by Albany, leading Walter to further flights of rhapsody: "A home with Mother, in Albany too!"

Grant is a marvelous cad, perpetually coiled in anticipation of the next surprise strike. Burns is a more respectable version of Grant's huckster from *Sylvia Scarlett*, quick with a scheme and fluent in the ways of the con. In a career of smooth-talking roles, Walter Burns is Grant's most effortless. He plays the rubes—who include everyone but Hildy—like so many xylophones. "Maybe she'll think kindly of me after I'm gone," he tells Bellamy, wiping a tear from his eye in mock-tenderness, and tapping his rival on the shoulder when he fails to pay adequate attention to the bravura performance.

Like a dull setting for a brilliant diamond, screwball required the efforts of a few good Ralph Bellamys to properly offset Grant. "He looks like, um, that fella in the movies, you know . . . ," Grant's Walter Burns tells a slinky blonde he has hired to gum up the works between Bellamy and his ex-wife in *His Girl Friday*, the name on the tip of his tongue: "Ralph Bellamy." Bellamy's kind-hearted but fatally slow dullards hinted at what the burgeoning genre favored: speed, wit, charm, and adaptability. The genre may have been birthed elsewhere, but the face of its emergent maturity is Grant's, and Grant's alone.

Screwball married the physical ingenuity of silent slapstick with the dazzling cascades of verbal wit associated with the New York stage. Famously taxing of its performers, screwball exposed those actors incapable of meeting its demands. Unique among his fellow stars, Grant could easily handle both the physical and verbal challenges of screwball. From his stable of costars, only Katharine Hepburn was a true equal, but Grant's radiance was generous, raising his fellow performers rather than diminishing them. Even a limited actress like Russell was near-miraculous in *His Girl Friday*, giving as good as she got for the film's ninety-one minutes.

There would be one more collaboration between Grant and Hepburn, before the actress was drawn into the orbit of Spencer Tracy: *The Philadelphia Story* (1940), also directed by Cukor, and costarring James Stewart. The film was Hepburn's, even with the glittering cast, devoted to her show-business redemption via ceremonial humiliation. Grant is present mostly as an onlooker, playing the reformed ex-husband who refuses to let Hepburn's Tracy Lord marry beneath her. The two stars are royalty, and everyone else— even Stewart's ham-fisted reporter—are commoners. Grant, resplendent in gray suit and black tie, discovered an elemental truth that would serve him well for the rest of his career: with his looks, and his charm, he could get away with anything—including playing an unpleasant shit like *Philadelphia*'s C. K. Dexter Haven.

Richard Schickel, in his monograph on the actor, references the "obvious decline" in Grant's work after his trifecta of 1940 classics (*The Philadelphia Story*, *His Girl Friday*, and *My Favorite Wife*). While the films do indeed grow weaker in spirit, Grant's performances hardly flag. Once invigorated by screwball, Grant never let go of its spirit, even in inhospitable circumstances. The boys' adventures *Only Angels Have Wings* (1939) and *Gunga Din* (1939) had been animated by Grant's frantic good cheer, and even the weepie *Penny Serenade* (1941) is enlivened by the sight of Grant lugging around a giant pile of records in the hope of wooing Irene Dunne's comely record-store clerk.

Grant's personality made requests of his film's scenarios that they other- wise might not have been inclined to concede. *Mr. Lucky* (1943), which set out as a *Casablanca*-esque wartime tale of belatedly assumed responsibil- ity, eschews its ostensible moral fervor in favor of Grant's clowning. Grant is another Walter Burns–ian amoral charmer: beguiling the leaders of a wom- en's organization into submission in the hopes of winning a coveted gam- bling commission, he is bedazzled in turn by do-gooder Laraine Day. "Never give a sucker an even break," he proclaims, echoing W. C. Fields, but Day plays Grant for a sucker, sticking a needle in each of his paws and entrusting him with the mission of knitting for the boys overseas. Soon enough, a grow- ing mass of men gather outside the window to watch his fumbling efforts, entranced by the sight of this 1A star's 4F efforts.

As quickly as it had appeared, screwball had departed, its energies spent and its aura of boisterous unruliness no longer appropriate for a nation at war. The magic of the 1930s had evaporated, and the comedies of the new decade had grown strained, hectic rather than energetic. *The Talk of the Town* (1942) was a strange hybrid of *Bringing Up Baby* and *I Am a Fugitive from a Chain Gang*, with Grant as a left-wing firebrand on the run from the police, educating Ronald Colman's future Supreme Court justice about the evils of the American judicial system. Anguished and idealistic was hardly Grant's forte, even when played partially for laughs, and George Stevens's film comes off as astoundingly misguided. *Arsenic and Old Lace*, shot in 1941 but held from theaters until the conclusion of the Broadway show's theatrical run in 1944, was a black comedy with bum notes of noir menace. Cary Grant and Peter Lorre hardly seemed to belong to the same Hollywood, let alone the same film. Director Frank Capra encourages Grant to overplay, his eyebrows permanently raised, his eyes practically popping out of their sockets, and a lone strand of hair hanging down his forehead like an exclamation mark.

Still, the spirit of screwball lingered. H. C. Potter's *Mr. Blandings Builds His Dream House* (1948) finds Grant burdened with wife, family, advertising job, and ramshackle Connecticut house—far too many possessions for the free-spirited ethos of classic screwball. (Considering how that state had treated him in *Bringing Up Baby*, he really should have known better than to purchase property in Connecticut.) The air of simmering frustration makes for a symbolic link with Grant's 1930s classics. Of all his films, *Mr. Blandings* is perhaps the most underappreciated. Grant and wife Myrna Loy, assisted by best friend and attorney Melvyn Douglas, set out for their patch of rural bliss, only to find they have purchased a sinkhole where ambitions, and paychecks, go to die. Wrestling with everything from rabbited lintels to Zuz-Zuz water filters, Grant embodies the slow-burning irritation of the home builder. *Blandings* is a domestic film, its pleasures and its trials equally modest: the opening morning ritual in Grant and Loy's New York City apartment, with everything in its wrong place, is a small masterpiece of frazzled physical comedy.

If screwball were really to make a full-fledged comeback, the master practitioner's assistance would be required. Howard Hawks's two late collaborations with Grant are self-conscious attempts to resuscitate the genre. They are postwar films played at 1930s speed. The paragon of masculinity is feminized in *I Was a Male War Bride* (1949), playing a French officer tormented by the U.S. Army's draconian rules regarding marriage. Blithe American in uniform Ann Sheridan abandons her new husband Grant to his own devices, scrabbling for a place to sleep, and a means of joining her in America. Sleeplessness substitutes for sexual frustration, with the bridegroom stumbling around in a state of ever-increasing agitation, unable to find a bed of his own. As the humiliations pile up, Grant smiles cheerily at his degradation, which culminates in his donning a bad Spinal Tap wig and a skirt and posing as his wife's wife. He graciously turns down an offer of lipstick to round out his outfit: "I'm more the outdoor type."

Sex had been withheld in *War Bride*, but in *Monkey Business* (1952) it is sublimated, replaced by more mature pursuits. Grant was once more the absent-minded scientist, revisiting *Bringing Up Baby*'s David Huxley and adding a distinct note of middle-aged regret. Having discovered the formula for reversing the aging process, Grant tests it out on himself, and promptly transforms into a sex-crazed adolescent. His out-of-control hormones meet their match in the voluptuous Marilyn Monroe, whose pendulous breasts point accusingly at him like an unanswered question. *Monkey Business* is a comedy of male anxiety over aging crammed with copious double entendres, mostly revolving around Monroe's luscious figure. Grant buys a loud sports coat and an even louder roadster, to the consternation of his wife (Ginger Rogers). Rogers swigs some formula too, and soon husband and wife are in a race of regression back to childhood, with Rogers channeling her performance as Su-Su in Billy Wilder's *The Major and the Minor*. *Monkey Business* is, as Grant says of his formula, nothing more than "a series of low-comedy disasters," but like *Bringing Up Baby*, its silliness is offset by an undercurrent of anomie: what happens when the formula wears off, and normal life returns?

Grant never aged, never changed; one could imagine a Picture of Archie Leach moldering horribly in some forgotten attic as Cary Grant maintained his looks well into his seventh decade. The actor had become a national treasure, his success unflagging, his films dedicated to the preservation of his mystique. If they also tread gingerly around Grant, that was only the price to be paid for his unparalleled achievement. Cary Grant could no longer play a Hawksian bumbler; from here on out, he could only play "Cary Grant," that silver-tongued, silver-haired charmer. The mask had hardened, enclosing him within it. The tail end of Grant's career saw some of his most notable triumphs—1959's *Operation Petticoat* was his biggest box-office hit, and the romantic comedy *That Touch of Mink* (1962), with Doris Day, his second-biggest—and a handful of noteworthy additions to his canon.

Of all his directors, none cherished Grant's abiding appeal so much as Alfred Hitchcock, who saw him as an idealized doppelganger. Grant had enlivened Hitchcock's taut dramas *Suspicion* (1941) and *Notorious* (1946), and would play the charming roué in two of Hitch's most sparkling sex comedies. Grant is only ostensibly the star of *To Catch a Thief* (1955); the eye is continually distracted by the magnificent French Riviera, which serves as the film's backdrop, and the even more magnificent Grace Kelly, who plays Grant's sparring partner. *Thief*'s exploding fireworks are matched by *North by Northwest*'s surging trains as unsubtle emblems of what could still, at this point, only be hinted at. The hints, however, were growing stronger; the whispers were now loud enough to be heard in the back row of the theater.

Kelly, unpacking a picnic basket, asks him: "Leg or breast?" *North by Northwest*'s Eva Marie Saint pursues him with yet more forceful ardor, brooking no debate in her assault: "It's a long night, and I don't particularly like the book I've started. You know what I mean?" The tension was itself an aphrodisiac. Hitchcock cuts from Grant pulling Saint up from the ledge of Mount Rushmore to her being hoisted into bed, all in one smooth motion.

Kelly, Saint, and *Charade*'s Audrey Hepburn were each paying tribute to the undimmed appeal of the man who had courted the screen's most beautiful women for thirty-five years. "Do you know what's wrong with you?" Hepburn asks, cooing sensually as she approaches Grant. "Nothing." These late films agreed with her assessment. *North by Northwest* was a terrifically inventive comic travelogue, embroiling Grant's Roger O. Thornhill in espionage and murder without ever soiling his perfectly pressed suit. The actor predetermined the jocular action; if this was Cary Grant, none of this could be all that serious.

Charade (1963), Stanley Donen's attempt at recreating Hitchcock's magic, is yet more playful. This was a comedy about the aura of Cary Grant, with copious MacGuffinry only momentarily diverting the eye from its primary object of contemplation. Hepburn gets into the spirit of worshipful study, gazing up at his famous cleft chin and wondering, "How do you shave in there?"

When not under the spell of Hitch, or his imitators, Grant's work grew timid. Neither *Operation Petticoat*, with Tony Curtis (who would contribute the best-ever imitation of the star to Billy Wilder's *Some Like It Hot*), nor *Houseboat* (1958), with the fetching Sophia Loren as his children's nanny, were particularly memorable, and *That Touch of Mink* was more Doris Day's picture, with Grant hired as a stand-in for noted Grant imitator Rock Hudson.

The sole exception to the trend was Donen's *Indiscreet* (1958), which reunited Grant with *Notorious* costar Ingrid Bergman. As a well-regarded stage actress whose love life has hit a rough patch, Bergman is literally frozen in her tracks by the entrance of Grant. There is a touch of Lubitsch to Donen's directorial restraint, as well as a hint of *Pillow Talk* whimsy to Grant and Bergman's split-screen phone call. Both screen legends are a bit old for this virginal claptrap, but *Indiscreet* hardly minds, entranced by their pairing, and winking at the old proprieties.

Stung by Bergman's (momentary) rejection in *Indiscreet*, Grant heads for the door, murmuring, "I've seen plays with wonderful good-bye lines in them. I'm trying to remember one." No such good-bye line was provided for Cary Grant's career, but when the time came when women would no longer naturally flock to him, he knew it was time to make his exit. Virtually alone among his comedic peers, Grant chose when to say good-bye, and did so before he ever had the chance to embarrass himself. He would spend the last twenty years of his life serving on corporate boards, collecting lifetime achievement awards (including that long-denied honorary Oscar, in 1970), and occasionally showing up on television, or at a local theater, to share the odd reminiscence. The notion was a strange one. A creation of the screen, who was Cary Grant without it? But it all made a certain kind of sense. While the man who played Cary Grant could age, and even die, Cary Grant never could. Leaving us when he did, Grant ensured that the man onscreen never would.

11

KATHARINE HEPBURN

SPENCER'S RIB

"Not much meat on her, but what's there is cherce."
—Spencer Tracy, *Pat and Mike*

"You're rather *short*, aren't you?" Tall, lanky Katharine Hepburn, her sharply etched cheekbones and patrician nose genetic proof of old-money New England hauteur, gazes down at stocky, lumpy Spencer Tracy, with his silly-putty face and barrel chest. It is their first meeting, before they begin shooting their first picture together, *Woman of the Year*, and Hepburn, already famous for her performances as high-society bluebloods, was in character, even with the cameras off. This time, though, the tables were to be

Hepburn studies Tracy in *Guess Who's Coming to Dinner?*

turned. "Don't worry, honey," the film's producer Joseph L. Mankiewicz told Hepburn, a twinkle in his eye, "he'll cut you down to size." Roll camera on the legendary partnership—onscreen and off—of Tracy and Hepburn, Hollywood's shining exemplars of love, marriage, and equality.

Or so the story goes. The setup, the dialogue, the promise of future fireworks—it all sounds like a scene from a script by Garson Kanin and Ruth Gordon, the screenwriters most famous for creating the Tracy and Hepburn mythos. And indeed, this story's most famous iteration comes from Kanin's tell-all memoir *Tracy and Hepburn*, source of so many of the legendary stories of the couple's offscreen hours. Legends appear to be just what they were, for the most part—cozy tales of domestic bliss and professional partnership, burnished to a dull glow by the couple's hagiographers. But as a character in onetime Hepburn flame John Ford's film *The Man Who Shot Liberty Valance* once said, "When the truth becomes legend, print the legend." In essence, the films have become proof of the veracity of the stories, and the stories proof of the veracity of the films.

In reality, the Tracy-Hepburn relationship was more complex, and less romantic, than the legends allowed for. Far from cozily curling up in front of the fire, Hepburn nestled at Tracy's feet, the two actors were more like platonic friends than committed lovers. Married, with two children, the devoutly Catholic Tracy never divorced his wife, returning nearly every weekend to their San Fernando Valley home. Hepburn, meanwhile, shuffled through a rotating cast of female assistants, bosom friends, and advisers, many of whom lived and traveled with her. The closest Tracy and Hepburn came to living together was in the early 1960s, when they resided in adjoining cottages on the property of director George Cukor. Hepburn helped nurse Tracy, who was then in failing health from a lifetime of alcoholism, until his death.

The legend of Hepburn and Tracy, timeless lovers, began to grow only after the actor's death in 1967, once Hepburn saw the value of letting others turn her complex relationship with her mercurial costar into the stuff of undying love. So goes the unattractive business of creating the folklore of American popular culture. To find the Hepburn and Tracy we know and care for, then, we can no longer turn to the lives, but must instead find them in that place where they were most truly themselves—or at least the selves we wanted them to be: the films.

Marriage, they say, is no laughing matter, and American films have mostly agreed with that sentiment. Comedies traditionally end in marriage—they don't begin with them. Sure, William Powell and Myrna Loy made a charming Nick and Nora Charles, fighting crime and throwing back martinis in the *Thin Man* series, but for the most part, comedy demanded the possibility of romance—not bickering over who would dry the dishes. Katharine Hepburn and Spencer Tracy, who would form the best-known and most beloved romantic duo of the 1940s and 1950s, made domesticity exciting by entertaining us with their squabbling.

Marriage is never bliss for Hepburn and Tracy in this series of films; instead, it presents the opportunity to spar, day in and day out, with a partner of your choosing, one capable of parrying any thrusts you made, and offering some sharp jabs of his or her own. It is something of a historical irony that the movie couple who came to best signify romantic bliss and domestic tranquility was hardly representative of either.

It is nearly always a fool's errand to read autobiography into performance, but one cannot help but picture the young Katharine Hepburn as Terry Randall from the acerbic backstage comedy *Stage Door* (1937), asking the fellow residents of her Manhattan boardinghouse, "The trouble with you is you're all trying to be comics. Don't you ever take anything seriously?" Like Terry, Hepburn had been drawn to the theater against the wishes of her upper-crust Connecticut family, who saw acting as a whim unsuited to her station in life. After graduating from Bryn Mawr, Hepburn headed to Baltimore to act in local theater, thereby earning the enmity of her father, who cut her off financially—just like Terry's father.

Baltimore gave way to New York, and a series of small roles, including one in a show Hepburn would later star in—Philip Barry's *Holiday*. She was, by her own estimation, a poor actress then, gawky and clumsy, but with an intensity that belied her then-meager abilities. One is tempted, once more, to picture Hepburn as Terry, the wealthy, stage-struck ingenue, combating the Shakespeare-hating masses, with her limber wit her only weapon. "If I can act," she breezily tells her friends, "I want the world to know." She is Connecticut royalty, with a touch of Old Country diction—it's "lahst," not "laast" year—and the world, she expects, will be her oyster.

By the time of her first meeting with Tracy, Hepburn had, in fact, been a movie star for some ten years. Audiences were partial to her in roles like *Alice Adams* (1935), a George Stevens–directed tearjerker where she was soft and pliable as a lovelorn wallflower, but Hepburn preferred pricklier, more unpredictable characters—the kind that would get her pegged as "box-office poison." Starring alongside Cary Grant in four films, Hepburn is the defining spirit of the screwball era: headstrong, imperious, idiosyncratic, and tempestuous.

Sylvia Scarlett (1935), directed by George Cukor, is accordingly Hepburn's film, its magnificent weirdness a product of her dramatic ambidextrousness. Unsure of whether it prefers comedy or drama, romantic farce or poetic melancholy, *Sylvia Scarlett* opts for all of the above. The entire film feels like a delicious transgression, with Hepburn, Cary Grant, and Edmund Gwenn (playing Hepburn's father) flitting from mood to mood, and scene to scene, on nothing more than a whim and an outline. As a result, *Sylvia Scarlett* makes absolutely no sense. But with Hepburn and Grant together, who needs sense?

Perhaps the most nonsensical of *Sylvia Scarlett*'s follies had been for Hepburn to end up with the free-spirited artist played by Brian Aherne, and not with Grant. The film argued fiercely for it, but the outcome felt forced and unsatisfying. Howard Hawks made no such mistake with *Bringing Up Baby* (1938), which begins with Hepburn swiping Grant from his charmless fiancée. David Thomson describes *Bringing Up Baby* as "a screwball comedy surrounded by darkness, forever on the brink of madness," and its air of frenzy comes courtesy of Hepburn, whose inability to comprehend Grant's objections is entirely feigned. Hepburn never catches Grant's retorts, but only because she doesn't want to, afraid of what rejection might mean. Hepburn represents the forces of chaos, and resist as he might, Grant cannot fend her off—nor, ultimately, does he want to.

Pauline Kael, for one, favorably compared Hepburn's collaborations with Grant to her later work with Spencer Tracy, noting that with Tracy "she was humanized but maybe also a little subjugated, and when we saw her through his eyes there seemed to be something the matter with her—she was too high-strung, had too much temperament. . . . She was more exciting with Cary Grant, who had a faint ambiguity and didn't want her to be more like ordinary women: Katharine Hepburn was a one-of-a-kind entertainment, and he could enjoy the show."

Holiday (1938) is a victory lap for Grant and Hepburn. This film is more Grant's than *Bringing Up Baby* had been, with Hepburn once more the liberating free spirit unlocking the gates of romantic bliss for constricted manhood. Her Linda Seton is more sloppily sentimental, and less of an anarchic force, than she had been in *Bringing Up Baby*, and Grant is more skilled at parrying her blows. *Holiday* lacks some of *Baby*'s propulsive, headlong force, but is remarkably charming drawing-room farce, a kooky-family comedy in the vein of that year's Best Picture winner, *You Can't Take It With You*. Hepburn is coolly, bemusedly herself, unwilling to abate or allay any part of her spiky, occasionally unlikable character. She knew it, too; when playwright Philip Barry (who had written *Holiday*) told Hepburn he was writing a new play called *The Philadelphia Story* with her as protagonist, she told him to "make her like me, but make her go all soft."

The Philadelphia Story (1940) is Hepburn's calculated penance for perceived crimes against the box office. Main Line socialite Tracy Lord (Hepburn) is set to remarry an up-by-the-bootstraps bore when her ex-husband C. K. Dexter Haven (Grant) shows up, accompanied by slick newspaperman Macaulay Connor (James Stewart). Tilted as it is toward frankly ludicrous mea culpas (Tracy is responsible for her father's infidelities, and her ex-husband's alcoholism!), *The Philadelphia Story* veers dangerously close to comedy of an unintentional sort. (The only thing the film fails to accuse Tracy of is stacking the Supreme Court.) Hepburn's crocodile tears—"I'm so sorry for being myself!"—are entirely disingenuous, and the film's desire to find ever-new avenues of attack on the helpless Tracy grows weary. Hepburn was to be castigated for the defects of her personality, but who wanted to see a kinder, gentler Katharine Hepburn? Tracy Lord is "simply a doppelganger of Katharine Hepburn," according to her biographer William J. Mann; the film "feels calculated and contrived," he concludes, "because it *is*."

Spencer Tracy, meanwhile, had been the gangster, the tough guy, the violent brawler. He was the Hearst-esque mogul in the *Citizen Kane* precursor *The Power and the Glory* (1933), written by Preston Sturges, and the survivor of a lynch mob whose vindictiveness sets him on a course for revenge in Fritz Lang's uncompromising *Fury* (1936). A fireplug with a squashed mug and a blunt, two-fisted approach to acting, Spencer Tracy made as unlikely a romantic hero as the gawky, asexual Hepburn made a romantic heroine.

Grant had been the absent-minded academic brought down to earth by Hepburn's flighty Susan Vance in *Bringing Up Baby*, and Tracy inherits his dilemma, if none of his characteristics, in the ebullient *Woman of the Year* (1942). A brief shot displaying two newspaper posters artfully delineates their non-overlapping spheres of influence: "HITLER WILL LOSE," read hers, while his screamed, in equally oversized block letters, "YANKEES WON'T LOSE." This wartime film hands over all matters of political import to Hepburn's imperious, much-in-demand pundit Tess Harding, while the small remainder of sporting superfluity is given over to Tracy's sportswriter Sam Craig. "WHAT DO YOU THINK?" another ad wondered. "TESS HARDING TELLS YOU DAILY."

Hepburn is no longer the sexually ambiguous pixie of *Sylvia Scarlett*, but an alluring, charming woman; the first glimpse we have of her here is of her

long, coltish leg. The foursquare Sam is immediately drawn to the aristocratic, brilliant Tess, but is tongue-tied in her presence. He literally lacks the
vocabulary needed to converse with her; their second date turns out to be
a fancy-dress cocktail party at which he seems to be the only monolingual
guest. Tess gabs easily in French, Russian, and Greek while Sam sticks his
hands into his pockets, tickled by his own discomfort.

This is Tracy's secret in all of his films with Hepburn; try as he might to
pretend otherwise, he is often surprised to find himself amused by his subser-
vience. There are outbursts, to be sure, and recriminations, but deep down, he
likes being Herr Harding, as one Teutonic well-wisher refers to him. *Woman
of the Year* hints—more than hints, in fact—that in their relationship, it is
Sam who is the woman, the secondary, passive figure.

Woman of the Year is a comedy of mutual conspiracy, in which two lovers form a united front—private, joshing, and complete—against the world.
Dating is bliss, with Sam good-naturedly enduring the lectures on Spengler
and interruptions by world leaders demanding a moment of Tess's time, but
marriage is another equation altogether. Crowned America's Outstanding
Woman of the Year, Tess is stung by Sam's unstated reproach that she is no
woman at all.

Tess is forced to repent for the crime of her presumption. She crawls back
to Sam, seeking to make amends by acting the housewife and preparing her
husband's breakfast. The result is an unmitigated disaster, in which Hepburn
is ritually debased for the temerity of her independence, *Philadelphia Story*
style. Sam reads the paper distractedly, napkin tucked into collar in hus-
bandly readiness, as Tess burns the coffee and mangles the toast. She watches
helplessly as the waffles bubble and hiss like some faceless ectoplasmic beast.
Tess, confidant of presidents and kings, pledges her allegiance to the chroni-
cler of the sporting world before he belatedly offers her an olive branch: "Why
can't you be Tess Harding Craig?" Masculine and feminine, blue-blood and
blue-collar, political giants and football Giants: the warring sexes reach a tentative but enduring peace through Tess's humiliation. Intended as *Woman
of the Year*'s comic highlight, this sequence is instead indication of something darker—something angry and dissatisfied—bubbling beneath the fizzy
surface.

After their starring turns in the turgid *Keeper of the Flame* (1942), which
miscast them as hunter and prey in a crude *Citizen Kane* knockoff, and the
melodramas *Without Love* (1945) and *The Sea of Grass* (1947), Hepburn and
Tracy were reunited for Frank Capra's political drama *State of the Union*

(1948). Tracy is a rock-ribbed conservative idealist mulling a run for the presidency, and Hepburn his estranged wife. Ludicrous as drama, *State of the Union* is better when viewed as another relationship comedy. Tracy's Grant Matthews has been stepping out with scheming newspaper baroness Angela Lansbury, and the tardy arrival of Hepburn's Mary Matthews partway into the film only complicates his dithering over whether to run for president.

Whatever their tangled history, there is still a lingering aura of domestic coziness between husband and wife: the very first thing she does upon seeing him is mend a hole on his tie. Tracy and Hepburn appear to be acting out private routines of their own devising, whatever the screenwriting credits might say. Mary calls Grant "Nappy"—short for Napoleon. "Looks a little like your brother Dick," Grant observes playfully about an anti-tax crank who sneaks into their hotel suite, and Mary laughs and kicks him in the shins.

State of the Union was immediately followed by the greatest and most enduring of the Tracy-Hepburn comedies, *Adam's Rib* (1949). Written by the husband-and-wife team of Garson Kanin (who had come up with the original idea for *Woman of the Year*) and Ruth Gordon, intimate friends of Hepburn and Tracy, *Adam's Rib* is a comedy of rivalry and manipulation, a mutual one-upmanship contest in which husband and wife are collaborators and competitors, at home and in the workplace. Tracy is an assistant district attorney prosecuting a gun-toting housewife (Judy Holliday) for attempting to kill her straying husband (Tom Ewell), and Hepburn is the proto-feminist defense lawyer who makes it her mission to win her client's freedom.

Adam's Rib is best at evoking the merry, freewheeling egalitarianism of Hepburn and Tracy's home. The couple refer to each other as Pinky (spelled with a *y* for him, and an *ie* for her), whip up gourmet dinners together, exchange backrubs and sloppy kisses, host intimate parties to show their home movies, and engage in a witty running debate on gender roles. Their good-natured marital altercations are transposed to the courtroom, where their dispute over the rights and responsibilities of men and women intensifies. Some of the whimsical energy of their home life carries over as well. Adam taps his pencil against the desk to signal to Amanda while court is in session, and they both dip their heads out of sight. They make faces at each other, and Amanda shows her husband a hint of petticoat. He gawps in mock-surprise before both get back to regularly scheduled business.

Kanin and Gordon's script is high-spirited in true screwball fashion, with Adam and Amanda at crossed purposes much of the time. Adam feels, with some justification, that Amanda is turning the courtroom into a three-ring circus, while Amanda argues that she is fighting with every tool in her arsenal for the equality of women before the law. Adam loses his case, and must endure the slings and arrows of outrageous fortune, as he so often does when Hepburn takes more than her fair share of the limelight. Knowing her man far better than he knows himself, Amanda's eyes dart nervously in Adam's direction as soon as the verdict is announced, calculating its cost to her marriage.

There is no conclusion to the jesting of *Adam's Rib*, which is the film's waggishly proffered solution for maintaining marital freshness. Their marriage reconciled after a brief scare, Adam tells his wife that he plans to run on the Republican line for a judgeship. "Adam!" she calls out, having briefly pondered his announcement. "Have they picked the Democratic candidate yet?" *Adam's Rib* ends, but not without the sensation that this jocular, rivalrous back-and-forth could be carried on indefinitely.

The last of the core Tracy and Hepburn films, *Pat and Mike* (1952), also directed by Cukor, is another clash of the class and the crass. The roles have grown more exaggerated; Hepburn is an upper-cruster who also happens to be a scratch athlete, and Tracy is a sporting promoter straight out of A. J. Liebling's Manhattan demimonde, all half-baked moneymaking schemes and bluff bonhomie. Pat is saddled with a demanding fiancé who shatters her sporting concentration, and Mike, in possession of an up-and-coming boxer and a half-decent thoroughbred, is looking to expand his stable. "I can wind up with the top man, the top horse, and the top woman!" he exclaims, presumably listing them by order of importance. For all his gruff oafishness, Mike offers Pat something her high-society fiancé never could: "We're equal. We're partners, see, 5-0, 5-0."

This promise—of sporting equality, of an untraditional alliance of kindred souls—is the animating spirit of *Pat and Mike*. The tennis sequences are not exactly Wimbledon-quality, but Tracy and Hepburn bat the ball back and forth with some dispatch. The mood is too jovial, too rollicking to allow for much serious emotion, which would spoil the fun. Instead, the bulk of the film is a struggle for control between two partners who enjoy the sparring more than the main event. "What you need is A, a manager, B, a promoter," Mike tells Pat. "And that's me—A and B."

Soon enough, Mike is managing not only her career but her life as well. At a restaurant, he changes her order—no martini, no coffee, steak done rare, not medium. Mike is motherly in his attentions, cutting up her dinner into small pieces, even if his interest is initially more fiscal than personal. Tracy is the epitome of loutish philistinism, his garish checked blazer and gold pinky ring testament to his lowbrow tastes. The comedy stems from their discovering unexpected strengths; even taking his wardrobe into account, there is still something soft, something womanly about the gruff Tracy, and Hepburn is a natural as a Babe Didrikson Zaharias–like jill-of-all-sporting-trades.

Unlike *Woman of the Year*, which had gone to great pains to make Hepburn sexy, *Pat and Mike* is content to leave her androgynous. Bursting in on Pat in a partial state of undress leaves Mike entirely unruffled, and Tracy makes sure to mention—twice—that she is "a beauty-full thing to watch—in action." The film's conflict, in fact, stems from Pat's overstepping her gender-mandated boundaries, whipping some angry gamblers with deftly rendered karate chops and judo flips. Mike is further emasculated at the police station, where Pat must demonstrate her actions once more, this time for the police officers. She had shoved Mike out of the way, she testifies, because "well, I didn't want him to get hurt."

Tracy's happy-go-lucky hustler, content to let Hepburn have her way, has again had his feelings ruffled by a perceived slight to his masculinity. "I like a he to be a he, and a she to be a she," he gruffly tells her, demanding the restoration of order. Pat, who had earlier knelt at Mike's feet in adoring supplication (a common position in these films), begs him once more for protection, but ultimately the two come to a new, richer accommodation. "I don't know if I can lick you or you can lick me," Mike grandly announces, "but I'll tell you one thing I do know: together we can lick 'em all." We know, of course, that if there was any licking to be done, Hepburn would be wiping the floor with Tracy, but this pronouncement—the definitive expression of their screen magic—is nonetheless soothing.

Hepburn's glamorous working women of the 1940s give way to the spinsters she would play in the 1950s, with her starring turn in John Huston's *The African Queen* (1951) the most representative. Playing to stereotype, as the frosty matron unexpectedly thawed by love, Hepburn taps a fruitful lode of self-mocking comedy. Costar Humphrey Bogart made for an intriguing contrast with Tracy. He accentuates the hint of slovenliness that often lingered in his performances, his unshaven face and wrinkled clothing a marked contrast with Hepburn's exaggerated primness. She herself had a bit of the *African Queen* in her; a battered old steamboat, Hepburn could still run smoothly when she put her mind to it. Comedy had also given way, for the most part, to drama, with little of the effortlessly charming Kate of *Holiday* to be found in serious later roles like *Suddenly, Last Summer* (1959), *Long Day's Journey into Night* (1962), and *The Lion in Winter* (1968). Hepburn was a great actress, beyond doubt, but many would forget that she had also been, once upon a time, a great comedian.

Tracy, meanwhile, was embracing his lighter side, playing harried father George Banks in a pair of frothy family comedies directed by Vincente Minnelli, *Father of the Bride* (1950) and *Father's Little Dividend* (1951). *Father of the Bride* is superb social comedy, with Tracy's natural fatherly bonhomie perpetually interrupted by petty frustration. George is constantly irritable—frustrated by bands, caterers, invitations, and all the other accoutrements of a middle-class American wedding. Tracy wins us over by his direct address to the camera, his professions of calm increasingly funny as he shows himself to be thoroughly unhinged by the prospect of his daughter's impending nuptials. *Father's Little Dividend* tackles parenthood with similar panache, but the film belongs more to Elizabeth Taylor, whose volcanic emotion nearly obliterates the peaceful, easy glow of Tracy's work.

Tracy and Hepburn grew close once more in 1956, after seven years spent mostly apart. Hepburn fully embraced her old role as the frail Tracy's nurse and protector once more. Under her watchful eye, he quit smoking, took up a regular exercise regimen, and ate a healthier diet. Hepburn made it her primary business to care for the ailing actor, making only four films during the last ten years of Tracy's life—including the two pictures they made together. Whatever legends were to form about the timeless love of Spencer Tracy and Katharine Hepburn, they would develop during this era, when Hepburn selflessly sacrificed her professional ambitions in the name of her longtime companion.

It would not be until five years after *Pat and Mike* that Hepburn and Tracy were reunited onscreen, for the decidedly inferior, although moderately pleasurable, *Desk Set* (1957). Cukor had been replaced by the less gifted Walter Lang (who had also directed Marilyn Monroe in *There's No Business Like Show Business*). The setting had shifted, too, to the skyscrapers of midtown Manhattan, where Bunny Watson (Hepburn) is mistress of the Federal Broadcasting Company's all-knowing research library. Bunny's wood-paneled office is a riot of unfurled maps, tottering piles of books, and messy ivy tendrils curling along the walls. Tracy's Richard Sumner is her diametric opposite: a Taylorite efficiency expert brought in to update the library for the computer age. Soon enough, the homey little office is dominated by the quiet humming and bleeping of his baby-blue monolith.

Rivals they are once more, but the squabbling of *Adam's Rib* has been replaced by a pairing of like minds, iconoclasts in a world of establishment pipsqueaks. Puttering around her apartment together, putting on an impromptu play about a Mediterranean cruise that she might have performed with Grant in *Sylvia Scarlett*, Hepburn and Tracy speak a private language of playful abandon that transcends any surface differences. The battle of the sexes has been muted, too, with Bunny more pliable—less Kate—than previous Hepburn roles.

The sparks of romance in *Desk Set* never ignite into a fully roaring blaze. Phoebe and Henry Ephron's script strains for the madcap adventure of *Pat and Mike*, or *Woman of the Year*, but ends up with a moderately amusing middle-aged romance. Hepburn and Tracy were simply too old to be falling in love—something their last collaboration, another decade in the future, would be all too aware of.

Guess Who's Coming to Dinner (1967) would primarily be regarded as a social-problem film, direct descendant of earlier Oscar-bait pictures like *I Am a Fugitive from a Chain Gang* and *Gentleman's Agreement*. Here, the problem to be analyzed, grappled with, and symbolically overcome was that of interracial romance, and race relations in general. Sidney Poitier, that paragon of African American dignity and restraint, was Dr. John Prentice, a scientific researcher brought home by the carefree Joanna (played by Katharine Houghton, Hepburn's niece) to meet her impeccably liberal parents Matt and Christina Drayton.

The type of man who has a framed photograph of Franklin Delano Roosevelt on his desk next to one of his wife, Matt is nonetheless rattled at the idea of Dr. Prentice (as everyone refers to him, his first name having dropped off as a vestigial remnant after medical school) becoming a member of the Drayton family. A black doctor, yes; a black friend, sure; a black son-in-law, absolutely not. *Guess Who's Coming to Dinner* is a tortured debate between Tracy and Hepburn (and assorted friends, hangers-on, and beloved African American housekeepers) on the relative merits of interracial marriage, but its pleasures are to be found less in the film's dated racial politics than in their uncomplicated marital back-and-forth. Audiences felt like they were getting a privileged glimpse inside Tracy and Hepburn's personal lives, and *Guess Who's Coming* makes no effort to contradict that assumption.

The tense drama of what to do with their unexpected guest is interrupted by a seemingly unconnected interlude in which Matt and Christina leave the house to get some ice cream. At a drive-in, Matt orders a dish of boysenberry ice cream, sure that is the flavor he had enjoyed on an earlier visit. It is not, and Tracy's work in this scene is a small masterpiece of understated acting.

The first bite provides him with nothing but irritation, as if he has just swallowed a toad. By the second bite, the pain has passed, replaced by an unexpected pleasure. It may not be what he had expected, or hoped for, but it is good nonetheless. There is symbolism in this scene too—an unpleasant taste revealing surprisingly gratifying facets—but there is also the unreserved pleasure at seeing Hepburn and Tracy jab and counter-jab once more.

Nonetheless, this is Tracy's film. The sixty-seven-year-old actor had been unwell for some time, and both he and Hepburn were aware that this was likely to be his last film. *Guess Who's Coming to Dinner* is Hepburn's last gift to Tracy, voluntarily ceding the limelight to her longtime screen partner. Director Stanley Kramer makes vivid use of Hepburn's expressive, often weepy face, but it is Tracy—whose brow is perpetually furrowed in puzzlement—who receives most of the film's best bits of business. Fed up with what he perceives to be Christina's unthinking liberalism, Matt mercilessly mocks Hepburn's patrician diction: "Oh, rally? Oh, how *won*-derful! Where will we get enough roses to fill the Rose Bowl?"

More than anything, *Guess Who's Coming to Dinner* is an unabashedly rose-colored portrait of a successful marriage. When Matt is first asked for his opinion of his daughter's plans to marry, he silently studies Christina's face, hoping to suss out some sense of her thoughts before offering his own. And in ultimately capitulating to the young couple's wishes, Matt alludes to his and Christina's long-standing happiness—and, by extension, Tracy and Hepburn's. "In the final analysis, it doesn't matter a damn what we think," Matt tells them. "If it's half of what we felt, that's everything."

Spencer Tracy died two weeks after shooting the final scene for *Guess Who's Coming to Dinner*. He would win a well-deserved Oscar for his performance, as would Hepburn. She would go on to live thirty-five more years, winning two more Oscars and countless accolades, but comedy, on the whole, would be left behind with Tracy's death. The legend of Katharine and Spencer would be told and retold, polished with every repetition, and Hepburn would serve as the prime keeper of their joint flame. Some said that had Tracy been alive to see it, he might not have recognized the life described. But the truest Tracy and Hepburn had always—would always—be the one onscreen. It would be there that their love would be expressed as banter, their boundless pleasure in affectionate conflict etched permanently in celluloid. It is, ultimately, what endures.

12

BILLY WILDER

"NOBODY'S PERFECT!"

> "Audiences don't know somebody sits down and writes a
> picture; they think the actors make it up as they go along."
> —William Holden, *Sunset Blvd.*

O f all the films Billy Wilder never got to make—a Cary Grant romance;
The Marx Brothers at the UN; that drama about the acclaimed Frenchman who could fart the Marseillaise—the one he regretted missing out on
most was *Schindler's List*. Having dreamt for years of telling Oskar Schindler's
story onscreen, Wilder even met with Steven Spielberg in the hopes of winning away the rights to the film. Instead, Spielberg held on to the project,

---

Lemmon strains his spaghetti with a tennis racket in Wilder's *The Apartment*.

Schindler's List (1993) won seven Oscars, and Billy Wilder never made another film before dying at age ninety-five in 2002.

A Wilder Holocaust film? The prospect, while tantalizing, is difficult to imagine. The legendary wit, whose barbed quips did much to define the post-Lubitsch era of sophisticated comedy, could be serious when the occasion called for it. *Double Indemnity* (1944) and *Ace in the Hole* (1951), magnificently lightless masterpieces of noir, were testament to what Wilder could accomplish when in a sober mood. And yet, the film Billy Wilder never made perhaps tells us more about the writer and director than any of the films he did make. The Auschwitz-shaped hole in his filmography was matched by an Auschwitz-shaped hole in his own life—one he rarely spoke about. ("The twentieth century!" a character exclaims in *Sabrina*. "I could pick a century out of a hat, blindfolded, and come up with a better one.") For Wilder was a refugee from a vanished world, fleeing a country that no longer existed for a wholly unfamiliar world, speaking (and writing) a new language in a city of refugees. Those he left behind were among the millions destroyed by Adolf Hitler's genocidal frenzy. Stranded and alone in a new country, Billy Wilder helped create an America after his own image.

Wilder's films are like the sauce at the Chinese joint Fred MacMurray and Shirley MacLaine regularly visit for dinner and drinks in *The Apartment* (1960)—sweet and sour. Frequently accused of cynicism (a trait hard to find in his work), Wilder's work is, more than anything, bittersweet. Wilder is a romantic tempered by acidity. His characters, be they *The Major and the Minor*'s Su-Su Applegate or *Some Like It Hot*'s Joe and Jerry, find themselves while pretending to be someone else entirely. Any resemblance between them and a certain Viennese newspaper hack turned American movie legend are, of course, entirely purposeful. The role reversals in his films—crime-busting police officer becomes pimp, tight-assed executive becomes laid-back lover— were themselves symbolic representations of his own unlikely transformations, whereby the journalist became the screenwriter, the screenwriter became the director, the German became the American, and the Jew pulled a Houdini and escaped Hitler's noose.

Trained as a journalist in Vienna (he claimed to have interviewed Sigmund Freud, Richard Strauss, and Arthur Schnitzler on the same day), Wilder turned his own lack of *zitsfleisch* and traditional Jewish-son ambition into a successful career as a writer and raconteur. "If we had done what we are supposed to do," he once said of himself and fellow future director Otto Preminger, "we could have become lawyers and stayed in Vienna, waiting for Mr.

Hitler." Instead, Vienna gave way to Berlin, and small newspapers to slightly larger ones. One job came his way when Wilder walked in on an editor having sex in his office; another required his working briefly as a dancer-for-hire, waltzing with lonely women in a forlorn nightclub.

More interested in making movies than copy, Wilder was finding his way toward Germany's UFA film studio like a pig on the hunt for truffles. Writing and collaborating on a number of UFA films, including the well-regarded *Menschen am Sonntag* (1930), Wilder's burgeoning career as the next Fritz Lang was cut short by the ascent of Hitler. Shortly after the Reichstag fire in 1933, Wilder sold his prized collection of Bauhaus furniture and used the proceeds to purchase a train ticket for Paris, with Los Angeles his eventual destination. He had hoped to convince his family to flee along with him, but none could be budged. Wilder's father died before the outbreak of the Second World War, and his mother, stepfather, and grandmother refused his pleas to join him in America.

Like Joseph Conrad, or Vladimir Nabokov, Wilder was an expatriate writer, forced to adapt to a language not his own in an unfamiliar country. The first few years, needless to say, were difficult. Wilder got his big Hollywood break, after a number of fruitless years, from fellow German-speaking expatriate Ernst Lubitsch. At one of their first meetings, Lubitsch asked Wilder for a clever way to have the protagonists of his latest film meet cute. Quick as a flash, Wilder suggested a meeting in a department store, where the man was looking to buy only the top from a pair of pajamas, and the woman only the bottom. Lubitsch was suitably impressed with Wilder's comic fluency, not knowing that he had been saving that particular gem for years as a great, Lubitsch-esque gag. Along with his partner Charles Brackett (a Harvard Law graduate whose father had served in New York's state senate), Wilder wrote that film (*Bluebeard's Eighth Wife*) and *Ninotchka* for Lubitsch, and the brilliant *Ball of Fire* (with Gary Cooper as an absent-minded professor, and Barbara Stanwyck as the showgirl who shakes up staid academia) for Howard Hawks.

For Wilder, Lubitsch's magical Touch was comprised of two elements: the desire to top every joke with an even better one, and the drive to come at a problem from an unusual angle. Wilder and Brackett unsuccessfully struggled to dramatize Soviet commissar Greta Garbo's slow thaw toward capitalist excess in *Ninotchka* until Lubitsch had a eureka moment: "It's the hat!" Eschewing unnecessary clutter like Marxist dialectics, Lubitsch structured Ninotchka's transition in three reactions to a characteristically ridiculous Parisian hat: hate the civilization that made the hat, disdain the hat, love the hat. Comedy was the simplicity of the unexpected. Letting audiences feel sophisticated was a surefire recipe for success.

By the time Wilder graduated to directing his own films, sick of directors like Mitchell Leisen mangling his work, he had studied long enough at the master's feet to comfortably be called a Lubitsch disciple. (Wilder would later commission a sign from designer Saul Bass to hang in his office that read "How would Lubitsch do it?") Wilder films were every bit as funny as Lubitsch's (or close enough for government work), but his work possesses a tart acidity unlike anything to be found in Lubitsch. In a world where Auschwitz could coexist with Paris, how could Paris ever again be the city of lovers?

Knowing that the studio expected him, as a lowly writer, to quickly find himself overwhelmed and overmatched in the director's chair, Wilder intentionally aimed for the gooey center with his directorial debut, *The Major and the Minor* (1942). Tamping down the more acerbic style he had perfected as a writer for Lubitsch, he cast Ginger Rogers as a down-on-her-luck city girl headed back to Iowa on a child's train ticket, posing as an overdeveloped twelve-year-old. The film is charming, if slight, but there are moments where Wilder's wit flashes through. A train conductor asks SuSu (posing as a husky Swede) to say something in Swedish, and Rogers does her best Garbo: "I vant to be alone."

The rest of the decade saw Wilder achieve his first string of successes as a straightforward dramatist, with *Double Indemnity* (1944) and 1945 Best Picture winner *The Lost Weekend* both near the pinnacle of the noir genre. *Lost Weekend* is a breathtakingly honest depiction of alcoholism, but its bleakness was alleviated by the Lubitschean charm of its supporting players, and star Ray Milland's jocularity about his own impasse. "Don't wipe it away, Nat," he tells a barkeep reaching to erase the profusion of rings left on the bar by an afternoon of drinking. "Let me have my little vicious circle." Even Milland's nadir has its own brand of grim comedy; desperate to hock his few remaining possessions while on the hunt for another bottle, he is stymied to discover that every pawn shop in Manhattan is closed. A passerby explains the Kafkaesque nightmare: it is Yom Kippur, and all the Jewish pawnbrokers are in synagogue, repenting of their sins.

After the war, Wilder returned to Germany to shoot a documentary about the concentration camps. Survivors told him they had seen his mother in Auschwitz. Auschwitz was a reality too horrific to come to terms with, or grasp: "I lost my mother, my family, my friends—Auschwitz, which I could not imagine because it was unimaginable. And here I am." Unlike his fellow filmmaker George Stevens (who had filmed the liberation of Dachau), Wilder did not return to Hollywood weighed down with the world's troubles, and convinced that big, serious films could heal the breach. Instead, movies became an expression of an outlook on the world: jaundiced, world-weary, with an aftertaste of ashes in the mouth, but retaining some residue of American optimism. The world might be irrevocably broken, but that didn't mean we couldn't laugh about it, did it?

At first, Wilder had intended to cast Mae West as the aging screen goddess in *Sunset Blvd.* (1950). West's vision of Norma Desmond, though, did not allow for a diminution in her sexual prowess: "And you think I'd ever have let Bill Holden leave *me*? He'd've been too tired to get from the bed to the swimming pool." While it is tantalizing to imagine the wisecracking West playing the pitiful, delusional Norma, the good of the film required a more dramatically attuned actress, and Wilder turned to onetime silent star Gloria Swanson. Latching onto Holden's screenwriter and accidental gigolo Joe Gillis, Swanson's Norma is hilariously overdramatic and overwrought. Every minor setback in her mostly imaginary comeback campaign is cause for wailing and gnashing of teeth. Norma, formed by the silents, acts as if she were starring in a silent film, even long after the cameras have stopped rolling. Overacting becomes a baroque form of black comedy, with the silent style unwittingly parodied by its former exemplar. The irony is that, sitting among Norma's kitchen cabinet of "Waxworks," as she calls them, is Norma's exact inverse: the stone-face of the silents himself, Buster Keaton.

As it had in *The Lost Weekend*, comedy helps to break up the claustrophobic tension of *Stalag 17* (1953). Holden returns as a sardonic, sneering, possibly traitorous antihero, an amoral wheeler-dealer in a Nazi POW camp. From the outset, we are convinced—or nearly so—that Holden's J. J. Sefton is selling out his fellow prisoners in exchange for special privileges. *Stalag 17* is a drama posing as a comedy, its broadly drawn supporting cast (led by Robert Strauss's lunk-headed Animal, and Harvey Lembeck's savvy Jewish grunt) a wonderful counterpoint to Holden's irritable iconoclasm. Sefton is a noir hero trapped in a raucous comedy. His plight—that of the wrongfully accused man, nearly convicted of a crime he did not commit—is cushioned by the rowdy boisterousness of democracy in action. The babel of competing voices, of favored GI pinup Betty Grable's legs jockeying for screen time with jackbooted Nazis, made for Wilder's most sincere mash note to his adopted homeland. Pessimism does battle with a sincerity new to Wilder, with neither emerging entirely triumphant. "If I ever run into any of you bums on a street corner," Sefton tells his fellow POWs before escaping, "just let's pretend we never met before." Holden disappears from sight, only to pop up once more and jauntily salute his fellow prisoners.

Both *Sabrina* (1954) and *Love in the Afternoon* (1957) are Audrey Hepburn romances whose leading men should have been, but were not, Cary Grant. Wilder offered Grant both roles, but was unable to convince the reticent actor to sign on. Instead, Humphrey Bogart is the wealthy industrialist who woos the chauffeur's daughter in *Sabrina*, and Gary Cooper the playboy in Wilder's most direct Lubitsch homage.

Bogart is stiff and unromantic in *Sabrina*, as if he were not quite familiar with the protocol in these kinds of stories. This is the character he is intended to play, but one cannot help but feel that Grant, the master lover, would have made for a better romantic incompetent than the genuinely uncomfortable Bogart. If he were ever to get married, Bogart tells an underling, "he would require "a Dictaphone, two secretaries, and four corporate counsels along on the honeymoon." Hepburn, meanwhile, is entranced by her closeness to William Holden's callow libertine; even when the music stops, they keep dancing to the beat of their own shared intoxication. The movie, likewise intoxicated by Hepburn and Holden's chemistry, never fully commits to Bogart, who dominates the film without ever truly being part of it.

Love in the Afternoon is Lubitschean to the roots, with its Parisian locales, and the presence of Maurice Chevalier as Hepburn's father. Its charms show that the student has studied the master's work carefully. *Love*'s Paris is a bacchanal of trysting lovers, with Chevalier (who looks a bit tousled, like a Sturges supporting player) the private detective documenting the merry-go-round of momentary passion for his personal files. The only one left out of the fun is his daughter, who makes good use of her father's dossiers to win over noted playboy Frank Flannagan (Cooper). "He's like a cowboy, or Abraham Lincoln," Hepburn enthuses about her swain. Lincoln's corpse is more like it: Wilder carefully keeps his leading man in the shadows, but in the few instances where Cooper's face is fully lit, audiences could see how much he had aged. One wishes helplessly for a better leading man, because *Love in the Afternoon* contains so much prime Wilder: Chevalier's wonderfully charming voiceover, the musical theme that recurs whenever she thinks of her callow lover, and Hepburn's wholly imaginary audio memoir of lovers past, which Cooper plays obsessively as a form of self-torture.

Perhaps it makes the most sense to think of Joe and Jerry (Tony Curtis and Jack Lemmon), the itinerant musicians of *Some Like It Hot* (1959), as the Rosencrantz and Guildenstern in Wilder's free replay of Howard Hawks's *Scarface*. Adrift in a gangster epic not their own, these comic fools have been cut loose from their moorings, left to their own devices in a distinctly hostile world. Accidental witnesses to the St. Valentine's Day Massacre of 1929, Joe and Jerry must flee suddenly inhospitable Chicago. The only gig available is in an all-girls' band touring Florida. Cut directly to "Josephine" and "Daphne," tottering unsteadily in high heels as they dash for a southbound train. "How do they walk in these things?" Daphne asks befuddledly. "It is so drafty!"

"When I was a kid, I had a dream I was locked in a pastry shop overnight," Lemmon muses to Curtis, a twinkle in his eye. "We're on a diet," Curtis firmly reminds him. "I'm a girl, I'm a girl," Lemmon repeats to himself like a mantra. "I wish I were dead."

Kids in a pastry shop whose mouths are wired firmly shut, Lemmon and Curtis agonize over the delights they are forbidden to sample, with none more perfectly named than Marilyn Monroe's Sugar Kane Kowalczyk. Sugar Kane is an incorrigible boozer whose terminal incapacity to show up on time, or stay away from men and liquor, keeps her in permanent hot water. Monroe (star of Wilder's *The Seven Year Itch*, about which more later) is sex in high heels, her every jounce and swish a further torment to the men's already-engorged libidos. "Boy, would I love to borrow a cup of that sugar!" Lemmon roars, as if he were the first man to ever think of that double-entendre.

Of all Wilder's films, *Some Like It Hot* is the most sparkling, and the most ebullient. "Party in number seven!" one girl shouts aboard the train to Florida, and the entire band piles into Lemmon's cramped sleeping compartment, bringing along crackers, vermouth, and salamis for the impromptu get-together. The moment is like an outtake from *A Night at the Opera*, with Wilder lifting the Marx Brothers' famous stateroom scene for his own over-the-top party of a movie.

Later in the film, Curtis's Joe trots out his own set of movie impressions, reinventing himself as wealthy playboy Junior, who woos Sugar Kane with a note-perfect imitation of Cary Grant. Curtis's faux-Cary would be the closest the director would come to having Grant star in one of his films (although there had been a brief, superb Grant imitation in *Stalag 17*, too). Curtis had long been known as a gifted mimic, but his Grant ventures out far beyond parody, and comes closer to sincere homage. After all, if a man wants to sweep a woman off her feet, who better to serve as a role model than Cary Grant?

The purportedly impotent Junior's halfhearted efforts to protest Sugar Kane's diligence in combating his ailment, and his not-so-secret desire to keep it coming, all tumble out in one fell swoop: "Look, it's terribly sweet of you to want to help out but it's no use I think the light switch is over there." Curtis uses body language to deliciously blur the line between masculine and feminine. Junior's loafer phallically rises during a passionate kiss, but so does his leg, daintily taking leave of the ground during another clinch.

Lemmon, meanwhile, is engaged to daffy millionaire Osgood Fielding III (Joe E. Brown). "Why would a guy want to marry a guy?" the bewildered Curtis asks (the notion of gay marriage apparently not being a commonplace one for 1929—or 1959, for that matter). "Security!" Lemmon retorts, hitting the punch line forcefully. "I'm a boy," Lemmon now reminds himself. "I wish I were dead. I'm a boy." The gangster film gives way to a gender-bending romantic comedy, and even the return of Raft and his henchmen cannot wrench the film back to 1929 Chicago.

Instead, the two men become Monroe-esque gold diggers, straight out of *How to Marry a Millionaire* or *Gentlemen Prefer Blondes*. After ditching the gangsters on their trail, the two couples end up on Fielding's yacht. Curtis and Monroe promptly settle accounts, but Fielding is unwilling to accept his girl's excuses. She may not be a natural blonde, she may be a smoker, she may have lived with a sax player for three years—he doesn't mind. "I'm a man," Lemmon finally announces, taking off his wig, and dropping his voice a few octaves. "Well, nobody's perfect," Fielding merrily trills, and the movie ends on this deliriously chipper note.

If *Some Like It Hot* is best known for its closing words, its successor *The Apartment* (1960)—the second of Wilder's two Best Picture winners—is remembered for four of its own: "Shut up and deal." Deranged hyperbole gives way to muted, somber comedy, and the film's closing words—which are meant to be tender—are emblematic of its cranky romanticism. *The Apartment* is a wintry movie, its chill a product of too much time spent outdoors in freezing weather, and too much time spent indoors in frosty workplaces. It is those white-collar blues that give the movie its bite. Jack Lemmon's C. C. Baxter is part woebegone weakling, part conniving schemer, his efforts to ascend the corporate ladder requiring the use of his conveniently located Manhattan apartment.

The film cribs the famous opening shot of King Vidor's *The Crowd* to set a mood, tracking along an endless row of desks in an aircraft-carrier-sized office before arriving at Baxter's desk. Baxter desperately wants to separate himself from the crowd, but his only resource is the home-based house of ill repute he has inadvertently founded. The job Baxter is paid for takes a back seat to the juggling of a dozen executives' extracurricular love lives, each of which requires the occasional use of his apartment for trysts. Among them is that of his boss Jeff Sheldrake (Fred MacMurray), whose paramour turns out to be Fran Kubelik (Shirley MacLaine), the same pixieish elevator operator C.C. has had his eyes on.

Working in the register most comfortable to him, Wilder is freed to indulge his inner Lubitsch. The bit of business whereby a compact with a cracked mirror passes from Baxter to Sheldrake to Fran, cluing C.C. in to their secret romance, is a wonderfully economic example of Wilder's Lubitschean touch (as is the tennis racket Baxter uses to strain his spaghetti).

The Apartment is Wilder's best-ever blend of the sweet and the sour. The sweet comes from the halting, stop-and-start romance that grows between C.C. and Fran, as he nurses her back to health following a suicide attempt. The sour comes from Sheldrake and his merry band of middle-aged Don Juans, wooing another in a never-ending fleet of willing working girls before catching the 7:14 to White Plains. *The Apartment* is like *The Seven Year Itch* from the perspective of the guy missing out on all the fun, and the good-humored amorality of the earlier Marilyn Monroe vehicle turns rancid when exposed to the harsh winter light of reality. Lemmon and MacLaine are the schmooks who stand in the way of Sheldrake's pursuit of happiness, and are flattened as a result. "Some people take, some people get took," Fran observes, and it is abundantly clear that both she and C.C. are of the latter category.

Audiences mostly fled after the success of *The Apartment*, but Wilder's comic facility stubbornly persisted. In fact, his follow-up to *The Apartment*, brutalized upon its release for being shamefully out of touch with contemporary geopolitics, now looks like one of his most brilliant comedies. *One, Two, Three* (1961) marked Wilder's second return to postwar Europe, but unlike 1948's bleak drama *A Foreign Affair*, Wilder was looking to reanimate the corpse of the 1930s screwball comedy. What could be funnier than the collision of Coca-Cola capitalism and Stalinist Communism in the divided city of Berlin, with machine-gun dialogue spitting fire on the no man's land between East and West? During postproduction on the film, the Berlin Wall went up, and what had seemed like an amusing farce became a ghoulishly inappropriate, tasteless joke.

Or so it seemed to many critics at the time. Some two decades after the fall of that same wall, *One, Two, Three* has regained all its verve, its smashing of Cold War pieties nearly the equal of *Dr. Strangelove* for sheer audacity. In one of his last roles, James Cagney is C. R. MacNamara, a Coke exec in Berlin unexpectedly burdened with babysitting the boss's wayward daughter Scarlett. A philandering executive with one eye on the bottom line and the other on his secretary's bottom, Cagney would make a perfect running buddy for *The Apartment*'s Jeff Sheldrake. When Scarlett falls in love with a boy from the wrong side of the Iron Curtain, MacNamara must turn a Communist firebrand into a capitalist extraordinaire in a matter of hours.

Otto Piffel (note the dismissively diminutive name) is an apprentice apparatchik, his best grades in school undoubtedly in Anti-Americanism 101. "I spit on your money," he tells McNamara. "I spit on Fort Knox. I spit on Wall Street!" ("Unsanitary little jerk," McNamara mutters to himself.) Otto has no shortage of West-baiting one-liners: "Capitalism is like a dead herring in the moonlight. It shines, but it stinks."

Wilder, remembering Cagney's machine-gun-patter heyday, has him rattle off whole paragraphs without pausing for breath. Cagney is virtuosic, the ugly American in stereophonic sound. He never seems to pause for thought, let alone breath. *One, Two, Three* takes aim at American money-lust, Soviet idiocy, and the tragic absurdity of German history with unerring accuracy. With such an abundance of targets, Wilder overstuffs the film with punch lines, wickedly funny asides, and inventive physical gags.

Fifteen years after the Nazis murdered his mother and stepfather, Wilder has his revenge on Germany, but takes his payment in comedy. His Germans are dolts and liars, camp followers looking for a Fuhrer and finding it in the person of C. R. MacNamara of the Coca-Cola Corporation. Americans, by contrast, are capable of a dazzling, improvisatory exuberance. MacNamara builds his boss an ideal German son-in-law from scratch, pausing along the way to pay homage to the glories of Western civilization: "Any world that can produce the Taj Mahal, William Shakespeare, and striped toothpaste can't be all bad."

With *Some Like It Hot* and *The Apartment*, Wilder had found an ideal alter ego in Lemmon. He would go on to cast the unassuming leading man in five more films. The director's later years would be synonymous with Lemmon, whose bruised decency and plainspokenness were ideal Wilder traits. In *Irma la Douce* (1963), he is a Parisian cop who unexpectedly becomes a pimp for Shirley MacLaine, and in *The Fortune Cookie* (1966), he is a cameraman shamming an injury at the behest of his shyster brother-in-law. Lemmon's weary exasperation with his newfound roles—brute, or con artist—made him the perfect Wilder antihero, but neither film is entirely successful. *Irma la Douce* had been Wilder's attempt to make Paris both romantic and real, being undoubtedly the only film ever set in the City of Lights to begin at the Les Halles meat market. The recipe was right, but the ingredients were off. *Fortune Cookie* featured a wonderfully tart supporting performance from Walter Matthau as an unprincipled ambulance chaser, but, by Wilder's standards, was surprisingly bloated after a vinegary opening sequence.

Nineteen sixty-four's *Kiss Me, Stupid* featured Kim Novak doing an ace imitation of Monroe—breathy, scatter-brained, and casually sexy—and Dean Martin doing an even better parody of himself. Playing Dino, legendary superstar and ladies' man stuck overnight in a no-horse Nevada town, Martin almost topped Jerry Lewis's Buddy Love from *The Nutty Professor.* Sex-obsessed, obscenely narcissistic, and convinced of his own magnificence, Dino is a walking, talking, rutting horror. The only thing that kept *Kiss Me, Stupid* from being another Wilder gem—and it was a big one—was the casting of Ray Walston in the lead role, as a music teacher and overly jealous husband. Peter Sellers had originally been supposed to star, but a heart attack had forced him to drop out, and Walston torpedoes the film with his eyeball-rolling antics.

Lemmon as a Parisian pimp strained credulity, but him playing a harried businessman dead set on remaining blind to Italy's charms, in *Avanti!* (1972), was a triumph, making for Wilder's last, and least-known, classic. Its Italy is a land of enchantment that fails to beguile a man too prosaic for its poetry. On his father's death in an auto accident, Wendell Armbruster Jr. (Lemmon) flies across the Atlantic to collect the body and bring it back to the United States in time to deliver his eulogy for the 216,000 employees watching via closed-circuit television. Brusque, rude, and unwilling to brook any un-American lack of diligence (three-hour Italian lunches have him howling like a banshee), Wendell Jr. is stymied by the presence of Pamela Piggott (Juliet Mills), whose mother has died in the same car crash. Logical conclusions take the prudish Wendell an absurdly long time to reach, and even then he is incredulous: "You mean all the time we thought he was getting cured, he was getting laid?"

Avanti! is a hotel farce in the tradition of the Marx Brothers' *Room Service* (although far wittier), with Wendell and Pamela assisted by unflappable proprietor Carlucci (Clive Revill) and a rotating cast of bellhops and maids. Mills is not quite right for the role, too slim (and too lovely) for the endless jokes about her weight. This elemental casting mistake notwithstanding, *Avanti!* is perhaps the ideal Wilder romance, appealing and acid in equal measure. "Love, Miss Piggott," Armbruster Jr. pompously pronounces, "is for filing clerks, not the head of a conglomerate," but by the end of the film he and

Pamela are making plans to visit every year from July 15 to August 15, just like their parents once had.

There were a few other movies after *Avanti!*—a mostly pointless remake of *The Front Page* (1974) with Lemmon and Matthau notable only for its filthy mouth, a quasi-update of *Sunset Blvd.* called *Fedora* (1978), the Lemmon-Matthau pairing *Buddy Buddy* (1981)—but mostly Billy Wilder turned into a national treasure. Lauded by film festivals and universities, sought out for interviews and books, Wilder was granted everything except what he wanted most: the opportunity to make another film. The director went to his Beverly Hills office every morning, but there was increasingly little to do there, other than reminisce and dream.

Schindler's List was not to be, nor the biopic of the acclaimed French farter. And perhaps the Holocaust would have been too difficult a task for the notorious wit. Even at his most dramatic, there was always a joke or a bon mot to lighten matters up, but who could find a comic silver lining in the catastrophe that had cost him his own family? Perhaps it was for the best that Spielberg kept *Schindler's List* for himself. For Billy Wilder was a tragic figure who took solace in comedy—a man whose suffering was transmuted, through some mysterious alchemical process, into its precise inverse. He kept the tragedy for himself, and gave us all the humor.

13

FUNNY BLONDE

"Story of my life. I always get the fuzzy end of the lollipop."
—Marilyn Monroe, *Some Like It Hot*

"Under ordinary circumstances, I would certainly not expect my wife, Audrey, to forgive me if I were unfaithful to her," Billy Wilder once told biographer Charlotte Chandler, "but she would have forgiven me if I had an affair with Marilyn Monroe—*more* than forgiven me! She would have gone to her beauty salon and proclaimed to all the women there that her husband was having an affair with Marilyn Monroe. It would have enhanced

---

A study in feminine contrasts: Josephine (Tony Curtis) and Sugar Kane Kowalczyk (Monroe) in *Some Like It Hot*.

her status. She would have notified the newspapers, like parents announcing the engagement of their daughter. It would have meant she was not married to an ordinary male. Both our images would have been improved. It would have given me mythic proportions, and that would have reflected on her—the man who could sleep with Marilyn Monroe had married *her*." One suspects that Audrey Wilder was not the only woman in America who might have felt similarly about the prospect of being two-timed with Marilyn Monroe. What is undoubtedly the case is that every man in America—hell, every man in the world—hoped that their wife would be as understanding as Wilder's, were similar circumstances to arise.

So many barrelfuls of ink have been spilled about Marilyn Monroe the sex symbol that Marilyn Monroe the comedian has been obscured in the process. Monroe has been studied, lauded, critiqued, and psychoanalyzed; she has been turned into a buffoon, a tragic feminist symbol, a burgeoning Method actor, and a screen goddess. She has rarely been treated as a worka-day actress—one aiming, above all, to amuse. She was "a comedienne *impersonating* the American idea of the Sex Goddess," as Lincoln Kirstein put it. The turn-on was a put-on.

Marilyn Monroe was one of the first screen icons defined by what they represented, not the roles they played. Like James Dean—another subject of hysterical affection who died tragically young—Monroe's true significance lay offscreen. She was the symbol of America's sexual awakening after the prudishness of the war years, her romances with Joe DiMaggio and Arthur Miller (and possibly the Kennedy brothers as well) ascending to the level of myth even as they were taking place. Monroe was Betty Kockenlocker of *The Miracle of Morgan's Creek* with much of the pretense ("I'm not drunk, I've only bumped my head") scraped away. She was sexy and silly and a bit loose. She was a figure of the American collective fantasy, and as such, the real Monroe could never compete with the dream-icon. She was worshipped, but rarely seen. The movie Monroe was too small to be the real Marilyn.

Monroe modeled her screen persona on Mae West, the original outlandish sex symbol, but there was a crucial difference. West turned the tables on men in her movies, chasing them with lustful abandon and abusing them with effortless wit. Monroe, in comparison, is often the gold digger extraordinaire, her pursuit of men strictly financial. Any notches on her bedpost were merely calculations of her suitors' net worth. Mae couldn't have cared less about where her next meal was coming from, as long as she knew there would be something to nibble on in bed; Marilyn was often content with white-haired pensioners as long as her own old-age pension was secure. Monroe's characters are dim-witted and incurious, funny in spite of themselves. If West was the "dirty blonde," as a 2001 play about the actress was titled, Monroe was the iconic dumb blonde. We laugh at her, not with her—at her failed attempts at sophistication, at her naivete, at her childish enthusiasms, at that deliciously breathy voice. Or at least we think we do. For anything more than a cursory look at Monroe's work tells us that she controlled and manipulated her image with scientific precision. Dumb she wasn't.

In part, she was a product of her era. No woman could afford to be as unsentimentally sexual as West in the 1950s. Instead, financial assurance—the picket fence and the new Buick—were the measurements of contentment, and Monroe is only out to get her fair share. She may have looked nothing like Doris Day, but at bottom, the two representatives of 1950s American womanhood were out for much the same thing. Day is the single woman on the make as seen by women, and Monroe is that same figure as imagined by men. She is a cartoon of sexuality for a cartoonish era, in which bigger truly was perceived as better. If the tailfins on Chevys grew larger every year, why shouldn't the headlights on Hollywood's actresses? Monroe was a walking dirty joke, according to film historian James Harvey, and every man who looked at her was intent on providing the punch line. Jayne Mansfield, Mamie Van Doren, and other overdeveloped blondes would follow in her wake, intent to capitalize on what she had begun, but only Monroe was possessed of any measurable gifts as an actor.

Monroe's death from an accidental overdose in 1962 has kept her young in the public memory. It has also permanently frozen her as an icon of unfulfilled potential, leaving biographers and fans to speculate endlessly about what Monroe might have accomplished—who she might have become—if only she had lived. The icon rarely corresponds with the real woman; Saint Marilyn she was not. Just ask one of the directors who worked with her most closely. "Working with her was like being a dentist," Billy Wilder told Chandler. "You know, pulling those lines out like teeth, except the dentist felt the pain." Monroe would show up hours after call time, reporting that she had gotten lost on the way to the same studio she had worked at for years. She was constitutionally incapable of remembering her lines. Once, Wilder went so far as to tape an index card with her line written out inside a drawer she was supposed to open during a scene. Monroe promptly opened the wrong drawer. She was always, always late. "Instead of studying with Lee Strasberg,"

Wilder acidly remarked, referring to the Method acting guru, "she should have studied in Switzerland with Patek Philippe."

"But no matter how much you suffered with Miss Monroe," Wilder said, concluding his thought, "she was totally natural on the screen, and that's what survived. She glowed." Whatever traumas Monroe experienced in her private life, whatever traumas she inflicted on those directing her, none made the final cut. An unusually tormented and conflicted young woman, her screen fame has endured because the filmed, cut-and-printed Monroe radiates good humor, health, and sexual pulchritude.

The good humor had little basis in Norma Jean Baker's early experiences. Born in 1926 in the very heart of the filmmaking industry, Norma Jean was bounced around between foster families, orphanages, family friends, and the occasional ministration of her mother Gladys, whose struggles with mental illness kept her shuttling in and out of institutions. Some of these temporary caregivers, like her mother's best friend Grace McKee, were mostly tolerant and decent, inculcating in young Norma Jean a belief in her incipient movie stardom; others, like the intensely strict foster family, or the sexually abusive foster fathers, were not so kind. ("I've known what I was doing since I was six years old!" Monroe good-naturedly shouts in 1954's *There's No Business Like Show Business*, and the line registers, for all the wrong reasons.)

At fifteen, Norma Jean was pressured into marrying a twenty-one-year-old neighbor by McKee, who was moving to another city and ill-inclined to take her ward along. It was either marriage or the orphanage once more, and Norma Jean chose marriage. Then the country entered World War II, and she found work at a local defense plant, where she was a glue-sprayer and chute-packer on an assembly line building radio-controlled airplanes. An Army photographer caught sight of her at work, took some modeling snapshots, and passed them on to a film agent, who helped her get a screen test at 20th Century Fox. The young woman—newly divorced, her name Hollywoodized into the more mellifluous Marilyn Monroe—was now a starlet-in-waiting.

Monroe got her start as little more than gravity-defying eye candy. She makes a brief cameo in the Marx Brothers' last hurrah *Love Happy* (1949) as a femme fatale who stops in to see Groucho's private eye. "Some men are following me," she tells him as she slinkily steps out of the frame, and Groucho's eyeballs practically roll back into his head: how about throwing me a tough pitch? "Really?" he leers. "I can't understand why." Groucho is older than we like to imagine him, and Monroe too young and unformed to truly be herself yet, but one can imagine the actress gleaning something from Marx's single-minded consistency of character, sustained after decades of playing essentially the same role.

The apprenticeship in walk-on parts was not complete; she would serve as a shyster's moll in John Huston's *The Asphalt Jungle* (1950), where her picture on the film's poster is larger than her role in the film, and theater critic George Sanders's latest project in Joseph L. Mankiewicz's indelible *All About Eve* (1951). Monroe's Miss Casswell is a graduate of the Copacabana School of Dramatic Arts—yuk, yuk—whose gleaming platinum-blonde helmet of hair and plunging décolletage are hardly the mark of the dramatic actor. Miss Casswell is a frank gold digger, salivating at the sight of a plush sable coat, if not the rabbity producers who appear to be her lot in life. Anne Baxter's Eve eyes her approvingly, seeing in Miss Casswell a more vulgar, less diabolically subtle version of herself. Miss Casswell is simply perfect until she parts her lips and expels air through them; her mouth appears to lack that high-speed link to her brain that would allow for intelligent conversation. "Well, I can't yell, 'Oh, butler,' can I?" she wonders aloud after calling for a drink. "Maybe somebody's name is Butler."

There was already a hint of playfulness to her cheesecake, a half-submerged awareness of her own ludicrousness. As the boss's secretary in the exceedingly modest pleasure *As Young as You Feel* (1951), Monroe never entirely stops waggling her butt—or her eyebrows, Groucho-style. She is once more playing the floozy to be enjoyed, and tossed to the curb; the happy family reunion at the end of the film elides just what might happen to her when husband and wife lovingly reunite. This role was one Monroe was quite familiar with from her own off-camera experience. In search of stardom, she had determinedly slept her way to the middle, using (and being used by) Hollywood players like director Elia Kazan, producer Joe Schenck, and agent Johnny Hyde to weasel her way into fourth- and sixth-billed semi-notoriety in forgettable fare.

His collaborator I. A. L. Diamond may have cowritten *Let's Make It Legal* (1951), but no one would mistake this execrable enterprise for a Billy Wilder gem. This smarmy attempt at resuscitating the 1930s comedy of remarriage is a lamentable career misstep for the usually magnificent Claudette Colbert, but Monroe is granted a few brief moments of inventiveness that hint at future comedic pleasures. Part-vamp, part-naif, we believe Marilyn's momentary, wordless confusion when she bumps bellies with her swain. Even more, we laugh at it, pleased that Monroe has found a way to lighten our discomfort with her too-uncomplicated role.

We're Not Married (1952) followed the next year, with Monroe mostly the punch line to a soggy joke. How do you end up married to Marilyn Monroe, and still miserable? *We're Not Married* offers an implausible theory. David Wayne (fresh from serving as Katharine Hepburn's unstinting ally in *Adam's Rib*) is a harried house-husband, outfitted in an apron and lackadaisically feeding their baby its dinner as Monroe sets out to win the Mrs. Mississippi contest.

The role of Lois Laurel, the voluptuous secretary who catches Cary Grant's eye in *Monkey Business* (1952), might have seemed, from a quick glance at the script, to be more of the same, well, monkey business. But director Howard Hawks had spotted something larger-than-life about Monroe, something ludicrously outsized that would play beautifully as comedy. Casting Monroe in dramatic roles, Hawks felt, was like hammering a beautifully rounded peg into an obstinately square hole. "She's a completely storybook character," he told Fox's Darryl F. Zanuck, "and you're trying to make real movies." Hawks's anti-aging comedy expertly utilizes Monroe as window dressing, her tantalizing allures the siren call for Cary Grant's serum-concocting scientist. "Is your motor running?" she calls out to Grant, lodged in the driver's seat of his latest purchase—a midlife-crisis coupe. "Is yours?" he responds. We can practically see the cartoon smoke coming out of his ears.

Naive and scheming, infantile but already calloused, Monroe's Lorelei Lee in Hawks's Technicolor musical *Gentlemen Prefer Blondes* (1953) established the template for Marilyn the star. A fortune-seeker with a built-in diamond tracker, Lorelei is searching for treasure on a ship crossing the Atlantic. Issuing pronouncements about her man-hunting philosophy with some regularity, the childish Lorelei is a veritable fount of accidental double-entendres, splitting the difference between suckling and succubus. Lorelei is paired with her best friend Dorothy Shaw (Jane Russell), the brunette to Lorelei's blonde. Dorothy prefers the process to the resolution, looking men over with a hungry, knowing glance. Monroe's Lorelei, by contrast, could care less about the package; she is only interested in the interior—of their wallets.

Lorelei knows how to use her gifts to her advantage, but seems curiously innocent about sex. She is "all *about* sex," as Molly Haskell puts it, "but *without* sex." She is the cause of desire in others, but appears curiously without desire herself. Monroe's Lorelei is liquid sex, so much so that pairing her with a flesh-and-blood leading man is carefully avoided. The men who chase her are grotesques: comically inappropriate suitors possessing none of her physical charms. Lorelei is romancing, and being romanced by, codgers and infants precisely because her own sexuality is so cartoonishly hyperbolic. *Gentlemen Prefer Blondes* contrasts Monroe with Russell, making Dorothy the brunette next door, and Lorelei the exaggerated sex fantasy. "Ain't there anyone here for love?" Russell sings, with the Busby Berkeley–esque backdrop composed of well-toned male athletes doing splits and sit-ups, their geometrically arrayed limbs a daring masculine inversion of the traditional female musical eye-candy. The women aboard ship are dazzled into incoherence at the sight of so much delectable male flesh, but Lorelei is conspicuously absent from the scene.

There are not one, but two girls next door in *How to Marry a Millionaire* (1953), a landlocked *Gentlemen Prefer Blondes* with Monroe, Lauren Bacall, and Betty Grable as three single ladies on the make in ritzy Manhattan. Pooling their resources to rent a luxury apartment, the trio set out to snag an oilman, or at least a rising executive.

Like her roommates, Monroe's Pola Debevoise is so doggedly realistic about relationships that she fights her natural inclinations toward romance. *Millionaire's* hearty amorality is repeatedly undercut by its moralizing fervor, and by Bacall and Grable's wet-blanket performances. Both actresses are too goody-two-shoes to pass for fortune-hunters, and only Monroe looks like she's having any fun at all. But Marilyn is the comic appetizer; it is the other women, we are encouraged to understand, that are the main course.

There's No Business Like Show Business (1954), a CinemaScope musical with a fistful of Irving Berlin songs, is a regression—a return to the days of Monroe playing nice, dull girls with a touch of vavoom. Here, she pines for second-generation song-and-dance man Donald O'Connor while waiting patiently for the film to get around to offering her a number of her own. When it comes, in the form of "Heat Wave," it is splendid—sultry and easy—but too much time is wasted on soppy familial drama. Monroe is nothing if not knowing about her appeal. Practicing her hellos in her dressing room before meeting a potential patron, she runs through approaches: flirty, mysterious, all-American. Monroe seeks to remind us, lest we forget, that this all was an act, calculated and precise.

The box-office success of *Blondes* and *Millionaire* helped boost Monroe into the stratosphere of stardom, but it was her brief marriage to legendary baseball star Joe DiMaggio that made her more celebrity than actress. The union of the iconic starlet and the iconic athlete was a match so obviously made in tabloid heaven that its lasting barely nine months hardly registered among the Monroe-besotted. DiMaggio was too possessive to be married to a bombshell like Monroe, whose appeal was predicated on the impression of her availability. (The shooting of *The Seven Year Itch*, out on Manhattan's Lexington Avenue, was agony for DiMaggio.) Monroe was no blonde bimbo, waving to the boys at spring training on the way to vacation in the Florida Keys. She saw herself as an artist. Men were to be her ticket out of the ghetto of comedy, be they third husband Arthur Miller or Laurence Olivier, whose *The Prince and the Showgirl* was going to elevate her to the status of Olivier's wife Vivien Leigh. Not until it was too late did Monroe realize that it, too, was a frothy romantic comedy—exactly what she had hoped to escape.

Zanuck had, contrary to Hawks's wishes, indeed been trying Monroe out in dramatic films like Fritz Lang's *Clash by Night* (1952), where she had a small role as a fish-cannery worker, and as a disturbed presence in *Don't Bother to Knock* (1952) and *Niagara* (1953). Psychotic babysitters and murderous wives were hardly the most logical roles, but no matter the evidence onscreen, no matter the clamoring among audiences and directors to make more Marilyn Monroe films—lighthearted comedies with a splash of romance—Monroe insisted on chasing that elusive genie of respectability. Monroe's dramatic coach Natasha Lytess, who would perch behind the director on the set, offering a nod after a well-played scene, was only the first emanation of this craving; later Lee and Paula Strasberg and the Actors Studio would take over.

Chasing a seriousness she only dimly understood, Monroe pictured herself starring as Grushenka in *The Brothers Karamazov*, when audiences wanted the charmer they had grown fond of. "Marilyn, don't play that part," Wilder told her after the enormous success of *The Seven Year Itch*. "Stay with the character you created. You'll be an actress and a star like Mae West. Eighty years old, you'll be playing lead parts with the character you created." Ignoring Wilder's advice, Monroe preferred the kind of fatally self-serious, psychologically fraught dramas that were a specialty of the decade. *River of No Return* (1954), with Monroe opposite Robert Mitchum in an Otto Preminger Western, and *Bus Stop* (1956), directed by Joshua Logan, were both the kind of prestige material Monroe craved—A-list directors, gorgeous photography, and talented leading men. Ironically, they manhandled Monroe far more than any crass comedy ever could, treating her like an inanimate hunk of flesh, to be snatched by the first available man.

River is pictorially splendid, posing Monroe against the huge, occasionally menacing beauty of the natural world. Singing and strumming her guitar like a frontier Marlene Dietrich, Monroe is her usual alluring self, but Preminger's film is intent on roughing her up. A half-cocked rape scene turns into a seduction, and Mitchum ends up hauling her off like a prize steer, draping her over his shoulder. *Bus Stop* is hardly more sophisticated, paying unending homage to Don Murray's ill-informed hooligan cowboy. Monroe, her cute blonde curls matched by a halfhearted attempt at a Southern accent, is helpless prisoner to Murray's will, allowing herself to be worn down by his endless barrage of demands and pleas. Monroe strains for something deeper than accidental farce, but George Axelrod's script is far too facile to allow for much in the way of nuance.

Later, after years of screenwriting toil by then-husband Arthur Miller, there would be *The Misfits* (1961). Billed as an instant masterpiece, it suffered from the letdown of overly inflated expectation. The film was likable enough, but critics wondered where all the effort had gone; could this flimsy, quasi-mythical contemporary Western have been the product of all that work? Monroe strains for poignancy, but the effects she achieves at so much cost here were accomplished with a single wink or shimmy in her comedies. A troubled young woman with dreams of seriousness, Monroe could not see her own strengths. Dissatisfaction plagued her, emphasizing what she lacked, and addiction—to uppers, to downers, to alcohol—filled the empty spaces.

If casual film fans are familiar with any single moment in Monroe's filmography, it is Marilyn in a billowing white dress in Billy Wilder's *The Seven Year Itch* (1955), standing over a subway grate as a train passes below, a cool breeze blowing her dress up around her head. It is also of a piece with its predecessors in turning her into a caricature of readily available, no-strings-attached sex. Richard Sherman (Tom Ewell) is a summer bachelor in stifling Manhattan, his wife and son spending a few weeks in the country as he trudges to and from the office. Monroe is his new upstairs neighbor (identified only as The Girl), luscious, unattached, and slightly daffy. Making herself at home with dazzling rapidity in his air-conditioned garden apartment, Monroe is unaware of the effect she has on her new friend. "When it gets hot like this, you know what I do?" she asks him. "I keep my undies in the icebox!" She laughs with the pleasure of a good shared joke, and he swallows with barely concealed dread, already aware that the image of her chilled panties will be difficult to excise from his restless mind.

The joke of *The Seven Year Itch*—a joke that rapidly grows stale—is Ewell's overactive fantasy life. His imagination has summoned his dream woman, but the very same organ refuses him any enjoyment of her presence. Wracked with guilt, sure that retribution for his dream-crimes is forthcoming, the self-aggrandizing Ewell imagines himself a desperado, a lothario, a drawing-room sophisticate, but cannot allow himself the pleasure of genuine pleasure. His dreams of Fairbanksian vim and vigor notwithstanding, Ewell is actually like a younger Edward Everett Horton: a fussy wallflower with a motor mouth that you just know will never wind up with the girl. Monroe is given little to do other than appear occasionally and top up Ewell's momentarily waning supply of sexual attraction, guilt, and panic.

Lavish pedigree and all, *The Prince and the Showgirl* (1957) is easily the worst of Monroe's starring efforts. Monroe is an American chorus girl in London summoned to meet the regent to the throne of Carpathia (Olivier), and never quite leaves. Unsurprisingly, the director of *Henry V* and *Hamlet* has a ham-fisted sense of humor. Olivier's direction of Monroe is colossally misguided, turning her into a plucky, feisty Judy Holliday type, while downplaying her obvious comedic gifts. The prince and the showgirl fall in love, although all evidence in favor of this conclusion has been assiduously wiped from the film itself. Monroe's showgirl is festooned with the Royal Carpathian Order of Perseverance, second class, for her service to the Carpathian throne. For having sat through this film, audiences should have been granted the same honor—first class.

Wilder had gone through his own Good War in wrestling a performance out of Monroe for *The Seven Year Itch*, so he surprised even himself when he offered her a starring role in *Some Like It Hot* five years later. For Wilder, working with Monroe was a deeply trying experience that pushed the limits of his patience and ingenuity. "There are more books on her than there are on World War II," he would later reminisce, "and I think that there's a great similarity." It ended up being every bit as difficult as he should have known it would be. "Mr. Wilder," she responded to one of the director's notes with Strasbergian hauteur, "I wish you would not explain that scene to me. It interferes with my conception of it." Director Curt Siodmak was also on the set of *Some Like It Hot*, and asked Wilder how he could stand it. "Because Miss Monroe has a brain of cheese, tits of steel, she is very good in her part, and I am getting paid a quarter of a million dollars." (P.S.: Never, ever mess with Billy Wilder.)

Early on during the shoot of *Some Like It Hot*, Wilder called in his two male leads, Jack Lemmon and Tony Curtis, for a conference. They would have to be on their toes in every scene, he informed them, never making a mistake, because Wilder would print *any* take in which Monroe was good. If they happened to flub their line—well, that was their problem. With all the drama surrounding its production, *Some Like It Hot* is Marilyn Monroe's unquestioned finest moment. As Sugar Kane Kowalczyk, Monroe is a fragile rose, convinced she has begun to wilt when in fact she is in her most glorious bloom. She is a romantic heroine with a self-deprecating streak, sister to fellow Wilder heroines like *The Apartment*'s Fran Kubelik and *Avanti!*'s Pamela Piggott. Joe and Jerry are both attracted by the exterior, but the more they see of Sugar Kane's interior—kind, generous, and with a distinct preference for saxophonists and men with glasses—the more they find to like.

Wilder and cinematographer Charles Lang photograph Monroe gloriously, with a steady diet of softly lit close-ups. Monroe had never looked so ripe, so desirable as when she climbs into the same train berth with Lemmon, warming his cold feet with her own. Monroe's voluptuousness—she is practically bursting out of her black negligee—makes her a walking punch line, but Sugar Kane's humanity complicates the joke. She is a sex object with a soul.

Monroe had been pigeonholed by many as a scatterbrained sexpot, confusing the role with the performer, but when given the opportunity, she proved herself a natural comedian. George Cukor, long known as a master director of women, was nearing the end of his sterling career when, in 1960, he directed Monroe in the charming, if sugary, backstage musical *Let's Make Love*.

From the very outset of the film, we are aware we are in markedly different territory from previous Monroe vehicles. Our first glimpse of Monroe is of her stocking-sheathed legs sliding slowly down a pole and into the frame. "Boys," she whispers, tossing a ball and playing with jacks, "my name is Lolita. And—uh—I'm not supposed to"—here she wiggles her ass, for emphasis—"play, with boys!" Monroe is posing as the nubile underage nymph, her name alone promising taboo pleasures, and she sets out to throw her suitors into utter confusion. Sex is no longer accidental, or incidental; here Monroe is consciously, explicitly offering herself up for our appreciation. There were moments, in her previous films, where Monroe's ripe sensuality was treated as something grotesque, or unnatural, but no longer. She is now in complete control.

The remainder of *Let's Make Love* lacks the assurance of its opening. It soon reveals itself to be a continental romance, with Yves Montand a cut-rate Maurice Chevalier for this bargain-basement attempt at Lubitsch. Montand is a wealthy playboy who falls in lust with Monroe's struggling actress, and resorts to chicanery in the hopes of winning her heart. He gets a job in a revue sending up celebrities due to his remarkable resemblance to himself, and sets out to steal Monroe away from her puppy-dog romance with a fellow actor. The joke is that the world-class sexpot is downright motherly offstage.

She knows that sex is what motivates everyone else—her acting proves it. It just doesn't motivate *her*.

Montand envisions himself taking the place of her leading man, his office turned into a boudoir Mae West's Leticia Van Allen might have designed for herself in *Myra Breckinridge*. Sex is another kind of spectacle, and Monroe is a master performer, in every sense. Every shimmy, every wink, every smile is an arrow, and they all hit their targets dead center. Monroe is a horny man's dream, as her films had always been clear about. *Let's Make Love* was different only in letting her, at last, indicate her fully formed comprehension of the nature of her stardom. The joke was on us.

Let's Make Love was a beginning, and an ending. There would be no more comedies, as Monroe's private life increasingly took on the dimensions of tragedy. The lessons she had wrung out of the form at such great cost would never again be put to practice. After the mixed reception for *The Misfits*, Monroe was to star in a remake of Garson Kanin's *My Favorite Wife*, this time called *Something's Got to Give*. Monroe was to be the long-missing wife returned to her recently remarried husband, the hypotenuse of a love triangle with Dean Martin (playing the Cary Grant role) and Cyd Charisse.

Screwball was dead, as everyone knew, but if anyone could have revived the moribund genre, it would have been Monroe. She lacked Dunne's long-limbed grace, or her Southern airs. What she did have—what could have electrified the American comedy into the 1960s and beyond—was a delightful sense of the limitations of her own persona. As an idealized, self-mocking romantic hero with a winning sense of humor, she could have been the female analogue to Cary Grant. Instead, she took her own life, swallowing a fatal cocktail of pills on the night of August 5, 1962. Marilyn Monroe was thirty-six years old. The film was never completed.

14

DORIS DAY

BATTLE OF
THE SEXLESS

"I told you sex would get you in nothing but trouble!"
—Tony Randall, *Lover Come Back*

There was a time, before the collapse of the studios and the rise of the sexual revolution, when virginity not only wasn't laughable but could serve as a legitimate movie plot point. In this long-ago era, the battle of the sexes was one whose only acceptable resolution—at least according to the movies—was marriage. Men and women scuffled with their wits, because more

---

Doris Day comforts Rock Hudson's gentlemanly "Rex Stetson" in *Pillow Talk*.

physical, intimate forms of combat were verboten onscreen. The incredible thing was they managed to make all this seem kind of—well, sexy.

Sexy is generally not a word associated with the collaboration of Doris Day and Rock Hudson, who have undeserved reputations as prim and wooden, respectively. Nonetheless, their movies from the late 1950s and early 1960s—with suggestive titles like *Pillow Talk* and *Lover Come Back*—are reminders of the charm and resourcefulness of the comedies of the late studio era. Day and Hudson were a mid-century-modern Hepburn and Tracy, enjoying the thrill of the chase, and the battle of wits, more than the comfort of being happily settled. Before ties were loosened, and comedy threw its doors wide open to the (highly liberating) forces of raunch and gross-out, Day and Hudson marked the last gasp of the old comic order. They made chastity fun.

We have come a long way from the days of man-eating Mae West, but Doris Day's schoolmarmish reputation is mostly undeserved. By the standards of the 1950s, the Day-Hudson films are downright raunchy. Sex is everywhere, and the prospect of sexual relations between consenting single adults is treated as perfectly acceptable, if a bit risqué. Hudson and Day are the perfect American couple of the era—the man hunky, crude, but ultimately redeemable, and the woman girl-next-door beautiful, charming, and a bit uptight, but capable of reforming.

Day and Hudson's three films together—*Pillow Talk* (1959), *Lover Come Back* (1961), and *Send Me No Flowers* (1964)—are crammed full of sexually charged double-entendres, role-playing, and intimations of the sexual revolution lurking just around the corner.

Scratch beneath the surface of Day and Hudson's onscreen personae, however, and the yawning gap between silver-screen fantasy and gloomy reality readily becomes apparent. The two halves of the archetypal Hollywood couple, chastely courting each other, were deeply troubled souls, one hiding a secret, utterly taboo personal life, and the other's onscreen persona deeply at odds with her own rocky, and unfulfilling, personal life. "I'm not the All-American Virgin Queen," Doris Day candidly remarked in her 1976 memoir *Her Own Story*. To all her friends, she is Clara; no one who has made her acquaintance would dream of calling her "Doris."

Packaged and presented as the anti–Marilyn Monroe—sweet, well-scrubbed, and virginal—Day had more in common with the 1950s screen goddess than might be apparent at first blush. Both lived troubled lives off-screen that had little to do with their onscreen air of unblemished perfection, and both offered fantasies of postwar female sexuality too rarefied to be matched by reality.

One pictures Doris Day eternally smiling, crooning "Que Sera, Sera" to her son in Alfred Hitchcock's *The Man Who Knew Too Much*, or allowing some charmer—Cary Grant, say, or Clark Gable—to sweep her off her feet. The image of Doris Day being beaten by her husband when eight months pregnant, or threatened with a gun to her belly, is rejected entirely, an intrusion from some other genre entirely, not at all in keeping with the Day who was four times the number-one American box-office star of the year. Nor do Day's romantic comedies customarily end in marriage to a cold, calculating businessman accustomed to referring to his wife as "Doris Day" in conversation, habitually cheating on and ignoring her while maintaining a facade of collegiality for the cameras.

And yet, these experiences were the real content of Doris Day's life, and the happily-ever-after fadeouts merely the subject matter of Americans' collective dream life. "You just don't get it, do you?" Day rhetorically asked an interviewer during a 1991 PBS documentary about her life and work. "It was not a dream come true. All I ever wanted is what you have right now: a baby, a husband who really loved me, a home, all the happiness they could bring. I never got that, and that's all I really wanted." For Doris Day, happiness was the thing with celluloid wings, floating away with the end titles.

Rock Hudson had a similar desire to break free of being "Rock Hudson"—or at least the imagined version of him did, the one narrating *Rock Hudson's Home Movies*, Mark Rappaport's politically charged 1992 documentary. "In the interest of truth and justice, I've set down the unvarnished facts," "Rock" informs us. "What I'd like to know is how come everyone didn't know. . . . It's not like it wasn't up there on the screen, if you watched the films carefully." "It," of course, was the barely concealed fact of Hudson's homosexuality—an open secret during the decades of his Hollywood stardom, and impossible to conceal after his untimely death from AIDS in 1985. For both Day and Hudson, their lives were the weeds sprouting, untamed, in the well-maintained gardens of their stardom.

The movies may have been attuned to the ringing of wedding bells, but Doris Day's characters were more energized by the ringing of alarm clocks. They insisted that all they were looking for was a warm hearth and a brood of children, but their actions told a markedly different story from their words. A model of virginal rectitude and wifely ambition during her 1950s and 1960s heyday, Doris Day is ripe for reinvention as a proto-feminist role model.

A singer, with hits like "Sentimental Journey" under her belt, Day came to the attention of Hollywood in the late 1940s, signing with Michael Curtiz's production company. Presented to audiences as a dewy young star, Day already had a lengthy, and mostly unpleasant, romantic history. First husband Al Jorden, a fellow musician, had been the violent one, and second husband George Weidler had fled their marriage in brief order. After a brief interlude that included a romance with *Winning Team* costar Ronald Reagan ("It really wasn't conversation, it was rather talking at you," she said of Reagan's attempts at chit-chat), Day ended up marrying her agent, Marty Melcher—a relationship that lasted until Melcher's untimely death in 1968.

Day and Melcher's relationship may have been long-lived, but it was not particularly placid, or happy. Melcher was a serial cheater, inclined to see his wife as more cash cow than beloved, and Day herself strayed numerous times—her tastes ran toward athletes, with base-stealing champ Maury Wills and Mickey Mantle among her conquests.

By the time Day was first paired with Rock Hudson by producer Ross Hunter, she had already carved out a niche as a chipper comic heroine. Her specialty had been lighthearted musical romances like *On Moonlight Bay* (1951) and *By the Light of the Silvery Moon* (1953)—the kind with a few frothy numbers and a puppy-dog peck at the conclusion. By the mid-1950s, Day had grown too old for these confections, and tentatively dipped a toe into dramatic waters. Day had been revelatory as singer Ruth Etting in the underappreciated biopic *Love Me or Leave Me* (1955), ferociously tangling with her gangster husband (James Cagney), and another in the line of cool blondes with which Alfred Hitchcock decorated his films, starring in his 1956 remake of *The Man Who Knew Too Much*.

Even the romances had changed; instead of being partnered with second-tier stars like Gordon MacRae, or Reagan, she was starring opposite Clark Gable in 1958's *Teacher's Pet*. Directed by George Seaton, *Teacher's Pet* establishes the template for the Rock Hudson films to come. Day is a professor of journalism attempting to recruit crusty newspaperman Gable to guest-lecture to her class, not knowing he is already enrolled as a student. Gable is a bit elderly for the role—you can see his hands shake when he thrusts a newspaper at Day—but the two work up a nice comic routine, with Day idealistic and sunny, and her foil cantankerous and vinegary, loving women without respecting them: "You mean to tell me that now they've got dames teaching unsuspecting suckers?"

Gable is most believable at his most crabbed; when he melts for Doris, the moment is hardly in keeping with the role, or with Gable himself, who never met a dame he didn't want to push around. Day, meanwhile, struggles to maintain the appropriate distance from her student, but physical contact, like the kiss Gable snatches in her office, leaves her a little woozy, and gasping for breath. We know Doris has sex on the brain because she spurns the advances of Nobel Prize–winning scientist and author Gig Young (this film's Tony Randall equivalent), preferring something in a more dashing cut.

Producer Ross Hunter had had the bright idea of pairing the biggest box office stars of 1958, and the chemistry between stiff Hudson and frosty Day belies their reputations. Hudson is macho, boorish, and charming; Day is cute, easily offended, and looking to be swept off her feet. These comedies take place just down the block from Marilyn Monroe's turns in *The Seven Year Itch* and *How to Marry a Millionaire*—sparkling big-city films set among sexy, upwardly mobile singles.

Pillow Talk (1959), directed by the previously undistinguished Michael Gordon, establishes the model for all future Day-Hudson comedies, as well as Day's collaborations with Rock stand-ins like Cary Grant (it is ironic that Hudson, in so many ways a student of Grant's bluff, good-natured charm, should be seen as the real thing, and Grant the understudy, when it came to Day). Day is Jan, a prosperous interior decorator driven to near-homicidal rage by sharing a party telephone line with occasional songwriter and full-time playboy Brad Allen (Hudson). Jan is simultaneously fascinated and revolted by Hudson's odious charmer. She reports him to the authorities (in this case, the telephone company) in the hopes of never again having to hear him croon his heartfelt original composition to another conquest whose name is carefully slotted in to the lyrics: "You are my inspiration— Eileen, Eileen." Brad is the kind of toxic bachelor who has a single switch in his living room that turns out the lights, puts on a romantic record, and locks the doors—and a second that automatically unfolds the bed in his sleeper couch.

Learning that Jan is the intended of his close friend and patron Jonathan (Tony Randall), and growing curious, Brad crafts a character intended to snare her away—"Rex Stetson," Texas businessman and perfect gentleman. Accurately pegging Jan as the type of woman looking for a desexed version of himself, Rex woos Jan with admirable restraint, never making an ungentlemanly move. Rex is so restrained that Jan must take the wheel of the relationship, plotting a course for land. "Rex, we're both over twenty-one," she gently chides him, after he tries to ask her to spend the weekend with him, and grows tongue-tied.

Day is breathy, kittenish, and willing to be seduced—in fact, practically egging Rex on to do the seducing. For all her virginal reputation, it is usually Day who has little problem with sex as a natural outgrowth of romance. It is her leading men who balk at the prospect of sex with a good girl like Day.

Hudson is here, as in the two films that follow, a split personality. He is both horndog and mama's boy. The mama's boy, with his courtly manners and reserve, is in danger of being perceived as limp-wristed, and *Pillow Talk* roars with pleasure at the prospect of the virile-looking Hudson drinking with his pinky finger extended, expressing delight at Jan's "working with all them colors and fabrics," and hoping to get a recipe to bring home to his mother. "What a vicious thing to say!" Jan hollers at Brad, after he implies that Rex may not be playing on Jan's team. One can only imagine how Hudson—a gay man pretending to be straight playing a straight man pretending to be gay—felt about acting out such scenes of gay panic.

The hollowness at the heart of Hudson's masculinity is implied by another running joke in *Pillow Talk*, in which an obstetrician is convinced that he is going to be giving birth to a baby. Hudson is the prototypical romantic hero—with his strong jaw and hulking physique, he is almost comically manly—but *Pillow Talk* implies a certain cavity in his machismo, as if, of the two roles he plays, Brad Allen is the bigger put-on.

Being a movie of its era, *Pillow Talk* can only imply so much; it must limit the potential fallout of any such innuendo about its leading man. And so we have Tony Randall as Brad's best friend—a quivering mass of pantywaisted insecurities. Jonathan is the type of man who breaks up with his girlfriend on his therapist's suggestion, who fruitlessly pleads with Jan to marry him, who serves his best friend as faithful valet and advisor. In short, Jonathan serves to inoculate Brad Allen, and by extension Rock Hudson, against any such claims of inadequate masculinity.

"I was having a rendezvous with Rock Hudson—me, David, George, Gabriel, Adam, and Hobo. All of us!" Airy romance with the heavenly Rock was rendered a mere housewife's daydream in *Please Don't Eat the Daisies* (1960), in which Day is weighed down by an unappreciative husband, four sons, and one oversized dog. There was a touch of *Mr. Blandings Builds His Dream House* to this escape-to-the-country domestic comedy, but the film was most useful as an object lesson in the peculiar perfection of the team of Day and Hudson. David Niven was like a wet blanket draped across the screen, his British reserve playing as aloof when paired with the bubbly Day. *Daisies* is mostly polite, tolerable if meandering, but there is a niggling implication that all of this—raucous children, messy house, country living, even Niven's professional troubles—all stem from Day's inability to properly keep a home. Whatever indications there might be to the contrary, domestic life did not agree with Doris Day.

Lover Come Back (1961) was both sequel and remake to *Pillow Talk*, with Day and Hudson returning as squabbling rivals and occasional lovers. Here, Day is Carol Templeton, a tightly wound advertising executive infuriated by the cheap-shot tactics of her competitor Jerry Webster (Hudson). The contrast between rock-ribbed Day and playboy Rock is underscored from the very first scenes, in which she arrives at the office in a taxi, bright-eyed and beehive-hatted, and he wakes up in the passenger seat of the convertible being driven by his latest conquest. "What kind of a goodnight kiss is that?" she squawks, as the worker drones stream into their assigned hives. "We're not married!"

Jerry Webster is most assuredly not married, and his intimate familiarity with the bachelor's lifestyle gives him the edge when competing for the account of entrepreneur J. Paxton Miller. Carol and Jerry are competing for his business, and Carol wants all the latest facts and figures on Miller so she can win him as a client. Jerry is looking for facts and figures, too, but of a different sort: the type of women Miller likes, his brand of liquor, and whether or not his wife will be joining the evening's festivities. Business and pleasure go head to head: "The agency that lands this account is the one that shows Mr. Miller the most attractive can," Carol announces, as director Delbert Mann cuts to dancers in bunny outfits wiggling their butts.

When her boss compares Jerry to the common cold—striking twice a year, no matter what—Day responds: "There are two ways to handle a cold: you can fight it, or you can give in and go to bed. I intend to fight it." Carol is intent on not taking anything to bed and sleeping with it, a fact that Jerry seizes on with alacrity. "I don't use sex to land an account," Carol tells him huffily when they speak on the telephone. "When do you use it?" he asks, a glint of enjoyment in his eyes, as if he sees a potential checkmate a few moves away. "I don't!" she huffily responds, and Jerry seizes the dagger and rams it home: "My condolences to your husband."

The second half of *Lover Come Back* has Hudson and Day switching roles once more, with Doris now the sexually experienced pursuer and Rock—posing as Dr. Tyler, a cloistered scientist purportedly working for the nefarious Jerry—the virginal, sheepish pursued. Hudson's unreconstructed, unapologetic masculinity becomes, if not quite the outright homosexuality of *Pillow Talk*, a similar brand of limp-wristed fearfulness. Randall, as ever, is present to protect

Hudson against any such claims of effeminacy, his prissy indecisiveness indicative of an essential asymmetry between the red-blooded Rock and himself.

Jerry's Dr. Tyler, brilliant and coddled, unable to assert himself in the boudoir as he does in the laboratory, is like Hudson doing his best version of Randall. Dressed in a suit that looks like grandma's couch cut into a forty-two long, "Tyler" tells Carol that he wants nothing more than to be . . . Jerry Webster. "You deserve a man," he sadly observes, "not a mass of neurotic doubts." Tough as nails at the office, Carol is trusting and downright gullible away from it, willing herself to believe in the saintly Dr. Tyler. "Knock at my door, and I shall take you in," Tyler worshipfully says to her, and Carol replies, "Dr. Tyler, I'm knocking." Tyler's response ("Miss Templeton, I'm taking you in") only registers for the audience.

Tyler is like a woman choosing between two suitors: nice Carol and naughty Jerry. Carol repeatedly stumbles on Tyler after he has purportedly escaped Jerry's clutches, retreating into the warm embrace of Carol's kindliness. Carol wants to give herself to Tyler, preferring the mass of neurotic doubts to crass, calculating Jerry Webster. In fact, Jerry and Carol never fall in love, precisely. *Lover Come Back* is a romantic comedy without a genuine romance to its name. Having created two diametrically opposite romantic leads, the film cannot figure out a way to ultimately bring them together, other than deception.

An overhauled version of *Please Don't Eat the Daisies*, 1963's *The Thrill of It All* (directed by Norman Jewison, from a script by Carl Reiner) was the best of Day's Hudson-less comedies. Harried housewife Day is unexpectedly recruited to star in a TV soap commercial. She stammers and fumbles her way through her pitch, sure she has blown her big opportunity at success. Her lack of polish strikes a chord with viewers, somehow, and she is hired as a permanent spokeswoman, for the hefty sum of eighty thousand dollars per year.

James Garner plays her husband, chagrined that she is no longer satisfied with being a doctor's wife. In one surprisingly intimate moment, Day limns the outlines of a barren homemaker's existence: "The PTA and home-bottled ketchup—that is it! And it's not very fulfilling." Day apologizes and Garner fumes, and the confusion of marital roles is unsettling to everyone. Garner has his comeuppance by doctoring evidence of an imaginary affair, in the hopes of making his wife jealous enough to leave her career behind. Garner is a far better actor than Hudson, but a less effective foil, and the film suffers as a result. Mostly, though, *Thrill* is bubbly good fun, effective at rendering the battles of the sexes as (mostly) harmless horseplay.

Garner and Day would be reteamed later the same year, stepping into the shoes of two legendary comedy stars for a remake of a screwball classic. "Poor Cary Grant thought his first wife was dead," Day wistfully reminisces, fondly remembering the plot of *My Favorite Wife*, but memories of *Move Over, Darling* (directed by Day's *Pillow Talk* collaborator, Michael Gordon) would be significantly less sentimental. *Move Over* is practically a shot-for-shot remake of Garson Kanin's 1940 gem (itself to have been remade by Marilyn Monroe before her untimely death), forcefully striking every note of the original while perversely emphasizing the story's melodramatic qualities. Exhibiting none of Irene Dunne's playful charm, Day lacks the twinkle in her predecessor's eye, turning a masterful farceur into a scorned woman on the warpath. And Garner, while undoubtedly game, is no Grant. By its absence, *Move Over, Darling* is a forceful reminder of what made the comedies of the 1930s and 1940s so brilliant: their light-footed grace. The battle of the sexes had grown bloodier without gaining an iota of maturity, or wit.

Speaking of Hudson, he was busy having his weaknesses poked and prodded by Howard Hawks in the accidentally revealing *Man's Favorite Sport?* (1964), which turned the role-playing of the Doris and Rock films into the stuff of psychic splintering and degradation. Hudson is a world-renowned fishing expert who, truth be told, has no idea how to catch a fish. Tomboy Paula Prentiss must teach Hudson how to comport himself on the river to save him from mortal embarrassment at a fishing contest. The symbolism was almost too fraught: this Rock was a sham, a man in name only, his aura of expertise pierced at the first jab.

Day and Hudson's third and final onscreen collaboration, the far inferior *Send Me No Flowers* (1964), begins after the "Happily Ever After." Hudson is George, a hypochondriac whose tender self-directed ministrations drive his wife Judy (Day) batty. Mishearing a doctor's pronouncements after his latest checkup, Rock is convinced he has just weeks to live, and strives to set his house in order. Furthering the furtive gay subtext of these films, Rock goes husband-hunting for his wife, scouting eligible men with best friend Arnold (Randall again) in the hopes of helping her score an appropriate mate. (Randall has a wife we never see, preempting any questions of why *he* doesn't marry her.) "George, he's loaded. He's loaded!" Arnold exclaims, like a teenage girl swooning over the quarterback of the football team.

A solution swiftly emerges in the form of Bert (Clint Walker), a granite-jawed Texas oilman who looks like a Neanderthal version of Hudson himself.

Bert blatantly romances Judy in George's presence, and George (after some initial, residual anger) hardly bats an eye. George is essentially letting a manlier version of *Pillow Talk*'s Rex Stetson steal his wife away. *Send Me No Flowers* comes dangerously close to giving away the game with Hudson, offering the specter of a husband unmoved by the prospect of his wife's getting into bed with another man.

In fact, it is George and Arnold who are the true married couple here, squabbling and making up with some regularity. "George, do me?" Arnold asks, handing him his cummerbund before a black-tie event. Later in the film, we see Hudson and Randall sharing a bed, and Hudson practically shrieking when Randall's cold feet give him an icy chill. Judy is little more than an encumbrance, and a problem to be solved.

Day, however, has the ground cut out from beneath her. *Pillow Talk* and *Lover Come Back* worked in large part because Day was so believable as a flinty career woman and tempered romantic. In *Send Me No Flowers*, Day is a married ditz, perfectly content to let her husband worry about the affairs of the world as she twitters around the house in her bathrobe. "What is amortization of a mortgage?" George demands of Judy, attempting to give her a crash course in microeconomics. "I don't care," Judy replies, "I really don't care." It is only when Judy believes she has caught George two-timing her, shoving his wheelchair out the door and locking him out, that a glimpse of the unflinching Doris of yore peeks out from beneath the dowdy attire and unflattering hairdo (which looks like a ferret has chosen to roost on her head).

Without Hudson to accompany her, Day's other romantic comedies offered diminishing returns. Even the prospect of starring opposite the real Cary Grant, in *That Touch of Mink* (1962), would not be enough to reverse the inevitable downward spiral of Day's career into providing a pretty face (in increasingly soft focus) for processed Hollywood cheese. *Mink* slots Grant into the traditional Rock role, as an industrialist playboy with a myriad of notches on his belt. Grant effortlessly romances Day, jetting her off to Philadelphia for a world-class bowl of fettuccine, and whisking her to Bermuda for the weekend. Grant's well-oiled seduction machine begins to sputter when Day breaks out in an ill-timed rash. Day's overheating psyche turns every object she looks at into a bed. "What do people do here at night?" she asks Grant, and he stares blankly in response, as if she had suddenly misplaced fifty points of IQ.

Swapping in Grant for one of his legions of imitators ("I thought you would have married someone like Cary Grant," a character told Day in *Send Me*

No Flowers) should have been a guaranteed improvement, but the fifty-eight-year-old actor was too old to be the playboy, and the romance falls flat as a result. It was much easier to believe Day ending up with Rock Hudson than with Grant, who looks terminally disinterested here, as if he had been hoping to make a better film than this one. Everything in *Mink* feels like a down-grade: Stanley Shapiro and Nate Monaster's script is a pale carbon copy of earlier Day-Hudson efforts, and Gig Young, while suitably fey, is hardly an adequate replacement for Tony Randall in the best-friend role.

Day was even more ill-suited when paired with director Frank Tashlin for *The Glass Bottom Boat* (1966) and *Caprice* (1967). Tashlin, who had helped make Jerry Lewis a superstar, was a cartoonist by trade, and his films were essentially live-action cartoons, preferring mechanical artifice to acting or dialogue. *Glass Bottom Boat* restricts Day to outraged yelps and klutzy she-nanigans, hoping to disguise her being at least ten years too old for the role with filters and gauzy lighting. Day is entirely upstaged by Dom DeLuise, who channels Lewis's spastic brand of physical comedy for his role as an inept spy. Tashlin is far more interested here in the comedy to be generated from technology run amok than his characters, and it shows; what other director would go so far out of his way to make Day this unappealingly stupid, and outfit her so unflatteringly?

Hard as it may be to imagine, Doris Day was offered one last role that could have rejuvenated her career, and cast all her prior work in a dramatic new light. Day was approached by Mike Nichols and offered the role of Mrs. Robinson in *The Graduate* (with ex-flame Ronald Reagan playing her hus-band!). Given Day and Melcher's strong preference for family-friendly enter-tainment, it comes as little surprise that Day could not see herself seducing a boy twenty-five years her junior onscreen.

The world was denied the ultimate stunt casting; instead, Day starred in *With Six You Get Eggroll* (1968), an extension of *Daisies'* vaguely raunchy brand of family comedy. Day is a widow running a lumberyard who unex-pectedly finds romance with a widower (played by Brian Keith). The adults prance around like lovestruck teens, as their children serve as their inquisi-tors and jailers. The film has a weird frisson of hepcat cool not at all in keep-ing with the plot, as if a smidge of the Summer of Love, and a few punch lines from George Carlin (playing an opinionated waiter) could save Day from ter-minal irrelevancy.

Hudson and Day had long since gone their separate ways, but there would be two more encounters—one real, and one symbolic—that would remind their fans of what Rock and Doris had once had together. In 1985, Hudson made one final public appearance, on his former costar's television show *Doris Day's Best Friends*. The public was unaware of it, but Hudson had only a few months to live. Sweaty, emaciated, and increasingly disoriented, Hudson was in the final stages of AIDS, and would be the first celebrity casualty of the disease. It was, as James Wolcott noted, a real-life remake of one of their pictures, but played for tragedy, not farce: "In truth, it wasn't *Pillow Talk* they were reprising, but *Send Me No Flowers*, this time for real, with no last-minute reprieve."

Hudson died later that year, his tragic loss galvanizing the fight against AIDS, and Day went into seclusion, mostly disappearing from the public eye. And then, in 2003, something strange took place: Doris and Rock were together again, starring in a new movie called *Down with Love*. The plot sounded familiar, like a hastily reworked *Pillow Talk*, the sets were sleek and mid-century modern, like 1960 all over again—hell, even Tony Randall was back!

To be more precise, Tony Randall was here twice over: first as the sexless, neurotic sidekick to the hero, looking none the worse for wear, given the passage of four decades, and then there was Randall himself, aged and weary, his presence the lone tangible link to the films *Down With Love* was so bountifully feting.

For, now that we looked a bit more carefully, it was David Hyde Pierce, not Randall, in the sidekick role. And Day and Hudson were present only as guardian angels, the inspiration for this lavish tribute to a bygone era. Peyton Reed's film was a candy-coated, over-the-top, delirious parody and testimonial. Renée Zellweger was an ideal Day manqué, and Ewan McGregor captured Hudson's macho appeal, if not his hidden reserves of wounded-child sensitivity. Zellweger was a proto-feminist author telling women to be more like men when it comes to romance, and McGregor the swashbuckling journalist intent on penetrating her defenses.

The film was knowing in ways its predecessors were not—suffice it to say that the earlier films' buried homoerotic charge no longer required a Ph.D. in gender studies to unearth—but the tone was endearingly unaffected. *Down with Love* is less a debunking than an encomium, a belated but all-too-necessary acknowledgement of Day and Hudson's winning chemistry. The match was not a precise one, the tone ever-so-slightly too arch, but if we unfocused our eyes, and let our imaginations wander, it would be easy enough to convince ourselves that this was, after all, the long-delayed reunion of Doris Day and Rock Hudson, the one that would end happily ever after.

15

JERRY LEWIS

THEY'RE CRAZY ABOUT
HIM IN FRANCE

"Ma!" —Jerry Lewis, *The Ladies Man*

By 1950, the era of the silent giants had long since come to an end. Buster Keaton was reduced to working as a gag consultant and glorified extra, Harold Lloyd was serving as Imperial Potentate of the Shriners, and Charlie Chaplin released new films with the regularity of appearances by Halley's Comet. The one-time gods had fallen to earth, and the films that had brought

Note the pinky ring: Dr. Julius Kelp, *The Nutty Professor*.

them to the Olympus of comic glory now gathered dust, residents of some moldering Hollywood warehouse.

Overnight, the brand of comedy meticulously developed by hundreds of funnymen in thousands of films had become obsolete, rendered useless by dialogue. Movie comedians now lived and died on the basis of what they said, not what they did. Physical comedy—until then the only kind of comedy there was—was now seen as lowbrow, lowest-common-denominator stuff. True comedy was Lubitsch, or the Marx Brothers, or Wilder: brilliant dialogue uttered by men in dinner jackets, or wags with cigars screwed into the corner of their mouths.

All the while, though, the hard-won truths of silent comedy, proved definitively in countless celluloid experiments, lay dormant. All they required was someone to make them fresh again. They were waiting for Jerry Lewis.

Like Chaplin, reared in the music halls of London, Jerome Levitch was a child of the theater. His father, who took the stage name Danny Lewis, was an itinerant vaudevillian, playing everywhere from weddings and birthday parties to the legendary burlesque houses of Newark, New Jersey. His mother, Rae, was a pianist of some middling success. Jerome, born in 1926, occasionally went on the road with his parents, but more often stayed behind with relatives.

By the time he was a teenager, his father had become a low-level headliner in that onetime-bastion of middle-class Jewish leisure, the Catskills. Jerry was a child of the burlesques—he told people he had lost his virginity as an eleven-year-old to a stripper named Marlene—and of the mountain resorts. His first appearance onstage as a comedian was in the Catskills, doing movie impressions with some of his waiter friends and lip-synching to records. By the time he was a teenager, Jerry Lewis—he had taken his father's stage name as his own—was sure that comedy would be his life as well. Maybe, if he was lucky, he would one day headline the clubs that his father had always dreamt of.

The traumas of a quasi-orphaned childhood were long-lasting. The adulation granted a successful performance was, for Lewis, the only balm for the parental absence that had so marked his early years: "An audience is nothing more than eight or nine hundred mamas and papas clapping their hands and saying, 'Good boy, baby.' That's all. You'll find that people who had enough 'Good boy, baby,' from their actual parents rarely turn to comedy." If the audience was composed of parents, rendering judgment with each round of applause, the performer forever remained a child, anxious, needy, and in search of attention.

While still a teenager, during World War II, Lewis was partnered with fellow 4F Dean Martin. Martin was a former boxer and blackjack dealer, a lazy nightlife habitue content to skate by on charm and fumes. Together, Martin and Lewis were magic. Martin was the consummate professional, the lover-man on the make; Lewis was his ball and chain, his curse, and his responsibility. He was, in the words of Lewis biographer Shawn Levy, the Putz to Martin's Playboy. Both men were outfitted in tuxedos, but Martin's was dapper, and Lewis's was ironic. In short order, they became the most popular comedy duo in the country. Jerry Lewis was headlining the swankiest clubs in the United States by the time he was legally old enough to drink, and radio and television success followed in short order. Where does a son go when he's surpassed his father before the age of twenty-five?

By the time of his splashy debut onscreen, a supporting role in 1949's *My Friend Irma*, Jerry Lewis was a big, bouncing, fully formed baby. Martin was father figure to Lewis's irrepressible toddlers, forces of uncontrollable destructive energy. Martin was the singer and Lewis the comic relief, and much of the pleasure of these slapdash efforts comes from the friction between these two seemingly mismatched stars. Try as he might, Dean could never rid himself of pestering, well-meaning Jerry.

Lewis's mental age in these films is approximately eleven. He is just old enough to appreciate women, if not quite mature enough to know what to do with them. On the whole, though, he prefers boyish pursuits—comic books, ray guns, six-shooters, and the like. Harvey, Myron, Melvin, Seymour, Virgil, Wilbur: the names of Lewis's characters alone limned his klutzy, nerdy, Jewish characters. His voice is a nasal whine occasionally rising to an uncontrolled screech. He maintains a constant stream of babble: near-words, helpless murmurings, yelps, gasps, and shrieks that convey meaning without being actual, unadulterated English.

To some critics and cultural custodians in the early 1950s, Jerry Lewis was a further sign of the apocalypse: a grinning, destructive man-child, mostly incapable of speech, charming undiscerning audiences into helpless laughter. Lewis, to those same naysayers, was symbolic of the devolution of comedy into mindless infantilism. To others, he was the sole attraction of the Martin & Lewis films, held back only by his singularly talentless compatriot.

The critics were not mistaken about Lewis's technique, only about his intent. The first film Jerry Lewis had ever seen was Chaplin's *The Circus*, and traces of the silents had remained in his bloodstream ever since. Lewis's idiocy was not the sign of a fool, only of a silent-comedian Rip Van Winkle, awoken in a time not his own. In Jerry Lewis, the silent comedy had found its rejuvenator.

The films Lewis and Martin made together—sixteen of them in seven years—were mostly interchangeable, their plots hypodermic needles designed to deliver the largest possible dose of Lewis's infantile shtick. Lewis was a bratty younger brother to the suave Martin, dogging his every step and foiling all his routines—both onstage and off.

Lewis may have been the sidekick onscreen, but he was the main event off it; *The Stooge* (1952), where Lewis was the underappreciated secret weapon of Martin's sophisticated entertainer, was a symbolically freighted comic version of the two performers' relationship. Martin was infinitely more polished than the still-gawky, unformed Lewis, but audiences greatly preferred the shrieking, hyperactive man-child, and were more than happy to tell him so. Martin was a useful reality principle for the effervescent Lewis; without him, Jerry Lewis would have to create him afresh—or even embody him himself.

Lewis was not only infantilized by these films, but feminized. The films regularly filched their scenarios from proven comic hits of the past, inverting the originals to cast Lewis in the submissive, female role. Billy Wilder's *The Major and the Minor*, with Ginger Rogers as a woman posing as a child aboard a train, became *You're Never Too Young* (1955); the Ben Hecht–scripted farce *Nothing Sacred* was transformed into *Living It Up* (1954), with Lewis in the Carole Lombard role as the rural homebody who parlays an imaginary illness into an all-expenses-paid New York vacation. (Even those films that were not explicit remakes often borrowed liberally from their predecessors. *That's My Boy* (1951) was essentially an updated version of Harold Lloyd's *The Freshman*, and *The Stooge* a loose adaptation of *All About Eve*, with Jerry as the scheming Eve.)

Lewis was putting his own distinctive stamp on film history, inscribing himself into the margins of Hollywood's past and shrieking to be heard over the dialogue. The effect was simultaneously mesmerizing and alarming, as if a mental patient had commandeered an otherwise normally functioning film set, and the final product was released to theaters. In addition to remaking comedy classics for his day job, Lewis and his actor pals (including Janet Leigh and Tony Curtis) shot Semiticized parodies of Hollywood classics for their own amusement on days off from the studio: *A Streetcar Named Repulsive*; *Come Back, Little Shiksa*; and best of all, *Fairfax Avenue*—a lampoon of Wilder's *Sunset Blvd.*, set on Los Angeles's Jewish Main Street. Screenwriter Joe Gillis becomes Yakov Popowitz, and the film's big reveal takes on a similarly Jewish flair: "Yakov Popowitz eats ham."

Lewis may have seen himself as the reincarnation of Chaplin's Tramp, but his true teacher was a six-foot-three, 220-pound former Los Angeles *Times* cartoonist and Harpo Marx gag writer named Frank Tashlin. Tashlin had broken into Hollywood as an animator, working for Disney and Columbia's animation studios. Transitioning to live-action direction hardly dimmed his enthusiasm for cartoon-like gags and routines. With his impossibly dexterous body and rubbery face, Jerry Lewis was a Tashlin fever dream come to fully formed life.

Artists and Models (1955), the first of the Martin & Lewis films with Tashlin as director, solved the problem of the stars' increasingly diverging interests by effectively cramming two films into one. Martin had always shoehorned a few musical numbers into their films, and *Artists* cast Martin in a romantic musical while Lewis was the star of a broad satire. Martin was the one who ended up seeming out of place, exuberantly crooning his way down the street like he was belting out a number in a Stanley Donen–Gene Kelly musical. Lewis, meanwhile, was an overgrown boy with a hyperactive imagination informed by—wouldn't you just know it?—comic books. Dino plunders Jerry's Technicolor dreams for the plots of the comics he draws, and sets off a HUAC-esque political imbroglio in the process. Lewis's Eugene Fullstack is essentially an oversized infant, as suggested by the repeated shots of him standing on his fire escape, its bars forming an oversized crib. The dialogue sounded like the contents of thought bubbles, too: "Oh-oh-oh-ah-ah-eeh-ahah!"

By the last few Martin & Lewis films, the ironic distance between the films' ecstatic tributes to friendship and the two performers' now-frosty personal relationship could not have been greater. "You and me will be the greatest pardners, buddies, and pals," went the lyric to the closing song of *Pardners* (1956), but any lingering hope on Lewis's part that the two actors could go on working together was by now thoroughly extinguished by Martin's withering cynicism. "The two worst things that happened to Jerry," Martin noted, taking dead aim at his partner's burgeoning artistic ambitions, "were taking a good picture with a Brownie and reading a book about Chaplin."

Stung by critics' assertions that Lewis was the comic genius and he merely the oafish sidekick, Martin pulled the curtain down on their long and immensely fruitful collaboration after 1956's tepid *Hollywood or Bust*. The two, though, had been breaking up for years—at least onscreen. In almost every film they had made together, Martin sought to shake childish, destructive, utterly impossible Jerry. This had been the joke all along, until it was a joke no longer, and Jerry was suddenly, unexpectedly left to his own devices.

(Lewis never really got over being dumped by his partner. He was still mulling over the breakup with Martin in 2005, when he published the surprisingly tender memoir *Dean & Me: (A Love Story)*.)

Tashlin provided continuity, helping Lewis to bridge his Martin and post-Martin eras. Their collaborations without Martin maintained the comic core of *Artists and Models*, while revealing a sentimental streak heretofore unknown to director or actor. In both *Rock-a-Bye Baby* (1958) and *The Geisha Boy* (1958), Lewis made for an unlikely father figure to needy children (perhaps anticipating his later work with the annual Muscular Dystrophy Telethon). The sentiment, so at odds with Lewis's traditional comedy, made for films that were like jury-rigged remakes of *Artists and Models*, with Lewis playing both ends of radically divergent plotlines.

A tamped-down version of *The Miracle of Morgan's Creek*, the quasi-musical *Rock-a-Bye Baby* revisits the boundary-pushing Preston Sturges film from the perspective of Eddie Bracken's patsy. Lewis's childhood love, now a movie star, unexpectedly gives birth to triplets after a brief Mexican marriage, and dumps the infants with Lewis's hapless handyman. Unsure whether it is a broad physical comedy or a tender family film, *Rock-a-Bye Baby* slops together syrupy and slapstick moments indiscriminately. Lewis is a brilliant mimic—a scene where he acts out an entire television broadcast to entertain his drunken quasi-father-in-law is a small masterpiece of quick-change inventiveness—but the film seems to prefer tugging at the audience's heartstrings.

The Geisha Boy mines similar ground, with Lewis a struggling magician who adopts a fatherless Japanese boy on an overseas tour. Sentimental and often maudlin, *Geisha* is a comedy aimed at pint-sized sensibilities. The men don't know, but the little kids understand: Lewis's destructiveness pleases the younger crowd, even as it discomfits the older generation. In an attempt to help a pushy starlet off an airplane, he tears off her dress, and rolls her up in the red carpet like the contents of an oversized, misshapen cigarette. The silent, unsmiling boy laughs for the first time in years, and a friendship is born of Lewis's naive good-heartedness.

Having labored under the tutelage of Tashlin, Lewis was ready to set out on his own as a director. *The Bellboy* (1960) is a disconnected series of vignettes, linked by Lewis's inept hotel porter Stanley. True to Lewis's appreciation for Chaplin, Stanley is a silent character in an all-too-cacophonous world. Perpetually on the verge of speech, Stanley is forever being crowded out of the conversation. He is a schlemiel of the sort embodied by French comedian

Jacques Tati's Mr. Hulot, bringing up the engine block of a Volkswagen to a guest's room when told to empty the trunk, or bringing a newly svelte dieter a box of candies as a gift.

The Bellboy is the most understated of Lewis's films—a series of comic experiments rather than the well-honed routines of his collaborations with Tashlin. Stanley conducts an imaginary orchestra to frantic applause; he hijacks an airliner and buzzes the hotel where he works; he watches confusedly as a man pretends to eat an apple, deafeningly. Lewis is marvelously confident for a first-time director, eschewing narrative in favor of a free-form series of sketches akin to a vaudeville show. Don't like this gag? No need to panic—another is on its way momentarily.

The Tashlin films were deliriously flat, as if the screen were merely a larger, more colorful comic strip. With *The Ladies Man* (1961), Lewis reveals a sophistication of technique well beyond Tashlin's capabilities, or inclinations. The film's dollhouse set serves as a physical manifestation of Lewis's goulash aesthetic—each closed door opens to reveal a new prop, or another costar. As a result, *The Ladies Man*, while not quite the funniest of his films, is unquestionably his most proficient effort as a director, nearly musical in its rhythm. For once, pathos does not pose awkwardly next to comedy, but is itself integrated into the comedy.

Lewis is Herbert H. Heebert (the H, of course, stands for Herbert), scarred by his college girlfriend's infidelity, and picking up the pieces as an all-purpose houseboy at a women's boarding house. Herbert, like so many other Lewis heroes, is schizophrenic, simultaneously childish and mature, a resourceful numbskull. The title is not descriptive so much as it is possessive; Herbert is not one for the ladies, but is himself their plaything, mascot, and punching bag. (Lewis has a one-word response to such indignities: "Ma!") The black-and-white of *The Bellboy* gives way to exuberant, eye-popping color here, whose unnatural vividness—like a comic-book panel—is an expression of Lewis's super-saturated, everything-and-two-kitchen-sinks style.

The Errand Boy (1961) picks up where *The Bellboy* leaves off, with Lewis once more a well-intentioned menace. Taking a first tentative step up the evolutionary ladder, Lewis's Morty Tashman is capable of speech, if just barely. A studio sign-painter hired by the executives of the Paramutual Film Corporation to be their on-set eyes and ears, Morty mangles names, sings braying gibberish-songs, and is deathly afraid of abuse at the hands of his employer-parents.

The idiot is also king: we first see Morty putting up a sign reading "Directed by Jerry Lewis," in case we had forgotten who the brains behind the foolishness might be. *The Errand Boy*'s episodic sketches are an extension of those in *The Bellboy*. Morty interrupts the business of the studio, disrupting battle scenes and Western cattle drives, overdubbing sappy ballads from romantic comedies with his own tuneless warbling. This being a Jerry Lewis film, Morty is rewarded for his artless virtue. Dim-witted genuineness triumphs over mean-spirited professionalism.

Even after he became a director, Lewis kept on working with his onetime mentor Tashlin. Their later collaborations lacked the audacious comedic radicalism of Lewis's solo efforts as a director, or even the no-frills charm of *Artists and Models*. Lewis was getting better and better as a performer, but there was something surprisingly feeble about *Cinderfella* (1960), *It'$ Only Money* (1963), and *Who's Minding the Store?* (1964). An inexplicable undercurrent of hostility runs through the films, casting Lewis as the unwitting defender of traditional values on behalf of aggrieved masculinity. *Cinderfella*, a gender-switched, jazz-inflected *Cinderella*, with Lewis playing another uncomplaining manservant, was warped by a series of unprompted, quasi-misogynistic outbursts. "I believe a man has got to be king in his own ranch-type-style tract house," Lewis tells his girlfriend's henpecked father in *Who's Minding the Store?*, and the entire film is a slow gathering of resources for revenge against overweening womanhood. Having studied at Chaplin's feet, Lewis had somehow twisted the great man's Victorian worship of women into a sardonic misogyny.

The best of the Tashlin-Lewis films bears the strongest resemblance to Lewis's own directorial work. *The Disorderly Orderly* (1964) is episodic after the fashion of *The Bellboy*, its string of disconnected routines structured around Lewis's bumbling medical-school dropout. The further Tashlin and Lewis stretch from the strictures of the realistic, the better off they are; *Disorderly* bears more than a faint whiff of absurdism. Brief, wildly exaggerated riffs are the norm here: the patient in a body cast who smashes into a million pieces, the tottering towers of cans that come spilling out of a supermarket with the force of gunshots. There is another lachrymose subplot, about an adolescent crush of Lewis's now hospitalized for depression, but *The Disorderly Orderly* deftly sidesteps maudlinity with perhaps the most unrestrained of Tashlin's patented revenge-of-technology endings.

Lewis, though still firmly associated with the dim-witted persona he had introduced with Martin, was insistent on regularly breaking character, and shoehorning some reminder of his offscreen self into his films. Why were his Stanleys and Herberts always wearing gaudy Vegas-style pinky rings, or wedding bands? There was something self-defeating about the gesture, as if Lewis could not set foot in front of the camera without a tangible reminder of the difference between himself and the characters he played.

The rings are also indicative of Lewis's desire to play another version of himself onscreen, one closer to the actual, offscreen Jerry: suave, tuxedo-clad, charming. The real Jerry Lewis was no schlemiel, we were to understand; or so Lewis had sought to remind us by appearing in a second role in *The Bellboy*: "Jerry Lewis," superstar.

Lewis is not averse to poking fun at his image—"Oh, mother used to take me to see him when I was just a kid," an elderly bellboy sourly notes when he appears—but the hapless schnook was balanced, and offset, by the Martinesque smoothie.

Stanley and "Jerry Lewis" stare at each other, silently, each flustered by the presence in close proximity of their doppelganger. It was as if the warring sides of Lewis's personality had burst loose, free to confront each other in a wordless joust for superiority.

With *The Nutty Professor* (1963), Lewis molds his preoccupation with multiple personalities into a meditation on his tempestuous relationship with Martin, and an acknowledgement of the dueling sides of his personality. Lewis had long been a comedic wunderkind; now, at last, he had something to say as well.

Geeky, accident-prone scientist Dr. Julius Kelp transforms himself, with the help of a magical potion he has developed in his laboratory, into Rat Pack nightclub swinger Buddy Love. Lewis, honest if not quite generous to his former partner, gives Buddy a snappy line of patter and a new set of threads. Singing and playing the piano, charming the coeds and bantering with the barkeeps, Buddy knows he's the life of the party. "Innkeeper," he shouts, "got sexy lights?"

Buddy is not quite Martin—for one, his singing voice is still too nasal to truly sound like Dean's—but the self-absorbed charm is all there. "The swingingest and the best," he says of himself. "You want on time too?" Buddy is a condescending, patronizing, self-aggrandizing lush—Dino as reflected in a cracked mirror. (Compare him with Martin's own version of himself in Billy Wilder's *Kiss Me, Stupid*, from the next year, and note the affection lavished on *Kiss Me*'s boozy woman-chaser, and its complete absence here.)

Kelp is every bit as brilliant a creation as Buddy. His speech a parade of verbal gaffes, his face dominated by a ridiculous pair of bifocals, he is the inarticulate geek transcendent—the summation of Lewis's career-long fascination with outcasts and screwballs.

Still wrestling with the specter of Martin, Lewis sought to exorcise the demon by summoning him. His Buddy is both the swinger his Stanleys and Juliuses dream of being, and a cautionary tale. For Buddy is Mr. Hyde and Frankenstein's monster rolled into one; once let loose, he cannot be controlled. There are psychic costs to being Buddy, and Kelp—read Lewis—has come to acknowledge them: "I don't want to be something that I'm not. I didn't like being someone else." We should not forget the hints provided by the profusion of pinky rings, either; Buddy is not only Dean Martin, but Jerry Lewis as well, and *The Nutty Professor* is a record of the conflict between Lewis's onscreen putz and his offscreen playboy.

After the career peak of *The Nutty Professor*, Lewis willingly shackled himself to pathos, at the expense of comedy. The prodigal bellboy returned for *The Patsy* (1964), but this time in markedly changed circumstances. Loosened up by *The Ladies Man*'s experimentation with color, decor, and cinematic space, *The Patsy* was like a steroid-enhanced sequel to Lewis's directorial debut: *The Bellboy Goes Hollywood or Bust*. Lewis's errant Stanley was now to be primped, polished, and prepared for incipient fame by a wily team of show-business veterans. The only hitch in the plan is Stanley.

The Patsy is clever, even inspired at moments (as when Stanley improvises a bit as a starstruck fan for an appearance on *The Ed Sullivan Show*), but Stanley exists mostly to reiterate Lewis's contempt for the trappings of fame. Stanley is a disaster as a star, with a gift for destruction, and the destructive mangling of the English language, but stardom beckons nonetheless. Lewis's treacly emotionalism, casting his lamblike innocent into the lions' den of scheming industry players, emphasized his belief in the arbitrariness of the fame game, even as his own career had been born of his own blood, sweat, and tears.

The Family Jewels (1965) transforms *The Nutty Professor*'s multiple-personality disorder into the stuff of family entertainment. Stealing a page from Peter Sellers's playbook, Lewis is Willard, kindly chauffeur to an underage heiress. After her parents' death, she must pick a new father from among her colorful array of uncles. Lewis, of course, plays all six uncles, who include a gap-toothed Chicago mobster, an aging sea captain, a high-fashion photographer, and a belligerent clown.

Lewis's characters are not fashioned from entirely new cloth—the photographer is a dead ringer for *The Nutty Professor*'s Julius Kelp, and the clown bears a distinct resemblance to Buddy Love. Lewis's creeping sentimentalism, which had been kept in check, for the most part, in previous films, begins to overflow its banks here. The tone was an expression of his

Chaplin-envy. *Family Jewels* is his version of *The Kid*, with Lewis as the protector of a helpless child adrift in an all-too-adult world. The biggest laughs come from the silliest bits: Willard backing his truck in and smashing it against a low-hanging ceiling; tweedy, pseudo-British Uncle Skylock beating a pool shark with aplomb; Willard ineptly manning a gas station. If Chaplin was the source for the material, Tashlin supplies the mise-en-scène; the color-coded compositions are lifted directly from Tashlin's 1950s work.

Playing out the string, Lewis's final two films of the 1960s were pale imitations of his earlier successes. All the fizz had gone out of his work, leaving only a flat concoction composed of stale ingredients: the Day-Glo Bergman of *Three on a Couch* (1966) and the familiar Buddy-Julius dichotomy of *The Big Mouth* (1967). Lewis had no shortage of funny hats and wigs to don, but the characters all feel tiresomely familiar. The ever-increasing hysterics of *Couch*, and the posturing of *Mouth*, were not enough to distract from the essential fact of Lewis's progressively soggier routines. Lewis had never been one to shy from repeating a successful gag, but nearly two decades of stardom had warped his sense of his own strengths. Lewis was still aping himself, but the furious comic invention that had made him such a dazzling performer had softened into a flailing vigorousness.

After the unremarkable *One More Time* (1970) and *Which Way to the Front?* (1971), Lewis planned to adapt Joan O'Brien and Charles Denton's story of a German clown who entertains Jewish children on their way to the gas chambers. After filming *The Day the Clown Cried* (1972), Lewis belatedly discovered that he had never actually acquired the rights to the story. The film was shelved, never to be screened, and Lewis did not work again for another eight years. The fizzled project was evidence of Lewis's monumental hubris, soothing the pain of mass extermination with the healing balm of his comedy, but his crass instincts were right-on; Roberto Benigni would win an Academy Award, twenty-five years later, for playing a version of Lewis's Helmut Doork in his *Life Is Beautiful* (1998).

"JERRY LEWIS IS HARDLY WORKING," reads the title card to *Hardly Working* (1980), and the announcement is a suppressed howl of outrage at his career setbacks—how could *I* not be working? —and a capsule summary of the film. His character—an unemployed clown with a familiarly Lewisesque proclivity for courting disaster—is ushered into a series of ill-fitting jobs (gas-station attendant, bartender, Japanese chef), each of which ends calamitously. The dialogue was risible, only rarely rising above the insipid, but something—perhaps the time away—had made the old Lewis routines charming once more. As a postal worker, Lewis scarfs down his boss's dough-nut and coffee, sets off a chain reaction of toppling mailboxes, and drives his mail truck like it is a Formula One racecar.

Lewis was scripting his own triumphant return, on his own terms. "I'm not a clown," his Bo Hooper tells a friend. "Not anymore." Lewis wants it both ways; he is the clown no longer, but *Hardly Working*'s triumphant conclu-sion has him donning the white makeup once more, delivering the mail to an adoring crowd. Never the subtlest of artists, Lewis was having his midlife crisis onscreen, and scripting his own happy ending.

There was an air of self-pity to *Cracking Up* (1983), as if Lewis had fallen out of step with the world he had long depended on for approbation, and no longer knew how to regain the rhythm. The film felt semi-autobiographical, much as *Hardly Working* had: a portrait of the artist as a middle-aged mis-fit. Lewis is the suicidal Warren Nefron, visiting a therapist's office in the hopes of acclimating himself to society. *Cracking Up* is a series of thematically linked flashbacks. Some are historical, like a one-man version of Mel Brooks's then-current *History of the World, Part I*, and some are updated versions of old gags from *The Bellboy* and *The Family Jewels*.

As a director, Lewis had grown increasingly amateurish; little of the luster of *The Ladies Man* remained. But as a performer, he had deliberately stripped away the polish, until all that remained was the man: wounded, haunted, and empty. Lewis douses himself with gasoline at the end of *Cracking Up*, then finds himself unable to light a match. (It is tempting, albeit unlikely, to read the scene as a reference to Richard Pryor's then-recent freebasing incident.) The moment's bleakness was practically Beckettian.

Jerry the clown had been summarily dismissed, a failed suicide and hapless jester. But what of the Jerry Lewis we were constantly being reminded of in the 1960s films—the suave entertainer, the living legend? He, too, was given a proper send-off, although the master of ceremonies was not Lewis, but Martin Scorsese. The director cast Lewis as legendary late-night host Jerry Langford in *The King of Comedy* (1982). The film was Scorsese's riposte to his critics after *Taxi Driver*'s accidental role in the shooting of President Ronald Reagan.

De Niro returns, following *Taxi Driver*'s Travis Bickle, as another fame-obsessed loner, a nobody whose fantasies of redemption require the divine intervention of Lewis's show-biz luminary. Lewis is the straight man for this bleakest of black comedies, his cool dispassion a response to a baffling world of unexpectedly intense encounters with fans. "You should only get can-cer!" a well-dressed matron shouts at him on the street after he rebuffs her entreaties, and Lewis silently blinks back his surprise. After a lifetime of wild-eyed, shrill buffoonery, Lewis was being asked to summon a muted dignity as everyone around him behaved with the lunatic unpredictability of a Jerry Lewis character. It was a fitting end to a storied career; having spent the better part of four decades tormenting the unsuspecting, Lewis was now tormented in turn by a world seemingly comprised entirely of Jerry Lewis imitators.

16

PETER SELLERS

THE MAN BEHIND
THE MASKS

"It would not be difficult, Mein Führer."
—Dr. Strangelove (Peter Sellers) to President
Merkin Muffley (Peter Sellers), *Dr. Strangelove*

Think of a Peter Sellers movie, and you almost undoubtedly will picture Sellers wearing a ridiculous costume, affecting a ridiculous accent, or both. For a time in the 1950s and 1960s, Sellers and Jerry Lewis were the reigning titans of American comedy, but where Lewis was neurotic, infantile,

---

The Angel of Death in the War Room in *Dr. Strangelove*.

and exaggerated, Sellers was cool, crisp, and gently absurdist—even as he engaged in the same knockabout humor that made Lewis a comic idol. One always pictured Lewis, away from the cameras, as more Professor Julius Kelp than Buddy Love, no matter how much he protested otherwise; but Sellers seemed to maintain a permanent private reserve of self bearing little resemblance to what we saw onscreen. Like Groucho Marx, the question was: would we recognize him offscreen? For Peter Sellers in particular, the question was also: would we want to?

Taking on three roles in Stanley Kubrick's *Dr. Strangelove*, or adopting an absurdly broad French drawl for the *Pink Panther* films, Sellers was uniquely plastic, disappearing into his roles until character took precedence over performer. We remember Inspector Clouseau, or Dr. Strangelove, as independent entities, existing separately from the actor who embodied them. Sellers may have been born in Britain, but his penchant for slipping out of an old skin, and into a more comfortable new one, marks him as profoundly American.

Like so many of the other great performers of American comedy, Peter Sellers's roots were in vaudeville. Like Charlie Chaplin in particular, Sellers came out of the crumbling English music hall, where his parents were third-tier performers—dad was a piano player and occasional confidence man, and mom wore a scanty mermaid costume and swam around a water tank for the edification of her overwhelmingly male audience. Young Peter made his first appearance onstage at two weeks old, when the audience serenaded him with "For He's a Jolly Good Fellow." "Most of my childhood," Sellers would remember later, "seemed to be spent curled up on my mother's lap in the back seat of a car, going from town to town, theatrical digs to theatrical digs. Into the car, out of the car, suitcases out of the trunk, clump, clump, clump up the stairs of some third-rate boardinghouse."

By his teens, Sellers had discovered that mimicry was the fastest way to girls' hearts. Learning that his schoolboy crush had a yen for Errol Flynn, he made a quick study of all Flynn's films, imitating his walk, his facial expressions, and his speech patterns; when she switched her affections to Robert Donat, Sellers mastered the staid British matinee idol too. Later, his fellow RAF airmen, during the Second World War, would enjoy his dead-on impersonation of an officer, surreptitiously inspecting the troops and asking after their creature comforts. A few short minutes later, Sellers would appear at dinner as himself, and no one would be any the wiser. There was a lesson to be learned. Imitation was not only the sincerest form of flattery; it was also the quickest way to disappear in a crowd.

After the war, Sellers slowly made his way through the lower echelons of British radio, offering an impression here and a song there, before linking up with two fellow veterans, Spike Milligan and Harry Secombe. The trio called themselves the Goons, and they offered a brand of proto–Monty Python lunacy, mime, music, and bawdy humor borne of Sellers's music-hall youth. *The Goon Show* (originally called *Crazy People* by a skittish BBC) premiered in 1951, and struck a chord with its utterly deranged, druggy humor. Episodes were given outlandish names like "The Dreaded Batter-Pudding Hurler (of Bexhill-on-Sea)," and the gags were mostly directed at the British Establishment. Sellers's characters included a bumbling British military officer prone to verbal mishaps, and the show developed a nonsense catchphrase: "Ying tong iddle I po."

Sellers was consciously operating in the shadow of his illustrious comedic forebears; one notorious *Goon Show* bit had him doing his best Groucho Marx impression, asking a waiter if a restaurant served crabs, and then bringing one out and requesting that it be served lunch. (The Goon style would be immortalized in the 1960 short *The Running, Jumping, and Standing Still Film*, codirected by Sellers and Richard Lester, and deeded over by Lester to the Beatles for *A Hard Day's Night*, which is essentially a feature-length remake.) Sellers was talented enough to actually replace his idols on occasion. He provided a raucous voice-over commentary to Chaplin's re-released silent short *Burlesque on Carmen*, and even dubbed Humphrey Bogart's voice for *Beat the Devil* (1953) after Bogart was injured in a car accident.

It would be appropriate, then, that Sellers had a small role in *The Ladykillers* (1955), in which Alec Guinness was a criminal mastermind planning a bank robbery. Sellers was a glum Teddy Boy named Harry, not given much of a chance to contribute much to the robbery, or the comedy, but his joint presence with Guinness marked the passing of a torch. Guinness, that chameleon given to disappearing into his roles, had found his successor. The torch was no longer there to be passed, though; Sellers might have made an ideal Ealing comedian, but the era of the dry British comedy had passed. In fact, Sellers's British comedies serve both as testament to his remarkable skill and as a reminder of the insufficiency of the stage. Sellers was following in the footsteps of Guinness, indeed, but his was a baroque variety of character acting, more suitable to the larger-than-life aesthetic of Hollywood than British film's temperamental modesty.

After a series of forgettable films (anyone seen *The Case of the Mukkinese Battle-Horn* recently?), Sellers formally donned Guinness's mantle, playing three roles in the gentle political satire *The Mouse That Roared* (1959).

Sellers is the clipped Etonian prime minister "Bobo" Mountjoy, soft-spoken country boy Tully Bascombe, and the fluting, demure Grand Duchess of the miniature European state of Grand Fenwick. The country decides to attack the United States in order to reap the benefits of postwar aid, only to find itself the unexpected victor on the battlefield. Anticipating *Dr. Strangelove*'s aggressive mobilization, *Mouse* deploys Sellers in nearly every scene—sometimes acting opposite himself.

Even when limited to a single role, Sellers preferred wholesale transformation to more limited alterations. With an ill-fitting suit, a brush cut, and a Hitler mustache, Sellers's Mr. Kite, shop steward and failed rabble-rouser in *I'm All Right Jack* (1959), looks older and chubbier than the actor would in later, more glamorous roles. Kite is an old man trapped in a young man's body, an elderly codger tramping around the confines of his too-small house and ranting drunkenly to himself. *I'm All Right Jack* is the record of Kite's abasement, his dreams of collective strikes and Communist glory disrupted by the unruly, homely conservatism of his employees. Sellers is still in his understated phase in these films, the rococo opulence of later character roles nowhere in evidence.

Sellers had always needed a particular voice, or a certain look, in order to find his way into a role. For the atrocious *The Millionairess* (1960), a broad Indian accent liberally coats all the surfaces of Sellers's performance, its intended hilarity meant to mask the film's gaping deficiencies. (What the Scottish accent would be for Mike Myers, the Indian accent is for Sellers.) The film itself is nearly unwatchable, a travesty that inexplicably casts Sellers as the straight man to the comically inept Sophia Loren. Sellers would return to the well one time too often (more like four times too often), but his taste of India gave him license to erase the grubby British character actor he had been, and become an unidentifiable man of the world.

Just to clear this up, once and for all: there really is no good reason why the series of films collectively known as *The Pink Panther* bears that name. The beloved comedies starring Peter Sellers as the bumbling Inspector Clouseau have become identified with the name, and with the charming animated title sequences, but the name itself comes from the original *Pink Panther*, from 1963. In that film, the Pink Panther is a world-famous diamond whose lone flaw, when held up to the light, appears to take the shape of a pink panther. Clouseau is not, nor ever would be, the Pink Panther, and yet the name and the character have become inseparable—so much so that four later films all included *Pink Panther* in their titles, for little particular reason. I thought I would mention this to indicate the world of illogic you have committed to settle into as soon as you enter the world of the Pink Panther.

Everyone is familiar with *The Pink Panther*, but it is the accoutrements that are more familiar than the films themselves. The troublemaking animated panther and Henry Mancini's slinky theme summon up a charming sense of sexual and criminal frisson that the films themselves often struggle mightily to match.

Clouseau was a sidebar in the original *Pink Panther* (1963)—an amusing diversion from the main action. David Niven plays Sir Charles Lytton, world-famous ladies' man and suspected jewel thief, romancing Pink Panther owner Princess Dala (Claudia Cardinale) as he woos the inspector's wife (Capucine). Peter Ustinov was originally booked to play the clumsy detective before bailing on the production three days before shooting began, and Sellers was his last-minute replacement. Clouseau is the unwitting cuckold, amorous and clueless as he tries, and continually fails, to achieve romantic bliss with his wife. He is put off by everything: cold feet, thin blankets, glasses of warm milk, exploding champagne bottles, screechy violins. There is a touch of Buster Keaton's stone-faced imperturbability, and a hint of Chaplin's misplaced dignity, in his Clouseau.

As funny as Clouseau gets, he is never as laughable as the purportedly romantic dialogue between Niven and Cardinale, who hardly generate romantic spark sufficient to light a miniature candle. Sellers is not yet buffoonish, only inept, and his Gallic mangling of the English language is not yet as pronounced as it becomes in the 1970s Pink Panther films.

The Pink Panther introduced the world to Clouseau, but it is not until the second film in the series, *A Shot in the Dark* (1964), that the natty French inspector with the grey trench coat and carefully trimmed mustache took center stage. Clouseau (no longer married, and on the prowl) is deadly sober, grim-faced as he approaches the task of homicide investigation. The facts of the case hardly matter; all anyone watches for is the wink-wink sexual suggestiveness (now rather dated), and Sellers's remarkable gift for physical comedy. Director Blake Edwards (who made all the *Pink Panther* films) has shifted gears here, from thriller with shades of sex farce to out-and-out comedy with a tinge of sex farce. Clouseau, who always seemed extraneous to *The Pink Panther* (or maybe it was everyone else who was out of place?), now has a scenario pegged to his strong suits.

Clouseau is still to be an object of ridicule in *A Shot in the Dark*, but he is now the actor, not the acted-upon. Having borne silent witness to the unerring superiority of Niven's sexual aristocrat in *The Pink Panther*, Sellers is granted the privilege of his own nemesis in Herbert Lom's increasingly unhinged Inspector Dreyfus. Dreyfus is competent where Clouseau is inept, precise where Clouseau is scattershot, and utterly unmoored by his rival's destructive capabilities. No longer an object of condescension, Clouseau is now a small-bore nuclear weapon of catastrophe, setting himself off at steady intervals in the name of scientifically assured detection. At first a dependable source of exasperation with Clouseau's slapstick ways, Dreyfus changes, over the course of the Pink Panther films, into a defender of preyed-upon mankind against Clouseau's cosmic ineptitude. In short, Clouseau drives him batshit insane.

Clouseau fancies himself Hercule Poirot, but is actually more akin to Jacques Tati's Mr. Hulot—a brilliant klutz masquerading as a great detective. His dignity never flags, though, whether he has just exited a taxi directly into a fountain, loudly slurped the ink from a pen, or torn up the felt on an elegant pool table. "I examine the facts," he loudly announces to a roomful of potential suspects, pontificating about his crime-solving method as he remains blissfully oblivious to the dollop of skin cream on his nose. "Give me ten men like Clouseau," Inspector Dreyfus mutters to himself, "and I could destroy the world."

Anticipating Austin Powers, Sellers's Clouseau is a master of the absurdist catchphrase: "This is my pistol-pen! Get your own pistol-pen!" "You fool, you've broken my pointing-stick! I've nothing to point with!" "It's a good job I was able to check my reflexes," he sputters at an underling after stumbling over him. "I could have killed you with a karate chop!" he shouts, his hand frozen in mid-chop.

The same year *Shot* was fired, Sellers had his most indelible success as the impish reigning spirit in Stanley Kubrick's midnight-black comedy *Dr. Strangelove, or How I Learned to Stop Worrying and Love the Bomb* (1964). *Dr. Strangelove* is a comedy of frustration, whose scramble to avoid nuclear calamity is repeatedly spoiled by homegrown idiocy, knavery, and right-wing quackery. Kubrick has been occasionally pilloried for his lack of human warmth, but *Dr. Strangelove* (which may be the chilliest Kubrick film of all) is rarely accused of inhumanity, due to Sellers's moderating presence. Sellers had initially been hired to play four of the film's major roles: President Merkin Muffley, Group Captain Lionel Mandrake, Major "King" Kong, and the eponymous Dr. Strangelove. A badly sprained ankle forced Sellers to abandon the role of Kong (which went to Slim Pickens), but his presence still looms large over Kubrick's film.

Kubrick had fallen in love with Sellers's talent on the set of *Lolita* (1962), where the actor had played the madly improvisatory Clare Quilty, nemesis of James Mason's Humbert Humbert. Sellers loved collaborating with Kubrick, enjoying their playful working through every permutation of a character before settling on an interpretation of a scene. As Quilty, Sellers was one character containing multitudes; for *Strangelove*, Sellers fractures, inhabiting multiple roles while taking up no psychic space of his own. Peter Sellers, for all intents and purposes, had ceased to exist.

Kubrick himself once said of the actor, "There is no such person." Seeing *Dr. Strangelove*, one begins to understand. Each character Sellers played bore so little relation to the others that it was nearly impossible to believe the same actor was behind them all. Mandrake, the British officer tasked with preventing Sterling Hayden's mad General Jack D. Ripper from unilaterally instigating World War III, was an extension of Sellers's comically inefficient *Goon Show* army men, his elongated nose and bushy mustache symbolic evidence of his typically English mediocrity. President Muffley is a liberal egghead a la Adlai Stevenson (to whom he bears a notable physical resemblance), reduced to helplessness by the incompetence and blood-thirst of his advisers. And Dr. Strangelove, the most memorable creation of all, is the post-Hiroshima Angel of Death.

Sellers invests Strangelove—the greatest of all his creations—with a mad, whirring glee. What Sellers gives Kubrick, more than anything else, is a purposeful confusion of tones. The threat of nuclear apocalypse keeps giving way, under Sellers's careful prodding, to some other mood, some other genre. "Jack, I'd love to come," Mandrake tells General Ripper when requested to feed the general's bazooka, "but, um, what's happened, you see, the string in my leg's gone. . . . I never told you, but you see, gamy leg, oh dear, gone and shot off." Sellers has transported Mandrake to another film entirely—the last scene of a second-rate British World War II film, perhaps.

President Muffley has a marvelous moment, too, where his normally Mr. Rogers-esque calm gives way to a shrill wail of helplessness. He is on the telephone with Soviet Premier Kissoff, and must break the news of a potential nuclear attack. Chuckling agitatedly, his voice having risen an octave in pitch, Muffley is talking to the second-most powerful man in the world as if he were a baby in need of soothing. "You know how we've always talked about the possibility of something going wrong with the bomb," Sellers begins, giving the words a singsong intonation, as if this were the introduction to a particularly unsettling children's tune. "The *bomb*, Dmitri . . . the *hydrogen* bomb."

For those who haven't seen *Dr. Strangelove* in some time, it may come as a surprise that the title character appears in only two scenes, the first of which does not occur until more than half the film has unspooled. For all that, Strangelove still owns the film. Possessed with a bursting enthusiasm for the glories of the post-apocalyptic, Strangelove is the dark angel of the mushroom cloud. In a wheelchair, with an enormous upswept quiff of hair and a single black glove, he is a lavishly ornamented peacock in a sea of buzzcuts. (Later wags saw Strangelove as a brutal parody of Henry Kissinger, but Kissinger was not yet the internationally famous figure he would soon become. Sellers would note in interviews that he had modeled his accent on crime photographer Weegee's impenetrable English, with a touch of ex-Nazi rocket scientist Wernher von Braun's chilly demeanor.)

Sellers's physical ingenuity turns Strangelove into a man halfheartedly wrestling with his own darkest impulses, and losing. His Strangelove is the barely repressed spirit of erotically charged destruction that Kubrick's film satirizes. Addressing President Muffley as "Mein Führer," forced to physically restrain his disobedient arm from shooting out in a Nazi salute, Strangelove is the genocide-lust reborn. More than anything, Sellers's Strangelove is a man of mismatched parts: the rebellious hand, the froggy croak of a voice, the terrifyingly deranged smile. His misbehaving fingers wrap themselves around his throat, seeking to choke the life out of anyone who would deny access to his untapped reservoirs of murderous glee.

Sometimes the characters themselves were patched together from mismatched parts. Sellers's concert pianist in *The World of Henry Orient* (1964), perpetually stymied in his romantic ardor by two nosy teenage girls, cannot make up his mind whether he is from France or Forest Hills. His elegant Parisian drawl occasionally gives way to a dees-and-does bray; appropriate for this schizophrenic film, which squeezes Sellers into an already-crammed tale of teenage friendship and romantic confusion.

Strangelove and Clouseau had made Peter Sellers an international star, but overblown, expensive messes like *What's New Pussycat?* and *Casino Royale* had given Sellers the unfortunate opportunity to indulge his lowest common denominator. The wastefulness of the films (should this scene feature elephants, or bagpipers?) was matched by the laziness of Sellers's performances, which coasted on his well-honed array of voices and characters.

Sellers is a lecherous Strangelove in *What's New Pussycat?* (1965), a drunken fumble of a movie whose purported pleasures are curiously joyless. The movie, written by Woody Allen, is a disastrous muddle, with Sellers wasted as a horndog shrink with a thick Austrian accent and dreams of ditching his shrewish wife. *After the Fox* (1966) is a brazen daylight robbery of *The Pink Panther*, including its immediately recognizable title sequence. Sellers is fine as an Italian crook with family trouble, but Vittorio De Sica, who had directed *Bicycle Thieves* and *Shoeshine*, should have known better. The James Bond spoof *Casino Royale* (1967) pre-empted Sellers, splintering 007 into a victim of multiple-personality disorder. Sellers, alongside David Niven, Ursula Andress, and cowriter Woody Allen, is one of the numerous Bonds hopscotching through this turgid mess of a film, which deflects all attempts at entertainment, or coherence, with persuasive thoroughness. And in the notably superior, but still muddled, *I Love You, Alice B. Toklas!* (1968), Sellers is an uptight Jewish white-collar drone in loosey-goosey L.A., belatedly tuning in and dropping out. With his beads and long hair, passing out newspapers on the street, he is a precursor to Albert Brooks's yuppie bohemian in *Lost in America*. Sellers's nasal American accent cuts in and out nearly as much as it had in *The World of Henry Orient*, matched only by the strained farce of Paul Mazursky and Larry Tucker's script.

Like Golda Meir once said of the Palestinians, Sellers never missed an opportunity to miss an opportunity. A mild heart attack forced him to drop out from Billy Wilder's *Kiss Me, Stupid* (his replacement Ray Walston ended up torpedoing the film, making it a missed opportunity for Wilder as well). The lead in Chaplin's valedictory *A Countess from Hong Kong* fell through, and Mel Brooks offered him a starring role in *The Producers*, which he immediately turned down. Later, his untimely death would keep him from starring in a remake of Preston Sturges's *Unfaithfully Yours*. Meaty roles were regularly turned down in favor of ones that would allow him to indulge his comedic sweet tooth.

Sellers was developing an unwanted reputation as a one-trick comedian, the man with the odd voices and funny costumes. The string of flops was broken only by reuniting with Blake Edwards for *The Party* (1968). Slathered in brown makeup, wielding an Indian accent that ranges anywhere from thick to entirely impenetrable, wreaking terrible havoc on a staid Hollywood party, Sellers's Hrundi V. Bakshi is a crude stereotype, even for 1968. With a bit of generosity, however, one can begin to grasp what Sellers and director Blake Edwards were intending with the masquerade. Scrub off the pancake makeup, and swap out the clipped Indian vowels for elongated Gallic ones, and Hrundi is none other than our old friend Inspector Clouseau in disguise.

Clouseau was on extended leave from the big screen, but *The Party* is practically a *Pink Panther* sequel, thrusting Sellers's bumbling, accident-prone protagonist into an extended version of the already-legendary nightclub sequence from Jacques Tati's *Playtime*, released the previous year. In the most memorable moment in Tati's masterpiece, Hulot had single-handedly dismantled a plush club on its opening night; Hrundi similarly stumbles from one disaster to another, sowing seeds of destruction with his every step. His shoe flies into the pool, and then onto a tray of hors d'ouevres; an errant stab with a fork sends his chicken breast flying into a woman's tiara; a mission to scrub an elephant clean floods the house with soap suds.

The Party is as near to pure physical comedy as the sound film could come. There is remarkably little dialogue, with the soundtrack composed primarily of background murmurings, and plot serves only as a bridge between one set-piece and its successor. For all its Hulot-esque fumbling, *The Party* is not quite *Playtime*, lacking Tati's formal rigor and eye for composition. Despite the offensiveness of Sellers's brownface routine, *The Party* is one of his very best films, and undoubtedly the least seen. It is a film of small pleasures—the squish of wet shoes interrupting a musical performance, Hrundi's nonsense phrase "birdie num num," repeated ad infinitum—that prefers to have its audience determine just what might be funny here. Taking a page out of Tati, this is neorealist comedy, purposefully lacking a director's guiding eye: look here, look there. The screen is crammed full of activity, and the audience's eyes are left to wander where they may.

The aimless free-jazz comedy of *The Magic Christian* (1969) was like *The Party* in reverse, all high-concept setup with no attendant punch line. It was exceedingly difficult to believe that the same Terry Southern who had written the magnificent *Strangelove* had penned this lumbering ode to the corrupting powers of money. Pity for Sellers, then, that *Magic Christian*, and not any of his earlier successes, would form the template for a series of disappointing early 1970s films.

Two messy divorces (including one from *After the Fox* costar Britt Ekland) and a newfound reputation for unpleasant on-set behavior had brought Sellers unwanted notoriety as a prima donna and tyrannical husband. The onset of fame had made Sellers more mercurial and temperamental than ever. He was demanding and petulant, prone to bouts of depression and loneliness. Sellers drove directors batty with his on-set demands, gave his employees migraines fulfilling his petty desires, and fell in and out of love with his wives and girlfriends with the utmost rapidity. Sellers had become the sort of man who insisted on having his suits tailored to his ideal weight, rather than his actual weight, and then had them redone when he couldn't button them. Having suffered a heart attack, Sellers grew morbid, convinced of his impending death. The offscreen Peter Sellers, it seemed, was no fun at all.

Sellers and Edwards took an eleven-year hiatus from Clouseau, but the desire for a surefire hit brought the Sûreté's best-known investigator back for another three cases. The holiday-romantic mood of the first two films gives way to an international-crime travelogue, as if Clouseau were a significantly less suave James Bond. Perhaps, having failed to properly inhabit 007 in *Casino Royale*, Sellers sought to compensate by making his most beloved character into a Bond manqué. The plot of *Return of the Pink Panther* (1975) made even less sense than the average Bond thriller, with the theft of the fabled Pink Panther diamond (there it goes again!) dragging back Sir Charles (with Christopher Plummer replacing Niven) and his wife Lady Lytton (Catherine Schell) into a murky world of double- and triple-crossing.

During his sabbatical, Clouseau has grown even more exaggerated, and a little predictable; the slow-motion fights with his houseboy Cato (Burt Kwouk) take on a familiar air by the time they have been trotted out for the third and fourth time. Sellers is waxy of pallor, and his energy has noticeably flagged since the last Clouseau outing, but his ability to provoke helpless fits of laughter is undiminished—and the proof is in the final print of the film. In a nightclub scene, where Clouseau is posing as a lounge lizard in a ear-piercingly loud red sports coat and mutton-chop sideburns, costar Schell erupts in uncontrollable hysterics, sputtering into her drink, when Sellers toasts her *Casablanca*-style: "Here's looking at you, kid." I'm not sure what it says about *Return* that Edwards left this scene in. Is the film charmingly shambling, or in dire need of a better editor?

By 1976's *The Pink Panther Strikes Again*, Clouseau is less buffoon than magical idiot, a precursor to Sellers's Chauncey Gardner in *Being There*. Clouseau's hair is now carrot-colored, and his trench coat has been matched with a herringbone fedora, but his mangling of English consonant sounds has remained. *Robber* comes out as "ghebber," and *challenge* is "sha-longe." The Bond allusions are now explicit, with Lom's Inspector Dreyfus now playing the villain to Clouseau's inept 007. Clouseau has ascended to the realm of holy fool, not only protected from harm but assured, in all instances, of ultimate triumph.

"Diminishing returns" would be too kind a description of the remaining films in the series, with 1982's posthumous *Trail of the Pink Panther*, composed out of stray remaining bits of Clouseau, particularly, ghoulishly egregious. Clouseau's strangely out-of-touch Eastern fetish had infected Sellers's other work; the rancid Asian jokes of *Revenge of the Pink Panther* (1978) were close kin to the inscrutable-Chinaman stereotype of Sellers's Charlie Chan manqué Sidney Wang in the limp Neil Simon adaptation *Murder by Death* (1976).

The *Pink Panther* brand, however, remains evergreen, with Steve Martin replacing Sellers in a 2006 remake, and a 2009 sequel. Martin is no sha-longe to Sellers as Clouseau. Sellers may have been spotty, but we prefer to remember him at his ingenious best. Watching these wildly inconsistent films prompts us to paste together our own mental highlight reels of the brilliant Sellers. When you hold *The Pink Panther* series up to the light, the rest just disappears.

Before Sellers's untimely death of a heart attack at the age of fifty-five, in 1980, he had one last conjuring trick up his sleeve. If his entire career had been one long, steady disappearing act into his characters, his valedictory role as Chauncey Gardiner in *Being There* (1979), directed by Hal Ashby, was the perfect summation of Sellers's eccentric charm. Concerned about aging, Sellers had had a facelift just prior to making the film, which suited his role perfectly. Chauncey Gardiner is a blank slate, unmarked by life, free to be written on by anyone and everyone. A gardener who has spent his entire life living and working on a multimillionaire's estate, Chauncey is forced out into the harsh, unfamiliar world after his boss's death. He is formed of equal parts gardening tips and life lessons gleaned from television, which serves as his sole source of information about the world he knows so little of.

An accident and a chance encounter steer him into the rarefied world of power couple Benjamin and Eve Rand (Melvyn Douglas and Shirley MacLaine). In short order, Chauncey, and his array of horticultural metaphors, are fodder for television talk shows and wielders of behind-the-scenes political influence. Sellers's Chauncey does nothing other than talk about plants and seeds, and take tips from everyone else. If the president of the United States shakes hands a certain way, then so does he. Being blank, Chauncey is read differently by different audiences. To the housekeeper who has long taken care of him, he is little more than a child; to African American gang members, he is the Man, representing invisible, nefarious white power; to Ben Rand, he is a shaman, offering koans of economic advice. Chauncey is a Rorschach test. What people read in him says more about them than about him. Sellers's Chauncey is asexual, uneducated, and lacking in affect. His face registers only minuscule changes, like the flicker of laughter that darts across his eyes while watching a cartoon. Chauncey is a nonentity in a three-piece suit.

Ashby's film is a rip-roaring political screed disguised as a gentle comedy. Sellers, playing a naif, assigns no moral value to his Chauncey Gardiner. Chauncey is merely a beneficiary of unpredictable circumstance, the projection of others' hopes and desires with none of his own beyond the immediate: a hot meal, a warm television. *Being There* is simply too much—a comedy far too exaggerated to possibly swallow—until one remembers that the very next year, a Gardiner-esque blank slate would be elected the fortieth President of the United States. If there is a reason that no feature-film biopic of Ronald Reagan has yet been made, it is perhaps because Peter Sellers has already embodied him here.

As if to confound our understanding of this deceptively simple character, Sellers's final act in *Being There* is to calmly, quietly walk on water. It is as if having studied his filmography with some care, Chauncey were embodying the ethos of another Sellers character, Hrundi V. Bakshi: "Wisdom is the province of the aged, but the heart of a child is pure." Sellers's characters had rarely been wise, but they had always maintained the purity of childhood. Each mask, when slipped on, offered the possibility of transcendence, of the ideal self he had always sought and never found; until, for his final act, Sellers became, simply, no one at all.

17

DUSTIN HOFFMAN

STARDOM, REVISED

"Plastics." —The most famous bit of career advice in film
history, supplied to Dustin Hoffman in *The Graduate*

"What can we do about his nose? What can we do about his eyebrows?"
Mike Nichols, the thirty-four-year-old directorial wunderkind,
fresh off the success of his *Who's Afraid of Virginia Woolf?* (1966), looked at
the face of the actor in the makeup chair—the potential leading man for his
second picture—and didn't like what he saw. Dustin Hoffman looked like
a comedian. With his small frame, generously proportioned nose, squeaky

Hoffman's all-American woman, *Tootsie.*

voice, and lack of leading-man stature, the thirty-year-old theater actor was hardly the second coming of Cary Grant—or even Spencer Tracy.

Hoffman ended up getting the role, for a film called *The Graduate* (1967), and the axis of American film history began, ever so slightly, to shift. "The press couldn't believe that a movie actor could look like that," the film's screenwriter Buck Henry observed, "and soon, *every* movie actor looked like that." Not every actor, exactly, but enough to make a difference. Soon, even the ones good-looking enough to have made a go of it in the studios' heyday found themselves aping Dustin Hoffman—this schlemiel, this puffed-up character actor.

With others' harsh physical assessments kept carefully in mind (and sometimes stoked by Nichols on the set of *The Graduate*), Hoffman was able to preserve the tradition of the comedy of effete awkwardness, transmitted in a nearly unbroken line from Stan Laurel to Peter Sellers to himself. Dustin Hoffman was more, though, than just the schlemiel redux. Like Grant, or Katharine Hepburn, Hoffman was equally comfortable with comedy and drama. His performances brooked no distinction between the two; Hoffman's dramas made us laugh, and his comedic roles sometimes made us cry. His template would be one emulated by nearly every other actor of his generation.

Hoffman would eventually win two Academy Awards for his dramatic work, but the movies that would make his name would, like the actor himself, blend the ridiculous and the sublime, the bleak and the sunny. In part, these movies were products of their era: a time of mass concerts and mass death, youth revolt and "silent majority" backlash. *The Graduate*, *Bonnie and Clyde*, *Butch Cassidy and the Sundance Kid*, and the other notable films of the late 1960s and early 1970s placed comedy in uncomfortably close proximity to discomfort, violence, and death. Busting through the unnatural limitations imposed on the Western, the gangster film, the musical, and other hoary Hollywood genres, the new batch of films sought to complicate—in a manner much like what Robert Altman would accomplish with his own work—what they saw as the simplistic narratives of the classic studio era. These new movies were serious endeavors and playful larks, all at once, and the comedic riffs that dotted their surfaces were proof of the new mood.

The Graduate had initially been headed in a markedly different direction. Charles Webb's novel of post-collegiate angst had been a hot property, intended to star one of the young Turks of late–studio era Hollywood: Warren Beatty as Benjamin Braddock, perhaps, or Robert Redford. But Beatty rejected the script, and when Nichols was brought on as director, he dismissed all thought of Redford after a telling encounter with the golden-boy actor, to whom the concept of romantic rejection was clearly a foreign concept.

Dustin Hoffman, in comparison, looked like he might never have gotten lucky with a woman, ever. Presentable-looking enough, like the president of the Future Accountants of America chapter at his college, Hoffman radiated a colorless blandness that made him both an unlikely movie star and an implausible generational icon. Nichols was placing his own imprint on *The Graduate* via the casting of Hoffman, and in so doing, helping to create a new kind of movie star: self-mocking, sardonic, and comically gifted. In short, Hoffman was the first of the Jewish movie stars. "My unconscious was making this movie," Nichols would later observe. "It took me years before I got what I had been doing all along—that I was turning Benjamin into a Jew. I didn't get it until I saw this hilarious issue of *Mad* magazine after the movie came out, in which the caricature of Dustin says to the caricature of Elizabeth Wilson, 'Mom, how come I'm Jewish and you and Dad aren't?'"

The half-buried religious subtext—Jew adrift in WASP paradise—was only a small part of *The Graduate*'s enormous, unexpected success in the fall of 1967. Nichols's film was the first of what would soon be an onslaught of groundbreaking comedies. Call them post-Hays films—movies whose amusement stemmed directly from their flouting of the onetime Production Code's most inviolable tenets. With its extramarital affair, brief snatches of nudity, and lack of bad-guys-finish-last moral rigor, *The Graduate* would have been an impossible movie to make in Hollywood anytime before the late 1960s.

A college man seduced by a cougar on the prowl, who then ditches the mother in favor of her dewy, unformed daughter? Louis B. Mayer would have had apoplexy just thinking about it, and yet *The Graduate* touched a nerve among a younger generation of filmgoers left unmoved by a previous era's separate-beds-please sex comedies. It was entirely apropos that Doris Day had opted not to make *The Graduate*, for it spelled an end for the kind of sparkling but fatally inexplicit films she had made with Rock Hudson only a few years prior (the last of their pairings, *Send Me No Flowers*, had been released only three years earlier). There could be no returning to *Pillow Talk* after Ben and Mrs. Robinson had so frankly ceased to beat around the bush.

A canny manipulator of actors, Nichols used Hoffman's tentativeness and lack of confidence to his benefit. Hoffman's "dreadful certainty that the experience of making *The Graduate* would end in humiliation for him," as Mark Harris describes it in *Pictures at a Revolution*, was translated into a performance whose comedic notes are drawn from that very same lack of assertiveness. His Benjamin is convinced that the world is conspiring to crush him, even as it opens its petals for his delectation. "Are you here for an affair, sir?" a clerk (played by the film's screenwriter, Buck Henry) wonders as he lurks nervously in a hotel lobby. Like Hollywood itself, Benjamin was tentatively, wincingly submerging himself into the shallow end of human sexuality. The scuba mask and deep-sea diving gear would come later.

Ben's furtive sexual encounters with Mrs. Robinson (Anne Bancroft), a friend of his parents, are rewarding, but he still cannot bring himself to call her by her first name. Ben is flustered and passive, while Mrs. Robinson is effortlessly commanding. Ben can never quite break through his veneer of good manners with Mrs. Robinson; the polite Jewish boy to the last, he consistently, amusingly fails to grasp her meaning.

What begins as a charming sex farce rapidly enters more unsettling psychological territory, with the randy housewife transformed into a pathologically jealous mother, protecting her daughter Elaine (Katharine Ross) from the same intruder she so willingly allowed in. Buoyed by its soundtrack of pensive Simon & Garfunkel songs, *The Graduate* transforms into a wistful romance, with Ben chasing the luscious but terminally bland Elaine all the way to Berkeley. There are moments of charming wit—Hoffman passing himself off as a priest to a gas-station attendant, and fighting off wedding-goers with a deftly wielded crucifix—but the mood of *The Graduate* has subtly changed, with comedy giving way to (perhaps overly earnest) drama.

In its anxious intermingling of clashing tones, *The Graduate* would come to serve as a model for many of the films that would follow in its wake—including Hoffman's own. The Best Picture-winning *Midnight Cowboy* (1969) stars Hoffman alongside Jon Voight as threadbare Manhattan hustlers on the make. Hoffman's Ratso Rizzo was the true hustler of the pair—a slippery-tongued devil with a thick-as-egg-cream outer-borough accent and an eye for the short con. Wheedling, whiny, with a mangled walk and a battered white suit, Ratso is a comically ludicrous figure. Hoffman perfectly captures his pathos, and his accidental charm. Even as Ratso is sweaty and pale, nearing death on a Florida-bound bus, his winsome monologue epitomizes *Midnight Cowboy*'s admixture of tones: "Here I am going to Florida, my leg hurts, my butt hurts, my chest hurts, my face hurts, and like that ain't enough, I gotta *pee* all over myself!" Ratso's face is a mask of pain, but his rant still makes Voight break up in laughter. "That's funny?" Hoffman demands. "I'm fallin' apaht heah!"

Still playing the callow youngster, albeit in drastically changed circumstances, Hoffman is the heart of Arthur Penn's terrifically entertaining upside-down picaresque *Little Big Man* (1970). Penn's film is a Western whose audacity begins with the casting of Hoffman as its ageless protagonist and helpless victim of circumstance. His Jack Crabb is like Benjamin Braddock as a Wild West Tom Jones, hopscotching from Native American warrior to confidence man to gunslinger to scout for General George Armstrong Custer. With its unlikely reversals and unexpected plot twists, *Little Big Man* is a tall tale, but it winks and asks us to go along with the joke. Hoffman, brilliant as ever, serves as the punch line—the polite Jewish boy turned Western hero. *Little Big Man* has a winning sense of humor, unendingly amused by life's unpredictability, but like Penn's other revisionist genre exercises (including *Bonnie and Clyde*), its laughter dies away, displaced by tragedy.

In the early sequences of Bob Fosse's fractured Lenny Bruce biopic *Lenny* (1974), Hoffman was playing a nice Jewish boy once more—Benjamin Braddock gone Hollywood, a rising star wooing audiences and a kind-hearted blonde stripper (played by Valerie Perrine) with equal finesse. Soon, though, Lenny Bruce is to become comedy's secular saint, a hipster Jesus dying so that his descendants—including those of us in the audience, the film more than implies—could speak more freely. *Lenny* is perhaps the most funereal movie ever made about a stand-up comic (Richard Pryor's *Jo Jo Dancer, Your Life Is Calling*, explicitly in the debt of Fosse's film, is a close second), its brief moments of humor echoing bleakly against the crushing sadness of the comic's life.

The lights come up on a close-up of Bruce's mouth—his gift, and source of all his problems. Hoffman's Bruce is a fearless trailblazer and a First Amendment pioneer, but is hardly a laugh machine—deliberately so. He is a tragic hero whose business is comedy. (*Lenny* is a movie so relentlessly dour that even copious amounts of sex and drugs cannot redeem it.) Hoffman clearly proves himself capable of being funny onstage (describing Jerry Lewis holding a telethon for victims of the clap, Hoffman does an able Bruce impersonation), but *Lenny* prefers to shine its spotlight on the dark side of Bruce's routine, with drug addiction, infidelity, and emotional callousness destroying his marriage and his career, and ultimately taking his life. If drama, in the post-*Graduate* era, was rarely without its lighthearted moments, then *Lenny* was its inverse, ultimately losing track of the comedy in what was, among other things, the story of a famous comedian.

Dustin Hoffman had been a model comic star for the post-studio generation because he had looked too much the character actor to pass for a matinee idol. As his influence spread, the mocking, self-deprecating style became de rigueur for a new generation of leading men. From the very start, Warren Beatty and Paul Newman had looked and sounded like the last of the matinee idols, which made it all the more refreshing that in their films, they so clearly preferred to undercut their own authority.

Playing the leading man in such iconic American New Wave films as *Bonnie and Clyde* (1967) and Robert Altman's *McCabe & Mrs. Miller* (1971), Beatty's sexual swagger was undone by a perceived hollowness at his core. His Clyde Barrow, in *Bonnie and Clyde*, is a Depression-era Robin Hood whose own gun shoots only blanks, and McCabe is one of Robert Altman's signature delusional heroes, playing by the rules of a world (and a genre) whose only rule is chaos.

Newman, meanwhile, was the cad as swashbuckling hero, turning in a series of variations on the theme of the reluctant antihero. He would go on to collaborate with Robert Altman on the eclectic historical pageant *Buffalo Bill and the Indians* (1976), and provide the Coen brothers with a cigar-chomping, scenery-chewing antagonist to Tim Robbins's cloddish Norville J. Barnes in *The Hudsucker Proxy* (1994).

The romantic-comedy meet cute of *Bonnie and Clyde* (1967) was a revisionist version of Lubitsch and Wilder's *Bluebeard's Eighth Wife*. The lovers meet, not at the pajama counter of a department store, but when Bonnie catches Clyde in the act of stealing her mother's car. Bonnie dreamily strokes Clyde's pistol, the sexual symbolism so blatant as to become a punch line in its own right. Comedy and sexuality and violence are all jumbled together into a single unbroken whole; one can see why more conservative film critics, like Bosley Crowther of the *New York Times*, were mortally offended by the movie.

Bonnie and Clyde uses comedy provocatively, its amusement spilling over into darker territory. The film's single funniest moment is also its most unsettling: sidekick C. W. Moss (Michael J. Pollard) parallel parks the getaway car during a bank robbery, and cannot navigate out of his spot. A bank teller leaps onto the back of the car, and Clyde shoots him point-blank in the face—the film's first truly violent act. Director Arthur Penn (a superb genre revisionist) lets laughter explode into violence, surreally juxtaposing the film's funniest and bloodiest moments.

Like a lighter-hearted, friendlier version of *Bonnie and Clyde* that mostly ditched the aura of overhanging dread, *Butch Cassidy and the Sundance Kid* (1969) was an existential buddy comedy. Katharine Ross, fresh off *The

Graduate, was present as the ostensible love interest, but there was no doubt that the true romance was between partners in crime Paul Newman and Robert Redford. There is a joshing quality to *Butch Cassidy*, as if Newman and Redford were little boys enjoying an elaborate game of dress-up, exchanging wisecracks between bank robberies. Butch and Sundance's criminal mayhem is played for laughs; "Well, that ought to do it," Newman mutters after a stack of dynamite blows a train car to bits, scattering greenbacks across the countryside. Later on, Redford and Newman stand at the edge of a cliff, tracked by their faceless, fury-like pursuers, needing to leap into the water to escape. Redford tells his partner that he can't swim, and Newman cackles mirthfully. "Why, you crazy? The fall'll probably kill ya!"

Like its predecessor *Bonnie and Clyde*, death—initially absent from the proceedings—wrestles its way to the center ring of *Butch Cassidy*, but the film never sheds its playfulness. Butch and Sundance bicker till the very end. And considering the way the film sidesteps the actual moment of their death, one can presume they go on the same way forever. For all intents and purposes, they do, with 1973's *The Sting* (also directed by George Roy Hill) a sequel in all but name. Butch and Sundance are now Henry Gondorff and Johnny Hooker, a grizzled Depression-era Chicago con man and his untutored colleague, joining forces to pull the ultimate scam. Redford once again manages to star in a comedy without betraying any apparent sense of humor, but delivers his lines with enough snap to serve as a passable foil for the superb Newman. "Luther said I could learn something from you," Redford lazily observes, jabbing at his teeth with a toothpick. "I already know how to drink."

The grift is the humor of *The Sting*, which takes elaborate pleasure in the preparations for the con. The film's dirty-Chicago ambience is like a colorized version of the first reel of *Some Like It Hot*, all speakeasies, hot jazz, and bloody street wars. The grifters are like actors preparing for a role—getting into costume, preparing their lines, shaking pre-performance jitters—and the wit of *The Sting* is found in the pleasure of being thrust together with the schemers.

Beatty's own 1970s efforts as a producer and star, 1975's *Shampoo* (directed by Hal Ashby, from a script by Beatty and Robert Towne) and 1978's *Heaven Can Wait* (which he codirected with Buck Henry), betray a similarly purposeful sabotaging of the star game. *Shampoo* is a gentle comedy with an acrid aftertaste—a Gallic sex farce with a wicked political bite. Beatty is a hairdressing Lothario in Beverly Hills posing as gay to avoid the ire of his sex-starved clients' husbands. The film, cowritten by Beatty, wittily shuttles him between his lovers, but *Shampoo* is a comedy with an aching emptiness at its center—the absence of meaning, or permanence. *Shampoo* takes place in the hours immediately before and after Election Day of 1968, and Nixon's ascendancy is a harsh reminder that the good times depicted here had long since come to an end, though its characters might be the last to know it.

Heaven Can Wait, a remake of a 1940s hit called *Here Comes Mr. Jordan* (and not the Ernst Lubitsch film of the same name), is a clever football comedy about a washed-up quarterback for the Los Angeles Rams who is taken before his time, and returns to Earth in the body of a rapacious billionaire. The sports film and the drawing-room comedy intermingle, with a touch of the supernatural as the topping to this sundae of divergent genres. The film veers precipitously, from farce to romance to the Super Bowl. The deliberate confusion of tones—is this a comedy? a romance? a fantasy?—was essential to *Heaven Can Wait*'s appeal, its whiplash shifts in mood elemental, in true post-*Graduate* fashion, to its success.

Meanwhile, Hoffman himself was introducing new shadings to his actorly palette. He ended the decade with *Kramer vs. Kramer* (1979), written and directed by *Bonnie and Clyde* screenwriter Robert Benton. *Kramer* is a male weepie about the fallout of divorce—a reverse empowerment story in which an abandoned husband discovers unexpected reserves of feminine initiative. Hoffman's Ted Kramer serves powdered doughnuts for breakfast and occasionally forgets what grade his son is in, but the implied emasculation of single fatherhood makes way for enlightenment. Hoffman (who won an Academy Award for the role) plays the material mostly for dramatic effect, but cannot help goosing the film with the occasional sliver of physical humor, like the moment when he lugs two armfuls of groceries into the office, like a harried housewife who has lost her way home.

Kramer vs. Kramer had Hoffman playing both mother and father to his son, and *Tootsie* (1982) is a sustained embrace of his no-longer-so-secret feminine side. Hoffman's perennially unemployable actor Michael Dorsey re-creates himself as brassy Dorothy Michaels, and wins a plum role on a ridiculous hospital soap opera. Perhaps channeling his own lengthy apprenticeship as a struggling actor, Hoffman's Michael is charmingly, touchingly neurotic. "Nobody does vegetables like me!" Michael shouts at his agent (played by the film's director, Sydney Pollack). "I did an endive salad that knocked the critics on their ass!" Transforming himself into Dorothy, in a single shock cut reminiscent of the male-to-female metamorphosis of Jack Lemmon and Tony Curtis in *Some Like It Hot*, has the unexpected side effect of changing his personality for the better: "I think Dorothy's smarter than I am."

Like it had for Lemmon and Curtis, Hoffman's cross-dressing gives him the temporary freedom to be both man and woman, straight and gay, hard-bitten Manhattan actor and frumpy Southern belle. Hoffman brilliantly channels the frustrations of womanhood, his newly acquired primness transforming vexation into comedy. Michael/Dorothy stares into the mirror while dressing for dinner with costar Julie (Jessica Lange), outfitted in a pair of control-top pantyhose, and assesses his meager wardrobe possibilities: "I don't have the right shoes for it, I don't like the way the horizontal lines makes me look hippy, and it cuts me across the bust." *Tootsie* is screwball comedy for the era of television; a movie about a television show with the sensibilities of a television sitcom. (Screenwriter Larry Gelbart had, in fact, served as a writer on the television series *M*A*S*H*.)

Mike Nichols's onetime stand-up partner Elaine May, who had cowritten *Heaven Can Wait*, directed Hoffman and Beatty in the buddy-pic adventure *Ishtar* (1987), considered upon release to be one of Hollywood's all-time biggest flops, and only recently re-evaluated by critics like Jonathan Rosenbaum. Hoffman is another failed entertainer—this time an untalented songwriter and wannabe pop star—and Beatty his dim-witted sidekick, drawn into Middle Eastern intelligence-service skullduggery without their consent, or their awareness. *Ishtar* is a big-budget comedy in the Albert Brooksian mode, restlessly intelligent and moderately repellent. Part showbiz parody and part geopolitical satire, the differing strands of *Ishtar* never intertwine to any satisfaction. The true highlight of the film is Hoffman and Beatty sharing a piano bench, trading off lines with manic delight while composing their execrable songs. One senses the glint of another, far better, film in these moments—one that might have played more strongly to these two actors' strengths.

Beatty's most recent efforts as a director, both charming if relatively slight, adeptly wield comedy as a counterpoint: to popcorn-movie thrills in one case, and Capra-esque political preachiness in the other. *Dick Tracy* (1990), a summer blockbuster well aware of its own ludicrousness, casts Beatty's square-jawed detective as a stolid straight man for the cast of eccentrics led by Hoffman's incoherent stool pigeon, Mumbles. *Dick Tracy* is a production designer's wet dream, all sleek skyscrapers, rain-slicked streets, and color-coordinated sets, and its performances come courtesy of the makeup artists, whose big-nosed, misshapen-chinned grotesques are the film's primary special effect. Mumbles is Hoffman in partial *Rain Man* mode (the nearly unwatchable travesty of a film that won Hoffman his second Academy Award), self-absorbed, slow-witted, and sweaty. A stenographer puts her pencil down in dismay after attempting to transcribe Mumbles's testimony, watching each sentence inevitably leak away into incoherence. *Dick Tracy* is Beatty's swing for the summer-blockbuster fences, a transcription of Chester Gould's beloved comic strip that retains much of its exuberant weirdness.

The smarmily populist *Bulworth* (1998) also makes canny use of Beatty's inherent limitations, casting him as an empty suit rejuvenated by an encounter with the common man—or more precisely, Halle Berry's decidedly uncommon woman. His Senator Jay Bulworth is a recovered 1960s liberal whose suicidal urges liberate him from a lifetime of focus-grouped doublespeak. *Bulworth*'s brand of gleeful political incorrectness has the senator remarking to a well-heeled West L.A. crowd that his staff always put "the big Jews on my schedule," and chiding African American churchgoers that "if you don't put down that malt liquor and chicken wings and get behind somebody other than a running back who stabs his wife, you're never going to get rid of somebody like me!"

The senator's unlikely salvation comes via hip-hop, with Bulworth penning sophomoric rhymes about the corruption of the political establishment he has come to disdain: "Over here we got our friends from oil/They don't give a shit how much wilderness they spoil." This nursery-rhyme couplet offers a sense of the sophistication of Bulworth's midlife-crisis artistry, with Beatty's musical performances every bit as cringe-making as those in *Ishtar*. *Bulworth* was a novel idea that arrived a few crucial years too late; the soundtrack and the sentiments might have been daring had they come out in 1990, not 1998. Instead, *Bulworth* is as embarrassing as watching your father get up at a school talent show and break-dance.

After a mostly misbegotten decade of high-minded misfires (*Hook*, *Billy Bathgate*, *Hero*), Hoffman returned to comedy, and garnered his seventh Oscar nomination, for *Wag the Dog* (1997). This remarkably prescient satire (whose political smarts exposed the likes of *Bulworth* as unsalvageably juvenile) anticipated the soon-to-develop Monica Lewinsky saga: a president, caught with his pants down, engineers a fantasy conflict (with Albania) to distract attention from his peccadilloes on the eve of an election. Hoffman is Stanley Motss, the twinkly-eyed Hollywood mogul—think Lew Wasserman with incurable diarrhea of the mouth—brought in to produce the war.

"This is nothing, this is nothing," Hoffman affably burbles, as one unforeseen obstacle after another emerges. No amount of Oval Office interference, he tells his associates, can compare to the time he produced *Four Horsemen of the Apocalypse*, and three of the horsemen died before the end of the shoot.

For Motss, a producer's authority trumps that of any politician, and Hollywood runs roughshod over Washington, its powers of persuasion greater by leaps and bounds. He may never vote in presidential elections, but Stanley always casts his ballot for the Academy Awards.

By the new decade, Hoffman was a twinkly-eyed elder statesman, an eminence brought in to liven up young auteurs' comedic fantasies. For both David O. Russell's *I Heart Huckabees* (2004) and Marc Forster's *Stranger than Fiction* (2006), Hoffman is an *eminence grise*, possessed of the wisdom borne of age and experience. Hoffman and *Huckabees* costar Lily Tomlin are a twenty-first-century Nick and Nora for the era of corporate subversion and damaged personalities. Hoffman is the avuncular sage of Russell's existential detective comedy, a shaggy-haired ex-hippie with a fondness for using blankets and body bags to illustrate his philosophical parables. And in Forster's Charlie Kaufman–esque comedy of ideas, Hoffman is the English professor instructing IRS drone Will Ferrell, who has discovered himself to be a character in a writer's novel, in the intricacies of literary theory. He is an expert on obscure modes of narration, gushing excitedly to Ferrell's Harold Crick that "I've written papers on 'little did he know.'" In between stints as lifeguard at the faculty pool, Hoffman serves as a literary therapist, interrogating hapless Harold to uncover just who might be telling his story.

Breaking through as the studios, and their perverse unwillingness to acknowledge ethnicity of any kind, were slowly dying, Hoffman celebrated his innate awkwardness, rather than covering it up. In his hands, comedy had become something less Cary Grant–smooth, something more . . . Jewish. It would be no accident that, some thirty-five years after *The Graduate*, when casting about for the perfect Jewish father for Ben Stiller in the sequel *Meet the Fockers* (2004), an ideal foil to Stiller's uber-WASP father-in-law (played by Robert De Niro), the producers called on Dustin Hoffman. In many ways, *Fockers* was anticlimactic, for Hoffman had already served as Stiller's cinematic father, his work paving the way for Stiller's, and numerous other leading men who could never have passed for movie stars before Dustin Hoffman arrived.

Consider Hoffman's ever-at-ease Bernie Focker, then, a tip of the hat from one generation to the next, a sly acknowledgement of paternity in the metaphysical, if not the literal, sense. It is Stiller ("Can you believe I conceived him with one testicle?" Hoffman crows) who plays the Hoffman role in *Fockers*: anxious, intense, perpetually expecting the inevitable onset of disaster. Hoffman coasts on charm and the unflappable insouciance that can only come from having jettisoned, at long last, the crippling burden of Jewish anxiety, renouncing it as a testament for the next generation. It would be left to Stiller, and the other sons of Dustin Hoffman, to carry on the work of sweaty-palmed panic.

18

ROBERT ALTMAN

OVERLAPPING DIALOGUE

"I find that people always talk at the same time."
—Robert Altman

The filmmakers of the mid-to-late 1960s had begun the process of updating the American film for contemporary sensibilities, but their makeover had been only skin-deep. Films like *The Graduate* (1967) and *Bonnie and Clyde* (1967) had reinvigorated the moribund studios, their daring subject matter embraced by audiences and critics, but had left the DNA of mainstream Hollywood filmmaking—the three-act structure, the unobtrusive directorial style—mostly untouched. To be sure, films like Arthur

Donald Sutherland and Elliott Gould prepare for eighteen holes in Altman's *MASH*.

Penn's *Mickey One* (1965) began the process of cinematic splintering, violating chronological order, bleeding sound from one scene into the next, and employing the editing room as a directorial commentary on the action. But these films were mostly show-offy exercises in cinematic erudition, sloppy homages to the French New Wave auteurs they worshipped. It would take a latecomer to the American New Wave, older than his compatriots, and with an unlikely apprenticeship in the art of filmmaking, to truly revolutionize the American film.

Robert Altman was less a comedian than an artist possessed of an essentially comic sensibility: one that acknowledged the absurdity and futility of a world where communication was near-impossible. Altman perfected a style uniquely his own, where actors spoke in unison, their lines lost beneath a maelstrom of meaningless verbiage. Everyone spoke and no one listened; no lessons were learned and no conclusions reached. Instead of well-wrought urns, Altman's films were pieces of homemade pottery, deliberately sloppy and unpolished. The comedy in films like *MASH* (1970) and *The Long Goodbye* (1973) came from Altman's purposeful messiness, from the degree to which the director had seemingly let his characters loose in a disordered, fractured narrative under no one's control.

Like his New Wave colleagues Hal Ashby and Mike Nichols, Altman was no slapstick filmmaker; his sense of comedy was intimately tied to character and place. His humor was not something separate from drama, to be cordoned off and ghettoized in its own discrete works. Comedy was simply part of life, and Altman's recipe for making a comedy was the deceptively basic one formulated by one of his Hollywood predecessors, Howard Hawks: merely begin with a fully fledged drama, and then add a splash of humor.

Robert Altman would serve an unusually long apprenticeship before ascending to mainstream filmmaking. Born to a wealthy family in Kansas City (his grandfather had made a fortune, first in jewelry, then in real estate), he had been an indifferent student, first at a Catholic school, then at a nearby military academy. Skipping college, he enlisted in the Air Force at age nineteen, and served in the Pacific at the tail end of World War II as a B-24 copilot. Altman flew nearly fifty missions under perilous, life-threatening conditions, but his military duty was more *MASH* than *Saving Private Ryan*, consisting (at least in the director's later reminiscences) of an endlessly rewound reel of wine and women, only broken up by the movies screened nightly. Seeing the neorealist classic *Bicycle Thieves*, and, later, *Brief Encounter*, had set his fertile mind buzzing: there was someone behind the camera, he realized, and it was their sensibility, more than those of the actors, which formed the images on the screen.

After brief stints as a songwriter, screenwriter for hire, and dog-tattooer (he branded President Truman's dog), Altman took a job with the Calvin Company, a Kansas City producer of industrial films. Initially hired to drive the generator truck, he quickly proved himself a trustworthy and efficient craftsman as a director. Working rapidly, Altman would leave himself enough time to experiment with his crew, playing with zooms and elaborate camera moves to keep himself from dying of boredom on repetitive shoots. Altman would alternate stints at Calvin with briefer jaunts to Hollywood, where he would wash up with some regularity. There was work to be had, especially in television, but Los Angeles never welcomed Robert Altman with open arms, and inevitably he would return to Kansas City, and Calvin, chastened but unbowed.

Eventually, Hollywood beckoned more seriously, and Altman recreated his Kansas City success as a superlative craftsman working in a self-effacing field. Initially employed on the television series *Alfred Hitchcock Presents*, Altman went on to direct episodes of *The Whirlybirds, U.S. Marshal, The Millionaire, Maverick*, and *Bonanza*. Even at this stage, Altman's approach was cinematic; he described his work on *Bonanza* as Sturgesian screwball, and his pioneering work on the WWII series *Combat!* served as an embryonic version of *MASH*'s idiosyncratic style. *Combat!* earned kudos for an episode, directed by Altman, in which a dazed American soldier stumbled around in a post-skirmish fog, unknowingly surrendering to a dead German, but Altman's ambition of becoming a first-rate film director was evaporating with the remorseless passage of time. (His attitude toward his superiors may not have helped; one famous communique to his bosses at Universal read, in its entirety, "Fuck you. Rude letter follows.") The young Turks of television were being granted opportunities, but Sydney Pollack and John Frankenheimer were from the legitimate, live-theater side of TV production, not the crass commercial world of nighttime dramas. Robert Altman was over forty, and the future was receding into the distance.

Altman had already directed a number of little-seen, low-budget films in the late 1950s, but the tide began to turn with 1968's low-budget *Countdown*, a space-race drama starring James Caan and Robert Duvall notable for its muddy, distinctly overlapping dialogue. Studio head Jack Warner was not enamored with Altman's work, believing him incapable of recording clean sound, but when screenwriter Ring Lardner Jr. and producer Ingo Preminger

(Otto's brother) were casting about for a director for their next film, a Korean War drama about harried surgeons, Altman's name popped up.

From the very first shot of *MASH* (1970)—a bloody body on a stretcher—there was little doubt that the director had placed his own stamp on overly familiar material. The sole diversions available to the staff of the Mobile Army Surgical Hospital, other than sex and booze, are the slate of forgettable World War II films screened nightly. *MASH* is a rebuke to those faux-humane revels in bloodshed, and a romp in the killing fields of the war film. Playing by none of the rules of his adopted genre, Altman's war film is not only a comedy—it is a smutty, profane comedy.

Taking place at a remove from the front, *MASH* is a combat film with no combat, a war film whose war intrudes only at the margins. This is due not only to its willful confusion of time frames—like Joseph Heller's novel *Catch-22*, this is a Vietnam story transposed onto an earlier war—but its aura of hollow revelry. Hawkeye Pierce (Donald Sutherland) and Trapper McIntyre (Elliott Gould, an Altman favorite) are the ringleaders of the tormentors, shepherding their squad into daily battle with the grinds and drips of the U.S. Army. There is little amusement here that is not tinged with cruelty. The boys' sidekick Radar (Gary Burghoff) sticks a microphone under the bed of their nemesis Major O'Houlihan (Sally Kellerman), catching her in bed with goody-goody surgeon Major Burns (Robert Duvall) and inadvertently granting her a self-appointed nickname: Hot Lips. Later on, they exchange twenty-dollar bets on the burning question of whether Hot Lips' carpet matches her drapes, and settle in outside the communal showers with folding chairs, guitars, and high-powered binoculars, like theatergoers anxiously awaiting the raising of the curtain.

MASH recreates the theater of war—its callousness, its separation into good and bad guys, its oft-senseless designation of arbitrary enemies—but its conflict is internecine, taking place between the squad's liberals and conservatives, hipsters and squares. The good guys pass out nudie mags in lieu of Bibles, taunt the religious Major Burns with raunchy versions of "Onward Christian Soldiers," and put on a mock Last Supper for a colleague whose sexual impotence has led him to contemplate suicide.

MASH was an enormous hit upon its release (although Altman's son Michael, who wrote the film's famous theme song, made far more money from the film than his father did). It garnered five Academy Award nominations, but its ability to amuse has notably dimmed with the passage of time. Its sexism in particular is off-putting, with the film implicitly endorsing, and egging on, its male protagonists' dismal view of women as bimbos and playthings. What remains fresh about *MASH*, and what Altman would carry with him to future films, was its stylistic audacity. Altman's camera was untethered, roaming the expanses of its set without preordained plan. The microphones roved too, with Altman using selectively chosen sound to direct the audience's attention. Voices piled atop each other, lines of dialogue were lost amidst the bedlam, and Altman smiled, pleased with his creation.

Gould and Sutherland had sought to have Altman fired from *MASH*, feeling they were being ignored in favor of glorified extras, but that metaphorical rack focus, shifting attention from foreground to background, was the heart of Altman's style. The star system was burned out, and from its ashes had sprung a glorious cacophony of competing voices. The effect was Renoir-esque, offering a dazzling glimpse of a topsy-turvy world in which everyone had their reasons—and demanded to be heard. Altman was the redactor, sifting through the endless raw material and cobbling together a messy, lively, inescapably comic babel of competing voices. On set, too, Altman was less dictator than chief collaborator, telling his cast and crew, in an assistant director's recollection, "Anybody can come up to me at any time and give me any ideas they have or discuss anything they want. Sometimes I'll use them and sometimes I won't. I may not always have time to tell you why I'm not going to use your idea, but I'll always listen."

"I was always trying to get away with this thing of actors talking at the same time," Altman would later tell an interviewer, "but putting individual mikes on actors finally allowed me to handle the whole thing the way I wanted." The whole project was self-aware, winking at its movieness: "Attention," a familiar voice on the loudspeaker announced, "tonight's movie has been *MASH* . . . snatching laughs and loves between amputations and penicillin." (These it's-just-a-movie reminders, playfully tweaking the authority of the form, were recurrent in Altman's work: witness the use of the song "Hooray for Hollywood" and the *Third Man* reference at the close of *The Long Goodbye*, the faux-infomercial that opened *Nashville*, or the *Touch of Evil* homage at the start of *The Player*.)

The underrated *Brewster McCloud* (1970) is another counterculture comedy, with pigs and stiffs thoroughly outwitted by a loose band of hipsters and freaks. Bud Cort's contemporary Icarus and Michael Murphy's iconoclastic police detective are Trapper and Hawkeye redux, coolly repulsing the charmless, brainless hordes. *Brewster* is a murder-mystery-musical, its soundtrack the thrum of multiple simultaneous conversations. There is more than a hint of Keystone-style slapstick to *Brewster*'s anarchic sensibility, but as with *MASH*, Altman was hinting at something dank and unpleasant at the heart of the American character in the era of Nixon: a wet splatter of bird shit obliterates a political headline, and a scatologist—an expert in the study of shit—is named Agnew. Death had become entertainment of an unremarkably commonplace sort.

The long shot with close-up sound, first introduced in *MASH*, became the iconic Altman shot, with *McCabe & Mrs. Miller* (1971) a revisionist Western whose ragged zooms and smudged look were an implicit rebuke to the prim, clean proprieties of the genre. Warren Beatty is the burgeoning entrepreneur, dreaming of empires of sin in the untamed West, and Julie Christie the British madam brought in to manage his stable of prostitutes. Altman's Western is deliberately unkempt, its heroes compromised, its women less than virginal, its America rife with senseless, horrific violence.

Altman was subverting genre once more, trusting in audiences' familiarity with the well-rehearsed rituals of the form in order to playfully undermine them. The director was less interested in revisiting the traditional plots than in the color and noise to be found at its margins. "So everybody knows the movie, those characters, and the plot," he would say of his genre excursions, "which means they're comfortable with it, and gives them an anchor. And I can really deal with the background." No longer a symbolic testing ground for American values, the Western becomes an expression of something dark and untamed lying deep in the nation's heart. Flashing the film stock (on the recommendation of cinematographer Vilmos Zsigmond) for a yellowish tinge, muddying the sound track into inaudibility, Altman was, in his own words, "doing everything to destroy the clarity of the film." Technique was metaphorically standing in for content; the muddy, washed-out picture and sound were echoing a set of beliefs—in American exceptionalism, in the purity of the frontier—that had themselves faded into indistinctness.

The Long Goodbye (1973) makes explicit what had only been subtext for *McCabe & Mrs. Miller*. The era of studio plenty had evaporated, leaving behind only the dried-out husks of genre. Altman and screenwriter Leigh Brackett's revisiting of Raymond Chandler's last novel, and his eternally popular gumshoe Philip Marlowe (immortalized by Humphrey Bogart in *The Big Sleep*), turn him into "Rip Van Marlowe," ludicrously unsuitable for the slouchy 1970s. Dressed in his dark suit and white shirt, driving his 1948 Lincoln Continental, Elliott Gould's Marlowe is a walking anachronism. He is a stoic surrounded by shameless hedonists, laughably out of place in the yoga-and-joints Southern California of the Me Decade. As embodied by the star of *MASH*, Altman's private eye is also the anti-Bogart—a curly-haired, scrawny, self-effacing (Jewish) Marlowe.

The Long Goodbye is acutely aware of its own movieness, its characters pickled in the brine of movie culture. The security guard who entertains drivers with dead-on impressions of Barbara Stanwyck in *Double Indemnity* and Cary Grant ("Juu-dy, Juu-dy, Juu-dy!") is only the most explicit of its film-snob winks. But Altman is doing more than paying homage to a beloved genre; he is compromising its integrity, tearing away what he can use and jettisoning the rest.

Like W. C. Fields's lovable smartasses, Gould's Marlowe is an inveterate backtalker, keeping up a steady stream of muttered asides directed at no one in particular: "It's OK with me," he keeps telling himself, as sure a sign as any that it is most assuredly not OK with him. Alone among the figures that populate the film, Marlowe is aware that he is just another character in a movie, mumbling the same familiar lines and sleepwalking through the same hackneyed situations. *The Long Goodbye* is funny because of its winking, self-reflexive knowingness; we have seen this movie before, and the film knows it.

The Long Goodbye's camera roved and darted, twisted and poked. Altman's jittery style of filming had cozied up to his unusual method of sound recording, with multiple microphones capturing the dialogue of not only the film's protagonists but its walk-on performers as well. Actors had to remain on their toes with Altman, never knowing when they might be press-ganged into service.

The sound was reflective of Altman's priorities; the main characters of *California Split* (1974) are often tuned out in favor of strangers, nobodies, and supporting players. Gould and George Segal are a pair of degenerate gamblers whiling away their days at racetracks and casinos, hustling the yokels and dreaming of a big payday. *MASH* had turned the war film into a rambunctious blast of rude energy, and *California Split* plays the opposite hand. Gould and Segal's hijinks ring terribly hollow, its fun smacking of terrible desperation. There is, nonetheless, an infectious charm to Gould's rambling commentary on the oddballs he encounters, as if he were more audience member than protagonist. "Lyndon Johnson is definitely his hero," he notes of one potential competitor he spots in the distance, while another had clearly "seen *The Cincinnati Kid* too many times."

All the preceding films, all the years of television and industrial work, were building up to Altman's towering masterpiece, in which there were no protagonists, only supporting characters, and dialogue was a kind of hand-to-hand combat. *Nashville* (1975) had first emerged out of screenwriter Joan Tewkesbury's firsthand impressions of the country-music scene. Released the year before the U.S. bicentennial, Altman's sprawling film about the intersection of musicians, political operatives, and assorted loners and oddballs over three days in the country-music capital of the world was intended as a filmmaker's state of the union. "We must be doing something right to last two hundred years," country star Haven Hamilton (Henry Gibson) croons, and the bulk of *Nashville* is devoted to drolly disproving his lazy assertion.

With twenty-four characters and a running time of nearly three hours, *Nashville* is deliberately grandiose, but other than its masterfully ambiguous conclusion (about which more momentarily), the film deliberately undercuts itself. It is an epic whose characters are users, hangers-on, charlatans, and phonies, in love with the sound of their own voices and ill-used to listening to anyone else's. Its jumbled sound mix only captures snatches of dialogue—overlapping, muddled, and deliberately confusing. Cutting between characters, rapidly alternating between storylines, Altman enjoys the juxtaposition of dark and light, the serious and the ridiculous. *Nashville* allows its characters to hang themselves with ropes of their own making. It is a mirthful social comedy that unexpectedly, belatedly turns dark.

It is also another revisionist version of a well-thumbed genre, with Altman using the familiar rituals of the musical (rehearsals, diva antics, the big show) to expose its inadequacies; what can a musical—onetime playground of Fred and Ginger and Busby and Judy—say about America in the age of political assassination?

The film is overstuffed: with sound, with people, with activity, with competing storylines. Geraldine Chaplin (Charlie's daughter, and a perennial Altman favorite) is the directorial stand-in, her orotund musings a pitch-perfect parody of breathless American travelogue: "I'm wandering in a graveyard. The dead here have no crosses, nor tombstones, nor wreaths to sing of their past glory, but lie in rusting, decaying heaps, their innards ripped out by greedy, vulturous hands." (Listening in voyeuristically to his characters' conversations, Altman cherry-picks the choicest bits of dialogue, in a fashion soon to be emulated by another comic director working in a profoundly different style: Christopher Guest.)

This, then, is the mood of *Nashville* as a whole: a joke that peters out into mirthlessness, that is shocked into tragedy. Its characters are simultaneously hilarious and appalling. Keith Carradine's Tom is a charming cad who calls an old flame as his latest conquest is still in the process of packing her things; Shelley Duvall's New Age space cadet never manages to visit her dying aunt in the hospital, distracted by the city's abundance of available men; Chaplin's British journalist is fussy and clueless, her commentary insipid and her snobbishness repulsive. Even the third-party presidential candidate Hal Philip Walker, with a platform consisting of banning lawyers from politics and adopting a more tuneful national anthem, is as much stand-up comedian as statesman.

But as the film progresses, and the strands of the plot are drawn ever-tighter, its inexorable progress toward a single fateful meeting is matched by a growing sobriety of tone. Violence is in the air, on the lips of its characters, and all the discussion of assassins, and the betrayed promise of the Kennedys, suggests that it is Walker who is to be killed. Instead, it is the helpless country diva Barbara Jean (Ronee Blakley) who is shot, an entertainer standing in for a politician as sacrificial lamb (in horrifically prescient anticipation of John Lennon's death some five years later). A singer is dead, and this *is* a musical, so what else is there to do but sing? Just follow the bouncing ball . . .

Nashville was a peak Altman would never climb again, his maximalism growing increasingly exaggerated with success. The sardonic fervor of Altman's masterpiece would also trickle into its successors, subtly poisoning them with some of the director's devilish mirth. If *Nashville* had been an unambiguous success with twenty-four characters, then why not forty-eight? If it had been acclaimed for its grasp of American history, then why not a film that effectively was a historical pageant? *Buffalo Bill and the Indians, or Sitting Bull's History Lesson* (1976) is history as self-aware spectacle, its once-notorious personages reliving past glories for an audience's knowing edification. Close kin to *Nashville* and *McCabe & Mrs. Miller*, *Buffalo Bill* is another revisionist exercise, its Wild West legends (Annie Oakley, Sitting Bull, Paul Newman's legendary gunslinger Buffalo Bill Cody) all newly enrolled in "the show business." The film is a battle of wills between Newman's cheerily amoral killer-turned-businessman and the silent Sitting Bull, who stubbornly insists on accurately reflecting the tragedy of history. Eventually, the chief is replaced by his hulking assistant, who fits the part of terrifying Indian scalper far better than the scrawny Sitting Bull. The pseudo–Sitting Bull is brought on to fight a symbolic (rigged) duel with Buffalo Bill. The audience cheers.

Altman's target was bloated American ritual, returning time and again to familiar gatherings—weddings, elections—in order to undercut their pomp. Sticking whoopee cushions under the guests of honor, Altman prefers raucous truthfulness to dishonest order. *A Wedding* (1978) eventually shed some of its intended four dozen characters, but its boisterous nuptials are testament to the director's passionate commitment to the happy babble of conversation. There are too many characters, and not enough time, for Altman's preferred leisureliness, and certain plot developments (especially the death of two supporting characters in a car crash) feel rushed. But *A Wedding* is genially cutting, its deconstruction of the rotting institution of marriage blithely savage.

After *Health* (1980), a simultaneous parody of the burgeoning health-food movement, and another of his indictments of American electoral politics, Altman took another swing at an already-familiar genre. *Popeye* (1980) is one of the stranger examples of the musical form ever recorded to celluloid, its fastidious live-action recreations of R. C. Segar's characters conjoined to a set of songs penned by Harry Nilsson. Robin Williams's Popeye is like Elliott Gould's Marlowe—a muttering loner at odds with the world—but a children's film made for inhospitable ground for Altman's cinema of alienation. (Producer Robert Evans had originally wanted to cast Dustin Hoffman in the leading role, and writer Jules Feiffer had tailored his script for the star, who might have given the film a bite it otherwise lacked.) The spinach-eating sailor's enormous forearms were a special-effect of their own, but other than the sublime casting of Altman regular Shelley Duvall as Olive Oyl (could any other actress have embodied her so perfectly?), *Popeye* suffers from the precise inverse of Altman's perpetual narrative problem: there is not enough going on here, rather than too much.

His reputation in tatters after the perceived failure of *Popeye* (which had actually turned a profit), Altman moved to New York, and then to Paris, and made a series of low-budget theatrical adaptations. Some, like the Richard Nixon one-man show *Secret Honor* (1984), were superb; others, like his versions of David Rabe's *Streamers* (1983) and Sam Shepard's *Fool for Love* (1985), went mostly unnoticed. The 1980s were Altman's lost decade, his reputation in eclipse and his projects (like a planned version of *Ragtime*, an ideal property for the director) as likely as not nixed by jittery studio executives. Salvation arrived in the form of *Doonesbury* cartoonist Garry Trudeau, who was at work on an HBO series about the upcoming 1988 presidential primaries, and looking for a director. *Tanner '88* (1988), with Altman regular Michael Murphy as a Michigan congressman seeking the Democratic presidential nomination, was a triumph, and granted the director a second shot at big-budget filmmaking. There was talk of a *Nashville* sequel, which never came to fruition, and a large-canvas adaptation of Raymond Carver short stories set in Los Angeles.

While Altman cobbled together the financing for the latter film, which would become *Short Cuts*, he was brought in as a director-for-hire on *The Player* (1992), a crafty burlesque of Hollywood mores. There is a *Sunset Blvd.* tartness to Michael Tolkin's script (based on his own novel) about hotshot studio executive Griffin Mill's fatal run-in with an embittered writer. (The film explicitly nods toward its famous predecessor with a phone message delivered to Griffin: "a guy named Joe Gillis called.")

The film's opening shot pays homage to Orson Welles's legendary six-and-a-half-minute tracking shot from *Touch of Evil* (1958), and the plot echoes not only Wilder's classic but also Nicholas Ray's paranoid thriller *In a Lonely Place* (1950), starring Humphrey Bogart as a screenwriter suspected of murder. The movies have chipped away at the world, eroding any reality beyond the one on the screen. Even Griffin's attorney, representing him on official business, references another twisty Wilder thriller, *Witness for the Prosecution*, in his defense. "Can we talk about something other than Hollywood for a change?" Griffin moans to his friends over lunch. A hushed silence ensues, followed by laughter; there is nothing other than Hollywood to talk about. There is nothing else, period.

Altman's trademark slow zooms sneak up on the action, eavesdropping on the characters, catching their vapidity, self-obsession, and absurdity. The best part of the film—the part everyone remembers—is the opening sequence, with Griffin pelted with ludicrous movie pitches: "Goldie goes to Africa. . . . It's *Out of Africa* meets *Pretty Woman*." Buck Henry stops by, too, to pitch a sequel to *The Graduate*, in which Ben and Elaine, some twenty years later, are living together in a rambling New Hampshire house, where they are joined by the still-frisky Mrs. Robinson. Once the film veers from lacerating insider comedy to comic crime thriller, *The Player* never quite regains the verve of its opening reels until its art-imitates-life-imitates art finale.

The Player is a movie about Hollywood endings: those imposed by its executives on messy, unpleasant real life, and the one it cynically grants to Robbins's murderous boy wonder. "What took you so long?" Julia Roberts's death row inmate, only seconds from execution, asks Bruce Willis in *The Player*'s film-within-a-film. "Traffic was a bitch," Willis responds, his trademark grin telegraphing a punch line as he triumphs over the massed force of the American criminal-justice system. Hollywood, *The Player* forces us to acknowledge, is nothing more than a reassuring lie, and we are its playthings. So what does that make *The Player*? A distressing truth?

Distressing truths are the stock in trade of Altman's panoramic *Short Cuts* (1993), an L.A.-basin update to *Nashville* made possible by the success of *The Player*. An enormous cast (including Robbins, Jack Lemmon, Lily Tomlin, and Coen brothers regular Frances McDormand) drives an unwieldy, top-heavy vehicle across three hours of unsteady emotional terrain. Betrayal and infidelity are in the air, and the mood is tense, irritable, and crabbed. Like so many of Altman's other efforts, *Short Cuts'* good humor gives way to an exceedingly bleak vision of human nature, but still makes for a surprisingly funny study of life's essential grubbiness.

Its unpleasant clashes between friends, spouses, and strangers are tempered by Altman's twinkly-eyed enjoyment of everyday absurdity. Robbins's tyrannical cop escorts his nemesis—the yappy family dog—on his motorcycle to a remote street corner and abandons him, shouting, "Run away, we don't want you anymore." Jennifer Jason Leigh is a phone-sex operator whose cooing entreaties ("my panties are getting a little wet") are delivered as she changes her daughter's diaper. Even Lemmon's admission of marital infidelity with his sister-in-law is leavened with unintentional comedy: "I didn't want to hurt her feelings," he tells his disheartened son. "After all, it was your mother's sister." Altman's characters are only accidentally funny, their emotional messiness unknowingly comic.

Short Cuts, like *The Player*, garnered Altman another Oscar nomination for best director (although no Oscar), and the opportunity to continue making sprawling, lavishly cast films. In its aftermath, the director had settled into a comfortable final act, his films genial and leisurely, but lacking some of the grit of his most beloved 1970s work. *Ready to Wear* (1994) takes in the world of contemporary fashion with a gimlet eye (the fashion-show finale featured models strutting the catwalk in the buff). The otherwise somber jazz picture *Kansas City* (1996) is livened up by Jennifer Jason Leigh's flinty, scheming kidnapper Blondie, her style a tribute to her big-screen idol: "If Jean Harlow's cheap, then I'm a monkey's uncle!" The underrated *The Company* (2003) offers a deliberately meager dollop of narrative in order to concentrate more forcefully on the rapturous beauty of its dance sequences.

The prime exception was 2001's remarkable *Gosford Park*, an upstairs-downstairs British murder mystery stemming from a conversation Altman had had with character actor and Christopher Guest collaborator Bob Balaban (who plays an American movie producer in the film). The style was borrowed directly from *The Long Goodbye*, with a jittery camera roving indiscriminately between the lavish public rooms and servants' quarters of an elegant British manor, but *Gosford Park* was more homage than revamping. There is a death—as there always is in Altman films—but the mystery is only an afterthought, a side effect of *Gosford Park*'s initial desire to pay tribute to the Agatha Christie detective story. "I make a point never to gossip with servants," Geraldine Chaplin had haughtily informed her driver in *Nashville*, but *Gosford Park* breaks that vow, with masters and minions thrown together, and the invisible steel of the British class system binding and separating the well-born and the meek.

Ten Little Indians might have been the initial inspiration for *Gosford Park*, but it is Jean Renoir, once more, who is the reigning spirit. Altman's final masterpiece is his own *Rules of the Game*, his beautifully crafted portrait of an orderly world, maintained only at fearful cost, on the brink of its permanent collapse. Sound and image are wrenched apart, with Altman refusing to underline crucial moments visually. Everything—even death—is rendered in a low key, easily missed by the inattentive eye. Altman, with the assistance of editor Tim Squyres, cuts against the grain, eschewing carefully matched visual and aural close-ups in favor of a jauntier rhythm.

A good portion of the film's charm emerges from the collision of classes ("It's nobody!" a well-heeled wooer tells his girl as a servant rounds a corner), but it is Maggie Smith's penniless snob who provides its funniest moments. It is a cruel, callous sort of humor, born of self-absorption and a native lack of sympathy for others. "Do you think he'll be as long as he usually is?" she wonders as film star Ivor Novello (Jeremy Northam), fresh off an appearance in Alfred Hitchcock's *The Lodger*, settles in at the piano. After one of Novello's numbers, a smattering of polite applause is heard, and Smith instantly seeks to dampen it: "Don't—please don't encourage him." Like Gould's Philip Marlowe, it is her muttered asides that are the funniest of all; she is an elderly child, having never outgrown her youthful enthusiasms and disdains.

After returning to his onetime presidential candidate for the television special *Tanner on Tanner* (2004), in time for the 2004 election, Altman got to make one last film. *A Prairie Home Companion* (2006) is hardly his best work, or even particularly noteworthy, but Altman's death later that year tinted memories of the film an unexpected sepia. The loss of the master put even the hardest-hearted critics in a forgiving mood. *Prairie* was the last of Altman's musicals, its drama (last night of a beloved radio show) cut with funny, sentimental songs. Comparisons to *Nashville* were inevitable, but Altman had softened. No judgment was being rendered on the American soul, no knives twisted in the guts of its characters. Instead, a well-honed ritual is performed one last time, every note carefully struck, and everyone playing their part.

The metaphorical appositeness was overwhelming. Garrison Keillor (the film's screenwriter) offers a taste of his down-home Midwestern cornpone. Woody Harrelson and John C. Reilly are lovably profane cowpokes with songs like "Lovin' You Ain't Easy, but Your Sister Is" and "I'll Give You Some Moonshine If You Show Me Your Jugs." The dialogue is fast, Dadaist, incomplete, with Altman's trademark fractured editing often cutting his characters off in mid-thought. People talk the way we know them to, with nary a complete sentence to be heard, and the gentle humor is funnier for feeling so recognizable. A mysterious woman (Virginia Madsen) seeks to intercede with the heartless corporate drudge brought in to close down the show, telling him that "When I used to listen to them, it was like they were all my really good friends." The twinkly-eyed truth-teller of the American cinema had gone ever-so-slightly soft in his old age, but Madsen's tribute would serve Altman's oeuvre just as well. It was in the listening that we recognized them.

19

MEL BROOKS

THE 2000-YEAR-OLD
PARODIST

"Never Give a Saga an Even Break." —Subtitle, *Blazing Saddles*

The threadbare set of a 1930s Art Deco musical. A staircase is dotted with men in top hats and tails, whirling their canes and wiggling their behinds. The dancers, prodded by their tyrannical director, are running through take two when a sudden commotion is heard below. A wall gives way, and the set is overrun with cowboys, horses, cold-blooded varmints, damsels in distress, a black sheriff, and his alcoholic sidekick. The musical and the

Brooks's Wild West governor enjoys a quiet moment with his secretary in *Blazing Saddles*.

Western do pitched battle on Fred and Ginger's turf, but there is no contest: the manly men thoroughly thrash the fey pantywaists. "Piss on you," says one goon, before delivering the knockout blow, "I'm workin' for Mel Brooks!"

This pregnant moment of cinematic civil war takes place near the end of Brooks's 1974 mock-Western *Blazing Saddles*, which has already devoted much of its running time to challenging its chosen genre's carefully honed cliches. Dueling genres, and genres duly exploded; such is the oddly febrile world of Mel Brooks, who for nearly four decades has fought his own pitched battles with the moldering traditions of a Hollywood he simultaneously mocks and honors. Brooks could not exist without the industry whose hand he bites. If you've ever suffered through some slapdash *Scary Movie* or *Not Another Teen Movie*, here's my cellphone; give Mel Brooks a call and a piece of your mind for creating a comic sub-genre that has managed to consistently deliver minimal returns.

After the phenomenal Broadway success of the recent musical version of *The Producers*, starring Nathan Lane and Matthew Broderick, Mel Brooks is, following a substantial hiatus, a cinematic icon once more. Mentioned in the same breath with Woody Allen as an elder statesman of American comedy, lauded for his contributions to the form, Brooks is a living legend. And yet, there is a nagging reality that must be acknowledged. Mel Brooks is over-rated. There—I've said it, and there's no taking it back. Comedy is idiosyn-cratic, one man's gold is another's crap, and for me, Mel Brooks is someone to admire without particularly enjoying. His best-regarded movies, like *The Producers* (1968) and *Young Frankenstein* (1974), have aged poorly, and his cinematic output over the past twenty years has been sporadic and spotty. All of which is not to say that Brooks is anything less than a comic legend, or unworthy of recognition—it merely illustrates the fundamental difficulty of writing about comedy. If a comic tells you a joke, and you don't laugh, is there really anything further to be said?

I think there is. Brooks may not tickle my personal funny bone on a con-sistent basis, but his shtick-heavy, gag-filled films simultaneously look back to traditions older than film itself—vaudeville and the self-deprecating humor of the European Jewish ghettos—and to the potty humor of the post-*SNL* era. Brooks helped define the postmodern comedy in all its self-referential, pastiche-drenched irony, and for that alone, he is an icon of contemporary comedy.

Brooks's movies are gag machines—one-armed bandits that pay off in nonstop punch lines. There are times that one might wish Brooks would stop finding comedy so easy. Being a gag machine also means recycling the same jokes time and again, and certain Brooks routines become wearisomely familiar. To a cynic, writing a Mel Brooks movie may appear to consist of reaching into a well-handled sack of familiar bits and shuffling them around into a new formation. We won't be quite so cynical, but permit us to say that watching a Mel Brooks movie can often trigger profound feelings of déjà vu.

Like Woody Allen, Brooks (born Melvin Kaminsky) was a product of working-class Jewish Brooklyn in the years before the Second World War. Comedy was an effort to diminish the loneliness of outsiderdom, and a response to the exclusion Brooks felt as a Jew. Melvin Kaminsky would become Mel Brooks, the same way Joseph Levitch de-Semiticized himself into Jerry Lewis, and Allen Konigsberg turned into Woody Allen, but being Jewish would nonetheless be the cornerstone of Brooks the comedian. "My comedy," he once noted, "comes from the feeling that, as a Jew, and as a person, you don't fit into the mainstream of American society. It comes from the realization that even though you're better and smarter, you'll never belong."

Fatherless and impoverished, young Melvin turned to comedy as his protector in the mean streets of Williamsburg. "If your enemy is laughing," he later noted, "how can he bludgeon you to death?" Melvin's first love was Buster Keaton ("He wore a flat pancake of a hat, and I just couldn't believe the man's grace"), and by the time he was a teenager he was a tummler at a Catskills hotel. Tummlers, who wandered the grounds entertaining guests, were required to be tireless provocateurs, equipped with enough gags to convince a restless audience of vacationing middle-class Jews that they were getting their money's worth. There could hardly have been a better comedic trial by fire for Brooks than these fussy patrons in need of entertainment, or more unequivocal proof that there was no time for setups, just an unending array of punch lines.

After a brief time in the military, where his service primarily consisted of entertaining troops, Brooks became an unpaid errand boy and yes-man for Sid Caesar, star of the television show *Admiral Broadway Revue*, and later *Your Show of Shows*. Persisting beyond all rational expectation, Brooks lingered, offering encouragement and the occasional gag until Caesar began paying for his services out of his own pocket. Eventually, Brooks was hired as a staff writer, on salary, for *Your Show of Shows*, whose brilliant staff included Carl Reiner, Neil Simon, and briefly, Woody Allen.

Following his rendering of service unto Caesar, Brooks spent a number of years in the show-business wilderness. He worked as a Broadway script doctor and unsuccessfully collaborated with Jerry Lewis on his film *The Ladies Man* before being fired for disobedience. Concerted effort got him nowhere, but a project initially conceived as a lark turned Mel Brooks into a household name. Brooks and Reiner had made a habit of entertaining at parties by trotting out a favorite character: a spry codger double the age of Methuselah. The sage with the heavy Yiddish accent became known as the 2,000 Year Old Man, and the resulting records featuring his musings made Brooks an icon of the new comedy.

Brooks would go on to cocreate the spy satire *Get Smart* with Buck Henry, which would have a successful run on CBS from 1965 to 1970. All the while, Brooks had an idea for a satirical novel about Nazism that he was tentatively calling *Springtime for Hitler*. The novel eventually became a play, and then a movie script, and the storyline shifted from Hitler himself to Broadway producers putting on a show about him, but Brooks's initial germ of an idea would serve as the basis of his first feature film: *The Producers* (1968).

Max Bialystock (Zero Mostel) is an over-the-hill Broadway producer reduced to cobbling together checks wrenched from the hands of the lonely old ladies he seduces. Max is a pseudo-Lothario with a cabinet full of framed photographs of grannies, each one removed from its storage place and relocated to a prominent place on his desk before a visit. All of Max's hair appears to grow from a single spot at the back of his skull, and his finances are in even greater disarray than his follicles. Nebbishy accountant Leo Bloom (Gene Wilder) stops in one day to bring order to his books, and finds himself instead drafted as chief plotter on a scheme to make a mint through an epic theatrical failure.

The pieces are all there: the Hitler-loving musical book contributed by Fuhrer fanatic Franz Liebkind (Kenneth Mars); the paranoid, drug-addled hippie named LSD (Dick Shawn) hired to play the lead; Christopher Hewett's brain-dead director, Roger De Bris ("I never *realized* that the Third Reich meant Germany," he says of Franz's play. "I mean it's *drenched* with historical goodies like that"). *The Producers* is in love with its own absurdist shock value; when Roger asks, "Will the dancing Hitlers please wait in the wings? We are only seeing singing Hitlers," Brooks's offscreen laughter is practically audible.

Only the show itself redeems the movie, revealing Brooks's gift for musical comedy. Dancing Nazi soldiers and their jackbooted *frauen* elegantly spin and twirl for the opening number. The camera lifts to an overhead shot for the Busby Berkeley–esque geometrical formation at its conclusion, with the Hitler fanatics forming an undulating swastika. LSD unexpectedly saves the show, transforming Hitler into a Summer of Love hepcat, reigning over a Haight-Ashbury on the Spree. "I lieb ya, baby, I lieb ya," he tells Eva Braun. "Now lieb me alone!"

The Producers purposefully muffles its intended blows, putting us firmly on the side of the con men intending to make a killing by putting on the worst, most offensive Broadway show of all time. The joke is not on us, with-it hipsters that we are; rather, it is on the unwitting schlemiels who might be offended by something as absurd as a charming musical about Nazism. Brooks also intended it to serve as his revenge on a world he saw as deeply inhospitable to Jews. "*The Producers*," Brooks would wryly note, "made me the first Jew in history to make a buck out of Hitler."

One can hear the typical Brooks gag achieving its ideal form here, soon to be repeated endlessly, with Jews or African Americans or Native Americans coming in for similar ribbing. The brief snippets of *Springtime for Hitler* are like a perfectly executed gag from *Your Show of Shows*. Brooks had turned the comedy film into an extended sketch, stringing together a series of unrelated scenes and praying that mood would suffice where plot dwindled away to nothing.

It is tempting to imagine what the film might have been like had Brooks had his druthers and cast Peter Sellers as Leo Bloom, and an unknown young actor named Dustin Hoffman as Franz Liebkind. Hoffman agreed to take the role before dropping out to star in *The Graduate*, and Sellers was too addled and self-absorbed to take Brooks's offer seriously. Sellers would eventually reward Brooks for his efforts. Happening to screen *The Producers* for his film club (the scheduled film had gotten misplaced, and the projectionist offered to screen an obscure new picture instead), Sellers took out a trade advertisement extolling it as "the essence of all great comedy combined in a single motion picture." Avco Embassy, which had been planning to shelve the film, instead released *The Producers* to great acclaim, and overwhelming success. Brooks took home the Academy Award for Best Original Screenplay, beating out *2001: A Space Odyssey* and *Battle of Algiers*.

The Twelve Chairs (1970) mistakenly assumed that the success of *The Producers* had stemmed less from the cleverness of its framing device than its tummler tirelessness. This stolen-jewels thriller set in Soviet Russia substitutes ceaseless, frantic motion for any sense of coherence, or zest, and is accordingly dragged down to the level of dull farce. Brooks himself is wonderful as the faithfully stupid servant of Ron Moody's former aristocrat, but the rest of the film is sorely lacking in character, its unusual setting notwithstanding.

After the misstep of *The Twelve Chairs*, Brooks returned with a pair of enormous successes in 1974. *Blazing Saddles*, the first of his twin box-office triumphs, is the Brooks film least contaminated by preciousness or saddled (pardon the pun) with groan-inducing humor. It is an energetic demolition of the Western, planting dynamite under its rotting pillars and blowing the entire set of familiar locales to high heaven. Brooks's Western shares a fundamental purpose, if not a mood or tone, with Robert Altman's *McCabe & Mrs. Miller*. *McCabe* had sought to undercut the nourishing myths of the Western, and *Blazing Saddles* lustily finishes the job.

The proposed subtitle paraphrased W. C. Fields, but the tone is definitively Marxian. Some characters are in on the joke, and others are decidedly not. The wreckers are led by Bart (Cleavon Little), the unlikely new black sheriff of the town of Rockridge. (Richard Pryor had worked on the film's screenplay with Brooks, and the role of Bart had initially been intended for him.) A wised-up urban cowboy surrounded by dim whites, Bart knows exactly how to play their prejudice to his own benefit. As he approaches, the music and church bells welcoming the new sheriff's arrival unceremoniously cease, the banner in his honor abruptly curls, and the introductory speaker is surprised mid-sentence: "As chairman of the welcoming committee, it is my privilege to extend the laurel and hearty handshake to our new . . . *nigger*."

Bart is a Pryor-esque racial anachronism, and *Blazing Saddles* is animated by his disruptive presence in the conservative Western genre. "Excuse me while I whip this out," Bart begins his opening remarks, reaching toward his waistband. Ladies shriek and men grab for their six-shooters as he pulls out—a piece of paper. Surrounded by hostile racists with itchy trigger fingers, Bart craftily summons up the ghost of lily-livered Stepin Fetchit to make his escape. "Oh lawdy, he's desperate!" he shouts, slowly backing away toward safety as he holds a gun to his own head. "Do what he say, do what he say!" Spotted by a pair of Ku Klux Klan gunmen later in the film, Bart is unmasked with the perfect inflammatory aperçu waiting on his lips: "Hey, where da white women at?" (The Coen brothers would later steal Brooks's KKK gag in their 2000 *O Brother, Where Art Thou?*—to distinctly lesser effect.)

Blazing Saddles cannily undercuts the Western by exposing it to unexpected bits and pieces of other genres. Brooks contributes a pitch-perfect Dietrich cabaret number for his own mini-Marlene, Lily Von Shtupp (played with energetic abandon by the Oscar-nominated Madeline Kahn). With her long, stocking-sheathed legs, sexual banter, and notable lisp, Lily is like a

Frankenstein monster created out of Dietrich's most memorable traits. Even her handwritten notes have a lisp.

Kahn does a freehand imitation of Dietrich's Western turn in *Destry Rides Again*. "Oh, it's twue, it's twue, it's twue," she exclaims upon unzipping Bart's fly, her excitement growing with each repetition. The next morning, she serves her lover a gigantic, absurdly phallic *schnitzengruben*, presumably in confirmation of his impressive manhood. Outside the window of the rapscallion governor (Brooks), a medieval holdover with a lisp and a hunch, clad in chainmail, oversees the process of hanging criminals, as if Mel had called Monty Python for a bit of assistance with a pokey gag. Brooks himself is wicked fun as a Yiddish-speaking Indian chief, and as the pleasure-seeking governor, who signs a bill while chatting with his scantily clad "secretary's" breasts, and demands a full-throated "harrumph" from a hanger-on who fails to adequately express his mock indignation at a gubernatorial pet peeve.

Brooks's other success of 1974 also treats its adopted genre as a tear-down. *Young Frankenstein* revisits James Whale's *Frankenstein*, recycling old-movie tropes by the fistful. The mad scientist, the dank castle, the steam-enshrouded train station, the rampaging villagers—all are present and accounted for.

Blazing Saddles had cleverly inverted the genre expectations of the Western, injecting a dose of Pryor-esque racial humor into its bloodstream and observing the results. *Young Frankenstein* has no such agenda, and instead settles for passively undercutting horror cliches. Believing itself to be wittily undermining its genre of choice, *Young Frankenstein* mostly reintroduces soggy, overly familiar tropes, at a loss for how to exploit them properly. Gene Wilder (who also wrote the script) is the famous doctor's grandson—Fronken-steen not Frankenstein—a medical professor obsessed with recreating his legendary ancestor's experiments. Brooks and Wilder stock the film with all manner of gags, from the horses' whinnying every time they hear the name of the intimidating Frau Blucher (Cloris Leachman), to the monster's soft-shoe performance of "Puttin' on the Ritz," but the tone is too frantic and uneven. *Frankenstein*'s individual moments of genius (many of which seem to include Kenneth Mars's mostly mechanical Inspector Kemp) are lost in the muddle of inoffensive mediocrity.

It takes a healthy sense of self-regard to consider following in the footsteps of Charlie Chaplin and Buster Keaton. It requires a near-lunatic degree of audacity to envision making a silent comedy in 1976, forty-nine years after the advent of sound. Brooks's earlier hits had only required an elementary understanding of the genres they mocked; *Silent Movie* asks audiences to sit through an actual silent film. Comedy audiences have rarely been amenable to high-concept experimentation, and *Silent Movie* does not offer enough in the way of surprise or vigor to overcome that essential inhospitability. It is a bravura experiment, inexpertly rendered.

Brooks plays a has-been director shopping an idea for a silent picture to the studios, who tell him that they'll be happy to do it as long as he recruits some A-list stars. Unsurprisingly, given the setup, *Silent Movie* is one uninterrupted walk-on cameo, with Burt Reynolds, James Caan, Liza Minnelli, Paul Newman, and Anne Bancroft (Brooks's wife) making brief appearances as themselves. Brooks has some fun with silent technique. Characters mouth noticeably different lines than what the intertitles have them saying. Mostly, though, the engine of the film is as antiquated as the classic roadster Mel and his friends drive. Gags like the trick Coke machine that fires soda-bullets were rusty when Harold Lloyd was still in short pants. Brooks borrows gags from the heyday of slapstick, like the roadster that tips over from the added burden of a hefty pregnant woman, but there is little of Chaplin or Keaton's improvisatory magic visible here. In fact, *Silent Movie* plays just like a Mel Brooks film minus the dialogue.

The film's best joke requires its lone word of spoken dialogue. Brooks calls legendary French mime Marcel Marceau to ask him to appear in his film, and receives a curt rejection: "No!" If only the rest of the film had been as inventive, or unexpected.

The next year's Hitchcock pastiche *High Anxiety* (1977) similarly squanders a sterling opportunity for comedic deconstruction. Whose work could be riper for parody than that of Alfred Hitchcock—especially his occasionally ridiculous, Salvador Dalí–assisted tribute to Freud, *Spellbound*? *High Anxiety* borrows the plot of that Gregory Peck–Ingrid Bergman thriller, undercutting Hitchcockian tension with Brooksian levity.

The principle of the bean dinner still applies here; in *Blazing Saddles*, Brooks had wondered how it could be that, after all those thousands of plates of beans consumed in Westerns, no one had ever let loose a fart. In *High Anxiety*, a swelling burst of suspense music after a dramatic announcement of potential foul play turns out to be a passing bus filled with members of the Los Angeles Symphony Orchestra. Cameras delicately glide in from the exterior to observe a dinner scene, only to crash into a window and break the glass. Waiting in the north by northwest corner of a public park, Brooks is suddenly set upon by a flock of ominous birds, who proceed to shit all over him. Best of all, Brooks takes over the Janet Leigh role from *Psycho*, delicately soaping his chest in the shower before a lunatic bellboy attacks him with a rolled-up newspaper. A close-up reveals black newsprint running into the drain, and Brooks's unblinking eye as he mutters, "that kid gets no tip."

The brief *Psycho* parody encapsulates everything *High Anxiety* could have been, and is not. This single moment exhibits a careful understanding of Hitchcock's work—his framing, his cutting, his masterful use of tension and surprise—and reveals its weak spots. Pity, then, that so much of *High Anxiety* is dedicated to weak tea—like characters named MacGuffin and Thorndyke, and lazily rehashed scenes from *Vertigo* and *The Birds*.

Truly the son of Sid Caesar, Mel Brooks was better suited to brief snippets than feature films. A quick, snappy sketch, lights out, and then a new setup. *History of the World, Part I* (1981) gives Brooks the freedom to leave narrative behind, and this loosely structured jaunt through history's high points contains some of his more inspired riffs. *History of the World, Part I* is essentially a long-form episode of *Your Show of Shows*, its sketches loosely strung around historical themes but otherwise unconnected. Brooks and his usual collaborators (Dom DeLuise, Harvey Korman, Madeline Kahn, Caesar himself) romp through ten thousand years of recorded history, beginning with Orson Welles sonorously intoning Brooks's laughably ornate narration, over music lifted from *2001: A Space Odyssey*.

The entire film plays like a rapid-fire re-creation of human history by some harried Catskills comics. Everyone here, from Moses to Roman centurions to Torquemada, has a distinctly Yiddishy tone, and the film is essentially an extended Purim *spiel*, swiftly disarming history of its majesty. Moses parting the Red Sea, arms cast to the sky, is a harried old man being robbed ("They don't let you live, they don't let you breathe!"). Torquemada pulls the lever of a slot machine whose wheels are covered with Jews on the rack, and Brooks's Comicus is an overbearing waiter at the Last Supper ("Are you all together, or is it separate checks?").

History of the World, Part I is like a ten-course dinner: if you don't like this joke, stick around a minute, and something better will come around. The film ends with a preview of *Part II*, with the *Producers*-esque "Hitler on Ice" and the Star of David–shaped spaceships of "Jews in Space." "When goyim attack us," their jaunty musical number goes, "we give 'em a smack, we slap 'em right back in the face."

It was quite a transition, but the Brooks-produced remake of Ernst Lubitsch's *To Be or Not to Be* (1983) was like another long-form sketch from *History of the World, Part 1*. Brooks and Bancroft stepped into the Jack Benny and Carole Lombard roles as Polish actors drafted into the anti-Nazi resistance. Brooks was starring in yet another Hitler lampoon; not only had he guaranteed himself a place in the record books as the first Jew to make a buck from Hitler, he was also gunning to be the Jew who had made the most money off the Fuhrer.

To Be gives Brooks the opportunity to show off his gifts as a ham, and to play with the costumes and disguises that had always been his stock in trade. For the bulk of the audience, who may not have been familiar with Lubitsch's original, *To Be or Not to Be* is a merry romp, lacking the original's sense of encroaching darkness. The original *To Be or Not to Be* had been so good that tampering with it would have been a crime, and so Brooks and director Alan Johnson (Brooks's longtime choreographer) mostly leave it as is. But would you rather watch Lubitsch's *To Be or Not to Be*, or Alan Johnson's?

The yarmulkes and ritual fringes may have vanished somewhere along the way, but Brooks's next film as a director was essentially "Jews in Space" blown up to feature length. *Spaceballs* (1987) had Brooks releasing all the hot air from George Lucas's lumbering giant *Star Wars*, but it was also an opportunity to revisit his favored retinue of yuks: the *Mad*-magazine-caliber jokes about Pizza the Hutt and Dark Helmet, the flaming-homosexual stereotypes, the unrelated movie parodies (*Lawrence of Arabia* and *Alien* get the full Brooks treatment here), the numerous characters who sound like Brooklyn garment manufacturers named Morty.

Like *Blazing Saddles*, *Spaceballs* exposes the hidden joints of a well-constructed, well-loved cinematic form, parodying it so ruthlessly that it becomes difficult to ever again take the films it mocks seriously. *Star Wars*' magic, and its menace, are rendered equally ridiculous by Brooks's slashing style of parody. *Spaceballs* is especially adamant about mocking *Star Wars*' phallic worship. Dark Helmet (Rick Moranis) and Lone Starr (Bill Pullman) size up the competition like men eyeballing each other at a urinal: "I see your Schwartz is as big as mine." Yogurt, *Spaceballs*' Yoda, is the film's designated Jew (played, of course, by Brooks's all-purpose Jewish jester: himself), his explanations of the Schwartz broken up by "moichandising" opportunities: *Spaceballs* towels, shaving cream, toilet paper, and placemats.

The recycling of familiar Brooks jokes; the jibes about tie-ins; Yogurt's wish that "God willing, we'll all meet in *Spaceballs 2: The Search for More Money*": it all added up to a typical Mel Brooks experience, in which the sense of the movie as an entertainment machine, slick and expert, was never far from the surface. Brecht he was not, but part of Brooks's charm is the constant reminder that all this is only silliness. Having devoted his film career to undercutting others' work, Brooks could hardly draw the line at his own movies.

The 1990s were a far less successful decade for Brooks. Brooks was now a straightforward parodist in the *Spaceballs* mode, mocking a single film in careful, occasionally wearying detail. *Life Stinks* (1991), with Brooks as an L.A. hobo, had been tasteless even by the director's own standards, and *Robin Hood: Men in Tights* (1993), passed off laziness as self-parody. Another thwarted-wedding conclusion, another black man appointed sheriff ("And why not? It worked in *Blazing Saddles*," observes one character), Brooks as the Yid out of water. Well, actually, Brooks is pretty terrific as Rabbi Tuchman, the traveling mohel ("CIRCUMCISIONS: SPECIAL OFFER, HALF OFF!") who assists Robin and his merry men. And Dave Chappelle, years before *Chappelle's Show* would make him a household name, is superb as Brooks's latest mock-Pryor, taking a beating from the medieval equivalent of the LAPD and delivering a rabble-rousing speech a la *Malcolm X*: "We didn't land on Sherwood Forest, Sherwood Forest landed on us!" The remainder of *Men in Tights*, with Cary Elwes as the legendary redistributor of wealth, is frightfully pallid.

Dracula: Dead and Loving It (1995), with Leslie Nielsen, of *Naked Gun* renown, the latest to don the cape and fangs, was mostly ignored by Brooks's once-loyal audience, but made for a marked improvement on *Robin Hood*. This note-for-note parody of Francis Ford Coppola's *Bram Stoker's Dracula* is so faithful at times that the film almost seems like a straightforward remake. Nonetheless, Nielsen makes a winning Dracula, like *The Naked Gun*'s Frank Drebin with a Transylanian accent, and Brooks is witty as ever as the vampire-hunting Van Helsing, for whom this is all frightfully old hat. As an associate pounds a stake into a vampire's heart, sending torrents of blood shooting everywhere, he mutters regretfully: "We should have put newspaper down."

Brooks had reached a nadir in his career, but redemption came from an unlikely benefactor: Broadway. Brooks had always enjoyed smuggling a song or two into his films—the Sinatra-esque "High Anxiety" in his film of the same name, "The Spanish Inquisition" and "Jews in Space" in *History of the World, Part I*, the acrobatic musical number "Men in Tights" in *Robin Hood: Men in Tights*—but the idea of Mel Brooks as a paragon of the musical theater would likely have been viewed by most Broadway denizens as an elaborate practical joke. Nonetheless, Brooks's musical version of *The Producers*, starring Nathan Lane and Matthew Broderick as Bialystock and Bloom, was a Broadway smash in 2001, running for more than twenty-five hundred performances.

A film version was inevitable, creating the wheels-within-wheels scenario of a movie based on a play based on a movie. *The Producers* (2005) was vaguely reminiscent of past Mel Brooks work—its Yiddish humor, the lines cribbed from *To Be or Not to Be*, not to mention the characters and scenario from the original film—but its Broadway roots are entirely too evident. Directed by Susan Stroman (who oversaw the stage version), *The Producers* is essentially a filmed 135-minute theatrical extravaganza with little sense of cinematic oomph. Brooks, however, proves himself a surprisingly solid tunesmith, with songs like "I Wanna Be a Producer" and "Der Guten Tag Hop Clop" smoothly translating the original film's madcap tone into music.

Will Ferrell is clever as unrepentant Nazi playwright Franz Liebkind, and Uma Thurman provides the requisite va-va-voom with a showstopping number of her own as Brooks's requisite dim-bulb European sexpot. More than anything, however, this *Producers* feels dutiful: loyal to the musical, loyal to the original film, scrupulously preserving the mood of Brooks's debut. Unfortunately for Brooks, what had been funny in 1968 was now significantly less so. The jokes about Roger De Bris and his fey bunch of limp-wristed associates (immortalized in the song "Keep It Gay") play as the tired banter of a comedian whose finger was too consumed with taking his own pulse to take that of his audience. One could only be thankful that Brooks had not cast a black actor as Hitler, for the opportunity to order up a new batch of *Blazing Saddles*–esque jokes.

Still and all, this second, self-referential version of *The Producers* made for an ideal finale to Mel Brooks's career, if finale it was. A film of a musical of a film, paying deferential obeisance to what had been initially been intended as an offhand lark, *The Producers* was precisely the sort of inside-show-biz absurdity that Mel Brooks might, in other circumstances, have lavishly mocked. The hall of mirrors had caught Brooks in a less-than-flattering pose, but he was man enough to take the joke: perhaps for his next project, Mel Brooks might attempt a no-holds-barred satiric takedown of aging Jewish parodists turned musical-theater wunderkinds.

20

WOODY ALLEN

HOPE AND BERGMAN

> "I had heard that 'Commentary' and 'Dissent' had merged
> and formed 'Dysentery.'" —Woody Allen, *Annie Hall*

Woody Allen's two heroes, nurtured since his Brooklyn youth, are Bob Hope and Ingmar Bergman. Allow that fact to sink in for a moment. On the one hand, the gawky "super-schnook," as Allen describes him, with the permanent stream of one-liners and hastily muttered asides; on the other, the prince of Scandinavian darkness, his films portentous, symbolically freighted musings on human impermanence and the absence of God. How

---

Allen lists a few of his favorite things in *Manhattan*.

can one filmmaker balance his Hope side and his Bergman side? How can the two even coexist? Funny you should ask.

Allen has been making films for more than forty years now. The arrival of a new Woody Allen film every year has become an expected ritual, treated as a naturally occurring phenomenon rather than a small miracle of unceasing consistency. For those four decades, we have been privy to the inner struggle of a gifted artist, torn between his strengths and his ambitions. Comedy has wrestled with drama, his talents for the former facing off against his desires to succeed with the latter. Would Hope be ascendant, or Bergman? "There's no question that comedy is harder to do than serious stuff," Woody Allen told an interviewer in 1972. "There's also no question in my mind that comedy is less valuable than serious stuff."

Let us not, however, make the same mistake that Allen makes in assessing his own work, and assume that complex, gnarled dramas are art, while the easy pleasures of comedy are something lesser. Woody Allen's comedy is art, as all good comedy is. The fact of Allen's seeming ease in creation is only testament to his genius. Nonetheless, Allen's yearning for gravity is hardly unfamiliar; we have already borne witness to similar ambitions from Charlie Chaplin, Jerry Lewis, and numerous others. To penetrate deeper into comedy, one must grow more serious; Walter Kerr's stipulation is as true for Woody Allen as it had been for his predecessors. Wherever his restless muse took him, Woody Allen was always a comedian at heart.

Whatever would follow, it was comedy that gave Woody Allen—or actually Allen Konigsberg, the boy wit of Avenue J—his first leg up. While still in high school, Konigsberg was hired to write jokes for a newspaper columnist on the strength of some unsolicited gags he had submitted. After school, he would take the train from Brooklyn's Midwood neighborhood into the enchanted borough of Manhattan, and spend three hours writing jokes that would later be credited to various celebrities. At nights, Allen would head to Manhattan again: the magical Manhattan of the movies, enraptured by the penthouse aeries, the sleekly elegant nightclubs, and the Art Deco decor. *The Purple Rose of Cairo*'s Cecilia (Mia Farrow), dreaming of escaping the dreariness of a dull existence by leaping headfirst into the movies, may actually be the most autobiographical of Allen's screen protagonists.

Konigsberg (who billed himself as Woody Allen to keep his comedic efforts a secret from friends and family) was a natural whiz with wisecracks. By nineteen, he had been hired by NBC for its young-writers program; at twenty-two, he was already writing for Sid Caesar.

Allen was mostly self-taught, having been expelled from NYU for poor grades. He studied playwriting and photography—useful pursuits for a future director—but his real education came at the Tamiment resort in Pennsylvania's Pocono mountains. This getaway for middle-class Jews was renowned for its theatrical productions, and the talented performers and writers (alumni included Caesar, Mel Brooks, Carl Reiner, Danny Kaye, and Neil Simon) recruited for summer stays. In the summer of 1956, Allen was a writer at Tamiment, penning short sketches like the one in which all the dialogue was replaced by the phrase "prune Danish."

On the basis of his successful Tamiment residency, Allen wrangled his dream job as a writer for Caesar, but was soon convinced by his managers to ditch writing and give stand-up a try. Performance was a terrible struggle. Allen thought of quitting constantly, angry that he had given up a comfortable living as a writer to humiliate himself nightly onstage. After a few years of fruitless efforts before sparse crowds, something clicked, and Woody Allen relaxed into his own material. The routines were surreal, parodic, a teetering edifice of absurdist non sequiturs. Allen was modeling himself after satirist Mort Sahl, but rather than Sahl's didja-see-this-article? shtick, Allen was punching above his intellectual weight, providing his own freewheeling annotations to Freud and Dostoyevsky.

Allen's stand up success brought him to the attention of well-regarded producer Charles Feldman, who saw the young writer as the ideal new talent for a slapstick comedy he had in mind. Allen was hired to write *What's New Pussycat?* (1965), about a reluctant Lothario's struggles with monogamy. There are shreds of what we now recognize as Allen's voice in the final film, but some combination of Feldman's decimation of the script, and star Peter O'Toole's inability to properly deliver his lines, renders *What's New Pussycat?* somewhere between a misfire and a complete disaster. The film, nonetheless, was an enormous box office hit. Allen wrote portions of another script for Feldman (1967's patchwork James Bond burlesque *Casino Royale*), but a lesson had been learned: if Allen wanted to work in the movies, and not see his hard work trashed by others, he would have to not only write, but direct.

Allen's early films show Hope ascendant. Allen had written the mordantly funny dubbed lines for *What's Up, Tiger Lily?* (1966), reworking a Japanese action film into a frantic chase after a much-desired egg-salad recipe. *Take the Money and Run* (1969), Allen's debut as a director (he had initially thought of hiring Jerry Lewis to direct), is an equally scattershot agglomeration of disconnected one-liners. The one-liners were, in essence, the fundamental point of the endeavor. The Groucho masks, the rapid-fire pastiches of other films, the 116 stolen veal cutlets—these isolated comic conceits are the essence of *Take the Money and Run*, whose buoyancy stems from the winning levity of Allen's non-sequitur-clad routine.

Allen stars as spectacularly incompetent criminal Virgil Starkwell, given to crafting guns out of bars of soap and misspelling holdup notes. There are brilliant moments here, like the bank robbery foiled by Virgil's poor penmanship ("What is 'abt naturally'?" one teller wonders), and Virgil's Chaplinesque preparations for a big date, removing his suit from the refrigerator and his shoes from the freezer. But by the standards of his later work, *Take the Money* is surprisingly slipshod; Allen is clearly still mastering the art of direction. Editing in particular was a challenge; Ralph Rosenblum, hired as editor, demonstrated to the despondent director that his supposedly disastrous rough cut only required a suitably up-tempo ragtime soundtrack to enliven seemingly dead scenes.

Woody was the Hope-esque unlikely hero, his razor-sharp wit his only weapon. Like Hope, Woody was a walking contradiction: a buffoon whose brilliant wit belied his supposed incompetence. How could anyone so adroit with a retort be such a schlemiel?

For pure comedy, Allen has never improved on the inspired riffs of *Bananas* (1971) and *Sleeper* (1973), masterful reanimations of the silent comedy welded to the inspired verbiage of Hope and Groucho Marx. They are triumphs of Woody Allen as performer; soon, having found his feet as a filmmaker, Allen would steadily cede center stage to his own burgeoning directorial vision. *Bananas'* loosely linked vignettes resembled *Take the Money and Run*, or Allen's hit-and-miss *Everything You Always Wanted to Know About Sex, but Were Afraid to Ask* (1972), but the writing had grown more assured, and Allen's understanding of film's capabilities to amuse had broadened. The faint air of slackness that marked *Take the Money* is nowhere to be found.

Allen's Fielding Mellish is a shlub accidentally drafted into a company of Latin American rebels, having packed all his Manhattan neuroses in his carry-on luggage. "I cannot suck anybody's leg who I am not engaged to," he tells a commander, chuckling at his own hang-ups. Fielding is another of Allen's chattering Jewish hysterics, now writ large as a Castro-esque revolutionary, his self-defeating foibles magically transformed into his greatest attributes. Plot takes a back seat to Allen's preferred brand of intellectual tomfoolery. Howard Cosell calls the play-by-play for a political assassination, and Allen works in a dream sequence about parallel-parking crucifixions before being sent on a mission to bring sandwiches back for the rebel forces: "490 on rye, let me have 110 on whole wheat, and 300 on white bread . . . and one on a roll."

With its comically exaggerated set pieces ("My God, I beat a man insensible with a strawberry," Allen marvels after romping in a patch of overgrown fruit) and its high-concept scenario, *Sleeper* has a silent-film feel, as if Allen had been studying Buster Keaton for clues. Set two hundred years in the future, with Miles Monroe (Allen) awoken from a multiple-century hibernation, the film is a hanger on which Allen drapes some of his wittiest riffs yet. The futuristic setup allows Allen the distance to bemusedly mock the ways of the East Coast chattering classes. Miles offers distinctly faulty information on the array of historical artifacts assembled by future generations: Charles De Gaulle was a French chef, Bela Lugosi the mayor of New York, and citizens, having been found guilty of a crime, were forced to endure broadcasts of Cosell's television programs. Buster's mathematical gags inform *Sleeper*'s slapstick, but another Keaton—costar Diane—is the genuine find, her air of cheerful battiness making her the ideal companion to the dour, self-absorbed Woody. She remains puzzled by her partner's point of view: "You don't believe in science. And you also don't believe in the political system's work. And you don't believe in God, huh? So then what do you believe in?" Allen responds as if he has been practicing this answer for two centuries: "Sex and death. Two things that come once in a lifetime. But at least after death you're not nauseous."

"My seconds will call on your seconds," a dueling partner tells Allen in *Love and Death* (1975). "Well, my seconds will be out," he responds, setting off a dazzling assault of Marx Brothers-inspired verbiage. "Have 'em call on my thirds. If my thirds are out, go directly to my fourths." Woody is a shabby New York Jew transposed to the nineteenth-century Russia of Tolstoy and Dostoyevsky, living out Allen's fantasy (later fleshed out in his celebrated short story "The Kugelmass Episode") of inserting himself bodily into the enduring classics of world literature. *Love and Death* is a Potemkin village, with the Russian landscape inexplicably peopled with stereotypical immigrant Jews. For its masterful conclusion, Allen and Keaton are twin Grouchos let loose in *War and Peace*, wreaking havoc on nineteenth-century history.

Allen's growth as a filmmaker was as rapid as his mastery of writing and performing had been. Through persistence, and the reassuring presence of collaborators like Marshall Brickman, the films grew tighter and more character-driven, the parade of gags replaced by an increasing emphasis on plot and characterization. *Annie Hall* (1977) had begun life as a loose-jointed mystery story, before preview screenings decisively demonstrated that audiences preferred the relationship drama to the ostensible suspense plot (which would later be resuscitated for 1993's *Manhattan Murder Mystery*).

Even without the mystery story, *Annie Hall* is still two films in one: one a loose-jointed comedy in the vein of *Sleeper*, and the other a tender romance offering the first glimmers of Allen's serious side. *Annie Hall* owes an enormous debt to Rosenblum, its editor, who devised the film's allusive, stream-of-consciousness cutting. The fractured narrative is not merely a matter of design; it is essential to *Annie Hall*'s air of unsettled melancholy. The film is a deft sleight-of-hand trick, structured around a series of anguished romantic confrontations between Allen's Alvy Singer and Keaton's Annie, and cushioned by broad comic set pieces. The looseness of Allen's earlier work is unchanged, but the Marshall McLuhan cameos, animated sequences, flashbacks, and direct addresses to the camera are now all newly relevant, puzzle pieces for *Annie Hall*'s mixed-up jigsaw of human frailty.

The entire film exhibits a heightened, frantic energy, its exaggerations (Alvy muttering distractedly about the second gunman at Dealey Plaza, the dust cloud of cocaine raised by an untimely sneeze) restrained by its surprising emotional kick. Allen begins and ends the film with borrowed jokes—including one from Groucho Marx—repurposed to serve as telling parables of personal and romantic neuroticism and fallibility. The humor, ultimately, is inseparable from the sentiment.

Annie Hall is one of Allen's funniest, and most touching, films, its sense of romantic disappointment underscored by the subtle ethnic differences between its protagonists. "You're what Granny Hall would call a real Jew," Annie offers as an awkward romantic ice-breaker, and Alvy's (admittedly untrustworthy) memory spits out a corresponding symbol of Annie as uber-WASP, ordering a pastrami sandwich on white bread with mayonnaise at a Jewish deli. And don't even get me started on Alvy's wrestling with the lobster; what more primal image of Jewish fear could possibly exist?

The addition of Annie and Alvy's charming, messy, unsalvageable relationship to the template established by *Bananas* and *Sleeper* transforms *Annie Hall* into something entirely new for Allen: a somber comedy. The film won four Academy Awards, including Best Picture, and remains, deservedly, his most admired picture.

The success of *Annie Hall* allowed Allen to embrace his European-auteur inclinations, to the broad dissatisfaction of his audience. *Interiors* (1978) and *Stardust Memories* (1980) were slavish appropriations of Bergman and

Fellini, respectively, their dialogue, as Allen later acknowledged, affected by the rhythms of those films' English subtitles. Allen was stretching himself as a dramatist, eschewing comedy as a lesser emotion. He knew the risks inherent in what he was attempting, and was voluntarily opting to leave some portion of his audience behind. The space aliens in *Stardust Memories* were not the only ones loudly professing their preference for "the early, funny ones," and not these stark, humorless academic exercises. Allen was paying homage to his heroes but had not quite mastered the fusion of their sensibilities with his own.

Manhattan (1979) begins with Allen's Ike Davis trotting out, and rejecting, potential opening sentences for his new novel: would it be romantic or realist? Open-minded or crabbed? *Manhattan* itself is similarly of two minds, melding its rhapsodic parade of New York imagery (Allen would have made a great ad man) to a muted version of *Annie Hall*'s romantic heartbreak. Gordon Willis's lavish black-and-white photography and the swoon-inducing George Gershwin soundtrack set the tone for this New York sonnet, more atmospheric than substantive. Keaton is back, this time as the anti–Annie Hall: outspoken, intellectual, and combative. (She and Allen are less oil and water than oil and oil.) The film's two love stories—between Allen and his two girlfriends, teenage Mariel Hemingway and the more age-appropriate Keaton—are both abortive and frustratingly incomplete, perhaps purposefully so. The film's true love is Manhattan itself, whose close-ups are far more glowing than those of either of its leading ladies.

In truth, Allen was neither Hope nor Bergman, but some heretofore unknown hybrid of the two. The Bergman-esque dourness of *Interiors* paved the way for the Allen dramas of the 1980s, in which the comforting familiarity of his own presence leavened the unstinting gloominess of his worldview. The past hangs heavily over Allen's 1980s films, be it the Depression-era fantasy of *The Purple Rose of Cairo* (1985), the refracted autobiography of *Radio Days* (1987), or Martin Landau's arguments with the ghosts of his youth in *Crimes and Misdemeanors* (1989). Unsatisfied with the simple pleasures of *Annie Hall* and *Manhattan*, Woody Allen was striving for something deeper, something less instantly gratifying.

If imitation is the sincerest form of flattery, then somewhere off the coast of Sweden, Ingmar Bergman was pleased as punch with *A Midsummer Night's Sex Comedy* (1982). Like *Stardust Memories*, it lifted a favored European auteur out of context, borrowing the sensibility of Bergman's *Smiles of a Summer Night* (a lovers' roundelay at a country home) without significant alteration. The humor, and the philosophy, were all Bergman's, and the result felt fevered and insufficiently personal, like a too-faithful cover version of a favorite song.

Allen was straining to find a style that paid sufficient homage to his own idols while remaining true to his own strengths, and *Zelig* (1983) was a first step toward something more nuanced, and less easily classifiable, than his earlier romantic comedies. Its protagonist is seen mostly in antique-seeming newsreel footage, its mockumentary construction looking back to *Take the Money and Run* and forward to the work of Christopher Guest. Zelig is a chameleon given to adapting to his surroundings, becoming obese or African American, all the while observing that "it's safe . . . to be like the others."

Zelig's observations about American conformism and its uneasy relation to fascism are trenchant, but its pleasures stem from its adroit use of cinematic technique, with Allen cleverly inserted into footage of Jack Dempsey, Herbert Hoover, and Nazi rallies, whose Hitler bears a notable resemblance to the rubbish-spouting tyrant of *The Great Dictator*. (*Forrest Gump* is essentially an extended homage to *Zelig*.) Allen had never been known for his cinematic wizardry, being of Chaplin's turn-on-the-camera-and-shoot school of filmmaking, but with *Manhattan* and now *Zelig*, he was developing a reputation as a stylistically resourceful director.

Broadway Danny Rose (1984) is, like *Zelig*, essentially an extended anecdote, barely sufficient for a feature film. It is a nostalgic showbiz tribute to a hustler lifted from the pages of A. J. Liebling's *Telephone Booth Indians* and deposited in the era of *Halloween II*. Allen is kindly disposed to his Danny Rose, representative of downtrodden entertainers everywhere, and *Broadway*, which deposits this "landlocked Hebrew" in a gangster picture not his own, is one of the most genial films of his career. Allen is superb as the energetic champion of one-armed jugglers and balloon-folders everywhere, and Farrow gives one of her best performances as a New Jersey mob princess, all shards and sharp edges.

The Purple Rose of Cairo (1985) returned to the 1930s of Allen's childhood, its fantasies of cinematic escape (filmed in one of the movie palaces of his Brooklyn childhood) tempered by memories of deprivation and want. The influence of Buster Keaton's *Sherlock Jr.* on the plot—movie star Tom Baxter (Jeff Daniels) steps off the screen and into the life of a lonely moviegoer (Farrow)—is clear, but another comedy classic, Preston Sturges's *Sullivan's Travels*, shadows the film's passionate advocacy for Hollywood fantasy. The movies are not merely another world, operating under rules contrary to those of mundane life—their essential strangeness exerts an influence on those dreaming in the dark. Allen milks much good-natured comedy from the existential oddity of his setup—Tom waits for the fadeout after a passionate clinch, and pays obeisance to his own personal gods, Hollywood screenwriters Irving Sachs and R. H. Levine—but at heart, *Purple Rose* is a boldly argued justification for Allen's own comedic work.

Like *Sullivan's Travels*, *Purple Rose* pays tribute to escapism as the best sort of balm for wounded souls. Astaire and Rogers take the place of *Sullivan's Travels'* Pluto cartoon, but the argument—that silliness is no luxury, but a necessity for those in pain—is much the same as Sturges's. *Radio Days* (1987) would be a reworking of many of *Purple Rose's* themes, its autobiographical resonances more clear-cut, its high-living radio celebrities another version of Tom Baxter's otherworldly assurance. The most heartfelt of Allen's films, *Radio Days* is highly uncharacteristic, modeled after Fellini's nostalgia-drenched *Amarcord* more than his own work. It is the closest Allen would come to returning to the uncomplicated pleasures of his early days.

In many ways, *Hannah and Her Sisters* (1986) continues the same discussion begun by *Purple Rose* in radically different circumstances. In an empty universe, where God is dead and morality a human construct, where do we find meaning? Allen had returned to his familiar Manhattan characters, but the light had grown heavy, and the yearning for truth more acute. Having wearied of the kinds of comedies he had once made, Allen relegates the Woody character to secondary status, eclipsed by a more dramatic central plotline of furtive sexual assignations, sibling rivalry, and romantic disappointment that was like Chekhov in modern dress. Farrow, Dianne Wiest, and Barbara Hershey are three sisters held together by affection and wrenched apart by petty grievances and the dissatisfactions of family. Allen, meanwhile, was Hannah's ex-husband, a self-pitying hypochondriac and searcher after eternal verities. Comedy echoes drama, shaping similar material in differing fashion. Allen squeezes in laughs about the Ice Capades, suicidal impulses ("my parents would be devastated. I would have to shoot them also"), and organized religion, with his Mickey giving Christianity and Hare Krishna a temporary tryout.

Religion is no solace for Mickey, but the movies are, as they were for *Purple Rose's* Cecilia and would be for *Crimes and Misdemeanors'* Cliff; the Marx Brothers are his gods, and *Duck Soup*—the film he watches in *Hannah's* final scene—his personal godhead. A skeptic and an atheist who saw Judaism as a highly effective guilt-injection mechanism, Allen's belief in the supernatural was limited to his love for the magic of the movies. Allen had grown as a filmmaker as well, his technique provocatively allusive in heretofore unseen ways. *Hannah*'s craft was its story in miniature, its frame fractured into a series of disjointed enclosures, its characters blocked from each other even in the same shot.

If *Hannah* was Chekhovian, *Crimes and Misdemeanors* (1989) was Dostoyevskian, its central storyline a modern-dress retelling of *Crime and Punishment*. Martin Landau was magnetic as the desperate doctor driven by his own entanglement with a jealous mistress (memorably played by Anjelica Huston) into the unthinkable act of murder. "I just wanted to illustrate in an entertaining way that there's no God, that we're alone in the universe, and that there is nobody out there to punish you," Allen said of his film. There was something of Bergman to the starkness of Allen's philosophy in *Crimes*, but the style was all his own. Allen once more tempers his unstinting vision by incorporating a comic subplot about his own romantic travails, but his failed courtship of Farrow's television producer—the misdemeanors, as opposed to the crimes, of a heartless universe—wittily echoes the film's diagnosis of a world devoid of significance or meaning. "If you want a happy ending," Landau tells Allen in the climactic scene, "you should go see a Hollywood movie."

By the time of 1991's *Shadows and Fog*, Allen and Farrow had made eleven films together, and been romantically linked for nearly a decade. Their relationship was a famously quirky union of opposites, with Allen and Farrow jointly raising two adopted children, and having a third, biological child together, while living in separate apartments on opposite sides of Central Park. In January 1992, Farrow discovered sexually explicit photos of her adopted daughter Soon-Yi in Allen's room. During divorce proceedings, Farrow accused Allen of sexually molesting their daughter Dylan—a charge that appeared to have no basis in fact—and Allen was forced to defend himself in the court of public opinion, and battle for custody of his children. He lost both cases; the children stayed with Farrow, and the public turned on Allen. His case was an unsympathetic one: he had taken up with a much younger woman who was, at best, his longtime girlfriend's daughter, and at worst his own stepdaughter. The links with his own work—the relationship with teenage Mariel Hemingway in *Manhattan*, *Zelig*'s persecution at the hands of those who resented his fame—were too obvious, and too delicious, for commentators to ignore. From comedic genius and New York icon to sleazeball and degenerate: Woody Allen's fall was precipitous.

The films that followed the split from Farrow reflected the chaos of this unsettled period acutely. The break came—consciously or otherwise—with

Husbands and Wives (1992), whose ugly, quasi–New Wave aesthetic is a deliberate counterpoint to his fluid, pictorially sensuous 1980s work. The sound—close-up even when the camera keeps its distance—is disarmingly near-at-hand, cutting is ragged and haphazard, and the camerawork deliberately shaky. The stylistic similarities to the work of Robert Altman were plentiful, even as the material was resolutely Allen's own. Allen claimed to have been working on the script of *Husbands* years before Soon-Yi, but the resonances—splintering middle-aged couples, marital sexual jealousy, the Allen character's tempestuous flirtation with a college-aged temptress—are all visible on the surface. Allen was peering behind the closed doors of ostensibly happy marriages, and uncovering hidden deposits of bubbling rage and simmering hostility. *Husbands* is insightful and vivid and painfully claustrophobic, like being trapped in someone else's therapy session.

Allen had achieved something unique with *Husbands and Wives*, something almost as stylistically groundbreaking, in its own way, as *Annie Hall* had been. Having unshackled himself from the burdens of pictorial beauty, one might have expected him to embrace the new cut-and-run aesthetic. But this would be to fundamentally misunderstand the director, who—unlike his admirers—has preferred never to look back.

Manhattan Murder Mystery (1993), split off from the original *Annie Hall* screenplay, was Allen's funniest film since *Broadway Danny Rose*, and an unexpected treat for *Annie Hall* fans hoping to see him reunited with Keaton. It was a sweet gift from a director whose work had grown increasingly stark and uncompromising, offering a glimpse of a future where Annie and Alvy not only had not split up, but got married and role-played as the crime-solving couple from *The Thin Man*.

Bullets Over Broadway (1994) offered a better sense of Allen's new proclivities. A warm, winning tribute to the glories of New York theater, *Bullets* was also the first in what would be a series of film-length defenses of the proposition that the artist—the true artist, that is—was above conventional notions of morality. John Cusack's well-heeled playwright believes himself an artist, but the true creator is an obnoxious, uncouth criminal named Cheech (Chazz Palminteri), hired to stand watch over the dim-witted starlet whose gangster boyfriend is bankrolling the production. Cheech eventually murders the starlet for damaging the new, much-improved play he has written, and *Bullets* cannot quite bring itself to condemn his act of aesthetic protectiveness, reflective of Allen's belief that "an artist creates his own moral universe."

The self-described fourth-worst person in the world (behind Hitler, Goering, and Goebbels, but presumably edging out Stalin and Pol Pot), novelist Harry Block (Allen) tours the wreckage of his own life while en route to accept an award from his alma mater. *Deconstructing Harry* (1997), an extended homage to Bergman's *Wild Strawberries*, is a lavish, extravagantly comic, heartfelt, bittersweet tribute to an egotistical monster of exculpatory self-justification. *Deconstructing* jaggedly alternates between stories from Harry's fiction and their real-life counterparts, employing *Husbands and Wives*' Godardian technique for another chronicle of artistic amorality.

Line for line, it may be Allen's funniest film, studded as it is with brilliant character studies, incongruous scenarios, and marvelous asides. It is a movie that bears a second watching, and a third; the humor never entirely recedes—who can help laughing at newly religious Demi Moore's solemnly uttering a prayer before giving her husband a blowjob?—but the melancholy of this excitable but forlorn film emerges. Ultimately, Harry Block—who, like one of his characters, has sought to remake the world to match the distortion he has become—is a man only his characters can love.

Having grown too old to play many of his protagonists, Allen had begun hiring younger actors to play roles that had clearly once been intended for the director. His influence was perhaps too strong; critics had carped that Cusack had embraced one too many Woodyisms in *Bullets Over Broadway*, aping Allen's speaking rhythms, his nervous energy, and his artful pauses with clinical fidelity. They had not yet seen Kenneth Branagh's near-slavish impression in *Celebrity* (1998), which loosely reworked Fellini's *La Dolce Vita* for the era of *People* magazine. For those who can get beyond Branagh's accidental Woody burlesque, *Celebrity* is a nifty satire of the cult of fame, one in which Orthodox Jews and KKK members rub shoulders amiably in the green rooms of TV shows ("The skinheads eat all the bagels already?" a rabbi grouses), and movies have joined TV journalism, media puff-piecery, modeling, and plastic surgery as symptoms of the mindless worship of fame. As he aged, Allen was growing angrier at the excesses of American society, usefully channeling his indignation into flights of comedic inspiration.

The past decade has found Woody Allen shifting gears once more, first back to the cheerful comedies he had so long disdained, and then, when domestic funding for his films dried up, to a series of dramas shot in Europe. The hype machine had perversely caught up with the least likely of its victims; each new Woody Allen film was greeted as a return to form, only to inevitably disappoint those fans expecting another *Manhattan*. These films were indeed not quite at the level of past Allen successes, but the director had not receded into irrelevance just yet. *Small Time Crooks* (2000) was charmingly scuzzy after the fashion of *Broadway Danny Rose*, with Allen endearing as a low-class hustler blessed with the ambiguous gift of great wealth. *Hollywood Ending* (2002) was a reasonably amusing trifle, and *Whatever Works* (2009)—reworked from an *Annie Hall*–era script—a return to the misanthropic charms of his heyday. Some of Allen's other efforts, like *The Curse of the Jade Scorpion* (2001), *Anything Else* (2003), and the Will Ferrell–starring *Melinda and Melinda* (2004), were painfully bad. Allen's comic conceits were growing thinner at the same time that his films were growing longer.

The untimely end of his longtime association with producer Jean Doumanian led to Allen's taking European financing for the series of films beginning with *Match Point* (2005), continuing through *Scoop* (2006), *Cassandra's Dream* (2007), and *Vicky Cristina Barcelona* (2008). The new settings freed Allen of the occasionally stale conventions of his New York work. With *Match Point*, his lifelong ambition of making a drama wholly untempered by comic subplots was realized. *Match Point* is essentially a remake of the Martin Landau section of *Crimes and Misdemeanors*, with Jonathan Rhys-Meyers as the reluctant murderer buffeted by the fates. The film takes place at an operatic pitch, its disquisition on the music of chance a symphony played solely in the darker timbers. Bergman was at last triumphantly in the ascendant, with no compensatory dose of Hope. *Cassandra's Dream* and *Vicky Cristina Barcelona* are lesser dramas, although the latter film was partially redeemed by Allen's unerring eye for Spanish architecture, and Penelope Cruz's Oscar-winning turn as an unhinged ex-wife.

How many fans of *Sleeper* would have guessed that thirty-five years later, Woody Allen would be directing a tempestuous melodrama set in Barcelona, with dialogue in Spanish? The conceit—neurotic Jewish intellectual from Manhattan exiled in the land of tapas and bullfighting—sounded like a *New Yorker* casual by Allen himself, but the juxtaposition was telling.

Woody Allen had always been a walking contradiction: a comic with pretensions to philosophic eminence, a self-taught intellectual playing a stooge, a shlubby New York Jew who envisioned himself as a matinee idol. From gagman to stand-up comedian, from actor to director, from descendant of Groucho Marx and Bob Hope to appointed successor to Bergman and Fellini, Allen had grown in stature by embracing his restlessness. What was *Barcelona*, then, but another unlikely outpost on the long, hard road to self-realization?

21

RICHARD PRYOR

REBEL WITHOUT A PAUSE

"Y'all know how black humor started. It started on the slave ships,
you know. Cat was on his way over here, rowing. You know, dude
said, what you laughing about? He said, yesterday I was a king."
—Richard Pryor, *Bicentennial Nigger*

There are ghosts that linger behind Richard Pryor. They are quiet
ghosts—we do not hear their names much, and their voices remain
mostly silent today—but they linger nonetheless. Look too closely at the
American films of the glorious past, and suddenly, the ghosts are everywhere, inescapable. They are the servants bearing Groucho Marx in on a

---

A study in contrasts: Pryor with Gene Wilder in *Stir Crazy*.

litter in *Animal Crackers*. They are Mae West's maids, Buster Keaton's foils, and Harold Lloyd's dim-witted sidekicks. They are Louise Beavers telling Cary Grant that "if you ain't eatin' WHAM, you ain't eatin' ham," in *Mr. Blandings Builds His Dream House*, and Rochester Anderson shaking his head mournfully when W. C. Fields is arrested in *You Can't Cheat an Honest Man*. They are housekeepers, mammies, faithful servants, and armchair wits. They are the American cinema's second-class citizens, relegated to the backbreaking work of reinforcing the very stereotypes that kept them down, and their ghosts do not rest easily.

The history of comedy has never run along a single track. For every new car added to the comedic train, a hoary tradition is decoupled, shunted off onto tracks leading nowhere except for the railyard of abandoned styles. And nothing is deader than what once made us laugh, and can no longer. Its claims to eternity notwithstanding, comedy is by its very nature ephemeral. What makes one group of people, in one time and place, chuckle heartily may leave another entirely unmoved. We call the works of Aristophanes comedies, but how many of us go to *Lysistrata* for a hearty belly laugh?

The American film comedy has some decoupled cars of its own, but this one in particular serves as an unsettling, sobering reminder of its power to render affliction to the afflicted. These African American performers not only have lost the power to make us laugh; they have, against all expectation, become tragic figures. They are the laughs that stick in our throats.

During the silent era, most African American roles had been one of two kinds: the tom ("hearty, submissive, generous, selfless, and oh-so-very kind," according to Donald Bogle's *Toms, Coons, Mulattoes, Mammies, and Bucks*) and the coon (who served as "amusement object and black buffoon"). The monumental success of D. W. Griffith's *The Birth of a Nation* (1915), and the African American backlash to its virulently racist depictions of black men as rapists and murderers, led to the general relegation of African American performers to comic supporting roles. They were present as lowbrow comedic fodder, counterpoint to the more sophisticated escapades of their white betters. Depending on the era, they were loyal servants, shucking-and-jiving nightclub entertainers, or easily rattled sidekicks, but their meaning remained constant: they were present to remind white audiences of their superiority to these dim-witted figures.

Stepin Fetchit, who starred opposite Will Rogers in *Judge Priest* and *Steamboat Round the Bend*, is the best-known of these names, but he was far from the only one. Actors like Clarence Muse, Bill "Bojangles" Robinson, and

Willie Best played harmless second bananas, the color of their skin immedi-ate and irrevocable proof of their essential foolishness. At the same time, But-terfly McQueen and Hattie McDaniel (the first black actor to win an Academy Award, for 1939's *Gone with the Wind*) were each variants on the loyal care-taker: McQueen fluttery and high-strung, McDaniel beefy, bad-tempered, and loving. None of the films these performers were featured in were explicitly, unabashedly racist, the way *Birth of a Nation* had been (although *Gone with the Wind*'s sepia-toned South comes close), which only makes their unthink-ing arrogance and viciousness all the more discomfiting.

When looking at Richard Pryor, we must imagine him standing at the very end of a long line, snaking back into the half-remembered past. Pryor is joined by Fetchit, and Best, and McQueen, and McDaniel, and Williams, and Robinson, and every African American performer forced into demeaning roles by time and circumstance. Pryor is the first major African American comic performer we encounter, but he is preceded by these black stars of the past, whom we might prefer to forget, or ignore. Pryor, though, knows them all; and his self-appointed task as a comedian is to revisit those ugly truths accidentally revealed by the stereotypes.

Cinematically speaking, the process truly begins with 1976's *Silver Streak*, in which Pryor crashes a Gene Wilder comic thriller halfway through the picture and never really gives it back, but the comedian had been working up to that moment for over a decade. Born in 1940 in that mythical hotbed of whitebread taste, Peoria, Illinois, Pryor's upbringing had been anything but commonplace. His grandmother and mother had run a string of brothels, and his father had been the proprietor of a nearby bar, the Famous Door. Childhood, as it is commonly understood, was something Richard Pryor never experienced; some of his earliest memories, recounted in his autobi-ography, include seeing a man, stabbed in the belly, crawl to a liquor store for a bottle of whiskey, and his mother clawing his father's testicles nearly off in a domestic squabble. Richard would break up his classmates with imita-tions of Jerry Lewis, but school would provide another form of education, too. Having given a white classmate a notepad as a gift while in elementary school, Pryor was surprised to be confronted by her father one day, wielding the same scratch pad: "Nigger, don't you ever give my daughter anything."

After a stint in the army, Pryor got his showbiz start as a low-rent nightclub emcee and Bill Cosby imitator. Having served his time in the strip clubs and rundown nightspots of Peoria, and other Midwestern locales, Pryor ventured to New York's Greenwich Village in the mid-1960s. There, he met Woody

Allen at the Bitter End, who suggested a program of careful study: "Stick around, watch me, and you'll learn something."

Inoffensive, racially neutral stand-up routines got him bookings on television programs like *The Merv Griffin Show* and *The Ed Sullivan Show*. He would do his impression of the first man on the sun, hopping around like a barefoot man on a noontime beach, and a baby being born, delicately pushing the door of the womb open to peer out into the bright, frightening world. Pryor had a safe, comfortable act that played well with crowds, but in September 1967, he threw it all away, walking off the stage at Las Vegas's Aladdin Hotel. He had been, depending on when you asked, either spooked by a future as a milquetoast Vegas act, or inspired by the new spirit of black militancy to craft a tougher, more truthful routine. Perhaps he had been moved by the words of Groucho Marx, who had cornered him at a party and asked him: "So, how do you want to end up? Have you thought about that? Do you want a career you're proud of? Or do you want to end up a spitting wad like Jerry Lewis?"

Either way, Richie Pryor was gone, and Richard Pryor, after a period of recharging and contemplation in Berkeley, California, would scale ever more dazzling heights as a fearless explorer of untouched comic continents. With his live show (documented in the little-seen 1971 film *Smokin'*) and his enormously successful records, including *Craps After Hours*, *That Nigger's Crazy*, and *Bicentennial Nigger*, Pryor became the most beloved American comic of the post–Lenny Bruce era. His routine was fearless, and deeply personal, making comedy out of sexual hang-ups, unpleasant childhood memories, and the specter of unstinting American racism. Pryor's "bicentennial nigger" pays wickedly barbed tribute to two hundred years of American democracy, lavishly thanking his white oppressors: "I'm so glad y'all took me out of Dahomey . . . I'm just so pleased America is going to last."

Pryor had already been featured in small roles in other stars' vehicles, faithful courtier to Diana Ross's Billie Holiday in *Lady Sings the Blues* (1972), sidekick and comic relief to Max Julien's Goldie in *The Mack* (1973), opposite Bill Cosby and Sidney Poitier in *Uptown Saturday Night* (1974), and alongside Billy Dee Williams and James Earl Jones in the Negro League baseball fantasia *The Bingo Long Traveling All-Stars and Motor Kings* (1976). None had quite captured Pryor's ferocious, incisive wit, or his emotional honesty. The films were mediocre, but Pryor had individual moments of grace.

In *The Mack*, he inoculates the film's star against accusations of cowardice, sobbing softly to himself after an encounter with racist cops: "He a punk,

Goldie!" His Charlie Snow, in *Bingo Long*, hopes to break the major-league color barrier by posing as Cuban star Carlos Nevada, practicing his Spanish-accented English. *Car Wash* (1976) had the poet of hustlers and shit-talkers playing evangelist Daddy Rich of the Church of Divine Economic Spirituality. "There's a good place in this world for money," he tells an assembled crowd of well-wishers, "and I know where it is: right here in my pocket!" Pryor's cameo in *Uptown Saturday Night* as private detective Sharp Eye Washington is the best of these brief appearances. Frazzled, drenched in sweat, his eye twitching uncontrollably, he is the private eye as paranoid con man, drizzling ice-cold water on all of Hollywood's Philip Marlowe fantasies: "I ain't had a woman in *how long*? MONTHS!"

The unbridled fury of Pryor's stand-up act had been channeled into brief bursts of genial silliness onscreen, as if his appeal still consisted of well-rendered impressions and little more. *Silver Streak* would change that. Directed by Arthur Hiller (who would later work with Pryor again, on *See No Evil, Hear No Evil*), *Silver Streak* is wrenched sideways by Pryor's entrance approximately one hour into the film. Prior to his arrival, it is a vaguely comic mystery-thriller in *Murder on the Orient Express* mode, with Wilder as book publisher George Caldwell, distracted from the prospect of a romantic encounter with Jill Clayburgh by the sight of a dead body hanging outside the window of his train compartment.

Pryor's Grover Muldoon, a petty criminal who pops up from the backseat of the police cruiser Wilder has stolen, is the return of the American film's repressed, offering an encyclopedic knowledge of its casual cruelties, and turning them around to work in his favor. Grover offers to disguise George as a stereotypical jive-talking black man to escape the notice of the police at a train station. Equipping him with a shoeshine man's knit cap and portable radio, Grover grabs a can of shoe polish and slaps it on George's face. "I can't pass for black," George petulantly notes, giving Grover the opportunity to slip in a subtle dig at Hollywood tradition: "Al Jolson made a million bucks looking like that."

Instructing George in the ways of blackness, Pryor takes control of the film. Grover keeps returning, even after we expect to have seen the last of him—even after he has made his good-byes, at some length, to the film's other characters. He shows up as the unexpected replacement for the train's waiter, shuffling into the compartment of the film's chief conspirator and taking his breakfast orders. "We aims to please," says Grover, summoning up the memories of hundreds of similarly servile Hollywood servants. No sooner are they recalled than they are dismissed, as Grover pulls a pistol on him and tells him he will "beat the white off yo' ass."

As a master manipulator (one can see the roots of Eddie Murphy's whip-smart con men from *48 Hrs.* and *Beverly Hills Cop* here), Pryor manipulates the well-established expectations of American society against itself. Having played both the faithful servant and the militant, Grover is once more the lily-livered steward, summoning the ghost of cowardly Stepin Fetchit. Pryor uses American film's checkered past jujitsu-style, confident that its history can be not only a shame but also a weapon. "This has been a nerve-shattering 'sperience for me, sir," he tells a police officer. That "'sperience" alone is proof enough of Pryor's politically charged genius; he has chewed up six decades of racist Hollywood depictions of fawning blacks, and spit them out, disgusted by the taste of submission. In Pryor's hands, the old stereotypes take on new, surprising force; no longer hateful, they are now a cudgel to be wielded, and a lesson to be taught. Watching Pryor, we see a dazzlingly gifted performer simultaneously playing and subverting the convention of the frightened Negro. Lying motionless on the ground after a shootout, Pryor is shaken by Wilder: "Are you all right?" He pauses for two beats, then opens his eyes: "Is it over?"

The trouble had only just begun, with Pryor the menial agricultural laborer turned hotshot executive in the seriocomic *Which Way Is Up?* (1977). Among its other queries, Michael Schultz's film seemed to be confused about its emphasis: was it a knockabout sex comedy, or a scathing satire of the black bourgeoisie? The movie was schizophrenically chaotic, half *The Jerk* and half—well, half Pryor's next film, *Blue Collar.* Both *Which Way* and *Blue Collar* reflected, if only obliquely, Pryor's own fears of being co-opted, of *becoming* the Man.

Pryor's lanky, cranky Zeke Brown in Paul Schrader's union noir *Blue Collar* (1978) is an assembly-line drone, building Checker cabs one bolt at a time. He is that rarest of Hollywood commodities—an honest-to-goodness working man, whose job is neither elided nor ignored. "It took me three years to pay for that motherfucker," Zeke grumbles at his wife, when she suggests they turn off a particularly dumb TV program. "We gonna watch everything they show on there. All the shit they show. And even the snow when the motherfucker go off—I'm gonna sit here and watch that." The wheels of Schrader's infernal machine, which begins as a jocular comedy and winds up a cracked, barren landscape of broken promises and squandered hopes, grind with relentless precision, but their noise is masked by the easy, unforced jesting of Pryor and his friends (played by Yaphet Kotto and Harvey Keitel) and the audience's familiarity with the star—then at the peak of his notoriety as a stand-up comedian. If Richard Pryor is in the movie, it must be a comedy—right?

Featured opposite his onetime hero Cosby in the Neil Simon adaptation *California Suite* (1978), Pryor is a vacationing Chicago physician whose dream trip to Los Angeles is spoiled by his impossible brother-in-law. A barely repressed fury smolders beneath Pryor's exaggerated calm. Each line is delivered with an icy cool that does little to mask his paralyzing anger. Wrestling on slippery hotel floors, engaging in a tennis grudge match to the death, Pryor and Cosby provide the slapstick energy for this talky comedy of manners. Perhaps Pryor was not merely following a script, but wrestling his own past incarnation—the imitation product he once dubbed "Richard Cosby."

It's hard to hear Richard Pryor these days. I don't mean because he passed away in 2005, although that undoubtedly complicates matters. I mean that Pryor rocked American comedy so thoroughly, remade it so thoroughly in his own image, that everything sounds like Pryor now. Racial humor? X-rated sex jokes? Liberal use of the word "nigger"? Check, check, and check. Pryor marked the return of comedy's repressed, in more ways than one—racially charged, unabashedly raunchy, and anything but family friendly. Pryor is the very performer the studio bosses had been afraid of when they locked his predecessors into shuffling, menial roles.

Pryor is so influential, that listening to him now—watching a performance film like *Richard Pryor: Live in Concert*, from 1979—is almost deflating (it all sounds so familiar!) until you remember that Pryor invented the entire shtick—from scratch. Instead, what stands out today when watching Pryor—whether in concert, or as an actor—is his tenderness, and his willingness to get deeply, embarrassingly personal.

"I don't wanna never see no more police in my life!" Pryor exclaims toward the beginning of *Live in Concert*, referencing a recent arrest. Pryor is the jester capable of tearing a giant gash in others, but preferring to jab at himself. He is the weenie, the coward, the merely competent sex machine: "I do about (lengthy pause) . . . three minutes of serious fucking. Then I need eight hours of sleep—and a bowl of Wheaties. . . . If you finish fucking, and your woman wants to talk about computer components, you've got some more fucking to do." Having already suffered a heart attack, Pryor is agonizingly conscious of death. "I'd like to die like my father died," he says of his father's post-coital shuffling off this mortal coil. "My father came and went at the same time." Turned inward, Pryor routines gesture at the deeply personal specifics of his own life. Tragedy is transformed into comedy, without losing sight of the surprising frailty of Pryor's persona.

Pryor's only superpower is his ferocious attention; under his gaze, no truth can go hidden for long. Pryor is nothing short of brilliant when dissecting the always-fraught complexities of race in America. Never quite so angry as billed, Pryor is amused by inequity, even as he is frazzled by it. Pryor's laugh sounds like nothing quite so much as a sob, and that unique yowl (a lob? a saugh?) is the perfect sound effect for *Live in Concert*, which prefers to chuckle at those things it deplores the most. The separation between black and white is one he imagines extending even beyond the grave. Seeing white doctors and nurses surrounding him after his heart attack, Pryor despairs of eternity: "I done died and wound up in the wrong motherfucking Heaven. Now I gotta listen to Lawrence Welk the rest of my days."

Before the Sidney Poitier–directed film breaks down by the side of the road, *Stir Crazy* (1980), which reunites the stars of *Silver Streak*, features some marvelous Pryor moments. Playing against type, Pryor is cast as the sensible one, and Wilder as the space cadet unaccountably thriving in the hostile world of maximum-security prison. A substantial part of *Stir Crazy*'s appeal is the friendship between Pryor and Wilder, which transcends both race and class. Wilder is the middle-class aesthete dimly aware of the harsh world outside his privileged cocoon, and Pryor the blue-collar hustler only too familiar with the aesthetics of the raw deal.

Given a script of only marginal wit, Pryor injects his own brand of physical comedy. Making his first appearance in prison, Pryor does a head-bopping, shoulder-rolling pimp strut all the funnier for its braggadocio-fueled ineptitude. Wilder, attempting the same, looks like he is rocking out to Creedence Clearwater Revival while simultaneously executing a series of fumbling karate chops.

Pryor's stand-up provided a blueprint for a nearly limitless array of visceral, personal, vividly funny films that would emerge organically from the comedian's persona. With the exception of the autobiographical *Jo Jo Dancer, Your Life is Calling*, however, none of these films would ever be made; the likes of *Richard Pryor Meets Muhammad Ali* would have to remain a figment of Pryor fans' imaginations.

Unfortunately, the movies he made remained depressingly familiar. Hollywood preferred taming the beast to letting him loose. There could be no question of a true Richard Pryor film, a fictional equivalent to *Live in Concert*; instead, like a once-fierce predator stripped of teeth and claws—or the ghost of Stepin Fetchit, reborn for the age of Reagan—Pryor was exhibited for our polite amusement.

The comedian was relegated (and relegated himself) to mannered dreck like *Bustin' Loose* (1981) and *The Toy* (1982). In *Bustin' Loose*, Pryor is a two-bit hustler out on parole, ordered by his parole officer to transport a busload of problem children from Philadelphia to Seattle. Pryor is in full-on heart-warming mode, his recidivist's fury tempered by the encounter with children far more troubled than him. Unfortunately, *Bustin' Loose* is at its most brilliant in its atmospherics; the film perfectly recreates the sensation of being trapped on a cramped school bus with some of the most unpleasant children on God's green earth. Pryor is once again channeling Cosby, this time with some tough-love racial uplift, years before *The Cosby Show* would hit the airwaves, but without the pleasurable buzz of that long-running television series' gently piercing insight.

Pryor is literally a consumer object in *The Toy*, purchased by magnate Jackie Gleason to entertain his spoiled son. The film gestures at social awareness, but for all its halfhearted attempts at racial sensitivity, and references to the legacy of slavery, *The Toy* is nothing short of appalling—a reminder of how Hollywood, with the best of intentions, could pervert Pryor's legacy. This mixed-up farce and social treatise had accidentally pegged Pryor's problem; he was being boxed and sold in the market, his own voice stifled in the rush to lucre.

Cosby had won America over with his calm, incisive wit; whatever the situation, we knew he would be unruffled. Pryor had never offered such reassuring bromides. He was a walking contradiction, a self-defined work in progress. His ambition, and his fragility, were a matter of public record. "Just needed a little water to relax," he tells the crowd for *Richard Pryor: Live on the Sunset Strip* (1982), pushing his hands down forcefully. "Calm down. Cause I feel the tension from y'all. Y'all want me to do *so* well, I want to do so well for you, but let's relax and enjoy *whatever* the fuck happens." The tension is the standard one faced by any stand-up performer, but it also stems from the elephant in the room: will he or won't he talk about it?

In June 1980, Pryor had set himself ablaze while under the influence of drugs. Initially described as an accident, in which he had caught flame while attempting to freebase cocaine, Pryor would later characterize the incident as a suicide attempt. In *Live on the Sunset Strip* (which he later said he filmed while high on cocaine), Pryor takes the opportunity to finally wrestle, in public, with his demons. "Yeah, I been burnt the fuck up!" he shouts, like a long-held breath finally released. Pryor asks the crowd if they want to hear the true story of what happened on that fateful day. Mocking their credulity, Pryor proceeds to spin a tale of settling in for his nightly snack of milk (low-fat, of course) and cookies. "And I dipped my cookie in, the shit blew up. I mean, the damnedest thing I ever heard in my life!"

Not one to hedge when the truth beckons, Pryor keeps circling back to his accident. He recounts the proofs of his having hit rock bottom: being turned away by drug dealers, attempting to smoke a piece of log in the hopes of getting high. His routine is the lament of the soul formerly in agony; every laugh here is one of bitter, cruel experience. "When that fire hits yo' ass, that will sober yo' ass up quick!" he enthuses. "Fire is *inspirational*. They should use it in the Olympics, cause I did the one-hundred-yard dash in 4.3!" If someone is going to transform his tragedy into comedy, Pryor prefers that it be him; under his expert eye, the fan seeking an autograph as smoke still rises from his burnt body, and the silent pantomime of excruciating pain as a nurse bathes his scarred chest, are fair game. "What's that?" he asks the crowd, his fingers gaily dancing through the air, a lit match gripped between thumb and forefinger. "Richard Pryor running down the street." Good night, folks—make sure to try the chicken a la king. . . .

All disguises had been removed from Pryor's routine, all masks stripped away, and audiences were left with the unsettling feeling of encountering a lone, frail individual onstage, literally and metaphorically scarred. The jokes were funny, but they also *hurt*.

Pain, and a bruised optimism, were the mark of Pryor's final concert film, *Richard Pryor: Here and Now* (1983). Here was a potent oxymoron: a comedy with almost no jokes in it. Pryor spars with a raucous crowd, raves about his time in Africa, and issues a tentative status report: "I haven't done any drugs now—it's been seven months." Pryor impersonates a junkie, seeking his fix and nodding off, and the crowd hoots appreciatively, but the moment is a terribly sad one. Comedy and pathos coil together like twin snakes, with Pryor himself the still-living symbol of the humor to be found in bleakness—the water-squirting rose that grew from concrete.

None of this—neither the pain nor the comedy—was reflected in Pryor's mainstream work. Cast opposite Christopher Reeve's Superman in the third installation of that superhero series, Pryor is an unemployed wastrel who finds his raison d'etre in computer-assisted embezzlement. Timid, stuttering, prone to fits of nervous laughter, Pryor was the stereotypical clueless Negro of yore, revived. Flying alongside Superman late in the film, Pryor channels the frightened servants of yore he had once mocked in *Silver Streak* with nary an iota of self-consciousness. For his ritual humiliation, Pryor was granted one sterling moment of comic inventiveness. Addressing the citizens of a hard-scrabble mining town in his Patton-esque military uniform, Pryor brilliantly, fleetingly channels *Dr. Strangelove*'s General Buck Turgidson: "We *cannot* afford a chemical plastics GAP!"

Brewster's Millions (1985) is better, if only marginally so, for giving Pryor the opportunity to exhibit his trademark coked-up exuberance. Pryor is a struggling minor-league baseball player who comes into a strange inheritance: he stands to gain three hundred million dollars if he can manage to spend thirty million dollars in thirty days without acquiring anything. Pryor and best buddy John Candy let loose their urge to spend, and the entirety of *Brewster's Millions* is like a feature-length version of a Rodeo Drive–Fifth Avenue shopping montage from some other movie. Occasionally awaking from the film's somnolent slumber, Pryor mocks the world of privilege to which he has accidentally, temporarily been admitted. "This is a business!" he shouts at his underlings, as if in imitation of the Wall Street moguls he may have glimpsed on television. "And we're in the business of being in business. And we're doing business. And nobody's business. Do it. Good. Business." The corrosive brilliance of Pryor's wit emerges, if only for the briefest of moments.

The contrast between the fierce honesty of Pryor's stand-up and the milque-toast insincerity of his acting roles was enormous, and unavoidable. Working in tandem with his longtime collaborator Paul Mooney (who had assisted in the writing of *Live in Concert* and *Live on the Sunset Strip*), Pryor sought to take matters in his own hands, transforming the raw material of his routine into a bittersweet comic biopic. The resulting film, *Jo Jo Dancer, Your Life Is Calling* (1986), was primal therapy, exorcising demons by exposing them to the light.

Pryor's doppelganger Jo Jo hangs between life and death in a hospital as his alter ego (also played by Pryor) offers a guided tour of his misbegotten life, whorehouse childhood and freebasing accident included. "I can't change anything," he tells himself, "but I can take you back through it so you can look at it." Jo Jo is a warts-and-all version of Pryor, cruel, prickly, and crippled by doubt. There is not much to laugh at in *Jo Jo Dancer*—purposefully so. Pryor the master alchemist had turned the unbearably harsh details of his own life into comedy, but with *Jo Jo Dancer* he could bear it no longer, and his self-made biopic is often searingly painful to watch.

Jo Jo's alter ego goes back to his childhood to visit his mother, interrupting her during a primal scene of sorts with a visiting john. Later, his father boots him out of the house for daring to dream of a career in show business: "This boy ain't shit, and his mama wasn't shit." Fame and fortune do little to erase the hurt of these astonishingly raw moments. Life is still cruel, unpredictable, and unbearably lonely, and comedy the process of translating these deflating moments into language, and thereby easing their sting. *Jo Jo Dancer* ends with a single freeze frame, Pryor basking in the glow of a crowd's roar of approval, his arms raised in triumph. It is the mixed achievement of this flawed but admirable film that at that moment, we taste the ashes more than the glory.

The remaining years would see a waning of Pryor's powers. Hoping to rejuvenate some of his lost box-office magic, Pryor reunited with Gene Wilder for two more films: *See No Evil, Hear No Evil* (1989) and *Another You* (1991). Pryor had already been diagnosed with multiple sclerosis, and these films offer copious, if inadvertent, documentary evidence of the infirmity that would render him a shell of his former self.

Neither of those Wilder collaborations were appropriate farewells for Richard Pryor, so let's end instead with two others. For his directorial debut, *Harlem Nights* (1989), Eddie Murphy cast Pryor as his mentor and surrogate father—a fitting role for the comic, who, more than anyone else, had influenced Murphy's work, and the work of an entire generation of younger comedians. Pryor's genial Sugar Ray is the ideal foil to Murphy's hotheaded Quick, quick with a joke and preferring to deflect the anger of others rather than attack it head-on. He is granted one beautiful moment, shaking his protégé by the shoulders and asking him to consider his legacy, his advice as much Pryor's as his character's: "What they gonna put on your tombstone? Here lies a man, twenty-seven years old. He died, but he ain't no punk?" For so long the figure of infinite jest, Richard Pryor is granted the opportunity to offer some of his own hard-fought wisdom. There was just enough to hint at the great roles he might have played, had he been given the chance.

We conclude with a performance that is not quite a performance, by an actor who is and is not Richard Pryor. The film is *Lost Highway* (1997)—the last he would ever make—and the disease that had been partially visible a few years prior was now inescapable. In his brilliant essay "David Lynch Keeps His Head," on the making of the film, David Foster Wallace described Pryor's presence as another of the mind games about identity that define Lynch's obsessively fixated puzzle-box mystery about the mutability of personality:

"Richard Pryor's infirmity is meant to be grotesque and to jar against all our old memories of the 'real' Pryor. Pryor's scenes are the part of *Lost Highway* where I like David Lynch least: Pryor's painful to watch, and not painful in a good way . . . and yet at the same time Pryor's symbolically perfect in this movie, in a way: the dissonance between the palsied husk on-screen and the vibrant man in our memory means that what we see in *Lost Highway* both is and is not the 'real' Richard Pryor." Pryor would die of the disease in December of 2005, lauded as a comic legend, but in *Lost Highway*, he is a liminal figure already, neither present nor absent, not dead, but not entirely alive, either—at least not in the way we once knew him. Like those predecessors he always carried with him, Pryor had become a ghost, haunting his own films.

22

ALBERT BROOKS

THE RETURN OF
SULLY SULLIVAN

"Why'd I pick reality? Why did I pick that, out of all the subjects?
I don't know anything about it!" —Albert Brooks, *Real Life*

A man sits alone in his apartment. *Sits* is perhaps not the optimal word;
he bounces off the walls, a product of the two Quaaludes he took and
the breakup he just initiated with his longtime, long-suffering girlfriend.
He lies down on his bed. "I can't sleep!" he wails, having closed his eyes for
approximately ten seconds. Wobbly, crashing into doors and furniture, he
flips through the vinyl albums on his bookshelf. "God, I have so many great
albums. . . . I love 'em, I love 'em!" He decides on the cheeseball-disco anthem

269

"A Fifth of Beethoven," flailing wildly before yanking the disc off the stereo, whining: "I don't like this song, it makes me sad." He riffles the entries in his Rolodex, intoning the phrase "Look how many friends I have" as if it were an incantation, protection against the onset of melancholy, or worse, boredom. Stopping at one entry, he picks up the telephone. "I have deep feelings for you," he tells Ellen, whose name had looked vaguely familiar. He offers to take her out on a date. "You're going to have the best time you ever had," he croons into the receiver. "And Ellen, this could be serious!" The man hangs up the telephone.

Blinkered optimists and monsters of emotionally needy narcissism, the heroes of Albert Brooks's movies are all brothers. The scene described above takes place near the start of Brooks's 1981 *Modern Romance*, but with only minor changes could be cut and pasted into any one of his films. Brooks's movies are all about different topics—moviemaking, relationships, the rat race, families—but they are all very much about the same character, one whom we'll call, for lack of a better appellation, Albert Brooks. Whether or not the actual Albert Brooks is himself an emotionally crippled, self-obsessed egotist is not up for discussion here; for the sake of friends and family members, one can hope he is caring, self-sacrificing, and given to adopting stray puppies. What is clear, though, beyond a shadow of a doubt, is that "Albert Brooks" is all of those things and more, and the films which Brooks has directed—*Real Life*, *Modern Romance*, *Lost in America*, and a handful of others—are separate entries in a single epic satire of yuppie ambition, confusion, and self-absorption.

Like Woody Allen, with whom he is often compared, Albert Brooks's films document a single milieu with obsessive rigor. For Brooks, it is the monied classes of West Los Angeles who are his kinfolk. Also like Allen, Brooks is given to playing variations on a single character—one who bears at least a surface resemblance to the man himself. Unlike Woody, Brooks prefers hitting the road to staying at home, and many of his films break out of L.A. in search of the world at large. Pity, then, that our guide remains stuck at home; you can take the yuppie out of Los Angeles, but you can't take Los Angeles out of the yuppie. Wherever Brooks's characters go, there they are; be it the Bay Area, New Delhi, or the afterlife, the miasma of L.A. ambition, entitlement, and selfishness trails behind like a noxious perfume.

His movies are also all failed experiments. Not for the filmmaker—considering the cohesion of his work, we can only assume that Albert Brooks has accomplished precisely what he had hoped to—but for his characters, who all set out in search of something they are too self-absorbed to find.

Brooks is not much of a technician—no one would ever mistake him for Allen as a director—but the blandness of his filmmaking technique only serves to belie the unity, simplicity, rigor, and pitilessness of his films. To watch an Albert Brooks film is to be a helpless onlooker to the utter degradation of a human soul. The joke is that only we, the audience, appear to be aware of that fact.

Imagine being young, curly-haired, and Jewish, attending Beverly Hills High School in the 1960s, and saddled with the name Albert Einstein. In addition to a thick skin, and a talent for fisticuffs, you might think about developing a robust sense of humor. You might figure that your bloodline carries a healthy dose of comic boisterousness—who else would give their kid that name?

For young Albert Einstein, comedy was in the blood, and in the air. His father, Harry Einstein, was a radio comic of some note, best known for his appearances on Eddie Cantor's radio show. His friends were from even more distinguished pedigrees; Rob Reiner (son of Carl) was a classmate, as was Joey Bishop's son Larry. Albert used to visit Reiner's house and entertain his father with new bits, like the one where he played Harry Houdini flustered by a screen door and unable to get in the house. Carl would usually end these bits laughing so hard he was crying; when during a *Tonight Show* appearance, Johnny Carson asked him who the funniest performers he'd ever seen were, he probably was only slightly exaggerating when he mentioned his son's sixteen-year-old friend.

Growing up in a showbiz family, among the glittering lights of Hollywood comedy, it was only natural that young Albert's routines would be a sort of meta-comedy, laughing at the absurdities of entertainment gone awry. Most of his early shtick was about bad performers, unaware of the ineptitude of their own routines. In "Danny and Dave," a ventriloquist visibly moved his lips while his dummy "spoke." The routine culminated in a deliriously odd bit—inverting a hoary ventriloquist's stereotype—by having Albert sing while the dummy drank a glass of water.

Other bits of business similarly reflected an interest in bringing back the bad old days of the long-vanished music hall, or variety show—the untalented ventriloquists, the incompetent mentalists, the mediocre mimes—in order to mock them for their cliched predictability. As Richard Zoglin says of Brooks's early career, "the joke was how bad the jokes were." Using a medium to poke fun at itself—pitilessly dismantling the foundations of the very building he worked out of—such was Brooks's goal as a stand-up comedian, and little changed in his transition to feature filmmaking.

Brooks essentially skipped the three-shows-a-night club phase of his career, graduating directly from amateur endeavors to television. Getting his first break on Dean Martin's variety show in 1965, Brooks was soon making regular appearances on *The Tonight Show*, where he announced a going-out-of-business sale of bargain-basement Albert Brooks routines, which he would personally deliver in the purchaser's home. On another occasion, he smashed an egg on his head and doused himself in whipped cream to offer an example of the lowest-common-denominator work he would never stoop to, all the while crying, "This isn't me!"

Brooks was preternaturally calm on television, but live performance was another matter entirely. One abortive live gig in Boston demonstrated incontrovertibly that all the nerves and shakiness Brooks so successfully tamped down for the small screen burst out when confronted with a live, paying crowd.

Television was more to his liking, and his performances there were joined in short order by comedy albums—*Comedy Minus One* and *A Star Is Bought*—and a series of appearances on a fledgling NBC show called *Saturday Night Live*. Brooks was the first person hired for *SNL*, brought in by Lorne Michaels to contribute short films that would alternate with the show's live material. He was given fifty thousand dollars to shoot six three-to-five-minute shorts, only to turn in a thirteen-minute segment called "Open-Heart Surgery" for the debut episode in October 1975. Brooks's films routinely ran long, and he refused all of Michaels's entreaties to cut them down. *Saturday Night Live* soon proved itself capable of functioning without Brooks's semi-independent operation, and his shorts were rapidly discontinued.

Having graduated from his *SNL* apprenticeship to feature filmmaking with 1979's *Real Life*, Brooks brought along his proclivity for self-referential meta-comedy. Instead of lampooning bad showbiz acts of yore, though, he had moved on to biting the hand of his newfound medium. Brooks was inspired by the groundbreaking 1972 PBS reality series *An American Family*, which had been the first television program to depict the mundane lives of everyday Americans. Brooks had once deflated the pretensions of mediocre comedians; now, expanding his purview to take in the film industry, he sought to pierce the pretensions of Hollywood's self-congratulation factory.

Albert Brooks—pardon me, "Albert Brooks"—is an entertainer craving something deeper, and his craving has pointed him in a new direction: real life. Like that other imaginary big-screen director, "Sully" Sullivan of Preston Sturges's *Sullivan's Travels*, "Albert" is searching for something beyond comedy—something lasting—and thinks he's found it. Borrowing from the premise of *An American Family*, Albert and his crew are going to document a year in the life of an average family: the Yeagers of Phoenix, Arizona. Trouble is, reality interferes with Albert's well-manicured showroom display of American life. Relationships go sour, cameras create, rather than reflect, reality, and the showbiz-bred director insists on injecting Hollywood pizzazz into whitebread, middle-class America.

With his debut film, Brooks was not only parodying himself—his "Albert Brooks" is delusional, self-obsessed, manically predisposed to entertain, and incapable of comprehending anything beyond the purview of show business—but, like Sturges, the comedian's inaptitude for the complexities of real life. *Real Life*, like *Sullivan's Travels*, is categorical proof of the inability of comedy and reality to coexist—while at the same time smuggling in copious amounts of that very same reality.

Like the Brooks heroes that would follow, "Albert" is a gifted dreamer whose grandiose schemes never quite pan out. Decked out in a brown and tan Western-style shirt and red cravat for his suburban-Phoenix crowd, backed up by the *Merv Griffin Show* band, Albert has blown into town to drum up excitement for his forthcoming reality film: "Hope you like the expensive buffet—two grand!" he shouts, two fingers held in the air to emphasize his point. (There is a bit of Jerry Lewis to Albert: the tireless intensity, the unblinking zaniness, the utter cluelessness.) With a team of scientists onboard, Albert is searching for the average American family, hoping to capture something of their lives onscreen. Questionnaires are filled out, computer-imaging tests are run to determine big-screen viability, and driving tests are proffered— "We wanted to make sure our family wasn't going to kill us." Exuberant and just a little unhinged, Albert is envisioning not just an Oscar but a Nobel Prize for his efforts on behalf of mankind.

"Be yourselves!" Albert shouts over and over again at the Yeagers, but his sense of reality has been warped by Hollywood. A limousine is dispatched to the airport to fetch the Yeagers from their vacation, and a huge crew, most of whom will have nothing to do with the production of the film, is introduced to the family for the sake of keeping up appearances. Warren Yeager (Charles Grodin) insists on serving as an impromptu assistant director, coaching his family through dinner and hamming it up for the cameras. Meanwhile, his wife Jeannette (Frances Lee McCain) is having a nervous breakdown prompted by the presence of the crew. Jeannette turns to Albert for guidance, wanting to leave her husband and hoping to seduce a Hollywood star to boot, but Albert is not entirely sympathetic. When she cries, Albert offers some halfhearted air-pats of her back; when she murmurs, "I think that I need to be alone now," he asks, "Can we come with you?"

Albert keeps promising to stop intruding and let nature take its course, but his showman's instincts demand more excitement than reality can provide. Disappointed at the dour footage of a family in crisis they have shot, Albert dons a clown costume, makes an unannounced appearance at the Yeager home, and asks them to stop "clamming up." "You're getting a false reality here," one of his scientific advisers informs him, but Albert is far more concerned with another doctor's comment that he looked a bit chubby onscreen. For Albert, the tragedy is what he has lost; everyone else is merely a supporting actor in his picture.

Albert, like Sully, comes to a realization after his failed experiment with reality. Sully embraces comedy as the last refuge of the downtrodden—the sole pleasure granted the voiceless. Albert, directly responsible for the calamitous meltdown of his project, lashes out, blaming the audience for preferring to avoid reality. "The studio is right," he wails. "The audience loves fake. They crave fake!" Seeking to provide the audience with the big thrill it apparently desires, Albert plans his own version of *Star Wars'* exploding planet, or *Jaws'* murderous shark. Throwing on his clown suit once more, Albert sets fire to the Yeagers' house, then heroically dashes into the flames to rescue—the cameraman. "This is a million times better than a big fish!" he exults.

Brooks was called Robert Cole in his next film, *Modern Romance* (1981), and was a film editor, not a director, but otherwise little had changed. The narcissism and self-absorption had been preserved untouched, with the focus shifting from crafting a film to crafting a line of patter to win a woman's affections. Robert breaks up with his longtime, on-again-off-again girlfriend Mary (played by Brooks's then-girlfriend, Kathryn Harrold), and then immediately regrets it. The Quaalude-fueled interlude is only the beginning of Robert's self-serving effort to simultaneously get over Mary and win her back. Robert is inordinately painful to watch, and Brooks derives a great deal of pleasure from watching us squirm. It is uncomfortable to see someone so uncomprehending of anyone other than himself, and so insistent on the supremacy of his own emotions. "I can't work now," he tells his assistant editor Jay (Bruno Kirby). "I'm a mess!" The joke is that Robert looks utterly unflappable, here and everywhere else in the film. His theoretical trauma hardly appears to touch him, which is why he must insist, in ever-louder tones, on the sincerity of his emotion.

Robert is utterly focused on winning back Mary, even though he has no conception of how to do so or why, exactly, he wants her back. Brooks's character is a manipulative, neurotic twerp with a tendency to shade the truth in his favor; one can be sure that Ben Stiller has carefully studied every Brooks move for his own discomfort-inducing pictures. No stumbling block can be allowed to stand in the pursuit of his goal of reclaiming Mary.

Mary, too, is finally just an impediment to Robert's pursuit of the greatest love of all: self-love. "There's something wrong with you," she bluntly tells him. "No, there isn't," he crisply responds, pulling out the sharpest arrow in his arsenal. "I'm in love." "It's over," Mary informs him. "Marry me," Robert responds, as if he were permanently hard of hearing—or utterly disinterested in what Mary has to say. More amazingly, Mary agrees. They go on to live happily ever after—at least until they get divorced. Presently, the closing crawl informs us, they are dating once more, with plans to remarry.

Brooks inverts another staple of American cinema and television with *Lost in America* (1985). That late 1960s classic of rebel culture, *Easy Rider*, is turned inside out for the go-go 1980s, becoming a parable of easily tempered yuppie rebellion. Brooks is David Howard, an L.A. advertising executive cruelly denied a promised promotion, and offered a transfer to New York. Distraught at the collapse of his ambitions—he'd picked out the new Mercedes and everything! —David manically bursts into his wife Linda's office, shouting at her to follow suit: "Quit right now!" Already dissatisfied with her too-comfortable middle-class existence ("I don't like my life, I don't like my house, I don't like anything"), she agrees to leave West L.A. comfort behind for the lure of America's wide-open spaces. David and Linda (Julie Hagerty, ideally cast as a self-destructive naif) hit the open road to the strains of Steppenwolf's "Born to Be Wild," and other *Easy Rider* hand-me-downs farcically stud the film. After gambling away the couple's entire savings in a single frenzied night at a Vegas casino, Linda insists that Captain America and Billy had no such nest egg; later in the film, David bonds with a cop intent on giving him a ticket over their shared love for the counterculture motorcyclists.

David and Linda's lived homage to *Easy Rider* is not scientifically precise. Twin Harleys have been replaced by a jumbo-size RV with full kitchen, and their rebellion seems to consist primarily of David's need to begin every conversation with "I've just dropped out of society, and . . ." After a brief panic attack following the loss of their savings—"You wanna go first, or should I?" David asks when they first spot the Hoover Dam—they settle in Arizona, and look to make ends meet. Linda instantly finds a job at Der Wienerschnitzel, slinging hot dogs, but David has more trouble. The employment officer he visits has never seen *Easy Rider*—only *Easy Money*, with Rodney Dangerfield—and ends up giving him a job as a crossing guard, where boys on bicycles torment him. Spotting the very Mercedes he was going to purchase approaching his corner, an angelic choir floods the soundtrack, and David has an epiphany. It is time to go to New York, eat shit, and beg for his job back.

Brooks is mocking the very foundations of the dream factory he works in. Truth, romance, freedom—these are only products the movies sell us. David and Linda are lost in America because there is no real America to find. The crashing and burning of their ambitions do not mark a failure of nerve on Brooks's part; rather, the failure is itself the comedy.

Between films, Brooks acted for his old friend James L. Brooks (who had made an appearance in *Modern Romance*) as a gifted reporter with a yen for Holly Hunter's wunderkind producer in *Broadcast News* (1987). Brooks had acted for other directors before—he had been the sardonic political operative in Martin Scorsese's *Taxi Driver* (1976), salivating over golden-haired Cybill Shepherd, and Goldie Hawn's not-long-for-this-world husband in *Private Benjamin* (1980)—but *Broadcast News* was Brooks's first meaty role in a film not his own. Brooks does a version of his regular shtick—brainy, self-critical, Jewish—but, this not being one of his own films, the whole package is far less unappetizing than usual. Brooks's Aaron Altman is downright heroic, and his epic meltdown when given the chance to anchor the weekend news (by the end of the half-hour, he is drenched in his own sweat and only partially coherent) is tragic at the same time that it is comedically apropos. James L. Brooks made him more charming, and less odious, than he had been in his own films, and the impact of seeing himself onscreen in a likable guise may have influenced the style of his next film.

It was six years from *Lost in America* until his next directorial effort, *Defending Your Life* (1991), which moved away from the now-familiar "man plans, and God laughs" Brooks plot and toward a scenario lifted in part from Lubitsch's *Heaven Can Wait* and in part from Michael Powell and Emeric Pressburger's *The Life and Death of Colonel Blimp*. The characters have hardly changed—brittle yuppies and micro-managing stress cases—but the focus has grown softer, and the comedy less cold-blooded. Brooks is Daniel Miller, another flinty executive buying another German car—a BMW this time—when he plays chicken with a city bus, and loses. Daniel finds himself in Judgment City, a way-station of the recently deceased on their way to eternal rest, or rebirth. Judgment City is some infernal combination of Disneyland and

Los Angeles's Century City commercial district, with tram cars at the ready to transport the judged to their trials, and faceless, impersonal skyscrapers ringing the city.

Ultimately, *Defending Your Life* is less concerned with its vision of the after-life, which is sketchy at best, than with the comic opportunities it provides. A comic's onstage patter has gone from "Where ya from?" to "Howdja die?" (Daniel shreds a hack comic who asks him that by responding "Onstage, like you"), and penis envy has been replaced by the brain envy of former earthlings toward their infinitely more intelligent Judgment City helpers. Charming in parts and never less than entertaining, *Defending Your Life* is nevertheless disappointing. The gauzy look, vaguely spiritual milieu, and heartwarming finale are so unlike the Albert Brooks of *Real Life* and *Lost in America* as to make one wonder what had happened to the caustic satirist of old. "Heart-warming" and "Albert Brooks" made for strange bedfellows.

Brooks had already made use of those most starry-eyed of 1960s dreamers, Simon and Garfunkel, in *Lost in America*; their hit "America" ("They've all come to look for America") served as a comic soundtrack to David and Linda's abortive adventure. Simon and Garfunkel returned, in spirit, for *Mother* (1996), where the lyrics to their classic "Mrs. Robinson," from *The Graduate*, were altered to reflect a new kind of baby-boomer dilemma: "Here's to you, Mrs. Henderson, your grown son is moving back today. . . . He needs to know you like him coming back, please when you see him try not to attack." John Henderson (Brooks) is a middle-aged novelist of middling accomplishment coming off a second divorce and plagued by a sense of utter futility. The source of his perpetual lack of success with women, he intuits, is the fact that his mother Beatrice (Debbie Reynolds) has never truly loved him, undercutting his every accomplishment. The solution to his psychic hang-up? Leaving Los Angeles and moving back in with his mother sounds just about right.

Like his predecessors as Brooks protagonists, John has a goal: to heal the wounds inflicted by his mother through a twenty-four-hour-a-day impromptu therapy session with her, and thus render himself fit for female companionship once more. Needless to say, the plan goes awry from the start. His mother offers her yuppie son week-old salad and ice-covered generic-brand ice cream for dinner ("Where'd you get this from, the Smithsonian commissary?" John chokes); she refuses to purchase a ten-dollar bottle of jam for John at the grocery store; she is concerned that her son's moving back into his childhood room might disturb her carefully assembled collection of broken chairs.

Brooks's character is once more a shallow narcissist whose sole concern is his betterment, but here he is faced with an adversary worthy of his gifts. In her absent-minded, sweet-voiced way, Beatrice is gifted at deflating her son's ceaseless complaints about grievances past and present. "Dear, I'm tired," she responds to one particularly pointed harangue. "We can berate me tomorrow."

Like *The Graduate*'s Benjamin Braddock, John is in a relationship with an older woman, and is not ashamed to admit it. There is a sexual undercurrent to their shacking up together, and Brooks ruthlessly exposes it to the light. After being humiliated by his mother in a mall pet store (she tells the clerk about his marital problems), John proceeds to drag her into Victoria's Secret. He informs the clerk there that he would like to buy his mother a pair of crotchless panties. John attacks his brother Jeff (Rob Morrow) by assaulting him with the specter of renewed Oedipal jealousy: "I love my mother, and I love having sex with her." Intent as ever on piercing the aura of smug self-satisfaction rampant among baby boomers, Brooks takes a sledgehammer to the fragile psyches of his generational cohort. Brooks has always been comfortable with our discomfort, and *Mother* stands as undoubtedly the most awkward Mother's Day film ever made.

Mother ventured so deeply into uncomfortable, *Curb Your Enthusiasm*-esque territory that Brooks's next film, *The Muse* (1999), was downright charming in comparison. A lighthearted Hollywood farce, the film is another self-reflexive comedy about the insecurities of the creative class in the vein of *Real Life*. Brooks plays a middle-aged screenwriter whom everyone insists has lost his edge. A successful buddy clues him in to the secret of his success: a muse, paid and pampered in order to inspire creative work. Brooks hires this muse (played by Sharon Stone), and is flummoxed by the seemingly endless list of her demands: a Four Seasons suite, a deluxe mattress, a late-night Waldorf salad.

Playing the corner-cutting cheapskate once more, Brooks hopes to purchase creativity at a discount. He heads to Tiffany's to buy Stone a gift, and settles on a Tiffany's-logo keychain, distressed by the exorbitant prices for the jewelry on display. *The Muse* is an artistic midlife crisis transfigured into comedy, its sharpest darts aimed at an industry that mistakes youthfulness for freshness, and half-baked stupidity for genuine revelation.

Brooks's most recent film is a brilliant idea in search of a coherent script. A has-been comedian named Albert Brooks, reduced to buttering up director Penny Marshall (*Big*) in the hopes of winning a role, is contacted by the State

Department. They would like to send him to the Muslim world on a mission to determine precisely what makes them laugh. *Looking for Comedy in the Muslim World* (2005) has all the makings of a great joke. Its setup is wonderful, but the punch line has gone missing.

At first hesitant about the mission ("I bet he thinks he's writing to Mel Brooks," he grouses), Albert gets into the spirit of scientific discovery once he arrives in India. Promises of the Presidential Medal of Freedom also help to pump him up. After experimenting with man-on-the-street interviews and visits to laughing-yoga groups, Albert finally settles on a surefire experiment: he will headline a comedy show in New Delhi, testing out every conceivable kind of joke on his audience. Their laughter will tell him what sorts of humor play in the Muslim world, and which don't.

As might be expected, the entire plan is a colossal flop. Albert bombs onstage, offering one absurd meta-comic gag after another to an audience hardly schooled in the ways of American stand-up comics. He even trots out the old ventriloquist gag from his *Tonight Show* days, to no appreciable response. His portly, middle-aged State Department minder reproaches him knowingly after the gig: "I just remember Lenny Bruce saying, 'know your audience.'"

Brooks milks the locale for a few good jokes. Workers in an Indian call center answer the phones everywhere from the William Morris Agency to the White House. Albert kills with an Indian-flavored joke: "Why is there no Halloween in India? Because they took away the Gandhi." (Try it in front of the mirror, with a stereotypical Indian accent.) Al Jazeera's new entertainment channel offers him a starring role in a new sitcom called *That Darn Jew.* The individual bits and jokes still work fine, but Brooks's sense of the unity of each joke to the enterprise as a whole has evaporated. *Looking for Comedy in the Muslim World* is a fistful of good gags in search of a premise.

Brooks leaves jokes on the table, and *Looking for Comedy* suffers as a result. The idea of this middle-aged Jew facing the collective wrath of the Muslim world, and hoping to assuage it with a few gags about improv comedy, is hilarious. The movie itself delivers on none of its promises: there is almost no glimpse of the Muslim world, and its comedy is fitful at best. This is, admittedly, the point; Brooks has always found his humor in failure and frustration.

Brooks had never wavered in the audaciousness of his lifelong project in alienating and disorienting audiences trained to expect comedy to be soothing and simple. It would be an irony that only Albert Brooks could appreciate that his greatest success would come as the disembodied voice of a cartoon fish in a family film. *Finding Nemo* (2003) may have found an audience infinitely larger than *Lost in America*, but Marlon is recognizably an Albert Brooks character: a low-grade hysteric, overbearing and burdensome. A clown fish, Marlon has every fish in the sea convinced he's a laugh riot. Unnerved by the high expectations, he relentlessly bungles his jokes, sapping them of all humor, and all meaning. This incidence of voiceover as autobiography has a happy ending, albeit one that Brooks himself might not have written for himself. Having tracked down his missing son, and learned to ease up on the helicopter parenting, Marlon also learns how to deliver a joke: "With fronds like these, who needs anemones?" Having never met a gag he hadn't preferred to step on, Brooks would have enjoyed the irony of the source of his belated success. He had finally, at long last, gotten to the punch line.

23

STEVE MARTIN

THE JERK AND
THE GENIUS

"He *hates* these cans!" —Steve Martin, *The Jerk*

Two snapshots from a charmed life in comedy: In the first, a young man stands before an audience, a fake arrow piercing his head, strumming a banjo. In the second, a middle-aged man sits alone in a suburban living room, the stale remnants of a wedding all around him, wearily holding his head in his hands. Left with only the photographic evidence, one might struggle to connect the dots. How had *this* boy turned into *that* man? From rebellious idiocy

---

"We are the Three Amigos": Chevy Chase, Steve Martin, and Martin Short in *¡Three Amigos!*

to Everyman emotion, from jester to family man, the career of Steve Martin has followed an unexpectedly direct path toward maturity (if not always toward sophistication). With the benefit of hindsight—the plays, the books, the well-wrought albums of his banjo playing, the copious *New Yorker* casuals—evidence of Martin's cosmopolitan savoir faire is everywhere in sight. But read in chronological order, Steve Martin's life bears the capacity to surprise.

What do you call a man who leads a crowd of college students into a drained pool, "swimming" across them by being passed from hand to hand? And if that same guy took another audience to the drive-in window at a nearby McDonald's, ordering three hundred hamburgers to go before canceling his order and asking for a single bag of French fries? Would *comedian* suffice?

Like Albert Brooks and Richard Pryor, Steve Martin was a comedian intent on redefining the parameters of the form. No longer was comedy telling a good joke well; now, it could also be telling a joke poorly—or not telling a joke at all.

Originality had not been first nature to Martin. A childhood job selling programs at Disneyland, just a few miles from his home in the Orange County suburb of Garden Grove, had first exposed him to his twin early loves of magic and comedy. Watching a comedian named Wally Boag, hired to entertain the crowds, taught him about timing and delivery; hanging out with a young man named Jim Barlow at Merlin's Magic Shop, located in the amusement park, gave Martin a taste for dazzling diversions. Barlow also, presumably, taught him something about the comical uses of fraudulence and insincerity: "Can I take your money—I mean help you?" he would pleasantly ask new customers.

Graduating to performances at another amusement park and magic shows for Cub Scout troops and Kiwanis Club gatherings, Martin perfected a brief, highly polished routine, part illusionist act (a silver-ball-and-silk-scarf effect called the Zombie played an important role) and part comedian's patter. Then a bomb dropped: the hugely popular comedy records of the early and mid-1960s, by acts like Mike Nichols and Elaine May, Lenny Bruce, and Tom Lehrer. All traces of the familiar had been scraped clean by these performers, supplanted by modernist self-referentiality and improvisatory daring. Not everything was hugely funny—Bruce was often rambling, more brilliant than hysterical—but absolutely nothing was hackneyed or secondhand. Steve Martin, aspiring stand-up comedian, realized that his entire act would have to be scrapped. "Any line or idea with even a vague feeling of familiarity or provenance had to be expunged," Martin would later write of this moment.

"There could be nothing that made the audience feel they weren't seeing something utterly new."

"I laugh in life," Martin would wonder, "so why not observe what it is that makes me laugh?" Rather than emerge with a new line of observational humor ("Didja ever notice . . . ?"), Martin crafted an act that was intentionally devoid of the usual laughs. Punch lines were swapped out, replaced by non-sequiturs. Martin's act would be close kin to Albert Brooks's in its portrayal of the comedian as self-deluded narcissist. Martin was no longer a comedian, but a parody of a comedian. The jokes were so bad, they were hilarious.

For a time in the late 1970s, Steve Martin was the king of the comedians, a son of Lenny Bruce who had ascended to the throne. Appearances on *The Tonight Show* led to a regular gig hosting the brand-new sketch comedy series *Saturday Night Live*, and a pair of platinum-selling albums. Martin had caught the first episode of *SNL* on television while living in Aspen, and had immediately been struck by the sensation of having comrades-in-arms he hadn't known about. "It came on, and I thought, 'they've done it!," he told interviewer Tom Shales. "They did the zeitgeist, they did what was out there, what we all had in our heads, this kind of new comedy." *SNL* writers took umbrage at Martin's hosting the show, believing that if he could, they could as well. They were both right and wrong; Martin's was a writerly sensibility, but he was also an inordinately gifted straight man, serving as comic foil to the Not Ready for Prime Time Players. Martin's stand-up translated well for the *Saturday Night Live* aesthetic; he debuted his novelty hit "King Tut," a ridiculously catchy song about the Egyptian king, on *SNL*. Serving as one-half of the clueless, horny Czech Brothers ("two wild and crazy guys") with Dan Aykroyd, Martin's good-natured, amiable zaniness was essential to the continued success of Lorne Michaels's late-night sensation.

Playing to record-breaking audiences across the country, Martin became a superstar, but the umbilical cord connecting performer and audience had been cut. You couldn't take twenty thousand people to McDonald's after the show. Martin's movie career was born of his stand-up work. His early movies, like his stand-up, were knowing, their sophisticated mockery requiring intimate knowledge of the forms they parodied. Martin's stand-up was funny only for people who had spent a lifetime watching mediocre comedians ply their trade; his early films similarly, gleefully mocked the bromides of old Hollywood chestnuts.

Attempting to preserve the intimate allure of being in on an unexplained joke, Martin took a single line—"I was born a poor black child"—from his stand-up routine, and crafted an entire film from it. *The Jerk* (1979) was a parody of whitebread culture, to be sure, but it is also an inverted picaresque, with Martin the tragic naif whose successes are as unwarranted, and unexpected, as his failures. Martin is Navin Johnson, the sole Caucasian member of a large, boisterous African American family. Navin is the ugly white duckling ("You mean I'm gonna stay this color?" he moans woefully to his mother), unable to master clapping and stomping in rhythm to his family's gutbucket blues numbers. His idea of a perfect birthday meal is a tuna fish salad sandwich on white bread with mayonnaise, a Tab, and a fistful of Twinkies for dessert. Lawrence Welk is his Chuck Berry, "Music in a Mellow Mood" revealing a great wide world beyond his limited purview. "I've never heard music like this before!" Navin raves. "It speaks to me!"

The Jerk, directed by Carl Reiner from Martin's script, makes Martin's clear superiority to his material part of the joke; he was too good for the foolishness, and that was what was so funny about it. Navin could not merely tell Martin's jokes; he had to somehow embody them. Martin lets comedy happen around him; content to play the fool, he allows Navin to plod on, oblivious to his surroundings, as he lurches from poverty to stability to success back to poverty. In essence, Martin was playing his own straight man, his film an extension of his stand-up high-wire act.

The Jerk is a rambling adventure with a fool for a hero. No lessons are learned, and none ventured. Navin remains chipper and optimistic, whether he is living in a room adjoining a public urinal, a mansion overstuffed with bric-a-brac, or on the street. Whatever the situation, Navin can be counted on to gloriously misunderstand. "St. Louis?" a passing driver asks, as Martin stands by the side of the road, his thumb cocked. Navin looks confused: "No, Navin Johnson." Later, a crazed gunman picks Navin's name out of the phone book and begins taking potshots at him at the gas station where he works. "Whatsa matter with these cans?" Navin exclaims, as one oilcan after another bursts open. "These cans are defective!"

After turning to musical drama for the underrated *Pennies from Heaven* (1981), in which he expertly played an unemployed sheet-music seller with delusions of grandeur, Martin reteamed with Reiner, writing and starring in *Dead Men Don't Wear Plaid* (1982). *Dead Men* is an archival work, doodling in the margins of film history. Martin is a hard-boiled private detective cast, via editing wizardry, opposite Humphrey Bogart, Barbara Stanwyck, Ava Gardner, Cary Grant (they share his train compartment from the 1941 Alfred Hitchcock film *Suspicion*), and other 1940s cinematic luminaries.

Lifting well-remembered sequences from classics like *The Big Sleep*, *The Killers*, and *Double Indemnity*, *Dead Men* has Martin insert himself, *Zelig*-style, into the familiar confines of Hollywood's noir past. He is picked up by Fred MacMurray in the famous supermarket scene from *Double Indemnity*, and attends the soiree thrown by Ingrid Bergman in *Notorious*. The most self-consciously portentous of Hollywood genres, noir is deflated by Martin's ludicrous sham of respectability. In *The Jerk*, Martin had mocked cinematic form, inverting our expectations; here he is mocking the films themselves. His burlesque of private-dick conventions eats away at the subject of its lampoon until all that is left is the hollow shell.

Dead Men Don't Wear Plaid facetiously promised a sequel, soon to make its way to a theater near you. *The Man With Two Brains* (1983) was nothing of the sort, but it similarly sought to demolish the hoary conventions of another genre. As a brilliant brain surgeon with the unlikely name of Dr. Michael Hfuhruhurr, inventor of the renowned cranial screw-top method, Martin is a successor to all the cinema's previous mad scientists—think Dr. Frankenstein driving a Mercedes. There are times where *The Man with Two Brains* plays like a loose remake of Mel Brooks's *Young Frankenstein*. Brooks had mocked horror by carefully inverting expectation; Martin and Reiner tear up the script and scatter the pieces. Fellow scientist Dr. Necessiter's laboratory lair is a Transylvanian castle recreated inside a faceless condominium complex, and Dr. Hfuhruhurr (don't worry, no one in the film can pronounce it either) is less restless striver after eternal truths than sex-starved husband, driven mad by his gold-digging wife (Kathleen Turner).

Frustration drives Martin into the arms—or the cranium, I suppose I should say—of Anne, a brain preserved by Dr. Necessiter for scientific research. Martin's yen for inventive physical comedy emerges in full bloom here. Tenderly romancing a brain pickled in a jar, Martin summons a daffy emotionalism that echoes and furthers his onetime embrace of the absurd. Returning from a late-night tryst with Anne, he is taking his pants off to get into bed with his wife when she stirs. He reverses direction and pulls his pants up, pantomiming having just risen from a night's slumber. Family life was a curse and a burden; somewhere, W. C. Fields was smiling ruefully.

All of Me (1984), the last of his screenplays to be directed by Reiner, is one of Martin's funniest films, but it also touches a dramatic nerve that none of its predecessors could have—or would have.

Dead Men Don't Wear Plaid had stuck a dress on him, but *All of Me* (1984) unleashes Steve Martin's inner woman. Martin is a man playing a woman playing a man. He is attorney Roger Cobb, assigned to attend to the dying Edwina Cutwater (Lily Tomlin), a domineering heiress accustomed to getting her way in all matters large and small. Edwina plans to transfer her soul to a younger receptacle with the help of a Buddhist shaman. Through a series of supernatural mishaps, Edwina's soul is instead transferred into Roger's significantly less delectable carcass.

Martin's body is the battlefield on which a particularly bloody civil-war skirmish is being fought. His left side battles his right, his body flailing about uncertainly before a carefully worked-out truce leads to a mincing walk borrowed from Monty Python's Ministry of Silly Walks. *All of Me* pits his body's owner against its accidental tenant, and much of the gleeful good cheer of the film stems from their differing approaches to the complexities of gender. Tomlin, posing as Martin, turns on the gruff, boorish masculinity: "good point, toots," her version of Roger tells his opposing counsel in court, spitting and picking his nose for emphasis. Martin, meanwhile, futilely combats the malign influence of the schoolmarmish Edwina, who is appalled to find herself in Roger's body as he is having sex, and calls his partner "a cheap sex tramp."

With his silver hair and noble profile, Martin is a comic in a leading man's body. *All of Me* knowingly plays Martin's own exterior against his interior. How could someone so conventionally handsome so willingly make a fool of himself? Our built-in disdain toward comedy worked in Martin's favor; we are charmed by his willingness to abase himself. Like Cary Grant had, Steve Martin makes being good-looking funny.

A similar process of transformation was taking place at the level of the films. *All of Me*, marking the end of Martin's collaboration with Reiner, also brought the first phase of his career to a close. Antic underground legend no longer, Martin would become what he had only recently mocked: a mainstream movie star.

Martin cowrote *¡Three Amigos!* (1986) with *Saturday Night Live* producer Lorne Michaels and singer-songwriter Randy Newman, and starred alongside Chevy Chase and Martin Short. The threesome are silent-era stars, pampered, sissified actors given to playing swashbuckling Spanish noblemen in their films. Fired by their studio, they are summoned to the Mexican village of Santo Poco to take on the evil El Guapo and his henchman Jefe. The actors are convinced they have been hired to put on a show, in which they symbolically overcome the local tyrants. Instead, they have been hired to fight, in entirely non-symbolic fashion.

What ¡*Three Amigos!* lacks in focus, it makes up for with the enormously gratifying chemistry between its three stars, and a script that, whatever its narrative faults, is overstuffed with delirious wordplay. There are some trademark Steve Martin moments, plumbing the depths of his feeble-mindedness. "Not so fast, El Guapo, or I'll fill you so full of lead you'll be using your dick for a pencil!" he announces, putting on his most officious white-man voice. "What do you mean?" El Guapo asks puzzledly. Martin pauses, and admits the truth without sacrificing an iota of his empty-headed intensity: "I don't know." ¡*Three Amigos!* has a giddy, rollicking silliness that is catching. Neither a great movie, nor a particularly good one, ¡*Three Amigos!* is a transcendent, endlessly rewatchable mediocrity.

Martin's next starring role, from another original script, was a further step on the path from Wild and Crazy Guy to soulful romantic-comedy heartthrob. A loose adaptation of Edmond Rostand's *Cyrano de Bergerac*, *Roxanne* (1987) stars Martin as C.D., the fire chief of a small California town. Summoned to rescue the cat of summer visitor Roxanne Kowalski (Daryl Hannah), C.D. falls for her immediately but finds that she is attracted to his younger, studlier underling. Martin agrees to serve as the mouthpiece for the tongue-tied youngster, aware that his own generously proportioned proboscis is a major hindrance to his competing for Hannah.

Roxanne wrings generous gobs of comedy from the oversized promontory on Martin's face. Every physical act becomes a challenge for C.D. A glass of wine requires attempting numerous angles of approach. Martin bends his nose this way and that, unsuccessfully, before slurping it up his nose and delicately patting it dry with a napkin. A kiss is a struggle with his encumbrance, C.D. striving to wrest enough of it out of the way to expose his lips for an embrace. Noses are on everyone else's mind as well. "Maybe you'd like some wine with your nose . . . cheese!" Hannah corrects herself at their first meeting.

C.D. is a performer too smart for his audience, composing rip-roaring monologues solely for his own edification. Martin deflates a barroom bully by unspooling twenty different varieties of joke about his nose: "Keep that guy away from my cocaine!" He thrives by pointing out his flaws before anyone else has the opportunity to do the same. "Laugh, and the world laughs with you," he informs the same crowd of drinkers. "Sneeze, and it's good-bye, Seattle!" *Roxanne* is a film about Martin the stand-up comedian, but C.D.'s routines are more playfully self-promoting than Martin's stand-up had once been. The self-deprecating jerk had becoming the self-deprecating genius.

Mainstream success allowed Martin to take middle-of-the-road roles any bankable actor could have starred in. These films were inevitably more milquetoast than those he had crafted himself, smoothing out the kinks in an effort to render Martin fit for mass consumption. *Planes, Trains, and Automobiles* (1987), *Dirty Rotten Scoundrels* (1988), and *Parenthood* (1989) exemplify this blandification process, with Martin the Dadaist jester now the jesting dad.

All of which is not to say that these films are uniformly terrible, or that Martin is not wickedly charming in spurts. *Planes*, directed by John Hughes, features Martin as the straight man to John Candy's well-intentioned hellion, good-naturedly wrecking his newfound friend's life as they trek across the Midwest together. For the first time, Martin plays the guy next door, no longer the kook himself, but the put-upon husband and father. Martin is chained to his accidental companion, and no amount of politesse or clumsy callousness is enough to shed himself of his burden. This is a buddy comedy whose joke is on the protagonist. His taxi to the airport stolen, his suitcases demolished, and his sleep persistently interrupted, Martin cackles uproariously at the sight of the car Candy rented furiously ablaze. At long last, a calamity for which he bears no responsibility! He has laughed too soon; Candy put the rental on Martin's credit card.

Scoundrels has the benefit of its exuberance, pitting Martin against Michael Caine in a battle of con men. Martin is an uncouth hustler on the rise, rough where his mentor is polished, gunning for the short take rather than the long haul. Martin is as glib as ever, but he allows us to see the gears visibly shifting, clicking into place for the next scam.

The exemplar of this newfound Martin is his starring role in *Parenthood*, directed by Ron Howard. The good-natured, well-meaning yuppie dad par excellence, Martin is the emotional center of this plot-heavy comic drama about the perils of parenting. The wild-man antics metamorphose before our eyes into the stuff of children's birthday-party entertainment; witness Martin's impromptu transformation into Cowboy Dan, charming the kiddies with tall tales of killing evildoers and slipping around in their guts.

Directed by Herbert Ross, who had served him so capably in *Pennies from Heaven*, and with a script by Nora Ephron, *My Blue Heaven* (1990) felt like a return to Martin's Carl Reiner glory days. As an Italian-American mobster exiled to sunny San Diego as part of the witness protection program, Martin is a New York fish out of water, lost in bland southern California with no chance of returning home. Arugula is a foreign word here, and Italian dinners consist of macaroni and cheese with Italian dressing. With his high-waisted pants, widow's peak, and cock-of-the-walk strut, Martin's Vinnie Antonelli (now Tod Wilkinson) is a disheveled peacock making his peace with exile. It is, needless to say, a work in progress. After hearing one too many super-market clerks wish him a nice day, Vinnie explodes like a true New Yorker: "*Fuck* you!" He is a reformed criminal who never quite reforms, and by the film's conclusion, when he breaks ground on the Vincent Antonelli (aka Tod Wilkinson) Stadium for Little League baseball, stubbornness has been ele-vated to a perverse sort of comic grace.

Stepping into Spencer Tracy's shoes as the overprotective father rattled by his daughter's impending marriage in *Father of the Bride* (1991), essentially reprising his role from *Parenthood*, Martin is the prototypical Everydad for Generation X. He is given his share of slapstick physical comedy (hanging from a second-floor balcony and chased by dogs at his future in-laws' Bel Air mansion) and giveaway verbal tics ("Don't forget to fasten your condom," he tells his daughter before she goes for a drive with her fiancé), but the vigorous horseplay of the original has been sapped. Billed as a comedy, this *Father of the Bride* might be more aptly described as a male weepie, its tiny violins no less audible for being cleverly hidden behind a comedian's pratfalls. Martin is quite good, but the film is hardly worthy of his talents.

Set in the same city as *Father of the Bride*, the Martin-penned *L.A. Story* might as well have taken place in an alternative universe. The hectic farce of Martin's early screenplays gives way to a relaxed, understated brand of satire that anticipated his charmingly goofy *New Yorker* casuals.

Martin's Los Angeles is a magical-absurdist wonderland: a place where freeway signs communicate with the lovelorn, and a weatherman named Harris K. Telemacher offers a daily Toupee Report. Martin is that showman, his wacky, meteorologically unhelpful performances dogged by a nagging sense of pointlessness. Yes, L.A. is the ideal place to get a half double decaf half-caf with a twist of lemon, just the way he likes it, but isn't there, like, something more? "L.A. WANTS 2 HELP U," a freeway sign tells him, and it is no lie; Los Angeles is conspiring to grant Harris K. Telemacher a glimpse of weightless happiness.

For the uninformed visitor, the underrated 1991 film, directed by Mick Jackson, is a visual tour guide to the City of Angels, offering a glimpse of what might be expected during their stay: pumped shotguns on the freeway, the Stationary Bike Riding Park, cars driven to visit a next-door neighbor, fluttery aspiring spokesmodels named SanDeE*. Before it descends into halfhearted hotel-room farce, *L.A. Story* is a wickedly precise parody of Angeleno mores. In this homage to *La Dolce Vita*, Fellini's statue of Christ, carried over the city by helicopter, has been replaced by a giant hot dog, with no one any the wiser.

L.A. Story lovingly mocks Los Angeles, but its jesting is an insider's; this is no *Annie Hall*, and Martin is no snotty Easterner with a bone to pick. The city's idea of high culture is Harris roller-skating through the Los Angeles County Museum of Art (thank you, *Band of Outsiders!*), and its denizens are devoted to shallowness with religious devotion, but Martin and *L.A. Story* love them nonetheless.

The mid-1990s witnessed the devolution of Martin's charms into mindless lowest-common-denominator fare, as if *Father of the Bride*, and not any of his other films, had been the quintessential expression of his charm and wit. There was another turn as the lovelorn, hapless father of the bride for the 1995 sequel (this one remaking Tracy's *Father's Little Dividend*), and *Sgt. Bilko* (1996) gave Martin the opportunity to step into the shoes of another comic legend, Phil Silvers. Needless to say, the latter film, directed by Jonathan Lynn, was not quite the equal of *The Phil Silvers Show*, although Martin does appear to enjoy his time as the gleefully amoral motor-pool boss. "All I ever wanted," he plaintively notes, "was an honest week's pay for an honest day's work."

As a palate cleanser from this increasingly sophomoric drudgery, Martin occasionally gave himself over to truly adult dramatic work. David Mamet's knotty suspense film *The Spanish Prisoner* (1997), with Martin as a shadowy entrepreneur, was the best of these forays, with his humdrum good looks revealed as a cover for unexplored continents of intrigue and chicanery. Martin was an unexpectedly capable actor, and the difference between the herky-jerky flailing of his early work and the calm dignity of dramas like *The Spanish Prisoner* lent Martin a mystery that had never before been present.

Martin was the beneficiary of the mixed blessing of a box-office resurgence, redefining himself as a family-friendly eminence in *Cheaper by the Dozen* (2003), *Cheaper by the Dozen 2* (2005), and a remake of *The Pink Panther* (2006). Perhaps they are best understood as payment in kind for the more idiosyncratic comedies Martin was privileged to make on his own. Without them, Martin might have lacked the clout to make *Bowfinger*, or *Shopgirl*.

Still, not all of Martin's middle-of-the-road work was completely embarrassing. *Bringing Down the House* (2003) took its revenge on Martin's newfound array of milquetoast householders, humiliating and ultimately transforming his buttoned-up tax attorney by the arrival of Queen Latifah's jailbird. Martin was impressively malleable; watching him strut through a nightclub in hip-hop gear, complimenting a woman by telling her to "back that booty up and put it on the glass" is a master class in his refusal to allow dignity to get in the way of comedy. The charmingly messy cartoon/live-action hybrid *Looney Tunes: Back in Action* (2003) transforms Martin into a live-action version of what is essentially a cartoon character: the spastic, charmless, Dr. Evil–esque chairman of the Acme Corporation.

Martin had the dubious distinction of replacing Peter Sellers as Inspector Clouseau for a *Pink Panther* reload. Martin gives it the old college try, but even having written the new script himself, this *Pink Panther* manages to get the physical comedy all wrong: Clouseau is intended to harm everyone *except* himself. His Clouseau surprisingly manages to wring some laughs out of that tired comic cliche, the exaggerated French accent. One scene with an exasperated accent coach teaching him to order dinner like an American sees Clouseau's efforts degrade from the inept to the surreal: "Hemburgar. Em-berr-gggair. Damburder. Hamdagger. Amburder." Sellers's Clouseau had been imbued with the surreal poetry of the buffoon. Martin's is merely a moron. A sequel, even less well-regarded than the first, followed.

Through the evolution of his onscreen persona, Steve Martin had found an unlikely second wind, recreating himself as a comic icon for the pre-pubescent set. Wild and crazy no longer, Martin became instead a permanent George Banks—the eccentric, daffy dad from *Father of the Bride*. The hits were dreck, but the little films—the ones he wrote, the ones between the blockbusters—retained some of the demented genius of old. His two best films of the last decade both emerged from his own word processor, each a successor to *L.A. Story* in their bemused, sympathetic admiration of the city Martin called home.

Bowfinger (1999), directed by Frank Oz and costarring Eddie Murphy in dual roles as a paranoid superstar and his doltish brother, is Martin's barbed tribute to Hollywood excess and oafishness. Martin is a grade-Z producer ("Cash, every movie costs $2,184") who casts screen idol Kit Ramsey (Murphy) in his latest production without the star's knowledge.

Moviemaking, in *Bowfinger*'s estimation, is a series of encounters with genial lunatics: narcissistic leading ladies, stars slavishly devoted to the tenets of their thoroughly ridiculous faiths, starlets sleeping their way to the middle, illegal-immigrant crew members leafing through the latest issue of *Cahiers du Cinema*. Martin's Bobby Bowfinger is the ringleader of the buffoons, his inextinguishable optimism the spark that lights the creative fire for the cast and crew of *Chubby Rain*. *Bowfinger* generously gives Murphy the bulk of its

most obvious laughs, although Martin's scene in an elegant eatery, oblivi-
ously pretending to hammer out deals on a cellphone whose car-phone cord
still dangles from its end, is nothing short of superb.

Shopgirl (2005), based on Martin's eponymous novella, is a sequel of sorts
to *L.A. Story*, with that movie's enchanted Los Angeles returning here in bittersweet form. Directed by Anand Tucker, *Shopgirl* is a bruised-romantic's
vision of urban alienation, its bleakness tempered by a profound generosity of spirit. "What Mirabelle needs," the film's narrator (Martin) informs
us about its protagonist, "is an omniscient voice to illuminate and spotlight
her." *Shopgirl* proceeds to provide just that, selecting Claire Danes's utterly
ordinary-seeming Saks sales assistant and ennobling her with its attentions.

The film marks a new elegance in Martin's work. Underlit and understated,
Shopgirl uses music as its repository of emotion, expressing what the dialogue
leaves unspoken. Martin's Ray is a well-heeled entrepreneur looking for companionship and little more. He and Mirabelle are two loners adrift in L.A.,
latching onto each other out of a shared desire to ease their solitude. Ray can
offer his financial bounteousness; Mirabelle, her emotional generosity. Ray
is fatherly toward Mirabelle, taking an interest in her future and buying her
thoughtful gifts. The money is easy for him, but the emotion is more difficult.
He has purchased a three-bedroom apartment in New York, he thoughtlessly
tells Mirabelle, "in case I meet someone and have kids."

Martin's writerly largesse means that *Shopgirl*'s appeal is to be found more
in its settings that in Ray himself. *Shopgirl* is a comedy mostly without punch
lines, preferring its whimsical-mystical metropolis, and Martin's self-aware,
writerly narration, to making another Steve Martin comedy. If *L.A. Story*
was Los Angeles's *La Dolce Vita*, then *Shopgirl* was its *La Notte*, with Martin
providing a provisionally happy ending to its minor-key tragedy of urban
anomie.

We are now confronted, then, with a third photograph for our thought
experiment, one that contains only a washed-out image of Steve Martin,
smudged and blurry. The conundrum had once been how to write Steve
Martin—all-knowing boy wonder of modernist comedy—into films without
spoiling his appeal. That challenge met, Martin sought to make himself over
into a no-frills movie star—the kind who might mope over his daughter's
wedding. And now, for a third act, Steve Martin was triumphing by writing
himself out of his own movies. Martin was still present, to be sure; but the
hectic amusements of yore had given way, in their time, to grown-up comedies that depended on the contents of his head, and not the arrow piercing it.

24

EDDIE MURPHY

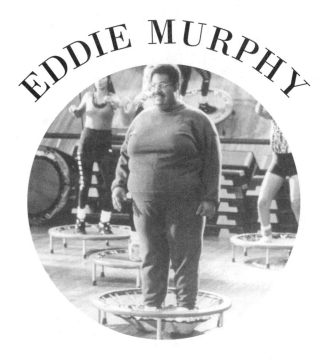

INCREDIBLE
SHRINKING COMIC

"White boys always get the Oscar. It's a known fact. Did I ever get a
nomination? No! You know why? 'Cause I hadn't played any of them
slave roles, and get my ass whipped. That's how you get the nomination. A black dude who plays a slave that gets his ass whipped gets
the nomination; a white guy who plays an idiot gets the Oscar. That's
what I need: I need to play a retarded slave, then I'll get the Oscar."
—Eddie Murphy, *Bowfinger*

Workout over: Dr. Sherman Klump, *The Nutty Professor.*

It is a safe bet that Eddie Murphy will never win an Academy Award. He came close once, with a 2006 nomination for his performance in *Dreamgirls*, but Murphy will likely never acquire a gold statuette for his bookshelf for the same reason nearly every other performer mentioned here has similarly failed: Hollywood likes comedy at the box office, but doesn't accord it any respect when it comes to commemorating and honoring itself. In a 2000 *New York Times* article, Steve Martin attempted to imagine "Where the Comedians Will Be on Oscar Night"; Murphy, he suggested, might be found "standing on a hilltop throwing stones into the ocean." (Martin himself would be "holding back the tears," presumably in his own living room.) *Dreamgirls* notwithstanding, Eddie Murphy has become a comic icon via that rarest of gifts: knowing his audience. Critics might lambaste him for the similarity of his recent movies (Eddie plays a dozen characters! Some of them are fat, women, or fat women!), but Murphy has found a middlebrow sweet spot that adds up to regular nine-figure grosses.

The first major African American comic star to emerge in the wake of Richard Pryor, Murphy was the anti-Pryor, even as he idolized the groundbreaking comic. In place of Pryor's fraught Peoria childhood, Murphy was born to a middle-class family in Rockville, Long Island. His father was a New York City transit cop, and his mother worked as a telephone operator. Murphy's parents divorced when he was three and his father was later killed by an ex-girlfriend, but home life for Eddie was stable and mostly unchanging. A brief opening skit at the start of Murphy's 1987 concert film *Raw* offers a hint at Murphy's childhood; at a boozy middle-class Thanksgiving party, circa 1968, a young Eddie shocks and entertains the adults with an off-color joke about a pissing, farting, shitting monkey. Murphy wanted to shock, but he also wanted everyone to go home pleased. No Pryor-esque cultural criticism for him.

Murphy, as he tells the *Raw* audience, grew up worshipping Pryor. He would sneak down to the basement, avoiding his eagle-eyed mother, to listen to Pryor's raunchy records. The studying paid off; Murphy does a wicked Pryor in *Raw*, doing scatological jokes in Richard's voice, complete with Pryor's trademark surprised guffaw. Murphy was hardly parroting his idol's routines, though. Pryor made race the explicit focus of his comedy, while for Murphy, the tangled webs of race were mostly something to be laughed off.

As a teenager, Murphy performed impromptu stand-up shows at school assemblies, to the adulation of his classmates. By fifteen, he was performing in local comedy clubs; by seventeen, he had taken his act to Manhattan. His own meager haul of material was supplemented by hastily memorized routines from Pryor's albums. In 1980, at the tender age of nineteen, Murphy was cast on *Saturday Night Live*. Murphy was hired as a featured player, rather than a cast member, during a time when *SNL* preferred to limit itself to one African American cast member at a time. At first, he was overlooked, even as he repeatedly proved himself to be the funniest person in the room—perhaps due to racism, or to the inherent bias of experienced comedians against a wet-behind-the-ears teenager.

The show's writers, always looking for the quickest route to airtime, soon came to understand, however, that locking yourself into a room with Eddie Murphy was the surest bet of all. "All you had to do with Eddie at that time," remembers writer Margaret Oberman in the *SNL* oral history *Live from New York*, "was be a real good stenographer. Because you'd get him in the office and he'd have the character down, and he'd have the voice down, and then if you had a good ear, you could kind of figure it out and give him the stuff right back, and he would just kick ass."

Murphy did, in fact, kick ass on *Saturday Night Live*, playing a dazzling array of characters: the adult Buckwheat, Mr. T., Gumby. In one memorable skit, he went undercover as the Caucasian Mr. White, discovering a heretofore unfamiliar world of privilege from which blacks were excluded: free newspapers, no-hassle loans, even drinks and dancing on the public bus after the last African American disembarked.

Murphy's virgin film appearance, made while still starring on *SNL*, set the tone for the bulk of his 1980s work. In *48 Hrs.* (1982), directed by Walter Hill, he is convict Reggie Hammond, sprung loose from prison to assist hard-bitten detective Jack Cates (Nick Nolte) in tracking down a pair of vicious killers. A go-it-alone San Francisco cop with a yen for phallic weaponry and a mouthful of bigoted tirades, Cates is a direct descendant of Clint Eastwood's Dirty Harry. Pity for him, then, that he is paired with motor-mouth Reggie, the embodiment of all his paranoid racist fantasies. *48 Hrs.* has a plot involving half a million dollars stashed in the trunk of Reggie's sports car, a kidnapping, and various other dastardly criminal plots, but mostly the film is an excuse for the energetic exchange of racial epithets. That Cates is given the bulk of the name-calling, and the upper hand in their battle of wills, is testament to Murphy's finely calibrated role. He is to be outspoken, but not too outspoken; combative, but within certain limits.

There is a certain word that dangles over *48 Hrs.*, a word left unspoken for much of its running time. It is all but implied, though, by every phrase and gesture Cates shoots Reggie's way. "We ain't got no deal," he tells Reggie, disturbed by talk of a quid pro quo during the convict's brief shore leave. "I *own* your ass." Cates is the movie's designated racial referee, intent on keeping the upstart Reggie in his place. "We ain't brothers, we ain't partners, and we ain't friends," he growls menacingly when Reggie oversteps his bounds. Eventually, Cates cracks, and the word that hangs so heavily over every scene here bursts out into the open. "Let me explain one thing to you, nigger," Cates begins, his thought quickly interrupted by the crunch of Reggie's fist meeting his face.

Murphy is the charming rapscallion, the shit-talker given a weekend pass to run his mouth. A two-bit hustler with a nose for the street, Reggie takes pleasure in his newfound authority. "You know what I am?" he rhetorically asks a bar full of rednecks. "I'm your worst fucking nightmare, man. I'm a nigger with a badge." Murphy's avuncular smile is his entree here, reassuring jittery moviegoers of his essential palatability. He disarms with charm, even as he is slamming a white hood's head into a car door, or pointing a pistol at a roomful of "Dixie"-whistlers. Reggie hardly seems to take offense at being called "spear-chucker" or "watermelon." Murphy's good-natured optimism enables him to stay above the fray, but it is hard to picture Sidney Poitier—or Pryor, for that matter—eating quite so much shit.

In the light of critic Donald Bogle's conclusion that "*48 Hrs.* makes racist jokes accessible," *Trading Places* (1983) is practically a sequel. Reggie knockoff Billy Ray Valentine is a scam artist posing as a legless Vietnam vet, skateboarding through Philadelphia's tonier districts and collecting handouts from card-carrying members of the old-boys' club. A chance run-in with titans of finance Randolph and Mortimer Duke (Don Ameche and Ralph Bellamy) turns Billy Ray into an unwitting participant in a social-science experiment testing the relative values of nature and nurture. What would happen if Billy Ray were to switch places—job, home, and everything else—with patrician Louis Winthorpe III (Dan Aykroyd)?

Murphy is once again a pawn in a white man's game, but his palpable sense of enjoyment at his newfound power and success are catching. *Trading Places* is good fun because we are allowed to vicariously participate in Billy Ray's unexpected coup, and revel in the prospect of exuberance triumphing over economics. The racial overtones of *Trading Places* are dated—wouldn't it be funny if it were a *black* man running a white-shoe firm?—but Murphy's braggadocio redeems the film, at least in part. Like Reggie, Billy Ray proves himself in unfamiliar terrain by falling back on his street smarts. He is positive that the price of pork bellies will fall on Christmas Eve—not because he knows the first thing about futures, but because he pictures traders sitting worriedly in their offices, concerned they won't be able to find that G.I. Joe with the kung-fu grip for Junior, and that their wives will deny them their rightful share of Yuletide nookie. And how wonderful is it to see Ralph Bellamy, the perennial also-ran of Cary Grant romantic comedies, as a scheming sonofabitch, for once?

Murphy, in his own estimation, was "a twenty-two-year-old black male onstage getting paid to hold his dick. God bless America!" *Eddie Murphy: Delirious* (1983), a concert film produced for television, should have been a well-deserved victory lap, and yet an unpleasant miasma dogged the scent of triumph. Murphy is a brilliant impressionist, his miniaturist portraits of childhood traumas—parentally administered beatings, fallen ice-cream cones—rendered with astonishing fidelity. He was not only holding his dick, though; he was downright obsessed with it, devoting much of *Delirious* to an overwrought fusillade of ad hominem attacks on gayness, both real and perceived. Murphy begins his performance by warning that "faggots aren't allowed to look at my ass while I'm onstage," then goes on to imagine *The Honeymooners'* Jackie Gleason and Art Carney as homosexual lovers, and express concern that his girlfriend might kiss a gay friend on the mouth and transact the AIDS virus. Gay-rights groups in particular were outraged by *Delirious*, but Murphy was unapologetically defiant.

Murphy's next hit—his biggest yet, and the one that branded him a superstar—begins somewhere even more hardscrabble than prison: Detroit. Again, a big part of the humor was the purported incongruity: how could Eddie Murphy, the epitome of ghetto survivalism, be an officer of the law? *Beverly Hills Cop* (1984) is not particularly groundbreaking, but we marvel at the superhuman verbal facility of Murphy's Axel Foley. Whatever the situation, whatever the consequences, Axel has a fully formed response at the ready. He is, like W. C. Fields, or Woody Allen, a savant of backtalk, keeping us entertained with a steady flow of patter.

Much like Murphy's earlier films, *Beverly Hills Cop* is a comedy whose implicit subject is race. Axel, like his predecessors, is adept at using it to his advantage. Marching into a hotel he knows is fully booked, he tells the clerk that he is a *Rolling Stone* reporter, at work on a story called "Michael Jackson Can Sit on Top of the World Just as Long as He Doesn't Sit in the Palm Hotel Because There's No Niggers Allowed in There." He gets a room. Later, he breaks into a tightly guarded warehouse, poses as a security consultant, and interrogates the guards about the lapse in judgment that allowed a black man like himself such unfettered access. Axel derives a childlike satisfaction from his prankish spirit, which leads him to do things like pose as a gay hustler named Ramon, informing a john that he is infected with herpes, or slip a banana into the exhaust pipe of a car tailing him. Axel is the lone improviser in a sea of performers reading directly from the script.

Eventually, *Beverly Hills Cop* dribbles its joyous life away with a series of utterly pointless shootouts and explosions. *Beverly Hills Cop II* (which followed the disastrous collision of Eastern spirituality and Murphy zingers that was 1986's *The Golden Child*), one of the standout box-office hits of 1987, ventured deeper into the awkward territory staked out by its predecessor. Director Tony Scott, filling in for Martin Brest, crams in three films' worth of violence and mayhem, all to the tune of Harold Faltermeyer's insidiously catchy techno anthem. Scott's trendy decor makes for an absurdly underlit film, with gloom darkening what little we can see of the action, as if this were the *Godfather* of slam-bang action films. What little comedy remains is mostly a tired rehash of the first *Beverly Hills Cop*. There are just enough brilliant asides, however, to keep the audience from collectively fleeing in disgust.

If Axel Foley was the audience-pleasing Eddie Murphy at his most genial, the "Eddie Murphy" on display in the stand-up concert film *Raw* (1987) was his dark twin, preferring hostility to pleasantries and repeatedly striking a raw nerve of ugly misanthropy. "The faggots were mad," he crows about the repercussions of his off-color jokes from *Delirious*. "I can't go to San Francisco—they have twenty-four-seven homo watch." The proceedings only degrade further from there. Women are rendered in stereoscopic depth, simultaneously avaricious, conniving whores and deluded hussies. Aiming for Pryor-esque bluntness, Murphy instead comes off as a severely misogynistic rageaholic. All men cheat, all women are greedy, and the only solution for an internationally beloved star like Eddie Murphy is to go to Africa and marry "some crazy, nek-kid zebra-bitch." Stardom was an elixir for Murphy, but its tonic proved it could be poisonous to his self-awareness as well. (The entire effort is so embarrassingly hackneyed that one wonders whether Murphy simply lifted some of his own unused *Raw* jokes for the hilariously inept material of Dave Chappelle's stand-up comic in his later *The Nutty Professor* ["Women be shopping!"].)

Murphy had always been fascinated by the act of disappearing into a role, of cloaking himself in the invisibility of another self. The apprenticeship with Lorne Michaels had planted the seed. With *Coming to America* (1988), a sweet fable that helped to erase *Raw*'s metallic aftertaste, Murphy began the transition to a fruitful second act to his career. Taking a page from Peter

Sellers and Jerry Lewis, Murphy would crack himself open, letting the dozens of characters huddling inside him spill out. Murphy was likable but featureless as a leading man; it was in his character roles, padded with rubber fat suits and swaddled in outlandish costumes, that he began to exhibit his remarkable gift for the quick change. In *Trading Places*, Murphy had briefly posed as a manically good-natured African exchange student, and *Coming to America* extends the impression to feature length. Part African fantasia, part adventure, and part musical, *Coming to America* is cobbled out of mismatched parts and held together by Murphy's geniality.

Murphy was Prince Akeem, the pampered heir to the throne of Zamunda. Tired of having his every need ministered to ("The royal penis is clean," a bare-breasted beauty calls out from the princely bath), Akeem desires to see the world beyond Zamunda, and find his own bride. And where better to find a woman fit for a king than Queens?

Akeem and his aide Semmi (Arsenio Hall) make the journey to New York's outer boroughs, taking lodgings in a rat-infested tenement, and employment at McDowell's, a dingy McDonald's knockoff. The romance with McDowell's scion Lisa (Shari Headley) is sweet, and Akeem amusingly accommodating, but *Coming to America*'s charge comes from its panoply of supporting characters, nearly all of whom are played by Murphy or Hall. Murphy was funketeer Randy Watson, with Prince's stage moves and Rick James's hair; barbershop owner Clarence, who stubbornly insists that boxer Joe Louis was actually 137 years old; and Clarence's sparring partner Saul, an elderly Jew with a perpetually hoarse voice, a Yiddish accent, and a fondness for debate ("A man has the right to change his name to vatever he vants to change it to. And if a man vants to be called Muhammad Ali, godammit this is a free country, you should respect his vishes, and call the man Muhammad Ali!").

Murphy's loving, enthusiastic embrace of these caricatures is palpable. Murphy was no Sellers; he didn't require the mask to succeed, as *Trading Places* and *Beverly Hills Cop* had demonstrably proven. But the masks had given him an opening to leave the bad-boy persona behind, and Murphy leapt at it. *Coming to America* would be the first of Eddie Murphy's films in which he devoted himself to the task of exploiting his multiple personalities. Once the would-be successor to Richard Pryor, Murphy would soon turn himself into the new Jerry Lewis—the man with a thousand faces.

Before he would rediscover himself in multiplicity, there would be an era of diminishing box-office returns, beginning with a film Murphy wrote and directed, *Harlem Nights* (1989). *Harlem* is more of a triumph for Murphy's talented supporting cast than for its star, wasted as a brash young gangster on the make. As a director, Murphy demonstrated an amateurish grip of technique (vertical wipes are pretty much the pinnacle of his sophistication), but *Harlem Nights* contained the kernel of his ambition to remake himself as a serious movie star. *Boomerang* (1992) is an upscale romantic comedy, with Murphy as a jaded Don Juan shocked out of his fuck-and-run lethargy by encountering Robin Givens's equally rapacious bad girl. Murphy is charming as a suave, well-dressed lothario, but *Boomerang* is two reels too long, and its plotting too confused, to be entirely effective as rebranding. A series of pointless, charmless sequels (*Another 48 Hrs.*, *Beverly Hills Cop III*) hardly did Murphy any favors, or any justice.

The Distinguished Gentleman (1992), by contrast, was a loose remake of *Mr. Smith Goes to Washington* in which the newcomer was not another idealistic Jimmy Stewart but an apprentice Claude Rains. Elected to Congress on the basis of having the same name as his deceased predecessor, Murphy's con artist Jefferson Johnson (shades of Stewart's Jefferson Smith) goes to Washington with visions of spending-bill pork and free-flowing lobbyist dollars dancing in his mind. Jeff doesn't ask for much, just a firmly planted finger in every governmental pie.

The Distinguished Gentleman is a surprisingly tart satire of Republican governance, with Murphy the ambitious black politico who gets ahead by playing the good ol' boy. Murphy, the master bullshitter, finds himself in the world capital of bullshit, and thrives by selling his services to the highest bidder. "I am not a yes man," he pertly informs a staffer. "When Dick says no, I say no." Murphy's oily self-satisfaction suits the boisterous Jeff to a T, and *The Distinguished Gentleman* succeeds in large part because of his ability to turn corruption into comedy. Murphy, the con man extraordinaire, sells cynicism and bleeding-heart idealism with equal aplomb.

Jerry Lewis's *The Nutty Professor*—the ur-text, if you will, of the multiple-personality film—had offered the spectacle of Lewis doing battle with his demons, fighting off his inner Dean Martin. Eddie Murphy's remake, directed by Tom Shadyac, seemingly made only for the crassest commercial purposes, is an unexpected triumph. The pinnacle of Murphy's experiments in multiplicity, this *Nutty Professor* is, against all odds, the greatest of his films. In superbly adapting Lewis's film to suit his own purposes, Murphy transforms the arid landscape of the original *Professor* (which seemed to possess no characters other than Lewis's Julius Kelp and Buddy Love) into one lushly peopled with kooks, freaks, and comic stereotypes.

Mustachioed, jowly, and roly-poly, with an ever-present bowtie, Murphy's Sherman Klump (the film's designated Julius stand-in) is a belly and butt in search of a waistline. Summoned to the college president's office, at the beginning of this new *Nutty Professor* (1996), for his latest infraction, we are more concerned with the sheer impossibility of his cramming his behind into the tiny office chair, and the suction-cup effect precluding its removal once he does squeeze himself in, than any possible punishment he might receive.

When Richard Simmons, acupuncture, and cutting out the candy bars don't cut it, Sherman turns to a formula he has been crafting in his laboratory, and voila! Out pops his skinny inner self, the svelte, suave dream-Sherman he had long been dreaming of. Buddy Love, as the new Sherman calls himself, is more than just trim. He is also a raging egomaniac lacking Sherman's intelligence or sweetness, a tightly coiled ball of imitation charm convinced, beyond a shadow of a doubt, that he is God's gift to women. Buddy is the id yearning to break free from Sherman's buttoned-up superego. He takes Sherman's scientific research and turns it into the latest diet fad, instantly eliminating gelatin arms, turkey neck, saddlebag syndrome, tank ass, and other Buddy-diagnosed body-image deficiencies.

Sherman and Buddy are not the only characters clamoring for attention here. In a bravura turn that expands on *Coming to America*'s gallimaufry of characters, Murphy plays nearly the entirety of the Klump family. He is irascible patriarch Papa Klump; cooing, perennially optimistic Mama Klump; Sherman's bitter brother Ernie; and Sherman's sexual dynamo Grandma Klump. As good as the Sherman-Buddy showdown is, it is the Klumps who are the unquestioned stars of *The Nutty Professor*, their unabashed crassness perpetually amusing. Murphy had given hints before, but with *The Nutty Professor* he was suddenly a magician, transforming unexpectedly into a one-man army of boldly expressive, Lewis-esque caricatures. Where Lewis had flirted dangerously with treacle in his panoply of impressions, Murphy's sweetness was endearing without being overly sentimental.

Sherman and Buddy ultimately must wrestle for control of the body they uneasily share. "Wrestling" is no metaphor; like Dr. Strangelove choking the life out of himself with one hand while the other shoots out in a Nazi salute, the two halves of the professor do battle inside the same body. For once, special effects are put to the uses required by story, rather than vice versa. Each slap and punch exchanged transforms Sherman's face into Buddy's, and then back again. One particularly ringing blow sends Sherman's face wobbling all the way down to his chest, like a clump of soggy cookie dough. (One might be tempted to see this final confrontation as representative of the turn taken in Murphy's own career, in which polite, unthreatening Sherman Klump chokes the life out of crass, brilliant Buddy Love.)

Soon after the triumph of *The Nutty Professor*, Murphy was embroiled in a career-threatening scandal. In May 1997, Murphy was pulled over by a police officer near Santa Monica Boulevard in West Hollywood, California, a transvestite prostitute in the passenger seat. Murphy claimed to be merely giving a needy soul a ride home: "This is an act of kindness that got turned into a fucking horror show." Given the time of night, and Murphy's presence in a known gay cruising ground, the explanation did not entirely hold water. For longtime students of the actor's career, the disjunction between persona and reality was puzzling: was the persistent, flagrant gay-baiting of Murphy's stand-up an instance of clever misdirection?

Much of the concern expressed over Murphy's arrest was for his future palatability as a family-friendly star. The naysayers needn't have worried; Murphy's next film, the kids' film *Dr. Dolittle* (1998), ended up grossing over $140 million at the domestic box office. The film, directed by Betty Thomas, cast Murphy as the straight man to a series of animal supporting acts like Chris Rock's rowdy guinea pig and the depressive tiger voiced by Albert Brooks. By all rights, *Dolittle* was better than it should have been, aided by Thomas's more-than-adequate direction, and by a winning team chemistry that de-emphasized Murphy in favor of his supporting cast.

Something similar would happen with his next film; the only difference would be that all the supporting roles would be played by Eddie Murphy. The subtitle of *The Nutty Professor II* (2000) hammed home the point. This one, it wanted us to know, was all about *The Klumps*. There was some nonsense about how "we all have a little Buddy Love inside us," and Buddy and Sherman dutifully returned, but *Nutty Professor II* only got truly jazzed about the Klumps.

Argumentative, profane, sexually inappropriate, and always, always hungry, the Klumps are a portrait of rowdy family togetherness, with everyone's foibles aired, displayed, and forgiven. Sherman's father is embarrassed by his sexual inadequacy and humiliated by others' insistence on discussing his impotence. Grandma, meanwhile, dreams of some freaky *9½ Weeks*–style passion with Buddy Love, picturing herself romping in an open meadow, her aged breasts juddering down to her waist. (The most prized member of Murphy's supporting cast, here as in 1999's *Shawshank Redemption*–meets–*O Brother, Where Art Thou?* prison buddy comedy *Life*, was master makeup artist Rick Baker.)

Grandma is once again the undoubted star of the film, her undimmed passion for her creaky new boyfriend ("the world's oldest Negro," one wag dubs him) and ardor for sharing embarrassing stories (one randomly chosen punch line: "I was standing on my own titty!") and sexual fantasies hugely charming and a tad icky. Wildly uneven, this second *Nutty Professor* could hardly be in danger of being confused with a classic, or even its predecessor, but Murphy's tender touch was surprising, and endearing.

Murphy was now the cinematic equivalent of Wal-Mart, offering two-for-one specials in the hopes of luring customers. *Bowfinger* (1999), written by Steve Martin and directed by Frank Oz, offered the prospect of double-duty Murphy, with him playing both paranoid superstar Kit Ramsey and his unassuming brother Jiff. Kit is a marvel of paranoid intensity, his brow permanently furrowed, convinced that each new script that crosses his desk hides a nefarious KKK plot to undermine him. Martin's script cleverly plays up the affinities between character and star; Kit's fondness for flashing Laker Girls is reminiscent of nothing so much as Murphy's recent transvestite troubles. His brother Jiff, in comparison, is Kit's inverse: an unassuming wallflower with a nonexistent resume. Hired as a fill-in star for Martin's bare-bones production on the basis of his resemblance to Kit, Jiff is more than content to do Starbucks runs between takes.

With *Nutty Professor* and *Bowfinger*, Murphy had solidified his role as a one-man studio stable, a star whose genius was as a character actor. Unfortunately, Murphy also took the eight-to-eighty success of *The Nutty Professor* and *Dr. Dolittle* as a permission slip to star in a series of brain-dead family comedies and adventures. Having once been a gleefully risqué comedy star, Eddie Murphy transformed himself into a lackluster purveyor of family-friendly yuks. *The Adventures of Pluto Nash* (2002), *Daddy Day Care* (2003), *The Haunted Mansion* (2003), *Meet Dave* (2008)—the parade of titles alone should serve as reminder enough of Murphy's descent into PG hell. Eddie Murphy had become that mystery: a still-successful comic star with no discernible fan base. Murphy was reduced to cannibalizing his own career; his distinctly unglamorous beat cop, in the reality-TV parody *Showtime* (2002), dreams of nothing so much as a few moments of Axel Foley glory, broadcast on national television.

Norbit (2007) was both proof of Murphy's diminishment and a reminder of his still-formidable comic gifts. For his multiple roles in the film, directed by Brian Robbins, Murphy garnished a record haul of awards, taking home prizes for actor, supporting actor, and supporting actress. Pity, then, that his were courtesy of the Razzies, dedicated to honoring the worst performances of the year. Revisiting what by now had come to be a familiar trope, Murphy is both the nebbishy, unhappily married, Jiff-like Norbit, and his demon-bride, Rasputia. Murphy was in an abusive relationship with himself, dominated by his overweight, tyrannical, undyingly crass wife. With its relentless barrage of racial and gender stereotypes, wielded with all the deftness of a polo mallet to the skull, *Norbit* single-handedly sets the cause of civil rights—nay, the cause of combating stupidity—back by two decades.

Rasputia in particular is a noxious creation, the anti–Sherman Klump. She is, as we first see her, an overgrown child, intent on having her way in all matters: shooting at terminal velocity down a water-park slide, leaping hungrily onto Norbit in a deftly rendered series of bedroom encounters. Her corpulence is taken as symbolic proof of her nefariousness, each undulating ribbon of fat coming in for its own individual ribbing. And yet, accepting its blatantly obvious flaws, *Norbit* is, at times, a surprisingly funny film. Murphy may not be working with his most vividly rendered material, but with Rasputia ("How *you* doin'!"), he is at the height of his powers of *Nutty Professor*–esque inventiveness. She is an untamed rapscallion, and Murphy (who cowrote the film's story with his brother Charlie) loves her unquestioningly, political correctness be damned.

The only exceptions to Murphy's post-*Klumps* box-office slide were the phenomenally popular *Shrek* (2001) and its sequels. Murphy contributed the voice for the perpetually panicky Donkey, aide-de-camp to Mike Myers's Shrek. Murphy's Donkey is a sweet-talking, child-friendly version of *48 Hrs.*' Reggie Hammond, talking fast to save his skin. Donkey is, in fact, the ideal Murphy role: the sidekick who subtly makes off with the film. By the time Donkey does a little Otis Redding call-and-response outside the church where Shrek's love Fiona is to be married, Murphy has become more like Buddy Love from *The Nutty Professor*, stealing the show with shameless compunction.

Would it be uncharitable, then, to view Eddie Murphy as a comic icon who had willingly transformed himself into a cartoon? Axel Foley had become, only too literally, an ass, all sting removed from his barbs. While justified, that would be somewhat too facile a response to the Shrek-ization of Murphy, who, after all, had had the foresight to see that Axel Foley was not a role he could keep playing on the wrong side of forty. There was something out of the ordinary, in fact—something remarkable—about Eddie Murphy's nearly unprecedented box-office hegemony, which stretched across three decades. Having begun as a motor-mouthed, fresh-faced upstart, Murphy had become a master of disguise, his every film another opportunity to recreate *The Nutty Professor*—or *Dr. Strangelove*. From the most beloved American comedian of his era, Eddie Murphy had become, quite possibly, the most underrated. How nutty is that?

25

BILL MURRAY

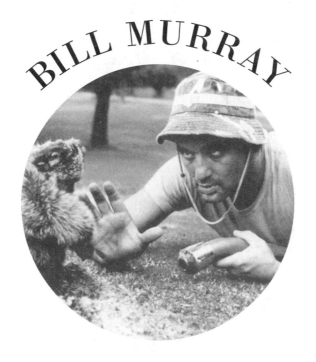

JUST THE USUAL COMIC INSPIRATION— FRUSTRATION, LOSS, AND DEATH

"Now if you'll excuse me, I'm going to go on an overnight drunk, and in ten days I'm going to set out to find the shark that ate my friend and destroy it. Anyone who wants to tag along is more than welcome."
—Bill Murray, *The Life Aquatic with Steve Zissou*

Carl Spackler seeks peace with his varmint enemy in *Caddyshack*.

There is a precise moment at which we can watch Bill Murray complete his transformation from lovable wiseass to actor. It is near the conclusion of Wes Anderson's 1998 film *Rushmore*, and Murray's bored industrialist Herman Blume shows up for a meeting with his friend, rival, and surrogate son Max Fischer (Jason Schwartzman) looking even more disheveled than usual: hair matted, clothing rumpled, shirt lapels jutting out awkwardly over a sports coat. Max ushers him into the barber shop whose window they have been chatting in front of, and introduces him to the dapper white-haired gent with the clippers: "Mr. Blume, this is my father, Bert Fischer."

Herman, who had been led to believe that his father was a prominent surgeon, immediately understands that Max is a dreamer, and a schemer, preferring the potential to the actual. Introducing Herman to his father is both an acknowledgement of their friendship and a painful admission of defeat. Blume shakes hands with Mr. Fischer (Seymour Cassel), takes a series of ragged breaths, blinks rapidly in short succession, and tilts his head slightly to the side. His eyes mist over, filling with emotion, but his face retains its masklike hardness. Those eyes transmit our sense of an internal earthquake; one Max has crumbled, and another has been rebuilt, in the space of a handshake. In a few brief seconds, without resort to language, Herman Blume has undergone a complete transformation.

Having dependably entertained audiences for more than thirty years, no single part of Bill Murray's career can be privileged over any other, nor can any era be dismissed as lacking in interest, or amusement. But were we to pinpoint the moment at which Murray became something greater than he had been—when he found a source for his comedy deeper than any he had ever tapped before—this scene from *Rushmore* would serve as well as any. Truthfully, though, the seeds of the transformation had been planted long before. For as long as Bill Murray has been acting, he has been doing battle with melancholy, thwarted ambition, and the imminence of death. Not the traditional sources of comedic inspiration, but then Bill Murray has never been much of a traditional comedian.

There was always something a little different about Bill Murray. Where other actors seemed to be sweating for every laugh, every response, Murray had floated above the fray, too good—or too lazy—to expend much effort. Rather than be castigated for his couch-potato brand of acting, Murray has been lauded—and rightly so. Murray has perfected a certain brand of insouciant—not acting, precisely, more like being—onscreen. In early films like *Meatballs* (1979) and *Ghostbusters* (1984), Murray was the wiseass as comic hero, never quite settling into the fabric of the narrative. Smirking, winking, commenting on rather than taking part in the action, Bill Murray was the ideal comic hero for a generation raised on dreams of rebellion but too unmotivated to rebel themselves.

In recent years, working with directors like Anderson, Jim Jarmusch, and Sofia Coppola, Murray uncovered a strain of melancholy buried beneath the surface of his acting. In *Rushmore*, *Lost in Translation* (2003), and *The Life Aquatic with Steve Zissou* (2004), Murray was weighed down by disappointment, failure, and loss. He made middle-aged frustration deeply, enduringly hilarious.

Rushmore had been the conclusion of the process, but another Murray gem had dramatized the very act of transformation. *Groundhog Day* (1993) had made the internal renovation from callow, cruel asshole to human being the centerpiece of its plot. Murray was Phil Connors, a self-centered Pittsburgh weatherman assigned to cover the annual Groundhog Day festivities in Punxsutawney, Pennsylvania. Phil is deeply chagrined to find himself reliving the same day, over and over, stuck in an endlessly recurring loop that begins with Sonny and Cher's "I Got You Babe" and manages to get even worse from there.

In order to escape the everlasting sameness, Phil has to shed his worn-out skin—a process similar to Murray's own metamorphosis. For *Groundhog Day*, in addition to being superlative comedy, is also a semi-autobiographical, allegorical retelling of Murray's career. The film is two separate movies stapled back to back: one starring the old Bill Murray, the other a new, as yet unformed actor of the same name. Entering as a wreck, a burned-out husk, Phil cannot leave until he changes into a human being. Murray, too, would have to find his humanity in order to grow as a comedian.

Before we can proceed any further with the new, improved Bill Murray, we must spend a bit more time with the shed skin. Murray was born in 1950 in suburban Chicago, the middle child of nine. His father was a lumber-company salesman, and Bill spent his summers caddying on a local golf course—preparation, perhaps, for his role in *Caddyshack* (1980). A smart kid with no patience for school, Murray followed his older brother Brian Doyle-Murray into acting. He joined the Second City improv group in Chicago, where he met John Belushi and future collaborator Harold Ramis, who would direct Murray in *Caddyshack* and *Groundhog Day*, and star alongside him in *Stripes* and *Ghostbusters*.

From Second City, Murray was hired by Belushi for the *National Lampoon Radio Hour* and eventually for the East Coast tour of the *National Lampoon*

Show. In 1975 two new late-night programs were up for casting: a glitzy ABC variety show hosted by Howard Cosell called *Saturday Night Live*, and a scruffy NBC variant called *Saturday Night*, produced by a young Canadian who had put together a handful of Lily Tomlin television specials. Lorne Michaels had intended to hire him for his program, but money was tight, and Murray was the last actor cut. Murray ended up joining his brother Brian, and Christopher Guest, with the Prime Time Players of Cosell's short-lived *Saturday Night Live*. "We were on with the Chinese acrobats and elephants and all sorts of crazy acts," Murray later remembered, "and we would get cut almost every other week."

After the first season of Michaels's *Saturday Night*, which became a phenomenon, making instant icons of its cast, Chevy Chase—who had been the show's breakout star—decided to leave for the greener pastures of Hollywood, and Bill Murray was hired as his replacement. *SNL* was never a forgiving environment for unproven talent, and the first few years of Murray's run consisted, in his recollection, of playing the second cop in others' routines. The breakthrough came with a fondly remembered sketch, in which the still-unheralded Murray engaged in a direct appeal to the show's audience for their attention. "There was a couple tablespoons of humility in it, I got laughs in it," Murray said, "and I think the combination of the two broke some sort of ice, not just for me, but for people watching." Murray would soon become one of *Saturday Night Live*'s defining stars, taking center stage after the departures of Aykroyd and Belushi.

Hollywood came calling in short order, with *Meatballs* (1979) Murray's first starring role. As Tripper, chief of the agitators at a middle-of-the-road summer camp, Murray fends off boredom, and a sea of whiny campers, with an uninterrupted stream of sardonic, mocking patter. Tripper is mostly out to entertain himself; an audience for his witticisms is only an unexpected bonus. Murray scores zingers off everyone: fellow counselors ("Roxanne, I have to tell you this as a friend: I can see right down your blouse"); campers ("You must be the short, depressed kid that we ordered. Glad you could make it"); even the camp's own mediocrity ("An update on tonight's dinner: it was veal").

An adult sex comedy and sentimental kids' story jumbled all together, *Meatballs* is nothing if not a hodgepodge of mismatched parts, but Murray plays every scene with the same undisguised glee. Clad in his ever-present Hawaiian shirt, red running shorts, and sneakers, his unkempt mop of hair party in the front and party in the back, Tripper is a character one can only imagine flourishing at camp. (What does he do in the off-season?)

Even when Tripper goes skinny-dipping with Roxanne, the part of his brain that controls his mouth refuses to cede control, cracking wise even as he gets lucky. And while *Meatballs* eventually goes limp, all soppy strings and sub–*Chariots of Fire* ending, it is Murray's limber wit that sticks in the memory. "Arts and crafts has been canceled due to bad taste," Tripper announces, and we smile, remembering counselors just like him—or wishing we did.

Being more of an ensemble piece, costarring Rodney Dangerfield and Chase, the man he had replaced on *SNL*, *Caddyshack* (1980) does not give Murray quite the same opportunity to dominate the mood of the film. Nonetheless, his deranged greenskeeper Carl Spackler is easily the most memorable figure in this golf comedy, cowritten by Murray's brother Brian, Doug Kenney, and Harold Ramis. A sweaty, disheveled loner, horny and creepy, Carl is the kind of guy who prefers to clean his apartment with a leaf blower. While Chase and Dangerfield wield putters and irons, demolishing the carefully maintained WASP gentility of a suburban country club, Murray appears to be acting in another film entirely. Given the task of eradicating the gopher population burrowing beneath the course, Carl is acting in his own Vietnam film, the course his personal Khe Sanh. "I smell varmint poontang," Murray mutters to himself, "and the only good varmint poontang is dead varmint poontang." With leaves stuck to his head, attempting a freehand imitation of John Wayne, Carl is a GI left behind in the forest to go native.

The repellent, imbecilic Carl shares little with the cuddly Tripper, but both Murray creations are driven by the desire to keep themselves entertained. Tripper does it with zingers; Carl does it by casting himself in ludicrous scenarios of his own devising. He is the lecher offering to play hide-the-salami with a foursome of middle-aged lady golfers; the television announcer, calling the golf tournament dominated by his own "incredible Cinderella story"; and the Travis Bickle manqué, washing away all the gopher scum from his course. He is even, for a brief moment, Bugs Bunny, getting all Acme on those pesky gophers with a squirrel stuffed full of explosives: "What's up, doc?"

Stripes (1981) continued the run of successes, with Murray a good-for-nothing Chicago slacker who joins the military on a whim and recasts the U.S. Army in his own image. Like *Meatballs*, *Stripes* is happiest when silliest; by the time the last third of the film rolls around, and incompetent soldiers John Winger and Russell Ziskey (Murray and Ramis) are fighting off the collective force of the Soviet Union while cruising around Czechoslovakia in an armed Winnebago, *Stripes* has lost its grip.

Before then, the rumpled, pasty, wisecracking Murray is given an ideal foil: the enormous, sclerotic, unthinking American military. Only a brief decade after the harried doctors of Robert Altman's *MASH* had symbolically suffered the torments of Vietnam, Murray was an American soldier for a newer, less consequential age. Army life was no longer an existential obstacle course, but instead a sequel to *Meatballs* in which summer camp was now year-round, and the campers were adults. "I'm part of a lost and restless generation," Winger says of himself, and the definition stuck. Murray's restlessness would loosen his tongue. The scenarios for films like *Stripes* and *Ghostbusters* would turn him into a latter-day Groucho Marx, scoring points off an endless array of patsies.

Limber tongue notwithstanding, Murray's John Winger was hardly the stuff of officer material. "I know I'm speaking for the entire platoon," a bleary-eyed Winger announces from his bed before an early-morning drill, "when I say this run should be postponed." Winger and Russell turn the military into a running joke, whose rules and regulations are good for mockery and nothing more. ("Got something in a low-rise bikini?" Murray asks when uniforms are handed out.) Eventually, Winger becomes the poster boy for a new patriotism—one defined by its self-mocking vigor. "We've been kicking ass for two hundred years!" he shouts to his platoon, pumping his fist. "We're ten and one!"

Murray was relegated to the supporting cast for Dustin Hoffman's triumphant *Tootsie* (1982), in which he played the struggling actor's equally flailing playwright roommate Jeff. There are traces of the already well-established Murray persona—Jeff appears to do less working at his restaurant job than distracted snacking—but he mostly serves as a distracted straight man bemused, and a little annoyed, by Hoffman's actorly shenanigans, which include forbidding his roommate to answer the telephone. "When you were playing Cyrano, and you stuck a saber underneath my armpit through the couch, you know, I didn't say anything," Murray tells Hoffman. "But I don't see any reason why I should just sit here pretending I'm not home just because you're not that kind of girl." Against his wishes, Jeff is dragged into the unexpected complications of his roommate's cross-dressing success. "I want you to know for the record, Jeff," Hoffman's male suitor tells Murray when he comes home unexpectedly, "that *nothing* happened here tonight." For a brief moment, Jeff taps invisible reserves of dignity, playing the long-suffering lover with weary gravitas.

Like so many other clowns, Murray craved the approval of dramatic success, and parlayed the box-office bonanzas of his comedies into a pet project:

an adaptation of W. Somerset Maugham's novel *The Razor's Edge* (1984). Columbia agreed to finance the film as the price for Murray's starring in *Ghostbusters* (1984), and the experience was a jarring one. "Ten days ago I was up there working with the high lamas in a *gompa*," Murray told a *Rolling Stone* interviewer, "and here I am removing ghosts from drugstores and painting slime on my body." To Murray's chagrin, the slime would be far more enduring than the lamas.

Along with Dan Aykroyd and Ramis, Murray is a paranormal investigator ridding New York City of its peskiest pests. Murray is doubly exposed: he is simultaneously in the movie, and at a remove from it. Approaching the film from a sidelong angle, Murray prefers to maintain an ironic distance from events, in order to properly mock them. We enjoy Dr. Venkman's shameless insincerity, his motor mouth, his unquenchable desire to entertain. Aykroyd and Ramis are straight men to Murray, who laughs at the movie even as he guides it along, scoring zingers off direct hits to the plot. Love interest Sigourney Weaver describes him as less scientist than game-show host, and that gets it just right; Dr. Venkman is endearingly, enduringly insincere.

This is jazzy comedy, with Murray's off-kilter line readings favoring unexpected words, employing a sing-songy tone improvisatory in their freshness. "*Human* sacrifice, *dogs* and cats, *living* together, mass hysteria," Peter says of the impending calamity set to strike the city, and its cleverness lies less in the words themselves than in Murray's incantatory rhythm. Some comedians are brilliant for their ability to disappear into their roles; Bill Murray always allowed characters to disappear into him. Scientist or slacker, counselor or charlatan, Murray was less chameleon than boa constrictor, swallowing roles whole and regurgitating them in his own image.

The late 1980s and early 1990s saw Bill Murray flirting dangerously with the prospect of becoming another Chevy Chase, or John Candy—an immensely gifted performer relegated to third-rate family comedies and supporting roles. The modern-day Dickens adaptation *Scrooged* (1988), with Murray as a television executive wakened to eternal truths by the Ghost of Christmas Past, was lightly likable—more than could truthfully be said for 1989's execrable, inevitable *Ghostbusters* sequel. *Mad Dog and Glory* (1993) was confused about whether it was a whimsical drama or a light comedy, and the confusion extended to the divvying up of roles, in which Murray was cast as the mobster and Robert De Niro as the lily-livered police officer. Murray was striking, his gangster dreaming of stand-up comedy success ("'Cosa Nostra' is Italian for 'cheap bastards'"), but the movie, directed by John McNaughton, is disastrously misguided. He was far better served by supporting roles in *Ed Wood* (1994), *Kingpin* (1996), *Wild Things* (1998), and *Charlie's Angels* (2000), each of which allowed Murray to surreptitiously make off with the film, snatching it from the grasp of his more prominently billed colleagues. But had Bill Murray been reduced to a character actor?

Groundhog Day's Phil Connors, on the other hand, is a typical Murray hero: sardonic, egocentric, and self-contained. The day in Punxsutawney is a minefield to be negotiated, and the mines all take the form of human beings, demanding engagement: companionship, warmth, and small talk. Phil, who prefers narcissistic self-absorption tinged with cruelty, gives none of these away readily. Colleagues are to be shunned; proprietors condescended to, acquaintances mocked. Forced to mingle with the grubby minions of the everyday, Phil prefers to keep an imaginary distance from mediocrity, as if his own rapier wit were protecting an invisible bubble shielding him from immersion.

Phil is another version of Bill Murray's most beloved past roles— *Ghostbusters'* Dr. Peter Venkman, *Stripes'* John Winger—but director Harold Ramis (who cowrote the *Groundhog* script with Danny Rubin) pulls back just far enough from Phil for us to feel, if only briefly, what it might be like to be on the business side of Murray's itchy trigger finger. (Phil owes something to *Scrooged*'s Frank Cross, another hardass softened by a glimpse of eternity.) He turns forcefully on a mild bed-and-breakfast proprietor, concluding a graduate-level disquisition on the weather after she makes the mistake of commenting on the impending snowstorm. "Did you *want* to talk about the weather, or were you just making chitchat?"

Ramis has Murray playing a slight variation on his familiar persona, but *Groundhog Day* subtly undermines his gift for mockery by shifting focus. Suddenly, Murray seems less hilarious than cruel, his routine a well-honed method of keeping intimacy away. When punishment strikes, Phil goes through a series of responses roughly corresponding to the stages of grief. He is shocked, he is angry, he acts out, he seeks atonement through good deeds, and ultimately, he embraces the only real thing there is: the present.

In rapid order, Phil tries on, and discards, a series of masks: the existential rebel ("I'm not gonna live by their rules anymore!"); the bad boy (filing away the name of a beautiful woman's homeroom teacher from high school, the better to feign friendship on some future day); the eternal student (studying the piano, and nineteenth-century French poetry); the jaded aesthete, afflicted with terminal ennui. "I'll give you a winter prediction," he tells the assembled Groundhog Day crowd. "It's going to be cold, it's going to be gray, and it's going to last the rest of your life." And what does one do, the film wants to know, once you've memorized the answer to every question on *Jeopardy*?

Groundhog Day takes enormous pleasure from these transmogrifications, milking them for maximal comic pleasure. Always a spoiled, self-indulgent child, Murray is wonderfully charming in these sequences. He is also, for the very first time, certifiably real. The spitball-thrower no longer, Murray is visibly wounded by life's slings and arrows—his romantic failures with Rita (Andie MacDowell), the ever-recurring death of the elderly man he finds daily, expiring in a tawdry back alley. The last vestiges of youth drain away from him, leaving a frazzled, disappointed middle-aged man, trapped in a life he never wanted. *Groundhog Day* ends on the expected upbeat note—the calendar page finally turns, the frosty Rita thaws, Phil rediscovers the exuberance of the present—but something of the film's surprisingly raw feeling lingers. "Anything different is good," a relieved Phil pronounces on finding Rita still in his bed the next morning, and Murray seemed to agree with the sentiment, for future roles would increasingly look like *Groundhog Day*'s later stretches. The old Phil was no longer.

Groundhog Day was a welcome diversion from the trend, but it took Wes Anderson's unerring eye for underutilized talent to fully resuscitate Murray's career. *Rushmore* provides confirmation of Murray's heretofore hidden talents, serving as the ideal segue into the darker, richer second half of his career. Anderson has the insight to see the frustrated, miserable middle-aged failure buried beneath the surface of the glib, flippant Murray. Swigging whiskey, lazily tossing golf balls into the pool at his sons' birthday party, a cigarette dangling from his lower lip as he aimlessly cannonballs into the swimming pool, Murray's Herman Blume is *The Graduate*'s Ben Braddock thirty years down the road. Saddled with a wife he doesn't love and children he hates, Herman also seeks refuge in the quiet, still depths, his knees pressed fetally to his chest.

Rushmore is a comedy unlike any Murray had ever done before: forlorn, whimsical, perfectly carved, not raggedly hewn. Herman Blume plays to Murray's strengths in a way that no other character, not even Phil Connors, ever had. There was the opportunity for typical Murray humor—dashing madly to block an elementary schooler's basketball shot, delivering a speech at an exclusive private school whose moral was to "take dead aim on the rich boys"—but it was all encased within a protective shield of sadness. Herman's eyes silently express a pain he prefers not to put into words.

The Bill Murray deadpan long familiar to moviegoers is revealed in *Rushmore* to be a dodge, an attempted escape from engaging too closely with a world intent on slicing him with its jagged edges. Herman is a surrogate father figure to the irrepressible Max Fischer (Jason Schwartzman), seeing in him a temperament far closer to his own than his own sons (grubby spoiled shits that they are). Conflict over the affections of a lonely, widowed schoolteacher (Olivia Williams) turns amity into rivalry. Herman is an overgrown child, perfectly willing to compete on an adolescent's playing field. Hiding behind a tree before approaching his crush, mirthfully crushing Max's bicycle underneath the wheels of his luxury sedan, practically snarfing up his drink at Max's boorish behavior during a formal dinner, Herman is hardly a paragon of middle-aged maturity. The movie pities him and admires him in equal part, and it is Murray's particular genius that he makes each facet equally plausible.

Rushmore would serve as the model for a new brand of Murray hero, inspiring similarly melancholic efforts by Coppola and Jarmusch. First, Murray would be reunited with Anderson, who cast him as Gwyneth Paltrow's long-suffering husband in *The Royal Tenenbaums* (2001). Perhaps deliberately, after being granted so meaty a role in their last collaboration, Murray's Raleigh St. Clair is notable only for his inoffensive blandness. Murray is mostly an afterthought amidst the jewel-box perfection and bittersweet beauty of Anderson's third film, and perhaps that, too, was part of the joke, for who would deliberately waste Bill Murray in this fashion?

Preferring the Murray of *Rushmore* to that of *The Royal Tenenbaums*, Coppola cast him as another melancholy drifter, bonding with fellow tourist Charlotte (Scarlett Johansson) through comfortably awkward silences and mutual sleepless nights in a distinctly foreign country. *Lost in Translation* (2003) is defined by its deadpan gaze, directed at Japan's utter strangeness. Coppola's camera is perpetually, creatively distracted, taking in billboards, passersby, parties, and popular culture with the same welcoming bemusement. Murray imitates its mood, observing everything with straight-faced detachment, as if the world were a practical joke that only he was in on.

His Bob Harris is a slightly over-the-hill movie star, reduced to starring in Japanese whiskey commercials for the sizable payday. "For relaxing times," he intones, practically rolling his eyes at the absurdity of the endeavor, "make it Suntory time." Hectored by belligerent directors, pummeled by the Johnny Carson of Japan for the amusement of television audiences, Bob endures his trials with grim good humor. Murray brilliantly uses his body to convey the disorientation of foreign travel. He bends his knees and cranes his neck to get below the chest-high hotel showerhead, and when the hotel's elliptical machine goes haywire, he briefly, brilliantly summons Jerry Lewis's manic physical grace. *Lost in Translation* is a quiet movie, preferring silence to chatter, and it demands of Murray that he act silently, with his body and with his eyes. He does so admirably; watching him sitting in a Tokyo gentlemen's club as strippers grind away passionlessly and a pornographic rap song blares through the speakers, we tangibly grasp his discomfort, and laugh at it, all at once.

With his puppy-dog eyes, hooded with exhaustion and melancholy, Bob is weighed down by a sadness we never fully grasp. His relationship with Charlotte is less sexual than parental, with Bob carrying the drunken beauty and tucking her into bed with fatherly tenderness. Murray serves as another unlikely father figure in the mode of *Rushmore*, coaxing her through a rough patch even as he endures one of his own. "Does it get easier?" he asks, echoing a question of Charlotte's. "No. Yes. It gets easier." Audiences clamored to know what Bob whispered to Charlotte before they separated, but Murray's eyes, brimming with emotion as Johansson walks away, are perfectly emblematic of Coppola's rich, layered, clever movie. Against all odds, Bill Murray had become an actor.

Murray was nominated for an Academy Award for *Lost in Translation*, and reunited the next year with Anderson for the melancholy boys' adventure *The Life Aquatic with Steve Zissou* (2004). Sumptuously photographed, production-designed to resemble a lavishly illustrated children's book, *Life Aquatic* was derided by some critics for its pretensions to grandeur; the *Village Voice*'s Michael Atkinson memorably described it as "a helium-tickled beach ball of a movie that struggles to stay inflated." Crabby critics notwithstanding, *Life Aquatic* was another miniaturist gem from Anderson: a madcap adventure with an international cast of wonderful weirdos. Murray—gone slightly to seed, his beard now gray, with only flecks of black remaining—is the director of this ramshackle film crew of damaged little boys living out their childhood dreams.

Once more the surrogate father (this time with the doubtful paternity of Owen Wilson's questing Ned hanging in the air like an unanswered question), Murray's undersea explorer Steve Zissou breathes every line like a weary sigh. *Life Aquatic* is simultaneously a depiction of the chaos and commotion of a film set—Anderson's self-reflexive portrait of moviemaking—and another tale of lost sons and inadequate fathers, scored to a looping motif of bittersweet regret. "I haven't been at my best this decade," Zissou tells his estranged wife (Anjelica Huston), and the sentiment could easily have been expressed by any of Murray's recent heroes. Anderson's is a film whose sense of adventure is deliberately amateurish; its action sequences are deliberately, bunglingly ridiculous. And who better to lead the band of madcap globetrotters than Bill Murray?

Bedlam gave way to solitude and stillness for Jarmusch's underrated *Broken Flowers* (2005), but the sentiments were the same. Murray was once more haunted by loss and regret for a life poorly lived. With a pink letter in his hands suggesting the existence of a twenty-year-old son he never knew about, onetime lothario Don Johnston (note the Don Juan–esque name) sets out across the country, tracking down old flames to determine the truth of his possible paternity. Jarmusch (who had previously used Murray in his episodic 2003 film *Coffee and Cigarettes*, trading health advice with the Wu-Tang Clan's RZA and GZA as he swigged directly from a pot of coffee) has crafted a nearly empty film, one whose exchanges of dialogue are less communicative than Don's silent time on the road, between destinations. Much is asked of Murray, who must carry the burden of all the film's submerged emotion on his shoulders. Every word Don utters falls into a bottomless pit of melancholy, weighed down by an undefined misery.

Don is another middle-aged Murray sad sack, on whose face only the ghost of past amusements lingers, but we are charmed nonetheless by Don's gaze, which offers us license to laugh at the distinctly American weirdness of the women—professional closet organizers, hippies turned real estate developers, animal therapists—he encounters on his travels. Jarmusch frames his star in a series of forlorn tableaus, with the symbols of past pleasure—flutes of champagne, Marvin Gaye ballads—now only conjuring up a pathetic loneliness. *Broken Flowers* is so mired in its melancholy that its humor is almost entirely implied; there is nothing particularly funny that can be articulated about the film, although its tone is one of gentle bemusement.

Broken Flowers was the logical extension of Murray's last decade of work—a comedy whose humor, and whose meaning, is to be found in silences. Only a trace of Murray's impetuous motor-mouthed past remained, but its vestiges—the faint memory of the wisecracks of a young man now mired in rueful middle age—were enough to convince us that even now, he was silently laughing at the world's absurdities.

26

THE COEN BROTHERS

ODDBALL AMERICA

"These blow up into funny shapes and all?"
"Well, no. Unless round is funny."
—Convenience store clerk to H. I. McDunnough
(Nicolas Cage), *Raising Arizona*

At one time, before they began hauling home Oscars by the bushel, Joel and Ethan Coen saw convenience store clerks as emissaries from their homeland in oddball America. By the time of *No Country for Old Men* (2007), Javier Bardem's psychopathic Anton Chigurh uses clerks for proof of his God-like powers over life and death, with coin flips determining their

---

The Dude abides: Jeff Bridges in the Coen brothers' *The Big Lebowski*.

fate, but some twenty years prior, in *Raising Arizona* (1987), register jockeys with impeccably deadpan delivery were proof of something entirely different: that the Coens, who had shot a film called "Henry Kissinger: Man on the Go" at the Minneapolis airport as youngsters, were the true children of Preston Sturges. The ebulliently strange characters, the back flips through genre, the cheerful demolishing of convention: the Sturges blueprint was all still in place, remodeled for the age of Reagan.

Emerging at roughly the same time as fellow indie auteurs Spike Lee and Jim Jarmusch, the Coens evinced a similar desire to avoid pigeonholing of all sorts; they were not comedians first or foremost, but like Robert Altman, comedy informed all of their work. Altman and his fellow disciples had revisited the genres that had become Hollywood staples, revising the Western, the noir, and the musical to properly reflect their pessimism and cynicism. Their successors preferred to stretch genre like taffy, creating pockets of space where the odd and the alluring could find a home.

If the discussion of the Coen brothers' work requires extensive discussion of the work of other filmmakers, there is simply no avoiding the necessity; the Coens are filmmaker-DJs, scratching, scuffing, and remixing American film until it plays a tune entirely of their own making. The task of revising genre had not been exhausted, but the motivation had changed. The Coen brothers preferred uncovering the hidden absurdity of heretofore-stolid genres, standing in ambiguous relation to the classic Hollywood they mined for material. Were they mocking their predecessors, or good-naturedly celebrating them? It depended on whether you thought round was funny.

The Coens had been raised in relative comfort in Minneapolis, Minnesota, where their father was a professor of economics and their mother a professor of fine arts. From an early age, the brothers had been fascinated by film. Fans of *Dr. Strangelove* and the Doris Day–Rock Hudson films of the early 1960s, Joel and Ethan preferred boldness and comic exaggeration to the dully distinguished. The brothers took a Super 8 camera into the backyard, and into the streets, shooting on-the-fly remakes of suspense films like *Advise and Consent* (1962). Not familiar with the concept of editing, they achieved a parallel-editing effect by cutting in the camera: "We'd shoot in one place," they told an interviewer, "then run over to the other and shoot that, then run back and shoot at the first spot again." Joel and Ethan, products of an intellectual Jewish household, were cultural magpies who weren't always familiar with their putative source material—a familiar scenario for their future work.

That remake of *Advise and Consent* was shot without seeing the Otto Preminger film, or reading the Allen Drury novel.

Joel went on to study film at NYU, and Ethan—three years younger—majored in philosophy at Princeton. Even while in school, the Coens collaborated on scripts together, like *Coast to Coast*, a screwball comedy in which twenty-eight Albert Einsteins were to be cloned by Chinese Communists. After graduation, Joel worked as a production assistant and editor on low-budget horror films, and Ethan took odd jobs as they dreamt of making a film of their own. To make their first film, *Blood Simple* (1984), the Coens turned to family friends, and a list of Jewish philanthropists wheedled from Hadassah, to fund the production. They wrote the script together, trading lines back and forth in front of a typewriter.

On set, Joel was nominally the director and Ethan the producer, but the division of labor was hardly precise. Like Billy Wilder with I. A. L. Diamond, Joel used Ethan as a sounding board, checking with his brother before calling "print" on any given scene. Having grown up as codirectors of their adolescent masterpieces, the Coens preferred to maintain joint control over their more mature productions, going so far as to edit their own films under the pseudonym Roderick Jaynes.

There was a nagging sense, with *Blood Simple*, that the Coens were somehow pulling our leg. Their credentials were impeccable, their cinematic references pitch-perfect, but something in the stone-faced noir revivalism of that violent Texas crime thriller indicated a playfulness mostly hidden from view. The film is a noir pastiche, a violent love triangle between Ray (John Getz), Abby (Frances McDormand), and Julian Marty (Dan Hedaya), but strangeness keeps creeping in at the margins, in the form of walk-on characters with agendas of their own. Like the oddballs that populated *The Lady Eve*, or *The Palm Beach Story*, there is a sense that these eccentrics are not supporting characters, but stars of other, unseen movies, of which we are only being provided the briefest of glimpses.

There is the Spanish-speaking landlord showing a potential tenant around an apartment while shouting at a disheveled man who, by all impressions, was still occupying the place: "Don't mind Mr. Garcia. He used to be my brother-in-law." There is the chatty African American bartender, intent on playing his favorite R&B classics on the jukebox of a redneck bar, lecturing Abby at epic length about volcanos. And at the film's very end, there is the midnight-black humor of a dying hit man, his last moments on earth cheered by Abby's stubborn insistence that the man she has just shot is her husband (long since dead): "I'm not afraid of you, Marty!" "Well, ma'am, if I see him," he wheezes, "I'll sure give him the message."

Blood Simple is more of a practice piece than a genuine film, a blood-soaked exercise in noir nostalgia, but hints of the Coens' Sturgesian sympathies were fully confirmed by the rip-roaring comedy of their follow-up. A parable of Reagan-era economic redistribution via armed robbery, the skewed banter, offbeat supporting characters, and bizarre premise of *Raising Arizona* (1987) telegraph its profound debt to Sturgesian screwball.

Recidivist convenience-store robber H. I. McDunnough (Nicolas Cage) is drawn to Ed (Holly Hunter), the corrections officer tasked with booking him after each of his scrapes with the law. Planning optimistically for a life together ("A brighter future lay ahead—a future that was only eight to fourteen months away"), H.I. and Ed marry, only to discover she cannot have children. H.I.'s deadpan narration is like a mock-Billy Wilder hero's: "Ed lost all interest in both criminal justice and housekeeping," he tells us, as the camera pans across a floor strewn with dirty clothes. Prodded by Ed, H.I. goes ahead and steals Nathan Jr., one of the famous Arizona family quintuplets. Money is tight, and soon enough H.I. is back to his old ways, a stocking on his head and Huggies under his arm as he dashes down the street, chased by trigger-happy cops, pimply teens with Dirty Harry weaponry, rampaging dogs, and worst of all, his furious wife.

Raising Arizona is simultaneously a cold-blooded farce, dropping a stick of dynamite at the foot of the white picket fence surrounding the American dream, and a tender comedy of marital sin and redemption, with Hunter and Cage (outfitted in an array of garish Hawaiian shirts, and with hair the color and texture of a dirty mop) finding their Zen through crime. It is a clamorous pastiche of clashing approaches, with differing narrative styles snatching control of the film like they were making off with Nathan Jr. H.I. and Ed are dim-witted lovers on the run out of *Bonnie and Clyde*, or Altman's *Thieves Like Us*; H.I.'s prison-escapee buddies Gale and Evelle are 1950s greasers from a grade-Z prison flick as filtered through the brainless hijinks of Laurel & Hardy; and the Lone Biker of the Apocalypse, who chases H.I. with demonic intensity, is channeled directly from *The Road Warrior*.

Synthesizing these jarring textures is the Coens' winking sensibility, best summarized by that convenience-store clerk and his deadpan judgment on the humorousness of balloons. *Raising Arizona* is the Coens' first stab at creating an oddball America full of losers, obsessives, neurotics, and misfits.

Attempting to revive screwball comedy for the 1980s, the Coen brothers began a tradition of tunneling out from underneath a well-established cinematic tradition. Genre was only a starting point, an easy-to-adapt template for their flights of wink-wink fantasy.

Miller's Crossing (1990) maintains the air of genre fidelity while mostly ditching the comedy. The Coens' most straight-faced film (at least until *No Country for Old Men*), *Miller's* is a somber gangster-film update, like *The Public Enemy* with a headache and a mild case of depression. The brothers' foray into James Cagney territory keeps its sense of humor firmly pinned to the ground, but loyalty to their predecessors erupts in an overabundance of deference. It is a movie filled with socks to the jaw, rattling tommy-guns, and smoke curling out of pistols, like a Dick Tracy cartoon strip come to rattling life. Like both of the Coens' preceding films, it is a tale of double- and triple-crosses, of conflicting loyalties and dueling responsibilities. Its pleasures are less in its deliberately familiar plot elements—feuding mob bosses, amoral, seductive molls, urban corruption (as if this were a loose remake of Sturges's *The Great McGinty*)—than its baroque love of the crime film's patter.

Miller's Crossing is drunk on language, suggesting an update of Abraham Polonsky's gloriously purple noir classic *Force of Evil*. The film drips with memorable lines. Jon Polito's crass, self-conscious boss Johnny Caspar in particular is a fount of fecund phrases. "What is this, the high hat?" he keeps asking, worried that someone—anyone—might be looking down their nose at him. There is a certain Yiddish gleam to the Coens' screenplay, dotted as it is with words like "shmatte" and "kaputnik," as if its Italian and Irish gangsters had all studied together at the same heder before taking to a life of crime.

Miller's Crossing was as much about its decor as anything else, and the Coen brothers were often accused of favoring style over substance. Their next film did little to discourage such detractors. Once again, the implicit subject was Jews adrift in somebody else's picture, somebody else's fantasy. The Coens had already demonstrated, in word and in spirit, a fondness for the 1940s, and *Barton Fink* (1991) picks up lock, stock, and barrel and sets up shop in Hollywood circa 1941. Barton (John Turturro, with thick eggshell glasses and an imposing tower of curls) is a Clifford Odets–like Broadway success transplanted to Los Angeles to write a Wallace Beery wrestling picture.

The Coens get a vicious kick out of writing Barton's overheated, symbolically top-heavy dialogue. ("It's late." "Not any more, Lil—it's early.") Tending to agree with Jack Warner that "if you want to send a message, call Western Union," the Coen brothers belittle their protagonist for his pretensions to social significance. *Barton Fink*, written and shot during a hiatus in the production of *Miller's Crossing*, is the blackest sort of comedy, one in which Barton's own fears of milking the destitute and despondent for fame and fortune are symbolically punished by the common man he so lavishly praises. Turturro is superb, and John Goodman is excellent as his working-class foil, but *Barton Fink* cannot help but feel, its abundance of well-tended historical detail notwithstanding, curiously empty.

Barton Fink is an industry satire, a mockery of writerly pretension, a Hollywood historical picture, and an Art Deco fantasia, all at once. These clashing goals jostle for space, much like in *Raising Arizona*, but unlike that extremely casual screwball adventure, *Barton Fink* struggles under the weight of the Coens' sneering indictment of their fellow scribes. Obsessively stylized, in the manner of *Miller's Crossing*, *Barton* is too pretty for its own good, subverting its own satirical bite with an excess of art-directorial lavishness.

The Hudsucker Proxy (1994) picks up where *Fink* leaves off, a 1940s Art Deco picture transplanted to the 1950s. Ransacking not just Sturges but Howard Hawks's rat-a-tat Cary Grant comedies and Frank Capra's common-man trilogy (*Mr. Deeds Goes to Town, Meet John Doe, Mr. Smith Goes to Washington*), *Hudsucker* pits 1940s noir pessimism against sunny Ike-era optimism, rigging the game so that Tim Robbins's gormless chump vanquishes Paul Newman's cigar-chomping schemer. It is a big-business film, crammed full of fast talkers, worriers, charmers, and connivers.

Overly full—there is plot enough for two films, and dialogue for three—*Hudsucker* is nonetheless an amiable, ramshackle affair. Following the suicide of company founder and Dick Cheney look-alike Waring Hudsucker ("Say, buddy, when's the sidewalk fully dressed? When it's Waring Hudsucker!"), eminence grise Sidney Musburger (Newman) plans to hire a schlemiel to run the business into the ground so he can make a killing on the stock market. That schlemiel presents himself in the form of Norville Barnes (Robbins), recent graduate of the Muncie College of Business Administration and part-time inventor. "For instance," he tells Musburger, showing him a drawing of a circle, "take a look at this sweet baby." After an uncomfortably long pause, he adds: "You know, for kids."

Norville's invention is, of course, the hula hoop, and the company death spiral becomes an unexpectedly graceful upward swoop. As wisecracking, multitasking reporter Amy Archer—think the Jean Arthur role, since this is a sort of Capra film, *Mr. Smith Goes to the Boardroom*—Jennifer Jason Leigh summons the spirit of Katharine Hepburn with her irrepressible, mile-a-minute stream of talk and her vaguely British, Cambridge, England-via-Cambridge, Massachusetts accent. Reviewers singled Leigh out for particular abuse, but in fact her performance is a sheer delight, taking this already-delirious film over the top.

Success goes to Norville's head, and *His Girl Friday* gives way to *It's a Wonderful Life*, with an amiable, quasi-mystical clock operator saving Norville and redeeming this gentle fable from irreversible tragedy. *Hudsucker*'s ending is supposed to be cornball, and we are intended to reject it. Knowing their audience of wised-up hipsters, the Coens had crafted a film intended to collapse under the weight of its own sugary pretensions. Postmodern Dr. Frankensteins, the Coens had reanimated the corpse of Capra-corn while ensuring that its heart could beat no longer.

Hudsucker was only a partial success, but its confident appropriation of genre and its mix-and-match aesthetic would lay the groundwork for the Coens' next two films, easily the most successful in their careers. *Fargo* (1996) and *The Big Lebowski* (1998) have little in common other than a sense of dependable genres having come entirely unmoored. Unlike *Hudsucker* or *Raising Arizona*, Joel and Ethan would not fold their hand partway through and burst into knowing laughter. Instead, the thriller and the private-detective film would be in for thorough renovations. In the case of the latter, the job was so thorough that not everyone would recognize the old jalopy.

At first, *Fargo* seems to have trouble deciding just what it is: a crime film, or a black comedy about Middle American dimwits. Half the joke appears to be the accents alone—broad Minnesotan vowels and aw-shucks mannerisms. *Fargo* is a cavalcade of "yahs" and a battalion of "jeezes," the hilarity of the characters' vocal inflections overshadowing, at first, the machinations of car dealer Jerry Lundegaard (William H. Macy), who hires two criminals (Steve Buscemi and Peter Stormare) to kidnap his wife and hold her for ransom. Macy's inept, desperate schemer is a successor to Jack Lemmon's sweaty-palmed Billy Wilder heroes, relocated to the Midwest, and stranded at the intersection of comedy and horror.

Pleased as punch by the underutilized Midwestern locale, reminiscent of their own Minnesota youth, the Coens embrace the inarticulate conversation, the relentless bad weather, the puffy coats, and the guileless sincerity of their characters. The crimes themselves are laughably peculiar, too; who can remember ever seeing a wood chipper put to so distinctly unorthodox a use as when Stormare disposes of his partner's body? *Fargo* occasionally condescends to its characters, treating them as objects of comic curiosity, but it is in the service of a larger purpose. The film sets up easy jokes but resolutely refuses to deliver the punch lines. It's a farce that silently, unexpectedly becomes a tragedy of American greed, desperation, and violence—*No Country for Old Men* without the air of ritualized formalism, wrapped in the cocoon of Carter Burwell's magnificent score.

Marge Gunderson (Frances McDormand), who does not even show up until more than a half hour of the film has elapsed, is herself an elegant piece of Coensian misdirection, appearing at the outset to be little more than another relentlessly chirpy local yokel. But the pregnant police chief, eating or drinking in nearly every scene she appears in, is ultimately *Fargo's* moral conscience, her sense of horror and pity outweighing its snarky comedy. McDormand (Joel Coen's wife) is magnificent as Marge, an indomitable hero whose exterior pudge hides interior steel.

Fargo brought the Coens their first Best Picture nomination, and won McDormand an Oscar for good measure. *The Big Lebowski*, in comparison, won no prizes, and received befuddled, if mostly pleasant, reviews. Lightly regarded on its initial release, the intervening decade has turned *Lebowski* into the quintessential cult film of the decade; Lebowski Fest, anyone? Since any discussion of *The Big Lebowski* could easily lead to line-by-line quotation of the film's brilliantly loopy screenplay, it is perhaps most sensible to begin with *Lebowski's* tone. Robert Altman's *The Long Goodbye* had resuscitated Raymond Chandler's legendary Philip Marlowe in order to lay bare the loneliness and moral ambiguity that had always lurked at the margins of the private-detective film. *The Big Lebowski* is a satiric overhaul of the genre, mocking its lone-man-on-a-mission sensibility as it hands over the investigation to an utter incompetent.

Stumbling into a scenario far too complex for his marijuana-and-White-Russian-addled brain, the Dude (Jeff Bridges) is a singularly inept private dick. The Dude—aka Jeffrey Lebowski—is an unreconstructed 1960s burnout stranded in the Gulf War–era 1990s, a floundering ex-radical equally disgusted by Reaganite economic mavens and Eurotrashy art-world dilettantes. Looking for the missing trophy wife of a wheelchair-bound industrialist also named Lebowski, the Dude encounters the Coens' broadest-ever array of screwballs and cranks: vaginally fixated performance artists, sex-offending bowlers, and wandering cowboys, drifted over from some other Wild West. He is aided in his quest by good buddy Walter Sobchak (John Goodman), a vet with a camouflage vest and a tendency to see everything as related, somehow, to 'Nam.

Lebowski is the fullest expression to date of the Coens' Sturgesian fascination with eccentrics. Everyone has a favorite; mine are the black-clad German nihilists who show up occasionally, demanding payment from the Dude while threatening to cut off his "chonson." John Turturro's Jesus is also an astounding creation, a strutting bantam rooster in royal purple who insists on talking shit to Walter and the Dude about their bowling game: "What's this day of rest shit? What's this bull*shit*? I don't fucking care. It don't matter to Jesus. . . . I would have fucked you in the ass Saturday. I will fuck you in the ass next Wednesday instead." Did I forget to mention that Walter considers himself an Orthodox Jew, and refuses to bowl on Saturdays? "I told that kraut a fuckin' thousand times," Walter rants, "I don't roll on Shabbes!" *The Big Lebowski* is a wormhole down which one can disappear and never return.

Lebowski is a marvel, being essentially a single, film-length shaggy-dog tale enclosed within an astonishingly tight script. With its incompetent scheming and iconoclastic detection, the film could be a remake of *Fargo*, but the mood has changed entirely. *Fargo*'s wintry fatalism has given way to Los Angeles's summery good vibes. The Dude and Walter, too, are a far cry from low-key, efficient Marge Gunderson. Walter alone manages to bungle a handoff of cash, purposefully upends a wheelchair-bound man, cracks a Corvette's windshield, pulls a pistol during a league bowling match, and sprinkles the Dude with the ashes of his closest friend Donny (Steve Buscemi, uncharacteristically blending into the scenery). *The Big Lebowski* is Chandler refracted through the perspective of a drug-addled hippie, *The Long Goodbye* if Elliott Gould's Marlowe had chosen not to refrain from smoking a couple of joints with his neighbors.

Bridges and Goodman are both brilliant here, Walter's manic belligerence the perfect complement to the Dude's muddled good cheer. Goodman had long been the Coens' secret weapon, but with *Lebowski* he outdoes himself, perfecting his blend of bland reassurance and unexpected savagery. And Bridges is nothing short of miraculous here, his Dude a lovable eccentric whose laser-like focus on the minutiae of his own life (room-tying rugs, Creedence tapes, White Russians in danger of being spilled by over-enthusiastic goons) is ultimately his saving grace. The Dude abides.

The Coens had paid homage to Sturges in their own idiosyncratic way in nearly all their films. As its title would indicate to those familiar with *Sullivan's Travels*, *O Brother, Where Art Thou?* (2000) is an attempt to hijack Sturges outright. Borrowing the title of Sully Sullivan's would-be magnum opus about the real America, *O Brother* is instead a magical-realist prison-escape movie, a Warner Bros. crime film shot by MGM's musical unit. *O Brother* pilfers the rambling gait and chain-gang milieu from *Sullivan's*, but otherwise entirely misreads the bittersweet perfection of Sturges's masterpiece.

George Clooney, John Turturro, and Tim Blake Nelson are escaped convicts on the run, their adventures (*very* loosely based on Homer's *Odyssey*) bringing them in contact with a hodgepodge of old-South tropes: revival meetings, Ku Klux Klan rallies, bluesman Robert Johnson, bank robber Baby Face Nelson, music-man governor Pappy O'Daniel. With its superb selection of revamped old-time ditties, *O Brother* is a soundtrack in search of a film. The maelstrom of action is as dense as *Lebowski*'s, but the air of condescension—of snickering at the yokels—tamped down in their two prior films, roars right back to the surface here. Even the Coens' trusty sense of humor fails them in *O Brother*. An attempted-lynching scene is played for comedy, as if a KKK rally could be merely another chuckle-inducing component of the hilarious Jim Crow South.

Even the homage to *Sullivan's Travels* is botched. The arrival of the chain gang to watch a movie is played strictly for suspense—the escapees think the guards have arrived to capture them—and the movie-love perfection of Sturges's ode to the power of comedy is crushed by the Coens' heavy-handedness.

The Coens' formula—playing nice with genre, only to thrash it mercilessly—was growing wearisome, requiring the rejuvenating touch of inspiration. *The Man Who Wasn't There* (2001) was another *Miller's Crossing*–esque attempt at noir, its somber mood punctured only occasionally by absurdities like the revolutionary new technology its characters discuss investing in: dry cleaning. *Intolerable Cruelty* (2003), like *Raising Arizona*, commandeers a comedic sub-genre of Hollywood's golden age, swiping the screwball comedy of remarriage and dashing for the exits.

Casting was of the essence here; as two of the most charming, most photogenic stars in Hollywood, Clooney and Catherine Zeta-Jones were ideal as the divorce lawyer who has written the industry's most ironclad prenuptial agreement and the gorgeous gold digger he falls in love with. *Intolerable Cruelty* is an old-fashioned battle of the sexes, a la *Adam's Rib*, but crammed full of grotesques like private eye Gus Petch (Cedric the Entertainer), proud progenitor of the catchphrase "I'm gonna nail yo' ass!" and asthmatic hit man Wheezy Joe, who fatally confuses his inhaler with his pistol.

Clooney is again all facial tics and spasms, scrunching his forehead and popping his eyes, but he makes a better mock Cary Grant than a mock Paul Muni. And in Zeta-Jones, he has found a worthy foil. Clooney is a verbally dexterous legal shark, swallowing opponents whole and spitting out their skeletons, and Zeta-Jones is a scheming hussy on the trail of an epochal payday. Their collision sends sparks flying. When Clooney, ironing out her prenup with the latest sucker-husband, pulls her aside for a private conference, his tone of voice belies his selection of words: "You fascinate me" comes out sounding more like "I hate your guts." *Intolerable Cruelty* is charmingly cynical about wedded bliss.

Intolerable Cruelty had reimagined *The Awful Truth* and *My Favorite Wife* as a crass financial squabble couched in the sweet nothings of love, and succeeded. As a remake of a British comedy classic, *The Ladykillers* (2004) should have been an easy smash for the Coens, but other than Roger Deakins's lovely photography, there was little to rave about. In what should have been a dream collaboration of filmmaker and leading man, Tom Hanks was miscast in the Alec Guinness role as the murderous impresario. And among the eclectic supporting cast (which included Marlon Wayans, J. K. Simmons, and Irma P. Hall), there was nary a Peter Sellers to be found. The Coens had always been metaphorically adapting others' films, but the task of actual adaptation proved ill-suited for the Coens, cramping their essential playfulness by imposing a solution where all they sought was an open-ended question.

After the terrifying, Best Picture–winning *No Country*, from which little laughter could be squeezed other than the inadvertent chuckles directed at Javier Bardem's ridiculous mop of hair, the Coens returned to screwball with *Burn After Reading* (2008). A comedy of personal and professional duplicity, *Burn* tweaks the spy thriller, depositing a pair of bumbling buffoons into a genre known for its chess-playing wizards. Linda and Chad (Frances McDormand and Brad Pitt), both employees of a Washington, D.C., gym, are dunces with an inflated sense of their own intellectual gifts. When they stumble on what appears to be a document containing sensitive government secrets, they contact the author, recently fired CIA spook Osbourne Cox (John Malkovich), hoping to blackmail him for a healthy payday.

Burn After Reading contains all the familiar elements of a Jason Bourne–variety spy thriller: great-power rivalry, satellite imagery, car chases, and much pseudo-insider gobbledygook about the significance of the film's designated MacGuffin. So why is it that, for all its momentary satirical pleasures, this *Burn* leaves an unpleasant taste? *Lebowski* was brilliant because, for all the myriad oddities glimpsed within (bowling Vikings, or porn films starring German nihilists), the entire gloriously messy hodgepodge revolved around a single, well-defined character. *Burn After Reading* has too many centers of attention—I haven't even begun to describe the adulterous affair between George Clooney and Tilda Swinton, or Richard Jenkins's unrequited passion for McDormand—and its intended mood of delirious, gleeful mayhem falls flat.

There are still pleasures to be had here, as with nearly every Coen Brothers picture. Pitt, always a better character actor than leading man, is charmingly goofy as an overgrown boy playing spy. A man whose most profound enthusiasm is reserved for the latest in treadmills, Chad miraculously transforms his stupidity into mystery. Outfitted with an ill-fitting blonde wig and an unflattering wardrobe, McDormand is a rare speck of warmth in this frigid atmosphere. All Linda dreams of is a little nip and tuck, and a suitor who does not look as if "his optometrist has a sense of humor." McDormand gave the potentially disastrous *Fargo* its soul; here, her profound humanity overloads a film not prepared for the presence of real, wounded souls.

All of which brings us, as if completing the circle, back to a familiar time and place: 1960s Minnesota. Returning to their childhood—that era of Jefferson Airplane on the radio and youngsters filming "Henry Kissinger: Man on the Go"—the Coens offer a twisted retelling of the Book of Job set under the endless skies and leafy streets of Midwestern suburbia. All the buried Jewish miserabilism of the Coens' oeuvre—the Yiddish-speaking gangsters and Orthodox Vietnam vets ("Three thousand years of beautiful tradition from Moses to Sandy Koufax," Goodman hollers in *Lebowski*, "you're goddamn right I'm living in the fucking *past!*")—has finally emerged. *A Serious Man* (2009) is a refracted memoir that is also an acknowledgement of the terrifying unknowability of the world.

Larry Gopnik (Michael Stuhlbarg) is a college professor and middle-class Jewish exemplar whose world unexpectedly, and without prior warning, falls to pieces: his wife plans to leave him, his tenure review is threatened by a blackmailing student, and someone named Dick Dutton from the Columbia Record Club keeps calling, hectoring him for overdue payment on some albums he never ordered.

Larry has been cursed by God, but even worse, he is cursed by Heisenbergian uncertainty: "It proves we can't ever really know what's going on," he tells his class, standing in front of a blackboard covered in mathematical formulae. "But even though you can't figure anything out, you will be responsible for it on the midterm."

A Serious Man is Larry's own spiritual midterm, a test of his moral progress played out against a backdrop of middle-class anomie and boredom. As usual, the Coens get every small detail correct; those viewers without a Jewish day-school education, or a Yiddish-to-English (and Hebrew-to-English) dictionary handy, are likely to feel somewhat stranded. But *A Serious Man*—like Woody Allen's *Crimes and Misdemeanors*, whose roundelay of doctors' visits and ministering rabbis this film echoes—is a lovingly rendered portrait of familiar, near-familial grotesques, a howl of terror stifled by a laugh.

The Coens' usual parade of crackpots—Mrs. Robinson–esque next-door neighbors, truth-seeking dentists, batty Hebrew-school teachers—are painted against a backdrop whose bleak blankness is seemingly borrowed from *No Country for Old Men*. The film is itself a proof of the very uncertainty it reflects on: just as its shaggy-dog story has been neatly resolved, the reunited parents *shepping naches* over their son the bar mitzvah boy, a tornado approaches. The huge gray cloud envelops the screen, and Larry, seemingly spared the worst in his trials, is symbolically condemned to death, the victim of God's terrible absence.

Having come home, the Coen brothers discover—to their evident aesthetic satisfaction, if not quite their pleasure—that even the realm of childhood is not spared from a glimpse of the abyss. The oddball America is as much their home as ever, but superficially charming as it may be, it provides no protection from *A Serious Man*'s austere desolation. Relentless pranksters of the American comedy film, the Coens had settled into middle-aged morbidity, their mischievous spirits now tempered by a sense of tragic pointlessness. The Coens had, at last, graduated to making their own *Sullivan's Travels* and sadly determined that, in their own estimation, laughter could offer little solace when the tornado beckoned.

27

CHRISTOPHER GUEST

THE BARON OF THE MOCKUMENTARY

"There was abuse in my family, but it was mostly musical in nature."
—John Michael Higgins, *A Mighty Wind*

T he list of prominent figures in American comedy who have also served as hereditary peers in the British House of Lords is rather short. In fact, it contains just one name: Christopher Guest, also known as Christopher Haden-Guest, fifth Baron of Saling in the county of Essex.

For Alan Barrows (Guest), a quiet moment before the performance in *A Mighty Wind*.

In contrast to his aristocratic lineage, Guest's films, as a writer, actor, and director, are primarily concerned with everyday people, hangers-on at the margins of fame believing themselves destined for greatness: dog lovers, community-theater performers, once-famous folkies. Guest has a tender interest in regular folks, taking pleasure in their ordinariness even as he enjoys savaging them. In the process, he has helped to create a new comic genre that would best accommodate his blend of the cruel and the kind: the mockumentary.

First trotted out for 1984's *This Is Spinal Tap*, which Guest cowrote and starred in, the mockumentary form gave Guest free reign to indulge his favorite pastime: watching intently as others hoisted themselves with their own petards. His characters are not stupid, exactly; they merely seem to have lost the ability to hear themselves speak. In films like *Waiting for Guffman*, *Best in Show*, and *For Your Consideration*, Guest revels in the foolishness of those barely surviving at the edges of celebrity, drowning in their own acute sense of self-importance: actors convinced that their ludicrous indie film is a surefire Oscar smash, delusional old folkies gathered for one last hootenanny, rockers whose amps go up to 11 but whose bulbs are permanently stuck on "dim." Guest is their poet-king, and they are his subjects.

Guest can be harsh at times. Placing his audience in the superior role of knowing cultural sophisticates, Guest grants them permission to chuckle, and occasionally sneer, at the cluelessness of the philistines. Guest's world is peopled with oddballs and scene-stealers who might have stepped from the pages of a Preston Sturges screenplay (as an actor, Guest is something of a Sturges oddball himself), but Guest lacks Sturges's benign admiration for eccentricity. He is every bit as likely as Sturges was to cede center stage to his beloved crackpots, but Guest can't resist kicking them in the behind for good measure. Does Guest love his characters, or does he exploit them for their absurdity? The answer varies from film to film, depending on the precise ratio of compassion to cruelty employed.

Like Sturges, Guest has an eye for the unusual face, or the funny voice, and a determined preference for working with the same stable of actors. The relation of star to supporting cast, familiar from the classical-Hollywood formula, however, has been entirely altered. Elliott Gould and Donald Sutherland had once complained, on the set of *MASH*, that director Robert Altman ignored them in favor of extras and character actors; but Guest goes that crucial extra step. There are no stars in Guest's world, only modestly familiar faces, trading roles from film to film. *Waiting for Guffman* would introduce many of the actors who would become regulars in Guest's stable, many of them veterans of improv comedy: Catherine O'Hara, Fred Willard, Eugene Levy, Parker Posey, Michael Hitchcock, Bob Balaban. Guest's *Spinal Tap* bandmates Michael McKean and Harry Shearer would soon join the fun, and Jane Lynch, Jennifer Coolidge, John Michael Higgins, and Ed Begley Jr. would eventually be added to Guest's stable.

The demands Guest places on his actors are intense: providing them with little more than a brief description, and a single motivating detail ("She's the sort of woman who wears pantyhose with open-toed sandals"), he asks them to mold their characters, supplying everything from costumes to accents. Guest sees the process as musical in nature, comparing his actors to jazz musicians: "We're actors and we're really jamming, with people soloing occasionally." Guest provides the stage, calls the key, and leaves his bandmates to figure out the tune.

The director himself is a featured actor in his own films, disappearing into roles to such an extent that even fans of his work might have trouble remembering what he looks like, or determining which role he might be playing in a given film. Guest has always been the kind of actor who preferred to remain anonymous. In this, he is emulating a childhood hero. Guest grew up in an artsy household in New York City, where his favorite actor was Peter Sellers. His father, Lord Peter Haden-Guest (eventually to be the fourth Baron of Saling), served as editorial director of the United Nations' publication arm, and his mother Jean Hindes was a vice president of casting and talent at CBS.

A musically limber adolescent, Guest picked up the guitar and mandolin, and occasionally backed up his high-school friend Arlo Guthrie at his Greenwich Village gigs. He went on to study theater at Bard and NYU, where he roomed, and wrote songs, with future collaborator and Spinal Tap bandmate Michael McKean. Guest also took a small part in a production of Jules Feiffer's play *Little Murders*, where his castmates included an up-and-coming actor named Fred Willard.

After college, Guest continued to act, with some success, and began writing sketches for *National Lampoon* magazine, the *National Lampoon Radio Hour* (which also nurtured the young Bill Murray), and *The Lily Tomlin Show*, for which he won an Emmy. He was nominated for three Grammys for his work on Lampoon comedy albums. Guest made regular television appearances, starring in a pilot for a program called *The TV Show* in 1978. The pilot was the only episode ever aired, but it included a skit featuring a heavy-metal band named Spinal Tap that would soon bear much fruit.

Guest is the mercurial guitarist Nigel Tufnel in *This Is Spinal Tap* (1984), which he cowrote with McKean (playing lead singer David St. Hubbins), Shearer (bassist Derek Smalls), and director Rob Reiner. The film introduces the style that Guest would soon make his own. There were precursors to *Spinal Tap* in the work of Woody Allen, whose *Take the Money and Run* and *Zelig* had also cleverly imitated newsreel footage, but here the style *was* the joke. Cinematographer Peter Smokler was hired on the basis of his work on the groundbreaking Rolling Stones documentary *Gimme Shelter* (1970), whose unpolished aesthetic *Spinal Tap* sought to purloin and mock.

Intrepid filmmaker Marty Di Bergi (played by Reiner) follows heavy-metal band Spinal Tap around on their sure-to-be-triumphant American tour. The "rockumentary," as Di Bergi dubs it, gives the impression of being shot on the fly, with herky-jerky camerawork, ragged zooms, and MTV-style editing contributing to the sensation of immediacy. The cutting-edge cool of *Spinal Tap*'s style is repeatedly undercut by the sense of an era coming to an end: Spinal Tap, so long a fixture of the metal scene, have come to the end of their run, hemorrhaging fans—or developing a more selective appeal, as their manager diplomatically puts it. The result is a portrait of a band in unexpected crisis, accidentally revealing far more than they might care to about themselves and their music.

Spinal Tap is an embarrassment of comic riches; nearly every scene contributes another aperçu to the pop-cultural treasury. "We've got armadillos in our trousers," Nigel says of his band's lack of appeal to young girls. "They run screaming." (Derek proves his bandmate partially correct later in the film, removing a foil-wrapped cucumber from his slacks at a metal detector, to the deep consternation of a security guard.) A critic offers an acerbic two-word review of a lackluster album, *Shark Sandwich*—"Shit sandwich." "If I told them once, I told them a hundred times," David's girlfriend rues on glimpsing the latest in a wave of dispiriting theater marquees. "Put Spinal Tap first, and puppet show last."

Best of all are the entirely absurd songs McKean, Guest, and Shearer dream up for their imaginary band, whose lyrics treat muddle-headed metaphors with hushed reverence. "I met her on Monday, 'twas my lucky bun day," goes a particularly subtle lyric from the Tap's smash hit "Big Bottom." "I like to sink her with my pink torpedo."

Spinal Tap is a deft musical parody, deflating heavy metal's pomposity and self-aggrandizement. *Spinal Tap* gets the music, and its enduring popularity is in large part due to its precision targeting of the unwitting absurdity (double basses! Marshall amps that go up to 11, not 10! Stonehenge backdrops!) of Deep Purple–style arena rock. *Spinal Tap*'s humor stems from its air of accidental revelation. The band and their handlers don't intend to reveal themselves as sub-moronic, sex-obsessed stooges whose brains, not just their eardrums, have been affected by years of high decibel levels. But the ever-present camera, and Reiner's faux-befuddled style of questioning, leaves them no other option. They simply aren't good enough actors to put on a show for that long.

On the strength of *Spinal Tap*, Guest (along with Shearer) was hired for the 1984–85 season of *Saturday Night Live*. At *SNL*, Guest was more of a mystery than a revelation. For a show used to the bright, brassy work of Eddie Murphy and Bill Murray, Guest was an unreserved flop (in much the same way Ben Stiller would be a few seasons later), lasting only one season before leaving. "Chris Guest is impossible to talk to," remembered a staff writer from the show. "The man is an emotional desert. He will not break his deadpan for any force on earth, so it's very hard to interact with him in a friendly way." There were, nonetheless, intimations of what was to come. A pseudo-documentary short film about the world of synchronized swimmers was *Spinal Tap*–esque in intent, looking forward to Guest's own investigations of tiny, self-enclosed communities of obsessives. The style was not a strong fit for the middle-of-the-road *SNL* of Billy Crystal and Martin Short, but was an effective test run for the pointillist aesthetic of *Waiting for Guffman*.

After being featured in Reiner's tongue-in-cheek fable *The Princess Bride* (1987), in which he was the villainous six-fingered count who killed Inigo Montoya's father, Guest made the transition from actor to director. His underrated directorial debut, *The Big Picture* (1989), is a gentle satire of movie-studio inanity. Its hero, fledgling director Nick Chapman (Kevin Bacon), is a student Academy Award winner with a script he is aching to shoot. Nick jumps on the studio merry-go-round, taking meetings with execs and signing on with a schmooze-happy agent (Guest's former *SNL* castmate Martin Short, effervescently inane). The studio takes his idea for a film—a love triangle at a snowed-in country house—and looks to jazz it up: how about a lesbian love triangle? How about stewardesses? How about fifteen or twenty pop hits to supplement the film? Bacon, young and impressionable, agrees to everything. Nick sells out his friends and becomes an obnoxious, Porsche-driving yuppie asshole before the ink is even dry on his contract, only to come crawling back to his old life once fame and fortune evaporate.

The Big Picture is not quite a great film, lacking the razor-sharp focus and unity of tone of Guest's mockumentaries to come. In its later moments, when Nick becomes a mensch once more, it flirts dangerously with sappiness. Nonetheless, Guest's portrait of clubby Hollywood dingbats drips with malice; the director's preferred medium is acid splashed against celluloid. Short's agent is an impish satyr with strawberry curls and attention deficit disorder, constantly pledging his faithfulness as his gaze flits to some other, more desirable potential client elsewhere. Dozens of comedies of the 1980s and 1990s, including *Bowfinger* and David Mamet's *State and Main*, would similarly gang-tackle the foolishness of the film industry, but few would come down so thoroughly on the side of the preyed-upon, independent-minded filmmaker.

The Big Picture is charmingly slight, with numerous jabs at the Hollywood rat race, and a well-honed sense of film history in its frequent fantasy sequences. What it is, above all, is a celluloid post-it note written by the director to himself: a reminder of what pitfalls Hollywood laid in his path, and a marker of his determination not to turn into another Nick Chapman, spit out and discarded by the film industry.

In the aftermath of *The Big Picture*, Guest briefly returned to playing Nigel Tufnel, releasing the surprisingly successful Spinal Tap reunion album *Break Like the Wind* in 1992, which spawned the hit single "Bitch School." He went on to direct the HBO film *Attack of the 50 Ft. Woman* (1993), which transforms the 1958 original into a feminist fable. *Fable* is the operative word; Guest plays up the hokiness of *Attack*'s science-fiction pastiche with deliberately artificial backdrops and cardboard spaceships. The film, starring Daryl Hannah as a beleaguered housewife who takes revenge on her manipulative, cheating husband, is entertaining if entirely predictable, but there are traces here of Guest's later style. The batty townsfolk—dipshit deputies and gold-prospecting hoboes—anticipate the down-home lunacy of *Waiting for Guffman*.

Some thirteen years after his first parodic jab at the unwittingly foolish, Guest returned to the comedic style he had played a part in creating. *Waiting for Guffman* (1997) establishes the template that future Guest films would follow. The director's style was purely improvisatory, with Guest providing no rehearsal and little preparation for his actors. The free-form process was enough to rattle the most experienced performers, but Guest's preference was to let his actors figure out the details. *Spinal Tap* borrowed extensively from Allen, but *Guffman*'s guiding spirit is unquestionably Robert Altman, whose improvisatory, democratic method had been co-opted by Guest and twisted toward more broadly comedic ends. (Guest had worked with Altman, acting in his little-seen 1987 film *Beyond Therapy*.) Guest's sets were improv sessions, with Guest the framer redacting the enormous mass of raw material into suitable shape. Eighty hours of film would become, after a nearly endless eighteen-month editing process, a brisk ninety-minute romp. Like Altman's, these are films *made* in the editing room.

Guffman is perhaps the flintiest of Guest's films, its portrait of the delusionally Broadway-bound lacking the sympathy and pathos that dot his later work. We are meant to enjoy our superiority over these Midwestern rubes so entirely lacking in self-awareness. The deadpan script crafted by Guest and Eugene Levy, and the film's no-frills style, ensures that we do so, but our pleasure in *Guffman* is partially undercut by its sometimes-ugly air of judgmental snarkiness.

An unseen, unheard documentary crew descends on Blaine, Missouri, to capture the celebratory theatrical spectacle for the sesquicentennial ("that's the hundred and fifty") of the town. The town fathers hire Broadway vet Corky St. Clair (Guest at his most fey) to oversee the show, and open tryouts bring in a slew of Blaine talents: showbiz couple Ron and Sheila Albertson (O'Hara and Willard), whose pre-performance ritual is as complex as their acting is crude; dentist and funnyman Allan Pearl (Levy); and Dairy Queen employee Libby Mae Brown (Parker Posey, who auditions with a breathy version of Doris Day's "Teacher's Pet").

Red, White, and Blaine, the show Corky directs, is part nostalgia trip, part Americana spectacle, and part local-yokel historical epic, livened up by dotty, *Spinal Tap*–esque musical numbers—"Stool Boom," "Covered Wagons, Open-Toed Shoes." High hopes, and the prospect of an opening-night visit from a New York producer, convince Corky and his actors of the possibility of their inept demonstration soon headlining on the Great White Way.

Guest doesn't just stab his characters in the back; he makes sure to twist the knife for good measure. Levy's dentist does a medley of Stephen Foster ditties, insists on doing terrible impressions of Johnny Carson routines, and has a lazy eye to boot. Willard and O'Hara are even worse: the former blustery and superficially charming, the latter submissive and imagining herself clued-in to theatrical ritual. Between the flattened Midwestern accents and the lack of any discernible onstage talent, *Guffman* is a coast dweller's backhanded slap at the foolishness of flyover country. "I'd like to meet some guys, Italian guys, you know," Libby Mae imagines of her new life in the big city, "and watch TV and stuff."

Guest encourages us to chuckle at his characters' cluelessness, to enjoy the spectacle of their humiliation. This begins with his own character; with his

Judy Tenuta T-shirts and references to going home and biting his pillow, the ostensibly straight Corky is prone to verbal tics hinting at a sexual proclivity more in keeping with Broadway musical theater. He vigorously thrusts his pelvis in a calamitous impression of a dancer, wearing backward baggy jeans as if he were the founder of the Missouri chapter of the Kris Kross fan club.

Guffman gives its characters just enough rope for them to hang themselves with, their delusions of grandeur securing the noose ever more tightly with each ludicrous utterance. Guest's mockumentary, at its most heartless, is less comedy than mass shaming through laughter. Altman's improvisatory looseness inexorably leads to Guest's occasional flashes of heartlessness toward his creations, as if the camera were an observer from some alien planet.

Guffman's characters aren't quite dumb; mostly, they just don't know any better. They are the type of people who would, in all seriousness, open a Manhattan store selling *My Dinner with Andre* action figures and *Remains of the Day* lunchboxes, as Corky's fate would have it. Guest's next mockumentary, 2000's *Best in Show* (in the intervening years, he directed the utterly forgettable Matthew Perry–Chris Farley explorers buddy comedy, *Almost Heroes*), tones down the snark in favor of a distinctly more charming brand of silliness. The setting is now New York, home to the annual Westminster Kennel Club dog show, and the subjects are all manner of dog enthusiasts—owners, breeders, trainers, and general dog fanatics. *Guffman*'s structure is retained, but the mood has mellowed, with gentle ribbing replacing that earlier film's occasionally noxious air of superiority.

Best in Show is the peak of Guest's efforts, providing the ideal balance of exaggerated mockery and low-key satire. The film shares the laughs in democratic fashion, with no one performer dominating the proceedings. Garish clothes and unflattering hairdos still abound—evidently dog owners dress no better than community-theater performers—but Guest's satire is loving, exploring a mysterious, utterly compelling subculture. Guest expands his focus to take in more than mere dreams of Westminster glory. *Best in Show* is a relationship film as much as anything else. "We both have so much in common," an Anna Nicole Smith–esque gold digger played by Jennifer Coolidge enthuses about her elderly, doddering husband. "We both love soup. . . . Talking—and not talking."

Other relationships are equally grounded in miscommunication, paranoia, and low-grade hostility. Eugene Levy's buck-toothed Gerry Fleck, who croons "God Loves a Terrier" at their pre-Westminster party, is increasingly discomfited by the racy past of his wife Cookie (Catherine O'Hara), which apparently included a one-night stand with every swinging bachelor on the Eastern seaboard. Uptight, panicky yuppies Meg and Hamilton Swan (Parker Posey and Michael Hitchcock) are first seen in a therapist's office helping their Weimaraner Beatrice get over the trauma of seeing her "parents" having sex.

Most memorable of all is Fred Willard's non-sequitur-prone dog show announcer Buck Laughlin. Buck interrupts the broadcast to wonder whether dogs from different countries bark differently, asks his partner how much he thinks he can bench-press, and proposes a book of beautiful women bathing dogs called "Doin' It Doggystyle." Willard is radiantly loony (and would play variants on Buck in both *A Mighty Wind* and *For Your Consideration*), but Guest's other characters are granted similar moments of unhinged brilliance. Levy's utterly uncoordinated Gerry (who literally has two left feet) does a wonderfully inept, stiff-shouldered, tight-assed walk on unexpectedly being drafted to show his West Highland terrier, Winky. Jane Lynch's cocky handler Christy Cummings gives the crowd a Mussolini-esque salute after her dog wins best of breed. And Guest's country-boy Harlan Pepper lopes with exactly the same gait as his bloodhound.

Guest is a performer in the Sellers mold, using the actor's toolkit of disguises and hairdos and voices to vanish entirely. His roles are never the showiest, or funniest, in any given film, and he prefers disappearing entirely into his characters, invisible in full sight. As a director, Guest encourages his cast to do precisely the opposite. His films are ensemble works not because no one leaps out to take center stage, but because every character, from those played by his cowriter Eugene Levy to the smallest walk-on role, has a life of their own. In part, this is due to the Altman-esque plethora of raw material; where Altman roves with his camera, cherry-picking favored bits, Guest merely leaves his running, allowing actors to improvise until something captivating emerges. As in the films of Lubitsch and Sturges, one can imagine any of these supporting players becoming the sole subject of their own films, with no noticeable diminution in entertainment value.

A Mighty Wind (2003) returns to the milieu of *This is Spinal Tap*, trading in one self-aggrandizing musical subculture for another. The death of a beloved folk impresario brings all of his favorite acts back together for a gala concert at New York's Town Hall. Once again, Guest introduces his audience to an insular subculture with its own brand of mythology and narcissism, with music as accompaniment to the cocktail of bruised feelings and misguided fantasy.

Three folk groups reunite for the evening, hoping to reclaim some of the fame that had once been theirs. The New Main Street Singers, successors to a once-popular 1960s group, are now headlining at amusement parks, where their harmonies are drowned out by the roar of roller coaster riders. The Folksmen, composed of *Spinal Tap* alums Guest, McKean, and Shearer, have aged into hand-cream enthusiasts and frustrated cross-dressers. And Mitch and Mickey (Levy and O'Hara), onetime favorites of knowledgeable folkies everywhere, have not seen each other for years since Mitch took a decided turn for the worse.

Levy's Mitch is part Dylan, part hobo—a psychiatric patient whose every word requires a careful inhalation of breath, as if protracted speech were a particular challenge. Sadness is in the air, for the first time ever in Guest's oeuvre. "There's a deception here," Mitch tells an anxious promoter. "The audience, they're expecting to see a man who no longer exists." Guest, usually intent on ending every scene with a punch line, offers none here.

Having carefully researched its milieu, *Wind*'s numerous in-jokes about the folk scene add to its verisimilitude, like a display of faux-folksy album covers with names like *Wishin'* and *Pickin'*; the tension between toothy, well-scrubbed groups like the New Main Street Singers and "real" folkies like the Folksmen; and the hyperbolic music historian who calls Mitch and Mickey's "A Kiss at the End of the Rainbow" "a superb moment in the history of folk music—and maybe, maybe a great moment in the history of humans." The musical form is ideal for Guest's preferred mode of realistic fakery. Assigning his performers the task of writing their own songs (and learning how to play their instruments), Guest's musical is endearingly ramshackle, comic, and heartfelt in roughly equivalent doses. "Not since *Nashville*," observed the *Hollywood Reporter* in their review of the film, "has a cast done such a good job of providing their own tunes."

Spinal Tap had struck a power chord with music fans for its uncanny impersonations of brain-dead metal anthems, and *A Mighty Wind* betrays a similarly well-honed ear for retro folk tunes. The movie lives and dies on the basis of its music; a single false note would wreck its ambitions to folkie authenticity. But the songs are just right, particularly Mitch and Mickey's beloved hit "A Kiss at the End of the Rainbow." Written by McKean and Annette O'Toole, "Kiss" garnered an unexpected Oscar nomination for Best Original Song, giving Levy and O'Hara an opportunity to perform in character as Mitch and Mickey for a billion-plus television watchers worldwide, alongside the likes of Alison Krauss and Elvis Costello. It made for great television, was an unlikely triumph for Guest's deadpan comedy, and was quite possibly "a great moment in the history of humans."

For Your Consideration (2006), in comparison, was a step backward. All the familiar ingredients are here: show-business imbecility, left-field Yiddishisms, Fred Willard as a nincompoop with a microphone. But *A Mighty Wind*'s heart does battle with *Guffman*'s callousness for supremacy here, with the final result a strange amalgam of good and evil Guest.

Operating close to home, taking on his own profession a la *The Big Picture*, Guest is in his comfort zone—perhaps too much so. *For Your Consideration* is on its strongest ground when jabbing at the Hollywood hype machine: PR spinmeisters, clueless talk-show hosts, and the blissfully naive actors themselves. Willard is brilliant once more as a moronic *Entertainment Tonight*-esque host prone to ludicrous getups, and Eugene Levy is superb as Shearer's opportunistic agent. The criminally underrated Jennifer Coolidge sparkles as the film's producer: "Someone's killed their children and made them into cookies," she says of one proposed film poster, "and I want to go see that." But Guest's direction is as flat as ever here—every one of his films could be converted into stage shows without much fuss—and the film suffers from a notable diminution of focus, especially when compared to its predecessors.

Guest savages the roller-coaster mentality of the Oscar season, his film echoing the unexpected rise and calamitous fall of one low-budget award contender, the Southern-fried Jewish melodrama *Home for Purim* ("Your coming home today was a *dang mitzvah*"). Shearer and O'Hara, veteran actors with little to show for it, are both hideously transformed by their moment in the Oscar-hype sun. O'Hara's Marilyn Hack appears on television as a sexed-up parody of herself, her breasts spilling out of a low-cut top, her makeup applied with a steamroller, her face frozen in a post-surgical rictus. Shearer's comic comeuppance, on a BET-esque youth program called "Chillaxin'," is hardly more flattering. "In every actor, there lives a tiger, a pig, an ass, and a nightingale," a moderately deranged PR hack tells an underling, but Guest is mostly content with making asses of his performers.

There is, once more, a hint of emotion buried amidst the mélange of flustered hopes. Marilyn sits in front of the television on the morning of the nominations, her Botoxed face impassive as she softly pleads with the screen: "Just say Marilyn Hack." The moment is fleeting, with Guest quickly moving on to the next scene, but even this briefest of interludes is nearly enough to avoid *Guffman*'s bullying aura.

Having been through the mockumentary wringer five times now, there seems to be little Christopher Guest can do with the form he helped to popularize other than repeat himself. Guest's films are a model of accessible high-concept comedy, consciously intended to be a cut above the sophomoric hijinks of the Eddie Murphys of the world. Whatever their faults, Guest's mockumentaries are a distinct, uniform body of work, offering contemporary comedy the closest figure it has to an auteur (along with Judd Apatow). His style has been father to numerous successors, none possessing the wit or panache of Guest himself. Cinematic nobility, Guest himself is both defined and limited by their successes. Unlike Altman, with whom he shares so much stylistically, Guest can only take his films so far. The baron of the mockumentary has become its prisoner as well.

28

BEN STILLER

GOOD JEWISH BOYS

"I'm pretty sure there's a lot more to life than being really, really good looking. And I plan on finding out what that is."
—Ben Stiller, *Zoolander*

Ben Stiller is Jewish. This is a fact about the actor himself, but it is also true of the characters he plays, even when it goes unacknowledged. Those icons of neurotic Jewish comedy, Woody Allen and Dustin Hoffman, are the bookends of Ben Stiller's career. They are the forefathers of his work, their influence directly encoded in Stiller's comedy. Having begun as a Woody parodist—one of the better sketches on his short-lived Fox television series

---

Stiller is hooked on Mary (Cameron Diaz) in *There's Something About Mary*.

The Ben Stiller Show was a note-perfect lampoon of Allen's jerky-camera *Husbands and Wives*, for an imaginary blockbuster called *Woody Allen's Bride of Frankenstein*—Stiller is the comedic heir to Hoffman's Jewish Everyman.

There is undoubtedly a noxious element of racial or ethnic stereotyping in Stiller's performances, which depend on his embodying certain traits of stereotypical Jewishness. He is nebbishy, sexually frustrated, paralyzed by rage; a mama's boy imprisoned in his own neuroses (except when, as in *Zoolander* (2001) and *Dodgeball* (2004), he oscillates to the other extreme and plays monsters of runaway ego). Stiller is so over-the-top, so clearly the embodiment of all the cliches about Jewish men, that he transcends stereotyping to become a parody of the stereotypes. Unlike Allen, Stiller rarely seeks to charm or flatter his audience. Stiller thrives on alienation, on presenting unpleasant, in-your-face characters without apology. He refuses to insert himself between his character and the audience, to remind them that he isn't *really* like that, that all this standoffishness is just an act.

Celebrity was mother's milk for Stiller. His parents are the well-regarded performers Jerry Stiller and Anne Meara. Growing up in its midst (there are home movies of tiny tot Stiller being held by Rodney Dangerfield, and he was taught to swim by the Pips), he was attracted to it himself; it is no accident that his dream project, for a number of years, has been a film version of a novel by another privileged Hollywood scion—Budd Schulberg's *What Makes Sammy Run?* Stiller grew up in New York, kept away from Hollywood distractions by his parents, but he found himself pulled toward the movies. As a child, he and his sister would shoot short films together, with titles like *They Called It Murder*, or *Murder in the Park*. Stiller thought he might be a cinematographer, but after a brief stint at UCLA, he wangled a role in a local production of John Guare's *The House of Blue Leaves*. During breaks between performances, Stiller cajoled the play's cast into shooting a waggish parody of Martin Scorsese's *The Color of Money* called *The Hustler of Money*. The short won him a slot on *Saturday Night Live* at the tender age of twenty-three—a disastrous tenure that lasted only five episodes. Like his comic idol, Albert Brooks, Stiller had dreamt of his own mini-empire within *SNL*, and discovered to his chagrin that Lorne Michaels approved of no vice-regents to his throne.

Stiller was a team player only so long as he was managing the team, and his own 1992 Fox sketch-comedy series, *The Ben Stiller Show* (produced by Judd Apatow), was a far more artistically successful endeavor. *The Ben Stiller Show*—which, in addition, to its namesake, also introduced future comic stars Janeane Garofalo, Andy Dick, and Bob Odenkirk—borrowed the *Saturday*

Night Live model while adapting it to Stiller's own Hollywood-formed tastes. Sketches were brief and punchy, and comic conceits were often grounded in absurdist juxtaposition: what if Al Pacino auditioned for the shaggy-dog film *Beethoven*? What if Fox's then-biggest hit, *Cops*, were set in medieval times?

The show's emphasis was on parodies and spoofs, as if the world were comprised entirely of pop-culture detritus. *The Ben Stiller Show*'s preferred mode of attack was mocking its own irrelevance. Ratings were abysmal, and much of the series' short run was given over to nervous joking about when Fox might finally pull the plug. Guest Dennis Miller genially offered greetings "to the six to eight people in America who watch this show," and in later episodes, the series poked fun at Fox's crass, lowest-common-denominator programming with spoofs like *Skank*, starring a foul-mouthed sock puppet. Needless to say, Fox did not pick up the show for a second season. Stiller received an Emmy as a consolation prize.

Emerging unharmed from the wreckage, Stiller moved on to filmmaking, not only playing a flinty executive at an MTV-esque television channel in *Reality Bites* (1994), but directing the film as well. Stiller's directorial debut epitomizes a now-vanished moment of Generation X ascendancy, defined by romantic confusion, economic insecurity, television-fed nostalgia, and the aggressive wielding of irony. Old friends Lelaina (Winona Ryder) and Troy (Ethan Hawke) are over-educated, underemployed slobs preferring intensive debate over the relative merits of *Good Times*, and the simmering sexual tension between Bonnie Franklin and Schneider on *One Day at a Time*, to adulthood.

Reality Bites is the quintessential Gen X movie, equal parts relationship comedy and generational manifesto. That manifesto is defined by aimlessness and a vague preference for the pleasures of childhood, pierced by an awareness of those pleasures' insufficiency for the complex 1990s. Michael (Stiller) is the artless yuppie in this twentysomething soap opera, overly ambitious (at least by the film's meager standards) and rattled by Hawke's unflappable, sardonic wit. Even at his most assertive, Michael is grasping. When he finally loses his patience with Troy, shouting "Hey, what is your glitch, huh?" one can practically feel the sweat stains forming under his armpits. Michael is the guy who will never—could never—be cool. Blasting gangsta rap out of the speakers of his Audi convertible, he is the epitome of cluelessness. (That "glitch" speaks volumes; Michael cannot even be trusted to get his lingo straight.)

Stiller's clueless-yuppie routine carries over to his next starring role, in David O. Russell's sterling screwball update *Flirting with Disaster* (1996). He is once more the flinty urban professional in search of meaning, this time on a cross-country hunt for his birth parents. The joke is in Stiller's gullible naivete when confronted by purported parental figures; how could his agitated, neurotic Mel Coplin be anything but the son of his adopted parents, the equally agitated, equally neurotic George Segal and Mary Tyler Moore? "I'm Finnish," the first of his potential mothers tells him, by way of genetic explanation. "I knew that!" Mel gratefully exclaims, as if finally grasping his lifelong appreciation of herring and Sibelius.

Summoned away at each stop just before he gets carried away and names his son after a Confederate general, or engages in some long-overdue sibling bonding with the Aryan-goddess volleyball players who are supposed to be his half-sisters, Mel, his wife Nancy (Patricia Arquette), and their adoption adviser Tina (Téa Leoni) are American wanderers, taking in gay-baiting, possibly anti-Semitic truck drivers; Gerald Ford-loving bed-and-breakfast matrons; and other exemplars of homegrown weirdness. In the meantime, *Flirting with Disaster* has unexpectedly become a sex farce, with Mel lusting not-so-secretly after the gorgeous Tina, and the awkward threesome joined by a pair of gay federal agents (played by Josh Brolin and Richard Jenkins). Stiller and Leoni, both superb physical comedians, have a series of abortive sexual encounters that always seem to result in property damage. The neurotics, Jewish in thought if not deed, are thrown together as Arquette and Brolin's sunny Gentiles form a new couple, genially discussing the challenges of nipple-pull while nursing.

That same year, Stiller directed *The Cable Guy* (1996), with Judd Apatow producing and delivering an uncredited polish to the script. The film left critics mostly befuddled and audiences unsatisfied, but is far better than its reputation would have it. Jim Carrey, earning his first twenty-million-dollar payday, is disarmingly creepy as cable repairman Chip Douglas, exposing the psychopath lurking inside his Ace Ventura. A brief sketch on *The Ben Stiller Show* had imagined Wilford Brimley as *Taxi Driver*'s Travis Bickle, blowing kids away with his .32. Chip is a bravura extension of the conceit, a killer with a smile. Manic Chip hooks up the cable for brittle yuppie Steven (Matthew Broderick), and then refuses to go away. At first, the lonely Steven is amenable to Chip's friendly overtures, but soon enough Chip is like a spurned lover, skulking outside Steven's apartment and ignoring all hints about his busy social calendar. *Single White Repairman*, anyone?

Carrey is genuinely unsettling as Chip. A bundled mass of coiled energy in a powder-blue jumpsuit, the mercurial Chip is capable of bounding from friend to foe, from medieval warrior to karaoke-spouting party animal to radical lawyer to therapist, almost instantly, as if an invisible remote control were flicking from channel to channel. Chip is little more than an overgrown child, raised by TV, and like the twentysomethings in *Reality Bites*, he yearns for the soothing homilies of the sitcom. His source material is always television, be it the relationship insights lifted from *The Jerry Springer Show,* or his name, taken from the youngest of the offspring on *My Three Sons*. Steven, with whom we are ostensibly meant to identify, is hardly more likable, using Chip and then discarding him when he can serve no further purpose. The only surprise is that Stiller would have given the role to another actor rather than keeping it for himself.

For fear anyone might have thought Ben Stiller insufficiently committed to the cause of warts-and-all comedy, a cursory glimpse at the opening sequence of *There's Something About Mary* (1998) should have been more than enough to dispel any such concerns. The Farrelly brothers' breakout hit begins with an instant-classic mishap that made *The Cable Guy*'s severe discomfort seem a mere flesh wound. Stiller's Ted is a vision in puce, his strawberry-colored shag and braces completing the picture of 1970s adolescent gawkiness as he awkwardly asks Mary (Cameron Diaz) to the prom. Ted ventures over to Mary's house to pick her up for prom, where he is tormented by her father and caught as a peeper by her mother. Hurriedly zipping up in the bathroom, he gets his privates snagged in the zipper, and unleashes a blood-curdling banshee wail. "Is it the frank," Mary's father anxiously queries, "or the beans?"

The remainder of *There's Something About Mary* cannot possibly match the bravura absurdity of its opening scenes, but the Farrellys do their utmost to try. Ted, now an adult, gullibly agrees that it would be wise to, as pal Chris Elliott suggests, "flog the dolphin" before his big reunion date with Mary. Stiller cannot find the incriminating evidence after the dolphin has been suitably flogged, and it is Mary who eventually locates it on his ear. "Is that hair gel?" she wonders, as she runs it through her locks, forming a stiff artificial cowlick.

Diaz is the infinitely desirable bait, and Stiller and his fellow lonely-guy conspirators (who include weaselly private detective Matt Dillon) seek to wheedle their way into her affections. The result is a warped romantic comedy, in which love is confused with the paranoid scheming of the unhinged. Hardly the traditional romantic-comedy hero, Stiller backs into romantic success after stumbling every step of the way.

By way of contrast, Stiller's next notable film (after a series of misadventures that included Neil LaBute's laughably misguided drama *Your Friends*

& *Neighbors*, and the revisionist costumed-superhero comedy *Mystery Men*) was a romantic comedy of the most straightforward kind. *Keeping the Faith* (2000), directed by Edward Norton (who costars), begins as a self-aware setup for a joke: a priest walks into a bar . . .

Norton is the priest, driven to drink by his unrequited crush on Anna (Jenna Elfman), the childhood friend who has recently blown back into the lives of Father Brian and Rabbi Jake (Stiller). Before departing for the angst-ridden territory of teary girlfriends, hostile Jewish mothers, and fraternal rivalry, *Keeping the Faith* is a likable enough charmer. Stiller is the rabbi as stand-up comic, jauntily assailing his Friday night audience for not displaying appropriate levels of "Shabbat-shalominess." (Confident and romantically successful, Rabbi Jake is, ironically, among the least "Jewish" of Stiller's characters.)

As with so many other love-triangle films, *Keeping the Faith*'s chemistry is far stronger between its male leads than its lovers. Stiller and Norton mesh nicely as old friends thrust into unfamiliarly rivalrous territory, but Stiller is not given enough to work with in this well-written but very traditional genre exercise. Stiller is a fighter, not a lover, equipped mostly for combat, and self-inflicted embarrassment is his specialty, not the warm and fuzzy stuff *Keeping the Faith* feeds him.

"It's not like I'm a rabbi or something." Gathered around the Byrnes family table for dinner, Greg Focker has been asked to say grace, and hurriedly agrees. The hilariously painful *Meet the Parents* (2000) is ostensibly an excruciatingly precise investigation of the unbearable awkwardness of parental visits, but given that Stiller was the star, it is also a study of a lone urban Jew adrift in the wilds of the WASP suburbs. Greg is brought home by girlfriend Pam (Teri Polo) for her sister's wedding. Forewarned of the uncompromising standards of her father Jack (Robert De Niro), Greg comes prepared to impress. Surrounded by so much healthy, well-adjusted American normalcy, Stiller defensively looks to prove his own bona fides, finding nothing but unyielding humiliation instead.

Meet the Parents, written by John Hamburg and directed by Jay Roach (*Austin Powers: International Man of Mystery*) is a comedy of emasculation, with each new scene unveiling a new facet to Greg's abasement. Not only is his last name Focker, not only is he a nurse, not only does he wear his girlfriend's floral bathrobe and a Speedo bathing suit, Greg also bloodies the bride-to-be's nose, floods the backyard with the contents of the house's septic tank, and sets the handmade wedding altar ablaze. There is no winning with the Byrnes crew. When he is jocular, they are somber; when he is competitive, they are laid-back; when he is friendly, they are mistrustful.

Meet the Parents is a Kafka-esque nightmare, in which the only guarantee is that of impending disaster. There is a sinking feeling, about twenty or thirty minutes in, when you realize things aren't going to get any better—that Greg Focker will continue screwing up, and getting caught, in an eternal cycle of well-meaning idiocy and haughty distrust. *Meet the Parents* uses the pain to its advantage, with Stiller maximally comfortable with the maximum possible discomfort. *There's Something About Mary* cast Stiller as the eternal patsy, subject to the cruel whims of fate. *Meet the Parents* only intensifies the process, but with a whiff of class and religious difference that adds tremendously to the sense of hilarious conflict. Ben Stiller was an underdog, and let no one forget it.

"Just got to do one more thing," De Niro observes, finally placated by Stiller's good intentions. "Meet his parents." The inevitable sequel *Meet the Fockers* (2004) casts Stiller once more into enemy territory, beset by traps on all sides and tormented by the possibility of utter calamity. For a brief moment, all appears to be well: taxis are voluntarily given up by strangers, lights turn green as far as the eye can see, first-class upgrades are free. Soon enough, however, we return to the forbidding landscape of the original, in which good intentions pave the road to hell.

Meet the Fockers is less a fully fledged film than a symbolic passing of the torch, with one master of neurotic Jewish comedy graciously sharing the spotlight with another. The best thing—by far—about this otherwise toned-down rehash of the original is the presence of those two echt-Jewish performers as Stiller's parents: Barbra Streisand and Dustin Hoffman. In sandals, a floppy, untucked shirt, and a fabric bracelet, his frosted-grey hair and leathery skin proof of his permanent-snowbird status, Hoffman is a walking punch line: the hippie Florida Jew, liberated from the oppressive Northeast. Hoffman plays against type as a loosey-goosey hippie, inclined to oversharing and inappropriate kissing.

After thoroughly humiliating himself in his first tête-à-tête with De Niro, Stiller is now in the position of standing by helplessly as his parents humiliate him in front of his future in-laws. They have loud, messy sex; they bring out Greg's snipped foreskin for ritual inspection; they torment the Byrneses with their blend of New Age hogwash and Jewish parental pride. By the time De Niro injects Stiller with sodium pentothal during an engagement party, and he begins to uncontrollably spill his secrets to the gathered crowd, we understand: the truth serum has merely turned him into his parents.

Just before *Meet the Fockers*, Stiller had been reunited with the man who created Gaylord Focker for another ode to romantically motivated humiliation. *Along Came Polly* (2004), written and directed by John Hamburg (who wrote both *Meets*), stars Stiller as Reuben Feffer, a buttoned-up risk analyst whose marriage turns out to be a chancy proposition. Hardly have the last strains of "Hava Nagila" faded when Reuben walks in on his wife getting a very private lesson from a scuba instructor on their honeymoon. Embracing the risk he has always avoided, Reuben chases the flighty, sexy Polly (Jennifer Aniston), and is promptly punished for his daring. A first date at a Moroccan restaurant leads to an acute case of gastrointestinal distress and a flooded toilet (given his movie track record, Stiller is probably best off avoiding bathrooms altogether). Future dates are equally punishing. "Since we've been together," Reuben tells Polly, "I've felt more uncomfortable, out of place, embarrassed, and just physically sick than I have in my entire life." He means it as a compliment.

Along Came Polly is nowhere near as awkward or discomfiting as *Meet the Parents*, but its air of waggish dread is aided by a marvelous supporting cast that includes Alec Baldwin as Reuben's boss, Hank Azaria as the rival for his wife's affections, and especially Philip Seymour Hoffman as his best friend, a washed-up child star with an E! camera crew following his every step. Hoffman is so brilliant as a barely functional wreck still capable of laughing at his own ineptitude that he swipes the film from Stiller. Polly is supposed to be the free spirit who, at long last, lets Reuben loosen up; but how can any man whose best friend hustles him out of a party because he has tried to fart, and accidentally loosened his bowels (a mishap he calls "sharting") be that much of a tightass?

Stiller is forever a member of the younger generation; even when playing a father, as in Wes Anderson's *The Royal Tenenbaums* (2001), he is defined by his fruitless striving for the paternal authority his own father, played by Gene Hackman, effortlessly embodies. Still suffering from the unexpected loss of his wife in a plane crash, Stiller's Chas Tenenbaum is an emotional wreck, coping with tragedy by moving back in with his mother and drilling his sons in emergency maneuvers. (Stiller's David Starsky, in the broad buddy picture *Starsky and Hutch* [2004], is like a sibling to Chas Tenenbaum, a tightly coiled ball of suppressed hostility tormented by partner Owen Wilson's loosey-goosey police work.)

Shoulders hunched, neck tensed with bottled-up rage, Chas is another of the once-prodigal Tenenbaums, burned out by early success and the steady drip of tragedy. Stiller's is only a supporting character here, taking third billing behind Hackman and the film's storybook aura of slightly dented magic, but it is Chas's slow shedding of his burdens that signal *The Royal Tenenbaums'* shift from quirky family comedy to transcendently cathartic family story. "I've had a rough year, Dad," Chas tells his father, his voice cracking from the force of pent-up emotion. The headstone on Hackman's grave reads "DIED TRAGICALLY RESCUING HIS FAMILY FROM THE WRECKAGE OF A DESTROYED SINKING BATTLESHIP," and it is Chas's unmistakable anguish which makes the inscription less a joke than a metaphoric truth.

Meanwhile, Stiller had crafted an alternate persona, an anti-Ben of sorts—inspired, perhaps, by his famous impression of noted egomaniac Tom Cruise on *The Ben Stiller Show*. In *Zoolander* (2001) and *Dodgeball* (2004), Stiller plays raging madmen of the id, lost in contemplation of their own splendor. Part of the joke lies in Stiller's self-referential wink; these monsters of masculine self-absorption are a study in contrasts with Stiller's traditional shrimpy, all-too-cerebral yuppies. Derek Zoolander enjoys nothing as much as looking at himself in a mirror, and his White Goodman in *Dodgeball* is overly enamored with his own buffed, toned body.

Zoolander began life as a series of sketches penned for the MTV Movie Awards, with Stiller as a dim-witted male supermodel besotted by his own chiseled good looks. In the feature-length version, world-famous Derek Zoolander must cope with a fresh-faced rival, Hansel (Owen Wilson), while fending off the *Manchurian Candidate* machinations of an evil fashionista (Will Ferrell, channeling *Austin Powers*'s Dr. Evil) to have him assassinate the prime minister of Malaysia. Derek cannot spell, is physically incapable of turning right on the catwalk, and has trouble with words of more than one syllable. For all the talk of his long-in-the-making new look (successor to the beloved Blue Steel and Ferrari), he seems to only have a single, vaguely flatulent, pose for the cameras.

Easily the best of Stiller's directorial efforts, *Zoolander* is exceptionally clever about exceptional stupidity. Stiller wrings an inordinate amount of comedy out of Zoolander's narcissistic feeble-mindedness. "Moisture," Stiller meaningfully intones while hawking a beauty product, "is the essence of wetness." With his hair blowing gently in the breeze, his lips pouting and his forehead carefully knit in mock-contemplation, Zoolander is the blank slate on which fashion's empty haikus are written.

Derek's own pronunciamentos are hardly more coherent. "What is this?" he roars while looking at an architectural model of his proposed Derek

Zoolander Institute for Kids Who Can't Read Good, before smashing it to pieces. "How can we be expected to teach children to learn how to read if they can't even fit inside the building? . . . The center has to be *at least*," he pauses to calculate, "*three* times bigger than this!" After his friends' tragic death in a gasoline-fight mishap, Derek's manager (played by his father, Jerry Stiller) asks him rhetorically, "What do we do when we fall off the horse?" Zoolander's brow furrows, pondering the words in a hopeless attempt to unearth some sliver of meaning from the convoluted query. *Zoolander* is the record of Derek's verbal gaffes, intellectual shortcomings, and physical mishaps, but unlike *Flirting with Disaster*'s Mel Coplin, or Greg Focker, he is never flustered by his failings. Zoolander never learns, nor does he ever see the need to.

Derek Zoolander might have passed for runway royalty, but with his Farrah Fawcett hair and Rollie Fingers mustache, Stiller's White Goodman in *Dodgeball* is unlikely to sweep anyone off her feet. What White lacks in sartorial elegance, he compensates for with a titanic sense of his own importance. Owner of a growing empire of workout palaces, White plans to take over Vince Vaughn's grubby neighborhood gym. In order to come up with the money to save the place, Vaughn and his tubby, out-of-shape friends enter a big-bucks dodgeball tournament, where they must vanquish Stiller's band of gladiators.

Once obese, White torments himself, and drives himself relentlessly, with the shameful memory of his blubber; he is likely the only character you'll ever see pleasuring himself with one hand while sniffing a hot slice of pizza in the other hand. Too bad that the rest of *Dodgeball* could not be so fresh. An inexplicable success at the box office, *Dodgeball* is weighed down by a cliche-ridden plot, and a lamentably phoned-in performance by the usually dependable Vaughn. Stiller wildly overacts, his portrayal of egotistical buffoonery a cartoonish amplification of his *Zoolander* antics. By the end of the film, Charles Atlas has become Sherman Klump once more, belly fat spilling out onto his sofa as he snacks on a chicken leg. A valuable cross-marketing sequel bonanza with Eddie Murphy's equally overweight couch potato was lamentably squandered.

Stiller was now recognizable box-office royalty, with the one-hundred-million-dollar-plus-grossing *Dodgeball* followed in short order by the even more successful comic fantasy *Night at the Museum* (2006). Stiller is a museum guard stuck with the unenviable job of keeping Roman centurions, Wild West gunslingers, Mayan warriors, dinosaurs, and Teddy Roosevelt under wraps when they emerge from their centuries-long sleep each night.

Other than his vigorous version of "Eye of the Tiger," belted out over the museum's loudspeaker, there is not much of the Stiller that we have come to know and love in *Night at the Museum*. There is little to *Night at the Museum* that specifically requires Stiller's talents; he seems to be here more for the familiarity of his name on the marquee than anything he might contribute to the film itself. A sequel (featuring Christopher Guest in a small role as Ivan the Terrible) inevitably followed.

Stiller had always been paired with statuesque blondes (including his wife Christine Taylor, costar of *Zoolander* and *Dodgeball*), offering the prospect of a golden-haired escape from traditional Jewish anxiety and misery. *There's Something About Mary*'s Cameron Diaz, *Keeping the Faith*'s Jenna Elfman, and *Meet the Parents*' Teri Polo had all fit the description, and at first, Malin Akerman, the willowy beauty he meets and marries in *The Heartbreak Kid* (2007) appears to be of a piece with her predecessors. Akerman's voluptuous good looks are a ruse, a sleight-of-hand trick meant to distract from her all-around noxiousness.

The Farrelly brothers' remake of Elaine May's classic 1972 comedy erases the class and religious conflicts of the original, in which newly married Charles Grodin lusts after shiksa goddess Cybill Shepherd while on his honeymoon. Stiller is still the Jewish commitment-phobe (he once broke it off with a fiancée because she hated *Caddyshack*), but now his wife is the blonde goddess, and the object of his affection distracting him on his Caribbean honeymoon is a vaguely ethnic-looking brunette (played by Michelle Monaghan).

Stiller is not given much to do here other than look embarrassed as he seeks to weasel out of a mistaken marriage. The overhanging dread of the original is noticeably lacking. What could have been another *Meet the Parents* is instead only a moderately diverting endeavor. Luckily, Stiller's father Jerry plays his father here, asking the question every son needs to hear: "You been crushin' any pussy?"

There was little pussy to be crushed in the epic war parody *Tropic Thunder* (2008), a sort of *Apocalypse Now* on the backlot cowritten and directed by Stiller. Stiller has always been generous as a filmmaker, leaving the choicest roles for other performers. For this story of misguided actors shooting a combat film accidentally dropped into a real-life war (shades of *¡Three Amigos!*), Stiller cedes the spotlight to his costars: Jack Black's whiny, drug-addicted star unfit for the rigors of battle; Tom Cruise, whose brief cameo as a studio boss alternately amuses and rankles; and especially Robert Downey Jr., in an Oscar-nominated turn as an intense Australian actor who insists on playing his role in blackface, never breaking character even when the cameras stop rolling. Stiller's script, written with Justin Theroux and Etan Cohen, slyly resuscitates blackface humor while acknowledging it as the ultimate taboo joke.

Downey's performance ruffled a few feathers, but it is also the undoubted highlight of this otherwise-soggy film, which squanders a potentially brilliant comic setup. As the muscle-bound egomaniac Tugg Speedman, fighting a real war with fake weapons, Stiller channels his earlier performances in *Zoolander* and *Dodgeball*, but with a few extra digs at Hollywood insularity. *Tropic Thunder* might easily have been a superlative sketch on *The Ben Stiller Show*; as a feature-length film, the initial burst of brilliance rapidly flagged.

The movie itself is outflanked by the mock trailers that bookend it, offering delights like Tugg's action-hero classic *Scorcher*, his shameless Oscar bid *Simple Jack*, and Jack Black in full *Nutty Professor* homage, playing an entire family of farting, squabbling butterballs in *The Fatties*.

He may be the love child of Dustin Hoffman and Woody Allen, but in his affect, Stiller is like the more socially successful offspring of Albert Brooks. Stiller's alchemical brilliance transformed Brooks's career-long mockery of yuppie entitlement and ennui into the stuff of multiplex fare. Somewhere, in a manner possibly visible only to himself, Albert Brooks was smiling.

Budd Schulberg, that Hollywood scion, had written *What Makes Sammy Run?* as a jaded insider's satire, a rip-roaring critique of the prototypical nobody-made-good's amoral hucksterism. Ben Stiller has yet to play Sammy. Astringent and remorseless as a performer, he is probably better suited for playing Schulberg himself. But in the cruel vitality of his reformed stereotypes, Stiller has managed a feat akin to Schulberg's own, transforming misshapen, ill-fitting sentiments—pettiness, jealousy, dyspepsia—into the stuff of comedy. In so doing, he exposes much of Hollywood for what it is—a clique of lowbrow mediocrities issuing endless variations on the likes of *The Fatties*. Anyone not affronted by Ben Stiller's comedy is likely not paying close enough attention.

29

WILL FERRELL

"A PRETTY NICE LITTLE SATURDAY"

"I have many leather-bound books and my apartment smells of rich mahogany." —Will Ferrell, *Anchorman*

Scene: a fraternity house filled with drunken, rowdy college students. The kitchen is crammed with frenzied young men crowded around a keg of beer, to which a funnel has been attached for easy access. The sea of youthful faces is notable for one older gentleman, looking to be in his mid-to-late thirties, whose mien is already marked with the first lines of worry and age,

---

"Stay classy, San Diego": Ferrell in *Anchorman: The Legend of Ron Burgundy*.

and whose party-hearty demeanor is more studied than those of his younger compatriots. His college-age friends encourage him to take a drink, and he demurs, saying, "I told my wife I wouldn't drink tonight. Besides, I've got a big day tomorrow." "A big day? Doing what?" his new friends want to know. "Well, um, actually a pretty nice little Saturday, we're going to go to Home Depot. Yeah, buy some wallpaper, maybe get some flooring, stuff like that. Maybe Bed Bath & Beyond, I don't know. I don't know if we'll have enough time."

The film, of course, is the 2003 comedy *Old School*, and the performer is Will Ferrell, who has made a career out of awkward encounters, misplaced enthusiasm, and manic intensity. Here, he is an adolescent posing as a family man, paying halfhearted lip service to the joys of happily settled marital bliss before breaking down and admitting defeat in the arms of (hops-infused) Morpheus. In films like *Anchorman* (2004) and *Talladega Nights* (2006), Ferrell was a cheerfully oblivious man-child, a little boy adrift in an adult world. The comedy stemmed from Ferrell's utter ridiculousness, his inability to cope with the most basic requirements of everyday life. The rest comes from Ferrell's giving us permission to laugh at all those things—sexism, cloddishness, all-around dimwittedness—that society officially pooh-poohs. Comedy is rarely polite.

Will Ferrell's is a gift that thrives in mundane surroundings. His movies—or at least the successful ones—place Ferrell against a plain-vanilla backdrop of middle-class uniformity. In that, he is a grandson of W. C. Fields, who in another time and era similarly revolted, with equally ineffectual results, against the strictures of family life. And how could anyone miss the family resemblance, when Fields and Ferrell are the American cinema's two great exemplars of the non sequitur exclamation?

There are certain moments we have come to expect in a Will Ferrell film. He will either get naked or appear in a ludicrous pair of underpants. There will be a musical number. Taunts will be exchanged, and dares fulfilled. Just like any nine-year-old, Ferrell will have an enemy, whom he will ultimately vanquish. In film after film, Ferrell is the boy who never grew up—sometimes explicitly, as in the sweet fantasy *Elf* (2003), and sometimes only implicitly, as with his petulant has-beens in *Anchorman* (2004) and *Blades of Glory* (2004).

So long the province of boys being boys, comedy was still, at the turn of the new century, a treehouse with a "NO GIRLZ ALLOWED" sign tacked to its entrance. The films—Judd Apatow's, Adam Sandler's, and above all Ferrell's—engaged in a complex series of exchanges with its audiences. They asked us to laugh at men behaving badly—nothing remotely new for comedy, which had been doing much the same since the days of Laurel & Hardy—but now requested our acquiescence in a ritual show of disgust at their antics. We disdained the brainless, politically incorrect, socially recidivist behavior of Ferrell's heroes out of one side of our mouths while snickering out of the other. We laughed even though we knew better; more than that, we laughed precisely *because* we knew better.

Will Ferrell had known he had an urge to be funny since a day in first grade when a math teacher announced that the class would now do some exercises. Will leapt out of his chair and did some jumping jacks, to the amusement of his classmates. By fourth grade, Ferrell was pretending to walk into doors in order to make girls laugh. Growing up in Irvine, deep in the heart of conservative Orange County, Ferrell was amused by the silliness of suburbia: police officers pulling over bicyclists to give them tickets. Show business was family business—Ferrell's father was a saxophonist and keyboard player for the Righteous Brothers—but the financial and familial insecurity of life as a performer pushed him away from his natural gifts as a clown toward a more stable profession. Attending USC, Ferrell pictured himself as a sportscaster—a natural profession for someone with his affinity for sports, and a propensity for making bizarre announcements over the PA system at his high school. Suburbia, high-school popularity, private college, fraternity membership—where is the private pain that is usually the province of comedians everywhere, the base metal they transmute into comic gold? Apparently nowhere to be found. "Will is unique in that his process isn't fueled by suffering," observed Judd Apatow in an interview.

After graduation, Ferrell took a job working on a local television program called "Around and About Orange County News," but found that he preferred riffing on the news to reporting it. He joined legendary local sketch-comedy troupe the Groundlings on a whim in 1992, where he quickly proved himself among the most gifted of their performers. Three years later, he had graduated to *Saturday Night Live*—arriving the same year as future *SNL* head writer and *Anchorman* director Adam McKay.

McKay and the other *SNL* writers pegged the gangly, polite Ferrell as a quintessential Southern California golden boy, a straight man if they had ever seen one. In relatively short order, though, the show's writers learned that if they wanted a sketch to air, they were best off writing it for Will Ferrell. He became well-known on the show for playing an irritating cheerleader and *Jeopardy* host Alex Trebek, but it was his loose-limbed impression of

President George W. Bush that catapulted Ferrell to cultural ubiquity. Ferrell's W. was less an impression than a free-form riff, cutting but also audaciously absurdist. His Bush was more like Chevy Chase's Gerald Ford than Darrell Hammond's Bill Clinton—a majestically dim master of the malaprop, only loosely related to the real man. Ferrell is to be saluted for introducing a new word to the English language, one that dogged Bush through his two terms in the Oval Office as the quintessential summation of the president's intellectual gifts: "strategery." (Ferrell enjoyed playing the forty-third president so much that he revived him for a well-received Broadway one-man show and HBO special in 2008, satirically titled *You're Welcome America: A Final Night with George W. Bush*.)

Ferrell had been amusing in small film parts slotted into his *SNL* breaks. He was the inept assassin Mustafa in *Austin Powers* (1997), cast into the fiery depths by Dr. Evil ("I'm very badly burnt," he moans from offscreen); Bob Woodward in the clever political parody *Dick* (1999); and downright marvelous as Ben Stiller's high-fashion nemesis Mugatu in *Zoolander* (2001). The rigors of his *Saturday Night Live* schedule, and the slow build of his career, meant that it would not be until 2003, some eight years after his *SNL* debut, that Ferrell was granted a role onscreen that measured up to his talents.

Old School's Frank Rickard—aka Frank the Tank—is well-meaning, gamely doing his best to pass for an adult, but failing miserably. Married to Marissa (the wonderfully tart Perrey Reeves), Frank is a reformed party animal on the straight and narrow. The prospect of beer far outweighs that of Bed Bath & Beyond, and Frank agrees to do just one funnel's worth. "FILL IT UP AGAIN! Once it hits your lips, it's so good!" (Frank, like so many Ferrell heroes to come, has a bit of a problem with voice modulation, and certain phrases, sentences, and entire speeches sometimes come out as strangled shouts.)

A few funnels into the future, Frank is crashing the stage, grabbing the mic from Snoop Dogg, and shouting to the packed audience of college students that "we're going streaking!" Ferrell's call is heeded by no one else; but nude or near-nude streaking would be a feature of future films, with the actor's pasty, untoned body unfurled and displayed for *Talladega Nights*, *Blades of Glory*, and *Semi-Pro*, among others. The flab sets Ferrell apart from his fellow comedians. Unlike Ben Stiller, whose aggressively toned abdominal muscles serve as a reminder (much as Jerry Lewis's gaudy pinky ring once had) that he was not to be defined by the characters he played, Ferrell literally embodies his saggy, gone-to-seed characters.

For Frank and his thirtysomething accomplices Beanie (Vince Vaughn) and Mitch (Luke Wilson), the quickest route to reclaiming lost youth runs right down Fraternity Row. *Old School* is a fantasy of youthful indiscretion lovingly recreated for adulthood. Their fraternity of elderly misfits, middle-aged stress cases, and college-age outcasts is a guild of rejects, and the enthusiasm that Frank, whose marriage is crumbling, brings to the project is contagious. The film contrasts Frank's sour interactions with his wife, where he always seems to be putting his foot in his mouth (musing about the color of a waitress's panties during a therapy session, leaving a message on her voicemail suggesting they meet for "frozen yogurt sometime, or maybe even a whole meal of food"), with the unalloyed pleasure-in-manliness of fraternity living.

A boy posing as a man in his adult life, Frank revels in his new role as fraternity elder. Kidnapping middle-aged men from supermarket parking lots while ransacking their wives' groceries, accidentally shooting himself with horse tranquilizers, Frank discovers heretofore unknown talents. In the film's single funniest transition, director Todd Phillips cuts from the collapse of a senior citizen pledge during a coed wrestling match to Frank belting out Kansas's "Dust in the Wind" at his funeral. "You're my boy, Blue!" he shouts to the heavens, his voice shaking with soulful melisma. Ferrell's faux intensity throughout—his playful imitation of seriousness—is terrifically endearing.

At first glance, *Old School* would seem to have little in common with the sweet-natured Christmas parable *Elf* (2003), in which Ferrell is a North Pole human, raised as a gift-manufacturing elf, who searches for the true meaning of the holiday in frosty, buttoned-down New York City. But his Buddy, much like Frank the Tank, is an adult in name only. Laughably out of synch with the rhythms and rigors of adulthood, Buddy ventures from the North Pole to New York in the hopes of tracking down his long-lost father (a gruff James Caan). Buddy has the natural ebullience of childhood—he's jazzed about everything from a diner advertising the world's best cup of coffee to the impending arrival of Santa Claus at Gimbel's, where Buddy works, naturally, as an elf. (At six-foot-three, Ferrell makes for a comically unlikely helper to Santa.) His juvenile enthusiasm is matched by equally amusing childish tantrums. Chuffed to find that the real North Pole Santa of his acquaintance won't be making an appearance at the department store, Buddy shouts at the impostor: "You sit on a throne of lies!"

Elf eventually settles in for a treacly series of lessons about Christmas cheer, with Ferrell teaching grumpy-Gus Caan about the true meaning of the holiday. Elves may not have to concern themselves with overdosing on sugar, but we humans do, and *Elf* liberally douses itself with fairy dust, until we are ripe to gag. Before we reach the sea of swirly gumdrops, though, most of Jon Favreau's film is surprisingly palatable. Buddy has a touch of Frank the Tank in him (his cruel, if unintended, mocking of the height-challenged children's-book luminary played by Peter Dinklage is mondo Ferrell), his destructive innocence the essence of Ferrell's comic appeal. His characters can't help but louse things up.

Ferrell suddenly had family-friendly movie stardom in his grasp, and the nine-figure grosses for *Elf* proved his crossover appeal. There was a fundamental sweetness and decency to Ferrell, as if at heart he really wanted to pass out swirly gumdrops to everybody—even his victims. In the meantime, though, Ferrell would take further pleasure in the delights of recidivism. Reunited with *Saturday Night Live* head writer Adam McKay (who would also direct him in *Talladega Nights: The Ballad of Ricky Bobby* and *Step Brothers*), *Anchorman: The Legend of Ron Burgundy* (2004) was a luminously subversive tribute to misplaced masculine aggression.

Ferrell is Ron Burgundy, a legendary 1970s newscaster famed for his nightly sign-off: "Stay classy, San Diego." Burgundy's own classiness comes under threat when faced with Veronica Corningstone (Christina Applegate), a young female upstart in the newscasting game who challenges Ron on his own turf. After a brief fling, which comes to an unceremonious end after Veronica has the audacity to anchor a broadcast in his stead ("You read my news!"), the battle begins: Men vs. Women, or—to be more precise—Boys vs. Girls.

Comedies like *Anchorman* step in to fill the vacuum created by the triumph of feminism, providing viewers with the opportunity to laugh alongside, and sympathize with, the harried, tread-upon middle-class white male, and to enjoy his moment of revenge against the women who insist upon stealing his rightful place in society. Ron's comeuppance is richly deserved, and *Anchorman* knows it, but it prefers to dawdle en route to political correctness, lavishing its attention on Ron and his workplace buddies' retrograde antics.

Ferrell's performance is nothing short of brilliant, with notes of carefully honed self-absorption mingling with defensiveness, clumsy aggression, and a trace of wounded romanticism. Ron is the kind of guy who, when summoned onstage at a jazz club, professes surprise as he pulls a flute out of his jacket pocket. He is also in love with his own romantic ardor. He kisses Veronica and moans: "Oh, I'm storming your castle on my steed, milady," as if a lone peck had turned him into a medieval knight dying from the wounds of love. Ferrell's term in office as George W. Bush on *Saturday Night Live* had prepared him well; no one did addled befuddlement and failed pretensions to intellectual agility better.

Veronica made an ideal foil for Ron, piercing his pretensions to knowledge-ability. Contrary to Ferrell's assertion, "San Diego" is not actually German for "a whale's vagina." Ron tears into Veronica with relish ("You are a smelly pirate hooker," "I'm gonna punch you in the ovary"), but she always delivers the knockout blow: "Jazz flute is for little fairy boys." Ron is a numbskull, and a louse, but his ignorance is so thorough, and his cluelessness so complete, that all crimes are forgiven.

Ferrell is the ringmaster here, his parody of oily self-assurance putting the entire film into air-quotes of a sort. Are we laughing at his jokes, or are we laughing at Ron's telling them? Are his woman-hating jokes funny, or is it funny that he is such a woman-hater? Either way, Ron Burgundy is the ne plus ultra of Ferrell's dunderheads. And I haven't even mentioned his usual prob-lems with controlling the volume of his voice, his vocal exercises ("the Human Torch was denied a bank loan"), or his mock-erudite, Fields-esque exclama-tions: "Great Odin's raven!" "Knights of Columbus!" "By the beard of Zeus!"

It was a substantial journey from wielding a bedpost in a back-alley show-down with rival newscaster Ben Stiller to cooking a Chilean sea bass lightly dusted with lime, but as with most actors in Hollywood, when Woody Allen calls, all you ask is where to show up. As an underemployed actor named Hobey in Allen's *Melinda and Melinda* (2004), Ferrell ably—too ably—imi-tates Woody's stutter-step line reading. *Melinda and Melinda* is an amplifi-cation of Allen's *Broadway Danny Rose*, this time laid out as a dinner-table debate between rival dramatists: is life fundamentally comic or tragic? The film lays out dueling versions of the same story, one lighthearted and the other heartrending. Ferrell, taking pleasure in each well-delivered bon mot, is asked to provide the comic relief, lusting in flailing fashion after a neurotic neighbor (Radha Mitchell) while enduring the breakup of his marriage.

Like so many Allen protagonists, Hobey is a tangled bag of neuroses: "I dream of myself kissing Melinda, and then I'm immediately on trial at Nuremberg," he confides to a friend. Unfortunately, like so many other late-Allen heroes (John Cusack in *Bullets Over Broadway*, Kenneth Branagh in *Celebrity*, Jason Biggs in *Anything Else*), he falls into the trap of channeling Woody rather than his character. Ferrell does what he can here (a sly bit of physical comedy involving a robe trapped in Melinda's door is charming), but he is out of his element. Still the boy from the suburbs, Ferrell's com-edy requires an overlay of mundane middle-class blandness to kick against.

Allen's thirtysomethings are stuck in a time warp, still discussing Stravinsky and Chekhov, and sobbing over Mahler. Google and Jay-Z might as well not exist.

Ferrell was a ringleader of the so-called Frat Pack, and cameo appearances were the currency whereby stars returned favors and bestowed distinction on their peers. Ferrell himself had dropped in on Judd Apatow's short-lived television series *Undeclared* and joined Ben Stiller and Owen Wilson in *Starsky & Hutch* (2004), but his brief appearance in *Wedding Crashers* (2005) is an undoubted career highlight.

Introduced with a swell of strings, Ferrell is Chazz Reinhold, the original inventor of the wedding-crashing gambit. Chazz has now moved on to yet more fertile ground: funerals. Ferrell touts the limitless possibilities of graveside pickups to Wilson, all the while shouting to his mother to serve his guest a snack: "Hey ma, the meatloaf, we want it now. The meatloaf!" (Ferrell's brilliance is not always adequately conveyed by the printed word; the disturbingly feral way his voice cracks as he shouts "meatloaf" is nothing short of inspired.) *Wedding Crashers* introduces Chazz to inoculate its heroes against accusations of callousness, but Ferrell is marvelously insincere. We cannot help but be charmed by Ferrell's gumption, and when we spot him, inconsolable, at a funeral, shouting at the heavens ("Damn you, Roger!"), we forgive all his excesses.

Ferrell had what amounted to an extended cameo in the film version of Mel Brooks's musical *The Producers* (2005) as Hitler-loving playwright Franz Liebkind. Ferrell is a Nazi straight out of Lubitsch's *To Be or Not to Be*—or maybe Brooks's version of the film: rant-prone and hysterical, with a hint of menace. Ferrell is one of the funnier presences here, but his persona—so utterly contemporary—is at odds with the vaguely 1960s setting of the film. One could hardly picture Will Ferrell in period costume.

In the wake of *Wedding Crashers*, Ferrell's career proceeded on two tracks, with unequal results: one where he is the charming degenerate of *Anchorman* fame, and a second where he is a standard-issue comic leading man. Ferrell is in full family-man mode in 2005's Oedipally charged kids'-soccer comedy *Kicking and Screaming* (no relation to Noah Baumbach's post-graduation gem of the same name, and pity for it), and the jokes venture no further than his newfound taste for coffee and a montage of the youthful Ferrell's athletic exploits set to the theme music from *Chariots of Fire*. (The only good joke in the movie is an insider's dig: Ferrell gets mauled by a little brat whose soccer jersey reads "APATOW," in honor of the film's producer.) *Bewitched* (2005), in which Ferrell was married to Nicole Kidman's sorceress Samantha in a feature version of the 1960s television show, was a well-publicized flop, and *Land of the Lost* (2009) similarly neutered Ferrell by seeking to target all quadrants of the moviegoing audience. *Elf* distinctly notwithstanding, Will Ferrell was not a movie star for children.

Talladega Nights: The Ballad of Ricky Bobby (2006), Ferrell's second collaboration with Adam McKay, is undoubtedly in the charming-degenerate vein. Some might dismiss the movie as an extended product-placement opportunity, with shameless plugs for Pizza Hut, KFC, and Applebee's occasionally interrupted by some sort of racing-themed story. But to characterize it as such is to do a disservice to *Talladega Nights*, which is another scrappy McKay-Ferrell effort. Ricky Bobby is another of McKay and Ferrell's unapologetic chowderheads, a master of the race car hardly able to steer his own life. Reigning unchallenged atop the NASCAR heap alongside best friend Cal (John C. Reilly), Ricky Bobby's dominance is challenged by jazz-playing, suit-wearing, macchiato-sipping French driver Jean Girard (a nearly unrecognizable Sacha Baron Cohen).

Ricky Bobby goes from surprise success to entitled superstar to has-been with dazzling rapidity. No sooner has Ricky Bobby finished telling a television interviewer that "I wake up in the morning, I piss excellence," than he finds himself drummed out of the sport, delivering pizzas on a bicycle. *Talladega Nights* flirts with sentimentality about Ricky Bobby's plight at the same time that it pisses excellence all over such saccharine sloppiness.

Cohen is like Sellers's Pink Panther updated for the era of freedom fries, his every gesture and vocal inflection designed to serve as contrast to Ricky and Cal's unadorned American-ness. The farcical showdown between American populism and French sophistication is taken to extreme lengths: Jean is not only into jazz, he drives a car endorsed by Perrier, and is married—to a man. Ricky Bobby is the last defender of true-blue American values, and the movie knows it: "Don't you say it, Ricky!" Cal implores him, after Jean has demanded that he vocalize his love for crepes. "These colors don't run!"

That Ricky Bobby sounds like he might be a redneck cousin of President Bush is hardly coincidental; Ferrell is simultaneously mocking and celebrating the hegemony of heartland stupidity. He and fellow driver, best friend, and homewrecker Reilly are the Bush-Cheney of auto racing: wrong-headed, buffoonish, and childishly pledged to each other, to the bitter end and beyond.

When asked, Cal likes to think of Jesus as a figure skater in white, doing interpretive dances of his life journey on the ice. Ferrell's Chazz Michael

Michaels is hardly Christ-like. However, for a brief moment at the start of *Blades of Glory* (2007), Ferrell's champion figure skater does have a religious following of his own, at least among fans of crotch-thrusting, groupie-licking hair-metal rejects in leather vests.

The bad-boy outlaw fallen on hard times was Ferrell's bread and butter, with Ron Burgundy and Ricky Bobby followed in short order by Chazz, whose reign atop the world of competitive figure skating is brought to an unfortunate conclusion by a brawl on the medal platform at the Olympics. Banned for life from men's figure skating, he is matched with nemesis Jimmy MacElroy (Jon Heder), forming the first-ever all-male pairs team. Ferrell is the star here, but the rhythms are mostly Heder's; much of the dialogue sounds as if it had been excised at the last minute from *Napoleon Dynamite*.

In case the men's figure skating angle had not alerted you, *Blades of Glory* is unendingly amused by the homoerotic possibilities of its plot. The skating sequences manage to squeeze references to every possible permutation of gay sex into their brief routines. Ladies, don't be alarmed; Chazz is no queer, but rather a sex addict with a raging libido. "You an official here?" he asks Olympic medalist Nancy Kerrigan (practically the only American skater who doesn't cameo in *Blades of Glory* is Tonya Harding). "Because you've officially given me a boner."

The entirety of *Blades of Glory* plays as a marginally superior version of Ben Stiller's *Dodgeball*: ridiculous sport, mismatched team, and unexpected triumph. It can safely be said that this is, without doubt, the only film in history to feature a speed-skating chase as a dramatic peak. Ferrell may never have become a sportscaster, but that sports-information degree was being put to good use nonetheless.

Anchorman had tackled the 1970s (Ferrell occasionally seemed like an extended, loving parody of the Me Decade himself), and Ferrell had made the daffy sports film a successful repeat enterprise. What could be better, then, than a sports film set in the 1970s? Ferrell stars in *Semi-Pro* (2008) as Jackie Moon, disco singer extraordinaire turned owner-coach-star of the American Basketball Association's Flint Tropics. Jackie is part Bill Veeck and part Barry White, regularly trotting out his red-light anthem "Love Me Sexy" to perk up teammates, fire up fans, and impress the ladies. When rumors of a merger with the NBA become reality, the ragtag Tropics band together to battle for a fourth-place finish and a transfer to the big time.

Semi-Pro had all the makings of a brilliant Will Ferrell effort. Its instantly recognizable setting, dripping with comic potential, was ripe for Ferrell's patented shtick. So why is this ABA-nostalgia picture such an unpleasant drag? Screenwriter Scot Armstrong and director Kent Alterman waste all their best jokes on the opening credits, with Jackie sponsoring events like Free Gerbil Night and Dime Beer Night, which in retrospect might not have been the best of ideas. Ferrell has some inspired moments, like when he does an Evel Knievel on roller skates over forty-seven feet worth of leggy ball girls, but the film expends so much of its effort on tired subplots and pointless diversions that the quintessential punch line of the movie—Will Ferrell in short shorts, thigh-high socks, copious facial hair, and flowing locks—is lost in the morass. *Semi-Pro* is edited with little respect for the attention spans of its audience, so scenes drag on unendingly and are pasted together with a minimum of care.

Any future highlight reel of magnificent Ferrellian mania, though, would have to include the scene where Jackie, wrestling a bear in the name of boosting attendance, watches it escape: "Everybody panic! Oh my God, there's a bear loose in the coliseum. There will be no refunds! Your refund will be escaping this death trap with your life. If you have a small child, use it as a shield. They love the tender meat."

Boys like nothing more than to squabble with other boys, and Ferrell milks the possibilities of sibling rivalry in *Talladega Nights* and *Blades of Glory*. *Step Brothers* (2008), Ferrell's third collaboration with Adam McKay, reunites him with race-car rival John C. Reilly. This time, the brotherly combat is literal, with Ferrell's mother (Mary Steenburgen) and Reilly's father (Richard Jenkins) tying the knot, forcing the forty-year-old failures to share a home. Much of *Step Brothers*' mirth is front-loaded, with the opening twenty minutes pitting one cranky, boozy, tantrum-throwing mess against his doppelganger. The fun is in seeing middle-aged men behave like ill-tempered third graders, yelping with outrage when their television-watching privileges are taken away. By the time Ferrell and Reilly bond over shared interests (vintage pornography, velociraptors, masturbating to *Good Housekeeping* magazine), the film has lost much of its verve. *Step Brothers* would have been best off, like Ferrell's acclaimed short "The Landlord," as a viral hit on his Web site Funnyordie.com—three minutes of inspired yuks.

There was something near-tragic, though, about seeing Ferrell and Reilly groaning under the burden of demanding jobs, or belatedly learning the utility of baby aspirin and car insurance. *Step Brothers* was a reminder that, as much as the eternal infantilism of Ferrell's comedy might spur a desire to see him, at last, grow up, the results could bear an unexpected tinge of sadness.

Seeing Ferrell as a gray IRS agent in Marc Forster's *Stranger than Fiction* (2006) was a charming diversion from his ordinary work, but was discomfiting too, in a way that only the unexpected seriousness of comedians can be. Ferrell's countenance is impassive in *Stranger than Fiction*, his brow furrowed, his shoulders slumped with the strain of existence. His Harold Crick is the kind of man who not only wouldn't get the joke—he wouldn't be aware that a joke had been told.

In the film, Ferrell discovers, with the help of Dustin Hoffman's English professor, that he is a literary construct, a character in a reclusive British novelist's latest book, meant to be killed off in the story's final pages. *Stranger than Fiction* is, like Woody Allen's *Deconstructing Harry*, the story of an author's confrontation with her creations. Only here, it is the character who tracks down his creator, in search of answers about an empty life. Harold must acknowledge and accept his imminent death, sacrificing his own life so that others' existences can be enriched by the enduring satisfactions of triumphant art. *Stranger than Fiction* was not so much a comedy as a metaphor for the life of the comedian, and the sorcery that transformed drudgery into genius. And wasn't that, ultimately, what the great comedians did—sacrifice themselves for the perfection of a single moment, of an enduring gag?

30

JUDD APATOW

PETER PANS AND
FRAT BROTHERS

"You know they say don't drink and drive? Don't
drink and bone." —Seth Rogen, *Knocked Up*

It is doubtful that the collected films of Judd Apatow inspire much thought of the Bible, but as Samuel L. Jackson's Jules Winnfield says in *Pulp Fiction*, "There's a passage I got memorized, seems appropriate for the situation." Genesis 2:24: "Therefore a man leaves his father and his mother and cleaves to his wife, and they become one flesh." The becoming of one flesh is

---

"Don't drink and bone": Katherine Heigl and Seth Rogen in Apatow's *Knocked Up*.

predicated on the abandonment of those who had once loved and cared for you. In the time of Adam, this meant one's parents. For Judd Apatow's man-boys, it means saying a painful farewell to the guys.

Before taking leave of comedy and entrusting it into the hands of the future, we must acknowledge the ever-growing influence of Apatow, whose films have come to define the 2000s like Woody Allen's did the 1970s. Apatow has become more than a writer or director; he has become a CEO, and a brand. A Judd Apatow film no longer has to be written or directed by the man himself. *Superbad*, written by Apatow stalwart Seth Rogen and Evan Goldberg and directed by Greg Mottola, or *Pineapple Express*, written by Rogen and Goldberg and directed by David Gordon Green, are Apatow works just as much as any of the films he has signed. Apatow's blend of no-holds-barred raunch, discreetly rendered emotion, and bromance brilliantly tweaked the formula established by *Old School* and its minions.

Born in 1967 in Syosset, Long Island, not far from Eddie Murphy, Apatow was a *Saturday Night Live* baby. In the days before his family owned a VCR, he would use a tape deck to record the show's audio, transcribing the dialogue and picking apart the comic DNA of its sketches. The Marx Brothers were his first love—"I think on some level I was attracted to people telling authority figures to fuck off," Apatow once said of them—and Steve Martin's unapologetic weirdness and taste for high-concept laughs was also a formative influence. Apatow once wrote Martin an angry letter after the star refused to sign an autograph outside his L.A. home, complaining that it was dedicated fans like him who had granted Martin his success. Martin sent back an autographed copy of his book *Cruel Shoes*, and a note: "I'm sorry. I didn't realize I was talking to *the* Judd Apatow."

As a high-school student, Apatow hosted a radio show dedicated to comedy and comedians, wangling interviews with well-known stand-up performers like Jay Leno, Garry Shandling, and Jerry Seinfeld. Apatow moved west to enroll at USC, where he studied screenwriting, but he preferred doing stand-up gigs and hanging out with other young comics like Paul Feig and Adam Sandler to the classroom. Apatow and Sandler were roommates after he dropped out of school; the home-video footage of a young Sandler making crank calls that opens Apatow's film *Funny People* was shot by the director in the apartment they shared.

Like that film's up-and-coming comic, played by Seth Rogen, Apatow was hired by a well-regarded older comic to write jokes for a big gig. In his case, it was Shandling, who was looking for assistance before hosting the Emmys.

None of Apatow's jokes made the broadcast, but he took to television. By twenty-three, he was producing *The Ben Stiller Show*, skimming *The Seven Habits of Highly Effective People* between meetings in the hopes of figuring out how to handle his responsibilities. The show lasted only one season, receiving copious critical acclaim on its way to the television dustbin. This would not be the last time Apatow would receive a combination kick in the ass and pat on the back.

Following *The Ben Stiller Show*'s demise, Apatow took a job writing for the HBO comedy series *The Larry Sanders Show*, starring Shandling as a late-night talk-show host. Eventually, Apatow would produce a television show of his own, about teenage misfits in 1980 Michigan. The series would be an unceremonious flop. It would also make Judd Apatow a star.

It was comedy that made you cry as often as it made you laugh, and never hesitated to make you cringe. The freaks, led by drone-turned-dropout Lindsay Weir (Linda Cardellini), fight off the sneers of their classmates and the hostility of their parents; while the geeks, whose king was Lindsay's younger brother Sam (John Francis Daley), hope to survive another day in the unfriendly confines of high school. With *Freaks and Geeks*, Apatow began assembling the stable of actors he would use in his films, with Seth Rogen, James Franco, Martin Starr, and Jason Segel included in the show's gifted ensemble.

For a rapidly cooling corpse, *Freaks and Geeks* had an impressive amount of doctors ready to conduct the autopsy. It was too smart. It was too weird. It had too many characters. Why couldn't there be more, you know, hot chicks? Or happy endings? *Freaks and Geeks* failed for the same reason it would eventually triumph, rediscovered by a discerning audience on DVD: it was all too real. Unlike so many other movies and TV shows about adolescence, *Freaks and Geeks* was disarmingly painful. Some of the pain was Apatow's own: one geeky character's solitary after-school routine, laughing at Shandling routines, the television his only friend, was adapted from his memories of a lonely childhood.

Cancelled after one brief season in 1999–2000, the show was soon replaced by *Undeclared*, which was essentially *Freaks and Geeks* gone to college. Critically adored and ratings-neglected, the show lasted—you guessed it—one season. It was even canceled by the same executive who had axed *The Ben Stiller Show*, leading an incensed Apatow to send Fox a framed copy of a *Time* magazine rave, along with a pithy note: "How can you fuck me in the ass again when your dick is still in there from last time?"

Freaks and Geeks and *Undeclared* had proceeded in orderly fashion through the rites of adolescence, navigating the choppy waters of first high school and then college. For his debut as a director, Apatow pushes the clock forward to adulthood. He had been impressed by Steve Carell while producing *Anchorman*, and solicited screenplay ideas from the actor. Carell suggested an old skit about a poker game with one member who desperately hopes to keep his extremely belated virginity a secret, and Apatow was off.

Andy (Carell), the middle-aged big-box store employee of *The 40-Year-Old Virgin* (2005), is the unfortunate successor to *Freaks and Geeks'* dorks. One could picture Martin Starr's Bill Haverchuck, he of the lonesome TV evenings and awkward encounters with Mom's boyfriends, moving out to L.A. and, losing himself in a haze of nostalgic childhood pleasures, never quite growing up. Andy is sweet and gentle, kind to neighbors and deferential to customers. He is also deathly afraid of women, and petrified of an adult world he does not entirely grasp. "I respect women, I love women," Andy says in his own defense. "I respect them so much that I completely stay away from them."

Apatow's debut is a comedy of panic and inexperience, a bildungsroman of contemporary American sexual mores. Resigned to monkish solitude, Andy is surrounded by a world saturated in sex. In a world where *Canoe Times* magazine has a *Playboy*-esque cover, and perfume ads insist that "you know you want it," what chance does Andy's preserved-in-amber innocence have?

The appallingly misinformed Carell (who believes that breasts have the heft and consistency of a bag of sand) is awkwardly paired with a trio of sex-crazed co-workers who, once they have discovered his secret, insist on co-teaching an impromptu crash course in the dark arts of seduction. David (Paul Rudd), Jay (Romany Malco), and Cal (Seth Rogen) are founts of misinformation, guiding Andy with laser precision down the path of zipless sex and conscienceless one-night stands. More than teachers, the three Lotharios are shit-talkers, filling empty moments at work with an effortlessly witty drizzle of insults, braggadocio, and ready-made banter. Sex is not so much on their minds as it is the entirety of their mind. Everything else is banished to the margins.

Sex comedy gives way to romance when Andy meets Trish (Catherine Keener), who works at the We Sell It on eBay store across the street. Trish not only has three kids; she's a grandmother, too. His friends love the idea of sex with a grandmother ("Fuck her while she watches *Murder, She Wrote*," one suggests), but Andy prefers to keep things platonic after a disastrous initial encounter. This, then, is the Apatovian style: the battle of the sexes, with jovial but emotionally immature men fighting, and then embracing, commitment with women. What had first appeared to be a raucous comedy of late-blooming sexual awakening becomes a more serious relationship drama. Love means leaving childish things behind, be they genuine *Star Wars* action figures or awkward jokes about "you know how I know that you're gay?" (answers include "You macraméd yourself a pair of jeans shorts" and "You have a rainbow bumper sticker on your car that says 'I love it when balls are in my face'").

Carell masterfully modulates his voice, hollowing it out to indicate Andy's cluelessness and emphasizing words at random at moments of increased stress. He parrots his friends' catchphrases ("I don't want to cram pimpage," "I need some *poon!*") without any grasp of what they might mean. Surrounded by frat brothers, Andy is more of a Peter Pan, his toys and his solitude keeping him forever boyish. Andy makes a woeful guy, which eventually makes him an ideal man.

The 40-Year-Old Virgin was a surprise box-office hit in the summer of 2005, eventually grossing over one hundred million dollars. Apatow, who had sweated anonymously for so long in comedy's boiler room, was an overnight success. His next film as a director, *Knocked Up* (2007), was even more of the moment. Along with Best Picture nominee *Juno*, it formed part of the year of the abortion comedy in Hollywood. *Juno* received the bulk of the acclaim, but it is *Knocked Up* that is by far the superior work. Eschewing the overly safe, PG-friendly direction mainstream comedy had taken, *Knocked Up* is an unapologetically adult film. What else could a film about unprotected sex, abortion, and out-of-wedlock birth be?

Alison (Katherine Heigl) goes out to a club with her older sister Debbie (Leslie Mann) to celebrate a promotion at work. She meets unemployed slacker Ben (Seth Rogen), and drunkenly dances and flirts with him. They end up having sex back at her place. The next morning, Apatow cuts to a tight close-up of Rogen's pillowy butt, whose flabby paleness seems to epitomize everything slack and unfocused about him. Cut to six weeks later, when Alison realizes she is pregnant. Much, much awkwardness ensues.

Knocked Up is a misalliance of incompatible personalities. Alison is a star-in-the-making, a TV producer moving in front of the camera, and into the limelight. Ben is a layabout whose most cherished possession is his bong, and whose career, such as it is, consists of documenting the exact location and duration of Hollywood starlets' nude scenes. Alison and Ben do not have the makings of a successful couple, which is precisely why *Knocked Up* throws them together. "*Knocked Up*," Apatow observed of his film, "is about a guy who gets a girl pregnant who would never consider being in a relationship with him."

Knocked Up is the prototypical Apatow film, arguing heatedly for maturity as it must be dragged, kicking and screaming, from its own embrace of childishness. Good thing, too; without the leavening presence of its raunchy male bonding, *Knocked Up* might have come perilously close to the type of preachy, message-heavy film that once would have been shown as an After-School Special.

Ben's friends, raucously cheering on his unlikely romantic success, are distinctly uncomfortable with the idea of fatherhood, offering their own suggestions for avoiding being permanently tied down: "It rhymes with shmushmortion," Jonah (Jonah Hill) recommends. Debbie's husband Pete (the virtuoso Paul Rudd), while glad to have Ben around, drops similarly anvil-sized hints warning him about getting in too deep. "Marriage is like that show *Everybody Loves Raymond*," he tells him, "but it's not funny. All the problems are the same, but instead of all that funny, pithy dialogue, everybody's just really pissed off and tense. Marriage is like an unfunny, tense version of *Everybody Loves Raymond*, but it doesn't last twenty-two minutes. It lasts forever." The fact that Pete is married to Apatow's real-life wife, Leslie Mann, is lost on no one; in interviews, Apatow and Mann acknowledged that *Knocked Up*'s marital squabbles were transcribed practically verbatim from their own disputes.

The film's romance is as much between Ben and Pete as Ben and Alison. Rogen and Rudd go out on man-dates, they parry flirtatiously at family get-togethers, they sneak away from their women for a glamorous Vegas weekend. Pete is Ben with an extra ten years of frustration and disappointment strapped to his back. Rudd, whose brilliance is white-hot here, turns heartache into humor, tagging a punch line onto every acidic expression of hopelessness. He is a man crushed by marriage, but he has been flattened into an amusing shape, and he knows it. Every setback is a chance for another laugh at his own expense. "So what do you think," he asks his wife, "should we have sex tonight?" "Sounds awful," Mann responds, "I'm just really constipated. Do you really want to?" Pete lets loose a brilliant smile, pleased at another disappointment: "Well, now!" Debbie latches onto her husband's affection for Ben, and tears into him at a restaurant double date. "Why don't the two of you get into your time machine, go back in time, and fuck each other?" Pete puts on his suavest PBS-host voice, and instantly responds: "Who needs a time machine?"

Knocked Up unabashedly adores Pete, even at his pig-headed worst. The film has more conflicted feelings toward Alison and Debbie, whom it admires in chilly, hands-off fashion. By its conclusion, when Ben and Alison have reconciled, and he has taken command of his child's birth, *Knocked Up* has come around (at least partially) to the feminine point of view. But its heart remains with its lost boys. Perhaps the funniest, and saddest, moment in the film, comes soon after Pete and Ben trade lighthearted barbs at a children's birthday party. Pete tells Ben he looks like "Babe Ruth's gay brother, Gabe Ruth." Ben unexpectedly lashes out furiously at Pete, telling him that Alison rejected him because of Pete's inadequacies: "'Cause you're such a shitty husband, she thinks I'm gonna turn into a shitty husband." There is a lengthy, intensely awkward pause, and then Pete marches out into the backyard, birthday hat affixed to his head and cake cradled in his arms, singing: "Happy birthday to you . . ." That's the thing about being an adult: even after the punch line, life must go on.

Apatow's other massive success of 2007 loops back, returning to a posse of sex-starved boys much like Ben and his friends, capturing them at the precise moment when girls begin to dog their Peter Pan adventures. Seth (Jonah Hill) and Evan (Michael Cera), and their occasional accomplice Fogell (Christopher Mintz-Plasse), are the younger brothers of *Knocked Up*'s stoner crew, parlaying perfectly timed insults and sex jokes among themselves but utterly tongue-tied when faced with a flesh-and-blood girl. Seth and Evan are a marriage of opposites, with Hill the dirty-minded shit-talker and Cera amiable and well-intentioned. And a marriage is what it is: with their rituals, their routines, and their squabbles, Evan and Seth are as conjoined as any couple that ever exchanged rings and vows.

At its best, *Superbad* is a reminder of why the rewind button was invented. Taking a page out of the screwball comedy, *Superbad* is a dazzling display of virtuosic talk, piled up in such profusion that one gem is no sooner unfurled than the next is exposed. Hill is vigorously, furiously profane (the Richard Pryor T-shirt he wears is hardly accidental). "Ah, I was so shitfaced last night,'" Seth says to Evan, flailing his arms in wobbly imitation of a hungover girl. "'I shouldn't have fucked that guy.' WE COULD BE THAT MISTAKE!" The all-caps are a lamentable necessity; Hill, enjoyable in small roles in *40-Year-Old Virgin* and *Knocked Up*, is far too much of a good thing in *Superbad*. He can only act in two modes—overheated and undernourished—and the bulk of *Superbad* has Hill threatening to spontaneously combust.

Cera, by contrast, is his typically brilliant self as meek Evan, desperately seeking to muster the courage to believe in his own studliness. "She likes you," he tells his mirror reflection. "She wants to suck on your penis. It's a good thing." Both Evan and Seth are flustered by the prospect of girls as sex-besotted and foul-mouthed as they are. Assigned to pair up with her for home economics class, Seth asks "Hey Jules, your partner didn't come today?" "That's kind of a personal question," she replies, and it takes Seth a handful of beats before he realizes she has made a joke, and an off-color one at that. Evan can't handle women talking dirty to him either. When a drunken Becca tells him, mid-hookup, "You have such a smooth cock," he pauses before offering this astounding attempt at a compliment: "You would too, if you were a man."

Ultimately, the relationship that truly matters here is the one between Seth and Evan. Beginning a process that would come to full fruition in *Pineapple Express*, *Superbad* lavishes the bulk of its affection on the tender bromance between Cera and Hill. The pair lovingly bicker, break up, get back together, and have a fond night of amour before heading their separate ways. "I love you," Seth tells Evan, testing the words haltingly before repeating them again, this time more forcefully. "I'm not even embarrassed to say it." "Why can't we say it more often?" Evan wonders. Seth playfully bops Evan's nose, and the pair cuddle in their sleeping bags before falling off to sleep.

The next morning is like the awkward aftermath of a drunken one-night stand. Seth is the regretful guy desperate to bail, and Evan is the woman, cajoling her man to stay a little bit longer. They end up at the mall, where they run into their new girlfriends. After a serial round of apologies for the previous night's shenanigans, they split off into couples. Childhood has ended, and as Seth and Jules head down the escalator, Cera takes a single look back at Hill, receding into the distance at the top. Both boys are more sad than thrilled, and the moment is played dramatically, as if this were the final scene of *Brief Encounter*, and Seth and Evan were renouncing each other eternally. The rest of Apatow's work, with its endless guy love, is a rejoinder to that very possibility, but the surprising bittersweetness of its conclusion gives *Superbad* a heft that it might otherwise have lacked.

Apatow's absurdly busy 2007 (which also included producing the John C. Reilly–starring *Walk the Line* parody *Walk Hard*) segued into a yet more ludicrous 2008. He produced Ferrell's *Step Brothers*, the forgettable *Drillbit Taylor*, and the Jason Segel–penned sleeper *Forgetting Sarah Marshall*. Segel stars as a lovelorn bachelor desperate to reunite with his starlet girlfriend (Kristen Bell). *Forgetting Sarah Marshall* amplifies the embarrassment factor of *The 40-Year-Old Virgin* and *Superbad* drastically, with Segel completely, startlingly nude for the breakup scene with his girlfriend. The film, directed by Nicholas Stoller, is never quite as rollicking as its Apatovian predecessors, but there is enough good humor to go around. Segel is quite good as the gormless chump, as is Russell Brand as the ludicrous, dim-witted superstar musician Sarah takes up with, and Mila Kunis as Peter's new flame. And how many films can you think of that end with Dracula-themed puppet musicals?

Practically everyone has had the experience of flipping channels late at night and settling on a mediocre action flick: absurd dialogue, hyper-stylized violence, aggressively cheesy synthesizer music, and comically evil villains. These grade-Z movies are made for just such occasions; mindless and filling, they are the cinematic equivalent of fast food. So what happens when grade-A filmmakers and actors decide to pay homage, in loving detail, to the kind of movie that might have been in featured rotation on Cinemax in 1988? The woefully underappreciated *Pineapple Express* (2008), written by Rogen and Evan Goldberg from a story by Apatow (who also produced), and directed by indie icon David Gordon Green, sought to answer that question. *Pineapple* did only middling box-office business, but in some ways it is the most perfect distillation of Apatow's cinematic style. It is also an indication of the Apatow technique's maturation. Having perfected a certain kind of boys-will-be-boys romantic comedy, Apatow welds his self-created genre to the brainless action shoot-'em-up and marvels at the unpredictable results.

Saul and Dale (James Franco and Rogen), two milquetoast outlaws more comfortable handling a bong than a Berretta, struggle to stay a step ahead of ruthless drug kingpin Ted Jones (Gary Cole) and his police-officer henchman (Rosie Perez) while remaining childishly trusting of everyone they encounter, including Saul's double-dealing buddy Red (Danny McBride, channeling John C. Reilly). Everything about *Pineapple Express*, from its bloody U.S.-Chinese drug war to its pounding, synthesizer-heavy soundtrack, screams parody, and yet the film is not quite that. Instead, it is the result of a comic experiment: what happens when Apatow's heroes find themselves cut adrift in a genre not their own, having dropped out of *Knocked Up 2: The Weed Years* and into a Steven Seagal film?

The film is a mash-up of Green's low-key realism and Apatow's potty-mouthed guy comedy. Saul and Dale are standard-issue Apatow heroes—charming, crass, sexually immature—but rather than struggle with their far more mature girlfriends, or come to terms with adulthood, they must flee for their lives. Saul and Dale try their best to be action heroes, and repeatedly fail. Saul attempts to kick out a police car's windshield and instead gets his foot firmly planted in the glass; Dale battles a drug dealer and gets clobbered in the head with an ashtray. Saul pulls out a gun in slow-motion and fires at Perez's evil cop, screaming "Fuck the police!" He misses her entirely. Even the criminals are less than fully professional: "I look like Hamburglar!" a baddie moans after being clocked in the face with a coffee pot. A chase is interrupted by calls of "Time out," "Time in," and "Cheater!" as if this life-and-death struggle were the province of eight-year-old boys on the school playground.

Pineapple Express also takes the half-submerged brotherly love of Apatow's earlier films and fully exposes it to daylight. The twentysomethings of *Knocked Up* and the teenagers of *Superbad* clearly preferred the company of their friends to that of their girlfriends, but were clever enough to pretend otherwise. The heroes of *Pineapple Express* are perfectly content to while away what little might remain of their lives in the company of men. The "bromosexuality," as the film calls it, is explicit, repeated, and without letup. "I want to be inside you," McBride plaintively moans at the end of the film, his man-love rushing to the surface. There are declarations of undying love, scenes of mock intercourse, and a call for three-way detachable best-friend candies. These men are not leaving each other behind for adulthood; they are leaving any semblance of adulthood behind for each other.

The comedy extends past the script and actors, and into Green's creative choices in the editing room. The panoply of wipes and transitions that Green and editor Craig Alpert utilize are funny in themselves, a canny reference to the slam-bang MTV cutting of the mid-1980s. Graeme Revell's score knowingly echoes the synthesizer symphonies of that era's cop films, like Harold Faltermeyer's *Beverly Hills Cop* theme "Axel F." *Pineapple Express* loves 1980s action comedies so much it recreates them, down to the last whiz-bang cut and synth solo, in order to hijack them. It is like a fan-fiction remake of *Beverly Hills Cop II* (the original is too clever to be properly parodied) that has excised Axel Foley and replaced him with two aimless stoners, one of whom must stop in at his grandmother's to change her clocks, and the other a process server whose not-quite-Schwarzenegger-esque catch phrase is "You've been served." The film is like a younger brother to *The Big Lebowski*, replacing White Russians with tightly rolled joints and noir cliches with their action-flick counterparts.

With *Pineapple Express*, Apatow had reached the logical conclusion of his aesthetic. As Chaplin and Sturges and Lubitsch and Woody Allen had all discovered, the only way to get funnier was to get more serious. *Funny People* (2009) maintains the framework of Apatow's previous efforts while setting course for far choppier emotional waters. The film stars Adam Sandler as a massively successful comedian who is diagnosed with a terminal illness, and Rogen as the up-and-coming performer who is hired to help him write jokes. It is an amalgam of comedy and drama whose explicit subject is itself comedy. Rogen's apartment walls are covered with photographs of great comedians past—Peter Sellers in *Dr. Strangelove*, Lenny Bruce, John Belushi—and its fractious, squabbling characters bond through in-depth discussions of the nuts and bolts of comedy.

"Dramedy," that awkward hybrid of a word, is perhaps the wrong description for *Funny People*. It would be more accurate to describe the film as a stand-up drama, whose haunting emotional core is leavened by a steady stream of jokes and asides. Its characters are themselves comedians, more comfortable with laughter than other, less predictable emotions. Apatow grounds his own distinct preference for levity in the sensibilities of his protagonists. Its whiplash emotions are reflected in the piecemeal assemblage of the film—a somber guitar tune one moment, a crass sex joke the next. It is the kind of film where Sandler's character, awaiting potentially life-changing news, finds the energy to jest with his Scandinavian doctor, observing that "I keep thinking you're going to be torturing James Bond later." In his own fumbling, joshing fashion, Apatow is stretching for something just beyond his reach—something nakedly poignant.

Funny People is simultaneously a comedy wrestling with serious issues and a film whose characters are comedians struggling with problems far beyond the ken of their stand-up. It is a drama that never loses its sense of humor, but the director's sense of pacing and rhythm, so assured in the comedic sequences, mostly deserts him in the misguided dramatic finale. *Funny People* touches a deeper chord than Apatow's previous work, wrestling fitfully with the connections between comedy and mortality, but its drama is halting, lacking the preternatural assurance of its well-honed routines.

As an artist, Judd Apatow bears little resemblance to Woody Allen, but the question he poses here is remarkably similar to the one that has animated many of Allen's later works: what good is being funny when the same fate awaits us all—and sooner than we think? *Funny People* ends on an ambiguously optimistic note, with Sandler and Rogen, estranged no more, renewing their bond by trading jokes. Apatow has come full circle, inscribing himself and his work into his film. As *Funny People* suggests, humor is cold comfort for the afflicted, but the act of making others laugh—be it bantering with a friend, standing on a stage, or acting in front of cameras—is itself a holy pursuit. Laughter is evanescent, as fleeting as orgasm and with equally limited capabilities for permanent fulfillment. And yet, it is a task that grown men and women set themselves to, plunging time and again into the abyss of discomfort, uncertainty, and potential humiliation, in the hopes of emerging, triumphant, with a single good laugh.

SHORT ENTRIES

Abbott & Costello

NOTABLE FILMS: *ABBOTT AND COSTELLO MEET FRANKENSTEIN; BUCK PRIVATES*

The team of Abbott and Costello present a conundrum that serves as a corollary to the central critical challenge of writing about comedy. If there is, ultimately, no rejoinder to the naysayers who find any given performer or director simply not funny, what does the critic do with the performers who fail to amuse him? Abbott & Costello are still much-loved, and their films (especially *Abbott and Costello Meet Frankenstein*) have been welcomed into the limited fraternity of pre-color comedies tolerated by contemporary mainstream audiences. So why is it that I find Abbott and Costello so thoroughly unamusing?

Bud Abbott and Lou Costello were both vaudeville vets, their skills honed in the brutal training grounds of the burlesque houses of the Eastern seaboard. Abbott was a producer who hired himself to replace his company's straight man, figuring he could do the job and save himself fifty dollars a week. Costello was an ex-boxer turned Hollywood stuntman giving comedy a go. A 1938 appearance on the *Kate Smith Radio Hour* introduced America to "Who's on First?" (a routine so popular it has its own plaque at the Baseball Hall of Fame), and Hollywood soon came calling.

Buck Privates (1941), with Abbott and Costello forcibly enrolled in boot camp, made them stars. Too much of their work, though, feels like recycled Laurel & Hardy, minus the delicacy and charm of that other pairing. In fact, they picked up where Laurel & Hardy left off, rocketing to big-screen success at the precise moment that Stan and Ollie lost their box-office mojo for good.

A look at *Abbott and Costello Meet Frankenstein* (1948) can only confirm the nagging sensation of laziness. The film is an extended horror parody, one painfully familiar setup after another, with Frankenstein, Dracula, and the Wolf Man present to justify the ransacking of their films. The movie was an enormous hit, and established the genre-tweaking routine that they would beat into the ground: *Abbott and Costello Go to Mars*, anyone? In their defense, Abbott and Costello were saddled with third-rate directors like Charles Barton and Charles Lamont for much of their career. What might Leo McCarey, that resuscitator of moribund comic careers, done for them?

Wes Anderson

NOTABLE FILMS: *RUSHMORE; THE ROYAL TENENBAUMS*

It has become a popular critics' drinking game to think of creative new ways to slag Wes Anderson. They call him pretentious; an unrepentant hipster; ostentatious; overly precious. The grinchy critics have proven themselves unable, or unwilling, to acknowledge that Anderson has become the most gifted, playful, near-miraculous filmmaker currently at work in the United States, and (with the exception of 2007's misguided *The Darjeeling Limited*) creator of an unbroken string of masterpieces and near-masterpieces. Anderson's films are cinematic dollhouses: their wonder is in the perfection of their recreation of the larger world outside their frames. Music, framing, editing, comic rhythm—all are utilized to precisely calibrate an aura that is Anderson's alone. A remarkably gifted manipulator of sound and image, Anderson's films are overstuffed with jokes, asides, and blink-and-you-miss-it details. The mood in Anderson's movies is bittersweet, tinged with regret and marked by loss; but the sheer inventive energy of his jewel-box films, and the comic engine that drives them, gives them a vigor not necessarily found in their plots.

Anderson began with the clever robbery-film sendup *Bottle Rocket* (1996), but the first true emanation of his inimitable style remains its pinnacle: the inextinguishably brilliant *Rushmore* (1998). *Rushmore* floats on the endlessly witty jockeying between Jason Schwartzman's Max and Bill Murray's Herman over the affections of an elementary-school teacher, and Anderson's Truffaut-esque direction. Max is a playwright, and the film is structured like a play, with three acts, and three seasons, moving from optimism to pessimism to a new, restrained kind of hope.

Royal Tenenbaums (2001) further gilds *Rushmore*'s Fabergé egg, its tale of a particularly unhappy family of former prodigies taking place in a fantasy

New York entirely of Anderson's imagination. *The Life Aquatic with Steve Zissou* (2003), returning Bill Murray to his proper place in the center ring of Anderson's traveling circus, is Fellini-esque in its warped reflection of the life of the artist. Anderson's is an exuberant brand of filmmaking tied to frequently somber themes. Perhaps it is this whiplash juxtaposition that sets off the naysayers, sure that Anderson's is a shallow talent. It is not; Anderson is merely exhibiting sufficient confidence in his artistry to let form and content proceed on distinct but intertwined tracks. And what is *Fantastic Mr. Fox* (2009)—that adaptation of Roald Dahl that also serves as a loose remake of his own Bottle Rocket—but the most dazzling demonstration yet of Anderson's childlike absorption in the all-too-adult bittersweetness of the world?

Jennifer Aniston

NOTABLE FILMS: *OFFICE SPACE; ALONG CAME POLLY*

I know, I know. Jennifer Aniston hardly deserves more mention here than Lucille Ball, her fellow television comedian turned movie star. Her monumental success on *Friends* notwithstanding, Aniston's career has proceeded in fits and starts, every triumph followed by two misfires: anyone remember *Picture Perfect* (1997) or *Rumor Has It* (2005)? And yet, Aniston's willingness to venture beyond bland star vehicles has demonstrated a becoming fearlessness.

Cherry-picking prickly, complex roles in unaffected films, Aniston has escaped the ghettoization that so often serves as the second act of successful television actors. *The Good Girl* (2002) and *Friends with Money* (2006) are indie charmers about the way we live now that grant Aniston the opportunity to undercut her well-scrubbed persona. Stepping out with the barely legal cashier at her dead-end job, scrubbing toilets in other people's houses as her well-heeled friends gawp indiscriminately, she is the middle-class misanthrope as minor-key revolutionary, insouciantly tossing bombs and skipping sidelong away from the impact.

Her adventures in the cinematic mainstream have been pokier, with bland roles in *Bruce Almighty* (2003), opposite Jim Carrey, and *The Break-Up* (2006) not doing justice to her unpredictability. Playing the firebrand to Ben Stiller's nebbishy accountant in *Along Came Polly* (2004) was a better fit, although one might have wished for Aniston to have been given slightly wackier pursuits than salsa dancing and ethnic cuisine. Aniston's best role yet, despite its humble size, remains the wage-slave waitress at a nightmarish theme restaurant in Mike Judge's epochal *Office Space* (1999), the working-class counterpart to Ron Livingston's oppressed desk jockey. Aniston is not given much to work with, other than a ludicrous costume and instructions to look suitably downtrodden, but it is her air of frustrated ambition that sells this work-sucks gem, belatedly discovered and embraced by a nation of disaffected white-collar workers.

Roscoe "Fatty" Arbuckle
NOTABLE FILMS: *THE GARAGE*; *THE ROUNDERS*

If the name of Fatty Arbuckle rings any bells today, it is far more likely to be linked with that of Virginia Rappe than with any of the films he made. Arbuckle was among the most gifted of the silent comedians. He was the secret link between Chaplin and Keaton, mentoring both before watching them outstrip and surpass him. He worked with Chaplin at Keystone, helping to introduce the green British comic to an American audience. Later, after leaving Keystone, Arbuckle hired the young Buster Keaton as his sidekick for a series of films.

In his own work, Arbuckle was a grotesque: an overgrown, petulant, confused baby whose speechlessness appears to stem less from a technological limitation than a constitutional defect. He was a mountain opposite Chaplin in *The Rounders* (1914), the film's humor accentuated by the obvious contrast between its two stars. Arbuckle, drunk and disorderly, staggers into a swanky restaurant and swipes a tablecloth to serve as a blanket. Resting his legs atop an ashtray, he looks peaceful, as if Mama had just tucked him into bed for the night. In *The Garage* (1920), Arbuckle is nominally the leading man, but actually functions, selflessly, as Keaton's sidekick. For so large a man, he was surprisingly agile; the nifty spin move he executes, whirling around to cover Buster's exposed backside after a rabid dog tears off his pants, has some of Chaplin's lithe deftness.

Arbuckle was an inspiration to both Chaplin and Keaton, serving as an example of a comic auteur capable of overseeing all aspects of his work. He was also doomed by his own attitude toward the audience; in one much-quoted exchange with Keaton, Arbuckle ventured a guess that the average age of his audience, intellectually speaking, was about twelve. Keaton, already primed for much greater things, retorted that anyone who felt that way would not be making films much longer. He was right about Arbuckle, but for reasons having little to do with the quality of his work.

His filmography has become secondary, eclipsed by the slow, grinding gears of tragedy. Because of it, as Walter Kerr notes, "we are looking not at what he does but at *him*." Today Fatty Arbuckle is best remembered for his fatal liaison with Rappe in 1921. Rappe was a model and aspiring actress who died of a ruptured bladder after suffering convulsions during one of Arbuckle's well-known, multiple-day parties. Rumor had it that Arbuckle had sexually assaulted Rappe, his more than three-hundred-pound girth contributing to the damage to her internal organs. Arbuckle was indicted for manslaughter and, after two hung juries, was ultimately acquitted.

Hollywood never forgot the scandal, though, and Fatty Arbuckle was banned from acting. His older films were also taken out of circulation. With some help from Keaton, who regarded him as a mentor, Arbuckle worked occasionally as a director under the name of William B. Goodrich. In the early 1930s, his scandal no longer fresh in audience's minds, Arbuckle directed a series of shorts for Warner Bros. Arbuckle would die in 1933, his work forgotten and only his scandal fresh in the minds of the public.

Jean Arthur

NOTABLE FILMS: *THE MORE THE MERRIER*; *MR. SMITH GOES TO WASHINGTON*

The studio era's shortcomings in depicting adult relationships between men and women were copious. The strictures imposed by the Hays code prevented much in the way of forthrightness about sexuality, stranding characters in an awkward limbo in which unbounded passion was signaled by a sustained embrace. The era's saving grace was its assortment of witty, unabashedly intelligent heroines, many of which were played by the same actress: Jean Arthur.

The screwball comedy required a particular brand of heroine, and Arthur was its exemplar. Not a sexpot like Jean Harlow, or a ditz like Carole Lombard, Arthur is a no-nonsense working girl able to trade punches with her leading man. One sees her, in the mind's eye, forever a reporter (like in *Mr. Deeds Goes to Town*) or clued-in political insider (like in *Mr. Smith Goes to Washington*), a step ahead of the clueless heroes and not particularly anxious to let them close the gap. Her world-weariness requires a specific sort of all-American dopiness as accompaniment; hence the success of her Capra pictures, where she worked with those exemplars of gullibility, Gary Cooper and Jimmy Stewart.

Arthur's best role, however, came the next decade, with 1944's *The More the Merrier*, directed by George Stevens. This wartime D.C. housing comedy features Arthur and Joel McCrea as accidental roommates. Arthur battles valiantly against the charming stranger, in favor of her colorless fiancé, but temptation ultimately proves too strong. Who can say no to a man who makes her laugh? The 1930s were a golden age for women's roles, and Arthur defined the decade's celebration of undiluted feminine assertiveness. Just think of her as Katharine Hepburn's spunky little sister.

Fred Astaire & Ginger Rogers
NOTABLE FILMS: *SWING TIME*; *TOP HAT*

Their dancing alone would be enough to catapult them into cinematic immortality, but people forget just how funny Fred and Ginger could be. The perennially mismatched pair recreate the same slow melt in film after film: flinty, tough Ginger repulsed by, and eventually attracted to, Fred's goofy good humor.

Aided by an able crew of regulars that included two of the best second bananas to ever steal a scene, Edward Everett Horton and Eric Blore, Astaire and Rogers make it all look easy. Astaire is cool, calm, and prone to getting into terrible scrapes; Rogers is confrontational, feisty, and unafraid to mix it up. They hit it off like oil and water. Their battles were all part of the charade; we knew they'd be perfect for each other, as soon as Ginger was in Fred's arms. But the combativeness was the source of the comedy. If they got along from the start, the dancing would be every bit as beautiful, but the films nowhere near as memorable. Good dancing, like sex, requires playing hard to get, and these films tease us mercilessly before giving in to pleasure.

As a dancer, a singer, and an actor, Astaire (real name Frederick Austerlitz; no relation, unfortunately) was the embodiment of effortless charm. Balding, short, with a pronounced nose and jug ears, Astaire was no one's idea of a matinee idol. Instead, he was a 1930s version of a superhero, the dance floor his quick-change telephone booth. Is there a more joyous moment in the entire decade than Astaire, having cadged a free lesson from dance instructor Rogers in *Swing Time* (1936), ditching the two-left-feet act and effortlessly whirling across the floor? Along with Cary Grant, Audrey Hepburn, and Jack Lemmon, Astaire is a performer who cannot help but make us smile.

Best when they were dancing, Fred and Ginger's offscreen relationship was frostier than we prefer to imagine. Both Astaire and Rogers would go on to fruitful second acts. Astaire would guide the musical into its more baroque, self-aware 1950s phase, bonhomie and good cheer giving way to the melancholia of *The Band Wagon* (1953) and the Cold-War-as-musical *Ninotchka* remake *Silk Stockings* (1957). Rogers, meanwhile, would win an Oscar for *Kitty Foyle* (1940), but would be better remembered as Su-Su in Billy Wilder's *The Major and the Minor* (1942), and as Cary Grant's ever-younger wife in Howard Hawks's *Monkey Business* (1952). What did it say about their partnership that Astaire's roles became ever more mature and adult, while Rogers won acclaim for playing characters barely old enough to cross the street on their own?

Lauren Bacall
NOTABLE FILMS: *THE BIG SLEEP; TO HAVE AND HAVE NOT*

When Lauren Bacall made her big-screen debut across from Humphrey Bogart in 1944's *To Have and Have Not*, she was hardly twenty years old, a model with essentially no acting experience. Skeptics could have been forgiven for assuming that the grizzled Bogie would run circles around her. It came as a pleasant surprise to see, then, that not only did Bacall keep up, stride for stride, with her costar, she actually set the pace: "You know how to whistle, don't you, Steve? You just put your lips together and . . . blow."

Bacall was at her best with Bogart and director Howard Hawks, who brought out her joshing, playful quality at the same time that they emphasized her raw youth. *The Big Sleep*, from 1946, is even better—a jury-rigged film noir recalibrated as a sly sex comedy, with Bogart and Bacall trading raunchy double-entendres while professing to be cracking a murder case. No one knew the solution, and no one cared.

The 1950s saw Bacall transformed into a grande dame, but she was unsuited for the role. An overabundance of seriousness made Bacall pinched and humorless—a surprising transformation for someone who had mastered the art of playful banter so early. She put a damper on the good cheer of *How to Marry a Millionaire* (1953), attempting to steer the film when she would have been better off taking her cues from Marilyn Monroe. And melodramas like Vincente Minnelli's madhouse *The Cobweb* (1955) and Douglas Sirk's *Written on the Wind* (1956), whatever their virtues, are hardly showcases for Bacall. In truth, Bacall never regained the comic verve of her all-too-brief collaboration with Bogart and Hawks, but those two films were enough. Bacall will be, for fans of comedy, forever young, forever trading lines with her future husband, her eyes forever twinkling with the joy of having found a partner in crime.

Anne Bancroft

NOTABLE FILMS: *THE GRADUATE*; *TO BE OR NOT TO BE*

For some reason—perhaps having something to do with her turn as Helen Keller in *The Miracle Worker* (1962)—no one could ever remember how funny Anne Bancroft was for very long. How could someone so regal in her bearing, so effortless in her authority, ever make us laugh? A near-throw-away moment from *The Graduate* (1967), in which Bancroft plays the calculating, libidinous Mrs. Robinson, epitomizes her subtle gifts. Mrs. Robinson and Benjamin (Dustin Hoffman) stand awkwardly in the hotel room their first night together, him charmingly fumbling, her coolly impassive. Impulsively, Benjamin makes the first move, sharply kissing her. All we can see of Bancroft is her rapidly blinking left eye, twitching in sharply escalating panic. Benjamin pulls away, and we see what has actually been troubling her: a mouth full of cigarette smoke, which she exhales with relief. The contrast between the psychological chaos we read on Bancroft's face and her genuine physical discomfort is jarring, and hilarious. We'll have to keep our eye on this one—she's unpredictable.

Offscreen, Bancroft was married to Mel Brooks, a union whose mismatched parts—queenly Catholic, antic Jew—suggested the collision of tragedy with comedy. But Bancroft and Brooks were kindred comedic spirits. She makes a brief but memorable appearance as herself in Brooks's mostly forgettable *Silent Movie* (1976), her arrival at a trendy restaurant greeted by applause, and a maitre d's passionately kissing her feet. Bancroft welcomes the attention as her natural due as showbiz royalty—a befitting status for the actress stepping into the shoes of the legendary Carole Lombard for the 1983 remake of *To Be or Not to Be*. The film was a genial but bloodless rehash of Lubitsch's tightrope-walking classic, but Bancroft was worthy of the original. To be good enough for Lubitsch—what higher praise could there be for an actor?

Drew Barrymore

NOTABLE FILMS: *THE WEDDING SINGER*; *FEVER PITCH*

Barrymore has been a presence onscreen for so long it is hard to believe that she is still nowhere near forty. Having gotten her start as a child star in films like *E.T.* (1982), Barrymore nimbly reinvented herself as a joyous gamine, a sprite forever young and forever game. Barrymore is not quite a comedian, but her lightness of tone—a perky, detached affectlessness—links her to her

Charlie's Angels castmate Cameron Diaz as a poster child for Southern California living.

She got her start as a third-generation scion of Hollywood—her father John Drew Barrymore had worked with Fritz Lang and Joseph Losey, and her grandfather was the legendary John Barrymore. In addition to talent, Barrymore also inherited a self-destructive streak from her forebears which nearly imploded her career before she had even reached the age of majority. Instead, she recovered, and transformed herself into a genuine actor, bridging the notoriously tricky gap between child star and adult performer.

She was miscast as an Upper East Side princess in Woody Allen's musical *Everyone Says I Love You* (1996), and provided the sole illumination for dreary exercises like *Boys on the Side* (1995) and *Ever After* (1998). But she was perfect in the Janet Leigh role in Wes Craven's clever, self-reflexive horror tribute *Scream* (1996), and winningly sinewy as the ass-kicking Dylan in the two *Charlie's Angels* films. The MTV editing of those pictures left them open to criticism, but Barrymore and Diaz make feminism flirty and fun, turning girl power into box-office power.

The Wedding Singer (1998) and *50 First Dates* (2004) are acclaimed by enthusiasts of Adam Sandler as being among his best films, but what they share is Barrymore's watchful, occasionally guarded openness. She provides the ever-necessary balance to Sandler's juvenile antics, her presence a reminder of an adult world these films grasp only incompletely. Barrymore was lovable, yes, but she was also surprisingly tough—a quality that served her well in the Farrelly brothers' *Fever Pitch* (2005), in which she heroically drags Jimmy Fallon's well-meaning, Red Sox–loving doofus into fully fledged maturity.

Noah Baumbach

NOTABLE FILMS: *KICKING AND SCREAMING*; *MR. JEALOUSY*

If arch, aimless chatter is not your cup of tea, then Noah Baumbach is likely not your favorite contemporary American director. Beginning with the perennial undergraduates of *Kicking and Screaming* (1995), continuing through the Truffaut-esque romance *Mr. Jealousy* (1997) and the de-nuclearized family of *The Squid and the Whale* (2005), Baumbach's worldview is epitomized by overly articulate squabbling. No two of Baumbach's films have taken up with the same characters, or milieu (although it is hard to imagine them being anything other than autobiographical), but any single scene from any one of his movies would be enough to identify its author.

Along with Whit Stillman and Wes Anderson (his cowriter on 2003's *The Life Aquatic with Steve Zissou*), Baumbach is an exemplar of the new, hyper-literate, cinematically savvy American comedy. Baumbach is perhaps the most self-consciously literary of the filmmakers, his work marked less by a noticeable directorial style (his films tend to be visually flat) than by a certain alertness to nuance that one might call novelistic if it weren't so trite. Writing runs in the blood—Baumbach's father is the novelist Jonathan Baumbach, and his mother the film critic Georgia Brown.

There are times where Baumbach's proclivities get him into hot water. See *Margot at the Wedding* (2007), where he briefly fancies himself John Cassavetes, for just how wrong things can go, even with every line of dialogue polished to a dull glow. Still, Baumbach's silver-tongued scripts, whose characters personify futility at the same time that their munificent talk embodies an opulent abundance of intelligence, are marvels. Critics and savvy art-house attendees duly celebrated *The Squid and the Whale*, but Baumbach's less lauded efforts, *Kicking and Screaming* and *Mr. Jealousy*, are his enduring works to date.

Baumbach specializes in pillorying and parodying a certain brand of self-aware, well-educated charmers who are most gifted at deluding themselves. The sardonic college graduates of *Kicking and Screaming* are dragged, in titular fashion, away from campus comfort and toward the rough waters of adulthood. And *Mr. Jealousy*, which is a love triangle along the lines of *Jules and Jim* (even borrowing Georges Delerue's haunting score from that film), turns the affair of two men and one woman into a mordant study of self-tormenting foolishness. This, at last, is what unites Baumbach's heroes; they have no one to blame other than themselves for their predicaments.

Ralph Bellamy

NOTABLE FILMS: *HIS GIRL FRIDAY*; *THE AWFUL TRUTH*

Poor Ralph Bellamy. Tall, good-looking, well-dressed, rich: there simply was no reason why he should not have been able to attract any woman he wanted. And he often did. There was merely one problem for him—the man he was wrestling with for his love's affections was usually Cary Grant. And who could conceivably compete with Cary Grant?

Bellamy is the perfect symbol of the comedy of remarriage, the screwball subgenre that flourished in the 1930s as an end run around the Hays code. How could movies acknowledge the obvious (that adult men and women have sex) when even married couples had to sleep in separate beds? The solution was the comedy of remarriage, in which a once-loving married couple, reduced to acrimony, is brought back together by the prospect of the woman's remarrying a solid citizen of the Bellamy model.

The comedy of remarriage was the genre that made being an adult look like fun. Wearing a suit, working, even getting married; all these could be rejuvenated by the prospect of constant loving combat. *The Awful Truth* (1937), *His Girl Friday* (1940), *My Favorite Wife* (1940)—the comedies of remarriage celebrated adulthood as an opportunity to *really* start enjoying yourself.

And who was left holding the bag? Why, none other than Bellamy, whose sole crime was being too slow to keep up. For these movies were celebrations of love in which compatibility was determined by wit. Bellamy and his stand-ins could never be clever enough for the women they loved; only the Cary Grants of the world, rogues that they might have been, could whir and twirl with sufficient speed.

Bellamy—dutiful, polite, confused, fatally Midwestern—was only one of the brilliant character actors whose silent labors did so much to create comedy's golden era. Where would the filmmakers of the 1930s have been without him—and Eugene Pallette, and Franklin Pangborn, and Felix Bressart, and Eric Blore, and William Demarest, and the countless other memorable faces whose names no one can ever remember?

John Belushi
NOTABLE FILMS: *ANIMAL HOUSE*; *1941*

When he was a writer for *Saturday Night Live*, now-senator Al Franken used to keep a veritable mountain of cocaine on his desk as tangible proof of his professional success (God bless America!). The only drawback to Franken's conspicuous drug consumption (at least, other than its destructiveness) was its visibility to the coke-hungry stars of the show, who would gobble the writer's stash without compunction. The worst offender—need I mention this to anyone even vaguely familiar with his life?—was John Belushi, and his limitless capacity to snort, swallow, and ingest all manner of licit and illicit poisons.

The first star to emerge from the orbit of *Saturday Night Live*, Belushi was the show's manic wild child, the ranting, raving, roaring maniac with the motor mouth. Audiences loved him, but there was something morbidly apropos that in the very opening skit of the very first episode of *SNL*, Belushi mimed dying of a heart attack.

SNL fame was shortly followed by two wildly successful movies, *Animal House* (1978) and *The Blues Brothers* (1980), and one notorious flop which has recently come in for critical reevaluation. As part of the ensemble in the fraternity comedy *Animal House*, Belushi's Bluto Blutarsky is the drink-sodden master of ceremonies, permanent inspiration for decades of college students to come. One eyebrow permanently raised, his gaze devilishly directed into the camera, Belushi demands our complicity in his prankish antics.

The Blues Brothers is less a comedy than a high-spirited musical, with Belushi and Dan Aykroyd as the outlaws on "a mission from God." John Landis's film is essentially a creaky 1940s musical played at warp speed, with tempo and a pounding soundtrack of blues classics substituting for a well-crafted script. He is far better in a supporting role in Steven Spielberg's *1941* (1979), the tone-deaf war comedy whose cartoonish lack of affect finds its ideal mascot in Belushi's indestructible, cigar-chewing flyboy. *1941* is like a scholar's careful recreation of a Frank Tashlin comedy—rigorous but bloodless—but Belushi, dogfighting above Hollywood Boulevard and single-handedly taking on a Japanese submarine, is an avatar of menacing cool.

On his thirtieth birthday, John Belushi had the #1 movie in America and the #1 album, and was the star of the country's highest-rated late-night television show. But even among the hedonistic cast members of *SNL*, Belushi stood out for his hard-partying ways. Like Richard Pryor, Belushi's public persona could not easily be untangled from the private demons consuming him. The speedball that killed him in March 1982, at the age of thirty-three, was the inevitable tragic conclusion.

Humphrey Bogart

NOTABLE FILMS: *THE BIG SLEEP*; *BEAT THE DEVIL*

Having begun his career as a bad-seed character actor, playing all manner of gangsters, criminals, and psychopaths, Humphrey Bogart hardly seemed the stuff of which great comedians are made. Bogart's plug-ugly face was made for drama. For him, any comedy would be reached only by a process of elaborate misdirection. Bogart was, in truth, one of the great wits of Hollywood's golden age, his comic facility born of his ability to trade banter with speed and precision. Working with costar and future wife Lauren Bacall, then a coltish teenager, on *To Have and Have Not* (1944) and *The Big Sleep* (1946), the couple's sexual chemistry translated into the machine-gun exchanges of coded double and triple entendres, turning horse racing into an elaborate metaphor for an entirely different kind of ride.

The Big Sleep is hilarious because it isn't supposed to be, having begun as a straightforward noir brawler and run off the rails. Bogart's macho wise-cracking dovetailed perfectly with the sensibilities of a man's-man director like Howard Hawks; teaming with Katharine Hepburn in *The African Queen* (1951) was like mixing vinegar with Chianti. And yet, the taste is surprisingly smooth. In fact, the film is itself about the sheer unlikeliness of their pairing, with Bogart quietly muttering to himself as Hepburn drives him batty with helpful hints.

For all his prowess, Bogart rarely appeared in a straightforward comedy. *Beat the Devil* (1953) is the best of them—a thriller with a false bottom. The film is an elaborate practical joke played on its audience. Bogart delivers his lines ever so slightly too fast, his insouciance our best indication that this John Huston film was a wafer-thin lark. In comparison, Bogart was entirely wrong for Billy Wilder's romantic fable *Sabrina* (1954), his gruffness the lead weight attached to Audrey Hepburn's lighter-than-air charm. Bogart preferred moonlighting as a comedian to taking it on as a full-time occupation.

Bugs Bunny

NOTABLE FILMS. *HIGH DIVING HARE*; *RABBIT OF SEVILLE*

It is jarring to think that the truest successor to the mantle of Charlie Chaplin's Tramp was a cartoon rabbit with a James Cagney accent and a penchant for cross-dressing. But Chaplin was notoriously difficult to successfully burlesque—even Harold Lloyd couldn't hack it as an imitator—and Bugs Bunny was a brilliant gloss on the wizardly, ingenious, indestructible Tramp. There are no tears where Bugs Bunny is concerned, only the inevitable working out of yet another brilliant escape from danger. Bugs, unlike his frequent costar Daffy Duck, is never frazzled. Every test—the shotguns to the face, the pistols at the back—is greeted with equanimity, and a pleased expression, as if taunting death were a favorite pastime.

Bugs Bunny is also a wordsmith. A master of manipulating language, Bugs enjoys twisting words around until his opponents—dumb hunters, circus animals, bullying jerks—are tied into knots formed of their own idiocy. Fleeing the hunter is an existential state for Bugs Bunny, as perpetual as the rising sun, or the cops that chase the Tramp. It is his attitude—mocking, wised-up, carrot-chomping—that defines his brilliance.

What Bugs borrows from Chaplin, more than anything, is an agility that is itself a form of genius. (Of course, the difference is that Chaplin had to physically work out these masterful moments, while Bugs, being a cartoon drawn on paper, is capable of anything his cartoonists can draw.) In *High Diving Hare* (1949), Bugs matches wits with Yosemite Sam, cajoling him into leaping from the high dive with a series of feints and artfully designed illusions. After a few repetitions, we no longer see the trick—we just hear the muffled whine of displaced air, and the splash.

The magpie bunny does not limit himself to aping Chaplin. There are jokes here that are borrowed from Keaton, as well: when Bugs sleepwalks through an underwater house in *Water, Water Every Hare* (1952), and pours himself a glass of water to drink, we are briefly back in the realm of *The Navigator*.

Frank Capra
NOTABLE FILMS: *IT HAPPENED ONE NIGHT; YOU CAN'T TAKE IT WITH YOU*

Before he became a director of uplifting, semi-political, occasionally comic social-message films, before he became Preston Sturges's bête noire and occasional inspiration, before he made the darkest, most despairing family film ever made, Frank Capra invented the screwball comedy. The year was 1934, sound was still in its relative infancy, and Ernst Lubitsch and the Marx Brothers were just beginning to explore the possibilities of dialogue as humor. Capra brought together firebrand Claudette Colbert and icy-cool Clark Gable, threw them together on an impromptu road trip, and called the resulting picture *It Happened One Night*. The outcome was not exactly a movie, the way moviegoers had known it; for one, it didn't really go anywhere. It was a story of people cracking wise, more about its digressions than its ostensible plot. The attraction was seeing two genuine movie stars batting the ball back and forth with dazzling rapidity, flirting and fighting all at the same time.

Capra had, somewhat accidentally, invented the genre that would carry Grant and Hepburn, Sturges, Powell and Loy, and the other stars of screwball. The film would make Capra himself a star, one of the small handful of directors whose names were familiar to the era's moviegoers. Detractors called it "Capra-corn," and Sturges specifically sought to deflate the director's inflated ambitions with *Sullivan's Travels*. These days, it is mostly the more dramatic later films that are fondly remembered; *Mr. Smith Goes to Washington* (1939) and 1946's *It's a Wonderful Life* (which is far, far more unsettling than its cozy

Christmastime reputation would have it) are the Capra films that make the rounds, but it is the early comedies—like the Jean Harlow vehicle *Platinum Blonde* (1931) and the gleefully cynical *Lady for a Day* (1933)—that retain some of their amoral sizzle.

Jim Carrey

NOTABLE FILMS: *ACE VENTURA: PET DETECTIVE*;
ETERNAL SUNSHINE OF THE SPOTLESS MIND

After the release of Jim Carrey's breakthrough film, *Ace Ventura: Pet Detective* (1994), esteemed film critic Jonathan Rosenbaum, who had panned the movie, went to see it a second time—this time with a paying audience. Tracking the audience's reaction to the film, Rosenbaum determined that the "aggressive, hyperbolic, and infantile" Carrey had a hold on his audience, although he found it difficult to explain why. To his mind, Carrey's Ace was a hot-dogging showboat, prone to swinging off chandeliers and catching bullets between his teeth when not frolicking with his animal menagerie.

Rosenbaum comes close to putting his finger on things, if only in passing, when he remarks that "Ventura's prime weapon in the corrupt world of grown-ups is the gross-out, for which a good many preteen boys feel a special affinity." Rosenbaum is correct to note that Carrey's popularity stemmed from his opposition to the adult world, but it is not only the gross-out scenes that cemented his fame—it is his principled opposition to treating the world of grown-ups with the respect it demands. Rosenbaum compares Carrey (unfavorably) with Jerry Lewis, and regardless of differing opinions on the two comics' relative quality, Carrey undoubtedly shares with Lewis a taste for the childish and the disgusting, and a complete disregard for the strictures of the straight world. When Carrey emerges from the bathroom at a party drenched with water, and announces to an appalled crowd "Do *not* go in there!" an enormous smirk stealing across his face, he is a child using bathroom humor to take his revenge on a world he rejects entirely.

Jim Carrey is a child's dream of adulthood. The rubber-faced Canadian comedian makes buffoons of the adult world he purports to belong to. For a time in the mid-1990s, Carrey was the face of a new, brash, utterly juvenile brand of comedy, with films like *The Mask* (1994) and *Dumb and Dumber* (1994) the epitome of imbecilic goofiness. With the passage of time, and the accruing of numerous twenty-million-dollar paydays, Carrey decided to go serious. He was quite good as the unknowing television star in Peter Weir's

The Truman Show (1998), putting his rubbery features and echt-Canadian amiability to dramatic purpose. For a comic, Carrey rarely seems to be having much of a good time, which is one of the reasons why his starring turn in *Eternal Sunshine of the Spotless Mind* (2004), as a man desperately trying to preserve his memories, is so guilelessly affecting.

Chevy Chase
NOTABLE FILMS: *FLETCH; NATIONAL LAMPOON'S VACATION*

Everything about *Fletch* (1985), from its setting to its wisecracking hero to its synthesizer score, pegs it as a carbon copy of *Beverly Hills Cop*. And yet, while *Fletch* may be the imitation and *Beverly Hills Cop* the original, the passage of time has substantially diminished the charms of Eddie Murphy's 1984 film, and Chevy Chase's knockoff has come to be one of the most effervescent comedies of the 1980s.

This is, in large part, due to Chase's nonchalant genius. Passing himself off as an aircraft mechanic, insurance salesman, or officer in the mattress police, Fletch is a glorious fraud. Fletch is a brilliant amalgam of Groucho Marx and W. C. Fields, the man of a thousand masks with a quip for each one. Employing deadpan to amusingly persuasive effect, Chase was the wisecracking wizard putting one over on a world of dim-witted goons.

Chase was the hepcat sneering at the straights, flicking zinger after zinger off the cinderblock foreheads of morons. *Fletch*, the best of his films, is a brilliant amalgamation of one-liners, as if Chase were being provided with an endlessly tempting array of dolts merely awaiting his insults.

Chase had already been a proto-Fletch in *Caddyshack* (1980), gleefully insincere as he partnered with Rodney Dangerfield to bulldoze the members of a snooty golf club. *Fletch* could have been the template for a dozen similar films; instead, Chase settled for one dishearteningly poor sequel and little more.

Chase was so nonchalant about his talent, in fact, that he tossed his career away—a career that had once, after his enormously successful *Saturday Night Live* run, seemed pregnant with promise. *Fletch* would be Chase's one unalloyed triumph, but his turns as movie star Dusty Bottoms in ¡*Three Amigos!* (1986), and the eternally optimistic dad in the *Vacation* films have their own charms, too. As hapless Clark Griswold in *National Lampoon's Vacation* (1983), *European Vacation* (1985), and *Christmas Vacation* (1989), Chase was a Gerald Fordian muddler, botching his family's attempts at recreational bliss. *Vacation*, directed by Harold Ramis from a script by John Hughes, charts the unending string of calamities that befall the Griswold family on their way to the Walley World amusement park. Clark is the quintessential gormless tourist, happy to tie the corpse of his wife's aunt to the roof rack if it means making better time on the highway. *European Vacation*, directed by Amy Heckerling (*Clueless*), exports the Griswolds overseas, allowing them to play the ugly Americans for an appreciative international audience.

Cheech & Chong (Cheech Marin and Tommy Chong)
NOTABLE FILMS: *UP IN SMOKE*; *NICE DREAMS*

The original stoner comedians, inspiration to a generation of joint-rollers and bong-tokers, Cheech Marin and Tommy Chong got their start in much the same way Albert Brooks and Steve Martin had: by cutting successful comedy records. With albums like *Big Bambu* (named after a brand of rolling paper) under their belts, the duo progressed to the big screen, where the joints got fatter and the jokes broader.

The druggy, whacked-out *Up in Smoke* (1978) is like a revamped version of Buster Keaton's *Cops* as seen through a filter of marijuana smoke, with the combined Los Angeles and Tijuana police forces chasing Cheech and Chong as they chase that high. In *Cheech & Chong's Next Movie* (1980), they levitate on the wings of some seriously trippy "space coke," and *Nice Dreams* (1981) finds the two budding entrepreneurs selling marijuana popsicles from the back of an ice-cream van, raking in a cool seventeen-million-dollar profit in their first month on the job.

Before them, marijuana had been a cinematic subject mostly fit for hushed tones and dire warnings; after them, the stoner comedy came into being as a micro-genre of its own. Cheech & Chong's films were not only about getting high; they felt as if the very celluloid they were printed on was capable of giving off a contact high.

Cheech & Chong may have gotten the party started, but the drug-themed film made a major comeback in the 1990s. Everywhere from Richard Linklater's *Dazed and Confused* to *Half Baked*, people were getting, well, baked onscreen. Why was smoking weed suddenly funny again? In part, because it fit so snugly with the conventions of the comedy of delayed adulthood: as a relatively innocuous form of rebellion, it was part and parcel of the trend toward endless adolescence onscreen.

The original fully baked wiseacres, Cheech & Chong made comedy simple again. Shorn of all its unnecessary accoutrements, their films took on a kind of purity, their chase quests as streamlined as Keaton's had been. Without them, Harold and Kumar (who borrow not only their drug-lust but their sense of minority pride from their predecessors) might never have existed.

Maurice Chevalier

NOTABLE FILMS: *LOVE ME TONIGHT; ONE HOUR WITH YOU*

Has anyone, other than presidents, been parodied quite so much as Maurice Chevalier? Mocked by the Marx Brothers in *Monkey Business*, imitated by Warner Bros. (whose cartoon character Pepe Le Pew was a portrait of the Gallic loverman as smooth-talking skunk), spoofed by generations of singers, Chevalier has become the default Frenchman, his tone, and his manner, having made the transition, like Xerox or Kleenex, from the trademarked to the generic. When people mock the French today, they're mostly imitating Maurice Chevalier, whether they know it or not.

Chevalier was Cary Grant when Grant was still knocking around in railroad flats, drizzling his oily European charm on Ernst Lubitsch's films of the late 1920s and early 1930s, and that mock-Lubitsch masterpiece, *Love Me Tonight* (1932). Chevalier was the exemplar, and benefactor, of that strange Hollywood rule that exempts the French from all rules of sexual propriety. Granted permission to misbehave, he is the roué par excellence, paired with the limited but charming Jeanette MacDonald in a series of Ruritanian operettas, including *The Merry Widow* (1934), in which he is usually the commoner pursuing her queen. Chevalier was funny because we *always* knew what he was thinking.

One suspects Chevalier was merely playing a version of himself onscreen. One would be entirely wrong. A notorious skinflint and sourpuss, Chevalier was no fun at all offscreen. Lubitsch used to while hours away on his sets dreaming up new ways to ensure that Chevalier would be stuck with the bill for lunch.

In the mid-1930s, Lubitsch began to prefer a more realistic, vigorous brand of comedy, for which the lackadaisical Chevalier would have been anachronistic. He went back to Paris, and after World War II was accused of collaborating with the Nazi-aligned Vichy government. Chevalier was not a collaborator, per se; merely someone who had made the frightful mistake of reaching a tolerable accommodation with fascism. The late 1950s saw a Chevalier revival on American screens, with the actor cast brilliantly against type as Audrey Hepburn's overprotective private-detective father in Billy Wilder's

Love in the Afternoon (1957), and crooning "Thank Heaven for Little Girls" in Vincente Minnelli's Best Picture winner *Gigi* (1958).

Claudette Colbert

NOTABLE FILMS: *IT HAPPENED ONE NIGHT; THE PALM BEACH STORY*

Colbert was present at the creation of the screwball comedy, hitching up her skirt to attract the attention of passing cars in 1934's *It Happened One Night*. By the standards of screwball to come—including pictures Colbert herself would star in, like *Midnight* (1939) and Preston Sturges's *The Palm Beach Story* (1942), *It Happened One Night* is downright stately. Colbert, though, is a revelation: sassy, self-possessed, regal, and with her heart-shaped face, simultaneously beautiful and believably ordinary.

Colbert was the spoiled heiress introduced to the glories of dunking one's doughnuts, and in Ernst Lubitsch's *Bluebeard's Eighth Wife* (1938), she returned the favor to wealthy lothario Gary Cooper. After the cutest of all meet-cute scenarios (this one scripted by Billy Wilder), Colbert settles down to the increasingly grim business of withholding sex from her philandering husband, in the hopes of returning him to monogamy.

Colbert is delightfully blunt in *Palm Beach*, willing to utilize all manner of feminine wiles to snag a rich second husband—all the while still married to her first, all-too-present husband. Starring in an Art Deco comedy about genteel poverty, Colbert's well-meaning gold digger is maddeningly matter-of-fact. She loves her husband so much she hopes to divorce him, in search of new means of bankrolling his dreams. She allows us entree into the joke of her manipulative allure (which makes her spiritual kin to *The Lady Eve*'s Barbara Stanwyck), and we are charmed by her cold-blooded calculation.

Gary Cooper

NOTABLE FILMS: *THE PRIDE OF THE YANKEES; BALL OF FIRE*

Even the stiffest of male lips has been known to quiver toward the conclusion of 1942's *The Pride of the Yankees*, when Gary Cooper as the dying Lou Gehrig steps to a microphone in order to inform a hushed Yankee Stadium crowd that "today, I consider myself the luckiest man on the face of the earth." Drowned in the lake of tears prompted by its mournful ending is any recognition that the first half of Sam Wood's film is a comedy, and a rather broad one at that. Cooper's Gehrig is the rube surrounded by clued-in pranksters, preyed upon by team superstar Babe Ruth and victim to numerous practical jokes. Gehrig is hardly the center of the antics—Babe Ruth, playing himself, demonstrates dangerous levels of charisma—but Cooper is clever enough to play the bumbling hero, alternately inspirational and ridiculous.

Pride's raucousness sets up audiences for the unexpected solemnity of Gehrig's illness and death, but the film still works today because Cooper makes so absolutely perfect a corn-fed yokel. Tall, gawky, with limbs only under loose advisement from his brain, Cooper was an ideal Everyman: bigger, stronger, and better-looking than any of us, but ungainly enough to draw a laugh. Audiences had more trouble with Cooper as a romantic lead. Both Ernst Lubitsch and Billy Wilder had cast Cooper as the jaded libertine, in *Bluebeard's Eighth Wife* and *Love in the Afternoon*, respectively, and nearly torpedoed their films in the process. Who would believe Gary Cooper as anything other than the all-American hero?

Cooper was superb as Frank Capra's emblem of American can-do enthusiasm and gormless intelligence in *Mr. Deeds Goes to Town* (1936) and 1941's *Meet John Doe* (although the latter runs into notably darker waters toward its conclusion), but his best comic work came as the absent-minded professor in Howard Hawks's *Ball of Fire* (1941). This loose remake of *Snow White and the Seven Dwarfs* casts Cooper as a bookish academic confronted with Barbara Stanwyck's wised-up, exotic-dancing Snow White. Hardly the likeliest candidate to play the pedantic scholar, Cooper convinces us with his gift for self-mockery. He may not radiate evidence of the life of learning, but he is just clumsy enough to make us believe him nonetheless. And seeing the endlessly charming Stanwyck run circles around him only emphasizes Cooper's sporting willingness to cede the limelight to his costars.

Bill Cosby

NOTABLE FILMS: *UPTOWN SATURDAY NIGHT; LET'S DO IT AGAIN*

A legendary comedian and television star, Cosby belongs in that pantheon of great comedy figures who never established a firm beachhead on the big screen, alongside Lucille Ball, Jack Benny, and Milton Berle. For a few years, though, Cosby partnered up with Sidney Poitier on a series of uproarious comedies (all directed by Poitier): *Uptown Saturday Night* (1974), *Let's Do It Again* (1975), and *A Piece of the Action* (1978).

Like 1970s versions of the Hope-Crosby *Road* films, these buddy comedies were gleefully slapdash two-man adventures, with Cosby filling Hope's irreverent shoes. Cosby is the motor-mouthed troublemaker, getting his partner in crime into trouble with his penchant for disastrous decision-making. One continually expects Cosby's characters in *Uptown* and *Again* to receive, at long last, the terrible beating he so richly deserves, but his pugilistic bravado and linguistic agility give him a Groucho-esque impermeability. (Poitier later replicated the straight-man-and-loon dynamic, with Richard Pryor and Gene Wilder substituting for himself and Cosby in *Stir Crazy* (1980).)

Cosby parried deftly with Pryor when Pryor played a twitchy private eye in *Uptown Saturday Night*, and the pair butt heads once more in the Neil Simon adaptation *California Suite* (1978). Cosby and Pryor were doctors visiting from Chicago who end up wrecking a hotel suite while taking out their vacation anxiety on each other—and the furniture.

Ascending into television immortality as *The Cosby Show*'s Dr. Cliff Huxtable, Cosby could never recreate his most beloved character's mixture of the sweet and the tart onscreen. Instead, he starred in legendarily inept films like *Leonard Part 6* (1987) and *Ghost Dad* (1990) before giving up movie acting entirely. Having become the epitome of the lovable television dad, Cosby could never go back to playing bad boys out for a dangerous good time. And Cliff Huxtable could not be replicated.

Billy Crystal

NOTABLE FILMS: *WHEN HARRY MET SALLY . . .; ANALYZE THIS*

Billy Crystal has made a career out of playing the sardonic, wisecracking Everyguy, set upon by lunatics, free spirits, and outrageous fortune. Crystal is the sensible urbanite adrift in unfamiliar surroundings, the Jew surrounded by crazy Gentiles intent on robbing him of his equanimity. Crystal plays a legendary Borscht Belt comedian in 1992's *Mr. Saturday Night* (which he also wrote and directed), and something of that Grossinger's-fed Semitic sensibility carries over to his other roles. Crystal was, like Woody Allen, a New York Jew gone mainstream. Billy Crystal was Woody without the rough edges, and lacking much of the insight into human character. Inevitably, Crystal would serve as one of his many doppelgangers, romantic rival to Woody's beleaguered novelist in one of Allen's best films, *Deconstructing Harry* (1997).

Often mentioned in the same breath as fellow 1980s comic superstars Robin Williams and Whoopi Goldberg, Crystal was far more measured in his approach. No antics for him when a raised eyebrow and a witty rejoinder would do. Crystal's film roles differed from his stand-up in lacking the pedal-to-the-metal drive of his own material. Onscreen, Billy Crystal was intended to be ideal boyfriend material: sweet, funny, and ever-so-slightly bland.

Crystal was at his best when wrestling with maniacs: crazed killers in the Hitchcock-gone-comic *Throw Momma from the Train* (1987), weathered cowboy Jack Palance in the smash hit *City Slickers* (1991), depressed mob boss Robert De Niro in Harold Ramis's assured *Analyze This* (1999). "I crap bigger than you," Palance tells him in *City Slickers*, and that sense of shrimpy Jews taking on the world is at the heart of Crystal's best performances. Even that perennial favorite *When Harry Met Sally . . .* (1989) pits Crystal against uber-WASP Meg Ryan. And what is Sally unleashing an orgasmic wail at Katz's Deli other than a New York Jew's worst nightmare, squared?

George Cukor

NOTABLE FILMS: *ADAM'S RIB*; *HOLIDAY*

During his more than thirty-five years as an A-list Hollywood director, George Cukor was best known for three things: getting fired from *Gone with the Wind*, directing that paragon of overblown 1960s musical epics, *My Fair Lady*, and turning Katharine Hepburn from "box-office poison" to grand dame. Cukor's reach is vast. His filmography includes the subcontinental romance *Bhowani Junction* (1956), pre–Hays code scandal sheet *Girls About Town* (1931), that weepie for the ages, *Camille* (1936), and Hollywood's best-loved adaptations of both *Little Women* (1933) and *Romeo and Juliet* (1936).

More than anything, though, Cukor was a comic director, and Hepburn his muse. Beginning in the 1930s, when Hepburn was paired with Cary Grant, and continuing through her legendary partnership with Spencer Tracy, Cukor molded the actress into the best version of herself: footloose Connecticut royalty, fiercely intelligent and unexpectedly romantic.

Cukor is not a particular favorite of the auteurists; working so regularly, in so many different styles, he lacks the unifying grace of a John Ford, or the cohesive thematics of a Howard Hawks (Hepburn's other great 1930s champion). What he was, however, and what cost him the chance to sign his name to *Gone with the Wind*, was a champion of actresses. Cukor's films are chock-full of meaty female roles. As a primarily comic director, then, it should come as no surprise that so many of Cukor's films are battles of the sexes, pitting male against female in order to establish, once and for all, who reigns supreme. Hepburn-Tracy duels like *Adam's Rib* (1949) and *Pat and Mike* (1952) fit this bill, but so does the romantic comedy *Born Yester-day* (1950), in which William Holden educates dumb blonde Judy Holliday about the finer things in life and receives an education of his own in return, and the *Rashomon*-as-musical *Les Girls* (1957), in which Gene Kelly and two showgirls trade their flawed recollections of furtive affairs that may or may not have taken place.

Outside of his work with Hepburn, Cukor's best film, and one of his least regarded, is *The Marrying Kind* (1952), written by regular collaborators Garson Kanin and Ruth Gordon. Holliday and the bumptious Aldo Ray are a bickering couple appearing in divorce court. Under the prodding of a kindly judge, Holliday and Ray go over the petty details of a life lived together. Petty details, in fact, are all there are: spilled ball bearings and pointless arguments and brief moments of snatched happiness. Among the studio filmmakers, Cukor had always been the most inclined to add a dollop of unvarnished realism to his carefully polished scenarios, but *The Marrying Kind* is much like life itself: funny and exasperating and sad and ultimately wearying. There is tragedy in *The Marrying Kind*, sneaking up unexpectedly on us in the middle of a film otherwise reinforced by the strength of trivial, workaday concerns, but it is of a piece with the comedy here. We laugh, less because anything here is all that funny, but because we recognize it all.

Cameron Diaz

NOTABLE FILMS: *THERE'S SOMETHING ABOUT MARY; IN HER SHOES*

Less actor than acted upon, Cameron Diaz was introduced to the American public via two notorious special effects: Jim Carrey's rubber tongue unrolling like a red carpet at the sight of the blonde beauty in *The Mask* (1994), and the string of ejaculate hanging from her earlobe like a translucent earring in *There's Something About Mary* (1998). Diaz was a special effect in her own right, her exquisite allure seemingly trumping all other, less immediate, considerations. And yet, Diaz's relaxed posture onscreen—always sounding as if she were hanging out with her girlfriends, shooting the shit—make her more than a pretty face.

With the tone and posture of a sun-bleached California girl, Diaz is good-natured even as she is in the midst of embarrassing herself; has any other actress with so poor a voice agreed to sing in so many films? *Mary* was her breakthrough, an opportunity to demonstrate her slapstick skill opposite accident-prone Ben Stiller. Beautiful but clumsy, her loveliness compounded by her alacrity in chancing humiliation, she is an ideal romantic heroine for the potty-mouthed Farrelly brothers. Her Natalie in the not-nearly-as-bad-as-advertised *Charlie's Angels* films is an older sister to Mary, her bubbly girl-next-door appeal augmented by a surprising girl-power toughness.

Diaz was frumpy, and out of her depth, in *Being John Malkovich* (1999), not up to the task of Charlie Kaufman's twisty scenario. She is a mainstream actress, not suited for the indies. This should be no humiliation. Diaz is superb in the underrated *In Her Shoes* (2005), in which she was the bratty, messy, slutty sister to Toni Collette's pulled-together lawyer. It is a thankless role, requiring a willingness to tamp down her natural charms in favor of selfish petulance, and Diaz executes beautifully. Watching her tangle with grandma Shirley MacLaine was an especial delight, for hadn't MacLaine—dazzling and down-to-earth all at once—been the Cameron Diaz of her day?

Marlene Dietrich

NOTABLE FILMS: *DESTRY RIDES AGAIN*; *ANGEL*

The line between camp and comedy is a thin one. Introduced to American audiences by Josef von Sternberg, who never met a smoke machine he didn't like, Marlene Dietrich was a Central European sex symbol swathed in silk and cloaked in shadow. Audiences embraced her as a soul sister to Greta Garbo, that other international representative of forbidden sensuality, but there was something different about Dietrich, whose come-ons were so lavish that one couldn't help but feel that she was tweaking our collective noses. With her slight lisp and tendency to burst into song, Dietrich pre-empted all parody of herself; Madeline Kahn's version of her in *Blazing Saddles* is only a partial exaggeration.

If Ernst Lubitsch had been able to make an ebullient comic heroine out of the dour Garbo in *Ninotchka*, what possessed him to take the vivacious Dietrich and cast her in the glummest of his comedies: *Angel* (1937)? Dietrich and Lubitsch could have made beautiful music together, but *Angel* is a limp ballad that hints at prostitution while paying obeisance to the old platitudes. Dietrich had been a better Lubitsch heroine in that mock-Lubitschean romance *Desire* (1936), produced by the master himself, in which she was a jewel thief straight out of *Trouble in Paradise*, entangled romantically with straight man Gary Cooper even as she picks his pockets. Better yet is George Marshall's *Destry Rides Again* (1939), a crafty Western parody that allows Dietrich the opportunity to demonstrate her finely calibrated sense of irony. Against the backdrop of the lumpish horse opera, Dietrich's European sophistication is itself comic, a deftly wielded mixed metaphor.

Dietrich had been one of the earliest and most ferocious of the Hollywood anti-Nazis, which made it all the more ironic that Billy Wilder cast her as an ex-Nazi chanteuse tempting American soldier John Lund in the Berlin-set *A Foreign Affair* (1948). Dietrich, to her credit, bites into the part with gusto. Her amoral exuberance is easily the best thing about this fascinatingly flawed study of postwar Germany from two German exiles condemned by Adolf Hitler to American stardom. ·

Stanley Donen
NOTABLE FILMS: *SINGIN' IN THE RAIN; FUNNY FACE*

In addition to being, without doubt, the greatest American musical ever made, *Singin' in the Rain* (1952) is also a pretty nifty comedy. Playfully tweaking the story of its shaky transition from silence to sound, Stanley Donen's masterpiece is a sneakily clever Hollywood satire, an insider comedy about the studios' struggle to incorporate music and dialogue—in short, those gifts which the self-reflexive *Singin' in the Rain* possesses in such profusion. Music and comedy are seamlessly intertwined; this is a musical in which the songs, in addition to being contagiously catchy, are truly funny. Codirecting with Gene Kelly (with whom he had also collaborated on 1949's *On the Town*), Donen and screenwriters Adolph Green and Betty Comden give the American comedy its first and only commandment, courtesy of the preternaturally skilled Donald O'Connor: "Make 'Em Laugh."

This, then, was Donen's way. His musicals were also comedies, and his comedies had pretensions to the musical's grandeur. *Funny Face* (1957), like *Singin'*, is a nearly perfect melding of the two forms, its burlesque (this time of high fashion) stingingly precise and its musical grace effortless. (Working with the likes of Kelly, Fred Astaire, and Audrey Hepburn was no hindrance, either.)

By the early 1960s, Donen had tired of the musical, even in its new hybridized form, preferring to smuggle comedy into other, more hostile genres. Not every experiment is a smashing success; the quasi-British upper-crust comedy *The Grass Is Greener* (1960) is one of Cary Grant's lesser films, and the overrated *Two for the Road* (1967), with Hepburn and Albert Finney as perpetually squabbling lovers, is one genre hybrid that should have picked a side, and stuck with it. But after Howard Hawks, and possibly Alfred Hitchcock,

Donen was the director with the best grasp of how to make use of Cary Grant, and the result was two singular late-career triumphs: *Indiscreet* (1958) and *Charade* (1963). *Charade* in particular is a victory lap for both star and director, a flirtatiously jaunty tribute to Grant's preternatural charm with a verve all its own, and distinctly Donen's.

Margaret Dumont

NOTABLE FILMS: *DUCK SOUP; NEVER GIVE A SUCKER AN EVEN BREAK*

It's the question everyone wants to ask: did she get it? Did Margaret Dumont, that paragon of overstuffed dignity, begging for the prick of the needle, realize that the Marx Brothers were using her as a comic punching bag, lacerating her with an unending blast of jabs and asides? Some dedicated Marxists insist that Dumont had no clue that she was making comedies at all, seeing the Marxes' verbal assaults as unnecessary intrusions into otherwise respectable pictures.

Even a cursory look at Dumont's filmography should settle the question permanently. How could anyone who worked with not only the Marx Brothers but also W. C. Fields and Laurel & Hardy remain so blissfully unaware? In crediting the Marx Brothers, a disservice has been done to Dumont, one of the great straight men of comedy's golden era. Her string of grand dames are enduring symbols of all the Marx Brothers hold in contempt: wealth, authority, polite society. Never breaking character, never hitting back, Dumont served with such diligence that her labor has been mistaken for simplicity. Hardly. The list of great male character actors of the era is so lengthy that we struggle to recognize their female equals, of which Dumont is perhaps the foremost luminary.

The mention of Fields is a reminder of the oddity of seeing her as Mrs. Hemogloben in 1941's *Never Give a Sucker an Even Break*, Fields's final film. In our minds, Dumont is a fixed property, a dim moon forever orbiting the planets Groucho, Chico, and Harpo. Her interaction with Fields is oblique, forever at an angle, as if they did not know quite yet the other's preferred modes of engagement. What might another film or two together done for them? Perhaps today we would think of Dumont as being Fields's faithful servant, as much as that of the Marxes.

Blake Edwards

NOTABLE FILMS: *"10"*; *VICTOR/VICTORIA*

Blake Edwards and Peter Sellers jointly collaborated in clobbering Inspector Jacques Clouseau to death, pummeling him with a seemingly never-ending series of unfunny plots and repetitive gags. The cause of death was childish loyalty to familiar jokes, denting the aura of the director of *Operation Petticoat* (1959), with Cary Grant and Tony Curtis as randy sailors, *Breakfast at Tiffany's* (1961), and *Days of Wine and Roses* (1962). But for a brief moment in the late 1970s and early 1980s, Edwards rejuvenated his career with a pair of forcefully adult romances about inexplicable longing.

Successful composer Dudley Moore is stricken by the vision of a gorgeous blonde in a wedding dress in *"10"* (1979). Macho businessman James Garner finds himself moved by a woman posing as a female impersonator (played by Edwards's wife Julie Andrews) in *Victor/Victoria* (1982), and is convinced she is not what she claims to be. The result is hectic bedroom farce of the sort that Cary Grant might once have starred in.

Farce is the order of the day in both films—Clouseau would not be entirely out of place getting stung by a bee in church in *"10,"* and the roundelay of lovers and locked doors in *Victor/Victoria* is straight out of *A Shot in the Dark*'s opening sequence—but the stakes are far higher. We laughed at Clouseau because he was so inhumanly impervious to criticism or derision; we laugh at Moore, or Garner, with our hearts in our mouths, their humanity rendering Edwards's maniacal slapstick all the more wondrous.

Nora Ephron

NOTABLE FILMS: *YOU'VE GOT MAIL*; *JULIE AND JULIA*

In order to attempt a remake of Ernst Lubitsch's *The Shop Around the Corner*, a filmmaker must possess two things: a perpetually refilling reservoir of audacity, and a higher-than-average tolerance for critiques that begin "Nice try, but . . ." Far be it from me to stand out from the crowd: let me express my strongly held opinion—more akin to a religious belief—that *The Shop Around the Corner* was, is, and will be among the greatest American films ever made, and that Nora Ephron's *You've Got Mail* (1998), in comparison, could only be the merest of trifles. This is no dis of Ephron—who could live up to Lubitsch?—but rather a sneaky compliment. Having pilfered from Lubitsch, with some of its best lines borrowed from Samson Raphaelson's original script, *You've Got Mail* is enough its own film to be likable in its own right.

Ephron retains the bickering rivals and secret pen pals, with AOL mailboxes replacing the post office's, and Tom Hanks and Meg Ryan stepping in for James Stewart and Margaret Sullavan. *You've Got Mail* is wise enough not to reach for *Shop*'s bittersweet perfection, settling for an autumnal melancholy ditched at the first bloom of romance. Ephron, daughter of screenwriting team Henry and Phoebe Ephron (they wrote the Hepburn-and-Tracy comedy *Desk Set*), makes the act of writing essential to romance. It is when they face the blinking cursor that Hanks and Ryan offer up the best of themselves; real life, in comparison, is by turns dull and disappointing.

Ephron already had experience in furtive remakes of Hollywood classics, with *Sleepless in Seattle* (1993) a quasi-revival of Leo McCarey's legendary weepie *An Affair to Remember*. There, the original film functioned as a lodestone, a reminder of the overwhelming emotional force of love for its lonely contemporary characters. Ephron keeps her lovers apart for as long as humanly possible—in both films, Hanks and Ryan literally get together in the very last scene—preferring the snap and crackle of doubt to the dullness of certainty.

Ephron's best film is no adaptation at all—or rather, an adaptation of two women's memoirs of their love affairs with food. *Julie and Julia* (2009) is two biopics in one, documenting the early years of budding French cook Julia Child and a restless blogger who devotes a year to cooking the entirety of Child's *Mastering the Art of French Cooking*. Meryl Streep's marvelous Julia overshadows Amy Adams's Julie, but Ephron's direction has grown markedly in confidence. The result is a witty, confident, insightful comedy about women's struggle for self-definition, past and present.

Bobby & Peter Farrelly

NOTABLE FILMS: *THERE'S SOMETHING ABOUT MARY*; *FEVER PITCH*

It's funny how the passage of time can radically change our views. When the Farrelly brothers, native Rhode Islanders with a taste for the scatological and the graphic, first scared highbrows and delighted children of all ages with deliriously foolish entertainments like *Dumb and Dumber* (1994) and *Kingpin* (1996), all anyone could or would notice were the money shots (so to speak): the beer bottles full of piss in *Dumb and Dumber*, Ben Stiller's spunk providing Cameron Diaz with a helpful dollop of hair gel in *There's Something About*

Mary, or Stiller's frank and beans getting caught in his zipper. The Farrellys were crowned the kings of coarseness, the prime representatives (along with frequent star Jim Carrey) of rapidly encroaching American vulgarity. The naysayers were fearsome, pouncing on every new Farrelly film as the new nadir of the glorious American comic tradition of Chaplin and Keaton, etc., etc.

What they missed was the disarming sweetness of the Farrellys' work, and their soft spot for outcasts and misfits of all sorts. Whether the multiple personalities of Carrey's cop in *Me, Myself, and Irene* (2000), Gwyneth Paltrow's fat girl in *Shallow Hal* (2001), or the conjoined twins of *Stuck on You* (2003), the Farrellys showed a compassion and consideration for oddballs profoundly lacking in the average comedy. Having begun with jism and farts, the Farrellys slowly ventured away from teenage-boy humor toward the sweet spot of romantic comedy. *Mary* marked the first step of the journey, and the pinnacle of the Farrellys' antic jesting.

By the time of 2005's Red Sox–loving *Fever Pitch*, the ick factor had dropped to nearly nil. The Farrellys' fan base had similarly diminished, too, which was too bad, since *Fever Pitch* is good fun: a charming movie about sports love that is also a surprisingly adult relationship film. The Farrellys had finally grown up, but was anyone still around to care?

Tina Fey

NOTABLE FILMS: *MEAN GIRLS*; *BABY MAMA*

Consider this a placeholder for a future entry. The star of only two films to date, Fey is the brightest of a younger generation of comic auteurs yet to fully blaze a trail onscreen. Like so many of the other luminaries profiled here, Fey received her on-the-job training on *Saturday Night Live*, where she was the first woman to ascend to the post of head writer. Fey has since gone on to star in, and write for, the brilliantly batty NBC series *30 Rock*, which documents the antic goings-on of a show bearing a remarkable resemblance to *Saturday Night Live*. She has also written perhaps the only worthy high-school comedy of the past decade, *Mean Girls* (2004), starring the oft-intolerable Lindsay Lohan.

Mainstream superstardom has as of yet eluded her, although her wickedly perfect impression of then vice-presidential candidate Sarah Palin (to whom she bore a notable resemblance) made Fey, briefly, a household name. In this era of guy comedy, when women are mostly relegated to attractive appendages to the eternal boys, nagging them toward enlightenment, the quirky, sardonic, self-deprecating Fey (who never hesitates to make herself the butt of the joke on *30 Rock*) is an acquired taste. She is the missing female equivalent to Judd Apatow: the unabashed celebrant of unfiltered, flaky femininity. Her 2008 film *Baby Mama*, in which she costars with fellow *SNL* alumnus Amy Poehler as a harried white-collar single woman who employs a crass emissary from the *Jerry Springer* classes as a surrogate mother, was a critical success but a commercial flop, leaving one to wonder: what does Tina Fey have to do to become a star?

Whoopi Goldberg
NOTABLE FILMS: *GHOST; THE PLAYER*

Full disclosure: I struggled mightily over the decision to include Whoopi Goldberg in this book. As a stand-up comedian, she is an undoubted legend; as a movie star, significantly less so. Goldberg has never had a role worthy of her gifts, wasted in limp comedies and trashy action films until audiences were convinced she could do no better. Whether this is a product of Goldberg's poor selection of roles, or indication of the paucity of decent films offered to her, is difficult to say.

Goldberg's film career peaked in the early 1990s, with her Oscar-winning role as a psychic assisting Demi Moore's supernatural romantic quest in *Ghost* (1990). The movie is sappy and limp, but Goldberg is sassy and irreverent, a cleverly updated stereotype for a film that trafficked in little else. And Paul Rudnick's *New Yorker* essay on the making of *Sister Act* (1992) is significantly more entertaining than the film itself, a hodgepodge of Catholic jokes and Motown numbers. Perhaps the only quality comedy Goldberg ever made was Robert Altman's *The Player* (1992), in which she is a sardonic police detective tasked with investigating murderous studio exec Tim Robbins. Goldberg fairly disappears into the role, but for once, we actually feel the warmth and wit of her presence, even as it lies coiled, mostly hidden offscreen.

Since hanging up her wimple, Goldberg has been an increasingly rare presence onscreen. Her absence, as well as her hit-and-miss career as a whole, stands as a rebuke to the constricted vision of the American comedy—and the American film in general. Having come of age with films made by and about white men only, the American comedy still struggles mightily to define itself any other way. Goldberg, on that basis, is doubly excluded. Her loss is ours as well.

Elliott Gould

NOTABLE FILMS: *THE LONG GOODBYE*; *CALIFORNIA SPLIT*

For a time, Elliott Gould was Robert Altman's cinematic doppelganger, his one-man wrecking crew sent to decimate the studio film, one genre at a time. Curly-haired, broad-nosed, olive-skinned, Gould was the nightmare vision of the Eastern European immigrants who had once run the movie industry: *Jewasaurus rex*, fifty feet high and ravenous for Gentile flesh. He made his first splash as part of the more cautious pair of a quartet of swingers in Paul Mazursky's halting step into the counterculture, *Bob & Carol & Ted & Alice* (1969). Altman made him the star of *MASH* (1970), in which the Korean War was relocated to Vietnam and rewritten by Joseph Heller. Gould was the film's Yossarian, an army surgeon seemingly only just arrived from a Haight-Ashbury brownie bakeoff, or a Soho Happening. He trampled—with heavy army boots—on all the conventions of the war film, his cool insouciance sneering at all the muscle-bound John Waynes busily refighting World War II.

Altman preferred Warren Beatty to Gould for *McCabe & Mrs. Miller* (1971), but could anyone else have played the Me Decade Philip Marlowe of *The Long Goodbye* (1973) so well? Gould was filling Humphrey Bogart's shoes, but with no desire to imitate or compete; his was a new rendering, undermining all the carefully preserved assumptions the movies had established about private eyes like Marlowe. Beyond good and evil, Gould's Marlowe was powerless, a pushy slob in a town of well-manicured monsters.

Stardom had gone to the actor's head, and Gould developed a reputation as difficult and moody. Altman returned to Gould for the underrated gambling picture *California Split* (1974), another pitiless examination of the grubby realities only partially buried underneath the American dream, but other than a brief cameo in *Nashville* (1975), never worked with the actor again. Gould drifted, working the margins of the industry for years, until his admirers caught up with him once more. He was Josh Hamilton's father in Noah Baumbach's *Kicking and Screaming* (1995), a Vegas eminence in Steven Soderbergh's *Ocean's* trilogy, and father to David Schwimmer and Courteney Cox on the television series *Friends*. A loop had been completed: the prodigal Jew had returned to father the next generation of lovable neurotics.

Jean Harlow

NOTABLE FILMS: *PLATINUM BLONDE*; *BOMBSHELL*

Harlow was the original bimbo arriviste. Looking like a cheap good-time girl gone unexpectedly upscale, Harlow's characters devote themselves to protecting their flimsy respectability against all enemies—including the men who had pegged them only too well. By contemporary eyes, Harlow is not beautiful, or even sexy; the passage of time has erased most of the allures the audiences of the 1930s found in abundance. What remains is Harlow's jittery energy, and her willingness to cannily play to all the stereotypes about those platinum blondes. Without her, there might not have been any Marilyn Monroe or Jayne Mansfield. Contemporary of and colleague to Mae West, she inhabited similar psychic terrain, albeit from a different point of view. Audiences laughed with Mae, but they laughed at Harlow.

Harlow's preferred mood as an actor is not sultriness, but frustration. She is forever lashing out at a world inhospitable to her desires, be they for a man or for—well, usually they were for a man. She was crass and anything but coy, and audiences loved her for her frankness. Without her unpleasantness, George Cukor's *Dinner at Eight* (1933) would be fatally dull. Harlow was rarely given the opportunity to triumph; MGM preferred her as the wrong woman, whose magnetism inveigled otherwise-upstanding men like *Red Dust*'s Clark Gable and *Platinum Blonde*'s Robert Williams to stray.

Bombshell (1933), Harlow's best picture, was the inspiration for Mae West's later *Go West Young Man*, with Harlow as the harried movie star whose extracurricular activities are impeded, then exaggerated, by press agent Lee Tracy. The inside-Hollywood gossip is entertaining, but it is Harlow's hood-rat princess who provides the bulk of the excitement. Coming at the very tail end of the pre–Hays code era, *Bombshell* is one of the last of the risqué comedies before sex was smothered in a heavy blanket. West's version is tame in comparison. Harlow died in 1937 of uremic poisoning, only twenty-six years old. What might Preston Sturges have made of her, had she lived?

Howard Hawks

NOTABLE FILMS: *BRINGING UP BABY*; *HIS GIRL FRIDAY*

Howard Hawks did many things, all of them well: gangster films, Westerns, action pictures, detective films. Favoring the clash and clamor of men at work, Hawks was the American cinema's poet laureate of masculinity. What he did best, though, was make people laugh. No matter the genre in question—whether it was the noir atmospherics of *The Big Sleep* (1946) or the African-safari adventure of *Hatari!* (1962)—Hawks tweaked tradition by playfully mangling orthodoxy. Working with John Wayne, Humphrey Bogart, or Gary Cooper, Hawks demanded that they be both macho and blithe, entertaining us with their farcical good humor.

In the process, genres themselves were transformed. *The Big Sleep*'s famously convoluted plot becomes merely another punch line, sublimated beneath the perverse good cheer of Hawks's pseudo-noir. Similarly, *Rio Bravo* (1959), which can reasonably claim to be the greatest of all Westerns, is a good-natured parody of the genre at the same time that it honors those very same archetypes. Hawks, upon closer study, is cinematic godfather to Quentin Tarantino, honoring and pilfering from every genre in sight while remaining stubbornly dedicated to the comedic possibilities of confidently bantering dialogue.

Hawks was a brilliant comic director; who has ever evinced so many marvelously funny performances from actors known for anything but comedy? Having made one of the very first screwball comedies, *Twentieth Century* (1934), Hawks had been present from the very start. Hawks would return to comedy with some regularity: for the stripper Snow White of his academics' fairy-tale *Ball of Fire* (1941), the Technicolor fantasia *Gentlemen Prefer Blondes* (1953), and that masterful metaphorical study of Rock Hudson's hollow appeal, *Man's Favorite Sport?* (1964).

Hawks's reputation as a comic giant, though, can confidently be summarized in his possession of the home telephone number of one Cary Grant. Hawks proved his bona fides over and over, but working with Grant made it all seem easy. Hawks asked more of Grant, too, than he normally gave. Of all Grant's directors, Hawks best understood his appeal. Consequently, Hawks was also the one most likely to cast Grant against type: as the callous flyboy in *Only Angels Have Wings* (1939), the conniving huckster in *His Girl Friday* (1940), or the asexual researchers of *Bringing Up Baby* (1938) and *Monkey Business* (1952).

Ben Hecht

NOTABLE FILMS: *DESIGN FOR LIVING; MONKEY BUSINESS*

There are the movies Ben Hecht wrote; there are those he had a hand in creating; and then there are those he said he wrote. A notorious credit-hoarder, Hecht had a shadow career as a script doctor, purportedly performing surgery on sick scripts for Ernst Lubitsch, Howard Hawks, and the Marx Brothers. Barring extensive correspondence between the relevant parties, it is exceedingly difficult to know just how much credit to assign Hecht for the success of, say, *The Shop Around the Corner*, or the Marx Brothers' *Monkey Business*.

What we can safely ascertain is the extent to which the music of Hecht's characters—slangy, irreverent, cynical—became the soundtrack to an entire era of comedy. The fast, loose banter of the Chicago newspapermen who had once been his colleagues becomes the language of his celebrated play *The Front Page*, recorded for posterity in a 1931 film adaptation by Lewis Milestone, and later—gender-switched and adapted for the purposes of romance—Howard Hawks's classic *His Girl Friday* (1940). In the meantime, Hecht's style had become the standard for the new genre known as screwball, where language whizzed by at a clip too fast to properly parse, or deflect.

Hecht not only inspired screwball, he helped build it, writing three of its defining texts: the Carole Lombard–starring *Twentieth Century* (1934) and *Nothing Sacred* (1937), and the film that stands as the very last gasp of the genre, Hawks's *Monkey Business* (1952). The films share a breathless vigor, a passion for limber wordplay, and a contempt for the squares unable to keep up.

A man of a thousand faces, Ben Hecht also contributed the script for the superlative suspense thriller of the 1940s (*Notorious*), helped run guns to Palestine during the Israeli War of Independence, and wrote *We Will Never Die*, a play (starring a very young Marlon Brando, no less) arguing for American intervention to prevent the Nazi genocide of Jews during World War II. Why has there never been a Ben Hecht biopic?

Amy Heckerling

NOTABLE FILMS: *FAST TIMES AT RIDGEMONT HIGH; CLUELESS*

Teen comedies are close kin to pop singles, offering the same melodies, time and again, with a constantly renewed store of lyrics. Like pop songs, teen comedies are rote, by-the-numbers, and generally trite; but these comedies touch a place deeper than intellect, more resonant than we might care to admit. They are movies to be worshipped in the sickly private comfort of our own personal chambers of emotional confusion, offering an opportunity to relive all the delirium and despondence that forms adolescence in perpetuity. It is the bittersweet tune, not the words, that keep us coming back.

Fast Times at Ridgemont High (1982), directed by Amy Heckerling, may not have been the first teen comedy, but it is the first in the form we have come to recognize as our own. It is about the way we live now, teen style. Unlike *American Graffiti* (1973), its obvious predecessor and influence, it is not nostalgic; and unlike the teen comedies of the 1950s and 1960s, it is intended for a primarily teenage audience interested in hearing it talk to itself.

The boys of *American Graffiti* may have been sex-starved, but it would have been near-impossible for them to picture their female successors in *Fast Times at Ridgemont High* practicing fellatio on carrots in the school lunch room. *Ridgemont's* adolescents are consumed by sex: worrying over it, finding it, having it, dealing with it. But *Fast Times at Ridgemont High* is more than just another raunchy teen film; it is a surprisingly delicate exploration of what it really feels like to be young, horny, and stupid. Screenwriter Cameron Crowe, little older than a teenager at the time himself, had spent a year in a Southern California high school, and written about what he found for *Rolling Stone*. *Ridgemont* is no documentary, but its blend of the serious and the shallow, and its mellow, stoned banter, captures something that teenagers recognized in themselves.

All anyone remembers of *Ridgemont* (other than Phoebe Cates's legendary nude scene) is Sean Penn's Jeff Spicoli, the blond-haired surfer for whom every clock always reads 4:20, but the film is actually a great deal more than a compilation of weed jokes. The real heart of *Ridgemont* is Stacy Hamilton (Jennifer Jason Leigh), whose bittersweet induction into the mysteries of sexuality and teenage romance is the film's primary concern. Stacy is a mall wage slave, serving slices and sodas with one eye on the clock and the other on potential Romeos galloping in to the rescue. Sex is everywhere, but romance hard to come by; the guys Stacy meets are looking to get into her pants, and then back into their own, with record speed. Stacy is looking for something a bit more lasting, but as Cates's Linda reminds her: "Romance in Ridgemont? We can't even get cable TV."

Legions of imitators and successors emerged in the wake of *Fast Times at Ridgemont High*, many slavish and some quite good, but only Heckerling was capable of exceeding *Ridgemont's* rowdy charm. And the stakes were consistently escalating—I'll see your pool scene and raise you one apple pie. In the years between her two gems, Heckerling had directed Chevy Chase in *National Lampoon's European Vacation* (1985) and overseen all three entries in the inexplicably popular *Look Who's Talking* series, in which aggressively clever babies emitted streams of wisecracks like so much spittle.

These trifles were shrugged off as so much detritus when Heckerling returned to high school, an entirely new syllabus in hand. *Clueless* (1995) had little in common with *Ridgemont*—ritzy where its predecessor was resolutely middle-class, floridly comic instead of understated, eschewing realism for unmoored fantasy. Adapting (loosely) Jane Austen's *Emma*, Heckerling was also looking back to the golden era of bickering lovers epitomized by Cary Grant and Katharine Hepburn.

We laugh at Cher (Alicia Silverstone) for her Beverly Hills-centric take on life, where parking is a pointless skill ("What's the point? Everywhere you go has valet"), the Nixon era is ancient ("Isn't my house classic? The columns date all the way back to 1972"), and the mall is "a place where I could gather my thoughts and regain my strength." Her foil is Paul Rudd's archly contemptuous slacker, intent on rubbing her face in the world beyond Contempo Casual. *Clueless*'s high-school milieu is every bit as rich as *Ridgemont*'s, crammed full of strivers, dopers, deviants, and adolescent aristocrats, but its universe has expanded to take in entire spheres of sophistication excluded from its predecessor. Breathless and extravagant in ways *Ridgemont* would have scorned, *Clueless* is exuberant, pitch-perfect comedy. Its true colleagues are *His Girl Friday* and *Adam's Rib*, not *Can't Hardly Wait*.

Audrey Hepburn

NOTABLE FILMS: *BREAKFAST AT TIFFANY'S*; *FUNNY FACE*

Audrey Hepburn was a dream of womanhood: elegant, sophisticated, unerringly charming, and absolutely enchanting. As Hollywood was endorsing the bigger-means-better philosophy for its leading women, Marilyn Monroe leading to Jayne Mansfield, the boyish, elfin Hepburn made for an unlikely icon of femininity. As numerous directors and studio executives testified, she was simply all wrong: too gawky, too unformed, the planes of her face misaligned for the harsh mirror of the silver screen. And yet, every time Audrey Hepburn appeared up there, larger than life, we sighed, assured we had just seen the most ravishing woman in the whole world.

Not content to please only our eyes, Audrey Hepburn was a personality in addition to a face. Daffy and headstrong, if a bit undeveloped, Audrey was the perpetual ingenue. She was a gifted actress—see her splendid turn opposite Fred Astaire in *Funny Face* (1957) for proof—but like Astaire, or Cary Grant (with whom she starred in *Charade*), she made it look too easy for her work to be taken seriously. Not quite a comedian, Hepburn nevertheless had timing and showmanship enough to delight us.

Billy Wilder made her his romantic beau ideal for *Sabrina* (1954) and *Love in the Afternoon* (1957), a melting brunette counterpart to the firm blonde allure of his other favored female star, Monroe, and the wised-up fatigue of Shirley MacLaine. Hepburn sleepwalks her way through these films in a romantic haze, her fantasies a bulwark against the onslaught of ugly reality. She dreamily forgets her cello in the hall outside aging Romeo Gary Cooper's room in *Love in the Afternoon*, then just as dreamily steps out and hauls it in. In both films, Hepburn must belatedly acclimate to a world in which love is merely another currency, and a devalued one at that.

Of all her iconic performances, only one has ascended into the realm of myth, a name standing in for a difficult-to-quantify blend of flightiness and yearning and bruised romanticism: Holly Golightly, in 1961's *Breakfast at Tiffany's* (directed by Blake Edwards). Holly's hardness is unexpected, coming after Hepburn's work with Wilder, in which she is so soft and yielding that we worry she will be torn apart at the first jab of the outside world. Even Hepburn's callousness can be charming. The scene in *Charade* (1963) where she coolly rebuffs Grant's advances is enormously winning: "I already know an awful lot of people, and until one of them dies, I couldn't possibly meet anyone else."

Alfred Hitchcock

NOTABLE FILMS: *NORTH BY NORTHWEST; TO CATCH A THIEF*

Cruelty and humor are more closely related than you might think. As the all-time master of cinematic suspense, Alfred Hitchcock derived enormous pleasure from tormenting his audiences; just think of the unbearable tension of Jimmy Stewart's solitary lookout in *Rear Window* (1954), or the skin-crawling creepiness of the Bates Motel in *Psycho* (1960). Hitchcock often tickles us with taboo, his humor inseparable from his eagerness to unsettle. *The 39 Steps* (1935), the preeminent film of Hitchcock's British era, is suspense welded to screwball's vigor, literally tying its romantic leads together. We are not so much laughing with the film as being laughed at by the film, and its director.

After a few years in Hollywood, Hitchcock's work becomes looser, jazzier, more willing to tweak expectation. Cary Grant may have had something to do with the change. Hitch had given Grant his most successful dramatic role to date in *Notorious* (1946), but their two 1950s collaborations are peaks in both men's careers. *To Catch a Thief* (1955) is a trifle, but oh, that all trifles should feature Cary Grant, Grace Kelly, the French Riviera, and a never-ending array of tongue-in-cheek double-entendres. Fireworks were rarely this explosive, and Hitchcock derives enormous pleasure from the sexual gamesmanship of his inordinately attractive stars.

North by Northwest (1959) was a more challenging task for Hitchcock, attempting to maintain the jocular good spirits of its predecessor while amplifying and extending the mostly-irrelevant suspense plotline of *Thief*. The differing tones never clash, with Grant's whimsical good cheer when faced with the unexpected—be it a plot against his life or the dazzling, eminently available blonde beauty played by Eva Marie Saint—sustaining the mood of frantic levity. The entire film is an epic of delayed gratification, with lusty banter taking the place of the old in-out-in-out. Grant and Saint are romantic-comedy figures straight out of Lubitsch, deposited in the wrong film and struggling for their lives. Somewhere behind the camera, Hitch was laughing his head off.

Judy Holliday

NOTABLE FILMS: *THE MARRYING KIND*; *BORN YESTERDAY*

If Katharine Hepburn was George Cukor's vision of American aristocracy, Judy Holliday was Cukor's plebeian—crass, brassy, and invested with a particularly American brand of moxie. The director gave Holliday her first meaty film role, in 1949's *Adam's Rib*, supposedly as an advertisement for the actress's charms, in the hope of her winning the lead role in Cukor's next film, *Born Yesterday* (1950). In a film stocked with superlative supporting performances, Holliday's is perhaps best of all: accused of taking a potshot at her straying husband, she and attorney Hepburn mount a vigorous counterattack in defense of harried womanhood. Holliday was the ditzy commoner to Hepburn's polished aristocrat, a stance carried over to her Oscar-winning performance in *Born Yesterday*, where William Holden provided her trophy floozy with an impromptu education in elegance. Holliday was the ideal putty for Cukor's fables of the common woman; something about the timber of her voice, piercing and occasionally shrill, permanently defined her as the anti-Hepburn—the Brooklyn to Kate's Connecticut.

She was the ironic counterpoint to Hepburn and Tracy's fruitful, combative partnership in *Adam's Rib*, but Cukor was intrigued enough by her character to essentially revisit it for *The Marrying Kind* (1952), still one of the most cutting comic indictments of marital discord ever recorded on celluloid. The film is a marvel, and it is impossible to imagine anyone else in the starring role. Holliday worked again with Cukor on *It Should Happen to You* (1954), opposite Jack Lemmon, and with Vincente Minnelli on the pleasant musical *Bells Are Ringing* (1960), costarring her antipode, the permanently laid-back Dean Martin. Holliday might have made an ideal comic heroine for the 1960s, but *Bells* was her last film; she died of cancer in 1965, only forty-three years old.

Bob Hope
NOTABLE FILMS: *ROAD TO MOROCCO; SON OF PALEFACE*

You mean that old guy who used to host the Oscars? The one with the creaky jokes who used to entertain the troops in Vietnam? The one who used to crack wise about golfing? That guy? Yeah, that guy. For better or for worse, in this life you are remembered for what you've done recently. Bob Hope may have admirably served his country through his numerous USO tours, but by doing so he also erased memories of his service as Hollywood's most gifted nebbish. Paired with straight-man Bing Crosby on the underrated *Road* films (*Road to Morocco, Road to Singapore, Road to Zanzibar*), the British-born Hope was the schlemiel as hero: cowardly, sex-starved, and relentlessly sarcastic.

Before he became a tired purveyor of jokes about nagging wives, Hope was a master alchemist, taking all his personal weaknesses—tall, gangly, pushy, and unheroic—and turning them into comic gold. *Monsieur Beaucaire* (1946) was a breathless cavalcade of one-liners, with Hope as the French barber-cum-aristocrat, extravagantly besmirching an entire genre of powdered-wig pictures. The charm was in the mismatched alliance of player and part; Hope was an empty suit in a tan trench coat in the private-eye parody *My Favorite Brunette* (1947), his best jibes pointed in his own direction. "I know a sniveling coward when I see one," Hope announces, spotting his own reflection in the mirror. "Hi, sniv."

Comedy fans who think that Woody Allen invented self-mockery would be advised to see any of the Hope-Crosby films, which remain fresh and irreverent some sixty years later. Allen would, in fact, credit Hope (along with Groucho Marx) as a major influence on his own style. The *Road* films were spotty but charming, as perpetually aware of their own deficiencies as Hope was of his own.

Hope's most lasting legacy might be in the two cutting parodies Frank Tashlin wrote for him (directing the second): *The Paleface* (1948) and *Son of Paleface* (1952). Tashlin, guilty of cartoonish excess even in his most restrained moments, constructs a workable scale model of the Western, reserving all the absurdity for Hope's puffed-up, delusional egotists. With its undercurrent of filial anxiety, *Son of Paleface* is a film-length practical joke played on its protagonist, who never realizes his father was every bit the dolt he is, with or without the Harvard pennant.

Edward Everett Horton

NOTABLE FILMS: *TROUBLE IN PARADISE; TOP HAT*

It may at first seem like a figment of the imagination that Edward Everett Horton—fussy, dyspeptic, perpetually flustered—was second banana in practically every movie made between 1930 and 1940. A cursory look at his filmography, however, reveals that first impressions are not mistaken: Horton really did play a supporting role in an inordinate number of comedies in the years before Pearl Harbor.

The 1930s and 1940s were a golden age for character actors, with the likes of Peter Lorre, Felix Bressart, and Eric Blore (often Horton's foil in the Astaire-Rogers pictures) providing idiosyncratic counterpoint to straight-arrow actors and leading ladies. Of all its character actors, none so thoroughly exemplifies the era as Horton, who served both Ernst Lubitsch and Fred & Ginger as an ideal straight man. Whatever the film, whatever the situation, Horton kidnaps every scene he appears in, his fidgety discomfort winningly amusing. Lubitsch customarily had Horton playing over-the-hill white-collar executives (although how someone so incompetent could ever have risen to a position of influence is anyone's guess), toothless romantic rival to the leading man. Astaire usually had Horton as an adviser: one who starts more fires than he puts out.

The argument has been made that Horton's fussiness is Hollywood code for homosexuality. While not entirely baseless (Horton is Fred's sidekick, among other reasons, to inoculate Astaire against charges of effeminacy), the brush is too broad. Horton, like his eventual successor as the screen's most deliciously self-deluded hero, Ralph Bellamy, is a dupe.

John Hughes

NOTABLE FILMS: *FERRIS BUELLER'S DAY OFF; SIXTEEN CANDLES*

Teenage poet laureate of the Reagan years, John Hughes churned out well-crafted high-school comedies with such regularity that one might have assumed he had developed a secret formula for hit films. In a way, he had. The same pieces continually recurred: the Chicago settings, the compressed time frames, the iron-clad high-school hierarchy, the ebullient musical numbers, and—of course—Molly Ringwald. Hughes's reign was short-lived, book-ended by Amy Heckerling's equally iconic *Fast Times at Ridgemont High* and *Clueless*, but his quartet of *Sixteen Candles* (1984), *The Breakfast Club* (1985), *Pretty in Pink* (1986), and *Ferris Bueller's Day Off* (1986) have ascended into the pantheon of the teen film, their humor and pathos a renewable source of energy for each new generation of hormonal teens.

Hughes has been lauded for the wit and delicacy of his dialogue, but his is a highly stylized form of aimless chatter. As a result, his protagonists—Ferris Bueller, *Sixteen Candles*' acerbic Samantha Baker—are prone to break into well-crafted monologues, reaching over the heads of their fellow characters to directly address the audience. Hughes's two best films are essentially inverses of the other: *Bueller*'s perfect day, and *Sixteen Candles*' terrible, horrible, no good, very bad one. Hughes's sense of humor is broad, and his characterization occasionally borders on the crude, but in his case, simplicity is a virtue. *Sixteen Candles* is a teenage love story that acts as if its reversals of fortune had no precedent in recorded history; which, come to think of it, is how most teenagers think of themselves, no?

Ferris Bueller is easily the best of Hughes's films, its charm and that of its perpetually scheming protagonist and namesake both stemming from an unforced confidence in the ingeniousness of its carefully constructed mousetraps. *Ferris* owes an unmistakable debt to the Warner Bros. cartoons of the 1940s and 1950s. Like Bugs Bunny, we are entirely confident that Ferris (Matthew Broderick) will triumph; the only question is how his enemies—scheming principals and jealous sisters—will be vanquished. Lip-synching atop a parade float manned by German oompah musicians, catching a foul ball at Wrigley Field, gunning a Ferrari through the streets of the Windy City, Ferris has escaped the bounds of dreary high-school drudgery embodied by Ben Stein's monotonal economics teacher for a screwball fantasy of his own making.

Hughes would later go on to oversee another set of films, aimed at an even younger set of moviegoers: the *Home Alone* trilogy. *Home Alone* (1990) was primarily a chance for adorable, pre-pubescent Macaulay Culkin to take his revenge on klutzy thieves Joe Pesci and Daniel Stern via all manner of slapstick carnage. Pesci must have shed a tear thinking of all the Martin Scorsese masterpieces he had to turn down for these crass paydays. Hughes was still a successful filmmaker, but the mad burst of inspiration that had allowed him to embody a generation's youth onscreen had evaporated, never to return.

Jim Jarmusch

NOTABLE FILMS: *GHOST DOG: THE WAY OF THE SAMURAI*; *DEAD MAN*

Categorizing Jim Jarmusch feels wrong. Dub him as comedian, dramatist, or farceur, poet of native-born kookiness or postmodern hipster, and some remainder of Jarmusch's work lingers, a square peg for a round hole. But viewing Jarmusch as a comic filmmaker—albeit one with some very serious philosophical fixations and an abiding fascination with death—is placing his work in the most logical category. Whatever the aura of his films—the aimless travelogue of *Stranger than Paradise* (1984), the absurdist Southern romances *Down by Law* (1986) and *Mystery Train* (1989), the existentialist, esoteric *Dead Man* (1995) and *Ghost Dog: The Way of the Samurai* (1999)— Jarmusch scatters comic bits of business like so many rose petals, or pebbles meant to mark the road home. His given mode is the deadpan. Using actors like Tom Waits, John Lurie, Forest Whitaker, Johnny Depp, and Bill Murray, Jarmusch hires funny actors and then makes them eschew all their most favored bits of business. A Jim Jarmusch film plays by a separate set of rules.

The line between the humorous and the numinous is blurred, so that a jarring moment like Whitaker's spotting a boat being built atop a roof in *Ghost Dog*, or the sudden outbursts of violence in *Dead Man* (Jarmusch's masterpiece), are simultaneously funny and chilling. Lacking sureness in our responses, we are disarmed. Jarmusch's funniest film (if not quite his best) is *Down by Law*, in which three mismatched misfits all wind up in the same Louisiana prison cell. The spirit of half-forgotten 1930s Warner Bros. jail pictures is summoned, but *Down by Law* is more concerned with its throwaway moments of fraternal bonding and bickering than with its ostensible plot. One cannot help but feel, in fact, that Jarmusch builds his films around his non sequiturs, smuggling in the beautiful and the ridiculous by draping the rudiments of a narrative over them.

Chuck Jones

NOTABLE FILMS: *WHAT'S OPERA, DOC?*; *DUCK AMUCK*

As a child, Chuck Jones lived two blocks from Charlie Chaplin's studio. After school, Jones would trek over to see Chaplin work his magic, naively assuming that any child his age could see Chaplin at work, or glimpse Mary Pickford at the head of a regiment of soldiers marching off to the First World War. Years later, when he was an animator creating Warner Bros.' legendary Looney

Tunes and Merrie Melodies cartoons, Jones granted his characters—irrepressible, impish Bugs Bunny, colicky Daffy Duck, amorous Pepe Le Pew—some of Chaplin's allure. Bugs in particular would take on Chaplin's aura, his Tramp a perennial winner, outsmarting the cloddish masses with carrot-chewing panache. Jones was assisted by fellow directors Tex Avery (whose work, like *Red Hot Riding Hood*, tended to be more raucous than Jones's) and Friz Freleng, composer Carl Stalling, and the man of a thousand voices, Mel Blanc.

Jones's WB cartoons were unashamedly sophisticated, transposing Wagnerian opera, the geometric figuration of Oskar Fischinger, and the process of animation itself into vernacular forms. *Duck Amuck*, from 1953, is an ideal reflection of Jones's audience-friendly modernism. Daffy is a saber-wielding musketeer who accidentally wanders into a blank frame. "Psst!" he hisses, embarrassed. "Whoever's in charge here—the scenery!" Jones, as Daffy's off-screen God, puts the hotheaded duck through a series of paces that extend and enrich Buster Keaton's other-side-of-the-screen magic in *Sherlock Jr.* Backdrops unexpectedly shift, sound falls out of sync with action, and a giant pencil emerges to erase Daffy entirely. "Buster," the dyspeptic Daffy spits, "it may come as a surprise to you to learn this is an animated cartoon." It may come as a similar surprise to audiences, who realize they have been put through the paces of creating an animated cartoon themselves. Where does Daffy go when that eraser does its work? Even grown-ups, seeing Jones carving himself into the stone of his most beloved work, may be unsettled, and awed, by the reminder of that blank screen, and the hand that fills it.

While lacking the freewheeling genius of the Looney Tunes (and their instantly recognizable characters), later Jones efforts like the Oscar-winning *The Dot and the Line* (1965), the Dr. Seuss adaptation *How the Grinch Stole Christmas* (1966), and *The Bear That Wasn't* (1967), based on a Frank Tashlin children's story, are similar expressions of Jones's multivalent gifts: showcases for the capabilities of animation disguised as lighthearted entertainments.

Garson Kanin & Ruth Gordon

NOTABLE FILMS: *ADAM'S RIB; THE MARRYING KIND*

With the assistance of his wife, Ruth Gordon, Garson Kanin created Katharine Hepburn and Spencer Tracy. The two stars were already well-known names in their own right by the time of *Woman of the Year* (1942), their first pairing, but it was Kanin and Gordon who invented Hepburn-and-Tracy as an ideal expression of Hollywood romance. As a husband-and-wife writing team, Kanin and Gordon were at their best in writing about marriage. *Adam's Rib* (1949) is brilliant in its perception, borrowed from *The Thin Man*, that marriage can be not only placid contentment but rip-roaring fun. Marriage was not all fun and games, though; Kanin and Gordon were also responsible for one of the most disarmingly bleak marital comedies of the 1950s, *The Marrying Kind* (1952). Having offered Judy Holliday and Tom Ewell's squabbling, gun-toting couple as evidence of the rarity of Hepburn and Tracy's blessed alliance in *Adam's Rib*, Kanin and Gordon were compelled to return to the scene of the crime, retelling the same story—this time from the inside.

Kanin was not only Hepburn and Tracy's most gifted writer for the screen; he was also the prime hagiographer of their private lives. His memoir *Tracy and Hepburn*, published a few years after Tracy's death, led to a rift between Hepburn and her onetime close friends. What Hepburn later came to understand was that Kanin was bronzing the official legend of Spencer and Kate—the timeless love story that had the two actors recreating *Adam's Rib* in private, for their own amusement. Whether there was any truth to the tale, he would never say. Kanin could not help but create love stories, whatever the form.

Charlie Kaufman

NOTABLE FILMS: *ETERNAL SUNSHINE OF THE SPOTLESS MIND; ADAPTATION*

What to make of Charlie Kaufman? The reclusive screenwriter has re-energized the American independent film with his defiantly quirky puzzle-boxes. Without him, the occasionally stifling air of plodding realism that has dogged the Sundance classes in recent years might have become terminal. And yet, like amateur medical practitioners identifying a sure-fire case of hemianopsia—a neurological condition that causes a severely impaired field of vision—Kaufman must be diagnosed with a similar malady, cinematically speaking.

Each of his films as a screenwriter—beginning with *Being John Malkovich* (1999) and proceeding through his directorial debut, *Synecdoche, New York* (2008)—suffer from a bizarre ailment in which an artfully introduced, immediately compelling theme slowly and unexpectedly withers away in the films' second halves. There appears to be no cure for the disease; *Synecdoche*, which begins so promisingly as a study of an artist in crisis, unexplainedly collapses under the weight of its own ambitions.

Even *Eternal Sunshine of the Spotless Mind* (2004), easily Kaufman's best script, partially crumbles, burdened by its excessive ambition, before reaching its guardedly optimistic conclusion. Kaufman at his worst—which is to say in the third act of any of his scripts, or the entirety of *Human Nature* (2001)—is nearly intolerable, his self-reflexive desire to offer commentary on his work, even as it is in the midst of unfolding, indicative of a fatal self-consciousness.

This, in some perverse way, is Kaufman's point; he wants his movies to be more than movies—or is it less than movies? A master of highbrow wackiness, Kaufman ultimately prefers to undercut his own carefully crafted premises, enjoying the sensation of things falling apart. And so *Adaptation* (2002), which begins as a portrait of the screenwriter as rebel, eventually becomes everything its "Charlie Kaufman" (beautifully played by Nicolas Cage) despises. "I don't want to cram in sex or guns or car chases, you know," Charlie shouts in frustration, "or characters, you know, learning profound life lessons or growing or coming to like each other or overcoming obstacles to succeed in the end, you know. The book isn't like that, and life isn't like that." Kaufman is illustrating, in his own perverse way, the ways in which the movies fail life; but can failure ever be triumphant?

Diane Keaton and Mia Farrow

NOTABLE FILMS: *ANNIE HALL* (KEATON); *THE PURPLE ROSE OF CAIRO* (FARROW)

Like counting the rings on a tree, identifying the leading lady is the most trusted method of scientifically dating a Woody Allen film. If it's Diane Keaton, then it's likely the mid-1970s. If it's Mia Farrow, it's the 1980s. (If it's neither, check the size of Woody's bald spot; it may be the early 1970s, or the 1990s and 2000s, and the extent of Allen's male-pattern baldness will provide an easy hint as to which is the more likely).

Keaton and Farrow are the two actresses most closely associated with Allen; both were romantically as well as professionally involved with the actor and director. Keaton was present for the best of Allen's "early, funny" years, culminating in *Annie Hall* (1977) and *Manhattan* (1979), while Farrow (who had memorably played the pregnant bride in Robert Altman's *A Wedding*) oversaw the period stretching from *A Midsummer Night's Sex Comedy* (1982) to *Husbands and Wives* (1992).

Of the two, Keaton is easily the more natural comedian, lightening the emotional forthrightness of *Annie Hall* with her skittish self-abasement, and winning a well-deserved Oscar for her efforts. She is a beautiful clown unafraid to appear ridiculous; one can only imagine what Chaplin, or Lubitsch, might have done with her. She was more actress, though, than comedian, and her presence urged Allen away from the broad comedy of *Bananas* and *Sleeper* to the more mature, humane comedies of his middle period.

Allen and Keaton eventually parted ways, and she was replaced—both personally and professionally—with Farrow, an altogether different kind of onscreen presence. Farrow was not the laugh-getter Keaton had been; the comedy appeared to flow around, rather than through, her. She demanded a different kind of scenario, one more devoted to the ensemble than the lone performer. *The Purple Rose of Cairo* (1985) is Farrow's best performance, coming as it does in Allen's bittersweet ode to the dream-world of the movies. As good as *Zelig* or *A Midsummer Night's Sex Comedy* is, the comic sequences often seem too demanding for Farrow. Farrow is to be credited, however, for her fearlessness. She plays distinctly unsympathetic characters in *Broadway Danny Rose* (1984) and *Crimes and Misdemeanors* (1989), leagues away from Keaton's charming ditzes.

Allen and Farrow broke over allegations of child abuse, and Allen's taking up with stepdaughter Soon-Yi Previn. Keaton briefly returned to Allen's warm embrace for *Manhattan Murder Mystery* (1993), itself a nostalgic rejuvenation of the broad comedy of Allen's early years. In the years since, Farrow has mostly vanished from the movies, making a brief, welcome return in Michel Gondry's *Be Kind Rewind* (2008), while Keaton has flourished in feather-light, modestly amusing roles in films like *Something's Gotta Give* (2003).

Stanley Kubrick

NOTABLE FILMS: *DR. STRANGELOVE; LOLITA*

Kubrick is really not much of a comedy director, having made only one outright comedy: 1964's *Dr. Strangelove, or How I Learned to Stop Worrying and Love the Bomb*. Since *Strangelove* is, with the possible exception of *Duck Soup*, the greatest political satire ever made, it is tantalizing to imagine what Kubrick might have done for comedy had he ever devoted himself fully to it. It is also worth remembering just how close Kubrick came to turning in a wholly dramatic nuclear-panic film. Adapting Peter George's novel *Red Alert*, Kubrick had intended to shoot a fictional counterpart to Peter Watkins's supremely chilling documentary *The War Game*. Somewhere along the way, though, the inherent absurdity of nuclear doomsday began to poke through, and Kubrick and cowriter Terry Southern turned *Red Alert* into a madcap, midnight-black farce.

Current events ended up intruding on *Strangelove*, in truly bizarre fashion. Look closely at the lips of Slim Pickens's Major Kong as he sorts through the contents of his emergency packet ("One hundred dollars in rubles. One hundred dollars in gold. Nine packs of chewing gum. One issue of prophylactics."), and you'll see they don't line up properly with what we hear him conclude with: "Shoot, a fella could have a pretty good weekend in Vegas with all that stuff." Pickens had originally said "Dallas," but the assassination of President John F. Kennedy in Dallas in November 1963, between the completion of principal photography and the release of the film, had led to a hasty overdub of the line, to avoid giving accidental offense to Americans mourning the president's death.

Harry Langdon

NOTABLE FILMS: *THE STRONG MAN*; *TRAMP, TRAMP, TRAMP*

Chaplin and Keaton were wizards of manipulation, their appeal a product of their unexpectedly brilliant exploitation of dull objects. Harry Langdon, meanwhile, was a prisoner of circumstance. He works no magic, and contains nary a spark of hidden genius. This may be why Langdon is the least remembered of the silent giants. There being room for only three medalists on the reviewing stand, Langdon has been shunted into the dusty bin of forgotten silent clowns, his legacy a matter best left for academics and silent-film historians.

With his thickly applied white pancake makeup, Langdon's was a baroque, self-knowing clowning. His pants too long, his shirts hanging sloppily over his belt, a floppy hat on his head, he was an adjunct to Chaplin's Tramp, a naif lacking the Tramp's grace. His loose-limbed waddle was that of an infant only just learned how to walk, and still fearful of toppling over. In a precise inversion of his silent colleagues, Langdon was funny in direct relation to his helplessness. He was, as Walter Kerr describes it, "forever trying to *prevent* the comedy other men made."

Harry Langdon was an adult mimicking a prepubescent boy, an overgrown infant surrounded by knowing women. His father's bankruptcy in *Tramp, Tramp, Tramp* (1926) is greeted with disbelief: "Does that mean I don't get my new bicycle?" His energy, and his enthusiasm, are immature. Even when he is mooning over the billboards of Joan Crawford in *Tramp, Tramp, Tramp*, it is with a little boy's avidity, not a man's ardor.

Langdon is the most stylized of all the silent comedians, and perhaps this explains his diminished appeal. Hit on the head with a bottle, he curls up and goes to sleep. Spotting a nude model posing in *The Strong Man*, Langdon flees, crashing into a screen and tumbling down a flight of stairs in his retreat from sex. Adulthood was not to be his realm. In *The Strong Man* (1926), he plays with his girl's fingers, covering her hand with his hat before daring to kiss it. He slumps back, exhausted by his effort.

The Strong Man (1926), the most enduring of his films, is a precursor to *City Lights*, the tenderness of its romance between Langdon's Belgian WWI veteran and his blind pen pal a likely inspiration for Chaplin's epochal comedy. If Langdon could never transcend his occasional flashes of ingeniousness, well—not everyone could become one of the immortals.

Spike Lee

NOTABLE FILMS: *DO THE RIGHT THING; SHE'S GOTTA HAVE IT*

Woody Allen had taken New York's Jewish middle class and made their prickly, neurotic concerns a mainstream affair. Similarly finding the universal in the particular, Spike Lee took inspiration from African American life in New York City, making the Big Apple his unofficial capital and permanent favored location. Lee's career would branch off in very different directions, but for his first few films, at least, he appeared to be an inheritor of Allen's mantle. His debut film, *She's Gotta Have It* (1986), particularly resembled Woody: a superbly written romantic duel between well-heeled New Yorkers, with glossy photography and stylish performances. Lee even starred in his film, too, playing bike messenger Mars Blackmon, the least serious of the contenders for the charming Nola Darling. Foul-mouthed, outspoken, and fashionably bedecked in hip-hop gear, Mars is undoubtedly the only character from a low-budget independent film ever to later star in a line of Nike commercials with Michael Jordan.

Do the Right Thing (1989), still Lee's best film, is a quintessential my-crazy-day film, consumed with strange neighbors, irate girlfriends, and frazzled bosses before the ground gives way beneath the feet of Lee's Mookie, and mundanity unexpectedly transforms into tragedy.

Lee has always been a funny actor himself, enlivening his own films (even the epic *Malcolm X*) with his supporting performances, and comedy remained a fixation even as his directorial resume grew crammed with intimate, searching dramas like *25th Hour* (2002). He directed the masterful 2000 concert film *The Original Kings of Comedy*, which features brilliant stand-up routines from performers Steve Harvey, D.L. Hughley, Cedric the

Entertainer, and Bernie Mac. There is not much of Lee himself to be found in the film, but even if he is only wise enough to turn on the camera and stay out of the way, *Original Kings* is one of the funniest films of the past decade.

And for all of its many flaws, *Bamboozled* (2000) is a noble attempt to come to terms with the poisonous heritage of humor by and about African Americans, particularly the dubious legacy of the blackface routine. In Mantan and Sleep n' Eat, the lead performers of the film's smash-hit TV minstrel show, Spike Lee summons the restless ghost of racist comedy, and wonders: what do we do with a joke that has stopped being funny?

Mitchell Leisen

NOTABLE FILMS: *MIDNIGHT; EASY LIVING*

Fans of comedy's golden era owe a great debt of thanks to Mitchell Leisen, whose mangling of carefully crafted scripts roused both Billy Wilder and Preston Sturges to become directors. "I was inspired to become a director by a cockroach," Wilder once said of his career, and it was Leisen who set the cockroach in motion—or, more precisely, failed to do so. Shooting Wilder and Charles Brackett's script for *Hold Back the Dawn* (1941), actor Charles Boyer had elected to cut an entire speech delivered to a cockroach, deeming the scene illogical. "How can I talk to a cockroach if a cockroach cannot answer me?" Boyer wondered. Aghast at Leisen's inability to protect his words, Wilder decided he would never let another director mangle his work.

If only for the sake of his own reputation, it might have been wise to be kinder to Wilder (who cowrote *Midnight* and *Arise, My Love*) and Sturges (who wrote *Easy Living* and *Remember the Night*). But for all of Wilder and Sturges's well-justified grumbling, and whatever the provenance of their charms, Leisen's films are emblematic of screwball comedy's unmatched bench depth. Leisen is the backup quarterback of the screwball era, which only goes to show what a great team it really was. *Midnight* (1939) in particular is testament to the magical properties of Parisian backdrops for romantic comedies, and Claudette Colbert's vivacious charms in particular. If Leisen is a mediocre filmmaker, and the result is *Easy Living* (1937) and *Midnight* (1939), let me be the first to submit a petition for far, far more mediocrity in Hollywood.

As a director, Leisen had little of the panache of Wilder, or Sturges. His films are testament to the democratic impulse of screwball as a genre, as well as its durability. Their champagne fizz has yet to wear off, more than seventy years later. We can only guess how much better they might have been had he shot them as they were written, but we'll take the final product gladly. Anyone could do it—even Mitchell Leisen.

Jack Lemmon & Walter Matthau

NOTABLE FILMS: *THE FORTUNE COOKIE*; *THE FRONT PAGE*

Long before they were lovable codgers in search of romance, Jack Lemmon and Walter Matthau were the ideal Billy Wilder cocktail of delight and dyspepsia. Wilder had been drawn to each of them separately. He had unsuccessfully sought to cast Matthau in the Tom Ewell role in *The Seven Year Itch* (1955). Lemmon had been his frazzled antihero in *Some Like It Hot* (1959) and *The Apartment* (1960), finding unexpected grace under comic fire. Playing against the likes of Tony Curtis and Shirley MacLaine was good—they bickered like old friends—but being paired off with Walter Matthau was like duking it out with family.

It was more than apropos that the pair played brothers-in-law in their first collaboration, *The Fortune Cookie* (1965): that relationship perfectly encapsulates the vague sense of attachment and permanent air of disdain that define their relationship. Matthau is the scheming lawyer who convinces Lemmon's cameraman, injured at a football game, to fake a debilitating injury, dreaming of a sizable payday. Matthau, who won an Oscar for his performance, is another in a long line of charming Wilder scalawags, with Lemmon serving as both foil and prey.

The balance of power stayed much the same for Wilder's mostly unnecessary remake of *The Front Page* (1974), with Lemmon as soon-to-be-married reporter Hildy Johnson, and Matthau as his irrepressible editor Walter Burns. Matthau, reprising the Cary Grant role from *His Girl Friday*, is shameless in the pursuit of a hot story, taking a charlatan's delight in the journalist's dark arts of deception. Lemmon is cursed with the straight-man role in both films, but has there ever been a better one? Practically spritzing the camera with outrage, Lemmon is the little guy screaming at the top of his lungs about how he's not going to take this lying down, even as he fluffs the pillows and pulls back the sheets.

The Wilder collaborations are delicious, if little-seen these days, but the pairing everyone still remembers is *The Odd Couple* (1969), based on the Neil Simon play. Matthau had the showier role as gruff, sloppy sportswriter Oscar Madison, but Lemmon steals the show as the prim, occasionally suicidal Felix Unger, who cooks Oscar's dinners and reorganizes his poker games.

Both Lemmon and Matthau are easily forgotten when lists of great performers are assembled; they seem too humble, their work too comfortably familiar to laud. But each, in his own way, is an ideal example of the true craft of acting. In films as disparate as *Charade* (1963), *Charley Varrick* (1973), and *The Taking of Pelham One Two Three* (1974), Matthau was the epitome of crass good humor, his gruff plainspokenness deeply refreshing after years of moody Method-ists. And Lemmon was Wilder's go-to leading man for a reason; the actor, much like his occasional partner, seemed to be not so much acting as being. Lemmon was superb in other films, too, like the Simon adaptation *The Prisoner of Second Avenue* (1975) and *Glengarry Glen Ross* (1992), but he saved his best for Wilder. As the director once said of his favorite actor, "He was my Everyman."

Richard Linklater

NOTABLE FILMS: *DAZED AND CONFUSED; BEFORE SUNSET*

Richard Linklater's *Dazed and Confused* (1993) reconfigures the recent past as a wonderfully mellow, motor-mouthed nostalgia trip. A retro teen comedy in the vein of *American Graffiti*, *Dazed* is an all-night bacchanalia on the very first night of summer, 1976. No lives are permanently changed, no earth-shattering romances conceived. Like any good party, this one is all about the music. *Dazed and Confused* is a mix tape of Linklater's favorite hard-rock jams of the mid-1970s: Aerosmith's "Sweet Emotion," Kiss's "Rock & Roll All Night," Foghat's "Slow Ride," Alice Cooper's "School's Out." These songs become the expression of hormonally charged youth, in all its agony and ecstasy.

Dazed and Confused is a paean to youth as remembered in adulthood; its fondly traced remembrances are marked with the knowledge that the freedom of youth is irrevocably fleeting. Youth is constrained on all sides—by authority, by responsibility, by fate—but for a single moment, its anarchic energy reigns triumphant. No skirmishes are fought, no battles won—other than the right to bail on the football team, get high, and buy Aerosmith tickets. The open road beckons.

Linklater, perhaps the most assured American filmmaker of the past two decades, is, like Steven Soderbergh, a serious director with a comic bent. Having begun with the lackadaisical Ophuls-esque roundelay that was *Slacker* (1991), he cannot help but indulge his comedic sweet tooth, even in the midst of adventure films (*The Newton Boys*), talk-heavy adaptations of plays

(*Suburbia* and *Tape*), animated films (*Waking Life* and *A Scanner Darkly*), and even wide-angle dramas (*Fast Food Nation*). Straightforward comedies like *Dazed*, or the conjoined men-behaving-badly pictures *School of Rock* (2003) and *Bad News Bears* (2005), are Linklater embracing the rollicking mischief-making of eternal youth. And the paired romances *Before Sunrise* (1995) and *Before Sunset* (2004), in addition to being gloriously charming, are exemplars—no less than Tarantino's chatterfests—of the comic potential of well-wrought conversation.

Carole Lombard

NOTABLE FILMS: *MY MAN GODFREY*; *TO BE OR NOT TO BE*

As posthumous tributes go, it would be difficult to imagine a better one than Ernst Lubitsch's *To Be or Not to Be*. Lubitsch's 1942 anti-Nazi satire was a howl of protest against the culture of death swooping over Europe, but it was also mourning a loss of its own: that of its star Carole Lombard, killed in January of that year in a plane crash. Her death made the laughs heavier, but *To Be or Not to Be* was Lombard's masterwork in addition to her swan song. As Warsaw actress Maria Tura, wife to famed ham Josef Tura (Jack Benny), Lombard is a slippery fish, playing every scene according to her own private specifications. Onstage and offstage are meaningless terms to her; all the world is a stage, and every encounter another performance. Lubitsch luxuriates in Lombard's falsity, her willingness to oversell everything—romance, intrigue, despair—her essential charm. We never get to see the real Maria Tura, whoever she might be, and we never care.

Lombard's elegant blonde good looks were always being undercut by the tremors of silliness emanating from her presence. She was a comedian trapped in a leading lady's body, and good directors—like Howard Hawks (*Twentieth Century*) and Gregory La Cava (*My Man Godfrey*)—played up her essential incongruity. *My Man Godfrey* (1936) is prime screwball, with Lombard's bored high-society dame rescuing "forgotten man" William Powell and hiring him as her kooky family's butler. Lombard could only feign stupidity; her innate intelligence was too conspicuous to make anything else believable. In the elegant Ben Hecht–scripted trifle *Nothing Sacred* (1937), she was a small-town girl shamming her way to big-city success via a medical hoax. Who could blame her? Warsaw, Vermont, was hardly big enough to hold the likes of Carole Lombard.

Myrna Loy

NOTABLE FILMS: *THE THIN MAN; LOVE ME TONIGHT*

Hollywood likes to fade out as wedding bells ring. Marriages are either miserable, invisible, or imminent, but only rarely—as in *The Thin Man* (1934)—are contented partnerships actually present onscreen. Nick and Nora Charles, played by William Powell and a willowy brunette named Myrna Loy, are the screen exemplars of marital satisfaction, getting to the bottom of cases, be they cases of murder or cases of liquor. Powell's boozy antics attract the eye, but it is Loy who is the beating heart of *The Thin Man*. By not only tolerating but assisting her husband, Nora enables this fantasy of marriage as a never-ending adventure to bloom. The film has hardly aged at all; who wouldn't enjoy spending ninety minutes in the company of a couple having so much fun?

Loy would play Nora in five more *Thin Man* films of decreasing cleverness (although 1936's *After the Thin Man* is amusing). No matter the convoluted or third-rate plot, the sleepy-eyed Loy was worth watching. Appearing one beat behind the action, she was always a step ahead—the same trick she had used to wrestle scenes away from inveterate scene-stealer Maurice Chevalier in *Love Me Tonight* (1932).

Loy had an exceptionally long career by the standards of Hollywood actresses, spanning the period from the silents to the Reagan administration. Her last notable comedy, though, was 1948's *Mr. Blandings Builds His Dream House*, in which Loy is the subtly sardonic helpmeet to Cary Grant's weary homebuilder. Stripped of some of her sass—the egalitarian 1930s about to give way to the conformist 1950s onscreen—Loy nonetheless silently conveys her disdain for her husband's ill-begotten, grandiose plans, while proving herself equally prone to ill-fated schemes of her own.

Shirley MacLaine

NOTABLE FILMS: *THE APARTMENT; IRMA LA DOUCE*

Before the past lives and the chakra-boosting jewelry, before turning herself into a New Age laughingstock, Shirley MacLaine was a wised-up ingenue for the embittered 1950s. With her pixie haircut and sharp-toothed smile, MacLaine came off as the natural successor to good girls like Debbie Reynolds and Doris Day. The roles hinted at darker possibilities, though: prostitutes and good-time girls, plagued by self-loathing and dreaming of impossible escapes. MacLaine offered a splash of postwar darkness poured into an alluring, well-designed pitcher. The ugliness was masked, tragedy concealed behind a wry smile. Straightforward nice-girl roles were not her forte. Opposite Jerry Lewis and Dean Martin in *Artists and Models* (1955), MacLaine was wasted, a grown-up woman playing in the sandbox with the boys.

MacLaine craved the ambiguous and the in-between, caught between laughter and tears. "When you're in love with a married man," her Fran Kubelik tells Jack Lemmon's sad-sack C. C. Baxter in *The Apartment* (1960), "you shouldn't wear mascara." Billy Wilder was her truest admirer, and MacLaine his muse. Although what did it mean to be the ideal woman of someone with so jaundiced a view of the world? MacLaine the skeptic and Lemmon the schnook made an exceptional team, and Wilder reunited them for *Irma La Douce* (1963), in which she is a scheming French streetwalker who adopts Lemmon as her putative pimp. This is Parisian romance Wilder-style, the Eiffel Tower replaced by Les Halles as symbol of a city where romance was just another cut of meat. The film is Lemmon's, but MacLaine's is the voice of wised-up experience: "I'm sorry—I never remember a face." Only Wilder could make seven words so ambiguously suggestive, and only MacLaine could say them so sweetly.

Jayne Mansfield

NOTABLE FILMS: *THE GIRL CAN'T HELP IT; WILL SUCCESS SPOIL ROCK HUNTER?*

Giggling, yelping, cooing, the bubble-headed starlet deluxe, Jayne Mansfield was the ideal image of pulchritudinous excess for an era that celebrated it, and a director who craved it. Frank Tashlin made Mansfield a star with the two comedies he constructed for her, *The Girl Can't Help It* (1956) and *Will Success Spoil Rock Hunter?* (1957). In each, Mansfield is courting fame, and tempting the Tashlin hero—weak-chinned and wavering—to stray.

Mansfield was, in a way, parodying herself: the talentless bimbo doomed to success by virtue of her physical gifts. In *The Girl Can't Help It*, she dates a gangster who dreams of pop-star success for her. *Rock Hunter* transforms her into a global icon, her every titter the subject of feverish journalistic coverage. Exiting an airplane with a fur coat draped over a one-piece bathing suit, she seeks to dispel some of the rumors swirling around her private life: "All my lovers and I are just friends."

Tashlin transformed her into an icon of 1950s womanhood, an exaggerated, campy Marilyn Monroe stripped of the vulnerability. In *The Girl Can't Help It*, Mansfield is literally statuesque—an unspeaking statue of immense loveliness. We recognize her by the impact she has on men: the iceman melts two blocks with his hands, the milkman's bottles foam over, and an older gent's glasses crack after taking the sight of her in. Was she a goddess, or a lampoon of one?

Mansfield's stardom was exceedingly brief. Having collaborated with Tashlin, and starred opposite Cary Grant in Stanley Donen's *Kiss Them for Me* (1957), she bounced around in third-rate schlock for another decade before her death in an automobile accident in 1967. Unlike Monroe, Mansfield was hard-pressed to exceed the role that Nature (and Frank Tashlin) had granted her, lacking the skill—and perhaps the determination—to transcend caricature.

Dean Martin

NOTABLE FILMS: *ARTISTS AND MODELS*; *RIO BRAVO*

Of all the thankless roles in film history, few were less appreciated than serving as sidekick and straight man to that ambulatory poster child for attention deficit disorder, Jerry Lewis. Lewis was an infant, forcing anyone acting opposite him into frazzled adulthood and attempted guardianship. Over the course of sixteen films together, Martin patiently dogged Lewis, offering counsel and an older brother's steady hand, even as their pictures celebrated a pre-linguistic impulse to unmitigated destruction. Martin is the brake on Lewis's out-of-control car—a crucial safety feature nonetheless resented by those preferring no restraint to chaos.

Martin received a raw deal from fans and reviewers, who saw him as a clod holding his partner back from ever-wilder feats of lunatic prodigality. He was actually those films' reality principle, as well as a talented comedian in his own right. Lewis was the inventor, while Martin was the nightclub performer, singing, clowning, and telling jokes with Copacabana polish.

Martin and Lewis eventually split, riven apart by Lewis's appalling temper tantrums and Martin's simmering frustration. Without Martin, something basic—something human—had been lost from Lewis's work; something which would only return when he resorted to playing Dino himself, in *The Nutty Professor*.

Martin's twinkly-eyed geniality may have been the whiskey bottle in his back pocket, but he was not above gently prodding his own offscreen persona. He was a drunk redeemed by duty in that greatest of all Westerns, *Rio Bravo* (1959), and a funhouse-mirror version of himself in Billy Wilder's scabrous

Kiss Me, Stupid (1964). The film's "Dino" is a lush and a narcissist who gets trapped in the town of Climax, Nevada, while headed for a Vegas engagement, and finds his own climax with the wife of his impromptu host. The film is not quite great—one wishes Peter Sellers, and not Ray Walston, is starring opposite him, as had initially been planned before Sellers's heart attack—but Martin boldly, craftily caricatures himself. And why not? Everyone had been doing it for years.

Elaine May
NOTABLE FILMS: *THE HEARTBREAK KID; ISHTAR*

The links between *The Heartbreak Kid* and *The Graduate* are numerous and immediately notable. The mismatched Jewish-WASP romance, the confused antihero, the generational bloodshed—all the pieces of Mike Nichols's generation-defining film have been ported over to this 1972 comedy, directed by Nichols's onetime partner in stand-up comedy, Elaine May. But *The Heartbreak Kid* is a different sort of comedy, one infused by the spirit of John Cassavetes. Something of the coarse, oafish intensity of Cassavetes's *Husbands* and *Faces* is carried over into this unlikeliest of scenarios, with Charles Grodin as the smooth-talking Jewish newlywed blinded by the light of Cybill Shepherd's WASP princess. It is a storybook romance in which Grodin's wife nurses a sunburn in her hotel room as he dashes from one romantic engagement to the next. It is also a comedy whose awkward silences weigh more heavily than Neil Simon's deliberately artless dialogue (although Grodin does describe his bride as being "not really my type").

Nichols and May had been stand-up standouts of the Lenny Bruce era, their genial Dada routines deceptive in their simplicity. Both would go on to direct their own films, but where Nichols's career was a reminder of the days of the jack-of-all-trades craftsmen of the 1930s and 1940s, May's movies were true to the spirit of the American independents of which she belatedly found herself a part.

May would go on to recreate Cassavetes in more loving detail with *Mikey and Nicky* (1976), a roughly hewn drama starring the master himself, and his favored disciple Peter Falk. The results were Cassavetian in mood, if not in effect, and May would not direct again for over a decade. One wonders if May might have worked more had she been a young male wunderkind and not a middle-aged woman. *Ishtar* (1987) is one of Hollywood's legendary flops, but it is also another exercise in surprisingly fluid comic awkwardness, buoyed by the delightfully eccentric performances of Dustin Hoffman and Warren Beatty. Since then, May has been reunited with Nichols as a writer, contributing the screenplay for Nichols's two best films of the 1990s, *The Birdcage* (1996) and *Primary Colors* (1998).

May is an irregular presence onscreen as a performer, but a welcome one. She was one of the hotel guests in the Neil Simon omnibus *California Suite* (1978), and wonderfully daffy as one of Woody Allen's *Small Time Crooks* (2000), her stupidity revealed as a dazzling candor.

Leo McCarey

NOTABLE FILMS: *DUCK SOUP*; *THE AWFUL TRUTH*

Once upon a time, when movie directors were more jacks-of-all-trades than highly trained specialists, Leo McCarey directed it all. A former lawyer and copper miner, McCarey got his start during the silent era, writing gags for Hal Roach and shooting fly-by-night shorts for comedians like Charley Chase. It was McCarey who oversaw the first pairings of Stan Laurel with Oliver Hardy, seeing the possibilities in bringing the wickedly inventive little man together with the big-boned doofus.

McCarey left Hal Roach after seeing him dive into a pool. Roach, in his opinion, was too healthy for there to be any future at his studio. By the time sound came in, McCarey's experience gave him a leg up on the mostly mediocre run of comedy directors. There is a solid reason why *Duck Soup* (1933) is, hands down, the best Marx Brothers movie of all. The Marxes were wildmen, prone to run roughshod over any director assigned to them. McCarey hated the Marx Brothers ("They were too irresponsible and also I couldn't get them all together at the same time—one was always missing"), but he wrings genuine performances out of them, rather than disconnected clowning, and that (plus Bert Kalmar and Harry Ruby's script) is enough for immortality.

McCarey was a journeyman in the best sense of the word. He worked with many of comedy's all-time greats: Cary Grant in *The Awful Truth* (1937) and later, in a profoundly different register, three-hanky weepie *An Affair to Remember* (1957); Mae West in *Belle of the Nineties* (1934); W. C. Fields in *Six of a Kind* (1934); Harold Lloyd in *The Milky Way* (1936); Bing Crosby in Best Picture winner *Going My Way* (1944) and its sequel *The Bells of St. Mary's* (1945). Grant had been a dry-as-toast leading man before working for McCarey on *The Awful Truth*. Grant was so desperate to leave the picture that he offered Harry Cohn of Columbia five thousand dollars to offset any costs incurred by his departure. McCarey offered Cohn double that to give Grant the boot. Cohn turned them both down, and McCarey made him a superstar.

McCarey won an Oscar for directing *The Awful Truth*, and another one for *Going My Way*. The 1944 priestly buddy picture is too pious to be unrestrainedly hilarious, but it remains one of McCarey's most charming films. Crosby and Barry Fitzgerald are simply splendid, better than they had ever been before or since. That was what McCarey did; he got the best out of you, whether you wanted to give it to him or not.

Joel McCrea

NOTABLE FILMS: *SULLIVAN'S TRAVELS; THE PALM BEACH STORY*

Preston Sturges's career had two halves: the Joel McCrea era and the Eddie Bracken era. McCrea was tall, rangy, and sleepy-eyed; Bracken was short, wiry, and gallon-of-Red-Bull hyper. Many connoisseurs of comedy prefer the Bracken comedies—*Hail the Conquering Hero* and *The Miracle of Morgan's Creek*—to the earlier films, seeing McCrea as a budget-rate Gary Cooper, a well-dressed empty sack. I would like to strenuously, vociferously disagree. The 1930s and 1940s were the era of star power—MGM sold itself as having "more stars than the sky"—and McCrea was one of the most unassuming. In film after film, he played the hunk next door, whose good looks were balanced by an appreciation of life's lumbering absurdities. Starring in *Sullivan's Travels* (1941), *The Palm Beach Story* (1942), and *The Great Moment* (1944), McCrea was Sturges's alter ego, a reflection of the director and man about town's best qualities: debonair, witty, and gregarious. (By extension, one could assume that nervous wreck Bracken is whom the director saw in the mirror at his darkest moments.) It is all too easy to mistake good-naturedness for disinterest, and McCrea's acting work can be misconstrued as lacking in passion.

McCrea could play drama more than adequately, as witnessed by his magnificent turn in Jacques Tourneur's nostalgic Western *Stars in My Crown* (1950), or his role as the idealistic architect tangling with gangster Humphrey Bogart in William Wyler's *Dead End* (1937), but comedy was his playground. McCrea worked nimbly with almost every director he was ever paired with, energizing one of Alfred Hitchcock's better light entertainments, *Foreign Correspondent* (1940), and as the illegal boarder turned love interest in George Stevens's charming wartime comedy *The More the Merrier* (1943).

Joel McCrea possessed the rare quality of self-possession. He was only rarely ruffled onscreen, and it required genuine distress of the sort only Sturges could provide—being stranded on a Southern chain gang, or required to turn over his secret formula for numbing pain—to dent his natural bemusement at the world's silliness. McCrea was Sturges's alter ego because he could easily be all of ours; like Cary Grant, he is the kind of man most men want to be.

Lorne Michaels

NOTABLE FILMS: *WAYNE'S WORLD*; *¡THREE AMIGOS!*

Has anyone been responsible for the cultivation of more comedic talent than Lorne Michaels? Bill Murray, Eddie Murphy, Mike Myers, Will Ferrell, Tina Fey, John Belushi, Dan Aykroyd, Chevy Chase, Christopher Guest, Adam Sandler, Ben Stiller, Chris Farley, Chris Rock—Michaels's eye for up-and-coming performers, recruited to his late-night sketch-comedy series *Saturday Night Live*, has been unstinting. There are hardly more than a handful of major comic performers of the past thirty years who have not felt the imprint, in some form or another, of Michaels's touch.

As talent scout alone, Lorne Michaels deserves a mention in any worthwhile history of the comedy film. Given that, and the sterling box-office records of *SNL* alums, how is it that Michaels's filmography has been so sketchy? *Coneheads* (1993), *Black Sheep* (1996), *A Night at the Roxbury* (1998), *The Ladies Man* (2000)—Michaels's record as a film producer reads like a nightmare compilation of mediocre *SNL* skits stretched to feature length.

Michaels's reign at *Saturday Night Live* has been inordinately, uncompromisingly successful, with the Canadian comic wizard serving as the stern, remote father to an ever-changing array of young performers craving approval, and the limelight. *SNL* has served as the stepping stone to glory for many comedians, but stepping stone it is. Few, if any, of the superstars Michaels nurtured have been much interested in returning to the nest; hence the list of credits whose stars tend to be *SNL* second-stringers like David Spade and Chris Kattan, or future stars like Ferrell. No one wants to disappoint Dad, but hardly anyone wants to move back home either. (Mike Myers denies it, but his colleagues unanimously agree that Dr. Evil, from the *Austin Powers* films, is at its heart a wicked impression of none other than Michaels.)

There are, however, some flecks of gold amidst the dross: *¡Three Amigos!* (1986), which Michaels cowrote with Steve Martin and Randy Newman, is a zany tribute to a previous generation's half-remembered oaters, and *Wayne's World* (1992) is the highest-grossing, and perhaps the most entertaining, of the numerous films spun off from *SNL* sketches. And Michaels's recent collaborations with Tina Fey, for her films *Mean Girls* (2004) and *Baby Mama* (2008), and her superb NBC series *30 Rock* (itself about the making of an *SNL*-esque sketch-comedy show), present the possibility of a better future class of Michaels-branded entertainment on the big screen.

Mike Myers
NOTABLE FILMS: *WAYNE'S WORLD*; *AUSTIN POWERS:*
INTERNATIONAL MAN OF MYSTERY

As a twelve-year-old boy in the Toronto suburb of Scarborough, Mike Myers watched the first episode of *Saturday Night Live* in 1975 and turned to his parents, a determined glint in his eye: he was going to be on this show someday. His was no idle boast; the day he graduated from high school, Myers got himself a job with the Second City troupe in Toronto. Toronto gave way to Chicago, and in 1989, at the ripe old age of twenty-six, Mike Myers was hired to appear as a performer on *Saturday Night Live*.

It was appropriate, in the final estimation, that the movie that made Mike Myers a bona fide movie star was an extended *Saturday Night Live* sketch. The hugely successful feature version of *Wayne's World* (1992), with metalloid dunderheads Wayne and Garth's public-access television show crashing the big time, was a metaphor for Myers's own conundrum, wondering if it were possible to grow fabulously successful without doing an injustice to the anarchic spirit that had gotten you there in the first place. If the 1990s were a long-held exercise in irony and self-deprecation, *Wayne's World* (along with its secret sharer, Ben Stiller's *Reality Bites*) is its most perfect expression. The film insists on reminding its audience of its own untrustworthiness, with the slightly queasy look on Myers's face symbolic of its pained self-consciousness.

The successor to *Wayne's World* is a Bay Area comic noir enlivened with a healthy dash of *Wayne's World*–esque silliness. There are times when *So I Married an Axe Murderer* (1993) feels like a supersized episode of *Friends*: the coffeehouse camaraderie, the melodious pop-rock soundtrack, the quirky relationship humor. As a unified whole, *Axe Murderer* is an ungodly mess; broken down into its constituent parts, the film achieves moments of near-perfection.

Austin Powers, from the 1997 film of the same name, is like a yet-more-exaggerated version of *The Big Lebowski*'s Dude—the lone survivor of the wreck of the 1960s, cast adrift in unfamiliar waters. Austin arrives in the 1990s bearing his copious assortment of sex gadgets and the volume he penned as a swinging, shagging bachelor: *Swedish-Made Penis Enlarger Pumps and Me: This Sort of Thing* Is *My Bag, Baby.* Austin is so childishly insistent on displaying his sexual valor that he achieves a certain illogical purity. *Austin Powers* is a film of glorious, near-Dadaist nonsensicality, amplifying *So I Married an Axe Murderer*'s brief glimpses of Marx Brothers–esque wordplay until Myers had become a Groucho for the Clinton years.

In the sequel, *Austin Powers: The Spy Who Shagged Me* (1999), Dr. Evil becomes a harried father to two squabbling sons—one a one-eighth-size clone—and a repository of utterly forgettable pop-culture references. Dr. Evil is a balder, more malevolent Wayne Campbell with a sentimental streak and a preference for world domination. (Dr. Evil even tips his hat to Charlie Chaplin, dribbling the globe like a basketball, after the manner of *The Great Dictator.*)

The extended product-placement opportunity *Austin Powers in Goldmember* (2002) was *Duck Soup* in comparison with 2008's fanatically misguided *The Love Guru.* In truth, the funniest Mike Myers moment of the decade was an entirely accidental one; during a post-Katrina benefit broadcast in September 2005, Myers was a copresenter when Kanye West bluntly told a nationwide television audience that "George Bush doesn't care about black people." Myers, caught unawares by West's outburst, does an impromptu double-take, like Austin Powers had just been told that Dr. Evil had swiped his mojo once again.

Mike Nichols
NOTABLE FILMS: *THE GRADUATE*; *WORKING GIRL*

Mike Nichols, one of the talented young men who overthrew the old studios for good, has ended up having a career which is itself a throwback to the classical era of Hollywood. In the old days, workmen like Michael Curtiz or Leo McCarey would handle a staggering array of genres with aplomb, bouncing around from screwball comedy to adventure to melodrama with no noticeable dip in quality. Nichols has also covered the waterfront in his more than four decades as an A-list director, handling everything from tony theatrical adaptations to space-alien farces.

Nichols got his start with the celebrated one-two punch of *Who's Afraid of Virginia Woolf?* (1966) and *The Graduate* (1967), two comedies with an unexpected emotional wallop. *Virginia Woolf*, with Elizabeth Taylor and Richard Burton as a squabbling academic couple, is an unsettling blend of black comedy and tragedy, held together by the real-life couple's uncanny magnetism. *The Graduate* was an instant icon of the 1960s counterculture, and Nichols followed up with two more films that mingled—some might say jumbled up—comedy and drama: 1970's *Catch-22* (adapted from the Joseph Heller novel) and 1971's *Carnal Knowledge*.

Nichols was striving to keep his finger on the pulse of youth culture by stirring anarchic, devil-may-care comedy with raw sentiment. *Catch-22* was as successful as any adaptation of such a beloved work could be, which is to say only partially; Nichols entirely misfires in straining to capture the novel's zany humor. (If only Groucho Marx had been available, and forty years younger, he might have been capable of embodying the unique absurdity of Captain Yossarian.) *Carnal Knowledge* was a sex comedy whose humor was lost on everyone except its truly rancid heroes, played by Jack Nicholson and Art Garfunkel.

Nichols would go on to direct melodramas, highbrow horror films, and political dramas, all bearing the crisp imprint of his subdued style. There were straightforward comedies, too, like the *La Cage aux Folles* remake *The Birdcage* (1996), but Nichols was at his best when playing mix and match with genre. *Working Girl* (1988) is a female-empowerment manifesto for the shoulder-padded 1980s, with savvy Staten Island chick Melanie Griffith triumphing over well-manicured Manhattanites. Griffith, whose ditzy-blonde looks and exaggerated curves are like a throwback to Jean Harlow, makes an ideal screwball heroine for this Wall Street farce. *Primary Colors* (1998) is a political thriller played with the rhythm of farce, and *Charlie Wilson's War* (2007) is a madcap Washington adventure whose Afghan-mujahedeen hilarity rings distinctly, and deliberately, hollow.

Jack Nicholson

NOTABLE FILMS: *THE LAST DETAIL; ABOUT SCHMIDT*

Before Jack Nicholson became a joker—and then the Joker—he was an actor of unparalleled nuance and sympathetic imagination. Once upon a time, before, like Narcissus, he fell in love with his own reflection, Nicholson worked with a tiny, dazzlingly precise brush on the celluloid canvas. Nicholson was part of the American New Wave's fleet of gifted young actors, alongside Robert De Niro, Al Pacino, Dustin Hoffman, and the rest. Like Hoffman, Nicholson possessed the gift of being able to chuckle at himself, and his best early roles—in films like *Five Easy Pieces* (1970), *Carnal Knowledge*

(1971), and *The Last Detail* (1973)—contained a hint of self-mockery, as if the actor were far too self-aware to ever take himself seriously. Nicholson shared with his colleagues a delight in blurring genre distinctions, so that even *Chinatown* (1974)—that darkest of neo-noirs—is occasionally lit by the slapstick exuberance of Nicholson's physicality. Of his early films, *The Last Detail*, directed by Hal Ashby, is unquestionably the most luminous showcase for Nicholson's comedic gifts. Ashby's film of Navy men escorting a prisoner to the brig is raunchy and raw, and Nicholson is the master of ceremonies, his trademark twinkle the prime indication of his lusty preference for all forms of the profane. Mike Nichols's *The Fortune* (1975) is a film in a similar key, if a different mood, with Nicholson endearingly schlemiel-like next to Warren Beatty's polished kidnapper.

It is hard to look back on Nicholson's later career with anything but a twinge of disappointment, for he has allowed Hollywood's bizarre love affair with him to derail his own work. *Batman* (1989), in which Nicholson played the ingratiating, coyly amused Joker, marked the beginning of the once-great actor's fall from grace into the stifling cocoon of Hollywood royalty. Nicholson's dramatic work has been hit-or-miss (2001's *The Pledge* a fine example of the former, and his grating, distracting performance in 2006's Best Picture–winning *The Departed* a textbook example of the latter), and his comedic work similarly mirthless. Only *About Schmidt* (2002), his collaboration with the gifted director Alexander Payne, proved an exception, with Nicholson summoning some measure of his once-abundant powers of subtlety for this somber travelogue of the American road, and the twilight years of a lonely man.

Alexander Payne
NOTABLE FILMS: *SIDEWAYS*; *ELECTION*

Alexander Payne has only made four films, and his legacy as a filmmaker is still unsettled. But in his brief career, Payne has demonstrated a remarkable empathetic gift for his characters. Grotesque though some of them might be, Payne loves them all, as he loves the blandly American landscapes through which they zig and zag. Payne prefers the mundane to the slam and bang of tumultuous eventfulness; his movies are farces paced by his preference for character over punch line.

Citizen Ruth (1996) is a bold wade into the eye of the abortion hurricane, and *Election* (1999) a satirical recasting of the 1992 presidential campaign as a hard-fought student council contest. Reese Witherspoon's Tracy Flick has ascended into the pantheon of characters whose very names signify a set of behaviors, in her case grinding, humorless ambition. *Election* is a film that has grown with the passage of time, but Payne's masterpiece to date is *Sideways* (2004).

Absconding from Payne's traditional Midwestern outpost in Omaha, *Sideways* is an uproarious, and sobering, jaunt through the wine country of the Napa Valley. The film is a drunken interlude and the next-morning hangover all at once; a strong cocktail of regret and anxiety and frustrated desire whose saving grace is its unerring eye for human absurdity. Paul Giamatti's pretentious oenophile is both a bold masterstroke of cutting satirical observation and a heartfelt ode to sadsack masculinity. And what other film can reasonably claim to have shifted the drinking patterns of so many Americans? Pinot noir growers everywhere must raise a glass nightly to Giamatti, and his brilliant speech arguing for pinot's subtle pleasures.

Tyler Perry
NOTABLE FILMS: *MADEA GOES TO JAIL; MADEA'S FAMILY REUNION*

Tyler Perry's movies are an impossible jumble of stories, moods, and styles: women's films cut with a taste of thug passion, melodramas leavened by low farce. Perry, who has become a one-man cottage industry, has remained largely incomprehensible to the mostly white coterie of American film critics. His appeal, and that of his films, can easily be summed up in a single word: Madea.

Perry's alter ego is a gun-toting grandmother with an anger-management problem and a propensity for fisticuffs. Conflating two hoary African American stereotypes, Madea is alternately a rock of feminine familial stability and an unrepentant gangster: "I'm a real thug," she warns in *Madea's Family Reunion* (2009). "I shot Tupac!"

As played by Perry in a white wig, oversized glasses, and a misshapen bust, clad in a variety of psychedelic-colored housedresses, Madea is an instantly recognizable variation on Eddie Murphy's Grandma Klump and Martin Lawrence's Big Momma. Madea is her own comic relief, an avenging angel and figure of motherly grit dispensing homespun wisdom to those who will listen, and furious beatdowns to those who choose not to.

First introduced as the scorned wife's tough-as-nails grandmother in the surprise hit *Diary of a Mad Black Woman* (2005), Madea emerged as the breakout star of Perry's films. There is an odd juxtaposition between Madea's scenes and the schmaltzy melodrama, as if these limited scenarios cannot properly contain her. She is the release valve for these occasionally gaseous efforts, her quiver of Southern-fried catchphrases ("Halleluj-er!," "Call the po-po, ho") a refreshing blast of terminally lowbrow silliness.

The dialogue in Perry's films betrays his roots in regional theater, and his direction often veers uncomfortably close to ludicrousness. Madea, and her brother and male doppelganger Joe, rescue the films from terminal slackness. As a writer and director, Perry is essentially reanimating the corpse of the women's film, but as he rapidly determined, no one would be willing to sit through the sermon without Madea's charming irascibility.

Pixar

NOTABLE FILMS: *TOY STORY 2*; *RATATOUILLE*

Animated films, Disney's in particular, have been many things—child-friendly, heartwarming, iconic—but funny has rarely been one of them. Steve Jobs and John Lasseter's mini–animation studio has been a marvel in so many ways that reviving animation's sense of humor is only one small aspect of Pixar's remarkable run of success. Beginning with *Toy Story* (1995), Pixar has offered entertainment for children designed to perk up adults' spirits. Perhaps the best way of defining what Pixar has done for animation is to clarify what it is not: multilevel storerooms of in-jokey humor, crammed full of Hollywood yuks meant to keep adults busy as the kids are mindlessly entertained.

Pixar has never been much interested in children alone; their films are truly family entertainment, as capable of thrilling the most jaded cineaste as the tiniest tot. They have achieved this lofty goal (something Disney has only been able to do intermittently since the heyday of Uncle Walt) by deploying wit instead of cleverness, awe instead of shock: the steady lift of a fleet of balloons, the dazzling insight trapped inside a bite of food.

Pixar films are as well-written as the tightest screwball comedy, every line clicking audibly into the whole. The plots have the simplicity of perfection—children's toys in their leisure hours; a family of superheroes; a rat who dreams of becoming a chef—and it is that very simplicity that sometimes causes Pixar's work to be overlooked. First-class voice actors (Tom Hanks and Tim Allen in *Toy Story*, Samuel L. Jackson and Holly Hunter in *The Incredibles*) are part of the equation, but Pixar owes the bulk of its success to

Lasseter's remarkable vision, and more recently to the genius (no other word would do him proper justice) of director Brad Bird, whose *The Incredibles* (2004) and *Ratatouille* (2007) are undeniable masterpieces.

Harold Ramis
NOTABLE FILMS: *GROUNDHOG DAY*; *CADDYSHACK*

Ramis, alone among his contemporaries, has had two mostly divergent careers as a writer and director, and as a performer. In both, he has had the good fortune, and the wisdom, to play second banana to Bill Murray. As an actor, Ramis was valet and foil to Murray in *Stripes* (1981), where he followed him into remodeling the U.S. Army as a slacker's paradise, and epitomized geek-chic in completing the trifecta of *Ghostbusters* (1984) alongside Murray and Dan Aykroyd. Ramis's performances blend capably into the background, overshadowed by Murray's flamboyant clowning.

Which makes it all the more understandable that he has achieved even greater success as a writer and director. Ramis was an essential player in the post–*Saturday Night Live* flourishing of the R-rated comedy. Once again, Murray was key to his success. After writing the era-defining fraternity comedy *Animal House* (1978), Ramis took Murray under his wing. He scripted the underrated *Meatballs* (1979), which gave Murray his first set of zingers, and the ensemble comedy *Caddyshack* (1980).

The best of Ramis and Murray's collaborations, though, is undoubtedly the brilliant *Groundhog Day* (1993), which ushered Murray into the thoroughly unexpected mature period of his career. Before Wes Anderson or Sofia Coppola had even caught wind of him, Ramis already saw the melancholy behind Murray's eyes, and expanded the scope of his comedy to make room for it.

Ramis went on to further directorial triumphs (the *Sopranos*-anticipating mobster-psychoanalysis comedy *Analyze This*) and a handful of disappointments (*Stuart Saves His Family*, *Multiplicity*), but all along maintained his own prickly iconoclasm—a character trait that allowed him to be one of his era's foremost talents without ever being entirely of his era.

Ramis, never quite a household name, has had an outsized impact on the American comedy. Judd Apatow cast him as Seth Rogen's father in *Knocked Up* (2007), no less clueless about relationships than his son, and the moment he shares with Rogen is an elegant, understated passing of the comedic torch from one generation of chroniclers of oblivious guys to the next.

Tony Randall

NOTABLE FILMS: *PILLOW TALK*; *LOVER COME BACK*

Effete, jittery, hysterical: Tony Randall was the second banana for the age of psychiatry. In film after film, Randall tenaciously insisted—his therapist had told him so—that he was the romantic hero of the story, conveniently ignoring the presence of Rock Hudson as his best friend, or the proximity of the surrealistically pneumatic Jayne Mansfield as his girl of choice. Replacing the Edward Everett Hortons of yore, Randall was delicious in precise relation to his own lack of self-awareness. He was the quasi-hero of Frank Tashlin's delirious *Will Success Spoil Rock Hunter?* (1957), but is best remembered as Hudson's sidekick, wingman, and domestic partner in the three comedies they made with Doris Day.

Randall and the similar but inferior Tom Ewell (*The Seven Year Itch*, *The Girl Can't Help It*) were interchangeable commodities for a decade that insisted on promoting a beefy masculine ideal. They were flaccid figures for an era that demanded erectness of its men. Their fatally unheroic figures were at odds with their own self-dramatizations; asexual in form, they insisted on playing the dashing roué, no matter how ill-fitting the costume.

Ewell quickly grew tiresome, but Randall was savvy enough to offer a series of prissy variations on a theme in the Doris-and-Rock films and the Marilyn Monroe–starring *Let's Make Love* (1960), his panty-waisted ne'er-do-wells all dreaming of a romantic fade-out of their own.

Randall would go on to fill Jack Lemmon's shoes as Felix Unger on the television version of *The Odd Couple* from 1970 to 1975. The year before his death, in 2004, Randall was granted one last opportunity to revisit his youth, in the Doris-and-Rock tribute *Down with Love*. Instead of playing the Tony Randall role (David Hyde Pierce capably filled in), Randall is granted the opportunity to play the big man for once: a book publisher intent on crushing proto-feminist author (and Day replacement) Renée Zellweger. It was a nice parting gift for a professional life spent watching others have all the fun.

Samson Raphaelson

NOTABLE FILMS: *THE SHOP AROUND THE CORNER*; *HEAVEN CAN WAIT*

Ernst Lubitsch is too large a figure to be entirely encompassed by the work of any one of his collaborators, but if one screenwriter deserves to share some of the credit for his success, it is Samson Raphaelson. A journalist and playwright (he wrote *The Jazz Singer*), Raphaelson penned the screenplays for eight Lubitsch films, from 1931's *The Smiling Lieutenant* to 1943's *Heaven Can Wait*. Lubitsch was the all-time master of the brilliant, economical sight gag, and required dialogue every bit as precise. A craftsman of dazzling talk, Raphaelson was the mouth to match Lubitsch's gimlet eye.

As *The Jazz Singer* might indicate, Raphaelson was known to flirt with maudlinity. As his collected body of work might indicate, Lubitsch was known to flirt with winsomeness. Together, they redeemed each other. Raphaelson was Lubitsch's heart, and his reminder that the truest comedy teeters on the edge of tragedy. Both *The Shop Around the Corner* and *Heaven Can Wait* are comedies that veer perilously close to darkness, occasionally enveloped by its cloak.

Lubitsch and Raphaelson gave outright drama a single try, with the legendary misfire *The Man I Killed* (1934), in which a French veteran of the First World War becomes entangled with the family, and fiancée, of a German soldier. The results were uncharacteristic, but the failed experiment was a useful reminder that for Lubitsch, comedy was the air that he breathed. He could no more function outside it than he could transform himself into an epic poet. What Raphaelson did was smuggle bits and pieces of the outside world into Lubitsch's tightly enclosed Ruritania, baking them into the crusts of Lubitsch's soufflés. We were nourished without our even noticing.

Carl Reiner
NOTABLE FILMS: *THE JERK; ALL OF ME*

Carl Reiner's is a name that comes up time and again, in a variety of guises, in telling the story of the American comedy. He played straight man to Mel Brooks's 2000 Year Old Man, talked up his son's friend Albert Einstein on *The Tonight Show* before he changed his name to Albert Brooks, and directed Steve Martin in four of his best early films. In fact, of all Reiner's roles, it is that of director that fits him best—perhaps because his is a talent that is strongest when not exposed to the bright light of day.

Reiner's collaborations with Martin are extended roasts of carefully selected genres, delving deep into Hollywood tradition in order to ridicule them from the inside. Unlike Mel Brooks's films, which are similar in intent, Reiner's best films—*The Jerk*, *The Man with Two Brains*, *All of Me*—are subtly mocking, genial without being frantic or ingratiating. Reiner's directorial track record without Martin is decidedly more mixed (although 1970's

Where's Poppa? has its admirers), suggesting that the collaboration of director and actor was a unique occurrence in both their careers. Reiner's post-Martin directorial work is mostly dismal; when your best effort is *Summer School* (1987), with Mark Harmon and Kirstie Alley, you know you've done something wrong. The Reiners are now a directorial dynasty; his son Rob is a comic standout in his own right, having directed *This is Spinal Tap, When Harry Met Sally . . .*, and *The American President.*

Reiner is equally unassuming as an actor, making Hitchcock-esque cameos in many of his own films, and similarly brief appearances in those of others. A dirt-encrusted ten-watt bulb, he manages to outshine the dazzling star power of George Clooney, Brad Pitt, and Matt Damon in Steven Soderbergh's lackadaisical heist caper *Ocean's Eleven* (2001), surprising the superstars with the hard-fought, wily bemusement of one who has seen everything and done everything—twice.

Rob Reiner

NOTABLE FILMS: *THIS IS SPINAL TAP; WHEN HARRY MET SALLY . . .*

Descended from Hollywood comic royalty (his father Carl had written for Sid Caesar, played straight man to Mel Brooks, and directed Steve Martin), Reiner made an early splash as Archie Bunker's son-in-law and nemesis Michael "Meathead" Stivic on the legendary television series *All in the Family.*

As it turned out, Rob's future was not in acting, but in directing. Having made his reputation helming *This Is Spinal Tap* (1984), the inspiration for cast member and co-screenwriter Christopher Guest's future directorial efforts, Reiner soon expanded into more mainstream efforts. *The Princess Bride* (1987) is the rare children's adventure unlikely to cause adults to heave with disgust, its reinvention of fairy-tale romance, and deft use of skilled comedic performers like Billy Crystal and Christopher Guest, doing justice to a well-worn genre. *When Harry Met Sally . . .* (1989) does much the same for the Woody Allen–style comedy, with Crystal and Meg Ryan as star-crossed lovers in this frothy romance. Ryan contributes the most genuine-sounding cinematic orgasm not recorded in the San Fernando Valley, and Crystal was never better than as a Woody-esque schlemiel, polished and rendered safe for mainstream audiences.

Reiner went in search of Oscar in the 1990s, with commercially successful dramas like *Misery* (1990) and *A Few Good Men* (1992) followed by flops like *Ghosts of Mississippi* (1996). Reiner had always had an eye for good scripts, and good screenwriters, and latched on to a doozy with the Aaron Sorkin–scripted *The American President* (1995). A romantic comedy set in the Oval Office, the film would inspire Sorkin's triumphant television drama *The West Wing*, whose mingling of comedy and drama, and walk-down-the-hall-with-me-as-I-explain-a-few-things style of exposition, would reinvent the form for the 1990s as *Spinal Tap* had for the 1980s.

Hal Roach

NOTABLE FILMS: *NEVER WEAKEN; BIG BUSINESS*

His IMDB credits list him as the producer of more than twelve hundred films. OK, so most of them were one- or two-reel shorts, made on the cheap and on the fly. But still—twelve hundred films? Hal Roach was a one-man comedy factory, the 1910s and 1920s his testing ground, his experiments utilizing the same limited complement of elements—girls, cops, animals, babies, parks, tenements, and the wild boys wreaking havoc on them all. Roach was a blatant imitator of Mack Sennett, co-opting Sennett's formula but minus the star hierarchy. Roach's preference was to hire past-their-prime greats—once-luminous performers like Will Rogers and Theda Bara—and milk their waning talents dry. There would be no stars in Roach's stable, no Chaplin to overshadow all the others—or so Roach thought.

Roach discovered Harold Lloyd when both were extras on the Universal set in 1914, although *discover* might be too strong a word. Roach saw no particular talent in Lloyd, glimpsed no unseen reservoir of comic genius wasted in menial roles. He needed an unassuming, hard-working young actor, and Lloyd had the theatrical training to handle anything thrown his way. Lloyd made hundreds of shorts with Roach, steadily occupying more of the spotlight as he left his extended Chaplin imitation behind and crafted his own character.

Roach generously allowed Lloyd to take over the production of his own films, too busy to give them the proper attention they deserved. Later, when Lloyd was a major star, Roach took the credit for his success, attributing the addition of Lloyd's trademark glasses to his own intercession. Based on his handling of the other comic luminaries to appear in Roach's stable, one would have to assume the contrary. Roach had both Stan Laurel and Oliver Hardy under contract in the 1920s, and took years to even think of putting them together in the same film.

Julia Roberts

NOTABLE FILMS: *MY BEST FRIEND'S WEDDING*; *ERIN BROCKOVICH*

The pre-eminent female movie star of the past two decades, Julia Roberts has craftily molded the romantic-comedy form to her benefit. *Pretty Woman* (1990), *My Best Friend's Wedding* (1997), *Runaway Bride* (1999), *Notting Hill* (1999): Roberts has been America's sweetheart for so long it is difficult to see any longer how ill-suited she is for the role. Roberts is flinty, and more than a bit testy. Famous for her dazzling smile, she is a cold performer, inhabiting the frame without illuminating it. What's more, Roberts is an asexual presence onscreen, beautiful without any trace of seductiveness or sensuality. Woody Allen cast her in his musical *Everyone Says I Love You* (1996) to provide a frisson of beguiling allure that never arrived; one need only look over at Goldie Hawn, playing Allen's ex-wife, to get a glimpse of the sparkle Roberts has always lacked.

It is no accident that the one costar she truly clicked with was Rupert Everett's gay best friend in *My Best Friend's Wedding*. Freed from the pressure of romance, she was finally able to embrace her inner bitchiness, and shines as a result. Roberts's only unquestionably smashing performance is in Steven Soderbergh's semi-comic *Erin Brockovich* (2000). Roberts uses her clinical sexuality as a walking punch line, distracting a dismal series of lust-dazzled men with her cleavage into divulging the truth behind an energy-company cover-up. Jeffrey Kurland's costumes deserved much of the credit, but Roberts was bold enough to embrace the contradictions inherent in the role: half sexpot, half crusader.

Recently, as Roberts has aged beyond the bounds of the traditional romantic comedy (which generally puts women out to pasture as soon as they celebrate their thirty-fifth birthday), she has taken on more challenging roles with directors like Mike Nichols and Tony Gilroy. Not all have suited her equally, but *Duplicity* (2009)—itself only partially successful as a highbrow caper comedy—accentuates character notes unfamiliar to the romantic comedy. She made for a more believable spy than sexpot, her obvious pleasure in skullduggery a marked counterpoint to the tepidity of her romantic interludes.

Will Rogers

NOTABLE FILMS: *JUDGE PRIEST*; *STEAMBOAT ROUND THE BEND*

He seems to belong to a timeless America more suited to woodcuts, or tintypes, than cinematographs. His name conjures up thoughts of Mark Twain and Ambrose Bierce, not John Ford and Stepin Fetchit, and yet Will Rogers, in addition to his roles as humorist, political sage, and national icon, was also, with some moderate success, a movie star. It is an odd experience to see him there. His presence feels anachronistic, like those brief snippets of Eleonora Duse and Sarah Bernhardt captured for eternity by the film camera. Working in film from the height of the silent era until his death in 1935, he maintained a wry distance from Hollywood, even as he worked there. "I am the only man who came out of the movies," he noted, "with the same wife I started with."

The films he made, too, seem to take place in some idealized America of the then-recent past, where the corn grows high, the afternoons stretch long, and the South never really lost the Civil War—only postponed the conclusion of the engagement. *Judge Priest* (1934), one of John Ford's best-regarded and least-seen films, is fascinating and troubling, a comic *Gone with the Wind* all mixed up with *Young Mr. Lincoln* and *To Kill a Mockingbird*. Rogers is folksy, charming, and always a mite smarter than his compatriots: "First thing I learned in politics," he tells an acquaintance at a party, "is when to say 'ain't.'"

Is the judge's Southern chauvinism real, or is it as feigned as the all-black band playing "Dixie" outside the courtroom? *Judge Priest* wants to have it both ways, casting Rogers as a liberal Confederate, a friend to blacks riding a horse named after the founder of the Ku Klux Klan. It is finally the presence of Fetchit—obsequious, foolish, muttering, calculating, the raucous comic stereotype of an era so distant that its humor plays more like tragedy—that capsizes this almost-buoyant film, causing *Judge Priest* to sink under the weight of its contradictions.

Paul Rudd

NOTABLE FILMS: *KNOCKED UP*; *I LOVE YOU MAN*

Paul Rudd first came to our attention as the dreamboat stepbrother in *Clueless* (1995), trading barbs with Alicia Silverstone like Cary Grant had come back to life clad in a Radiohead T-shirt. Rudd promptly proceeded to spend the next decade trapped in drivel like *The Object of My Affection*, where he was adopting a baby with Madonna. The fault lay not in Rudd, but in his stars;

he had simply arrived a decade too early for the boys'-night-out comedies that would be his making. Will Ferrell, and then Judd Apatow, would rescue Rudd from his rut, seeing in him an ideal wingman for their Peter Pan comedies of eternal boyhood. With his leading-man looks and Southern California affability, Rudd is a masculine ideal for the era of post-feminism, his version of Cary Grant less domineering and more neurotic.

Rudd is the loosest of our contemporary actors, so relaxed onscreen that he makes the likes of Seth Rogen appear excessively formal. Rudd is forever misrepresenting himself, a thick layer of fraternal bonhomie pitted in sections by regret and a workaday brand of hilariously forthright melancholy. He was the shameless swinger selling lovelorn Steve Carell a bill of goods in *The 40-Year-Old Virgin* (2005) while pining after his ex-girlfriend, and in 2007's *Knocked Up* (for which, in a far better world than this one, Rudd would have won an Academy Award), he was the miserable husband sneaking off for fantasy-baseball evenings and Vegas weekends with future brother-in-law Rogen. Rudd's misery is our good fortune; even in the depths of despair, he is never anything less than affable.

Finally, with *I Love You Man* (2009), Rudd was granted a vehicle of his own, belatedly discovering man-love with fellow Apatovian Jason Segel. There were about a dozen too many tongue-tied mishaps for Rudd to plow through, but there he was: genial and amusing as ever, a romantic comedy hero for a romantic comedy that cut women out of the equation entirely.

David O. Russell

NOTABLE FILMS: *THREE KINGS*; *I HEART HUCKABEES*

The progression has been steady: from the interior to the exterior, from the local to the universal. David O. Russell has made all of four feature films in his fifteen-year career, but the leap from one project to the next has always been significant, unexpected, and amazingly assured. *Spanking the Monkey* (1994), Russell's debut, is a neurotic family comedy that plays incest for laughs. Its follow-up, *Flirting with Disaster* (1996), is pitch-perfect screwball pastiche stocked with superb comic performers like Ben Stiller, Téa Leoni, Alan Alda, and Lily Tomlin: the man had clearly been studying his Sturges.

Russell could have spent the rest of his career making variations of *Flirting*, but disappeared into the woodshed instead, and emerged with *Three Kings* (1999), a war comedy with an aching heart. It is a film in the vein of *Sullivan's Travels*: a romp that unexpectedly turns deadly serious, a weightless farce that takes on the burden of an irretrievably broken world. With *Flirting with Disaster* and the first half of *Three Kings*, Russell had proved himself to be among the preeminent comic filmmakers of the era; with its second half, he demonstrated himself no longer interested in empty laughs. The truest humor was to be found in going deeper.

Three Kings was itself no preparation for 2004's *I Heart Huckabees*, a magpie metaphysical comedy that borrowed Paul Thomas Anderson's mise-en-scène, Woody Allen's absurdism, and Wes Anderson's dollhouse perfectionism. The result was a philosophy lesson mined for laughs, or possibly a comedy whose subject was our place in a cold, hostile universe. Russell's characters had always been looking for themselves, and for answers about who they might be; the only thing that changed was where they were doing it. From the suburban home, to the American road, to the vast deserts of the Middle East, to the even vaster deserts of the mind. What does one do for an encore after taking on the universe? Perhaps head to Washington, D.C., site of his next, Kristin Gore–scripted film.

Rosalind Russell

NOTABLE FILMS: *HIS GIRL FRIDAY*; *AUNTIE MAME*

Rosalind Russell's two triumphs came nearly two decades apart. In the first, she was a working girl tardily attempting to prove she was more than her job; in the second, she was a lady of leisure who takes to work to prove herself worthy of surrogate motherhood. In both, she was more than an actress in a role—she was a genial storm, swirling across the screen.

Russell had made the rounds of second-tier pictures in the 1930s, culminating in the one-two punch of George Cukor's catty proto-feminist tangle *The Women* (1939), in which she was one of the divorcees, and Howard Hawks's epochal *His Girl Friday* (1940). Russell was a whirlwind bamboozled by a whirlwind, her every attempt to checkmate Cary Grant's acerbic, amoral Walter Burns and depart for a new life in Albany (or was it Oklahoma City?) stymied. Eventually, she bows, secure in the knowledge that she has been defeated by a grand master. We are secure, too, confident that whatever our initial misgivings (shouldn't Hepburn have played this role?), Russell's Hildy Johnson is every bit the equal of Cary Grant at his finest.

For her second go-round, Russell would not make the same mistake again. *Auntie Mame* (1958) is a two-and-a-half-hour comic slugfest in which Russell combats a series of puny featherweights. Russell's Auntie Mame represents every 1950s stereotype of bourgeois bohemianism, but she also stands for the triumph of the fabulous life over drab conformity. *Auntie Mame* is a midlife picaresque, with Russell's adventures—by turns glamorous and heart-wrenching—united by Mame's unflinchingly optimistic good cheer, as if life were all a cocktail party and everyone a delightful new guest. Russell's every motion is a theatrical one, as if she were always performing for some unseen audience. As it turned out, she was.

Winona Ryder
NOTABLE FILMS: *REALITY BITES; HEATHERS*

How quickly they forget: for a long moment in the late 1980s and early 1990s, Winona Ryder was the darling of the American cinema, the princess in waiting without whom no teenage comedy was complete. Replaced, and partially erased, by a later generation of Lindsays and Sarah Michelles who lacked her sardonic wit, or her flashes of fragile grace, Ryder was the beau ideal of the post–*Fast Times at Ridgemont High* generation, to whom a snappy comeback was twice as good as smooching the captain of the football team.

Ryder's best performance, and the one she will likely be remembered for, is as the murderous It Girl of 1988's *Heathers*—undoubtedly the sharpest-edged film ever made about high school. Having already served as the Goth teenager intrigued by the dead people in her attic in Tim Burton's *Beetlejuice* (1988), Ryder made the ideal cheerleader-killer. By turns snide, conniving, and loving helpmate to Christian Slater's Nietzschean *übermensch*, Ryder's fiery Veronica was dazzlingly contradictory.

Growing into her newly established prominence as the representative of a confused generation, Ryder was the obvious choice to star in Ben Stiller's Generation X epic *Reality Bites* (1994). Ryder was the film's soul, and its conscience, and without her, Stiller's attempt at summarizing the emotional needs of a nation of Kurt Cobain fans would have fallen irredeemably short. Contrary to all indications, *Reality Bites* was not a stepping-stone to bigger and better things, but a milestone in and of itself. Burned out by early success, Ryder became better known for a shoplifting incident, and the concomitant raft of "FREE WINONA" T-shirts, than her onscreen work. There were a few highlights, including a turn as Kenneth Branagh's upwardly mobile actress girlfriend in Woody Allen's *Celebrity* (1998), and playing opposite Adam Sandler in the loose Capra remake *Mr. Deeds* (2002), but Ryder appeared to be going through the motions. Whatever spark had animated her early work—the one that had caught everyone's eye—had long ago burnt out.

Morrie Ryskind, Bert Kalmar & Harry Ruby, George S. Kaufman, and S. J. Perelman

NOTABLE FILMS: *DUCK SOUP*; *ANIMAL CRACKERS*

Or, the necessity of reminding Marx Brothers fans that Groucho did not, actually, come up with all his lines as the cameras rolled. The task of parceling out credit for the dazzling flights of verbal fancy in the Marx Brothers' early films is a fiendishly difficult one; Groucho was a writer, not just a performer, and was responsible for a significant portion of his own dialogue. With the early films, the Marxes would take their scripts on the road, testing them in front of audiences and tinkering with the results themselves until they had a final product they were comfortable with. The loosely assembled team listed above, collaborating in different formations on each of the Marx Brothers' Paramount features, dragged the sensibility of Broadway and 42nd Street west to Hollywood and Vine.

Kaufman was a critically lauded playwright; Perelman a brilliant humorist; Kalmar and Ruby were lyricists (they wrote all of Groucho's most memorable songs, from "Hooray for Captain Spaulding" to "Whatever It Is, I'm Against It"). Ryskind would later write *My Man Godfrey*, *Stage Door*, and *Penny Serenade*; Perelman penned *Around the World in Eighty Days* (although whether anyone should take credit for that mess is another matter entirely); and Kaufman's plays served as the inspiration for the films *Dinner at Eight*, *You Can't Take It With You*, and *The Man Who Came to Dinner* (which featured a Harpo-esque character named Banjo).

Harpo was an early adoptee of the Algonquin Circle, and something of the Round Table sensibility lingered in the writers the Marxes employed. Kaufman and Ryskind manned the first handful of Marx Brothers films, with Kalmar and Ruby recruited to assist on *Horse Feathers* before arriving at the peak of *Duck Soup*. How those two former song pluggers went from "When Those Sweet Hawaiian Babies Roll Their Eyes" to "Hail Freedonia" is one of the great unexplained stories of that vast uncharted continent of film history—the work of screenwriters.

If we cannot arrive at an exact quantification of these writers' impact on the Marx Brothers' work, we can at least demonstrate that their presence was essential to the Marxes' success. It is no coincidence, after all, that the move to MGM coincided with the switch to a new stable of studio-approved writers, and a drastic fall-off in the quality of their pictures, or that the one decent MGM Marx picture is *A Night at the Opera*, with script by Kaufman and Ryskind. As momentarily disappointing as it may be to admit, the Marx Brothers went nowhere without their writers.

Adam Sandler
NOTABLE FILMS: *PUNCH-DRUNK LOVE*; *THE WEDDING SINGER*

Inexplicably, and without prior warning, Adam Sandler has become the pre-eminent comic star of his generation. Once a genial, inoffensively childish *Saturday Night Live* cast member, best remembered for charmingly infantile characters like Opera Man and Candy Man, Sandler has developed a fervent following, ensuring nine-figure grosses for every one of his films. The mystery is why. Sandler began with tepid films directed at a teen audience, composed of 70 percent fart jokes and 30 percent adolescent sex humor. Sandler operates in only two modes: steroidally exaggerated masculine hostility, and mushy emotion. Early films like *Billy Madison* (1995) and *Happy Gilmore* (1996) are purposefully insipid, movies for twelve-year-olds with a twelve-year-old's sensibility about the world. Lacking Jim Carrey's physical grace, or Mike Myers's wordsmithery, Sandler is mediocrity writ large.

Sandler is whatever the opposite of an acquired taste might be; he is a comedian for those whose sense of humor has never advanced beyond the flinging of one's own poo. My hesitation regarding Sandler has only partially been abrogated in recent years by a moderately increased willingness on his part to take roles outside his comfort zone. As he has ventured into middle age, Sandler's films have timidly dipped a toe into adulthood. Starring in Paul Thomas Anderson's cracked romance *Punch-Drunk Love* (2002), Sandler evinces a yearning, neurotic romanticism not at all in keeping with his prior work. The 2008 Zionist fantasia *You Don't Mess with the Zohan*, while silly for the most part, is a fitting tribute to Sandler's proudly Jewish brand of comedy. Judd Apatow's *Funny People* (2009) is an autobiographical portrait of Sandler through a mirror darkly, playing a bitter, unhappy superstar whose puerile entertainments (*MerMan*?) offer little more than empty cinematic calories. Sandler is to be saluted for his ability to laugh at his own shortcomings; I only wish I felt like laughing at Sandler quite as much.

Mack Sennett

NOTABLE FILMS: *TILLIE'S PUNCTURED ROMANCE; THE KNOCKOUT*

With Sennett, we venture back to the very creation of the movies: and on the sixth day, Mack Sennett created slapstick. Sennett had been an actor before joining D. W. Griffith's Biograph Pictures in 1908, beginning as an actor and writer before taking over production of Biograph's comedies. Griffith had never been much of a comedian, but Sennett possessed a native gift for knowing what would appeal to audiences still untutored in the possibilities of film comedy. Sennett's sensibility came out of vaudeville, but preferred not to linger in simple transposition of the old routines.

Sennett left Griffith and built up his own company, Keystone, where he was producer, director, editor, and head of production. Sennett's stable of comedians was vast (Charley Chase, Chester Conklin, Fatty Arbuckle, Ford Sterling, Mabel Normand, and Marie Dressler among them), but his collection of storylines distinctly less so.

Sennett's films are, to modern eyes, more raucous than hilarious. They are nonetheless worthy of study, their DNA the building blocks for not only Chaplin but Keaton and Lloyd too. What they lack in hilarity they attempt to make up for with nonstop, pinwheeling energy. They are anarchic, antiauthoritarian, and often shockingly violent. They are crude films—rough cave drawings to the subtler Renaissance arts of *The Kid* and *Grandma's Boy* and *Cops*. One imagines the cameras themselves must have been constructed out of flint and animal skins.

Chaplin gave Sennett a lightness, a gentility, that had never before been present in Keystone. The films they made together in 1914 are more Sennett's than Chaplin's, with the Tramp hastily inserted into Sennett's prefabricated array of setups, but there are hints, even then, of what was to come.

Sennett's studio was no frills, though, and the only superstar on the lot was Sennett himself. After his hugely successful first year at Keystone, Chaplin demanded the princely sum of one thousand dollars a week. Sennett, firmly believing that there was no "Charlie" in "team," turned him down flat. Chaplin left for Essanay, and greatness; Sennett hired Charlie's half-brother Syd as a replacement. His studio was never the same.

Neil Simon

NOTABLE FILMS: *THE ODD COUPLE*; *THE GOODBYE GIRL*

Simon's work is the theatrical equivalent of Chinese food—it's delicious, it goes down with the greatest of ease, and it leaves you hungry an hour later. No wonder Hollywood loved him. Nominated four times for a screenwriting Oscar, Simon is the author of films that are not much seen or discussed today. They have fallen into the oblivion of presumed mediocrity.

The onetime *Your Show of Shows* writer had become, by the 1970s, a staggeringly prolific Broadway playwright—a one-man Manhattan tourist board, drawing in theatergoers from Bangor to San Diego. At the same time, the process of transferring his light, lightning-quick shows from stage to screen established Simon as his own self-contained Hollywood cottage industry. Hardly a year went by, from the late 1960s to the mid-1980s, that a new film written by Neil Simon did not make its premiere. He was one of the very few writers whose name possessed the cachet necessary for it to be attached to his films' titles. By so advertising them, audiences knew what they were getting: two hours or so of literate squabbling, washed down by a barrelful of yuks and a chaser of sap.

Some of his efforts, like the *Grand Hotel*–esque omnibus *California Suite* (1978), have indeed shrunk with the passage of time. But the crackle of Simon's wit, honed, perhaps, by the effort of keeping up with Carl Reiner, Mel Brooks, Woody Allen, and the other *Your Show of Shows* luminaries, is still engaging. *The Odd Couple* (1968), with Jack Lemmon and Walter Matthau as bickering roommates, is a domestic buddy comedy both sharp and sweet, and *The Prisoner of Second Avenue* (1975) paired Lemmon with Anne Bancroft as a sort of married odd couple. The one unquestioned success of Simon's screenwriting career is also the least Simon-esque, astringent and deliberately charmless: *The Heartbreak Kid* (1972), directed by Elaine May with a pitilessness unique among the parade of middlebrow adaptations.

Kevin Smith

NOTABLE FILMS: *CLERKS*; *CHASING AMY*

Slackers. Richard Linklater first brought them to the screen, with the simply titled *Slacker* (1991), his portrait of aimless Austin twentysomethings, but in many ways Linklater's film was too complex, too . . . *thoughtful* to truly deserve the appellation. Lazy characters require a lazy, laid-back film, and no film could be lazier than Kevin Smith's ultra-low-budget debut *Clerks*, from 1993. Two aimless ne'er-do-wells, one a video-store clerk and the other a register jockey at a convenience store, waste the slowly ticking minutes of their directionless lives with bad jokes, dumb pranks, and sexual specula- tion. *Clerks* can best be defined by what it lacks: action, development, plot, or characters with a purpose. In its stead, we are presented with a torrent, a veritable avalanche, of verbiage: these slackers may lack career objectives, but they are surely well-endowed in the verbal department. Smith's slackers cele- brate their terminal adolescence, their dead-end lives becoming a rejection of a culture of success and accomplishment they refuse without fully grasping.

For a brief moment, now long eclipsed by a string of poor movies (like the misguided religious parable *Dogma* [1999] and the truly unfortunate sequel *Clerks II* [2006]) and unfortunate career choices, Smith was a purveyor of exquisitely funny, raunchy, deliberately scandalous films that pushed buttons as they entertained. Smith romanticized the aimless slacker in the same fash- ion that Woody Allen had celebrated the neurotic Jewish striver.

Smith toes the line between romantic-comedy masculine sensitivity and the raunchy, no-holds-barred blowjob jokes of lowbrow comedy. *Chasing Amy* (1997), in particular, is a triumph of fart-joke romantic comedy, its raunchy verbal excesses tightly integrated into the unlikely romance between quint- essential Smith hero Ben Affleck and lipstick lesbian Joey Lauren Adams. It is, at one and the same time, a tender love story and a crude comedy of male bonding, anticipating Judd Apatow's nearly a decade before *The 40-Year-Old Virgin*. *Chasing Amy* seemed to promise a new Allen in the making; instead, it would be Smith's last truly assured film.

Steven Soderbergh
NOTABLE FILMS: *OUT OF SIGHT; OCEAN'S ELEVEN*

This entry, by all rights, belongs not just to Steven Soderbergh, but to George Clooney, Brad Pitt, Luis Guzmán, Albert Finney, Don Cheadle, and the legions of admirable actors Soderbergh has employed during his two decades as an indie-film icon and master manipulator of the studio system. Soder- bergh has always been a superb director of actors, and his looseness—the room he allows for actors to breathe—is his films' saving grace. When Soder- bergh gets tight—see *Solaris* (2002) and *The Good German* (2006), or better yet, don't—the results are inevitably disappointing. Soderbergh yearns for seriousness, but his sensibility is essentially comic. He is usually content to let any amusing bit of business concocted by his actors make its way into the final cut of his films; in fact, when he doesn't, the films suffer for their absence.

Soderbergh got his start with the Palme d'Or–winning *sex, lies, and videotape* (1989), and something of that film's shagginess stuck with him, even as budgets ballooned and subject matter grew denser. *Out of Sight* (1998) is a terrifically casual thriller, its sensuality only amplified by the relaxed banter of George Clooney and Jennifer Lopez, even as they are locked together in the trunk of a car. (It is also one of the few films, other than Brooks's own, to make worthwhile use of Albert Brooks as an actor.) And *Traffic* (2000), for all its merits as an exploration of America's failed war on drugs, is also a showcase for a dazzling array of character actors. Soderbergh is to be commended for his willingness to allow for these digressions. Sometimes, in his lesser work, they can be his salvation. *The Limey* (1999) is a mostly forgettable rehash of John Boorman's *Point Blank*, but Nicky Katt's hilariously profane hit man lingers in the memory long after the remainder has faded into obscurity.

Barbara Stanwyck
NOTABLE FILMS: *THE LADY EVE; BALL OF FIRE*

Barbara Stanwyck was such a brilliant actress—if you haven't seen her in *Double Indemnity* (1944), or *Forty Guns* (1957), put down this book immediately and go rent them both—that it seems unduly limiting to discuss her as a comic performer. But comedian she was, so much so that one cannot help but wonder what she might have done for the form had she dedicated herself wholly to it. Instead, Stanwyck's comedic resume is vanishingly slim, but tantalizing.

She is the temptress in Preston Sturges's ageless *The Lady Eve* (1941), luring lumpish Henry Fonda into original sin with the first glimpse of her bare midriff and plunging décolletage. Stanwyck is effortless, commanding, and dazzling; Fonda never stands a chance against her. In one brilliant sequence early in the film, she lures him back to her stateroom, positions him by her side, knocks him to the floor, places her cheek next to his, and caresses his ears. Fonda can only swallow and primly tug her skirt back into place, grimly attempting to rescue some lingering trace of his masculine assurance by minimizing her feminine allure.

Having stolen his affections aboard a cruise ship, and absconded with them, along with a sizable amount of cash and valuables, Eve has the effrontery to show up again, nothing changed but her accent. Other actresses would have given in to the lure of winking at the audience, reminding them of their cleverness, but Stanwyck never does. Her bravura is complete, and self-contained.

Having been Eve to Fonda's Adam, Stanwyck also got to play Snow White to the Seven Dwarfs of academia in Howard Hawks's underrated *Ball of Fire* (1941). She is once more the reminder of the temptations of the flesh to those living the life of the mind, giving professor Gary Cooper a life lesson that life occasionally transpires outside the pages of books. There is something ironic in her best roles being these vamps and enchantresses, for has there ever been a smarter, wilier actress than Barbara Stanwyck?

James Stewart

NOTABLE FILMS: *THE SHOP AROUND THE CORNER; THE PHILADELPHIA STORY*

One customarily thinks of Jimmy Stewart in heroic mode, rescuing Bedford Falls from the greedy capitalist clutches of Mr. Potter or flying nobly across the Atlantic in the *Spirit of St. Louis*. Stewart's early comic roles, lacking the soft-spoken gallantry of his best-known performances, or the clammy, sickly intensity of Stewart's Hitchcock roles, do not register quite so strongly on the Stewart mythos, but are essential to understanding his enduring appeal.

Stewart's aw-shucks charm was a popgun whose barrel had been deliberately tampered with; where normally it might be expected to reliably peg its target, here it was just as likely to explode in his own face. There was something ever-so-slightly puffed-up about Stewart in these films, something unyielding that required the prodding of a good woman to pierce. Stewart was so plainly the archetype of unthreatening American masculinity (as opposed to more menacing models like Clark Gable) that the occasional ludicrousness of the roles he was asked to play hardly put a dent in his aura.

He is the scion of a family of WASP entrepreneurs who gets mixed up with Jean Arthur's kooky iconoclasts in Frank Capra's Oscar-winning *You Can't Take It With You* (1938), and Tom Destry in the parody Western *Destry Rides Again* (1939). Stewart is the hard-boiled reporter who comes between Katharine Hepburn and Cary Grant in *The Philadelphia Story* (1940), and most memorably, the lovelorn Alfred Kralik in Ernst Lubitsch's *The Shop Around the Corner* (1940), the unknowing romantic pen pal of workplace nemesis Margaret Sullavan.

Lubitsch and Samson Raphaelson were its architects, but it is hard to imagine *The Shop Around the Corner* existing in anything like its present form without Stewart. Stewart is the drudge who dreams of a little happiness of his own, and his unstinting belief in its possibility, in the face of all the obstacles Lubitsch and Raphaelson throw in his way, are the gossamer wings on which this magical film ascends to cinematic heaven. There are glints, already, of the near-maniacal obduracy of Stewart's postwar work—perhaps, if one looks closely enough, one can see *Vertigo*'s Scottie Ferguson, another hopeless romantic whose dreams fail to line up with grubby reality, as an American Kralik gone sour. Like that other great actor of his era, Cary Grant, Stewart is far more complex than the hagiographers allow for. Even his funniest moments are tinged with a hint of mania, as his later dramatic triumphs would be underscored by a touch of comic absurdity.

Whit Stillman
NOTABLE FILMS: *METROPOLITAN; BARCELONA*

Poet laureate of the white-collar classes, Whit Stillman was Wes Anderson before Wes Anderson was old enough to legally drink. Stillman has been eclipsed by more successful imitators like Noah Baumbach, but Stillman's three films, *Metropolitan* (1990), *Barcelona* (1994), and *The Last Days of Disco* (1998) are diamond-sharp studies of the well-heeled. Stillman's subject is the secret lives of WASPs, and he finds humor in the hidden nooks and crannies of WASP ambition, ritual, and routine. With *Metropolitan*, Stillman pulls off the unlikely trick of mining humor from a passel of uptight, stuffy proto-yuppies and their joyless round of soirees. Impoverished Tom Townsend (he lives on the middle-class Upper West Side, not the far wealthier East Side) inadvertently crashes the Manhattan debutante season, making his voice heard over the crucial issues of the moment: What parties are worth going to? What's preferable: books, or literary criticism? And is Rick Van Sloneker an entitled jerk?

Barcelona continues in the same amiable, layabout vein, moving the action to early 1980s Spain, where two young men on the make—a Navy officer and a businessman—find both romance and anti-Americanism. *Last Days of Disco* is a sophisticated comedy set to the beat of forgettable music, energized by Kate Beckinsale's manipulative, undermining nightclub princess.

Stillman's preferred mode is the deadpan. For the director, it is not his place to make assumptions for his audience about what might be funny.

Serious readings of Stillman are possible, even preferable—about the erosion of the East Coast elite's sense of superiority, about the deterioration of pro-American sentiment around the world—but he never insists on being taken earnestly. Stillman's gift for genial, witty, dialogue is an increasing rarity in American film, which makes it all the more regrettable that it has now been over a decade since his last film.

Meryl Streep

NOTABLE FILMS: *MANHATTAN; THE DEVIL WEARS PRADA*

Meryl Streep is the greatest living American actress. This is a statement of no particularly controversial import, for who would choose to disagree? What is a matter of less universal agreement, if only for lack of due consideration, is that Streep may also be our greatest comic actress, as well. When Streep first emerged, with films like *The Deer Hunter* (1978) and Woody Allen's *Manhattan* (1979), she was almost ethereal—a WASP princess possessed of a remarkable delicacy. Streep's early strength was in roles that demanded an unshakable inner strength and an exterior fragility, like the unyielding ex-wife she played in *Manhattan*, or her dual performances as scorned women past and present in *The French Lieutenant's Woman* (1981). Comedy was not necessarily her forte; even working with Allen, she appeared to be channeling *Interiors*, not *Sleeper*.

Streep rapidly became the most formidable of our dramatic actresses—her performance in *Sophie's Choice* (1982) alone has achieved legendary status—and slowly incorporated the occasional comic trifle into her repertoire. Some, like *She-Devil* (1989), were stillborn, but others, like Mike Nichols's *Postcards from the Edge* (1990), and her performance in Albert Brooks's *Defending Your Life* (1991), exhibited a heretofore-unfamiliar looseness and charm.

With the passage of time, Streep has grown lighter-hearted and steelier, all at once, and her best roles of the last decade—which include her marvelous turn in Robert Altman's *A Prairie Home Companion* (2006)—have exploited this unlikely duality. *The Devil Wears Prada* (2006) cast Streep as fashionista medusa Anna Wintour—or a version thereof—at once mercurial, callous, and brittle, like a steel-toed boot encased in porcelain. Playing opposite ingenue Anne Hathaway, Streep was an ideal antihero, her scenery-crunching zeal turning a forgettable popcorn movie into memorable pulp fiction. *Julie & Julia* (2009), with Streep as legendary chef Julia Child, was even better, with the actress's lusty enthusiasm—for food, for sex, for the raw ingredients of experience—overwhelming the presumptive past-and-present division of Nora Ephron's film. And *It's Complicated* (2009) made Streep the unlikely heroine of her own late-middle-aged romantic comedy. Streep has, if anything, grown more comfortable as an actress after thirty years. She now seems to be enjoying herself.

Barbra Streisand

NOTABLE FILMS: *FUNNY GIRL*; *WHAT'S UP, DOC?*

Barbra Streisand shared an Oscar for her portrayal of Fanny Brice in *Funny Girl* (1968), in an exceedingly rare Academy Award tie, with Katharine Hepburn in *The Lion in Winter*. The links between Streisand and Hepburn run deeper than mere voting irregularities. Streisand styled herself a successor to Hepburn—an intriguing blend of verve, moxie, and showmanship. Her performance in *Funny Girl*, alternating between nostalgia and stubborn resolve, held together with the glue of her brash, brassy voice, was Hepburn-esque in its sheer size.

By the time Peter Bogdanovich got the idea to cast Streisand alongside Ryan O'Neal in a loose remake of *Bringing Up Baby*, the parallels were firmly locked in place. Barbra gamely does her best to summon the spirit of Hepburn in *What's Up, Doc?* (1972), along with a touch of the irrepressible Bugs Bunny (note the title), but what Kate had made seem so easy was actually a great deal harder than it may have appeared.

What's Up, Doc? is notable today as a well-needed refresher course on the magic of the screwball comedy. Screwball was so abundant in the 1930s and 1940s that one could be forgiven for thinking that there was something just a little too easy about its charms. Watching Streisand and O'Neal hit all their marks precisely in Bogdanovich's well-crafted screwball tribute, and come up woefully short, only underscores just how good Hepburn and Cary Grant were. Aiming to be charmingly daffy, Streisand ends up exhausting our patience.

After a rather unnecessary *Funny Girl* sequel, *Funny Lady*, Streisand has mostly eschewed comedy, her few acting appearances in melodramas like her directorial efforts *Yentl* (1983) and *The Prince of Tides* (1991). Streisand is to be commended for re-emerging, after a lengthy absence, to mother Ben Stiller in *Meet the Fockers* (2004). On the merits of casting alone, could two Jewish parents be any more perfect than Streisand and Dustin Hoffman?

Quentin Tarantino

NOTABLE FILMS: *PULP FICTION*; *RESERVOIR DOGS*

Tarantino made his bones as a purveyor of elegantly framed viscera; who can forget the severed ear in *Reservoir Dogs* (1992), or the Grand Guignol carnage of *Pulp Fiction* (1994)? And yet, as a successor to the indie directorial gods of the 1980s, Tarantino inherited some of Spike Lee and Jim Jarmusch's deadpan sense of humor. More than shoot-em-ups, Tarantino's films are orgies of chatter: bored, stoned, tense, ironic, chilling.

Reservoir Dogs became as well known for its inspired exegesis of Madonna's "Like a Virgin" as its mayhem, and *Pulp Fiction*'s discussions of the differences between American and European fast food, Amsterdam hash bars, and the cleanliness of eating pork are the beating heart of the film. Tarantino's characters are hoary Hollywood archetypes (the crumbum boxer with one last fight, the chatty hit men, the gangster moll) given the opportunity to express themselves, and the results are charmingly askew, like a 1990s American version of Jean-Luc Godard's New Wave mash-ups of half-remembered gangster films. Christopher Walken's long monologue about Bruce Willis's father's watch, hoarded up his ass in a Vietnam POW camp, is one such priceless moment, as is John Travolta and Samuel L. Jackson's Talmudic debate over the propriety of foot massages.

Later efforts like the *Kill Bill* films eschewed humor in favor of genre pastiche, but Tarantino's dialogue has never fully discarded his motor-mouthed panache, and his scenarios their exaggerated menace. In *Inglourious Basterds* (2009), a Jewish revenge fantasy of World War II with a deliberately loose grasp of world history, a Nazi Jew-hunter pulls out a gigantic Alpine-horn tobacco pipe during a tense sequence, and a message is transmitted: this is all an elaborate provocation, Tarantino seems to be telling us, not to be treated with any seriousness. Tarantino's is a fundamentally jesting spirit, inclined to satirically embellish his scenarios with a touch of postmodern élan; that this might be less appropriate for, say, a film about Jews fleeing the Nazis than for one about samurai assassins is a thought that would likely never occur to him.

Frank Tashlin

NOTABLE FILMS: *ARTISTS AND MODELS*; *THE DISORDERLY ORDERLY*

Director and screenwriter Frank Tashlin was a paragon of the grotesque—the perfect tongue-in-cheek showman for the more-is-more 1950s. Jerry Lewis

(Tashlin's star in eight films) was never known for his underplaying, and Jayne Mansfield and her absurdly exaggerated figure make for the perfect Tashlin heroine in *The Girl Can't Help It* (1956) and *Will Success Spoil Rock Hunter?* (1957), a comic-book heroine come to eye-popping life. "Monroe *delivered* gag lines," Richard Corliss noted. "Mansfield *was* one." Even Bob Hope, who had made a career out of relentless self-deprecation, is rendered as a hilariously puffed-up caricature in *Son of Paleface* (1952), perhaps the best of Tashlin's efforts as a director.

Nineteen-fifties comedy, emerging in the valley after comedy's 1930s–1940s screwball peak, fell into critical and scholarly eclipse for many years, and Tashlin's reputation has suffered as a result. Tashlin's films are silly, illogical, sex-obsessed, and plagued by modernity; if a character introduces a new vacuum cleaner, or lawnmower, even money says it will go haywire by the third reel. Technology, in fact, behaves in increasingly human fashion, as people become more and more robotic. It is the machines, not the men, that are constantly ejaculating in Tashlin's films.

For so hysterically over-the-top a director, Tashlin's films are surprisingly sentimental, with his Jerry Lewis films (*Rock-a-Bye Baby* and *The Geisha Boy* in particular) coming dangerously close to cloying. It is the director's cynicism that is his saving grace. Whether grousing about Cinemascope and television, or HUAC and rampant consumerism, Tashlin's crabbiness is sublimated into lavishly orchestrated bedlam. Tashlin's films dependably conclude with a chaotic free-for-all, in which he symbolically extracts his revenge on an unforgivably crass world.

The Three Stooges

NOTABLE FILMS: *YOU NAZTY SPY!*; *OILY TO BED, OILY TO RISE*

How to account for the astonishing, multigenerational popularity of those hyper-violent klutzes known as the Three Stooges? The Stooges—Moe (Moses Horowitz), Larry (Larry Feinberg), and Shemp (Samuel Horowitz), later replaced by Curly (Jerome Horowitz)—were silent comedians for the era of sound. Other comedians, Laurel & Hardy among them, had adapted for new times by taking to dialogue. Borrowing heavily from their predecessors, the Three Stooges preferred to use the soundtrack as an amplifier and audience guide. Exaggerated sound served exaggerated action, permitting audiences to laugh at otherwise-excessive mayhem. Those sounds—the ukuleles, twittering birds, and ringing bells—have themselves entered the pantheon of comedy standards.

Having begun onscreen in the early 1930s, the Stooges were still making films as late as 1968's *Star Spangled Salesman*. The violence—punches, kicks, tweaks of the nose, and all manner of prop-assisted savagery—in these short films is immediate, unstinting, and circular. Moe does to Larry, who does to Curly, who returns the favor to Moe. As with their Keystone predecessors, logic is the commodity in shortest supply here, but the sheer persistence of the Three Stooges is incredible. How many times can you bonk the same guy on the head?

One of the most memorable of their films, 1940's *You Nazty Spy!*, took on the Nazis in the same year as Charlie Chaplin's far more celebrated jab at Adolf Hitler. Moe is a housepainter hired as the dictator of Moronica. With his greasepaint mustache and occasional lapse into gibberish German, he is a dead ringer, not only for Hitler but for Adenoid Hynkel, from *The Great Dictator*. (*Nazty* actually beat *Dictator* to theaters.)

Nazty is riddled with Jewish humor, as if ethnic and religious pride was the best comedic weapon in their arsenal of anti-Nazi munitions. Greeting their Nazi bosses, the Stooges leap back and salute: "Shalom aleichem!" Much of the film's wordplay is colored by a similar Jewish flavoring, having brought Brooklyn with them on their European grand tour.

Themselves entirely out of time, the Stooges appeared to be near the end of their careers in the late 1940s when they were unexpectedly saved by the arrival of a new medium. Columbia licensed their shorts to television, which was still hungry for anything to fill airspace, and discovered that the Stooges appealed to a generation of children unfamiliar with their work. Today, the Three Stooges seem to belong to no era at all. Their stupidity is timeless.

Vince Vaughn

NOTABLE FILMS: *SWINGERS*; *OLD SCHOOL*

Of all the members of the so-called Frat Pack, who elevated lackadaisicality to an art form, none were so relaxed in front of a camera as Vince Vaughn. An accidental comedy star, Vaughn had spent the first years after his breakout role in *Swingers* (1996) in quixotic pursuit of dramatic success. *Swingers* had been a left-field hit, with Vaughn and Jon Favreau as underemployed L.A. actors on the make. Favreau was charmingly shambling, but the picture was entirely Vaughn's. Tall and rangy, with a sly smile that bespoke copious debauched nights out, Vaughn's Trent gave the wannabe hipsters of 1996 a plethora of new catchphrases.

He was so money, and he didn't even know it; it was as if comedy came so easily to Vaughn that he refused to recognize it as a marketable skill. Vaughn made for a more than respectable actor, but his calling was as the leader of the Peter Pans, chasing youth even as adulthood wrapped its tentacles tightly around them. Will Ferrell may have been the breakout star of the bunch, but Vaughn was the unquestioned leader of the Frat Pack. His natural bonhomie made for a perfect complement to Ferrell's nervous intensity in *Old School* (2003), where Vaughn is a husband and father hoping to recapture some of the rebellious aura of youth.

After the unexpected success of *Old School*, Vaughn transformed into a dependable comic wingman in films like *Starsky & Hutch* (2004), *Dodgeball* (2004), *Wedding Crashers* (2005), and *The Break-Up* (2006). Even in the presence of such talented performers as Ben Stiller, Owen Wilson, and Jennifer Aniston, Vaughn stood out. The man was just so damn relaxed onscreen, as if filming a scene were merely a matter of having a pleasant chat with friends. *Wedding Crashers* is not quite as brilliant as its fans may have wished, its vaunted daring distinctly overstated, but Vaughn is terrifically charming as the nuptial con man unexpectedly bitten by the love bug.

John Waters

NOTABLE FILMS: *PINK FLAMINGOS*; *FEMALE TROUBLE*

The crown prince of Baltimore grotesquerie, John Waters's films were so amateurish that he made Andy Warhol seem like Alfred Hitchcock. Camerawork was rudimentary, the sound recording was choppy at best, and the acting was deliriously wooden. And yet, early Waters films like *Pink Flamingos* (1972) and *Female Trouble* (1974) have a charm that transcends any such cavilings about their technical shortcomings. In part, this is due to the fearlessness of star Divine, but it is Waters himself, and his exaggeratedly campy sense of excess, that remain the chief selling point of these still-scandalous films.

Pink Flamingos is not only about a competition for the filthiest person alive; it presents its director as a prime contender for the title. Any discussion of the film tends to break down into a litany of its offenses: the incest, the castration, the salami tied to a Peeping Tom's penis, and of course, the consumption (to the tune of "How Much Is That Doggie in the Window?") of dog shit. All of this would be only so much provocation if it were not for Waters's delirious embrace of immoderation. Confronted with so much by which to be revolted, we are instead charmed, amused by Waters's maximalist gross-out.

Female Trouble is, if anything, even better than *Pink Flamingos*, its plot more concise, its winking incitements to outrage more sharply etched. Waters is chiefly a provocateur, but he is not entirely defined by that term. He is also mocking a straight world (in all senses of that term) defined by drudgery, monotony, and closed-mindedness. "The world of the heterosexual," Divine observes, "is a sick and boring life." Waters's world is many things, but boring is not one of them. At the end of *Female Trouble*, Divine is sentenced to death for murder, which is, as she notes, "the biggest award I could get in my field."

In later years, Waters has toned down his transcendently bad taste, resulting first in films that kept his tawdry sense of humor and eliminated the tabloid antics (like *Hairspray* and *Cry-Baby*) and later in films that offered little of either. If there were lifetime-achievement awards for the ingenious deployment of vulgarity, though, John Waters would be the first to be honored.

Keenen Ivory Wayans
NOTABLE FILMS: *I'M GONNA GIT YOU SUCKA!*; *SCARY MOVIE*

Just as Mel Brooks was winding down into a post-*Spaceballs* terminal funk, Keenen Ivory Wayans was emerging as his successor as the premier parodist of his era. In many ways, the blaxploitation parody *I'm Gonna Git You Sucka!* (1988) is a film deeply indebted to Brooks: the broad stereotypes, the ludicrous names, and the exaggerated action all owe something to *Blazing Saddles'* burlesque of the Western.

And yet, Wayans was attempting something Brooks could not: he was parodying blaxploitation as an insider. Brooks had always been the antic Jew mocking genres which he had no business being a part of; Wayans was mocking a brand of filmmaking which he had studied carefully, and to which he retained a certain knowing fondness. He was also an African American lampooning an African American genre, and if the jokes felt too easy at times (weren't *The Mack* and *Shaft* already comedies, in a way?), the affection for a bygone era was palpable.

Wayans went on to create, along with several of his siblings, the groundbreaking television sketch-comedy series *In Living Color*. The show spawned a monster: Jim Carrey, one of the lone white cast members, and the only *In Living Color* regular to become a bankable movie star. Not one to whine, Wayans went on to resuscitate the *Airplane!/Naked Gun* model for the twenty-first century, directing the smash hits *Scary Movie* (2000) and *Scary Movie 2*

(2001). Mocking the likes of *Scream* and *I Know What You Did Last Summer* was like shooting teenage fish in a barrel, but the specificity of Wayans's parody, as a black man chortling over the bottomless stupidity of the white teenager, was a lively change from the usual state of comedic affairs.

John Wayne
NOTABLE FILMS: *THE QUIET MAN; RIO BRAVO*

This must be a misprint. John Wayne? The Duke? Any book on the Western could hardly call itself complete without a compendious entry on the man born Marion Morrison, but what could John Wayne possibly have to do with comedy? As it turns out, quite a bit.

John Ford had made Wayne a star by casting him as the Ringo Kid in *Stagecoach* (1939), where he had provided the first of what would be an entire career of portraits of square-jawed rectitude. *The Quiet Man* (1952) marks a turning point in Wayne's career—the first time he steps beyond the comfortable rut of Westerns and war films that he and Ford had been making together. A rollicking comic romance about an American who moves back to his native Ireland, *The Quiet Man* is one of Ford's most charming efforts.

The Quiet Man notwithstanding, Wayne was more comfortable joshing with his pals than romancing the lasses. Later Ford films like the magnificent *The Wings of Eagles* (1957) make fine use of his relaxed, just-one-of-the-guys posture, as if a film set were merely a larger poker table, and his costars the regulars at a weekly gathering. Ornery, pickled in his own juices, Wayne made for an unusual comic actor in such late Howard Hawks masterpieces as *Rio Bravo* (1959) and *Hatari!* (1962). *Rio Bravo* is not only the finest comic Western ever made; it might also be the finest Western, period.

By the time the Academy belatedly got around to granting Wayne the Oscar he had so richly deserved so many times, for *True Grit* (1969), he was playing a comic version of the same Western heroes he had once straight-facedly embodied. His teeth bared in a permanent snarl, strutting like a wounded peacock, his Rooster Cogburn was irascible, ornery, and ultimately lovable, like a declawed version of *The Searchers*' Ethan Edwards. The role was little more than a glorified supporting part, and Rooster was a caricature so overblown that he was practically parodying himself, in a film that was hardly better than a parody of the far superior Westerns he had once made, but if anyone was to roast John Wayne, who better than the man himself?

Gene Wilder

NOTABLE FILMS: *THE PRODUCERS*; *STIR CRAZY*

Gene Wilder was essential to the success of not one but two of the key figures of the 1970s: Mel Brooks and Richard Pryor. For Brooks, Wilder is the demented straight man of *The Producers* (1968), *Blazing Saddles* (1974), and *Young Frankenstein* (1974), the establishment figure whose three-piece suit is missing a few buttons. For Pryor, he is a more ambiguous presence, trading off opportunities to serve as designated wild man in their four films together.

Brooks saw Wilder as an ideal leading man for his films, his slack, sallow features a sight gag all their own. As Zero Mostel romances the elderly and hard-of-hearing, Wilder's Leo Bloom is the quiet center of *The Producers*. His overdue embrace of showbiz opens the floodgates for Brooks to unleash *Springtime for Hitler*. Stemming from his original screenplay, *Young Frankenstein* (1974) is more Wilder's picture than Brooks's. The fart jokes have been eschewed in favor of Wilder's patient prodding of the weak spots of the classic horror film. It is an energetic spoof, lively and pleasant, but like too many of Brooks's other films, *Young Frankenstein* is a dicey proposition, more filler than killer.

Wilder and Pryor paired up on four buddy comedies, easily divisible into two distinct pairs. Like an old married couple, or combatants having signed a mutual pact of non-aggression, they trade roles back and forth: OK, this time you be the pain in the ass, and I'll be the grind. The first two films—*Silver Streak* (1976) and *Stir Crazy* (1980)—are irreverent goofs, with the two actors trading off the roles of wild child and straight man. *Silver Streak* is a polite comic murder mystery hijacked halfway through by Pryor's dangerously charismatic thief. Its follow-up, *Stir Crazy*, is turned over to the bug-eyed Wilder, intent on living life to the fullest while serving time in maximum-security prison.

Robin Williams

NOTABLE FILMS: *GOOD MORNING, VIETNAM*; *ALADDIN*

For a major comic figure of unassailed reputation, Robin Williams's filmography is dismayingly mixed. Having devoted himself for too long to the Oscar hunt and having associated himself with more than his fair share of legendary flops, Williams is a comic giant without any universally beloved hits. And no, box-office grosses aside, *Mrs. Doubtfire* (1993) does not count.

After breaking big as a stand-up performer, and as the alien Mork on *Happy Days* and *Mork and Mindy*, Williams got his first film role as Popeye in Robert Altman's 1980 adaptation of E. C. Segar's comic strip. Williams mutters manfully through Altman's fractured musical, his artificially enhanced biceps the film's only memorable special effect. Williams did not really come into his own as an actor until Barry Levinson's *Good Morning, Vietnam* (1987), where the manic stream-of-consciousness rants from his stand-up work became an essential part of his performance as a disgruntled Armed Forces Radio DJ during the Vietnam War.

The Oscar nomination was well-deserved, but instead of looking for roles that allowed him the full run of his talents, Williams instead went in search of likely Oscar bait. Playing an inspirational, poetry-spouting teacher in *Dead Poets Society* (1989), a doctor treating catatonic patients in *Awakenings* (1990), and a homeless man in *The Fisher King* (1991) were good for his run of Oscar nominations, but twisted Williams out of shape. A passable dramatic actor, Robin Williams hardly made much sense without at least a taste of his Tasmanian deviltry. *The Birdcage* (1996), which contains one of his best performances, has its mushy moments (and its dated ones), but Williams is manically effeminate, giving his domestic partner Nathan Lane impromptu lessons in manliness imparted in a John Wayne drawl.

Williams's only fully satisfying role, strangely enough, was one where he neglected to appear onscreen. His strongest suit as a comedian had always come when feverishly flitting from one impression to the next, shape-shifting with lightning speed. Williams provides the voice of the Genie for *Aladdin* (1992), livening up an otherwise dull family film with flashes of his improvisatory genius. Mimicking Jack Nicholson, Ed Sullivan, and Arnold Schwarzenegger, in addition to a cheerleader, a tailor, and a tour guide, the genie is reminiscent of no one so much as Williams himself doing stand-up, bouncing from one riff to the next with coke-fueled abandon. His was a personality best suited to cartoons.

Oscar success finally came with *Good Will Hunting* (1997), where Williams was a psychotherapist with some issues of his own to work through. But comedy proved harder to pick up than it had been to leave off. Williams's post–*Good Will* streak of clunkers included *Patch Adams* (1998), *Bicentennial Man* (1999), and *Death to Smoochy* (2002), all of which were box-office failures in addition to being critically drubbed. In an era when the understated Jon Stewart is a comic god, Robin Williams is simply too much of a good thing. You can never be too rich or too thin, but perhaps you can be too funny.

Renée Zellweger

NOTABLE FILMS: *BRIDGET JONES'S DIARY*; *DOWN WITH LOVE*

The pouty, squinty, apple-cheeked visage of Renée Zellweger inspires more disagreement than practically any other American actor. Is Zellweger charming and down-to-earth, or an insipid soup of involuntary tics and neuroses? The answer varies from moviegoer to moviegoer, and from film to film, but even before taking over the Doris Day role in the Rock & Doris homage *Down with Love* (2003), it was clear that there was something of Day to her genetic makeup. Zellweger milked laughter from her averageness, her charm teetering on the edge of obsequiousness the way Day's once had.

Audiences felt they knew her personally. Having been introduced in *Jerry Maguire* (1996) as Tom Cruise's love interest, Zellweger never entirely shed the initial impression that she had been only another face in the crowd, discovered and nurtured by their affection. *Bridget Jones's Diary* (2001), based on Helen Fielding's chick-lit novel, transcends the shortcomings of its source material by the force of Zellweger's longing, and her charming willingness to patiently endure her humiliations. Playing opposite caddish Hugh Grant, she was marvelously frumpy, her doughy physique the film's most memorable special effect. She was believably drab in a way her fellow comic actresses (Julia Roberts, say, or Cameron Diaz) might not have been.

A beautiful woman brought low; such was the template of the American comedy of the 1990s and 2000s (at least those few with roles for women that featured actual dialogue and characterization). There was something self-worshipping about her proto-feminist author in *Down with Love*—some sense that she was recording her own words for posterity, even as they poured out of her mouth—that made the inevitable comeuppance delivered by playboy Ewan McGregor downright delicious. Zellweger was not quite the equal of her forebear; where Day feels steely, she is mushy, her resolve practically marshmallow-soft.

Jerry Zucker, Jim Abrahams, and David Zucker

NOTABLE FILMS: *AIRPLANE!*; *THE NAKED GUN*

Formally known as ZAZ, this three-person filmmaking team is responsible for some of the most juvenile, crass, uproarious movies of the 1980s and 1990s. Groan-inducing puns, sight gags, Keystone Kops slapstick—no bit was too lowbrow for the creators of *Airplane!* and *The Naked Gun*. ZAZ took the setups from mediocre old films and doodled in the margins, splicing in as many jokes as they could cram in, and then dumping in another couple gallons for good measure. ZAZ films were not for the polite, or those in search of gentle humor.

Raunchy and unpredictable, *Airplane!* (1980) is a brilliant parody of the disaster film, transforming a forgotten 1950s misadventure into a raucous, gloriously uncouth tour de force. *Airplane II: The Sequel* (1982), which ZAZ was not involved with, was a dud, but *The Naked Gun* (1988) and its sequel *Naked Gun 2½* (1991) are marvelous send-ups of the cop movie. Notwithstanding the strange casting choices (Priscilla Presley as a love interest? O. J. Simpson as a sidekick?), the *Naked Gun* films are astoundingly energetic in their puerility. They are films for the ten-year-old inside all of us.

More than anything, ZAZ films gave us the gift of the marvelous Leslie Nielsen. Nielsen had been, once upon a time, a romantic leading man in films like *Forbidden Planet* (1956). The Zuckers' truly inspired brainstorm was to transform him into a deadpan comic hero. Already in his sixties by the time of *The Naked Gun*, Nielsen was too dapper, too much the suave leading man to possibly be as vigorously idiotic as he is here. Butchering the national anthem at a baseball game, urinating at great length while wearing a microphone, getting randy with his girlfriend while cloaked in a full-body protective suit, Nielsen was impressively game for anything.

TOP 100 AMERICAN COMEDIES

The Pawnshop (Charlie Chaplin, 1916)

The Immigrant (Charlie Chaplin, 1917)

The Kid (Charlie Chaplin, 1921)

Safety Last (Fred C. Newmeyer & Sam Taylor, 1923)

Sherlock Jr. (Buster Keaton, 1924)

The Gold Rush (Charlie Chaplin, 1925)

The Freshman (Fred C. Newmeyer & Sam Taylor, 1925)

The General (Buster Keaton & Clyde Bruckman, 1926)

Steamboat Bill, Jr. (Charles Reisner, 1928)

The Circus (Charlie Chaplin, 1928)

Big Business (James W. Horne & Leo McCarey, 1929)

Animal Crackers (Victor Heerman, 1930)

Monkey Business (Norman Z. McLeod, 1931)

City Lights (Charlie Chaplin, 1931)

The Music Box (James Parrott, 1932)

One Hour with You (Ernst Lubitsch, 1932)

Love Me Tonight (Rouben Mamoulian, 1932)

Trouble in Paradise (Ernst Lubitsch, 1932)

Duck Soup (Leo McCarey, 1933)

It's a Gift (Norman Z. McLeod, 1934)

The Thin Man (W. S. Van Dyke, 1934)

It Happened One Night (Frank Capra, 1934)

A Night at the Opera (Sam Wood, 1935)

Ruggles of Red Gap (Leo McCarey, 1935)

Tit for Tat (Charley Rogers, 1935)

Bringing Up Baby (Howard Hawks, 1938)

Ninotchka (Ernst Lubitsch, 1939)

The Shop Around the Corner (Ernst Lubitsch, 1940)

His Girl Friday (Howard Hawks, 1940)

My Favorite Wife (Garson Kanin, 1940)

The Bank Dick (Edward F. Cline, 1940)

The Lady Eve (Preston Sturges, 1941)

Ball of Fire (Howard Hawks, 1941)

Sullivan's Travels (Preston Sturges, 1941)

The Palm Beach Story (Preston Sturges, 1942)

To Be or Not to Be (Ernst Lubitsch, 1942)

Heaven Can Wait (Ernst Lubitsch, 1943)

The More the Merrier (George Stevens, 1943)

Hail the Conquering Hero (Preston Sturges, 1944)

The Big Sleep (Howard Hawks, 1946)

Adam's Rib (George Cukor, 1949)

Singin' in the Rain (Stanley Donen & Gene Kelly, 1952)

Monkey Business (Howard Hawks, 1952)

The Marrying Kind (George Cukor, 1952)

Son of Paleface (Frank Tashlin, 1952)

Gentlemen Prefer Blondes (Howard Hawks, 1953)

Duck Amuck (Chuck Jones, 1953)

Funny Face (Stanley Donen, 1957)

Some Like It Hot (Billy Wilder, 1959)

Pillow Talk (Michael Gordon, 1959)

The Apartment (Billy Wilder, 1960)

The Bellboy (Jerry Lewis, 1960)

One, Two, Three (Billy Wilder, 1961)

The Nutty Professor (Jerry Lewis, 1963)

Charade (Stanley Donen, 1963)

A Shot in the Dark (Blake Edwards, 1964)

Dr. Strangelove (Stanley Kubrick, 1964)

The Party (Blake Edwards, 1968)

Avanti! (Billy Wilder, 1972)

The Long Goodbye (Robert Altman, 1973)

Sleeper (Woody Allen, 1973)

Female Trouble (John Waters, 1974)

Annie Hall (Woody Allen, 1977)

The Jerk (Carl Reiner, 1979)

Real Life (Albert Brooks, 1979)

Richard Pryor: Live in Concert (Jeff Margolis, 1979)

Being There (Hal Ashby, 1979)

Fast Times at Ridgemont High (Amy Heckerling, 1982)

Tootsie (Sydney Pollack, 1982)

Diner (Barry Levinson, 1982)

This Is Spinal Tap (Rob Reiner, 1984)

All of Me (Carl Reiner, 1984)

The Purple Rose of Cairo (Woody Allen, 1985)

Lost in America (Albert Brooks, 1985)

Fletch (Michael Ritchie, 1985)

Down by Law (Jim Jarmusch, 1986)

Ferris Bueller's Day Off (John Hughes, 1986)

The Naked Gun (David Zucker, 1988)

Do the Right Thing (Spike Lee, 1989)

Metropolitan (Whit Stillman, 1990)

Groundhog Day (Harold Ramis, 1993)

Dazed and Confused (Richard Linklater, 1993)

Clerks (Kevin Smith, 1993)

Pulp Fiction (Quentin Tarantino, 1994)

Clueless (Amy Heckerling, 1995)

Flirting with Disaster (David O. Russell, 1996)

The Nutty Professor (Tom Shadyac, 1996)

Deconstructing Harry (Woody Allen, 1997)

Austin Powers: International Man of Mystery (Jay Roach, 1997)

Rushmore (Wes Anderson, 1998)

The Big Lebowski (Joel Coen, 1998)

Toy Story 2 (John Lasseter, 1999)

South Park: Bigger, Longer, and Uncut (Trey Parker & Matt Stone, 1999)

The Royal Tenenbaums (Wes Anderson, 2001)

Old School (Todd Phillips, 2003)

Anchorman: The Legend of Ron Burgundy (Adam McKay, 2004)

Harold and Kumar Go to White Castle (Danny Leiner, 2004)

Sideways (Alexander Payne, 2004)

The Incredibles (Brad Bird, 2004)

Knocked Up (Judd Apatow, 2007)

BIBLIOGRAPHY

Agee, James. *Agee on Film*. New York: Modern Library, 2000.

Allen, William Rodney, ed. *The Coen Brothers: Interviews*. Jackson: University Press of Mississippi, 2006.

Bjorkman, Stig. *Woody Allen on Woody Allen*. New York: Grove Press, 2005.

Blesh, Rudi. *Keaton*. New York: Macmillan, 1966.

Bogdanovich, Peter. *Who the Devil Made It*. New York: Alfred A. Knopf, 1997.

Bogle, Donald. *Toms, Coons, Mulattoes, Mammies, and Bucks: An Interpretive History of Blacks in American Films*. New York: Continuum, 2003.

Chandler, Charlotte. *Nobody's Perfect: Billy Wilder, a Personal Biography*. New York: Simon & Schuster, 2002.

———. *She Always Knew How: Mae West, a Personal Biography*. New York: Simon & Schuster, 2009.

Corliss, Richard. *Talking Pictures*. New York: Penguin Books, 1975.

Crowe, Cameron. *Conversations with Wilder*. New York: Knopf, 1999.

Curtis, James. *Between Flops: A Biography of Preston Sturges*. New York: Harcourt Brace Jovanovich, 1982.

Dardis, Tom. *Harold Lloyd*. New York: Viking Press, 1983.

Eliot, Marc. *Cary Grant*. New York: Harmony Books, 2004.

Everson, William K. *The Films of Laurel & Hardy*. Secaucus, N.J.: Citadel Press, 1967.

Fleming, Michael. *The Three Stooges: An Illustrated History from Amalgamated Morons to American Icons*. New York: Doubleday, 1999.

Girgus, Sam. *The Films of Woody Allen*. Cambridge, U.K.: Cambridge University Press, 1993.

Gross, Edward. *The Films of Eddie Murphy*. Las Vegas: Pioneer Books, 1990.

Harris, Mark. *Pictures at a Revolution*. New York: Penguin Press, 2008.

Harvey, James. *Movie Love in the Fifties*. New York: Knopf, 2001.

———. *Romantic Comedy in Hollywood*. New York: Knopf, 1987.

Hayes, Kevin J., ed. *Charlie Chaplin: Interviews*. Jackson: University Press of Mississippi, 2005.

Higham, Charles. *Kate*. New York: Norton, 1981.

Kael, Pauline. *For Keeps*. New York: Dutton, 1994.

Kanin, Garson. *Tracy & Hepburn*. New York: Viking Press, 1971.

Kaufman, David. *Doris Day: The Untold Story of the Girl Next Door*. New York: Virgin Books, 2008.

Keaton, Eleanor, and Jeffrey Vance. *Buster Keaton Remembered*. New York: Abrams, 2001.

Kerr, Walter. *The Silent Clowns*. New York: Da Capo, 1975.

Lax, Eric. *Conversations with Woody Allen*. New York: Alfred A. Knopf, 2007.

———. *Woody Allen: A Biography*. New York: Alfred A. Knopf, 1991.

Lane, Anthony. *Nobody's Perfect*. New York: Alfred A. Knopf, 2002.

Leaming, Barbara. *Marilyn Monroe*. New York: Crown Publishers, 1998.

Levy, Shawn. *King of Comedy*. New York: St. Martin's Press, 1996.

Lewis, Jerry. *Dean & Me: (A Love Story)*. New York: Doubleday, 2005.

Louvish, Simon. *Mae West: It Ain't No Sin*. New York: Thomas Dunne Books, 2006.

———. *Man on the Flying Trapeze*. New York: W.W. Norton, 1997.

———. *Monkey Business*. New York: St. Martin's Press, 1999.

———. *Stan and Ollie: The Roots of Comedy: The Double Life of Laurel and Hardy*. New York: St. Martin's Press, 2002.

Maltin, Leonard. *The Great Movie Comedians*. New York: Harmony Books, 1982.

Mann, William J. *Kate*. New York: Holt, 2006.

Martin, Steve. *Born Standing Up*. New York: Scribner, 2007.

Maslon, Laurence, and Michael Kantor. *Make 'Em Laugh: The Funny Business of America*. New York: Twelve, 2008.

McGilligan, Patrick. *Robert Altman*. New York: St. Martin's Press, 1989.

Morgan, Michelle. *Marilyn Monroe: Private and Undisclosed*. New York: Da Capo, 2007.

Muir, John Kenneth. *Best in Show: The Films of Christopher Guest and Company*. New York: Applause Theatre, 2004.

Palmer, R. Barton. *Joel & Ethan Coen*. Urbana and Chicago: University of Illinois Press, 2004.

Parish, James Robert. *It's Good to Be King: The Seriously Funny Life of Mel Brooks*. Hoboken, N.J.: Wiley, 2007.

Pryor, Richard, with Todd Gold. *Pryor Convictions*. New York: Pantheon Books, 1995.

Robinson, David. *Chaplin: His Life and Art*. London: Collins, 1985.

Santopietro, Tom. *Considering Doris Day*. New York: Thomas Dunne Books, 2007.

Schickel, Richard. *Cary Grant: A Celebration*. New York: Applause Books, 1999.

———. *Harold Lloyd: The Shape of Laughter*. Boston: New York Graphic Society, 1974.

———. *Woody Allen: A Life in Film*. Chicago: Ivan R. Dee, 2003.

Schickel, Richard, ed. *The Essential Chaplin*. Chicago: Ivan R. Dee, 2006.

Shales, Tom, and James Andrew Miller. *Live from New York: An Uncensored History of* Saturday Night Live. Boston: Little, Brown, 2002.

Sikov, Ed. *Mr. Strangelove: A Biography of Peter Sellers*. New York: Hyperion, 2002.

———. *On Sunset Boulevard: The Life and Times of Billy Wilder*. New York: Hyperion, 1998.

Stevens, George Jr. *Conversations with the Great Moviemakers of Hollywood's Golden Age*. New York: Alfred A. Knopf, 2006.

Thomson, David. *A Biographical Dictionary of Film*. New York: Alfred A. Knopf, 1994.

———. *Have You Seen? A Personal Introduction to 1000 Films*. New York: Alfred A. Knopf, 2008.

Thompson, David, ed. *Altman on Altman*. London: Faber and Faber, 2006.

Vance, Jeffrey. *Chaplin: Genius of the Cinema*. New York: Abrams, 2003.

———. *Harold Lloyd: Master Comedian*. New York: Abrams, 2002.

Walker, Alexander. *Peter Sellers: The Authorized Biography*. London: Weidenfeld and Nicolson, 1981.

Wenner, Jann S., and Joe Levy, ed. *The Rolling Stone Interviews*. New York: Back Bay Books, 2007.

Yacowar, Maurice. *Method in Madness: The Comic Art of Mel Brooks*. New York: St. Martin's Press, 1981.

Zuckoff, Mitchell. *Robert Altman: The Oral Biography*. New York: Alfred A. Knopf, 2009.

INDEX

*Page number in **boldface** indicates main entry or short entry*